KABUKI ENCYCLOPEDIA

KABUKI ENCYCLOPEDIA

An English-Language Adaptation of *KABUKI JITEN*

SAMUEL L. LEITER

GREENWOOD PRESS
WESTPORT, CONNECTICUT • LONDON, ENGLAND

Library of Congress Cataloging in Publication Data

Leiter, Samuel L
Kabuki encyclopedia.

Bibliography: p.
Includes index.
1. Kabuki—Dictionaries. I. Yamamoto, Jirō, 1910- Kabuki jiten. II. Title.
PN2924.5.K3L44 895.6'2'003 78-73801
ISBN 0-313-20654-6

Library of Congress Catalog Card Number: 78-73801
ISBN: 0-313-20654-6

First published in 1979

Greenwood Press, Inc.
51 Riverside Avenue, Westport, Connecticut 06880

Printed in the United States of America

10 9 8 7 6 5 4 3 2 1

FOR BAMBI AND JUSTIN

Contents

List of Illustrations

Preface

Kabuki Encyclopedia is an English version of a Japanese reference work called the *Kabuki Jiten*, composed by Professors Jirō Yamamoto (1910-), Akira Kikuchi (1923-), and Kyōhei Hayashi (1925-). Professor Yamamoto, one of Japan's outstanding Kabuki specialists, teaches in the Department of Education at Waseda University in Tokyo. Professors Kikuchi and Hayashi are theatre specialists employed by the Waseda University Theatre Museum.

The present book is by no means a mirror image in English of its Japanese counterpart. As it is unlikely that most users of this book will compare it closely with the original, it is important that the major differences clearly be set forth. Perhaps the most important difference lies in the book's organization. *Kabuki Encyclopedia* is arranged so that all terms are listed alphabetically, regardless of subject, from A to Z. In the *Kabuki Jiten,* in contrast, listings are arranged according to subject matter, with chapters on play synopses, actors, plays and playwrights, acting and production, architecture, management, costumes, makeup, wigs, music, scenery, and properties, plus several appendixes. For those who wish to locate material by subject in this English version, a Subject Guide to Main Entries has been prepared and will be found near the back of the book. The detailed general index also should be helpful. *Kabuki Encyclopedia,* therefore, can be used in two ways.

Another important difference is that of cross-references, barely any of which are found in the *Kabuki Jiten.* Two types of cross-references are used here. In one type, terms that appear in the explanation of other terms and that are themselves defined as separate entries are indicated by an asterisk (*). No matter how often such a term is used throughout the book, it will be followed by an asterisk when it first appears in a particular entry. The second type of cross-reference is indicated by a phrase—for example, *see* AUDIENCES or (*See also* GEZA). In the former example, readers will note the use of an English term as a main entry. Many such terms have been incorporated into the book. If use of the term is restricted largely to Kabuki, the English title, essentially a literal translation, is included merely as an aid in finding the appropriate Japanese term. The reader who looks up FLOWER PATH, for instance, will be referred immediately to HANAMICHI. For more general subjects, the English title may introduce the entry.

It is unlikely that there will be a plethora of comparable works in English, so I have taken the liberty of making *Kabuki Encyclopedia* as thorough as possible, given the limitations of space. This has meant the inclusion of material not found in the *Kabuki Jiten.* New entries are of two types: those with their own independent listings and those subsumed under entries already found in the *Kabuki Jiten.* The latter are expansions of the original entries and are confined largely to the areas of actors and play synopses. Over 90 percent of the play synopses provide additional material on their original casts, the dates and theatres of Kabuki premieres of puppet theatre plays (the majority of Kabuki plays were first produced in the puppet theatre), and the background and performance methods of the plays. In some cases, the play synopses include fuller plot descriptions than the original. Most of the plot summaries, however, are extremely brief; since more than two hundred plays are included, more detailed summaries would have made the book unwieldy. The bibliography lists several works that offer more details on the plots of certain plays, though they do not contain as many play listings.

All information provided in *Kabuki Encyclopedia* is pertinent and, hopefully, concise. There are few entries that could not be expanded into articles of considerable length. In a book already bulging with pages, however, compactness becomes a necessity. Many terms frequently used in Kabuki do not have main entries here, as their discussion falls under other headings. The very thorough general index lists all such terms and directs the reader to the appropriate entries in which they are discussed.

Some material has been cut from the original work. Most of these omissions are in the area of technical matters, which would make little sense in English translation. I believe that the material added to the text far outweighs in value, for the English reader, those few sections that have been left out. It should not be assumed that all relevant and important Kabuki terms are included in this volume. It would be possible to compile a book-length, encyclopedic guide to each area into which the original Japanese work was subdivided. Nevertheless, there are few important terms, plays, names, or subjects that are not touched on in *Kabuki Encyclopedia*, if only briefly.

An omission that I greatly regret is the Japanese characters for each main entry. Unfortunately, technical considerations made their inclusion impossible. Another sacrifice was made in the number of photographs used. Although fifty photographs is a considerable number for any book, a subject such as Kabuki could easily be illustrated by several hundred pictures. I refer readers seeking additional photographic illustration to Masakatsu Gunji's *Kabuki* and Toita Yasuji's *Kabuki: The Popular Theatre.* Details can be found in the bibliography.

There are many other ways in which I have attempted to make the English version as useful as possible. These include the addition of dates for many names and works mentioned only in passing, the compilation of a bibliography of works on Kabuki in English, the provision of English titles for plays that have been translated into English, along with the name of the translator, and so on.

Readers seeking a historical overview of Kabuki will find it, not in a specific main entry, but in Appendix I, which provides a comprehensive chronological survey of the major events in Kabuki. Although a detailed list of all entries providing historical information would be too lengthy to include here, the entries on actors, playwrights, theatres, theatre management, and theatre architecture offer abundant historical background and may be read in conjunction with Appendix I. For a list of relevant terms, consult the Subject Guide to Main Entries.

Appendix II provides a list of the major plays in Kabuki's repertoire. Not all plays included there are described in the text; an asterisk marks those that are. Each play is listed in the appendix with the name of its author, the date of its first performance, and the theatre form for which it was created. An excellent perspective on the most popular playwrights and most common sources of Kabuki's plays may be gleaned from this listing.

The world of Kabuki play titles is often complex. Most plays have several titles—some formal, others more popular. Usage depends on taste and inclination. I have attempted to keep all title references uniform throughout the book to minimize confusion, but references in other books may not conform to my choices. *Kanadehon Chūshingura,* for example, is normally referred to simply as *Chūshingura.* Appendix III provides a list of major variations on play and act titles (plays often are known by the title of one of their acts). In this list, the more popular title variations are listed next to the formal names. Many of the latter are followed by the act number to which the popular title correctly belongs. The reader should be aware that many plays have additional titles that are not given here.

In Appendix IV, the reader will find genealogical trees for all major acting families of today. These trees have been simplified so that only the most important descendants are listed. By studying them, one can see vividly how crucial to Kabuki's development has been the transmission of artistic standards within the framework of familial inheritance. One can learn as well just who the antecedents of today's stars were and how the system of artistic transmission has survived through both blood relationships and adoption.

Please keep the following notes in mind when reading the entries:

1. *Kamigata* designates the cities of western Japan, notably Osaka and Kyoto. *Kansai* is another term for this region.
2. "Edo era" refers to the period from 1603 to 1868, during which time the city now known as Tokyo was called Edo. Japan was ruled for the entire Edo era by the Tokugawa military dictatorship (the shogunate), which fell in 1868 to the forces supporting the restoration of the Imperial line (under Emperor Meiji) to sovereign power. The Meiji era refers to the period from 1868 to 1912.
3. The Genroku era is given throughout with its precise chronological dates (1688-1703), but historians consider the period and its influence important enough to extend its dateline as far as the 1730s.
4. Names are given in the Japanese style, family name first (except for the authors of the *Kabuki Jiten*, whose names are given in Western style).
5. *Za* is used throughout to signify a theatre or theatre company. Thus *Nakamura-za* means the Nakamura Theatre; *Zenshin-za*, the Zenshin Company. The context invariably makes clear which *za* is being used.
6. Play synopsis entries open with the title of the play, followed by its author(s), any alternate titles by which it is known, its English title if available in translation, the translator's name, the genre to which it belongs, the form for which it was originally written, the musical style(s) if it is a dance play, the number of acts or scenes, the date and place of its first performance, and, of course, a précis of its action. Some titles have parentheses around the latter portion—for example, SUKEROKU (YUKARI NO EDO ZAKURA). In such cases the segment preceding the parentheses may be used alone, as an alternate title, in addition to any given in the entry.
7. Entries for deceased actors are followed by the years of their birth and death, if known. Living actors' names are followed by their "shop names," or *yago* (a type of nickname), and then by the year of their birth.

Many people helped to make this book a reality. In particular, I would like to thank Professor Andrew T. Tsubaki of the University of Kansas for his many helpful suggestions in translation matters. For his valuable criticisms and corrections, my thanks go to Professor Leonard C. Pronko of Pomona College. Professor William C. Young deserves my gratitude for bringing this work to the attention of Greenwood Press. Many of the organizational and stylistic features of the book were first suggested by my editor at Greenwood, Marilyn Brownstein. For these and for her patient attention to detail, I heartily thank her. Kensuke Haga, who acted as my agent in

Japan in arranging for the translation and adaptation rights, did an excellent job for which I will never be able to thank him enough. My thanks are also extended to Professor Kyōhei Hayashi for his help in obtaining the photographic illustrations. And for her help in proofreading the text, criticizing the writing, typing a large portion of the manuscript, and preparing the indexes, my wife, Marcia, earns the lion's share of my thanks.

Samuel L. Leiter
Howard Beach, N.Y.

Introduction

The sleek, air-conditioned comfort of Japan's plush National Theatre (Kokuritsu Gekijō, established in 1966) is a long way from the open-air stages of the early seventeenth century. At first glance, there seems to be little in common with the theatres depicted in colorful, old, woodblock prints, theatres jammed with spectators, actors, and theatre workers. Gone are the little boxed-off cubicles seating huddled groups of five or six around a charcoal brazier, chatting volubly, smoking pipes, eating snacks, and paying close but sporadic attention to the all-day performance. Gone are the teahouses, the barkers, the ornate signboards, the extra runway through the auditorium (except for special plays), the onstage seating areas. Electric lights have replaced the daylight streaming in from high windows. No longer does one see the huge fan clubs, which dressed identically when going to the theatre, the fuse-cord sellers, or the colorfully dressed ushers and security guards. Few are the shouts of encouragement from loving fans. Missing is the feeling that the theatre is as much a part of daily life as the air one breathes. Gone are these and many other things.

What remains beneath the gloss of stark modernity, however, still is sufficient to transport the spectator magically back to a time when the theatre faithfully reflected Japanese tastes and social values. Here are the fabled tales of noble samurai overcoming evil adversaries, of adulterous lovers consummating their bliss in double suicide, of parents sacrificing their children in the name of loyalty to a a superior, of children sacrificing themselves for the sake of their parents. Presented in a world of spectacular sets, costumes, makeup, and acting styles, these venerable dramas provide an aesthetic experience paralleled by few other world theatres.

Three and three-quarter centuries of vigorous life have made Kabuki a world apart, a world with its own special language, a world that retains a feudal outlook with a hierarchical power structure and a ritualistic code of protocol. The past is as much a part of Kabuki as the present, and the new is looked on skeptically until it can be shown to be an inherent part of the old. Actors today may play baseball and golf, but they continue to take the names of their forebears, changing only the ordinal number. Nakamura Kanzaburō XVII, Ichimura Uzaemon XVII, Kataoka Nizaemon XIII—for the West to match such traditions it would have to provide a Richard Burbage XVII, a David Garrick X, or a Molière XIV. Carefully rendered genealogies display a constant line of artistic tradition with which few actors dare to trifle.

Plays are selected from a classic repertoire that ceased to develop once Japan broke the chains of its two-and-a-half-century isolationist policy and began the surge toward Westernization. Production styles practically froze during the late nineteenth century, so that a Kabuki play viewed today is not greatly different from what it was a hundred years ago. Scenery, costumes, makeup, props, music, and acting methods recall vividly their Edo period prototypes, despite the selective incorporation of new methods of production. Still, the heartbeat of today's Kabuki only faintly resembles the throbbing pulse of the old-time theatre.

Kabuki was, during the Edo period, the theatre of the people. It was to its time what television and the movies are to the present. It was thought of not as a classical theatre, but as the theatre that mirrored the fears, aspirations, and beliefs of the average man. Late in the nineteenth century, however, a new attitude arose. The people's subjective love for Kabuki slowly began to turn to objective appreciation. Awareness of Kabuki's uniqueness became prevalent, and, for the first time, this artless art took on the aura of a serious art form. Kabuki never has recovered from the blow.

Today, Kabuki has little of relevance to say to its audiences, though some actors are striving to find contemporary pertinence in some of the old plays. The legions of modern Kabuki admirers, Japanese and foreigners alike, see things in it that never would have occurred to audiences of the past. Kabuki's entire history reveals a constant effort to bring the life on stage and the life in the auditorium into the closest possible relationship. The development of the *hanamichi* runways allowed the actors to come out among the spectators and practically to touch them. Audiences shouted out the actor's name or words of praise (and blame) without reservation and would do so even if they spotted a player passing in the street. Lavish gifts were bestowed on the actors, who, despite their lowly social status, reigned like gods in the imagination and dreams of the people. It is this spirit that has vanished.

Westernization brought new delights. As civilization advanced amid a rushing stream of technological improvements, Kabuki rusted in its place. After more than two hundred and fifty years of continued life, often in the face of the most oppressive circumstances, Kabuki was seen suddenly as an endangered species. Efforts to reform it, to bring it up-to-date, however, served only to wound it seriously; viewed as a relic, that is practically what it became.

Foreigners bring to Kabuki much the same attitude held by the contemporary Japanese. They see this theatre as exotic, as aesthetically compelling, as revealing of a nation's psyche as it once was. It is a phenomenon to be studied, to be appreciated, to be understood. Our scientific attitude makes us want to examine its mechanism, to discover its fundamentals, though we will be deceived if we convince ourselves that the ticking we hear is that of a vigorous heartbeat. Kabuki today is a luxury; it is no longer a necessity. Or perhaps we should say it is not the necessity that it used to be, for beauty such as Kabuki's will always be required in a world as marred as ours.

Kabuki Encyclopedia has been prepared with the hope of making Kabuki accessible to non-Japanese theatre lovers. If appreciation and understanding are to be achieved, it is necessary for a common language to be spoken. In this book will be found the vocabulary of that language. Hopefully, communication with Kabuki will result.

KABUKI ENCYCLOPEDIA

A

ABURA BENI. "Oil red," a red cosmetic used chiefly to create the *beni guma** makeup style, but also to depict bruises and represent blood. Using a bamboo spatula, one mixes fresh crimson or *edo beni* with the hard oil called *kata abura* to create this substance. The secret in the formula is said to be the addition of unrefined sugar. (*See also* KUMADORI.)

ABURA TSUKI. A male wig style seen mainly in history plays and named after the manner of its back-hair dressing, which is pomaded with oil (*abura*) and has a beautiful sheen. Contrasted to it is the realistically prepared *fukoro tsuki** used in domestic plays; this has a pouchlike back-hair arrangement. (*See also* WIGS.)

ACTORS. Actors in Japan today usually are called *haiyū* or *yakusha.* Until the Meiji period the first word was read as *wazaogi.* In the pre-Edo era, actors normally were called *geisha* or *yakusha,* words that came into use when Kabuki was born. It was also in the Meiji period that Japanese actors rose from the lowest stratum of society, where they were commonly considered "riverbed beggars" (*kawara mono** or *kawara kojiki*), to a position where they mingled with the highest echelons of society.

Kabuki began at the start of the seventeenth century with the "Kabuki dances" *(kabuki odori)* of the female temple dancer Izumo no Okuni*, it passed through a period in the same century when its materials were drawn mainly from the older types of entertaiment, Nō and Kyōgen theatre (whose plays it vulgarized), and reached a time in the 1680s when its own professional playwrights appeared and the content and form of Kabuki were enriched. This theatre art was handed down to successive generations of Kabuki artists on the basis of various patterns *(kata*),* which, through repetition, came to be fixed. Each later generation inherited the heart of its predecessor"s skills and, adding new ideas and techniques, set its eye toward artistic perfection.

It is a characteristic of Japanese theatre for one generation's art to be handed down to the succeeding generation; by passing on an art form to an equal or superior, one preserves and broadens it. Ideally, the successor should be a blood relative, preferably a son, but when no one in the immediate family is of sufficient merit, a successor is chosen from among the actor's apprentices *(deshi)* or relatives. This is the basis of what is often referred to as family art *(ie no gei)*, the handing down of a certain style of acting or a particular play or role in which the actor's family specializes. A Kabuki actor may look to this great specialty as another element of his heritage. When a superb actor appears and inherits his family and artistic lineage, his family becomes the recipient of great honor within the Kabuki world. In the past, playwrights, often wrote plays with such actors in mind for the leading roles. (*See also* PLAYWRITING.)

A rigid system of classification has been developed for Kabuki actors. If an actor is not from a famous family, he stands little chance of being noticed unless, in addition to possessing exceptional skill and striking personal characteristics, he also is the recipient of good fortune. Lacking these prerequisites, he must be resigned to remaining among the lower echelon of actors. Kabuki developed within a feudal society, and insofar as this society was organized according to a class system, it was only natural for Kabuki to create a class system of its own. Thus, the ranking of actors into separate categories is a major characteristic of the Kabuki actor's world (*See also* ACTORS' RANKS.)

Because the strict moral code of Confucianism was adopted by the Tokugawa government (1603-1868), Kabuki and its actors often were legislated against as corrupters of public morality. First there was a ban against women's Kabuki* *(onna kabuki)*, then one against young men's Kabuki* *(wakashu kabuki)*. Later, even the actors' private manners were controlled. Kabuki plays and theatres were the subject of strict censorship. The ban against women's Kabuki (1629) meant, above all, that women could no longer appear on the Kabuki stage. When this was followed some years later (1652) by a ban against young men's Kabuki, it became necessary for Kabuki to grow artistically if it was to survive. One condition for the redevelopment of dramatic content was that male actors had to play female roles. Moreover, it became necessary to apportion actors' roles: Actors were divided into the two major categories of *otokogata* (player of male roles) and *onnagata** (player of female roles), and there were various subdivisions of these as well. It became an actor's duty to concentrate primarily on one role type. From this evolved Kabuki's unique role-type system. (*See also* ROLE TYPES.)

The *onnagata* came to be regarded as one of the main distinguishing features of Kabuki. This acting form is said to have originated with Ukon Genzaemon* in the mid-seventeenth century. It achieved a state of near perfection during the Genroku period (1688-1703), which in many ways was one of the greatest periods in Kabuki's history.

Kabuki has received enthusiastic support because of its many exciting stars, beginning with Izumo no Okuni and her legendary cofounder, Nagoya Sanzaburō.* As early as Okuni's time, Kabuki showed promise of being an entertainment form centering on the actor's skill and personality. Even when Kabuki's dramatic content began to mature, audiences would gladly accept a dramatic character who had been given the name of a particular actor.

The perennial playwright's problem of how to display an actor to his best advantage in a new role is quickly solved by a popular and charming actor whose mere presence acts as a solution. This illustrates Kabuki's special qualities as an actor-centered theatre art. (*See also* STYLIZATION.)

For a list of actors whose biographies appear in the encyclopedia, consult the Subject Guide to Main Entries.

ACTORS' CRESTS. Each Japanese family has a traditional crest *(mon).* Although many families no longer use these crests, they continue to appear in Kabuki, where many customs of the Edo period still survive. Kabuki fans are familiar with the crests of all the leading actor families as well as those of the various theatres in which Kabuki is performed. Perhaps the most famous actor crest is that of the Ichikawa family. It consists of three square boxes, one inside the next. Branch families of the Ichikawa line often personalize this crest by placing an identifying initial in the central box. Thus, the syllabic character for *sa* may be seen at the center of the crest used by the Ichikawa Sadanji* line.

Each *mon* was originally selected for a very specific reason. The three boxes of the Ichikawa crest supposedly represent three measures *(masu*)* of rice given by a fan to Ichikawa Danjūrō I.* The twofold fan with a picture of overlapping oak leaves that constitutes the crest of the Onoe family (also known as the Otowaya line) is said to commemorate the gift of rice cakes, wrapped in oak leaves and placed on a fan, presented by the shogun to Onoe Kikugorō I.* An interesting crest is that of the Nakamura Utaemon* line; it shows two scrolls, one lying across the other, within a circular pattern that is styled after an amulet called a *gion mamori.* The crossed scrolls are thought to symbolize a crucifix, for Utaemon III was rumored to be a secret Christian.

Actors' crests are often depicted on their costumes, on the curtains leading into their dressing rooms, on books dealing with their lives, and on properties that they use in plays, such as hand towels *(tenugui).* Crests may even figure in the scene design for certain plays in which an outstanding actor is to appear. They play a significant role in the close relationship traditionally enjoyed between Kabuki actors and their fans.

ACTORS' PICTURES. *See* SHIBAI E; SHINI E; BUROMAIDO.

ACTORS' RANKS. Kabuki actors may be divided by rank into two main categories, *nadai** ("name actor") and *nadai shita* ("less than name actor").

A dance position taken in *Musume Dōjōji**. The dancer holds a hand towel on which is printed his personal crest. *Courtesy of Waseda University Tsubouchi Engeki Hakubutsukan (Tsubouchi Memorial Theatre Museum).*

Actors have both permanent crests *(mon*)* and alternative crests. Which ones are used depends on the occasion. The above are all permanent crests.

Nadai is short for *nadai yakusha,* which literally means actors whose names were written on theatre billboards *(kanban*)* during the Edo era. Among these actors is the *zagashira**; he is usually the leading actor of male roles *(tateyaku* or *tachiyaku*)* and the leader of the troupe. The major *onnagata** or female impersonator in the troupe is the *tate onnagata**.

Nadai shita actors, those whose names do not appear on billboards or in programs (also called *shitamawari*), are the lower rank of performers. They may be further subdivided into three groups called (in descending order) *aichū kamibun, aichū* (also *chūdori*), and *shita tachiyaku.* As soon as he has a chance, an actor from the lowest category will seek to be placed in a higher grouping, especially *aichū kamibun. Aichū* and *aichū kamibun* actors of the past customarily dressed and made up in a large room *(ōbeya*)* on the theatre's third floor; consequently, they are also called *ōbeya.* Lowest in status is the *shita tachiyaku* group, also called *shinaichū, wakaishū, inari machi**, and *oshita.* These actors dressed on the first floor in a communal dressing room.

Formerly, one of the only ways that an actor could go from *nadai shita* to *nadai* was by gaining recognition as an understudy for an ailing star. Backing from one's master was also important. Since the Meiji era, though, there has been a testing system *(nadai shiken)* developed for actors who wish to raise their position. The children of stars are granted the best opportunities; actors without family connections, however, rarely get the chance to demonstrate their ability.

ACTORS' RATINGS. *See* KURAI ZUKE; YAKUSHA HYŌBANKI.

ADAUCHI KYŌGEN. *See* REVENGE PLAYS.

AGEMAKU. A curtain hung at the rear end of the *hanamichi** and occasionally at the entranceway on stage left. It is a dark blue cloth on which the theatre's crest is dyed in white. The curtain hangs from metal rings and, as it is swished open to the left or right, makes a distinctive sound signaling to the audience that someone is about to enter. The room at the end of the *hanamichi* is called the *kobeya,* the *agemaku,* or the *toya,* and it provides access to and from the backstage area via a passageway *(naraku*)* under the theatre. Actors wait in this room to make their entrances on the *hanamichi.* The *toyaban* (also *agemakuban* and *kirimaku**) is the functionary employed here to open and close the curtain for the entering and exiting actors. The *hanamichi agemaku* curtain is similar to that on the Nō theatre bridgeway *(hashigakari),* though the Nō curtain is of five colors and opens and closes by being raised and lowered by a bamboo pole. However, the scenery for Kabuki plays adapted from the Nō *(matsubame mono*)* uses the same kind of *agemaku* as the Nō, placing it on a diagonal on the upstage right wall.

AGE NO TSUKI. The final clap *(chon)* of the *tsuke** clappers following the closing of the curtain, the last powerful beats of the *taiko** drum, and the departure of most of the spectators. There are actually two claps of the *tsuke,* one while the drum is still beating and one shortly after it has stopped. However, these final claps are not heard on the closing day of a run.

AIBIKI. A stool-like stage prop made of pawlonia wood and used by the chief actors as a seat. Its seat is square, and it is wider at the base than at the top. A small cushion is usually attached to the seat. There are several *aibiki* sizes. The tallest *(taka) aibiki* are used by leading actors of male roles in scenes in which they must stand in one place for a long time. Though they actually are sitting, the height of the *aibiki* allows them to give the impression of standing. Small and mid-size *aibiki* are used to give the actor seated on them the appearance of greater size; he would seem much smaller if he were seated on his knees with his posterior resting only on his ankles. Tall *aibiki* are built according to the size of the actors who are to use them. These often have a ledge at their rear for the placement of small items like tea cups.

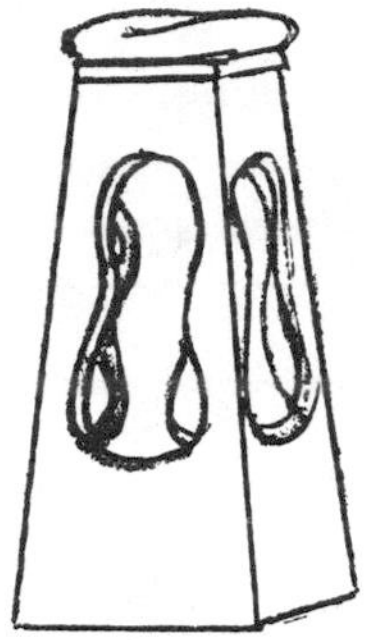
*Aibiki** stool.

AIGUMA. "Blue" *kuma,* a makeup term referring to a fearsome *kumadori** style of blue lines on a white base. It is used to express wickedness and treachery. The *hannya guma** and *kugeaku guma* are subtypes.

AIKATA. A musical term. The brief *shamisen** interlude between the singing parts of *nagauta** music are called *ainote**; the term *aikata* is used when this *ainote* has a specific theme and is performed as a longer, formalized piece. *Aikata*'s major characteristic is its lack of singing; thus, strictly speaking, passages with singing cannot be denoted by this word. *Aikata,* then, is the musical accompaniment played only by a *shamisen* following a passage combining voice and *shamisen.* It is played in the *geza** room during the opening and closing of the curtain, during a character's entrance, during conversations, and for a variety of dramatic situations. *Aikata* music produces emotional, psychological, and atmospheric effects. At the same time that the *aikata* allows the speech and acting to progress smoothly, its pitch serves to regulate the pitch of the dialogue. Its use extends to *nagauta, koto** music, *jiuta**, *hauta**, *kouta**—in fact, to almost all types of classical Japanese music. Set conventions have been established for the use of specific *aikata* in the various plays. Yet, some *aikata* are not fixed and are performed at the request of an actor who has his own preferences. *Aikata* that are specially

A climactic scene between Imakuni (on the steps) and Iruka in *Imoseyama Onna Teikin**. Iruka wears the *aiguma** makeup of the *kugeaku* villain (*see also* KATAKIYAKU), Iwakuni, Nakamura Ganjirō II*; Iruka, Jitsukawa Enjaku III*. *Courtesy of Waseda University Tsubouchi Engeki Hakubutsukan (Tsubouchi Memorial Theatre Museum).*

composed are called *atsurae* ("made-to-order") *aikata.* (*See also* GEZA: MUSICAL ACCOMPANIMENT CHART.)

AI KYŌGEN. The interlude section in a play. The device is derived from the Nō theatre *(matsubame mono*),* in which it is often employed as a linking device between the two halves of a play.

AIKYŌ O KURERU. "To charm"; when an actor speaks or acts on stage in a way suggesting great familiarity with his audience. For example, he may refer to himself or to another actor by name during a scene, as in the *Hamamatsuya* scene of *Aotozōshi Hana no Nishikie*.*

AINOTE. The *shamisen** accompaniment played as background music between sung passages. Its purposes include giving the singer an opportunity to regain his breath and allowing the *shamisen* player to display his artistry without having to share the spotlight with a singer. (*See also* AIKATA.)

AIZAMOTO. A term used during the Edo era when two or more managers (*zamoto**) ran a theatre. When a *zamoto* was unable to handle financial and other managerial matters by himself, this partnership system allowed him to set up other *zamoto* to assist him. The system began in 1651 when Murata Kuroemon, *zamoto* of Edo's Murayama-za, became ill and had to establish Ichimura Uzaemon* as his partner. (*See also* THEATRE MANAGEMENT.)

AJIROBEI. A traditional scenic element; it is constructed to resemble the wickerwork effect of a fence made of thin, pale beige boards crossed over and through one another at forty-five-degree angles. Each board is about three and one-half inches wide. *Ajirobei* is used mainly in history plays as an enclosure for the inner gardens of palaces and samurai residences.

AKAHIME. A princess role, which is also called *himegimi.* Because many Kabuki princesses wear red, long-sleeved kimono, the term *akahime*, meaning "red princess," is used to signify them. The *akahime's* costume consists of a kimono of red-figured silk or crepe on which designs of flowering plants, clouds, and flowing water are embroidered with gold and silk threads. The kimono is held together by an obi sash with a woven design; at the rear of the obi is a long hanging bow. The wig is a *fukiwa** type with a flower comb attached to it. (*See also* SANHIME.)

AKATERU. A special gunpowder used by the property men *(kodōgu kata)* to give the impression of the red light of the rising sun or of a conflagration. Ghost scenes use a green version called *aoteru.* These firelights burn at the ends of long poles *(sashidashi*)* held by stage assistants. Since the effects originally suggested by this technique can now be handled more realistically by modern lighting equipment, *akateru* is used only for plays that try to retain the naive quality of old-time Kabuki.

AKATTSURA. "Red-face," a character type noted for its reddish makeup. Such makeup originally was used during the Genroku period (1688-1703) by bold young warrior roles acted in the bravura *aragoto** style. Ichikawa Danjūrō I*, who originated *aragoto* acting, may have conceived it for his first *aragoto* role, Sakata Kintoki, a legendary superman traditionally depicted with a red face. Later, the convention became associated mainly with certain villain roles in the history plays. Among these are Shundō Gemba in the *Terakoya* scene of *Sugawara Denju Tenarai Kagami** and Iwanaga in *Dan no Ura Kabuto Gunki**. The red color is thought to add a touch of humor to such roles. Other characters seen with *akattsura* are the young men *(wakashu)* presented as the younger brothers or children of *jitsuaku* (*see* KATAKIYAKU) villains. Thus, Kitōta in the *Kinkakuji* act of *Gion Sairei Shinkoki** wears *akattsura* since he is the younger brother of the *jitsuaku,* Matsunaga Daizen. There is also a class of comical villains called *haradashi** who are acted with red faces. (*See also* KUMADORI.)

AKEGARASU (HANA NO NUREGINU). Sakurada Jisuke III*. *Sewamono**. Kabuki. One act. February 1851. Ichimura-za*, Edo.

This work was inspired by a popular Osaka piece in the musical style called *shinnai bushi*—Akegarasu Yume no Awayuki*—which described the lovers' suicides of Inosuke, son of a purveyor to the government, and Miyoshino, a prostitute. Jisuke's version, written in Edo, is performed with *kiyomoto** music. It was a great hit at its first performance, largely because of the beautiful voice of the *kiyomoto* singer, Kiyomoto Tahei, and the acting of Ichikawa Danjūrō VIII* as Tokijirō and Bandō Shūka I as Urazato.

In its first production, this play was part of a long work by Jisuke, based on the classic *Kanadehon Chūshingura**, but subsequent revivals omitted the connection with that play. There are a number of other well-known musical compositions based on the same story, as well as a puppet drama inspired by the Kabuki play and produced in Osaka in 1853. Known as *Akegarasu Yuki no Akebono,* it eventually was adapted for Kabuki as well.

Urazato, courtesan of the Yamana-ya, and her lover, Tokijirō, are the parents of Midori, a child maidservant at the brothel. Since a courtesan's having a permanent lover is considered an obstacle to the business operations of the Yamana-ya, an attempt is made to separate the pair. One snowy day an employee of the brothel discovers Urazato engaged in a secret rendezvous with Tokijirō. The latter is driven away, and the courtesan is tied to a pine tree in the garden and beaten. Urazato bemoans her ills for a time and weeps.

However, Tokijirō steals over the fence and rescues her; the lovers escape with Midori on her father's back.

Urazato's lamentation scene* *(kudoki)* and her love scene with Tokijirō are accompanied by melancholy *kiyomoto* music. At the heart of the piece is the gruesome beauty of the beating in the snow and its resultant pathos. This play was often performed to great acclaim by the outstanding trio of Ichimura Uzaemon XV* (as Tokijirō), Onoe Baikō VI* (as Urazato), and the musician Kiyomoto Enjudayū.

AKENANKO. "To speak clearly."

AKI KYŌGEN. *See* AUTUMN PLAYS.

AKUZUKI. A "bad month" at the box office. February and August are traditionally the poorest in attendance.

AMAI. "Sugary" or "slushy," a term applied to acting, plays, or productions that are not very deep, but appeal to popular tastes. *Karai**, or "pungent," is the opposite; it is used to refer to more difficult material or work of a high caliber. *Amai* also is used when a theatre has few spectators; a common phrase is "the audience is sweet" *(kenbutsu ga amai).*

AMAOCHI. Also called *kaburitsuki** and *koichi,* this is the first row of spectators. The term (meaning "falling rain") may derive from those occasions when people seated there got splashed with stage water or mud or from the fact that these theatregoers were doused by rainwater falling off the stage roof during the period when the pit area was uncovered.

AME. "Rain." Kabuki uses several devices to suggest a rainfall. The most realistic is called *hon ame** ("real water"); a water tank is placed above the stage, and water falls through holes drilled in a pipe behind the *ichimonji** border, which runs across the top of the stage. A more symbolic method is to attach silver strings, five or six feet in length, within a foot-wide space on a framework; this is lowered from above the stage. Another technique is to use a background painted with what looks like rain. The effect of rain also can be accomplished with lighting techniques using projections. The latter is frequently employed in newer plays.

ANA GA AKU. "A hole has opened," an expression used when an inadvertent pause has occurred during a performance, such as when an actor has forgotten a line or some other mishap has developed.

ANNAI NIN. The usherette who leads spectators to their seats. The usherette system first was introduced when the Teikoku Gekijō* opened in 1911.

ANTEN. The use of electric lighting to darken the house during a scene change, especially when the revolving stage* *(mawari butai)* is employed. Its first use in Japan was in 1905, during the premiere run of *Kiri Hitoha**.

AODA. "Green fields," an expression referring to the presence of numerous nonpaying spectators. The term derives from a farmers' phrase, "the fields have produced a poor harvest" *(aoda ni miirinashi)*.

AORIGAESHI. "Flap change," a quick-change scenic technique by which a painted flat *(harimono*)* is built with a separate section attached to its center by hinges. When the extra section is moved from one side to the other, like a page in a book, a new painted surface is revealed. It is often used in quick-change dances called transformation pieces* *(henge mono)*.

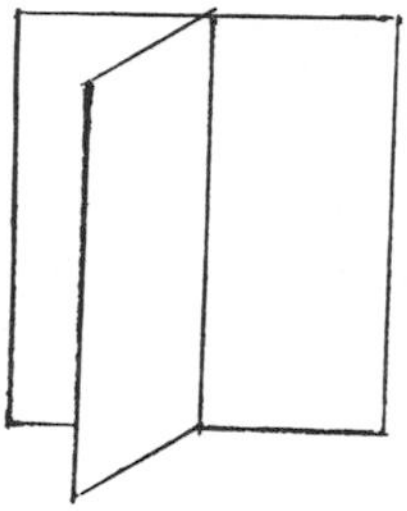

*Aorigaeshi** technique.

AOTOZŌSHI HANA NO NISHIKIE. Kawatake Mokuami*. Also called *Benten Kozō, Shiranami Gonin Otoko, Benten Musume Meono no Shiranami, Enoshima Sodachi Neoi no Chigokiku, Oto ni Kiku Benten Kozō.* English titles: *Benten the Thief* (Ernst), *Benten Kozō* (Leiter). *Sewamono**. Kabuki. Five acts, eight scenes. March 1862. Ichimura-za*, Edo.

Said to be based on a set of wood-blocks prints by Utagawa Toyokuni III (1786-1864), this play is a dramatization of the activities and fate of five bandits. The third act's *Hamamatsuya* scene, the fourth act's Inase River scene *(Seizoroi no Ba)*, and the finale at the Gokuraku Temple are often performed. The play's first production made the young actor Ichimura Uzaemon XIII (later known as Onoe Kikugorō V*), who played Benten, famous. Others in the outstanding cast were Nakamura Shikan IV* as Nango Rikimaru and Kawarazaki Gonjūrō (later Ichikawa Danjūrō IX*) as Tadanobu Rihei.

Posing as the daughter of a samurai and her attendant, two of the bandits, Benten Kozō and Nango Rikimaru, allow themselves to be discovered shoplifting at the *Hamamatsuya*, a textile shop. Benten is injured by a shop clerk and demands one hundred *ryō* in recompense. Tamashima Ittō just happens to be present and sees through Benten's female disguise. Later, when Ittō is rewarded for having saved the shop people from danger, he changes his manner and reveals that he is, in reality, Nippon Daemon, the bandit chief. Then Benten, Nango, and the other thieves appear and tie everyone up. But Kōbei, the shopowner, reveals that his son-in-law, Sōnosuke, is Nippon's true son and that Benten is his own son. Because of their crimes, the five bandits are pursued to the Inase River, where they gather and make good their escape. However, Benten is cornered later at the Gokuraku Temple, where he commits suicide; the others are captured.

From its first performance by Onoe Kikugorō V* to that by today's Kikugorō VII*, this play presents such audience-pleasing scenes as the discovery of Benten's disguise and the revelation of his blackmail schemes. One of Kabuki's most famous moments occurs when Benten removes the sleeve of his kimono from his arm and shoulder, revealing white flesh beautifully adorned with tattoos. The switch from female impersonation to straight male characterization has a truly unique theatrical effect. In the Inase River scene the colorful mustering of the thieves in gorgeous costumes offers an unforgettable visual display. The exciting musical accompaniment, thrilling rhythmical speech, and stylized abusive language provide vivid aural interest as well.

ARAGOTO. "Rough business," the distinctive Edo style of acting and production, in which the hero's superhuman strength and valor are stressed in a formalized manner. All aspects of production—costumes, makeup, voice, action, elocution, props, scenery—are unrealistically exaggerated. The style usually is said to have originated when the thirteen-year-old Ichikawa Danjūrō* made a big hit in the role of Sakata Kintoki in *Shitennō Osanadachi* at the Nakamura-za* in 1673. Legend relates that he performed in the fashion of the then popular Kinpira puppet shows *(kinpira joruri*)*. Danjūrō's stirring histrionics were so popular that *aragoto* was handed on to the later generations of his line, who continuously polished it and made it their family art* *(ie no gei)*. Examples of characters and plays performed in this style include *Yanone** and *Shibaraku** of the famous play collection, the *kabuki jūhachiban**; Watonai in *Kokusenya Kassen**; Umeomaru and Matsuomaru of the *Kuruma Biki* scene in *Sugawara Denju Tenarai Kagami**; Gorō in *Soga no Taimen**; and many others.

ARAKI YOJIBEI. 1637-1700. A troup leader *(zagashira*)* who was the first manager *(zamoto*)* at Osaka's Horie Shibai Theatre. Araki Yojibei became famous following his performance as the wounded outlaw in *Hinin no Katakiuchi* in 1664. Together with Arashi San'emon* and Sakata Koheiji, he was one of the leading stars of his time in the Kamigata area.

ARASHI HINASUKE X, *yago** Yoshidaya. 1913- . An *onnagata**, he debuted in February 1920 as Nakamura Chotarō, then took the name Hinasuke X in February 1943. Originally a student of Nakamura Kichiemon I*, he joined the Tōhō* troupe in the 1930s, but later returned to the Shōchiku* company. In 1941 he moved to the Kamigata area.

A superman *aragoto** type, Arajirō Otokonosuke, temporarily quells the evil Nikki Danjō, seen here in the guise of a huge rat, in the cellar scene *(Yukashita)* of *Meiboku Sendai Hagi**. Otokonosuke, Bandō Mitsugorō VIII*. He wears the *kumadori** makeup called *nihon guma**. At his knees are the pads called *sanriate**. *Courtesy of Waseda University Tsubouchi Engeki Hakubutsukan (Tsubouchi Memorial Theatre Museum).*

ARASHI RIKAKU V, *yago** Tomijimaya. 1897- . Born in Osaka, the son of Rikaku IV, he debuted in July 1903 as Arashi Katsunosuke, and took his present name in March 1945. He possesses the qualities of the old style and is an outstanding supporting actor in Kamigata Kabuki, being especially prized for his acting in *dōkegata** roles.

ARASHI SAN'EMON I. 1635-1690. He began his career as an Edo actor, but later moved to Osaka. San'emon was the most popular player of leading male roles in Osaka in the mid-seventeenth century. His specialty was the type of young lover called *yatsushi* (*see* NIMAIME), and he was an expert performer of *roppō** (a unique way of walking). He originated the family name of San'emon, which has come down to the present through eleven generations. The same line of actors includes Arashi Koroku, Arashi Sanjūrō, and Arashi Hinasuke*, illustrious names in Osaka Kabuki.

X, *yago** Tsunokuniya. 1908- . Born in Osaka, he debuted in January 1912. In January 1948 he changed his name from Nakamura Komanosuke to San'emon. He has been active as a supporting actor in Kamigata Kabuki.

ARASHI YOSHIŌ I, *yago** Tomijimaya. 1935- . He is the son of Arashi Yoshisaburō V*, with whom he acts in the company known as the Zenshin-za*. He debuted in 1939 as Arashi Ichitarō and joined the Zenshin-za in 1951.

ARASHI YOSHISABURŌ V, *yago** Tomijimiya. 1907- . An actor born in Tokyo and son of the actor Yoshisaburō IV. He debuted in March 1913, took his present name in 1927, and joined the Zenshin-za* troupe in 1934. He has displayed excellent talent in young lover *(nimaime*)* roles and as an *onnagata**.

ARAU. "To wash," a term that means tightening up a performance by eliminating any problem moments. It also refers to the practice of finding those playgoers who have entered without paying for their seats.

ARE. A wig device used to emphasize a change in character in history play scenes in which a male-role actor playing a conspirator or one who is planning to take revenge throws off his disguise suddenly and reveals his true nature. *Are* is the technique whereby the hair stands on end in a wildly disheveled fashion, making a striking impression. Examples are performances by Sadatō in *Ōshū Adachigahara** and Nikki Danjō in *Meiboku Sendai Hagi**. (*See also* WIGS.)

ARMOR. Known as *yoroi.* During the Edo era it was forbidden for actors to wear real samurai armor or even armor closely resembling it. This restriction was lifted with the establishment of the Meiji era, when all types of realistic armor began to appear on stage. One property type is the *surume yoroi*, an armor patterned after the ancient armor styles. It is made of a cardboard base on which metal or silver paper and colored cloth are applied. Today, only Kumagai and Atsumori in *Suma no Miyako Genpei Tsutsuji** wear *nui yoroi*, an armor made entirely of cloth to which small plates *(kozane)* are sewn with gold thread; it uses absolutely no metal fittings.

ASAMAGATAKE. Masuyama Kinpachi. Also called *Sono Omokage Asamagatake, Asamagatake Ironoyamagase, Sono Mama Asamagatake Shosagoto**. *Tomimoto**. March 1775. Ichimura-za*, Edo.

A dance piece based on a Chinese legend of an incense with fumes in which one may see the spirit of a departed lover. It is one of a group of works based on this theme; such works are termed *asama mono*. The first popular example of such a work was *Keisei Asamagatake*, produced in the Genroku era (1688-1703). Although it had not been performed for many years, a successful revival of *Asamagatake* was staged in 1926, and the piece has had several revivals since.

ASHIYA DŌMAN ŌUCHI KAGAMI. Takeda Izumo II*. Also called *Kuzu no Ha*. *Jidaimono**. *Jōruri**. Five acts. October 1734. Takemoto-za, Osaka.

This work is based on a Shinoda legend. Abe no Yasuna saves a white fox in the Shinoda Forest. To repay him, the fox turns into Princess Kuzu no Ha and visits him. They marry and have a child, Abe no Seimei, who in real life is said to have been a famous fortune-teller. The true Kuzu no Ha eventually appears, and the fox realizes that it must leave. It writes a farewell ode and returns to its forest haunts.

Customarily, the same actor plays both Kuzu no Ha roles. These roles are an important test of the *onnagata's** ability. Outstanding scenes are the lamentation* *(kudoki)*, performed when the fox must leave its child, and the writing of the ode, when the character uses its mouth and left hand. This unusual writing technique suggests the character's foxlike nature. The "child separation" scene of Act IV, the climax of the play, is frequently performed (the *Kowakare* scene), and another popular scene is one in which the fox turns into a servant and mocks a villainous character (the *Sashi Kago* scene). The present play is the most famous in a series of works based on the same legend, the earliest having been produced in 1678. Plays with supernatural occurrences provide effective material for puppet theatre dramatization. The three-man system of puppet manipulation found in the Japanese puppet theatre began with this play's first production. Kabuki's first version of the play was staged in 1737 at Edo's Nakamura-za*. The famous *kiyomoto** dance drama *Yasuna** is based on Act II of this play, called *Kosode Monogurui*.

ATARIGANE. A metal percussion instrument hung in the *geza** and struck with a small stick. It is heard in festival scenes and at entrances of dashing characters.

ATARU. A word used to refer to a successful production. In the past it was common for there to be a big celebration, the *atari iwai,* on such occasions. Celebration banquets were called *atari furimai.* They were held backstage, in a theatre dining room, or at a fancy restaurant. Current practice generally is to give each person concerned with the production a bonus envelope containing a small sum of money. An actor who achieves a notable success with his role *(yaku)* considers the role to be an *atari yaku.* (*See also* ŌIRI.) The word *ataru* also may be used to refer to the timing of an actor's movements to the sound of the *shamisen** or *tsuke**.

ATEBURI. The performance of excessively literal dance movements that imply more than is indicated in the line of the narration or song to which they are set. An extreme example is the line *"kiyabō usudon"* in the dance drama *Seki no To*:* A gesture signifying a tree branch *(ki)* is followed by actions representing notching an arrow *(ya),* working a pole *(bō)* through the hands, grinding with mortar and pestle *(usu),* and, finally, beating on a door *(don).* Most of these gestures imply a play on words, because the syllables that they enact—although homonyms—mean something other than the full words do.

ATEKOMU. Remarks interpolated into the regular dialogue. Usually such comments are in the nature of topical references. They are often ad-libbed by the actors.

ATSURAE. Anything unconventional or extraordinary requested by the actor for his performance. Usually used in the term *atsurae aikata,* to denote special music created at an actor's request instead of that conventionally used for a scene. (*See also* AIKATA; MIHAKARAI.)

ATSUWATA. An outer kimono *(kitsuke*)* stuffed with cotton and resembling a padded dressing gown *(dotera).* Seen mainly on *aragoto** characters, it is intended to show off the character's exaggerated physical attributes. Examples are Umeomaru in the *Kuruma Biki* scene of *Sugawara Denju Tenarai Kagami**, Gorō in *Yanone**, Sekibei in *Seki no To**, and Asahina in *Kusazuri Biki**.

AUDIENCES *(kankyaku.)* During the Edo era the greatest fans of Kabuki and puppet plays were the townspeople. These citizens took great delight in attending the theatres. Audiences had a close relationship with the stage and filled a crucial role in Kabuki's development.

One of Kabuki's characteristics is that it is actor-centered; the appeal of the individual actor frequently determines the pieces performed and the results of that performance. The popularity of certain actors led to the establishment of a patron system. Spectators belonging to an actor's fan club were called *hiiki**. Edo Kabuki was supported by such powerful cliques as the Yoshiwara, the Uogashi, and the Kuramae, while Osaka had its Ōte and Sasase backers' groups. In contrast to these more socially respectable backers, there were lower classes of patrons, such as those crowded into the *kiriotoshi** seating and the *denpō**, a clique who often bullied their way into the theatre without paying. The actors' fans were thus a conglomerate of types, ranging from the wealthiest to the poorest of townspeople.

Audiences were seriously regarded by theatre managements. This may be seen, for example, in the selection of plays to suit the tastes of the maidservants working for samurai families when these ladies visited the theatre on their annual spring vacation. There was a lively interchange between the stage and the audience, especially noticeable when the audience filled the theatre with shouts of encouragement. (*See also* DANTAI; HOME KOTOBA; KAKEGOE; KAWADŌRI; RENJŪ; THEATRE MANAGEMENT.)

AUTUMN PLAYS. Known as *aki kyōgen*, these were a regular feature of Kabuki's seasonal programming in the Edo era. They were usually performed from the time of the Chrysanthemum Festival, beginning the ninth day of the ninth month, to the fifteenth day of the tenth month. When the July performances *(bon kyōgen*)* were delayed and produced in August, they, too, were called *aki kyōgen.* As the last performances of the theatrical year were given in the fall, autumn plays were also called *onagori kyōgen,* or "farewell plays." The new season began a month later with the *kaomise** performances, in which a new lineup of actors was presented. (*See also* THEATRE MANAGEMENT.)

AWA NO NARUTO. Chikamatsu Hanji*, Takemoto Saburobei, others. Also called *Keisei Awa no Naruto. Jidai-sewamono.** *Jōruri**. Ten acts. May 1768. Takemoto-za, Osaka.

A revision of a play by Chikamatsu Monzaemon*, *Yūgiri Awa no Naruto* (1712), dealing with the love of Yūgiri and Izemon; several new plot strands are woven into the original story. The eighth act, *Junrei Uta,* remains.

Jūrobei of Awa and his wife, Oyumi, assume the appearance and behavior of bandits in order to seek out an heirloom stolen from the family of Jūrobei's master. Jūrobei is also desperate to obtain money for his samurai superior, Shuzen, who owes it to Fujiya Izaemon. One day, a young lady dressed as a pilgrim accidentally encounters Oyumi. The latter recognizes the girl as her daughter Otsuru; afraid to reveal her identity, Oyumi sends the girl away. She soon changes her mind and leaves to find Otsuru again. Meanwhile, her husband meets the girl and, not recognizing her, tries to rob her. In the struggle, he slays her. When Oyumi returns, she tells Jūrobei that the dead girl was their child, and the scene ends with the parents lamenting their tragic loss. Eventually, the missing heirloom, a sword, is recovered.

Kabuki's first production of this play was in 1789 at Edo's Nakamura-za*.

AYUMI. A feature of Kabuki theatre auditoriums when the pit *(doma*)* seating was divided into boxed-off sections *(masu*)*. The *ayumi* were the wooden walkways connecting the two *hanamichi**, and, though used by actors when crossing from one *hanamichi* to the other, they were mainly used by spectators as a means of getting to their seats and by hawkers selling their wares. *(See also* THEATRE ARCHITECTURE.)

B

BACKERS. *See* AUDIENCES; DANTAI; HIIKI; RENJŪ.

BACKSTAGE. The word *gakuya* comprises all the waiting rooms, lounges, and other backstage rooms in which actors, musicians, property men, and scene shifters relax and carry out their duties. This backstage area is now an architectural unit of the theatre building, although originally the *gakuya* was merely a place behind a closed upstage curtain. In the Edo period the audience, stage, and musicians were located within a unified architectural structure while the backstage rooms were part of a three-story system. However, since fire regulations led to the banning of three-story buildings, the second floor was called *chū nikai** or "mezzanine."

Edo period dressing rooms were distributed by the actors' rank and role type, according to a fixed system. Some received private rooms, some shared rooms with one or two other actors, and some were assigned to communal rooms, like the lowest class, *shitamawari,* and the low-ranking actors who shared the *ōbeya**, a large space on the third floor. Actors of male roles *(tachiyaku*)* were on the third floor, and the *onnagata** used the second floor. The first floor had a room for the *shitamawari;* it also was used for various purposes connected with the performances.

Actors use their dressing rooms to put on their makeup, wig, and costume, as well as to relax. Dressing rooms normally contain the actor's mirror (part of a low, legless vanity table) and personal belongings, such as art works or souvenirs. Today, dressing rooms are identified by a curtain at the entrance that bears the actor's name and crest *(mon)* on it (*See also* ACTORS' CRESTS); such curtains are gifts from the fans. A manservant *otokoshū** in the dressing room sees to the actor's personal property. Each major actor has his own personal vanity table and mirror, but the lower ranks must use the permanent ones placed in the *ōbeya.* (*See also* THEATRE ARCHITECTURE; ACTORS' RANKS.)

BAITEN. Shops located in the theatre's lobby; they sell mostly theatre souvenirs and food. *Baiten* were first used when the National Theatre of Japan* opened in 1911.

BANCHŌ SARAYASHIKI. Okamoto Kidō*. *Shin kabuki**. One act, two scenes. February 1916. Hongo-za, Tokyo.

A modern interpretation of the once popular puppet play, *Banshū Sarayashiki* (1741).

Okiku, a lady-in-waiting, has promised her favors to Aoyama Harima, a member of the troop of shogun's guards *(hatamoto)* called the Shiratsuka. Okiku is worried about a rumor that Harima is married. In order to determine his true feelings, she smashes a plate that is a treasured heirloom of his family. Thinking this an accident, he forgives her; however, when he learns her true motives, he grows angry at her suspicious nature and slays her. He runs out to rejoin a group of quarreling *otokodate* (the "street knights" of the Edo era).

The play skillfully presents the ways of a young *hatamoto* and the emotions of a female character. Ichikawa Sadanji II* counted this play among the most popular in his repertory and included it in his collection, the *kyōka gikyoku jūshu**.

BANDŌ HIKOSABURŌ I. 1693-1751. A player of leading male roles during the first half of the eighteenth century, he took the name of Hikosaburō in 1707. He, Ichikawa Danjūrō II*, Sawamura Sōjūrō I*, and Ōtani Hirōji were called the Four Heavenly Kings *(shittennō)* during their period of activity.

II. 1741-1768. A star of the Hōreki period (1751-63) who died young.

III. 1754-1828. Son of Ichimura Uzaemon* IX (1720-1785), he took the name of Hikosaburō in 1770. He was extolled as an expert in the romantic *wagoto** style during the latter part of the eighteenth century. In 1813 he retired and took the tonsure, was called Hansōan Rakuzen, and lived out the rest of his life as a priest. His greatest roles were Yuranosuke in *Kanadehon Chūshingura** and Kan Shōjō in *Sugawara Denju Tenarai Kagami**.

V. 1832-1877. Adopted son of Hikosaburō IV, he became Hikosaburō V in 1856 and was a representative actor of the late Edo and early Meiji eras. The possessor of good looks and an excellent voice, he was outstanding in history plays, domestic plays, dance plays, and so on, filling a wide variety of roles, from *wajitsu** to warriors to *onnagata**. His style is said to have been continued by Onoe Kikugorō V*.

VI. 1886-1938. Third son of Onoe Kikugorō V*, he took the name of Hikosaburō in 1915. He performed chiefly at the Ichimura-za* with his brother, the great Onoe Kikugorō VI*.

VII. *See* ICHIMURA UZAEMON XVII.

BANDŌ KAMEZŌ III, *yago** Otowaya. 1943- . Born in Tokyo, he is the son of Ichimura Uzaemon XVII*. He debuted as Bandō Kamesaburō in 1950, became Shinsui in 1965, and took his present name in 1972. A responsible player of leading male roles among the younger Kabuki actors, he greatly resembles his father and has a powerful voice.

BANDŌ KŌTARŌ, *yago** Yamatoya. 1911- . The son of Morita Kanya XIII*, he debuted in 1922 and took the name of Kōtarō in 1924. In 1931 he became a film actor, but returned to Kabuki in 1962. He acts as a villain and in supporting roles.

BANDŌ MINOSUKE, *yago** Yamatoya. 1929- . The son of Bandō Shūchō III, he was born in Tokyo and adopted by Bandō Mitsugorō VIII*, debuting soon afterwards as Bandō Mitsunobu (1932). In May 1955 he became Bandō Yaesuke and took his present name in 1964. Along with Ōgawa Hashizō (1929-), a former Kabuki actor who now performs mainly outside of Kabuki, he studied under Onoe Kikugorō VI*, beginning in his Mitsunobu days, and acquired a high degree of proficiency as a dancer. Collaboration with Hashizō and direction of a troupe of young Kabuki performers resulted in a fresh stage appeal. Onoe Shōroku II* became his teacher after Kikugorō's death. Possessing a steady and unostentatious style, he came to play leading roles at Toyoko Hall in Tokyo's Shibuya section. Bandō Yasosuke is his eldest son.

BANDŌ MITSUGORŌ I. 1745-1782. Adopted son of Bandō Sanpachi, he became Mitsugorō in 1766 and left Osaka for Edo. He specialized in leading male roles and young lovers *(nimaime*)*.

II. 1741-1828. Took the name in 1785. When the legitimate son of Mitsugorō I came of age, he changed his name to Ōgino Isaburō and handed the name of Mitsugorō III over to its rightful owner.

III. 1773-1831. The son of Mitsugorō I, he took the name in 1799. He achieved popularity during the first third of the nineteenth century when he engaged in artistic rivalry with Nakamura Utaemon III*. A good-looking man, he brought a tasteful elegance to his portrayal of *wagoto** and *wajitsu** roles, also being adept at dance dramas. As he had a home in Eiki in Edo's Fukugawa section, he was dubbed Eiki no Mitsugorō.

IV. 1800-1863. Adopted son of Mitsugorō III, he became the fourth in the line in 1832. He was particularly outstanding as the leading male in *sewamono** and in dance works. As his immediate predecessor had competed for preeminence, his rivalry with Nakamura Utaemon IV* filled the Edo theatre world with vigor. He later became Morita Kanya XI and managed the Morita-za*. Afflicted with palsy, he was nicknamed Yoi Mitsu ("Drunken Mitsu").

V. 1811-1855. Adopted son of Mitsugorō III, his first stage name was Bandō Tamasaburō, but for most of his career he was known as Bandō Shūka*. An *onnagata** of unusual beauty, he made an exceptionally popular team with Ichikawa Danjūrō VIII*. He died rather young and received the name of Mitsugorō posthumously.

VI. 1841-1873. The son of Mitsugorō V, he was active until the early Meiji era as an *onnagata.* His nickname was Aba Mitsu ("Pockmarked Mitsu") because of his scarred face.

VII. 1882-1961. Son of Morita Kanya XII*. In his youth he was taught by Nakamuro Shikan IV* and Ichikawa Danjūrō IX*, two of the top stars of the day. He became Mitsugorō VII in 1909 and performed with Onoe Kikugorō VI* and Nakamura Kichiemon I* during the Taishō period (1912-26). Mitsugorō VII was one of the best Kabuki dancers of his day and was considered on a par with the great Kikugorō.

VIII. 1906-1975. The adopted son of Mitsugorō VII. He debuted as Bandō Yasosuke in 1913, became Minosuke in June 1928, and participated in the Tōhō* troupe's work from 1935 to 1939. He switched to Kamigata Kabuki in 1940 and returned to Tokyo's Shōchiku* company in 1961, taking the name Mitsugorō in 1962. Mitsugorō was the best read of his generation of Kabuki actors and had an abundant love of learning. Adept at the tea ceremony, flower arrangement, and calligraphy, he presented a mature art backed by his knowledge of these traditional Japanese arts. Mitsugorō was also the author of a number of books. His death was caused by eating blowfish *(fugu),* a delicacy that, when improperly prepared, usually poisons those who eat it.

BANDŌ RYŪ. A school of Japanese dance founded in 1820 by Bandō Mitsugorō III*, who shared the dance limelight in Edo at the time with his rival, Nakamura Utaemon III*. The present head of the Bandō *ryu* (*see also* SŌKE) is Bandō Minosuke*, who took the dance name of Bandō Mitsugorō* on the death of his adopted father. The Bandō *ryū* popularized a number of dances in the genre known as *henge mono** or *henge buyō,* pieces requiring a mastery of quick-change techniques and a good deal of versatility.

BANDŌ SHŪCHŌ IV, *yago** Yamatoya. 1901- . The adopted son of Shūchō III, he debuted in 1905 and changed his name from Bandō Katsutarō to Shūchō in 1940. As an actor he is steadfast, but lacking in color. A thorough and correct *onnagata**, he plays supporting and old women's roles, as well as an occasional old man, and has a simple style.

BANDŌ SHŪKA I. 1813-1855. Adopted when young by Bandō Mitsugorō III*, he became Shūka in 1839. He rivaled Ichikawa Danjūrō VIII* in popularity during the mid-nineteenth century and specialized in *onnagata** roles.

II. d. 1893. Second son of Nakamura Karoku I*, he was an *onnagata* during the Meiji era. Shūka III was the previous name of Morita Kanya XIV*, and the fourth in the line is the adopted son of the latter.

BANDŌ TAMASABURŌ V, *yago** Yamatoya. 1950- . The adopted son of Morita Kanya XIV*, he debuted as Bandō Kinoji in December 1957 and took his present name in June 1964. He is one of the bright hopes among the young *onnagata** stars. Besides his old-fashioned face, which is just right for female parts, his acting shows great comprehension and he possesses the quality of boldness. His beauty and youth have propelled him to high popularity, and he is given one great role after another. In recent years he has garnered success as a Shakespearean star in parts such as Lady Macbeth.

BANDŌ YAENOSUKE I, *yago** Otowaya. 1909- . He debuted as the disciple of Nakamura Fukusuke IV in 1915, became a pupil of Bandō Hikosaburō VI* in 1924, and took his present name during the same year. He is very active as the fight choreographer and teacher *(tateshi*)* in the Kikugorō troupe, and his art has been designated an Important Intangible National Treasure.

BANDŌ YAGORŌ II, *yago** Yamatoya. 1909- . Born in Tokyo, he debuted in 1920, was a pupil of Morita Kanya XIII*, Sawamura Sōjūrō VII*, and Morita Kanya XIV*, and became Yagorō in 1941. He is a clever actor who is never wanting in supporting roles.

BANTACHI. A low-ranking actor who performed a daily dance of "purification" at three or four in the morning, when a theatre opened for the day. The subject of the dance dealt with the character Sanbasō*, still popular in dances bearing his name. *Bantachi* was also used to refer to the daily *Sanbasō* performance itself.

BANZUI CHŌBEI SHŌJIN NO MANAITA. Sakurada Jisuke I*. Also called *Manaita no Chōbei. Sewamono**. Four acts. August 1803, Nakamura-za*, Edo.

One of the many plays dealing with the famous Edo "street knight" *(otokodate)*, Banzui Chōbei. He was famed for helping the weak and standing up to the powerful. As was common in Kabuki playwriting, liberties were taken with the facts that the drama was based on. Gonpachi and Chōbei lived in different eras, but Kabuki was fond of intertwining their stories. Legend considers them to have been homosexual lovers. In the original production, Matsumoto Kōshirō V* played Chōbei, Nakayama Tomisaburō was Komurasaki, and Bandō Mitsugorō III* acted Shirai Gonpachi.

Shirai Gonpachi, supporter of Chōbei, has fallen deeply in love with the Yoshiwara courtesan, Komurasaki. Her client, Teranishi Kanshin, wants to purchase her bond, thereby redeeming her from her indenture, but she does not want to go with him. She elopes, therefore, with Gonpachi, and the pair take refuge at Chōbei's home. On their way back from a visit to the temple at Asakusa, Chōbei's son, Chōmatsu, and his apprentice quarrel with Teranishi's apprentice, Dotesuke, and wound him. Teranishi carries Dotesuke to Chōbei's home and falsely blames him for what has happened. Chōbei places his son on a huge chopping block *(manaita)* and sets this before Teranishi, telling him he may freely partake of this "meal." Teranishi now realizes Chōbei's true feelings and bestows upon him the miraculous sword for which Gonpachi has been searching.

BANZUKE. Program booklets in which plays were advertised and described. They contained a synopsis of the story and the cast list. *Banzuke* were first produced for *kaomise** performances. They were followed by the printing of poster programs *(tsuji banzuke)*, programs depicting the actor's crests *(mon banzuke* or *yakuwari banzuke)*, and picturebook programs *(ehon banzuke)*. The pattern differed from one period and region to another, but the basic program form was fixed in the mid-eighteenth century and continued up to the Meiji era. The modern program serves the same basic function.

kaomise banzuke. A program published for the annual *kaomise* performances. Besides listing the actors for the coming season, it provided the audience with the names of the chanters, the musicians, the choreographers, the playwrights, and so on. It was also called *yakushazuke, tsurazuke,* and *kiwamari banzuke.* The form varied from one major city to another. Edo used a large single sheet that was divided in two; the upper half contained names, and the lower half displayed a group picture of the acting company. The name section itself was divided in two; its upper half listed the newly hired personnel, while the lower gave the names of those members from the previous year's company who were back again. Also, the four chief *onnagata** were listed to the left and right of the manager's name. Small print above each actor's name gave his role type and acting specialty. The group picture showed the troupe leader *(zagashira*)* in the center; to his left and right were the chief *onnagata (tate onnagata*)* and the second-ranking *onnagata* (*see also* ACTORS' RANKS). Surrounding the troupe leader were the lower-ranking male-role actors *(tachiyaku*)*, the actors of villain roles *(katakiyaku*)*, and the like. The whole arrangement was fixed by tradition. Such *kaomise* programs were produced from the Kanbun era (1661-72) to the late Edo era. Kamigata programs had no group picture; they printed only the actors' names.

tsuji banzuke. Also called *tsuji bira*, these were Kabuki poster programs put up at city junctions *(tsuji)*, bathhouses, barber shops, and other gathering places. They consisted of one large sheet. The title was written in bold characters in the upper right-hand corner. The rest of the poster was in two parts, an upper and a lower. The upper portion was filled with illustrations of each scene in the play. Running along the bottom were the names of the actors. (Remember that Japanese writing runs in vertical columns.) At the extreme right was the name of the *kakidashi** actor, followed (to the left) by that of the supporting male role actors *(nimaime*)* or *onnagata.** In the central position was the name of the *nakajiku** (a star equal in prestige to the *zagashira**). At the extreme left side was the name of the *zagashira* himself. To his right was the *tate onnagata*'s name. All other actors' names were placed within the framework provided by *zagashira, nakajiku,* and *kakidashi,* in an alternating pattern based on troupe rank. Thus, before (to the right of) the *nakajiku*'s name was that of the actor closest in rank to the *kakidashi,* and following the *nakajiku*'s name was that of the actor closest in rank to the *zagashira.* The form deteriorated at the end of the Meiji era, when the posters were used to publish the cast lists of each act at the same time. Following the Taishō era (1912-26), *tsuji banzuke* gradually developed into the modern poster.

yakuwari banzuke. A program listing the actors' ranks, the play's title, the cast list, and so forth. As it displayed the actors' crests* *(mon),* it also was called a *mon banzuke; tōshi banzuke* ("straight-through" program) was yet another name for it. In Edo the form consisted of a three-sheet, bound, rice-paper booklet; the actors' names and crests were on the first sheet. These were listed so that their respective ranks could be discerned. Sheet two had the full titles of the main plays of the day, the titles of the acts, and the title of the narrative dance *(jōruri*)* to be performed. The third sheet contained, besides the cast list, the names of the playwrights, chanters, and *shamisen** players. In the Kamigata area these programs were mostly of a single sheet; in addition to carrying the cast list and titles, they usually printed names of the playwrights and chanters.

The accompanying chart duplicates the arrangement on page one of a typical *yakuwari banzuke* from the Edo period. It is derived from the program for the February 1805 performances at Edo's Nakamura-za*. In each box appears the crest and name of a specific actor in the cast. The topmost box in the center column contains the crest of the theatre itself. The large box beneath it gives the crest and name of the theatre's manager *(zamoto*).* The boxes on the sides give the names of each actor arranged by rank. The ranks begin with the troupe leader *(zagashira*)* and chief female impersonator *(tate onnagata*)* and descend in order as follows, *sanmaime*, yonmaime, gomaime, rokumaime, shichimaime, hachimaime, kyumaime, jūmaime, jūichimaime, jūnimaime, jūsanmaime, jūyonmaime, jūgomaime,* and *jūrokumaime.* The terms *tachiyaku** and *katakiyaku** refer to role types. Actors specializing in either one of these types might be placed in boxes bearing both terms. The names of lesser ranked actors in the company were printed on the rear of this page. In the chart, C represents "crest"; O, *"onnagata"*; T, *"tachiyaku"*; and K, *"katakiyaku."*

C *yonmaime* O	C *nimaime* O	theatre crest	C *tate* O	C *sanmaime* O
C *yonmaime* T-K	C *nimaime* T-K	*zamoto* crest and name	C *zagashira*	C *sanmaime* T-K
C *hachimaime* T-K	C *rokumaime* T-K		C *gomaime* T-K	C *shichimaime* T-K
C *jūnimaime* T-K	C *jūmaime* T-K		C *kyumaime* T—K	C *jūichimaime* T-K
C *jūrokumaime* T-K	C *jūyonmaime* T-K	C This box called *geta bako* (shoe box). *Yonmaime* T-K and others of similar rank.	C *jūsanmaime* T-K	C *jūgomaime* T-K

ehon banzuke. Also called *e banzuke,* these programs pictured the story of the play. They were booklets made of a special rice paper *(kogiku)* and consisting of six to ten sheets. They pictured each act from prologue to climax and printed the chief role names, the actors' names, and a simple explanation of the plot. Originally they were painted by famous artists, but in later years they were drawn rather roughly. The *ehon banzuke* were produced from the Kyōhō era (1716-35) to the Meiji, but were later merged with the *yakuwari banzuke* to become the *sujiyaki* ("synopses") *banzuke.*

BAREN. A gold and silver fringelike apron worn on the *yoten** costume by valorous role types. It is worn also by sumo wrestlers on their ornamental aprons. Characters wearing the *baren* include the bandits in pantomimes *(danmari*)* and the *gochūshin** soldier in the *Moritsuna Jinya* scene of *Ōmi Genji Senjin Yakata**. It also is a part of the *date sagari** costume worn by footmen.

BATABATA. A technique of beating the wooden clappers *(tsuke*)* to accentuate certain moments in the acting of history plays, dance plays, and classical domestic dramas. It is used for highly conventional pieces of acting, such as *mie** poses, fight scenes *(tachimawari*)*, and running scenes, especially when characters come dashing in on the *hanamichi**.

BATTARI. A double beat of the *tsuke** used to emphasize *mie** poses.

BENGARA GUMA. A makeup style devised by Ichikawa Danjūrō I*, this is the name of the *kumadori** formerly worn by Kamakura Gongorō, the leading character in the *aragoto** play *Shibaraku**. Gongorō originally had his hands, feet, and face painted in bright red ochre *(bengara)*, thus giving this style its name. *Bengara* has been replaced by the *suji guma** style.

BENI GUMA. Any *kumadori** makeup style using the *abura beni** cosmetic on a white base. Such styles as *ippon guma**, *suji guma**, *kaen guma*, and *saru guma** belong to the *beni guma* category.

BENI ITA. A beautifully covered, rectangular pocket compact of lacquered metal or cardboard into which rouge has been compressed. To use it, the actor licks a fingertip, rubs the rouge, and applies it to his lips.

BILLBOARDS. *See* KANBAN.

BIN. The sidelocks of a wig. Many wigs take their names from the style of their *bin*. There is the *kuruma bin**, for example, which resembles the spokes of a carriage's wheels *(kuruma)*; the square shaped "box," or *hako bin*; the *fukashi bin*, which are puffed out *(fukashi)* and rounded, and the *ita bin**, which are stiffly pomaded and pressed flat like boards *(ita)*. There also are such styles as the *yahazu bin**, or "arrow feather" style, and the *hishi kawa**, or "boar bristle" style. Wigs classified by their side locks are called by the general term of *bin mono*. (*See also* WIGS.)

BINTSUKE ABURA. Also called *kata abura* or simply *bintsuke*, this is a condensed oil or pomade applied to the side locks of the wig to prevent their coming undone. It often is used to give the finishing touch to Kabuki wigs. *Bintsuke abura* is also an indispensable item for making the silk *habutae** cloth, which is worn under the wig, stick to the head. This material serves a variety of makeup purposes, including the obliteration of the actor's natural eyebrows. (*See also* MAYU TSUBUSHI.)

BIRASHITA. "Under the bill"; complimentary tickets attached to posters displayed for small theatres. They are to be used by those who display the posters.

BITA. A word formed by reversing the syllables in *tabi* ("travel"). It refers to touring troupes.

BLACKMAIL SCENES. *Yusuriba*, or "extortion scenes," were a conventional type found in domestic plays: A villain or a gang of villains attempts to take advantage of someone's weakness by blackmailing him for money. These scenes flourished in the popular *shiranami mono* ("robber plays*") of the late Edo period. They were included in most domestic plays, in which they were considered among the major scenes. *Yusuriba* were the forte of Kawatake Mokuami*, who inserted them in various complex plots. Examples are the *Hamamatsuya* scene of *Aotozōshi Hana no Nishikie**, the *Genyadana* shop scene of *Yowa Nasake Ukina no Yokogushi**, and the *Iseya* shop scene of *Kanzen Chōaku Nozoki no Karikura.*

BOATS. Kabuki uses two main types of boats, or *fune*, in its stage settings; one kind is solidly built on a large scale and covers the entire stage; the other type, which is seen in dance dramas like *Sanja Matsuri**, *Inazuma*, and *Noriaibune**, is built as a cutout *(kiridashi*)* and has many variations. In *Hakata Kojōrō Nami Makura** the boat is a huge, solidly constructed one, set before a backdrop of the sea with a wave cloth *(nami nuno*; see* JIGASURI) spread on the floor beneath it. With the aid of the revolving stage* and trap doors, the boat seems to sway; when the stage is rotated ninety degrees, the boat turns from a side position so that it faces forward, its prow aiming at the audience. The boat in *Hachijin Shugo no Honjō** also looks as though it were moving. Boasting a red-lacquered cabin, the latter is called the "royal boat" *(gozabune)* because of the feudal lords and nobles who ride it. Pleasure boats have *shōji* rooms built on them. The *choki*, a flat-bottomed boat, has a pointed prow and is seen passing swiftly through the Yoshiwara pleasure quarters. At the end of *Shinpan Utazaemon** a boat is pulled offstage down the *hanamichi** by a rope, just as if it were on water; wheels are attached to its bottom to make it move easily. *(See also* SCENERY.)

BŌDARA. "Dried cod," a term used to describe a dull and untalented actor. (*See also* DAIKO.)

BON. "Tray"; refers to the shape of the revolving stage*. Also called *mawashi.*

BON KYŌGEN. During the Edo era, plays performed in July or August. It was the custom to open the summer season on July 7, the day of the Festival of the Weaver, but this occasionally was postponed to a later date, often in August. Many *bon kyōgen* were "water plays" *(mizu kyōgen*)* in which real water was used, ghost plays*, and revenge plays*; the latter two varieties

Kezori the bandit poses dramatically at the prow of his pirate ship in *Hakata Kojōrō Nami Makura**. Kezori, Onoe Shōroku II*. *Courtesy of Waseda University Tsubouchi Engeki Hakubutsukan (Tsubouchi Memorial Theatre Museum).*

employed an abundance of quick changes and other stage trickery to delight the audience. (*See also* SUMMER PLAYS; THEATRE MANAGEMENT.)

BONTEN. "Brahma-Deva," the religious offerings placed on either side of the *yagura** or drum tower that was formerly situated in front of Kabuki theatres; they were so placed in order to invite the protection of the gods for theatrical entertainments. They no longer were seen in Edo following the Kyōhō era (1716-35), but remained until a later date in the Kamigata region.

BŌSHIBARI. Okamura Shikō*. *Shosagoto**. *Nagauta**. January 1916. Ichimura-za*, Tokyo.

A Kabuki version of a Kyōgen play of the same name. The play's first cast consisted of Bandō Mitsugorō VII* as Tarō, Onoe Kikugorō VI* as Jirō, and Nakamura Kichiemon I* as the master. Kikugorō and Mitsugorō were so effective in this dance piece, for which they created the choreography, that they often appeared in it together in later years.

A feudal lord has departed, leaving his servants Tarō and Jirō tied to poles to prevent them from drinking his sake during his absence. Through various ingenious actions, the servants open the cask and drink all the wine. They then proceed to perform a lively dance. The master returns and, seeing his drunken servants, chases after them.

BUAI. A theatre that operates on a profit-sharing basis, giving actors and other theatre personnel a fixed percentage of the moneys earned at the box office. (*See also* BUKŌGYŌ.)

BUKKAERI. A quick-change technique, similar to the *hikinuki**. When certain threads of the costume's upper half are pulled out, it falls around the actor's waist so that the inside lining covers the lower half of the costume. The inner lining matches the top that is revealed when the threads are pulled, giving the impression that the whole costume has been changed. *Bukkaeri* is a powerful stage effect used when a disguised character reveals his true identity. Ghosts or spirits that have been masquerading as living persons employ it when the moment arrives for them to display their real natures. The technique is performed by Narukami in *Narukami**, Sasaki Takatsuna in *Kamakura Sandaiki**, Sadatō in *Ōshū Adachigahara**, and Sekibei in *Seki no To**. (*See also* HAYAGAWARI; COSTUMES.)

BUKŌGYŌ. A method, also called *bushibai,* by which the profits of a production were divided up among two or more investors according to the size of their investments. The investors in an Edo period production were called either *bukata* or *bumochi.* There also was a profit-sharing system called *sōbu* at small theatres where one production was no more important

The *bukkaeri** costume change technique illustrated by the role of Hayakumo no Ōji in *Narukami Fudō Kitayama Sakura. Courtesy of Waseda University Tsubouchi Engeki Hakubutsukan (Tsubouchi Memorial Theatre Musuem).*

than any other and the personnel were not on a fixed wage scale; here the profits were divided among everyone. (*See also* BUAI; THEATRE MANAGEMENT.)

BUNGO BUSHI. A narrative music style *(joruri*)* founded by Miyakoji Bungonojō (1660?-1740), who, as Miyakokunidayū Hanchu, had been the pupil of Kyoto's Miyakodayū Itchū (1650-1724) (*see also* ITCHŪ BUSHI). Together with his main disciples, Bungonojō moved to Edo late in the Kyōhō era (1716-35). Many of his narratives were lovers' suicide pieces; being rather passionate and suggestive, they were extremely popular. However, because they were considered a corrupting influence on public morals, *bungo bushi* was banned in 1739. Many narrative pieces were created in this style. *Bungo bushi* is used as a generic term for such styles as the *tokiwazu** created by Mojidayū, Bungonojō's disciple; the *tomimoto** of Komojidayū; and the *kiyomoto** that arose from the *tomimoto* school.

BUNRAKU MAWASHI. A small revolving stage set into a raised platform at stage left and used when a chanter and *shamisen** player are brought on; seen in plays derived from the puppet theatre, from which Kabuki borrowed the device. (*See also* YUKA; CHOBO.)

BUROMAIDO. "Bromide"; photographs of actors. Photography arrived in Japan during the late Edo era and actors soon were having their pictures taken in makeup and costume. Around 1887 the Moriyama Photographic Emporium opened in Shintomi-chō and the Genroku Emporium began operations in Kobiki-chō. Photographs of actors sold widely later, when the Shunyōdō and Kamigata-ya began to print collotype pictures; at the end of the Meiji period the wood-block prints of actors that had been so popular had nearly sunk into oblivion. After the great earthquake of 1923, photographic illustrations produced directly from the original plates became the fashion instead of collotypes. Most theatres today have flourishing stalls selling actors' photos. (*See also* SHIBAI E.)

BUTAI. The stage and its environs. (*See also* THEATRE ARCHITECTURE.)

BUTAI BAN. "Stage guard," a functionary who maintained order inside the Edo period playhouses. He wore a colorful costume to attract attention, piled up *tatami* mats on stage left, sat on top of them, and kept watch over the spectators in the auditorium. The *butai ban* also saw the actors off and greeted them on their return to the theatre.

BUTAI BANA. The front edge of the stage where it meets the auditorium.

BUTAI GAKI. Information found at the beginning of a playscript pertaining to the nature and disposition of the scenery. Edo scripts usually began with "An eighteen-foot-wide stage on which is set. . ." *(honbutai sanken no aida . . .)*, while Kamigata plays started with "The set pieces are . . ." *(tsukurimono . . .)*.

BUTAI GA MAWARU. "The stage revolves"; an expression used to explain that the revolving stage* has changed the scene and a new set of characters will now appear.

BUTAI URA. "Behind the stage"; the empty areas behind and to the left and right of the stage set—that is, the wings. The word varies in meaning and may be used to refer to the entire backstage* area, including the dressing rooms, or to only the area within the confines of the stage house that is not seen by the audience.

BUTA O AKERU. "The lid is open"; meaning that the show has begun. This term derives from the box-shaped entranceway of old-time theatres.

BUTSUDAN GAESHI. A trick stage device for aiding the appearance and disappearance of ghosts and spirits. It is a wheel hidden behind a Buddhist altar *(butsudan)* at the rear of the set. The wheel is large enough for an actor to be attached to it; depending on which direction the wheel is rotated, the actor can be made to appear or disappear through the wall. It is seen in *Tōkaidō Yotsuya Kaidan**.

BUYŌ. *See* DANCE.

BYAKU ROKU. Also called *ichidan*, this is an oblong scenic element, three to four feet wide, about ten inches high, and eleven inches deep. It is used as a step for access to and from the *tsune ashi* type of *nijū** platform.

C

CALLIGRAPHIC STYLES. *See* KANTEI RYŪ, TOKICHI RYŪ.

CHAKUTŌ ITA. "Arrival board," an employees' attendance record. It is a wooden board on which the names of the actors scheduled to perform are written; above each name is a small hole. When the actor arrives backstage, he puts a bamboo peg into the hole above his name. The *chakutō ita* is placed near the backstage entrance in the room used by the *tōdori**, or "backstage manager"; from this record he can learn exactly which actors have arrived at the theatre.

CHANI MUKURI. Said when an actor's words get tangled and he ruins a speech; used mainly in the Kamigata area.

CHANRIN. Excessive flattery expressed to a theatre person.

CHARIBA. A scene of comic relief. An example occurs in the *Terakoya* act of *Sugawara Denju Tenarai Kagami**, when Yodarekuri mimics the acting of the sad scene during which Chiyo leaves her son at the school, knowing he will be sacrificed.

CHASEN MAGE. A topknot shaped like the whisk used in the tea ceremony. The *hajiki chasen**, a version with the tip of the topknot flowing down behind the head, is worn both by young samurai before they have attained the ceremony marking manhood and by samurai-in-training. The *bō chasen*, the topknot standing erect, is seen on feudal lords in history plays. A paper cord *(motoyui)* is tied at the middle of the topknot and a little bit of hair protrudes at the end. The *mae jasen** is the opposite of the *hajiki chasen* and is a topknot that lies low toward the front of the head: it is worn by amorous *nimaime** characters and policemen in the history plays. The *nō chasen* is modeled after the wigs worn in the Nō theatre during the Edo period.

CHIECHIE KOMU. To be in a state of confusion and hurry.

CHIHAYA. A magnificent sleeveless coat worn over the simulated chain mail called *suami**. It is worn by messengers reporting from the battlefields *(gochūshin*)* or by brave warriors confronting the enemy.

CHIKAGORO KAWARA NO TATEHIKI. Tamegawa Sōsuke, Tsutsui Hanji, Nagawa Shimesuke. Also called *Oshun Denpei, Horikawa. Sewamono**. *Jōruri**. Three acts. January 1782. Geki-za, Edo.

Not much is known about the first productions of this play. It is based on an actual love suicide carried out in the seventeenth century. The Kabuki version came relatively late, when it was produced at Osaka's Naka no Shibai as *Sarumawashi Kado De no Hitofushi* in 1807; it soon became a staple of the repertory.

Izutsuya Denpei is in love with the courtesan Oshun. Because his rival—the evil samurai Yokofuchi Kanzaemon—has swindled Denpei out of 300 *ryō*, the two men get into a fight. As a result, Denpei kills his enemy and becomes a fugitive from justice. Meanwhile, Oshun is sent to her home in Horikawa, where her blind mother lives in poverty with Oshun's elder brother Yojirō, a monkey trainer. Aware that Denpei may come to Horikawa seeking Oshun, Yojirō is resolved to prevent the lovers from meeting; he fears that they will seek to commit double suicide. Denpei comes to the house at night and, after a series of complications, convinces Yojirō and his mother of the depth of his relationship with Oshun. They are sent off into the night, disguised as monkey trainers, after drinking a symbolic cup of water signifying their marriage. It is clear that they will resolve their problems by suicide.

The lamentation scene* *(kudoki)* in which Oshun's heart is laid bare is famous. The play beautifully depicts Yojirō's simple filial piety and his love for his mother and sister as well as Oshun's and Denpei's love for each other. Perhaps the most charming scene in the play is when Yojirō has his monkeys perform (puppets are used) as the lovers enact their nuptial rites.

CHIKAMATSU HANJI. 1725-1783. A puppet theatre playwright, he was the son of the Confucianist Hozumi Ikan, who was associated with the Takemoto-za puppet theatre and had been a friend of Chikamatsu Monzaemon*. Hanji wrote plays for about twenty years, from the late Hōreki period (1751-63) to the Tenmei (1781-89) era, leaving about fifty works behind. He adapted Kabuki methods, and his plays, which are known for their magnificent stage effects, are written in a highly skillful manner. At the time, the puppet theatre was beginning to topple from its position of great popularity as Kabuki gradually overtook it; with Hanji's activity, it managed a brief revival. Hanji is said to have been the last great puppet theatre playwright. His outstanding plays include *Imoseyama Onna Teikin**, *Honchō Nijūshikō**, *Ōmi Genji Senjin Yakata**, *Ōshū Adachigahara** and *Igagoe Dōchū Sugoroku**, most of which were made into Kabuki plays. Many of these hold a position of great importance in today's repertoire.

CHIKAMATSU MONZAEMON. 1653-1724. A puppet theatre and Kabuki playwright. His real name was Suginomori Nobumori, but he assumed several other names, including that by which he is best known. He was the son of a samurai retainer of Echizen and, after his childhood, went to the Kamigata area, where he served as a page to a feudal lord. Although facts about his youth are vague, he appears to have been educated by temple priests. In 1675 he became a writer of puppet plays under the guidance of Uji Kaganojō (1635-1711), a famous chanter who performed in the dry bed of the Kamo River in Kyoto. In 1683 Chikamatsu wrote *Yotsugi no Soga* and in 1685 created *Shusse Kagekiyo* for another famous chanter, Takemoto Gidayū* (1651-1714; *see also* GIDAYŪ BUSHI). These works firmly established him as a writer. Thereafter, until his death at seventy-two, he wrote about one hundred puppet plays and more than thirty for Kabuki. His Kabuki work was confined mainly to the years 1693-1704; he specialized in writing for a great actor, Sakata Tōjūrō*.

CHIKAMATSU TOKUSŌ. 1751-1810. A puppet theatre playwright and disciple of Chikamatsu Hanji*. Specializing in domestic plays, he dramatized news events, novels, and stories, rewrote old plays, and helped originate a new style of Kamigata Kabuki. His best works include *Ise Ondo Koi no Netaba** and *Meisaku Kiri Kono Akebono.*

CHIKARA GAMI. "Strong paper," a high-quality paper folded in the shape of large wings and used to tie the base of the topknot on the wigs worn by such characters as Gongorō in *Shibaraku**, Matsuomaru in the *Terakoya* scene of *Sugawara Denju Tenarai Kagami**, and Goemon in *Sanmon Gosan no Kiri**. It signifies the strength and masculinity of the samurai wearing it.

CHILDREN'S ROLES. Child actors and their roles are called *koyaku.* There are many roles in which one character must substitute for another *(migawari mono*)*; even though these are children's roles, considerable acting power must be displayed. Children from famous acting families play the best *koyaku* roles, but are not used for such minor parts as animals, groups of dancing children, or the schoolchildren in the *Terakoya* scene of *Sugawara Denju Tenarai Kagami**. Such parts are called *dakoyaku.* It has been the custom since the old days for *koyaku* to be trained in elocution and movement by the *onnagata**; thus, they have a distinctive manner about them on the stage.

The wicked spider fights its samurai attackers in *Tsuchigumo**. Note the weblike paper *(chisuji no ito*)* used by the spider. *Courtesy of Waseda University Tsubouchi Engeki Hakubutsukan (Tsubouchi Memorial Theatre Museum).*

CHISUJI NO ITO. "One thousand strings of thread," the threads spun by the spider in *Tsuchigumo**. They are made of thin, finely cut, rolled papers of the kind used as wicks for incense; the actor holds these curled up in his palm and then flings them about. They used to be prepared by a disciple of the actor playing the spider, but are now made by the property man *(kodōgu kata)*. Another term for them is *kumo no suso* ("spider's cobwebs").

CHIWATA. "Blood cotton," a cotton garment that occasionally is used to represent blood. It is worn by characters who are wounded in battle. When some of its threads are pulled out, an outer cloth falls off, revealing a bright red cotton, symbolizing blood. This highly stylized device, which is never used in realistic scenes, is utilized in *Suzugamori**. A slightly more realistic technique is called *chinori.*

CHOBO. The performers of *gidayū bushi**, who sit on a small platform at stage left or in a rattan-screened booth as they accompany the action of plays derived from the puppet theatre. The *gidayū* musicians relate the emotional states of the characters, and the actors recite the lines of dialogue. The *gidayū* also present narrative passages. The *gidayū* master *(tayū*)* marks in red the narrative passages in the script that he uses on stage with the notation *"chobo chobo,"* so the word *chobo* has come to refer to the *shamisen** player and chanter who comprise a *chobo* team. (*See also* YUKA,)

CHŌBUKU. To curse. Also, to do whatever one can to cause trouble for other actors on the stage.

CHŌKEN. Originally one of the formal costumes worn by nobles in Nō plays, it is a robe worn mainly by women in dances. The *chōken* is a silk, unlined kimono *(hitoe)* with the sides left open and with a long cord attached to the breast. *Azuma Bune* is one of the works in which it is seen.

CHŌMOTO. An Edo period theatre worker whose job encompassed many aspects of production; the general managers *(gekijō shihainin)* in today's theatres are comparable to him. He also may have acted as proxy for the manager *(zamoto*)*, procured money for the production, hired actors, settled the accounts, superintended the auditorium, and so on. (*See also* THEATRE MANAGEMENT.)

CHONCHON. The two final beats of the *hyōshigi** that are heard at the end of a production. An onomatopoeic expression.

CHŪ NIKAI. The second floor of dressing rooms in Edo theatres. Although the government forbade the erection of three-story theatres, the dressing

*Chūnori**, the *keren** technique of flying through the air used by the fox in *Yoshitsune Senbon Zakura**. Kitsune-Tadanobu, Ichikawa Ennosuke III*. *Courtesy of Waseda University Tsubouchi Engeki Hakubutsukan (Tsubouchi Memorial Theatre Museum).*

rooms were built in three stories, but evaded the prohibition by calling the second floor a "mezzanine" *(chū nikai)*. The term eventually came to be used for the lower-ranking *onnagata** who used the communal dressing room on this floor. Corresponding to them were the lower-ranking male-role actors called *sangai**, or "third floor." (*See also* ACTORS' RANKS; THEATRE ARCHITECTURE; BACKSTAGE.)

CHŪNORI. "Flying"; called *chūzuri* in the Kamigata area. It is a production technique by which a magical creature or ghost is made to fly through the air. A metal fitting on the actor's costume is fastened to a wire that lifts him off the stage and into the air over the *hanamichi** and sections of the auditorium. There used to be a delightful technique by which a character would be dropped from the air into a pool of real water. However, since this required special acrobatic skill and since such "trick" *(keren*)* plays fell out of favor some years back, Kabuki stages have been altered, making it rather difficult to perform such feats. The fox spirit in *Yoshitsune Senbon Zakura** provides a well-known example of *chūnori*. Dance plays such as *Modori Bashi** and *Hagoromo** also make use of it.

CHŪYAMONO. Someone in a traveling company who makes trouble or is dishonest.

CLAPPERS. *See* HYŌSHIGI; TSUKE.

COMIC ROLES. *See* DŌKEGATA.

COSTUMES. Known as *ishō*. Kabuki's three prime aesthetic elements are beauty of form, beauty of music, and beauty of color. Costumes and makeup contribute much to the important element of color beauty. The abundant variety of Kabuki's costume colors provides a veritable feast of hues. Even with a simple costume ensemble—an under and outer kimono, over which an *uchikake** robe, *kamishimo** formal vestments, or *haori** jacket is worn—there is a display of both variety and harmony among the respective patterns, colors, and styles. Further, variety and harmony are always preserved among all the costumes that may be worn in any one scene. Over the many years in which Kabuki plays have been performed, numerous creative costume ideas have accumulated.

Costumes, makeup, and wigs have a fixed style for each classical role. These conventional forms—like those of acting, production, and mechanical techniques—are called *kata**. For example, there is the *kata* for the role of the pre-Edo-period princess *(akahime*)* who figures in tales dealing with events occuring in medieval Japan; she always wears a red kimono and *fukiwa** style of wig. Conspirators wear the *ende** wig, evil men paint their faces red, lords wear the standing-collar robe called *omigoromo**, and so forth. Therefore, one can understand the nature of a particular character by examining his stage appearance. This is one of the most characteristic elements of the Kabuki art form.

Kabuki adapted, with great creativity, many of the artistic methods already perfected by the Nō, Kyōgen, and puppet theatre forms. It also assimilated almost everything that it could from the culture of the Edo period, within which it grew and developed as a theatre form. Of course, each social class of the Edo period was dressed appropriately when depicted on the stage, as were the characters from pre-Edo times. However, the method was not realistic, but stylized. This was especially true of the roles played in Edo's unique bravura style, *aragoto**. Although the female population of Edo had a marked influence on the costumes and wigs worn by Kabuki's female impersonators, it also is true that Kabuki costumes and styles often created great fads among the townspeople.

It is clear, then, that costumes play an invaluable role in Kabuki's spectacle and formal beauty; many of these costumes are recognized for their exquisite taste. In fact, the shogunate government of the Edo period, fearful that the lower classes might assume prerogatives reserved for their superiors, published numerous edicts and sumptuary laws designed to force the actors to diminish the splendor of their costumes. The custom at the time was for each actor to supply his own costume; this practice led to a stimulating competition among the better-paid actors to be the best-dressed actor on stage.

Performers were extremely conscious of the role played by color variety in Kabuki's aesthetic scheme; they paid careful attention to the relation between the outermost kimono *(kitsuke*)* and the overgarment *(uchikake)* and to the colors of the entire ensemble, including the undergarments. This is particularly evident in those scenes in which, one kimono being worn over the other, they are removed one by one with the aid of stage assistants, revealing a dazzling array of beauty. Kabuki often resorts to onstage costume changes and has several special techniques for helping the actor to make a complete or partial costume change quickly (*see also* HIKINUKI; BUKKAERI).

In some instances, audiences may witness an array of costumes representing both commoners and nobles at the same time. This indicates Kabuki's disregard for chronological accuracy or social class and its ability to choose the widest scope of possibilities. Even though they often show little regard for common sense, the diverse Kabuki costumes have achieved a marvelous quality of make-believe.

COURTESAN KABUKI. An early form of Kabuki growing out of the performances originated by Izumo no Okuni*, this was called *yūjo kabuki.*

CRITICISM. Known in Japan as *gekihyō*. It is common today for theatre critics to discuss their ideas in newspapers and magazines, as well as on television and the radio. The Edo period method of criticism, however, was embodied in annual critiques called the *yakusha hyōbanki**, which have a long history. The establishment of modern theatre criticism in Japan was pioneered during the Meiji period by Aeba Kōson and Jōno Saigiku. Other noted newspaper critics of the time were Okamoto Kidō*, Matsui Shōyō, Sugi Gan'ami, Oka Onitarō*, and Ihara Seiseien, all of whom were major litrary figures. Theatre criticism gained great prestige with the positivistic criticism of Miki Takeji and was furthered in its development by Tsubouchi Shōyō*, Mori Ōgai, and Osanai Kaoru. Miyake Shūtarō appeared in the Taishō era (1912-26) and endeavored to modernize theatre criticism even further.

CROPPED-HAIR PLAYS. *See* ZANGIRI MONO.

CURTAINS. A vital feature of Kabuki production, they are called *maku*. A number of different kinds of curtains are used, including the traveler show curtain *(jōshiki maku** or *hiki maku*)*, the drop curtain *(donchō; see also* DONCHŌ YAKUSHA), the *kuro maku**, and the *anten maku*. The *dōgu* ("property") *maku** is used to tie scenes together. It often has a landscape painted on it, although some depict *ajirobei** wicker fences, waves, mountains, clouds, or snow. When a scene ends, the appropriate *dōgu* curtain drops from above and covers the scenery (using the *furikabuse** method). When preparations for the succeeding scene are completed, the curtain falls swiftly by the *furiotoshi* technique (*see also* FURIDAKE), allowing the play to proceed. The *asagi maku* is a pale blue curtain that operates on the same principle. It may be employed for daytime scenes to contrast with the black curtain *(kuro maku)* representing night. Besides its use as an aid in scene changing, it is often hung behind the regular traveler curtain and, following that curtain's opening, is dropped suddenly (by the *furiotoshi* technique), creating a dazzling effect as the scenery is revealed. Kabuki's big, red and white striped *dandara maku** is used the same way.

The hanging border curtains over the stage, which hide the mechanical works on the stage grid, are the *mizuhiki** and *ichimonji**. Both borders and tormentors are black.

Other curtains include the small, hand-held "disappearance curtain" or *keshi maku**; the *kasumi maku**, used to hide onstage *jōruri** musicians; and the *agemaku**, which bear the theatre's crest.

D

DAIGANE. A copper framework that acts as the foundation for the actor's wig. It is made to fit the head precisely. The side and back locks and the topknot are affixed to it; or a silk cloth *(habutae*)* with hair sewn on as if it were growing there is attached to it. The *daigane* differs according to the various kinds of wigs. There are *daigane* for male and female wigs. Male-role *daigane* are *kōramono* or not: a *kōramono* has only the sides and back of a wig frame, as opposed to one that covers the entire hair-growing area of the head. The nature of the *daigane* also varies with the type of back-hair arrangement worn. Since the *daigane* forms the basis for the wig, the actor gives it serious consideration. The hairline may require an extreme change in keeping with the role or the actor's appearance; therefore, the making of the wig must be done well in advance, taking care to fit the *daigane* to the actor's head size and to consider his preferences. This is called the *katsura awase*, or "wig fitting." (*See also* WIGS; HABUTAE.)

DAIJIN BASHIRA. The so-called minister's pillar, located in the downstage left corner of a Nō stage; it is also called the *waki bashira**. Kabuki uses the same term to designate the pillar supporting the floor of the raised area on stage left where the chanter and *shamisen** player often sit to accompany certain plays (*see also* CHOBO). The pillar on stage right, incorporated into the structure of the *geza** music room that is found there, is also called *daijin bashira*. The two *daijin bashira* are distinguished from each other by calling them stage left *(kamite*) daijin bashira (kamidaijin* for short*)* and the stage right *(shimote*) daijin bashira (shimodaijin* for short*)*. The imaginary floor line connecting these pillars is the *jōshiki sen** or *daijin dōri*. The painted black panel connecting these pillars at the top of the stage is called the *oranma**. (*See also* THEATRE ARCHITECTURE.)

DAIJO. "Great opening," the *jomaku** or prelude scene of a play taken from the puppet theatre. Used for the more serious of such scenes.

DAIKO(N). "Radish"; a pejorative term describing poor acting. Its etymology is unclear; it may refer to the poor shape of a radish or to its unpleasant taste. (*See also* BŌDARA.)

DAIKYŌJI MUKASHI GOYOMI. Chikamatsu Monzaemon*. Also called *Osan Mohei, Koi Hakke Hashiragoyami.* English title: *The Almanac of Love* (Miyamori). *Sewamono*. Jōruri*. Three acts. Spring 1715. Takemoto-za, Osaka.

A dramatization of the true story of the adultery between Osan and Mohei that is depicted in Saikaku's novel *Kōshoku Gonnin Onna* (1686). Many others also treated the story before this play was written.

Osan, wife of the scroll mounter Isshun—finding herself in need of money to help her mother—approaches the gentle young clerk Mohei, seeking his help. Having access to his master's seal, Mohei uses it to forge a document aimed at gaining the needed money, but he is caught in the act by the craven assistant Sukeemon who reports the matter to Isshun. Mohei is confined to a storehouse and the maid Otama, who tried to intervene in the matter, is ordered to her room. Isshun, however, lusts after the maid and frequently attempts to take advantage of her in her room. She, in turn, is in love with Mohei. Osan, aware of her husband's attempted infidelities, decides to trap him by switching places with Otama. That very night, Mohei steals out of the storehouse and goes to spend the night with Otama. He and Osan discover their fatal error and flee to Mohei's hometown in Tanba. They are finally captured and are about to be executed as adulterers, but are saved at the last moment by Tōgan Oshyō of the Kurotani Temple.

This is one of three tales of adultery by Chikamatsu, the others being *Yari no Gonza Kasane Katabira** and *Horikawa Nami no Tsuzumi**. In these plays Chikamatsu attributes adultery to three causes: money, liquor, and jealousy. Each is a dominating influence in one of the plays. Contemporary attitudes precluded the use of love as an inciting force in such situations. In each case, the adultery occurs accidentally and not by design. A later version of the story has been dramatized by Kema Nanboku; Kawaguchi Shotarō has also written a play on the subject.

DAIMON. "Large crest," a ceremonial dress worn by samurai higher than the fifth rank during the Edo period. Five large family crests are dyed into the material at fixed places; trailing *hakama** trousers are worn with this kimono. It is seen on *daimyō* regardless of the period being depicted. In the prologue of *Kanadehon Chūshingura** it is worn by Wakasanosuke, Hangan, and Moronao. The *daimyō* in *Soga no Taimen** also wear it.

DAKIKO. A doll used to represent a baby. A *dakiko* also is used in *Tōkaidō Yotsuya Kaidan** when a stone image of the deity Jizō is substituted for a baby.

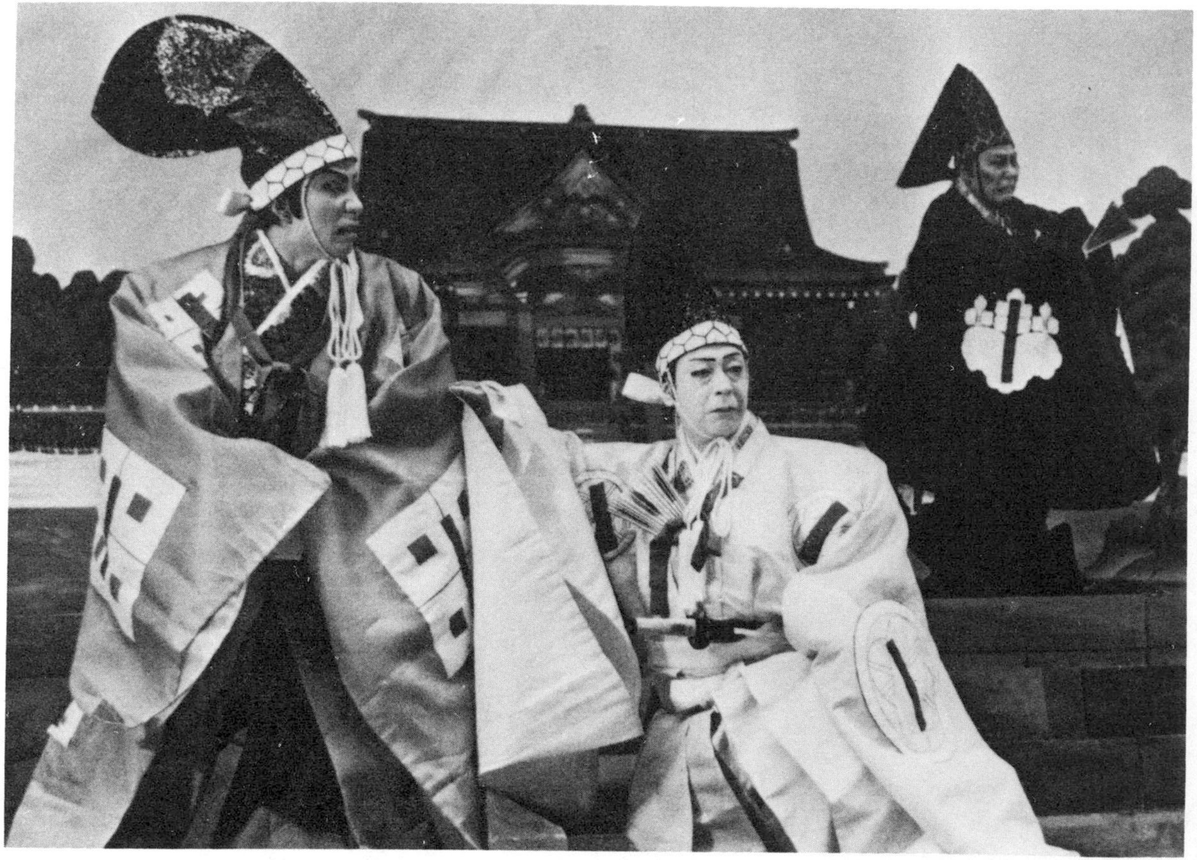

The opening scene of *Kanadehon Chūshingura**, in which the men wear the *daimon** costume. Left to right: Wakasanosuke, Ichikawa Ebizō X*; Hangan, Onoe Baikō VII*; Moronao, Onoe Shōroku II*. *Courtesy of Waseda University Tsubouchi Engeki Hakubutsukan (Tsubouchi Memorial Theatre Museum).*

DAME. "Bad"; a pejorative word used when something is lacking in the acting, production, script, props, music, or some other element of the performance.

DANCE. *Buyō* in Japanese. This word has many meanings in Japan, where there are numerous dance traditions going back to the beginnings of Japanese civilization. Dance is a central element in Kabuki. Kabuki dance *(kabuki buyō)* derived not from the highly polished dances of the Nō theatre, but from the more popular dances known as *nenbutsu odori, kaka odori,* and *yayako odori.* The latter all belong to a tradition known as *furyū odori,* which was extremely popular during the Muromachi period (1392-1568). Kabuki dance was originated during the period of Okuni Kabuki* early in the seventeenth century. It incorporated three principal stylistic features: *mai**, originally referring to a dance with circular movements; *odori**, a term deriving from dances with leaping and jumping; and *furi**, which denotes pantomime gestures. Another important element soon incorporated into Kabuki dance was the travel dance *(michiyuki*)*, which was a very important feature of the puppet theatre dance scenes called *keigoto** (often pronounced *keiji* today). The puppets also contributed a movement style to Kabuki dance; known as *ningyō buri**, it can still be seen in certain old plays.

Kabuki dance first was perfected by *onnagata**, especially during the Genroku (1688-1703) and Kyōhō (1716-35) periods. Such pieces as Ukon Genzaemon's* *Kaidō Sagari,* Mizuki Tatsunosuke's* *Yari Odori* and *Nanabake,* Nakamura Tomijūrō I* and Segawa Kikunojō I's* *Musume Dōjōji*, Shakkyō,* (*see also* SHAKKYŌ MONO), and *Sagi Musume*—nagauta** classics that are still performed—brought the art of *onnagata* dancing to unrivaled peaks. They developed the technique of sleeve and hem movements into uniquely satisfying patterns. Soon, however, male-role actors began to invade the field of Kabuki dance; artists such as Sadoshima Chōgorō appeared in the early eighteenth century and founded new schools of dance. Male-role dancing reached new heights with the appearance of Nakamura Nakazō I* in the same century, and audiences today are still grateful for the works that he introduced, including *Seki no To** and *Modori Kago**.

In the last part of the eighteenth century a new form arose, and it continued to garner popularity throughout the nineteenth century, up to the time of the shogun's downfall. This was the *henge mono* dance, or transformation piece*, a development of the quick-change dances pioneered during the Genroku era by Mizuki Tatsunosuke and Sadoshima Chōgorō. These works required the dancer to appear in several guises during the performance, presenting a display of variety and color. Major performers of the genre were Nakamura Utaemon III* and IV* and Bandō Mitsugorō III*. Later artists in these dances were Nakamura Shikan IV*, Ichikawa Danjūrō IX*, Bandō Mitsugorō VII*, and Onoe Kikugorō VI*.

It was customary for there to be one or two dance scenes in a day's program as well as a dance play performed between the two halves of the program (*see also* NAKAMAKU).

As Kabuki dance developed, so did the music accompanying it. This music is based on the performance of the *shamisen** and includes such styles as *nagauta* and the three main offshoots of *bungo bushi**—*tokiwazu**, *tomimoto**, and *kiyomoto**. Of these, only *tomimoto* is rarely heard, the others being the mainstays of Kabuki dance accompaniment. Occasionally, however, the puppet-theatre-derived style of *gidayū bushi** is employed as dance music.

During the Meiji period Kabuki dance took a new turn, as more and more works were based on the classics of the Nō and Kyōgen theatres. At the same time the theoretical writings of Tsubouchi Shōyō* led to the creation of Kabuki dances that were thought to be more in keeping with the modern temperament; such dances omitted the traditional themes of events transpiring in the pleasure quarters and concentrated less on fantasy and more on psychological realism. Shōyō himself contributed many of the new works that came to be called by the generic term *shin buyō* ("new dance").

Western ideas had a strong influence on the *shin buyō* genre. Many dance masters, not themselves Kabuki actors, began to explore *shin buyō* in new dance groups *(kai)* that they established. *Shin buyō* pieces often are seen on today's Kabuki programs. (*See also* SHOSAGOTO; FURITSUKE.)

DANCE DRAMA. *See* SHOSAGOTO; KEIGOTO; DANCE.

DANDARA MAKU. Also called *dan maku*, a big, red and white, horizontally striped curtain often seen in dance plays. It is hung across the stage during the first part of the dance, as the narrative singing introduces the story; it is then dropped and pulled off stage, revealing the lush scenery to be used for the remainder of the performance. It most commonly is seen in *Musume Dōjōji**. (*See also* CURTAINS.)

DANGIRE. The final musical passage in a dance play. Also the conclusion of the third act of a play derived from the puppet theatre. (*See also* GEZA: MUSICAL ACCOMPANIMENT CHART.)

DANGO O KUU. "To eat dumplings"; an expression signifying moments when an actor's words get fouled up and he puffs his cheeks in exasperation.

DAN-KIKU-SA. Ichikawa Danjūrō IX*, Onoe Kikugorō V*, and Ichikawa Sadanji I*, the three greatest actors of the Meiji period. As they created the golden age of Meiji Kabuki, this term—made up of the first element in each of their names—is used to denote them as the representative actors of their time.

DANMARI. A type of wordless pantomime in which a group of characters perform a battle as they grope for one another in the dark. Since the idea of the *danmari* is to introduce the actors of a troupe to the audience, it normally contains no plot. There are two main types of *danmari*, the historical *(jidai danmari)* and the domestic *(sewa danmari).*

jidai danmari. A pantomime scene usually set in a mountain clearing where various characters appear, including a bandit chief, a mountain ascetic, a young lord, a female thief, a chief retainer, a lady-in-waiting, a princess, a pilgrim, and so on. They struggle to capture a white flag or some family heirloom while accompanied by *ōsatsuma** type of *geza** music. The piece brims with Kabuki's formalistic acting techniques, such as the *hiki-nuki** quick-change, the "pillar wrapping" *(hashira maki no) mie**, and the *roppō** exit performed down the *hanamichi**. Famous examples are the *Miyajima Danmari* and the *Ichiharano no Danmari.* Many such *danmari* are performed as independent one-act plays.

sewa danmari. *Danmari* scenes included within domestic plays; they are never played independently. They lack the overt stylization of *jidai danmari* and have specific plots. *Sewa danmari* scenes are performed after a murder, a fight, or a mysterious occurrence. Famous instances are the Inbōbori scene of *Tōkaidō Yotsuya Kaidan** and the scene at Yatsuyamashita in *Kami no Megumi Wagō no Torikumi**. There also are such scenes as the "erotic," or *tsuya, danmari.* The *okashimi danmari* is a humorous subtype. In the old days, the entire company used to appear in the *ome mie danmari* when touring the provinces as well as the *kaomise danmari,* performed to announce the company's actors to the public.

danmari hodoki. Moments when a mystery posed by the events of a *danmari* scene are explained in a later scene of the play. Something picked up by a character in the *danmari* usually becomes the tool or clue (*hodoki*) with which the mystery is solved in a later "extortion scene" *(yusuriba*).* For example, in the *Ochanomizu Danmari* scene of *Mekura Nagoya Ume ga Kagatobi**, the evil Dōgen murders a man, but accidentally leaves his tobacco pouch at the scene of the crime. It is found by the fireman Matsuzō. Later, Dōgen attempts to blackmail a pawnshop owner, but when Matsuzō turns up and meaningfully brandishes Dōgen's lost pouch, the extortion attempt comes to an abrupt end.

DAN MONO. "Act piece," a term with several meanings.

First, it means a one-act dance piece, complete within itself, using *nagauta**, *tokiwazu**, or *kiyomoto** music and having a unified plot. The opposite would be a work that lacked a single plot and was made up of a number of *kouta** musical selections; such works are called *hamono**. An example of a *hamono* would be *Echigo Jishi**, while a *dan mono* would be *Kanjinchō**.

Second, it refers to a *michiyuki** or *keigoto** passage that has charming music, is extracted from a play originating in the puppet theatre, and is performed as a separate selection on a program.

Finally, a dance performed to *naguata, kiyomoto,* or *tokiwazu,* would be *dan mono,* while one performed to *hauta** music would be a *hamono.*

DANNA. "Master"; a word originally reserved for those who were entitled to be called *tayūmoto* (*see also* TAYŪ), it is now used for high-ranking actors.

DAN NO URA KABUTO GUNKI. Matsuda Bunkodō, Hasegawa Senshi. Also called *Akoya no Kotozeme, Akoya. Jidaimono*. Jōruri*.* Five acts. September 1732. Takemoto-za, Osaka.

A work dealing with the great general of feudal Japan, Taira Kagekiyo, and his mistress Akoya. Only Act III is still performed.

Since Hatakeyama Shigetada is seeking to learn the whereabouts of Kagekiyo—who, in turn, is pursuing Yoritomo—he interrogates Kagekiyo's mistress, the courtesan Akoya. Shigetada's colleague, Iwanaga Saemon, wants her to be tortured, but Shigetada applies his own kind of test. He forces her to play the *koto*, shamisen*,* and *kokyū,* musical instruments. Hearing no discordance in the music, he pardons the courtesan; he now believes that she has no idea of Kagekiyo's whereabouts.

The drama effectively contrasts the evil Saemon with the dignified Shigetada. The most popular scene of the play comes when Akoya is forced to play the musical instruments. Akoya must be played by an actor with great musical skill as well as a quality of profound dignity. Iwanaga, the *kataki-yaku** role, is played in a style that imitates the acting of the puppet theatre and is called *ningyō buri**. Shigetada is the classic example of the mature man of judgment (*sabaki yaku; see also* TACHIYAKU). The first Kabuki production of the play took place in 1733 at Osaka's Kado-za, with Yoshizawa Ayame II as Akoya, Fujikawa Heikurō as Iwanaga, and Arashi San'emon as Shigetada.

DANTAI. A theatre party. Japanese firms often send their workers and their families to the theatre as a sort of bonus or simply for their recreation. Large groups of school children attend the theatre as part of their education. The theatres, for their part, offer discounts and make special arrangements for groups over a certain size. Since many people participate in these theatre parties, the nature of the productions offered is frequently influenced by their presence. However, the *dantai* are certainly not limited to lovers of Kabuki, and their theatre manners actually have created a problem for theatre entrepreneurs. (*See also* AUDIENCES.)

DARAMAKU. Also called *honmaku** and *maku**, this is the most common manner of striking the *hyōshigi** at the end of an act. Following the beat called the *kigashira**, the *kyōgen kata** stage assistant begins beating the clappers gently, *"chon chon chon"*; as the curtain* *(maku)* is pulled across the stage, the pace rapidly increases. The term *daramaku* comes from the sound of the clappers going *"daradara"* at the same pitch as they are rapidly beaten.

DAREZUKI. A "bad month" at the box office. Also called *akuzuki**.

DATE ERI. "Fashionable collar"; a kind of cotton-padded collar that may be patterned like a horse's reins or have a spiral ropelike design. Footmen *(yakko)* in history and dance plays wear it. One may be seen on Chienai in the *Kikubatake* scene of *Kiichi Hōgen Sanryaku no Maki**, and the solo dancer in *Tomoyakko* also wears it.

DATE MUSUME KOI NO HIGANOKO. Suga Sensuke, Matsuda Wakichi, Wakatake Fuemi. Also called *Yagura no Oshichi, Yaoya Oshichi. Sewamono**. *Jōruri**. Eight acts. April 1773. Kita Horie-za, Osaka.

Today theatres present only the sixth act of this play, which presents the love story of Yaoya (Greengrocer) Oshichi and Kichisaburō, page at the Kisshoin Temple.

Because of the loss of a famous heirloom sword, which had been returned to the Imperial Palace by the young lord of the Takashima family, the sword's guardian, Yasumori Genjirō, must assume responsibility and commit ritual suicide *(seppuku)*. His son Kichisaburō has become a page at Edo's Kisshoin Temple in the Komagome district; having heard the news of his father's death, he is searching for the sword. Kichisaburō had fallen in love with Oshichi when her family had taken refuge at his temple after a fire had destroyed their house. The time limit for the sword's recovery expires on the following day, and Kichisaburō is resolved to die. Oshichi learns that the sword is in the hands of Kamaya Buhei. She must let Kichisaburō know this, but night has fallen and the wooden gates between the streets of Edo are shut. Understanding that her punishment for this act will be to be burned at the stake, she climbs the fire tower and rings the bell, hoping to get the gates opened.

Another Kabuki version of this story is Kawatake Mokuami's* *Shōchiku Baiyuki no Akebono*, staged in 1856 at Edo's Ichimura-za* with Ichikawa Kodanji IV*.

DATE SAGARI. "Fashionable apron," a costume element worn with the *yakko* or footman costume in history and dance plays. It is worn under the outer kimono *(kitsuke*)*, is tied around the waist, and hangs down in front like an apron. It has a beautiful gold and silver design and has fringes *(baren*)* hanging from its bottom.

The solo dancer in *Tomoyakko,* wearing the *date sagari**, *date eri**, and *baren**. Yakko, Nakamura Tomijūrō V*. *Courtesy of Waseda University Tsubouchi Engeki Hakubutsukan (Tsubouchi Memorial Theatre Museum).*

DE. The entrance of an actor in a play.

DEBA. Also *deha;* a kind of acting done on a character's entrance. It takes place at the spot on the *hanamichi** called the "seven-three" *(shichisan*),* which is seven-tenths of the distance from the rear of the *hanamichi* to the stage. Entrance speeches such as that of Gongorō in *Shibaraku** (*see also* TSURANE) are conventionally performed at the *shichisan.* For this reason, during the Kanbun era (1661-72), there was an attachment to the stage at this point; it was called the *nanoridai** or "name-saying platform." Dance plays often employ the *shichisan* for important business, too.

DEBAYASHI. Also *debayashigata,* the appearance on stage of *geza** musicians* *(hayashigata)* together with *nagauta** performers to provide the background music for dances and dance plays. According to the piece, only singing and *shamisen** playing may be required. Sometimes the *hayashi** musicians do not appear, but the term *debayashi* is still used. The *nagauta* orchestra sits on the special platform called *hinadan**; those on the right play the *shamisen,* and those on the left sing. The *hayashi* are ranged beneath them on the lower step. The smallest accompaniment group of *nagauta* performers may consist of one singer and two *shamisen* players, but the big playhouses invariably use ten or more of each. (*See also* GEZA; DEGATARI).

DEBESO. "Protruding navel"; an extension of the platform used in sets depicting interiors. The platforming thrusts forward toward the audience from the downstage edges of the room in order to improve the sight lines.

DEBUT. Known as *hatsu butai,* this is an actor's first stage appearance. It usually is said that he "treads the boards for the first time" *(hatsu butai o fumu).* Two- and three-year-old children often debut as Kabuki actors. A child who is the son of a famous actor is honored by a special greeting *(kōjō*)* given to him in the midst of the performance by his father, elder brothers, and relatives; even the play in which he acts is specially prepared for the debut.

DEGAICHŌ. A term referring to the performance by one theatre's troupe at another theatre.

DEGATARI. The appearance on stage of *jōruri** musicians *(kiyomoto*, tomimoto*,* or *tokiwazu*).* The word also denotes when the *gidayū** musicians appear onstage, as opposed to their performing from within the screened-in enclosure *(misu)* set up on stage left. In the latter instance they are called *misuuchi,* or "within the *misu.*" *Katō bushi** and *itchū bushi** musicians customarily perform within the enclosure. (*See also* YUKA; CHOBO; DEBAYASHI.)

DEKATA. An usher in Edo period theatres who aided spectators with their needs and served them food and drink. He also helped turn the revolving stage*, arranged the spectators' footwear, took the billboards in and out, and occasionally helped out the property men. After the Morita-za* moved to the heart of Tokyo in 1872, all *dekata* wore a standard striped kimono of blue cloth, the drawerlike trousers called *momohiki*, and white Japanese socks *(tabi)*. When the Kabuki-za* was opened in 1889, they wore hitched-up culotte trousers *(hakama*)*. The post of *dekata* was abolished after the great earthquake of 1923. (*See also* THEATRE MANAGEMENT.)

DENCHŪ. "In the palace"; a word taken from a speech by Moronao in Act III of *Kanadehon Chūshingura**; it refers to those moments when something is going wrong and one's stage partner brings it to one's attention by whispering the word.

DENDEN MONO. Kabuki plays adapted from the puppet theatre. The onomatopoeic name comes from the sound of the plectrum striking the skin of the puppet theatre *shamisen**. (*See also* GIDAYŪ KYŌGEN.)

DENGAKUGAESHI. A scene-changing method that calls for the background to be cut into separate sections and a shaft to be placed through the center of each section or flat, either vertically or horizontally. Each of these revolves on its axis so that the scene on the reverse side is visible, creating the effect of an instant scene change. It was originated in the puppet theatre in 1789. In addition to changing the scene, it also can be used to create the impression of magical characters appearing and disappearing through walls. Its name comes from its resemblance to a kind of bean curd that is eaten on a skewer and called *dengaku*.

DENPŌ. Edo period bullies who forced their way into theatres without paying for their admission. The term derives from the practice of those associated with Edo's Denpōin (Sosen Temple), who used their authority to see theatricals set up on the temple grounds without paying for their seats. The word eventually came to be used for anyone who inveigled his way into a theatre for free. (*See also* AUDIENCES.)

DEUCHI. "Appearance striking"; the Edo period custom of having the *kyōgen kata** appear in view of the audience to strike the *hyōshigi** for scene changes and final curtains. The post-Edo-period convention has been for the *kyōgen kata* to strike the clappers from the wings. According to the old method, he would come out shortly before the final curtain and sit in the downstage left corner facing upstage; this signaled the audience that the curtain was coming. On cue, he would rise and strike his clappers. This method is now used very rarely; it may be seen when old classics, such as plays in the *kabuki jūhachiban** collection, are staged.

DEZUPPARI. When an actor is onstage in a play from beginning to end, without a break. Also, when an actor appears in every scene of a play in every piece on a program.

DIALOGUE. *See* SERIFU.

DODEN. Also pronounced *donden*, an abbreviation of *dondengaeshi**, this is a scenic technique for turning a set over topsy-turvy. Used in the sense of something being overturned or of doing something over again.

DŌGU GAWARI. Warning signals provided by the *hyōshigi** that the set is about to change. The first *"chon"* is a warning to get ready, and the next marks the actual change.

DŌGU KATA. The men responsible for building, shifting, and maintaining scenery and scenic devices. (*See also* SCENERY.)

DŌGU MAKU. A scenic curtain on which mountains, waves, clouds, or fencing is painted and which is used as background scenery for a brief "front" scene. When the scene is concluded, the curtain is suddenly dropped and the scenery for the next scene revealed. (*See also* CURTAINS; FURIOTOSHI; FURIKABUSE.)

DŌJI GŌSHI. A costume pattern consisting of a bold, purple-and-white checkerboard design worn by valiant samurai in history and dance plays. The three brothers in the *Kuruma Biki* scene of *Sugawara Denju Tenarai Kagami** wear it, as does Kaidomaru in *Yamanba**.

DŌJŌJI MONO. Plays and dances that deal with the legend of Dōjō Temple. Ever since the original stage treatment given the legend by the Nō theatre, it has proved popular as material for dance dramas. Famous examples are *Musume* ("Young Lady") *Dōjōji**, *Keisei* ("Courtesan") *Dōjōji*, *Kishū Dōjōji*, *Ninin* ("Two People") *Dōjōji*, and *Yakko* ("Footman") *Dōjōji*.

DŌKEGATA. A comic role type, descended from the Saruwaka character who was an important feature of early Kabuki. Plays became more realistic from the late seventeenth century on, and the *dōkegata* came to emphasize a more subtle type of humor than formerly; this newer type of realistic

Sakuramaru in the *Kuruma Biki* scene of *Sugawara Denju Tenarai Kagami**, wearing the *atsuwata** robe with a *dōji gōshi** pattern. Sakuramaru, Onoe Baikō VII*. *Courtesy of Waseda University Tsubouchi Engeki Hakubutsukan (Tsubouchi Memorial Theatre Museum).*

clown was the *handō*. The *dōkegata* also is known as the *sanmaime**, a term that derives from his name's having been written on the third billboard in front of the theatre. (*Sanmaime* means "third flat thing"). (*See also* ROLE TYPES.)

DOKUGIN. A solo singing accompaniment in *meriyasu** style. Used as a background to heighten the emotional quality in long, quiet scenes.

DOKUHAKU. A monologue.

DOMA. "The pit," a name given to the seating in Edo theatres that contrasts with the galleries *(sajiki*)*—that is, the seats on the level ground floor facing the stage. During Kabuki's early days, when performances were outdoors, audiences spread mats on the floor to watch the play. The word *doma* (literally, "earth room") comes from the seating of the spectators on the ground. Later, the area was divided into sections by rope. After a regular theatre building was erected, square boxed-in areas partitioned off by wood barriers were installed. They were called *masu**. At a later period a slightly raised area of boxes was built just in front of the *sajiki* on the sides. It was known as the *takadoma*,* or "raised" *doma*. In contrast to the *takadoma*, the old *doma* now was called *hiradoma*, or "level" *doma*, and also seems to have been called *hiraba*. (*See also* THEATRE ARCHITECTURE.)

DŌMARU. An under kimono worn by *aragoto* roles such as the *oshimodoshi** ("queller of demons") and Watonai in *Kokusenya Kassen**. The upper part is a tight-sleeved, round-necked garment, the lower half being comprised of drawers *(momohiki)*. Round metal fittings are sewn against a red background. This costume, also called *hyōuchi*, is considered to be a type of stage armor.

DOMESTIC DRAMA. *See* SEWAMONO.

DONCHŌ YAKUSHA. "Drop-curtain actor," a pejorative term used to refer to actors at the small theatres *(koshibai*)*. In the old days, small-scale theatres and sheds set up on temple grounds *(miyachi shibai*)* were not allowed to use a traveler curtain, as in the major Kabuki playhouses, but had to use a drop curtain *(donchō)* instead. These theatres were termed *donchō shibai* ("drop-curtain theatres"), in contrast to the "big theatres," or *ōshibai**. Actors appearing in *donchō shibai* were spoken of contemptuously as *donchō yakusha*. Even the best of these players were not permitted to appear at the major playhouses. This manner of segregating actors apparently was relaxed when the Meiji era arrived, but, because of the former convention, small theatre actors were not respected for quite some time and were scorned by the rest of the Kabuki world.

DONTSUKU. Sakurada Jisuke III*. Also called *Kagura Uta Kumoi no Kyokumari. Shosagoto*. Tokiwazu*.* January 1846. Ichimura-za*, Edo.

All that remains of this work is a vaudeville-like series of turns performed at a Shinto street festival *(daikagura)* with humorous moments and acrobatic tricks; central is a dance by Dontsuku, a country servant. In the first production the leading parts were played by Nakamura Utaemon IV*, Ichimura Uzaemon XII, and Seki Sanjūrō III.

Daikagura was an Edo period street art; interwoven with it are dances of Edo manners, including the dance of a white-wine seller, a young lord, and a geisha.

DŌNUKI. An indoors kimono worn by courtesans, usually under an *uchikake** robe. The upper and lower portions are of different materials. Michitose in the *Naozamurai* segment of *Kumo ni Magō Ueno no Hatsuhana** wears one.

DORA. The striking of a bell to signify the marking of the hour.

DOROBUNE. "Mud boat," a muddy pond or rice paddy used as a scenic element. It is made by placing mud in a box that is set up at a specified area onstage. There used to be a hollow space called a *kariido* alongside the *hanamichi**, and this was used as the *dorobune.* A hollow cut in the stage floor was also used for this purpose. Stage mud is made by using wall plaster or by mixing a special type of soil with water.

DOROGIRE. "Mud cloth," a ground cloth. (*See* JIGASURI.)

DORON. A corruption of *dorodoro,* the drumming heard when a ghost disappears during a scene. This term refers to an actor's taking an unauthorized leave while in the midst of performing a play.

DŌSHI NO HITOBITO. Yamamoto Yuzō. *Shin kabuki**. One act. March 1925. Hōsaku-za, Tokyo.

This drama takes place during the period shortly after the 1868 restoration of the emperor to his position as ruler of Japan.

Ten allies of the defeated Teradaya rebellion are being escorted to Satsuma on a captured boat. Owing to unavoidable circumstances, Koreda Mansuke must assume the role of the killer of his friend and leader, Tanaka Kawachika. As Kawachika believes in the restoration of the emperor to sovereignty, he commits ritual suicide *(seppuku)* at Koreda's request.

The psychological depiction of the characters, especially Koreda, is skillfully handled as the story unfolds in the dark and narrow hold of the storm-tossed ship.

DRESSING ROOMS. *See* BACKSTAGE.

E

ECHIGO JISHI. Shinoda Kinji. Also called *Osozakura Teniha no Nanamoji*. *Shosagoto**. *Nagauta**. March 1811. Ichimura-za*, Edo.

One of seven dances that survives from a "transformation piece*" *(henge mono)*. Such works showed off the actor's virtuosity by allowing him to appear in a number of different guises; in each he did a characteristic dance. *Echigo Jishi* was produced by Nakamura Utaemon III* when he was temporarily eclipsed in popularity by his great rival, Bandō Mitsugorō III*, who had criticized Utaemon in his own current *henge mono* success. The work that comprises *Echigo Jishi* is said to have outstripped Mitsugorō's dance in popular favor.

Echigo Jishi is a folk dance depicting a lion, as performed by a street entertainer in Edo, Kakubei of Echigo. Displaying great verve and gaiety, it includes various Echigo folk songs and other popular features. At the dance's conclusion Kakubei does a turn with a long bleaching cloth.

EDO SANZA. "Edo's three theatres," the three representative playhouses of Edo. Edo's first theatre was the Saruwaka-za* (1624), followed by the Miyako-za*, the Murayama-za (later the Ichimura-za*), the Yamamura-za*, the Tamagawa-za, the Kawarazaki-za, the Kiri-za, and others, all of which obtained official licenses to produce plays. Gradually, the number of licensed theatres decreased, however, and by 1651 the number of Edo theatres was limited to four major playhouses called *ōshibai** ("big theatres"). In addition, there were small theatres set up on temple grounds on a temporary basis (the *koshibai** and *miyachi shibai**).

In 1714 occurred the notorious affair between the court lady Ejima and the Yamamura-za actor, Ikushima Shingorō (*see* EJIMA-IKUSHIMA INCIDENT), following which the government found it necessary to interfere with playhouse managements and actors; the Yamamura-za was closed down for good and its holdings confiscated. Thereafter, only the *Edo sanza* —the Nakamura-za, the Ichimura-za, and the Morita-za—were permitted to produce plays in Edo. When a theatre ran into some sort of trouble and could not put on plays, however, an alternate theatre was permitted to do so under the *hikae yagura** system. (*See also* THEATRE MANAGEMENT.)

EDO SODACHI OMATSURI SASHICHI. Kawatake Shinshichi III*. Also called *Omatsuri Sashichi. Sewamono**. Kabuki. Three acts. May 1898. Kabuki-za*, Tokyo.

The love story of Koito and Sashichi has been told by several Kabuki and puppet theatre writers, and plays dealing with their story are called *Koito Sashichi mono*. This particular version is a direct copy of Tsuruya Nanboku IV*s *Kokoro no Nazo Toketo Iroito*. The original cast included Onoe Kikugorō V* as Sashichi, Onoe Eizaburō (later known as Onoe Baikō VI*) as Koito, Onoe Matsusuke as Otetsu, and Kataoka Ichizō as Hanpei. Kikugorō played Sashichi in the manner created by his grandfather, Onoe Kikugorō III*, who acted the role in Nanboku's drama. Both Kikugorō and Baikō were so successful in their roles that they played them in many later revivals. Another outstanding Sashichi was Ichimura Uzaemon XV*.

Sashichi, a fireman, rescues the Yanagishima geisha Koito on the night of the Kamita festival and takes her home with him. Soon after they begin living together, Koito's scheming stepmother forces her against her will to speak harshly to her lover, breaking off their relationship (*see also* SEPARATION SCENES). However, as is typical of Kabuki plays, the rebuked lover kills his mistress. He soon learns of his mistake from a farewell note left by Koito and thereupon takes revenge on his enemy, Kurada Hanpei, who had plotted with Koito's stepmother.

The plot is rather conventional, from its separation scene, or *enkiri*, to its obligatory murder, and contains little that is new, but it overflows with the unique atmosphere of old Edo. Highlights include the vocal solo *(dokugin*)* sung in *meriyasu** style, the scene in which the farewell note is written, and the artistic effects of the murder scene.

EHON TAIKŌKI. Chikamatsu Yanagi, Chikamatsu Kosui, others. Also called *Taikōki, Taijū. Jidaimono**. *Jōruri**. Thirteen acts. July 1799. Wakadayū-za, Osaka.

Based on the chronicle of the same name, this play covers a period of thirteen days, each of which has its own act. This time span covers the events from the revolt of Mitsuhide to his death. Only the events of the tenth day (Act X) are presented today; this act is called *Amagasaki Kankyō*. Numerous puppet and Kabuki plays are based on the same material, and several of them influenced the writing of this play. The first Kabuki adaptation of the play was in 1800 at Osaka's Kado no Shibai. Asai Tamejūrō starred as Mitsuhide. Edo saw its first Kabuki version in 1841 at the Kawarazaki-za. The tradition developed for only the *zagashira** to act Mitsuhide and for the *tate onnagata** to play his wife, Misao, with Jūjirō enacted by the leading player of young male roles, Hatsugiku by the leading young *onnagata**, and Satsuki by the company's outstanding actor of old women.

The scene is a cottage at Amagasaki. Mitsuhide, formerly a vassal of Harunaga, has rebelled against Harunaga and slain him. Mitsuhide's mother, Satsuki, continually berates him for having been so disloyal to his overlord. Satsuki has left her son's abode and lives alone at Amagasaki during the war between Mitsuhide's forces and those of Hisayoshi, Harunaga's next in command. She is visited by Mitsuhide's wife Misao, and Hatsugiku, who is engaged to marry Jūjirō. Jūjirō and his bride take their nuptial vows, and Satsuki blesses them. Though his grandmother regrets his fighting in an unjust war, Jūjirō leaves for battle, determined to die with honor.

Meanwhile Mitsuhide has followed Hisayoshi to Satsuki's cottage and is determined to capture him. Believing Hisayoshi to be inside talking with Satsuki, Mitsuhide thrusts his lance through the paper door and pierces his mother. She pleads with him to cease his rebellion and to make peace, but he ignores her. Jūjirō returns, mortally wounded, tells his father that his forces have been defeated, and dies. Then Mitsuhide sees his mother pass away, and breaks down in tears. He soon recovers, however, and vows to meet Hisayoshi in battle again at Yamazaki.

Ehon Taikōki is famed as a *gidayū** narrative. When Mitsuhide is overcome with tears at the death of his mother and son, the acting reaches an emotional climax of great power.

EIRI KYŌGEN BON. Illustrated scenarios of Kabuki plays published in the mid-Genroku period (1688-1703). Also called *kyōgen bon* and *ehon kyōgen bon.* They were arranged like a scenario "reader," being similar in details to the regular playscript, but containing only a synopsis. Dialogue excerpts often were included. Of the examples known today, there are an estimated 150 from the Kamigata area and 50 from Edo. They are an invaluable source of material for study of Genroku Kabuki.

EJIMA-IKUSHIMA INCIDENT. The notorious affair between Lady Ejima and the actor Ikushima Shingorō. On the twelfth day of the New Year, 1714, Lady Ejima, a lady-in-waiting to the mother of the seventh shogun, Ietsugi, let it be known that she was visiting the Shizōjō Temple. In actuality, however, she went to the Yamamura-za* in Kobiki-chō, to have a rendezvous with the handsome actor Ikushima. Ejima's rendezvous was discovered and she was banished to faraway Shinshū; the actor was exiled to Miyakejima; and Ejima's attendants and others involved in the affair were severely punished. Further, the Yamamura-za was closed permanently. Because the Yamamura-za's teahouse had taken an active part in the affair, other teahouses were adversely affected. (*See* SHIBAIJAYA.) The event was the most notorious of all theatre occurrences during the Edo period. To understand the scandal, one must know that at that time the ladies of the shogun's inner chamber lived in an all-female society and had a strong interest in the Kabuki and its actors. The daughters of townsmen, in order to learn decorum and manners, often took service in the inner chamber or at a samurai's mansion; when they received their annual vacation in March, their chief pleasure came from visiting the Kabuki. The theatres catered to them and produced the so-called Spring Plays* *(yayoi kyōgen),* such as *Kagamiyama Kokyō no Nishikie** and *Shin Usuyuki Monogatari**, in which scenes of palace life concerning women were enacted. It was undoubtedly at such performances that Lady Ejima first felt the romantic sentiments that led to her tragic downfall. (*See also* EDO SANZA; THEATRE MANAGEMENT.)

ENDE(N). A wig showing that hair has grown in on the usually shaved pate; the hair is pulled back past the topknot on both sides, in the shape of a swallow's tail *(ende).* The *ende* wig is used for roles of fearful characters and villains such as Nikki Danjō in *Meiboku Sendai Hagi** and Mitsuhide in *Toki wa Ima Kikkyō no Hataage**.

ENKIRI. *See* SEPARATION SCENES.

EN'O JŪSHU. A collection of ten dance dramas originated by Ichikawa Ennosuke II (En'o I*); the collection was established by Ennosuke II and III*.

PLAY	DATE
Akutarō	1924
*Kurozuka**	1939
Takano Monogurui	1927
*Kokaji**	1939
Koma	1928
Ninin Sanbasō	1936
Nomitori Otoko	1929
Hanami Yakko	
Yoi Yakko	
Yoshinoyama Michiyuki	

(*See also* FAMILY ART.)

ENOMOTO TORAHIKO. 1866-1916. A playwright, born in Wakayama. He was a pupil of Fukuchi Ōchi*, joined Tokyo's Kabuki-za*, and succeeded to the position of chief playwright *(tate sakusha*)* in 1908, at Ōchi's death. He wrote few purely original plays, most of his works being revisions and adaptations of older works. Among his best creations are *Ataka no Seki, Meikō Kakiemon**, and *Minami Tsu Enjō.*

EXTORTION SCENES. *See* BLACKMAIL SCENES.

F

FACE-SHOWING PERFORMANCE. *See* KAOMISE KŌGYŌ.

FAMILY ART. Known as *ie no gei,* it comprises the acting style and plays handed down through the generations of an actor's family. The family's best roles and plays are chosen after careful consideration; they then form a collection that the family offers with pride. The most famous example is the *kabuki jūhachiban** collection of the Ichikawa Danjūrō* line. *Aragoto**, the style of acting represented by these plays, is the Ichikawa *ie no gei* as well. The Onoe family specializes in ghost plays, domestic plays, and dances; this family's favorite works are collected in the *shinko engeki jūshu**, ten dance pieces adapted from Nō or Kyōgen plays. The Kinokuniya family of Sawamura Sōjūrō*, specialists in *wagoto** acting, has the *kōga jūshu* collection; and the Kataoka Nizaemon* line, also experts in the Kamigata style of acting, has its representative works collected in the *Kataoka jūnishū**. (*See also* PLAY CATEGORIES.)

FEMALE IMPERSONATORS. *See* ONNAGATA.

FIGHT SCENES. *See* TACHIMAWARI.

FLOWER PATH. *See* HANAMICHI.

FOOTGEAR. Called *hakimono.* The most commonly seen footgear in Kabuki are the two-stepped wooden clogs *(geta)* worn at various heights, and the flat straw sandals with thongs *(zōri).* Either bifurcated socks *(tabi)* are worn with these or the actor wears them barefoot. Kabuki characters wear a wide variety of other shoes and sandals as well.

FORELOCKS. *See* MAEGAMI KATSURA.

FŪFŪ. The sound made when one blows into an envelope containing bonus money; the blowing is done to open the mouth of the envelope. (*See also* ŌIRI.)

FUIRI. "Poor houses"; said when attendance is low. (*See also* ŌIRI.)

FUJIMA RYŪ. A school of Kabuki dance, a marked feature of which is the use of long pauses. Fujima Kanbei founded the school in Edo in 1630. One of his most famous descendants was Kanbei III, who became famous as an Edo choreographer with his *Yamanba**, *Shiokumi**, *Urashima*, and other works in the early nineteenth century. This line continued up to the seventh Kanbei in the Meiji era. The Kanjūrō branch of the family began when Kanbei III temporarily took the name of Kanjūrō during his career; his adopted son later became Kanjūrō II and began that family line. During the first third of the nineteenth century he created the choreography for such works as *Yasuna**, *Komori**, *Kasane**, *Tomoyakko*, and *Sanja Matsuri**. With the appearance of Kanjūrō III, women began to specialize in the family art, and it soon became detached from the theatre world. The present family head is the seventh Kanjūrō; he frequently choreographs dances for actors belonging to the Kikugōrō troupe and also may be seen in frequent dance recitals.

Another important Fujima branch is the Kan'emon. Kan'emon I was a pupil of Kanjūrō II. Kan'emon II was responsible for such dances as *Kagamijishi** and *Onatsu Kyōran** in the late nineteenth and early twentieth centuries. Kan'emon III was the actor Matsumoto Kōshirō VII*; his son, Onoe Shōroku II*, one of today's leading actors, is Kan'emon IV.

FUJI MUSUME. Katsui Gonpachi. *Shosagoto**. *Nagauta**. September 1826. Nakamura-za*, Edo.

Fuji Musume is one section of a five-dance "transformation piece*" *(henge mono), Kaesu Gaesu Nagori no Ōtsue.* This plotless dance is based on the Ōtsu picture (a genre of Japanese art) of a maiden *(musume)* bearing a branch of wisteria *(fuji)* on her shoulder. The performance consists of a dance, on a stage completely decorated with wisteria blossoms, by a lovely maiden who wears a broad scarlet hat and carries a branch of wisteria on her shoulder, as in the picture. Onoe Kikugorō VI* interpreted the girl's role as being the spirit of the wisteria.

Fuji Musume was first presented by Seki Sanjūrō II who performed it as the conclusion to *Keisei Hangonkō**.

FUJINAMI YOHEI. The name of a family line of property masters. (*See* PROPERTIES.)

FUKIBOYA. Also *fukibi;* apparatus used to create the effect of fires. Pocket heater fuel and pine needles were placed at the bottom of a lamp. Then air was blown into the lamp through a pipe, so that flaming powder would be scattered in the air, giving the impression of a conflagration. The device was prohibited after a theatre was accidentally destroyed by means of this technique in 1958.

FUKIKAE. A "stand-in" or "double," the *fukikae* appears in scenes requiring a quick change when a single actor plays two or more roles. An individual who physically resembles the actor puts on an identical costume and makeup and substitutes for him as he makes his change. In order for the audience not to notice the switch, the stand-in turns his face toward the rear of the stage. Much use is made of the *fukikae* in the productions of Ichikawa Ennosuke III* and Jitsukawa Enjaku III*, both of whom specialize in quick-change techniques. In Ennosuke's case, his brother Ichikawa Danshirō IV* often makes an effective stand-in. (*See also* HAYAGAWARI.)

FUKIWA. A wig worn by princesses in history plays. The topknot is large, and flower combs are inserted at the front. Princess Yaegaki in *Honchō Nijūshikō**, Princess Yuki in *Gion Sairei Shinkōki**, and Princess Toki in *Kamakura Sandaiki** wear it. (*See also* SANHIME; AKAHIME.)

FUKORO TSUKI. The name of the back-hair portion of male wigs where the *tabo**, or section at the nape of the neck, has been dressed in a pouch style. Almost all townsmen in the domestic plays wear it. The opposite back-hair style is *abura tsuki**. (*See also* WIGS.)

FUKU. When an actor onstage "breaks up" over something funny.

FUKUCHI ŌCHI. 1841-1906. A Kabuki playwright. Originally a journalist, he founded the Kabuki-za* in 1889 with Chiba Katsugorō, became the resident playwright, and gained special prominence by writing living history* *(katsureki)* plays for Ichikawa Danjūrō IX*. He also wrote about forty domestic plays and dance dramas. *Haruhi Tsubone, Otokodate Harusame Gasa, Ōmori Hikoshichi**, and *Kagamijishi** are among his best works. His real name was Genichirō.

FUKUMI WATA. "Cotton stuffing," the cotton that actors formerly stuffed into their cheeks to make their faces look plumper for certain roles. It often was used by *onnagata**. Today, a kind of rubber has replaced the cotton.

FULL-LENGTH PRODUCTIONS. *Tōshi kyōgen* is the presentation of a whole play from beginning to end, as opposed to the more common contemporary practice of producing only one or two acts of a play at a time. In general, plays were performed in their entirety through the mid-Meiji era, but—among changes that occurred during this period—dramatic scenes came to be itemized and performed separately, a practice called *midori**. Nevertheless, unless there is a well-integrated cast and thorough understanding of the entire plot when a *tōshi kyōgen* is performed, the total effect will be inferior.

FUNA BENKEI. Kawatake Mokuami*. *Shosagoto**. *Nagauta**. November 1885. Shintomi-za, Tokyo.

A Kabuki dance version of the Nō play of the same name; like other adaptations from the Nō (*see* MATSUBAME MONO), the play is presented on a Kabuki version of the Nō stage. *Funa Benkei* belongs to the *shin kabuki jūhachiban** play collection created by Ichikawa Danjūrō IX*, who starred in its first performance.

The great general Yoshitsune departs from his mistress, Shizuka, and leaves on a boat from Daimotsu port. At sea a violent storm arises; the ghost of Taira Tomomori appears and troubles those on the boat, but the ghost is vanquished by the power of the prayers performed by Benkei, Yoshitsune's priest-attendant.

Shizuka and Tomomori usually are performed by the same actor, as the change from the gentle Shizuka to the violent ghost provides much of the play's interest. Following its first performances, the play was revived by Onoe Kikugorō VI*, who made it into a major dance drama.

FUNE. *See* BOATS.

FUNE E UCHIKOMU HASHIMA NO SHIRANAMI. Kawatake Mokuami*. Also called *Ikaku Matsu, Fuji to Mimasu Suehiro Soga*. *Sewamono**. Kabuki. Three acts. February 1866. Morita-za*, Edo.

A robber play* *(shiranami mono)* based on a well-known story. At its first production, Ichikawa Kodanji IV* played Matsugorō, Onoe Kikujirō II was Osaki, Bunzō was played by Seki Sanjūrō III, and others in the cast included Bandō Mitsugorō V* and Suketakaya Kōsuke IV.

Matsugorō, a tinker, envies the lifestyle of Shimaya Bunzō. While standing on Azuma Bridge, Matsugorō sees Bunzō floating by in a pleasure boat with the geisha Osaki. He decides to change his lifestyle and, throwing his tools into the river, turns to a life of crime. Later, breaking into Bunzō's home, Matsugorō recognizes Osaki as a woman with whom he has been in love; he now takes her as his wife. He gives the swordsmith, Moritoya Sōjirō, fifty *ryō* that he has stolen. But, learning that the money was marked for public use, Matsugorō commits suicide to wash the stain from Sōjirō's name.

The scene when Matsugorō throws away his tools and resolves to become a criminal is replete with the decadent atmosphere of the late Edo era; it has become one of Kabuki's most famous scenes. This play is considered a representative example of the *kizewamono** sub-genre, a classification to which all robber plays belong. This play strongly conveys the decadent atmosphere of mid-nineteenth-century Japanese urban life. Kodanji had one of his greatest hits in the role of Matsugorō. Famous successors to the role included Onoe Kikugorō V* and VI*, Ichikawa Sadanji II*, and Ichimura Uzaemon XV*.

FUNGOMI. Women's loose leggings of red silk that completely encase the legs. They are also worn by actors of young romantic male roles and add a very alluring touch to the performer. Such a role is Rikiya in *Kanadehon Chūshingura**.

FURI. An element of both *mai** and *odori**, in which rhythmic movements are mimed and feelings are depicted against a background of music and lyrics,—that is, the pantomime aspect of Kabuki dance. *Shigusa** means the same thing. (*See also* DANCE.)

FURIDAKE. A scenic device, it is a bamboo pole hung from the grid *(sunoko*)* parallel to the front edge of the stage; from its projecting fingers hang such curtains as the *asagi maku, dōgu maku*, kuro maku**, and *dandara maku**. (*See also* CURTAINS.) The bamboo fingers on the pole point upward on a diagonal; a rope is attached to a large projecting finger at one end. When the rope is pulled by a stage assistant, the pole rotates so that the fingers point downward, allowing the curtain loops to slide off and the curtain to fall swiftly to the ground. The technique is called *furiotoshi.* The opposite technique is *furikabuse**; here the curtain is packed onto the pole so that at the proper moment it can be quickly dropped, hiding the scenery above it.

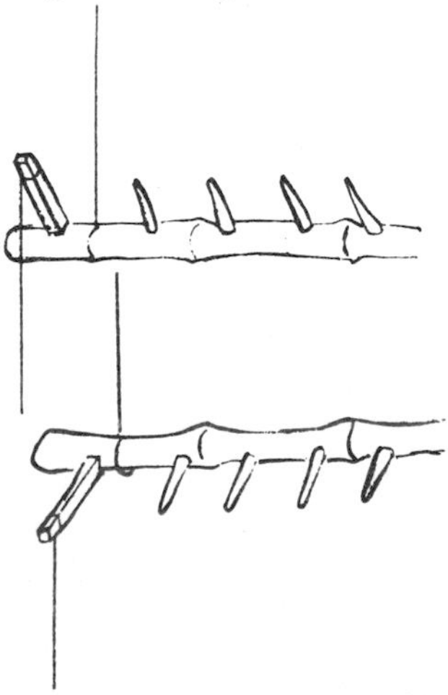

*Furidake** technique. After a drawing in Itō, *Butai Sōchi no Kenkyū.*

FURIGOTO. A performance in which dance, rather than speech and gesture, is central. (*See* SHOSAGOTO.)

FURIKABUSE. A scene-changing device. A curtain is tucked up above a bamboo pole hanging from the grid *(sunoko*);* when a rope hanging from the end of the pole is pulled, the curtain falls and conceals the set. (*See also* FURIDAKE.)

FURITSUKE. "Choreography"; executed by a choreographer *(furitsukeshi)*. Kabuki actors originally devised their own dance movements, but there gradually developed a specialization in choreography. Finally it became an independent endeavor. Shigayama Mansaku in the late seventeenth century is said to have been the ancestor of the Kabuki choreographer. After him there appeared Nakamura Denjirō, Katsuma Kanpei, Hasegawa Ogizō, Ichiyama Shichijūrō, and others, each of whom developed a new choreographic style. Those schools *(ryū)* flourishing today include the Katsuma, the Hanayagi*, the Bandō*, the Fujima*, and the Yamamura*. (*See* DANCE.)

FUTATATEME. Also known as *futatsume*, this is the piece following the *jobiraki** on an Edo period play program—the second play on the program. Like the *jobiraki*, it was performed by the apprentice class of actors and was written by apprentice playwrights *(minarai sakusha*)*. The contents dealt with such topics as the detection of a conspiracy; it was a curtain raiser that may or may not have had some relationship to the plot of the day's main play *(hon kyōgen*)*. Some of the *futatateme* took the form of prologues to the main play. Also like the *jobiraki*, it was staged early in the morning to barely any audience and with only the theatre personnel acting as spectators. However, high-ranking persons such as the troupe leader *(zagashira*)* occasionally were present, and an unknown actor's talents might very well have been discovered at such performances. Nakamura Nakazō I*, for instance, was first noticed while in a *futatateme* piece and was given the chance that led to a successful career. Following the *futatateme* on the program was the *mitateme**.

FUTATSU CHŌCHŌ (KURUWA NIKKI). Takeda Izumo II*, Miyoshi Shōraku, Namiki Sōsuke*. *Sewamono**. *Jōruri**. Nine acts. July 1749. Takemoto-za, Osaka.

Acts II *(Sumōba)*, IV *(Daihōji Machi Komeya)*, VI *(Nanpa Ura)*, and VIII *(Hikimado)* are usually presented together as a full-length production* *(tōshi kyōgen)*. A month after its puppet theatre debut, the play was produced by the Kabuki at Kyoto's Arashi San'emon-za. Osaka saw its first Kabuki production of the play at the Kado no Shibai in 1753, while Edo had to wait until 1774, when it was done at the Nakamura-za*. A number of later playwrights wrote their own versions, including at least four by Tsuruya Nanboku IV*.

The sumo wrestler Nuregami Chōgorō is trying to ransom the courtesan Azuma for Yogorō, in whose debt he stands. Hiraoka Goemon, who is at odds with Yogorō and Azuma, is the patron of the amateur wrestler Hanare-goma Chōkichi. Chōgorō purposely loses to Chōkichi and then asks the latter to stop Goemon's ransoming of Azuma; Chōkichi refuses, however, and they quarrel. Admonished for his dissipation by his sister Oseki, Chōkichi is going to commit ritual suicide *(seppuku)* as an apology for his behavior, but Chōgorō, who happens along just then, prevents him. The two men swear blood brotherhood. Later, hearing that Azuma has been kidnapped by Hiraoka, Chōgorō finds and kills Hiraoka and three other men. The wrestler puts his effects in the care of Chōkichi and flees to his mother's residence, at the home of Nan Yōhei in Yawata Village, Yamato Province. Chōgorō's mother had become the second wife of Yōhei's father; acting in concert with Yōhei's wife, Ohaya, she gives her son refuge. However, that very day Yōhei has been made his late father's successor in the post of village magistrate; he returns home in the dress of a samurai, which it is now his right to wear. He has been ordered to arrest the fugitive, if possible. Chōgorō's mother indirectly asks Yōhei to save her son. Yōhei behaves in a way that will allow the fugitive to escape, but the wrestler, feeling contrite, begs to be bound in ropes. Yōhei cuts his fetters, which had been tearfully applied by Chōgorō's mother. Since his tour of duty was to be only for the nighttime hours, Yōhei pretends that the light of the moon, shining in from the skylight to which Chōgorō had been bound, is the light of dawn and he shows Chōgorō the route of escape. Chōgorō disguises himself and departs.

The confrontation between Chōgorō and Chōkichi in the *Sumōba* scene, acted in the exaggerated style called *aragoto**, is a major highlight of the work. The scene in Yōhei's home, known as *Hikimado*, presents the unfolding of Kabuki's eternal conflict between duty and feelings, here represented by the act of opening the skylight *(hikimado)* to which Chōgorō is tied.

FUTATSU ORI. A topknot worn by actors in townsmen roles such as Koremori in *Yoshitsune Senbon Zakura**, Izaemon in *Kuruwa Bunshō**, and Yosaburō in *Yowa Nasake Ukina no Yokogushi**.

G

GAKUBUCHI. The proscenium arch that marks the borders surrounding the front of the stage. Adopted from the Western theatre's picture-frame stage, it is found today enclosing almost all theatre stages in Japan. Even in Japan it is correct to refer to this stage feature as the "proscenium arch" *(puroseniamu a-chi).* (*See also* THEATRE ARCHITECTURE.)

GAKUYA. *See* BACKSTAGE.

GAKUYA BURO. Actors' baths. After the actor removes his costume and makeup, he steps into a hot bath *(furo)* backstage. In the old days a wooden bathtub was placed for this purpose at the side of the theatre's rear entrance. The *onnagata**, however, did not use this tub; instead, a bath attendant scooped out hot water and carried it to the upstairs *onnagata* dressing room. All theatres have up-to-date baths today. (*See* BACKSTAGE.)

GAKUYA DANJŪRŌ. A "dressing-room Danjūrō," that is, an actor who makes a marvelous impression backstage in makeup and costume, but who fails to live up that impression when onstage. Danjūrō is the name of Kabuki's most famous line of actors. (*See* ICHIKAWA DANJŪRŌ.)

GAKUYA OCHI. Something understood only between close friends; an "in joke." Also, when a comment is made onstage that is meant only for the other actors onstage and not for the audience.

GAKUYA SUZUME. "Backstage sparrow," a theatre fan who constantly frequents the actors' dressing room area.

GAKUYA TONBI. "Backstage kite," someone who spends a great deal of time backstage with the actors. An avid fan.

GANDŌGAESHI. A scene-change technique that is also called *dondengaeshi.* The setting is placed on an axis and is flipped over backwards ninety degrees, revealing a new set on the bottom of the first. Supposedly, it was created by playwright Akita Jizō in 1762. In the Kamigata area it is called the *hako tenjin* technique.

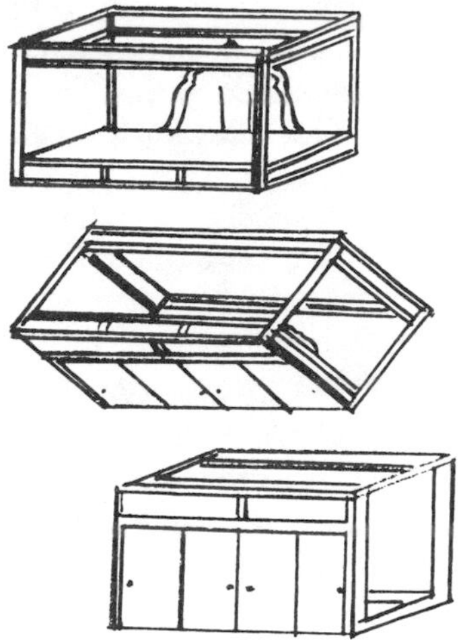

*Gandogaeshi** technique. After a drawing in Itō, *Butai Sōchi no Kenkyū.*

GANJIRŌ JŪNIKYOKU. A play collection established by Nakamura Ganjirō I*, composed chiefly of roles in the Kamigata style of *wagoto** acting. (*See also* FAMILY ART.)

1. Kawashō no Jihei in *Shinjū Ten no Amijima**.
2. Jihei in *Shigure no Kotatsu.*
3. Fuingiri no Chūbei in *Koi Bikyaku Yamato Orai.*
4. Harufuji Jirozaemon in *Katakiuchi Tsuzure no Nishiki.*
5. Akaneya Hanshichi in Ōmori Chisetsu's *Akanezome.*
6. Hanbei in Chisetsu's *Koi no Mizuumi.*
7. Oishi Kuranosuke in Watanabe Katei's *Goban Taiheiki**.
8. Tsuchiya Chikara in Katei's *Tsuchiya Chikara.*
9. Wankyū Sue no Matsuyama in Katei's *Wankyū Sue no Matsuyama.*
10. Sakata Tōjūrō in Kikuchi Kan's *Tōjūrō no Koi**.
11. Izaemon in *Kuruwa Bunshō**.
12. Yōhei in *Futatsu Chōchō Kuruwa Nikki**.

GATCHINKO. When an actor's words get twisted and he cannot get them out, or when he forgets his lines. Also called *zekku.*

GATTARI. A wig worn in fight scenes, among others; during the action the topknot comes undone and the hair falls loose in disarray. The trick is effected by pulling a peg inserted at the base of the topknot. It is used by Benten in the extortion scene of *Aotozōshi Hana no Nishikie**.

GEIURA. A seating location in Edo period theatres. It consisted of those seats in the rear and on the left side of the auditorium, by the *hanamichi**. The term comes from viewing the acting *(gei)* on the *hanamichi* from the rear *(ura).* (*See also* THEATRE ARCHITECTURE.)

GEKI BUSHI. A musical style made popular by Satsuma Geki after he moved from Kyoto to Edo sometime during the Keian and Meireki eras (1648-57).

At first it was employed in the puppet theatres, but in 1678 it was performed in Kabuki, where its masculine vigor made it a suitable accompaniment for the *aragoto** acting of Ichikawa Danjūrō I*. This style was soon merged with *ōsatsuma** music, created by a disciple of Geki, and was eventually absorbed by *nagauta**. *Nagauta* works in this mode include *Saru, Kairaishi,* and *Okina Sanbasō.* (*See* SANBASŌ.)

GEKIHYŌ. *See* CRITICISM.

GENPEI NUNOBIKI NO TAKI. Namiki Sōsuke*, Miyoshi Shōraku. Also called *Sanemori Monogatari. Jidaimono**. *Jōruri**. Five acts. November 1749. Takemoto-za, Osaka.

This play dramatizes events described in the narrative chronicles known as the *Genpei Seisuiki* and the *Heike Monogatari.* These events include the suicide of Minamoto Yoshikata; the oracle of the dragon god of the Nunobiki waterfall; the departure for the battlefront of Saito Sanemori, whose hair has been dyed black; and the birth of Kiso Yoshinaka.

The third act, set at Kurosuke's house, is often performed. Kabuki had produced a play based on these events in 1733; it bore the same title, and the similarity of the two plays suggests that the present one is an adaptation of the former.

From the play's earliest days, the first three acts, especially Act III, have been revived most frequently. Although the play is based on a Kabuki original, the Kabuki work that has come down to us is an adaptation of the puppet play. Its first staging was at Osaka's Kado no Shibai in 1757 and was followed soon after by the Kameya-za in Kyoto. Edo's first Kabuki production was at the Nakamura-za in 1793, with Sawamura Sōjūrō III* as Sanemori, supported by Nakamura Denkurō and Nakamura Sukegorō. Sanemori is now acted with *kata** developed by Bandō Mitsugorō III* and Bandō Hikosaburō III*, and enhanced by Onoe Kikugorō V* and Ichikawa Danzō VII*.

Minamoto Yoshikata's pregnant widow, Aoi Gozen, has come to take refuge at the home of a farmer, Kurosuke. Two envoys from the Heike faction, Senō Jurō and Saito Sanemori, demand that Aoi Gozen be turned over to them immediately, as they are after the child they know her to be bearing. Kurosuke's wife brings out a lady's severed arm, with which Kurosuke had returned earlier, and falsely claims that Aoi Gozen has given birth to it. Senō is amazed, but Sanemori offers an historical allusion to explain the event. Appeased, Senō leaves.

Sanemori's famous long narrative recital *(monogatari*)* is now spoken. Having come across the corpse of a girl whom he recognized as Kurosuke's daughter, he cut off her arm because her hand was gripping an important flag. Sanemori, having old ties to the Genji faction, realized that loss of the flag would have meant the downfall of the Genji. Senō, eavesdropping, understands that the dead girl, Kōman, was his own daughter, abandoned by him as an infant. He strikes Kōman's young son (his grandson), Tarokichi, deliberately forcing the boy to wound him and thus to prove himself worthy of serving the infant Komaomaru, who was born just then to Aoi Gozen.

Sanemori is a good example of the *wajitsu** type of role, a mature man with strong qualities of both reason and emotion. His *monogatari**, performed in a mixture of history and domestic dramatic styles, is a highlight of the play. Sanemori is valued among *tachiyaku** roles as a classic example of the eloquent samurai, torn between two camps in his allegiance to the Heike clan and respect for the Genji. His part is filled with thrilling moments of exceeding difficulty for the seasoned actor.

GENROKU CHŪSHINGURA. Mayama Seika*. *Shin kabuki**. Ten parts, twenty acts. September 1934. Kabuki-za*, Tokyo.

Mayama Seika's power was at its peak during the seven years, 1934-41, in which a serialized version of this work was produced by the Zenshin-za* troupe under Ichikawa Sadanji II*.

The play tells the familiar tale of Japan's loyal forty-seven masterless samurai, but differs from the classical account represented by *Kanadehon Chūshingura** in the modernity of its construction and its far greater emphasis on actual historical fact. A major example is the use of the real names of the characters who participated in the historical vendetta for which the forty-seven samurai were immortalized. *Kanadehon Chūshingura* was written at a time when it was forbidden to use the real names of contemporary samurai on the stage. *Genroku Chūshingura* also is much broader than the traditional Kabuki version in its coverage of the events surrounding the famous revenge. The author's depiction of the leading role of Oishi, based on an original view of samurai loyalty and on a careful consideration of psychological factors, shows the leading figure in the revenge plot less as an individual suffering from an agony of despair and more as a man of decisive action. Seika's dramatic skill is evident everywhere. This work was the masterpiece of his last years.

GENROKU HANAMI ODORI. Takeshiba Hyōsuke. Also called *Hanami Odori*. *Shosagoto**. *Nagauta**. June 1878. Shintomi-za, Tokyo.

A dance play performed as an entertainment at the opening ceremonies of the Shintomi-za (*see* MORITA-ZA), a theatre that contributed brilliantly to the world of theatre during the Meiji period. Iwai Hanshirō VIII* and Bandō Kakitsu were in its first performance.

Various characters—a samurai, a masseur, a youth, a city girl, a courtesan, and so on—all dressed in dazzling Genroku period (1688-1703) costumes, gather together on Mount Ueno, which is resplendent with cherry blossoms. They all dance with spirit and vivacity. The piece overflows with the charm of a flower-viewing excursion during the Genroku era.

"GENTLE STYLE." *See* WAGOTO.

GEZA. A room at stage right, facing the audience on a diagonal, it is also called the *kuromisu* and *hayashi beya**. Its interior is screened off by a rattan blind from the audience. The acting on stage and *hanamichi** can be seen perfectly from inside the *geza,* however. In this room the "stage effects" music *(geza ongaku)* and *aikata** background music is played. Central to this music is the *shamisen**, an instrument that is played in a complex variety of modes. In a sense, all music played within the *geza* during the performance of a play is called *geza ongaku.* It includes music performed by the chanters and instrumentalists who are collectively known as the *hayashigata** or *narimonoshi,* words that may be translated as "orchestra." The chanters all belong to the *nagauta** school of music. The *hayashigata* perform *shamisen,* vocal, or other instrumental music during the entrances and exits of stage characters, during the acting sequences, and in the intervals between scenes; they also produce sound effects, such as wind, rain, and snow. When, on occasion, the orchestra appears on stage to perform, its members sit either on a red-carpeted, stepped platform at the rear of the stage or on platforms designed to blend with the scenic background. This convention is termed *debayashigata* ("onstage orchestra"; *see* DEBAYASHI). Opposed to this is the *kage hayashi** ("in-the-wings orchestra").

Geza music is divided into two main classes, *aikata* and *narimono**. *Aikata* is an accompaniment by *shamisen* alone, no singing being used. *Narimono* makes use mainly of four instruments—the flute *(fue), kotsuzumi** drum, *ōtsuzumi** drum, and *taiko** drum—but may use more than thirty other instruments as well.

MUSICAL ACCOMPANIMENT CHART
(Note: Elements in parentheses are optional.)

AIKATA/ NARIMONO TERMS	INSTRUMENTS USED	SCENES IN WHICH USED
akabana aikata	*shamisen*	Murder scenes in domestic plays.
ame no oto	*ōdaiko**	Sound of rain.

AIKATA/ NARIMONO TERMS	INSTRUMENTS USED	SCENES IN WHICH USED
chakutō	*fue, taiko, ōdaiko*	A ceremonial music played thirty minutes before the curtain opens.
chidori no aikata	*shamisen, ōdaiko, ō* and *kotsuzumi*	Fight scenes on the beach. The *ōdaiko* provides the sound of waves.
chōren taiko	*taiko, shinobue**	Modeled after the Imperial Army parade music of the early Meiji era. Used in battle scenes dealing with the Meiji Restoration.
chōshi kawari no aikata	*shamisen*	A general term for music with a foreign mood; used in "living history" plays dealing with the early feudal period. Also called *hizen bushi* and *gaku no aikata.*
chū no mai (aikata)	*taiko, ō* and *kotsuzumi, fue, (shamisen)*	For entrance of history play characters; for example, when a shogun's envoy appears. It is somewhat faster than *jonomai.*
chūya aikata	*shamisen, ōdaiko*	Used for the police in *Keian Taiheiki**.
daishōiri aikata	*shamisen, ō* and *kotsuzumi*	Often used in fight scenes.
dangire	*taiko*	Chiefly used as two strong beats at the closing of the curtain in a history play.
donchan	*ōdaiko, dorafuchi*	Same as *tōyose.* For battle scenes.

AIKATA/ NARIMONO TERMS	INSTRUMENTS USED	SCENES IN WHICH USED
dontappo	*ōdaiko, kotsuzumi, shinobue*	Fighting scenes in history plays when someone is captured.
dorodoro	*ōdaiko*	Entrances and exits of spirits, ghosts, wizards, and the like. When the drum is lightly beaten, it is called *usudoro**.
ekiro	*suzu*	The sound of bells on a horse's trappings; used to suggest the feeling of traveling. Scenes on horseback, at inns, during the song of a pack-horse driver, and so on.
gaku no aikata	*fue, suzu, taiko, kotsuzumi, gakudaiko, shamisen*	Imitation of *gagaku* (court music). For entry of *kuge* nobles and dignitaries.
goshoku no aikata	*shamisen*	Intimate conversations in palace scenes.
gyōretsu sanjū	*taiko, shamisen*	Used in scenes of processions of feudal lords and for parades.
hachiningei no aikata	*doro, ōdaiko, taiko, atarigane*, shinobue*	For humorous acting.
hamabe uta	singing, *shamisen, ōdaiko*	Seaside scenes.
hatsunichi no aikata	*shamisen, ō* and *kotsuzumi*	Scenes of battle, group fighting, raids.
hayagane	*hontsurigane**	Scenes of calamities and disturbances at temples and for farmers' uprisings.

AIKATA/ NARIMONO TERMS	INSTRUMENTS USED	SCENES IN WHICH USED
haya kagura	*taiko, ōdaiko, shinobue*	For the opening of the prologue piece *(jomaku*)* on the *kaomise** program. Only those for *Shibaraku** and the *Kuruma Biki* scene of *Sugawara Denju Tenarai Kagami** still remain.
hayame no aikata	*shamisen*	For running characters and scenes of hot pursuit.
haya mokugyō aikata	*mokugyō*, shamisen*	Scenes of murder in such lonely places as temples, cemeteries, thickets, and embankments.
hayasōban	*sōban, ōdaiko*	Fight scenes among male comrades, footmen, and sumo wrestlers.
honchōshi no aikata	*shamisen*	Intervals between dialogue of feudal lords and shogunate retainers *(hatamoto)* at the mansions of powerful samurai.
hontsurigane	*hontsurigane*	For tolling the time and for assuming *mie** poses in fight scenes.
ichiban daiko	*ōdaiko*	A ceremonial style used to announce the theatre's opening. It was beaten in the *yagura** in the old days.
ichōiri no aikata	*shamisen, kotsuzumi*	For the entry of military leaders and feudal lords.

AIKATA/ NARIMONO TERMS	INSTRUMENTS USED	SCENES IN WHICH USED
idaten	*shamisen*	To indicate that someone is running quickly. When a courier or footman runs on stage, the *tsuke** clappers are used.
ishidan aikata	*shamisen*, *ō* and *kotsuzumi*	Fight scenes in history plays.
itsu gashira	*taiko*, *ō* and *kotsuzumi*, *ōdaiko*	Five beats in time with the movements of an *aragoto** *mie* pose. Used in the *Kuruma Biki* scene of *Sugawara Denju Tenarai Kagami*.
iwato kagura	*shinobue*, *taiko*, *ōdaiko*, (*shamisen*)	Used in scenes of *aragoto*, *danmari**, and dance fighting. Heard in *Soga no Taimen**.
jizō kyō	singing, *shamisen*, *matsumushi*	In mournful, lonely temple scenes.
jonomai	*taiko*, *ō* and *kotsuzumi*, *fue*, (*shamisen*)	A slow-tempo music for the entrance and exit of feudal lords and other samurai.
kagen	*ōdaiko*, *fue*, (*shamisen*)	Played at the opening of history play scenes and for the entrance and exit of characters.
kakeri	*ō* and *kotsuzumi*, *fue*	Played in battle scenes (for the entrance of crazed and maimed characters).
kakubei jishi	*shinobue*, *taiko*, (singing, *shamisen*)	Imitation of the Kakubei lion dance music, performed in the streets. Played at the opening of scenes in urban shops in domestic plays and for the entry of characters in these plays.

AIKATA/ NARIMONO TERMS	INSTRUMENTS USED	SCENES IN WHICH USED
kari to tsubame	*shamisen, atarigane*	Used for the entrances and exits of "street knights" *(otokodate)* and during their dialogue. This music has a bold and lively quality.
kassai nenbutsu	*taiko, matsumushi*	Imitates the sound of bell and drum used in reading aloud of Buddhist prayer. Used for desolate scenes of murder and struggle at farmhouses, at embankments, and in thickets.
kata shagiri	*taiko, ō* and *kotsuzumi, fue, (ōdaiko)*	Used at the beginning of dance pieces taken from the Nō and Kyōgen theatres, at the beginning of formal stage announcements *(kōjō*)*, and for the *mie* at the final curtain of certain history plays.
kawatta no aikata	*shamisen*	Combined with long speeches that are prefaced by the words, "Please listen to me" *(okiki kudasare).*
kaze no oto	*ōdaiko*	Sound of wind.
keiko uta	*shamisen,* singing	Used at the opening and closing of scenes in urban shops and homes; also for entrances and exits. It represents the sound of a neighborhood music master at practice.
kinuta	*kinuta*	A sound resembling the beating of the wooden fulling blocks that country people strike against cloth to soften it and make it shine. In scenes at country homes.

AIKATA/ NARIMONO TERMS	INSTRUMENTS USED	SCENES IN WHICH USED
kiyari	*shamisen*, singing	Used in scenes of festivals in domestic plays for the entrance of lively characters and geisha.
kodama	*kotsuzumi*	Depicts an echo resounding through mountains and valleys.
kōkyū iri no aikata	*shamisen, kōkyū*	Scenes in which a mistress reviles her lover and other scenes permeated by a feeling of pathos.
komadori no aikata	*shamisen*	Scenes in which children play tag and ponies romp about. Also when Yuranosuke cavorts in *Kanadehon Chūshingura**.
komearai	*shamisen, (kinuta, taiko, shinobue, atarigane)*	The name, meaning "rice washing," is used because the mode is often played as accompaniment to gestures of washing rice. It is heard in comical scenes.
koto uta	*shamisen*, singing, *(koto*)*	At the opening of palace scenes, for entrance and exit of court ladies, and so on.
kumiuchi no aikata	*shamisen, kotsuzumi*	Fight scenes in history plays.
magosa	*taiko, okedō, shinobue, atarigane*	The music for lion dances and other lively scenes.
maigo	*taiko, atarigane*	Modeled after the sound of a *taiko* drum, which was beaten during a search for a lost child. Used for scenes in which the police are searching for a fugitive.

AIKATA/ NARIMONO TERMS	INSTRUMENTS USED	SCENES IN WHICH USED
midare	*taiko, fue*	For exits and entrances of court ladies and princesses in palace scenes.
mikoshi taiko	*ōdaiko*	The music for lion dances and other lively scenes.
mitate no aikata	*shamisen*	Used in Act VII of *Kanadehon Chūshingura* when an entertainer and a waitress are chosen.
mitsu taiko	*ōdaiko*	Scenes of arrest. The term comes from the "three beats" *(mitsu)* given—*don, don, don.*
miya kagura	*taiko, ōdaiko, shinobue, chappa, shamisen*	Melodic variations of *kagura* shrine music. For scenes at shrines *(miya).*
mizu no oto	*ōdaiko*	Sound of water in scenes at riversides and embankments. Used when something is thrown into the river.
mokugyō iri no aikata	*mokugyō, shamisen*	For scenes in the vicinity of temples, graveyards, and lonely fields in domestic plays and for entrances, exits, and the intervals between dialogue.
momo no ki aikata	*shamisen, ō* and *kotsuzumi*	For calm entrances and exits in history plays by major roles and for intervals between dialogue.
monogi no aikata	*shamisen, (ō* and *kotsuzumi)*	Used in history plays to cover interludes while an actor changes costumes.

AIKATA/ NARIMONO TERMS	INSTRUMENTS USED	SCENES IN WHICH USED
mushi no aikata	*shamisen, (mushibue)*	Intervals in dialogue in scenes taking place in lonely fields.
namameki aikata	*shamisen*	Love scenes and the intervals between dialogue in such scenes.
nami no oto	*ōdaiko*	Sound of waves. When curtain opens and closes on seaside scenes and when characters enter and exit.
nedori	*fue*	The sound of wind blowing through crevices. For entrance of ghosts, apparitions, and evil spirits.
niban daiko	*ōdaiko*	Announces the opening of the theatre. A ceremonial type of music.
odoriji	*shamisen*, singing	Used for characters' entrances and at the beginning and end of scenes in the pleasure quarters of the Kamigata area.
oimawashi aikata	*shamisen, taiko*	Fight scenes in the pleasure quarters in history plays. Used near the final curtain.
okashimi aikata	*shamisen, ōdaiko, atarigane*	Used to accompany humorous behavior, such as fight scenes with *dōkegata** characters, fights between dead persons, and the like.
okuri sanjū	*shamisen*	Often employed after the *uresanjū* (see below) for sad exits.

AIKATA/ NARIMONO TERMS	INSTRUMENTS USED	SCENES IN WHICH USED
ongaku	*suzu, ōdaiko*	At temples and for the entrances of goddesses.
raijo	*fue, taiko, ōdaiko*	Used for the entry of a fox character. When a fox leaves quickly, a rapid version—*haya raijo*—is played.
rokudan no aikata	*shamisen*	Imitates a famous *koto* piece, *Rokudan*. For conversations between samurai.
roro no kosomichi	singing, *shamisen*	Murder and fight scenes.
sagari hata	*taiko, ō* and *kotsuzumi, fue*	This music follows that of the Nō orchestra and is used for solemn palace scenes, such as when nobles enter and exit.
sandanme aikata	*shamisen, ōdaiko*	For characters making rapid exits and entrances in history plays and during the intervals between hurried dialogue.
*sangesange**	singing, *shamisen*	A sung version of a high-ranking Buddhist priest's spoken prayer. At the opening of domestic play scenes and for entrance and exit of scamps.
sarashi	*fue, taiko, ō* and *kotsuzumi*	Bold fight scenes in *aragoto* and dance plays.
satsumasa	*shamisen*, singing	For entrances and exits of lively characters; also used without song for the passages between dialogue.

AIKATA/ NARIMONO TERMS	INSTRUMENTS USED	SCENES IN WHICH USED
seiten	*taiko*, *ō* and *kotsuzumi*, *shinobue*, *atarigane*, (singing, *shamisen*)	This derives from festival music. For opening scenes of festivals in domestic plays and for the exit and entrance of characters in these plays.
seri no aikata	*taiko*, *ō* and *kotsuzumi*, *fue*	This accompanies the use of the *seri** stage trap, and special music is composed for it.
shaden	*taiko*, *kodora fuchi*	Music patterned after the sound of rattling sabers. For scenes of flower viewing that erupt in confusion.
shagiri	*taiko*, *ōdaiko*, *fue*	Always played to accompany the end of an act, it is a ceremonial type.
shichome	*taiko*, *ō* and *kotsuzumi*, *shinobue*, *atarigane*	A melodic variation of festival music. For fight scenes among bold characters and for chase scenes.
shikoro no aikata	*shamisen*, *kankara taiko*, *taiko*, *atarigane*	Mingles with humorous acting. It is used for jugglers and acrobats, too.
shikoro sanjū	*shamisen*, *ō* and *kotsuzumi*	Also called *yoroitsuke*, it is played while a character puts on armor.
shinobi sanjū	*shamisen*	When characters quietly sound out each other's feelings.
shinoiri no aikata	*shinobue*, *shamisen*	Used in suicide *(seppuku)* scenes when a dying character remembers the past.

AIKATA/ NARIMONO TERMS	INSTRUMENTS USED	SCENES IN WHICH USED
shirabe	*taiko*, *ō* and *kotsuzumi*, *fue*	For entrances and exits from the hall of a samurai's residence.
shukuba sawagi	*dorafuchi*, *taiko*	Scenes in rural pleasure quarters and post-town teahouses. Also called *zaigo sawagi* and *inaka sawagi*.
shuntō no aikata	*shamisen*, *ō* and *kotsuzumi*	For exits by samurai outside the curtain.
shūra hayashi (aikata)	*ō* and *kotsuzumi*, *(shamisen)*	Fight scenes taking place in the gardens of samurai mansions, matches in arenas, and the like.
sōban	*sōban*, *taiko*	For the opening of scenes in temples and their environs and for the entry and exit of characters.
sōgaku	*shinobue*, *fue*, *taiko*, *atarigane*, *pipi*	Modeled after *gagaku* court music. Played in palace and temple scenes of plays placed in the early feudal period.
sorabue	*shinobue*	Blown mournfully at deathbed repentance scenes.
sugomi no aikata	*shamisen*	Played between speeches and action to depict the feeling of psychological and emotional desolation.
sumō no aikata	*shamisen*, *ōdaiko*, (singing)	For the acting out of sumo wrestling. *Komeyama kanku* is used for the wrestlers' entrance.
sumō taiko	*ōdaiko*, (singing)	A rhythmic version of the *yagura* drum. For sumo wrestling scenes.

AIKATA/ NARIMONO TERMS	INSTRUMENTS USED	SCENES IN WHICH USED
tada no aikata	*shamisen*	Played to fill the intervals of intimate dialogue in history and domestic plays, to mark characters' entrances and exits, and to represent the state of mind of the characters.
tadauta	singing, *shamisen*	Accompanies the exit of the lead role in history plays.
taimen sanjū	*ōdaiko*	For entrance of Gorō and Jurō in *Soga no Taimen.*
takano no aikata	*shamisen, kotsuzumi*	The processions of feudal lords going falconing in history plays. A type of *ichōiri no aikata* (see above).
takesu no aikata	*shamisen, taiko, kankara taiko, atarigane, shinobue, ōdaiko*, singing	Opening scenes at exhibition booths or at the Okuyama or Ryōkoku pleasure quarters in Asakusa.
taki no oto	*ōdaiko*	Sound of waterfalls.
tawara date no aikata	*shamisen, ōdaiko*	Played in the *Ga no Iwai* scene of *Sugawara Denju Tenarai Kagami* when the brothers Umēo and Matsuō battle with bags of straw.
tennō dachi	*fue, taiko, ō* and *kotsuzumi*	Opening of palace scenes in history plays.
tentsutsu	*shamisen*	When characters enter hurriedly.
teragaku no aikata	*shamisen, suzu, ōdaiko*	Temple scenes in history plays. Provides a quiet mood.

AIKATA/ NARIMONO TERMS	INSTRUMENTS USED	SCENES IN WHICH USED
teragane	*dorafuchi*	Copied after the sound of bells that report temple events. Used for scenes of temple environs at evening and for the close of scenes of sorrow.
tobisari	*taiko, ōdaiko, fue*	For flights of spirits, disappearances of wizards, or exits of *aragoto* supermen.
tohiyo	*fue*	The sound of bird voices.
toki no daiko	*ōdaiko*	Copies the sound of the drum beating the time in a castle. Used in castle scenes for the entrances of villains.
toki no kane	*hontsurigane, dora*	Represents the sound of a bell tolling the time.
tomomori no aikata	*shamisen*	The Daimotsu Beach scene in *Yoshitsune Senbon Zakura** in which the figure of Tomomori appears.
tōri kagura	*shinobue, okedō, (shamisen)*	New Year's in the pleasure quarters. Copied after the music of street entertainers.
tōyose	*ōdaiko, dorafuchi*	For battles. It used to be called *donshan*.
tsujiuchi no aikata	*shamisen, taiko*	The drum beating used to call people to a street junction. Used in the Kamigata pleasure quarters, at exhibition booths, and on temple grounds.

AIKATA/ NARIMONO TERMS	INSTRUMENTS USED	SCENES IN WHICH USED
tsukkake	*ōdaiko, (fue, taiko)*	Used for entrances of strong characters in battle scenes.
tsukuda no aikata	*shamisen*	River and riverbank scenes.
uchidashi	*ōdaiko*	To announce the end of a day's performance. A ceremonial type of music.
uresanjū	*shamisen*	A *shamisen* solo after a *hanamichi* exit, providing an expression of grief.
wasure gai no aikata	*shamisen*	When the ladies-in-waiting are seated in a row in the grand hall of a samurai mansion.
yachio hayashi no aikata	*shamisen, (koto, shinobue, ō* and *kotsuzumi)*	Fight scenes among jealous palace women.
yamaarai	*ōdaiko*	Gives the ill feeling of rumbling in the mountains.
yamaoroshi	*ōdaiko*	For the opening and closing of mountain scenes, the entrance and exit of characters, and the accompaniment to stage movement.
yatai hayashi	*taiko, ōdaiko, shinobue, atarigane*	For the opening and closing of festival scenes and fight scenes.
yoban taiko	*hiramaru taiko (hyōshigi, shamisen)*	To represent scenes taking place late at night in domestic plays.
yōkyū aikata	*shamisen, ōdaiko*	Scenes in the pleasure quarters. Also called *dokyū no aikata.*

AIKATA/ NARIMONO TERMS	INSTRUMENTS USED	SCENES IN WHICH USED
yotsu take aikata	*shamisen*, singing	For opening of scenes in a downtown section, in slums or at poor peoples' homes and for entrances and exits in these scenes.
yuki no aikata	*shamisen*	Quiet scenes in which snow *(yuki)* is falling.
yuki no oto	*ōdaiko*	Sound of snow. For opening and closing of scenes in which snow is falling, for entrances and exits, and for stage movement. A blizzard's sound effects are called *yuki oroshi.*
yū rei sanjū	*shamisen*	For entrances of angry ghosts.
zaigo uta	*shamisen*, singing	Country and farm scenes.
zai no aikata	*shamisen*	Country and farm scenes. It is the *zaigo uta* with only the *shamisen* playing.
zen no tsutome	*dorafuchi, ōdaiko*	Used for the entrance of priests in temples and their environs and in scenes taking place in thickets and lonely embankments.

GEZA TSUKE. A book in which the *geza** musicians' cues for a specific play are written. It is an abbreviated name for *geza tsukechō* (*see* TSUKECHŌ). The *geza tsuke* is usually oblong and made of rice paper folded lengthwise. The person in charge of the *geza* music decides on the *aikata**, song, and *narimono** selections in discussion with the actors and writers (at the *tsuketate* rehearsal: *see* REHEARSALS). These decisions are noted in the *geza tsuke*.

GHOST PLAYS. Known as *kaidan mono* (or *kyōgen*), these are eerie plays in which ghosts and apparitions appear. Angry ghosts and departed spirits figured in even the earliest period of Kabuki drama; the increased decadence in social affairs that arose in Japan with the Bunka-Bunsei era (1804-30) brought about the creation of many ghost plays in order to satisfy the demands of theatregoers who displayed a growing taste for the bizarre. The trend started with Tsuruya Nanboku IV's* *Tenjiku Tokubei Ikoku Banashi** (1804); Onoe Matsusuke I* was very successful in it with his startling stage tricks *(keren*)*. Thereafter, each of Nanboku's new plays showed an interweaving of intense love, torture, and murder scenes. Later actors perfected the genre, using new stage techniques that were created and passed on by Onoe Kikugorō III*. The great ghost plays include *Tōkaidō Yotsuya Kaidan** and *Tsuta Momiji Utsunoya Tōge**. *(See also* PLAY CATEGORIES.)

GIBA SURU. Sitting in a casual position, such as when one lounges to drink sake; a cross-legged position. Also said when an awkward fellow makes a big fuss about sitting down.

GIDAYŪ BUSHI. A narrative *(jōruri*)* musical style founded by Takemoto Gidayū. The son of a farmer in Tennōji Village, Osaka, he was a natural musician. He became the pupil of Kiyomizu Rihei, took the name of Kiyomizu Ridayū, and began to perform musical narratives in the puppet theatres of Osaka and Kyoto. He later changed his name to Takemoto Gidayū and in 1684 established the Takemoto-za puppet theatre in Osaka's Dōtonbori district. By combining the period's two outstanding schools of narrative recitation—the violent style of Inoue Harimanojō and the subtle style of Uji Kaganojō—he skillfully created the single most popular style of his time. As the *gidayū bushi,* this new style soon overwhelmed the others; finally, *gidayū* was interchangeable with *jōruri* as a word for narrative recital in the puppet theatre and Kabuki. One of Gidayū's pupils, Takemoto Uneme (Toyotake Wakadayū) set himself up as an independent performer and created the Toyotake-za. When this theatre became the rival of the Takemoto-za, the style of *gidayū bushi* really began to flourish. Kabuki absorbed many of the puppet theatre's *gidayū* plays, swelling its repertory. *Gidayū* *bushi* therefore occupies an extremely important place as a type of Kabuki music. (*See also* GIDAYŪ KYŌGEN.)

GIDAYŪ KYŌGEN. Plays written for the puppet theatre with a *gidayū bushi** style of chanting that have been adapted for Kabuki. These works are also called *jōruri**, *maruhon mono, maruhon kabuki, takemoto geki,* and *denden mono**. The first such play was Chikamatsu Monzaemon's *Matsuyo no Komuro Bushi* (1708), performed under a new title, *Tanba no Yosaku.* It was not until 1716, however, when Kabuki adopted the enormous *Kokusenya Kassen**, that the process of borrowing puppet plays became a serious commercial consideration. Eventually, puppet play adaptations became a principal source of Kabuki's repertoire. They generally are considered Kabuki's best examples of dramatic literature.

Known to the West as Bunraku, the puppet theatre is known by that and by several other terms in Japan. Perhaps the most common is *ningyō jōruri* ("puppet" *jōruri*). So great has been the interchange of techniques between Kabuki and the puppet theatre that they may be considered sister arts. Although related now, these arts spring from different sources, Kabuki from the folk and popular dances of the late sixteenth century, and the puppet theatre from the various types of narrative recitals known in medieval Japan. These recited styles joined together with the art of the itinerant puppeteer to produce the unique Japanese puppet theatre.

Both Kabuki and the puppet theatre made tremendous progress during the Genroku period (1688-1703), the former primarily because of its two great stars, Ichikawa Danjūrō I* and Sakata Tōjūrō I*, and the latter because of the playwright Chikamatsu Monzaemon and the chanter Takemoto Gidayū (*see also* GIDAYŪ BUSHI).

Following the death of Tōjūrō in 1709, Kabuki in the Kamigata area rapidly declined in popularity, while the puppet theatre reached new heights. The golden period of the puppet theatre lasted until the late eighteenth century; during this time the one-man-to-a-puppet system that Chikamatsu had written for changed to a technique of three men to a puppet, allowing for greater attention to realism in the puppets' movements. Numerous outstanding playwrights appeared and produced one fine puppet play after the other. Kamigata Kabuki, suffering a dearth of good new scripts, continued to strive for audiences with the puppets, borrowing not only their plays, but many of their acting techniques as well. In Edo the situation was rather different. Edo Kabuki was not as dependent on the puppet theatre for audience appeal and produced puppet-derived plays principally for visiting Kamigata actors and on special occasions. Edo was fortunate in being able to produce original scripts that local audiences were interested in seeing.

As the performances of the puppets grew more lifelike, puppeteers began to rely less on the puppets' intrinsic qualities and more on those of living actors. With the consequent shift in emphasis from a form in which the narrative recital was the principal ingredient to one in which the visual element vied for the spectator's attention, the puppet theatre soon was faced with a major problem: its performance style had approached too closely to that of the Kabuki. Given the choice, most spectators preferred actors of flesh and blood in this kind of theatre. The very plays created for the puppets came to be more effective in the hands of the Kabuki actors, and as a result, Kabuki rose again to a position of prominence, and the puppet theatre gradually lost ground. (*See also* PLAY CATEGORIES.)

GINBARU. "Silver-polished"; the sweaty shine on an actor's face when he has had to wear his makeup for a long time without getting a chance to fix it.

GINBŌ O FURIAGERU. "To brandish a silver truncheon." A term used to describe someone who is arrogant to others; it comes from the term used to describe the behavior of Kabuki policemen who brandish *(furiageru)* their silver truncheons *(jitte)* when they surround their prey. The *jitte* is made by applying silver paper to a wooden rod, thus giving it the name *ginbō* (literally, "silver stick").

GION SAIREI SHINKŌKI. Nakamura Akei, Asada Itchō, others. Also called *Kinkakuji. Jidaimono**. *Jōruri**. Five acts. December 1757. Toyotake-za, Osaka.

Today, theatres present only the fourth act, the *Kinkakuji* scene of this play, which is based on the *Shinchōki*, the record of Oda Nobunaga's life (1534-1582). Kabuki presented its adaptation of the play a year after its puppet theatre premiere, at Kyoto's Sawamura Somematsu-za. Edo's Morita-za* put the play on the same year with Nakamura Denkurō II as Tokichi.

Matsunaga Daizen has overthrown the shogunate and is living in luxury at the Temple of the Golden Pavilion (Kinkakuji). He has summoned Princess Yuki, daughter of Kano Sesson, a famous artist, to have her do his bidding. Aware that Daizen was her late father's enemy, she assaults him. As punishment for her effrontery, she is tied to the trunk of a cherry tree. With her feet she gathers the petals around the tree and with them draws a rat, which miraculously turns into the real thing and gnaws through her ropes. Meanwhile, Daizen's *go* (a chesslike game) partner, Kinoshita Tokichi, who plans to capture Daizen, rescues Keijuin, mother of the late shogun, from her imprisonment by Daizen. After a battle with Daizen, Tokichi leaves, vowing to meet up with Daizen once more, on the battlefield.

The magnificent use of the stage lift (*see* SERI) in this scene is famous. Princess Yuki is considered one of Kabuki's three main "princess" roles, the others being Princess Yaegaki and Princess Toki (*see also* AKAHIME; SANHIME); the role requires dignity and romantic feeling. The scene with the rat is often performed in puppet theatre fashion *(ningyō buri*)*. Among the play's other famous highlights is the moment when Tokichi fishes a *go* box out of the well into which it has been thrown.

GOBAN TAIHEIKI. Chikamatsu Monzaemon*. *Jidaimono**. *Jōruri**. Two acts. June 1706. Takemoto-za, Osaka.

This work deserves attention as one of the early works dealing with the Akō vendetta, later immortalized in *Kanadehon Chūshingura**. Today's script is the work of Watanabe Katei (1908). Chikamatsu's play is the second half of a drama he had produced in May of the same year.

The manservant Okahei, who is really an enemy spy named Teraoka Heiemon, is deceived by Oishi Kuranosuke's apparent dissipation. He reports it to Kuranosuke's enemies, the forces of Lord Kira, thus throwing them off their guard. However, suspecting the truth about Okahei, Kuranosuke has his son Chikara slay the servant. But before he dies, Okahei, moved by Kuranosuke's unflagging loyalty to the cause of avenging his master's death, provides information regarding the enemy's castle using *go* stones (a chesslike game). Hoping to encourage Kuranosuke in his plans, his mother and wife commit suicide. Together with Chikara, Kuranosuke leaves to carry out his revenge. The forty-seven like-minded samurai achieve their long-awaited desire in breaking into Kira's castle.

Outstanding actors of the leading role in this century were Nakamura Kichiemon I* and Nakamura Ganjirō I*.

GOCHISŌ. A "treat." When a highly popular or respected senior actor appears in a minor role. Also, when a usually unpopular speech or piece of business is performed.

GOCHŪSHIN. In history plays adapted from the puppet theatre, this is a soldier who enters to report conditions on the battlefield. Also, the word refers to the performance of such a role. Wearing a gorgeous net *yoten** costume, he runs in on the *hanamichi**, bearing a sword or spear and crying, *"gochūshin, gochūshin"* ("I have come to report, I have come to report"). He outlines the course of a battle supposedly raging offstage while performing a striking series of movements to the accompaniment of a chanter and *shamisen** player. When finished, he runs off, shouting, *"hayaosaraba"* ("I bid you a hasty farewell"). *Gochūshin* roles include Sagami Gorō and Irie Tanzō in the Daimotsu Beach scene of *Yoshitsune Senbon Zakura** and Shiragaki Tarō in *Ōmi Genji Senjin Yakata**.

Matsumoto Kōshirō VIII* as the *gochūshin** character, Shirosuka Rokuro, in *Honchō Nijūshikō**. He wears the *suami** and *chihaya**. *Courtesy of Waseda University Tsubouchi Engeki Hakubutsukan (Tsubouchi Memorial Theatre Museum).*

GODAIRIKI (KOI NO FŪJIME). Namiki Gohei I*. *Sewamono**. Three acts. May 1794, Nishi no Shibai, Kyoto.

This play dramatizes a 1737 incident in which the Satsuma retainer Sada Hachiemon killed the courtesan Kikuno and four other people in a fit of jealousy. Dramatizations of the event had appeared beginning in 1756, both in Kabuki and in the puppet theatre. In 1792 Gohei appears to have had two plays produced on the subject, one in Kyoto and one in Osaka. After the May 1794 production of *Godairiki Koi no Fūjime*, a shorter version was produced, in October of the same year, at Osaka's Naka no Shibai. It bore the title *Shima Meguri Uso no Kikigaki* and featured Onoe Shinshichi as Katsuma Gengobei, Arashi Koroku III as Sasano Sangobei, and Yamashita Yaozō as Kikuno. In these versions the actual name of the courtesan was used and the location of the action was at Sonezaki, where the murders took place. Gohei moved to Edo at the end of 1794, and in January 1795 the play was produced at Edo's Miyako-za, under the title *Edo Sunago Kichirei Soga*. The courtesan's name was changed from Kikuno to Koman, and the action was set in Fukagawa, which was more familiar to Edoites. Sawamura Sōjūrō II* played Gengobei and had an enormous success. Segawa Kikunojō III* played Koman.

The play's production in Edo was a landmark event. Up until its presentation, Edo productions had included both history and domestic style scenes in a single play produced with one title. Gohei introduced the Kamigata custom of presenting two separate plays on a program, a history play *(ichibanme mono*)* and a domestic play *(nibanme mono*)*. Though many followed his lead, the practice did not become a universal one in Edo.

Satsuma Gengobei has followed his young master to Osaka, where the latter has come to seek a family heirloom. His fellow retainer, Sasano Sangobei, persistently attempts to woo the courtesan Kikuno, but she shows no interest in him. To force him to leave her alone she entreats Gengobei to act the part of her lover for a time. However, Kikuno actually falls in love with Gengobei and, as a sign of her affections, writes the word *godairiki* on her *shamisen**. This word, which cannot be translated, was used by courtesans of the Edo period as a curse to prevent anyone other than their lovers from opening their love letters. It also was meant as a talisman against infidelity. However, because of a trick played on her by Sangobei, Kikuno heartlessly berates Gengobei. Seeing the word *godairiki* on the *shamisen*, Gengobei interprets it as being meant for Sangobei and kills the courtesan. He soon learns of her true feelings, though, and discovers that Sangobei has stolen the heirloom for which his master is searching. He slays Sangobei as well and retrieves the treasure.

The speech in which the courtesan reviles her lover is a familiar device and is found in many *sewamono:* it is known as *enkiri*, a separation scene*.

In some productions of this work the courtesan is called Koman instead of Kikuno. Many later adaptations of the play appeared in the puppet and Kabuki theatres. The original is thought to be Gohei's masterpiece.

GOHIIKI KANJINCHŌ. Sakurada Jisuke I*. Also called *Imo Arai Kanjinchō. Jidaimono**. Kabuki. Six acts. November 1773. Nakamura-za*, Edo.

Actors in the original cast of the play included Ichikawa Ebizō (later Ichikawa Danjūrō IV*) as Benkei, Ichikawa Danjūrō V* as Togashi, and Matsumoto Kōshirō IV* as Yoshitsune.

The famous flight of Yoshitsune, the great medieval general, into the provinces is the chief concern of this work. Yoshitsune and his men, disguised as priests, are fleeing from the forces of Yoshitsune's brother, Yoritomo, when they are stopped at the Ataka barrier gate. Benkei, the warrior-priest, is bound, but the others are permitted to proceed. Benkei bides his time, then tears the ropes with his superhuman strength, pulls off his captors' heads, puts them in a rain barrel, and mixes them around as if washing potatoes *(imo arai).* After behaving in this riotous fashion, Benkei leaves to join his master.

The scene in which the violent priest mixes the heads together with a pilgrim's staff is famous. *Gohiiki Kanjinchō* is still performed in the outlandish *aragoto** style that was popular when it was created. Although there is no published translation, Professor Leonard Pronko staged an English version of this play under the title *Old Time Kanjinchō* at Pomona College in the early 1970s. The play's modern history dates from its frequent revivals by Ichikawa Ennosuke II (*see* ICHIKAWA EN'O) early in the present century. He created an impressive *kumadori** makeup for Benkei by applying blue and black lines on a red background. (*See* AKATTSURA.)

GOJŪNICHI. "Fifty days"; a wig that gives the impression of fifty days' growth of hair on the pate. Matsuō wears it in the *Terakoya* scene of *Sugawara Denju Tenarai Kagami**. It suggests that the wearer has been too ill to trim his hair.

GONAN. "Troubles"; when a production's box office receipts have been so poor that there is no money to pay salaries.

GONJŌ. Fukumori Kiusuke. Also called: *Gonpachi, Sono Kouta Yume no Yoshiwara, Kamisuki Gonpachi, Hiyoku no Chō Yume no Yoshiwara. Shosagoto**. *Kiyomoto**. January 1816. Nakamura-za*, Edo.

The original work was divided into two halves; part I was called *Gonjō* and part II was *Gonke.* Part II is rarely staged.

Komurasaki, the courtesan, comes running from the Yoshiwara pleasure quarters to the side of her lover, Gonpachi, who is about to be executed at Suzugamori for murder. After exchanging nuptial cups at the execution site, Komurasaki cuts Gonpachi's bonds. All that has transpired, however, turns out to be a dream of Gonpachi as he travels in a palanquin to visit the pleasure quarters. The stage makes a complete scenic change from the gloom of the execution grounds to the glory of the Yoshiwara; similarly, Gonpachi makes a total change from the garments of a prisoner to those of a stylish visitor to the pleasure district.

Ichikawa Danjūrō VII* played the first Gonpachi and Onoe Kikugorō III* was Komurasaki.

GONKURŌ. The name of a clerk in the play *Kurote Gumi Sukeroku.* Used to refer to someone who is a ladies' man, but who is dishonest, uses people to serve his own ends, and will squeeze anything and anyone for money.

GONPACHI. A parasite. From the character named Shirai Gonpachi who lives at the home of Banzui Chōbei and sponges off him. (*See GONJŌ; BANZUI CHŌBEI SHŌJIN NO MANAITA.)*

GONTA. From the character Igami no Gonta in *Yoshitsune Senbon Zakura**; a villain.

GONZA TO SUKEJŪ. Okamoto Kidō*. *Shin kabuki**. Two acts. July 1926. Kabuki-za*, Tokyo.

A comical detective story based on a case solved by Ōoka, a famous magistrate in Japanese history.

Though the palanquin bearers Gonza and Sukejū are very good friends, they are always quarreling. They live in a rear tenement in Edo's Kanda section. One day, when the tenement's well is being cleaned, the Osaka haberdasher Kikosaburō visits the place. He states that he wants to do whatever he can to aid his father, Genbei, who has been arrested for murder. Out of public concern, Gonza and Sukejū examine the scene of the crime and manage to capture the villainous Suketarō, the true murderer. Genbei is safely released from prison.

Gonza to Sukejū depicts with great appeal the manners of Edo's citizens. It abounds with a feeling of summer, has a good deal of warmth, and is delightfully humorous.

GORŌ. Mimasuya Nisōji. Also called *Yae Kokonoe Hana no Sugata E, Ame no Gorō. Shosagoto**. *Nagauta**. July 1841. Nakamura-za*, Edo.

One scene remains from a nine-change "transformation piece*" *(henge mono)*, a dance depicting the young dandy and brothel frequenter, Gorō.

Onoe Takenzō created the role. Gorō wears the *kumadori** makeup style called *mukimi guma** and has a purple crepe scarf tied around his head and under his chin. This appearance suggests that, despite his *aragoto** nature, he has an element of the gentle *wagoto** style in his character.

GOSHŌ ZAKURA (HORIKAWA YOUCHI). Matsuda Bunkodō, Miyoshi Shōraku. Also called *Toyata Monogatari, Horikawa Youchi. Jidaimono**. *Jōruri**. Five acts. January 1737. Takemoto-za, Osaka.

A work based on materials in the chronicles the *Gikeiki* and the *Heike Monogatari.* Kabuki's first version of the play was staged at Kyoto's Sawamura-za in 1755. In 1773 Edo saw it at the Ichimura-za*. Act III is the most frequently performed part of this play; called *Benkei Jōshi,* it tells the legend of the warrior priest Benkei within a story about a dispute between two brothers, Yoritomo and Yoshitsune. Act IV, *Toyata Monogatari,* is also performed often.

Kyō no Kimi, wife of the Genji general Yoshitsune, is the daughter of an enemy general of the Heike clan. For this reason Yoritomo orders that she be killed. Benkei, acting as Yoshitsune's envoy, comes to the Horikawa palace of Chamberlain Tarō, in whose care Kyō no Kimi has been placed. Tarō would like to substitute the head of Shinobu, a lady-in-waiting, for Kyō no Kimi's, but Shinobu's mother, Owasa, cannot comply. She explains that according to a vow she made many years ago, Shinobu would not die before meeting the man who fathered her. Benkei stabs Shinobu from behind, stating that he was the very man to whom Owasa had made her vow; as proof, he shows her his sleeve, which matches one left with her by Shinobu's father. Knowing that Shinobu is his daughter, he carries out the substitution. To dispel any further doubts that Yoritomo may harbor, Tarō kills himself. His head, as that of Kyō no Kimi's guardian, will lend credence to the report that the other head really belonged to Yoshitsune's wife.

When Benkei makes his colorful confession, he shows abundant fatherly affection. Quite popular is the greatly exaggerated weeping of Benkei, who is acted in the bravado *aragoto** style and dresses in the grim costume of black robes with long trailing trousers *(nagabakama),* a formalized *kumadori** makeup, and a fanciful *kuruma bin** wig.

GOTAIHEIKI (SHIRAISHI BANASHI). Kino Jōtarō, Utei Enba, Yō Yodai. *Jidaimono**. *Jōruri**. Eleven acts. January 1780. Geki-za, Edo.

A play that combines the true stories of the attempted *coup d'etat* of Yui Shōsetsu in 1651 and that of a revenge carried out by two young sisters in the inner provinces in 1717. Act VII, the brothel scene *(Ageya),* is still frequently performed.

Shinobu, who has come from the provinces to visit her sister, is almost kidnapped by the evil Kankurō, but is saved by the Daikoku-ya's proprietor,

Soroku. Miyagino, the Daikoku-ya's favorite courtesan, is Shinobu's sister. The two resolve to revenge the murder of their father by Shiza Daishichi. Soroku compares the girls to the Soga brothers, who carried out a famous vendetta against their father's murderer; he rebukes them, though, for their overimpetuosity. Daishichi has been visiting Miyagino disguised as a guest, but he is discovered and flees. Soroku gives Miyagino her bond of indenture and a pass to the pleasure quarters so that she can come and go as she pleases. The sisters then depart.

The contrast of the rustic sister with her citified sister, leading courtesan of the Yoshiwara, is a fascinating conception and provides this scene with rich human qualities. Kabuki produced its version of the play in the same year as the puppet play premiered, at Edo's Morita-za*. Only the revenge theme was performed in later revivals.

H

HABA. A term first used in the puppet theatre; it refers to the moment when a play's performance begins.

HABUTAE. A silk cloth that the actor puts over his scalp in order to cover his hair and his hairline prior to donning the wig. The portion of the *habutae* that can be seen (on the forehead) when the wig is in place is made up in the same color as the face. There are two important varieties of *habutae;* one is the short *han* ("half") *habutae,* used when a wig that covers the whole head *(suppori*)* is worn; the other is the *maru* ("round") *habutae,* used with the kind of wig that is built on a copper framework and holds hair only on the side-lock portions so that the shaved pate can show. *Seitai**, the blue cosmetic, is applied to the crown to give it a shaved look. There is also the *metsuri habutae,* a short cloth tied tightly around the head to raise the eyes and make the actor's face more attractive.

HACHIJIN (SHUGO NO HONJŌ). Nakamura Gyōgan, Sagawa Tōta. *Jidaimono**. *Jōruri**. Eleven acts. September 1807. Dōtonobori Onishi no Shibai, Osaka.

A dramatization of the popular tale concerning the loyalty and subsequent poisoning of Katō Kiyomasa. Act IV, *Gozabune,* and Act VIII, *Honjō,* are still performed. The first Kabuki adaptation was staged in 1808 at Kyoto's Kitasoku no Shibai and Osaka's Nishi no Shibai, while Edo witnessed it at the Morita-za* in 1810.

The scene is at Nijō Castle. Satō Masakiyo, invited by Tokimasa (a theatrical substitute for the name of the Shogun Ieyasu) to drink what he knows to be secretly poisoned wine, does so because he feels deeply moved by the loyalty of Tokimasa's retainer, Mori Sanzaemon. The wine's effects are lethal, but not immediately fatal. While returning to his own castle by boat, Masakiyo, who is fighting the wine's potent effects, shares the company of his son, Kazuenosuke and his daughter-in-law Hinaginu, Sanzaemon's daughter. Attacked by a party of men sent by Tokimasa, Masakiyo valiantly kills them. Back at his castle Masakiyo secludes himself in his room. Since Hinaginu is the daughter of his father's enemy, Kazuenosuke must divorce her, an act that leads to her suicide. Masakiyo obtains the services of two noble generals, Kojima and Sasaki, and enlists them in the cause of his young master Haruwaka (a substitution for the name of the historical Hisayoshi). Masakiyo then dies with a clear mind.

The boat scene *(Gozabune)* boasts a splendid decor; Masakiyo is seen here as a truly heroic character. The scene at Honjō Castle (Masakiyo's home) is a complete change from the splendor of the boat scene; a gloomy atmosphere pervades the action taking place there.

HACHIMAKI. A headband. Kabuki characters wear a variety of *hachimaki* styles, each of which distinguishes a conventional character type.

HACHIMAN MATSURI YOMIYA NO NIGIWAI. Kawatake Mokuami*. Also called *Chijimiya Shinsuke, Sango Yachū Iro no Shingetsu. Sewamono**. Kabuki. Four acts. July 1860. Ichimura-za*, Edo.

Chijimiya Shinsuke of Echigo saves the courtesan Miyokichi from the annoying attentions of Akama Genzaemon. Later, when Eitai Bridge collapses, Shinsuke, who had been rowing in its vicinity, saves her again. When she thanks him as being the guardian of her life, he lays bare his true feelings and woos her. Miyokichi promises herself to him until her lover, Hōzumi Shinzaburō, is able to return to his lord's service with a censer for which he has been searching. Later, however, having been insulted by Shinzaburō, Miyokichi takes out her wounded feelings at Shinsuke's expense by humiliating him in front of others. Soon after, Shinsuke becomes possessed by the spirit of a bloodthirsty sword, which he purchased from a secondhand dealer, and goes on a murderous rampage, eventually killing the spiteful courtesan.

This drama is based on a true story. Mokuami wrote it for Ichikawa Kodanji IV*. Others in the original all-star cast were Seki Sanjūrō III, Iwai Kumesaburō (later Iwai Hanshirō VIII*), Kawarazaki Gonjūrō (later Ichikawa Danjūrō IX*), and Ichimura Uzaemon XIII (later Onoe Kikugorō V*). In form it is a rather conventional play, but the background of the Hachiman festival and the combination of the dry-goods dealer and the Fukugawa courtesan add an interest of their own.

HADE KURABE (ISE MONOGATARI). Nagawa Kamesuke*. Also called *Ise Monogatari, Hana Kurabe, Date Kurabe. Jidaimono**. Kabuki. Seven acts. April 1775. Naka no Shibai, Osaka.

A play that echoes various earlier plays dealing with the legend of Ariwara no Narihira, as told in the *Ise Monogatari.* The sixth act's scene at

Koyoshi's home is still performed. The cast of the first production included such Kamigata actors as Mimasu Tokujirō, Onoe Kumesuke, Fujikawa Yazō, Nakamura Utaemon I*, and Nakamura Tōzō.

Koretaka Shinnō, who wishes to attain the Imperial throne, searches for Narihira and Princess Izutsu. The pair are taking refuge in the home of Koyoshi, a farmer of Kasuga Village. Kino Aritsune, an old friend of Koyoshi, arrives there. Aritsune has entrusted his daughter Shinobu to Koyoshi, and she has grown up and married the handome Toshirō. As part of a plan that he has worked out, Aritsune cuts off the heads of the young couple in order to substitute them for those of Narihira and Izutsu. The sacred mirror that Shinobu has obtained at great sacrifice is now given to Narihira.

Highlights of the play include the scene in which Koyoshi and Aritsune become absorbed in reminiscence, while sipping hot barley flour tea. Also memorable is the scene of Toshirō's death and of the parting of Koyoshi from Shinobu, the sound of a *koto** and *kinuta** being heard in the background. It is usual for the actor who plays Narihira to double as Toshirō and for Izutsu to be played by whoever plays Shinobu.

HADE SUGATA ONNA MAIGINU. Takemoto Saburobei, Toyotake Oritsu, Yatami Heihachi. Based on a play by Ki no Kaion*. Also called *Sakaya. Sewamono*. Jōruri**. Three acts. December 1772. Toyotake-za, Osaka.

A dramatization of the true-life 1695 incident in which Akaneya Hanshichi and Minoya Sankatsu committed double suicide at the Sennichi Temple. Only the act described below is still performed.

Though Akaneya Hanshichi's wife, Osono, is faithful to him, he is in love with the courtesan Sankatsu, by whom he has had a child, Otsu. Further, he is said to have killed a man and has become a fugitive. His father, Hanbei, takes the blame for his son's crime and is bound in ropes at the bailiff's office. Osono's father has taken her home with him, but when he learns of her true feelings and those of Hanshichi's parents, he brings her back to her husband's home again. Osono feels that she is somehow to blame for all that has happened and wants to kill herself. Otsu appears and Osono takes a farewell note from Hanshichi out of the child's pocket. Everyone reads it and weeps.Outside the house, Sankatsu and Hanshichi murmur their apologies for their filial ingratitude and leave to commit double suicide. Soon after, proof of Hanshichi's innocence turns up and he and Sankatsu are saved.

Osono's speech of lamentation* *(kudoki)* provides the play's major highlight. Both the love of a father for his son and of a wife for her husband are stressed in this emotional work.

HAGATAKI. A minor villain's role. Opposed to major villain roles *(tate gataki*)*. (*See also* HARADASHI; KATAKIYAKU.)

HAGOROMO. Kawatake Shinschichi III*. *Shosagoto*. *Nagauta** and *tokiwazu**. January 1898. Kabuki-za*, Tokyo.

A dance play included in the play collection of the Onoe Kikugorō* line, *shinko engeki jūshu**. It was first performed by Onoe Kikugorō V* and the actor who later became Onoe Baikō VI*. Based on a famous Nō play of the same name, *Hagoromo* tells the classic legend of a fisherman who finds the robe of an angel on Miho Beach and gets the angel to dance for him before he will return her robe. Kabuki dances based on the *hagoromo* ("feather robe") legend date back to Segawa Kikunojō I's* performance in *Tenjin Hagoromo* at Edo's Nakamura-za* in 1745. A unique element of the present work is the use of the flying device called *chūnori**.

HAIKEI GA KAWARU. "The background changes"; an expression referring to the changing of scenery. It can also be used in the sense of an emotional transition.

HAIMYŌ, a haiku-writing pen name. Since Kabuki actors were often accomplished haiku poets, each had a special pen name with which he signed his poetic efforts. Later, all actors came to have *haimyō*, whether or not they were poets. Ichikawa Danjūrō I* became the pupil of Shiigamoto Saimarō and, taking the name of Saigō, began the *haimyō* custom for actors. Many of an actor's descendants took the same *haimyō* for themselves. There are a number of Kabuki actors whose stage names were originally *haimyō*, including Onoe Baikō*, Nakamura Shikan*, and Onoe Shōroku*. As a rule, the *haimyō* is written on the cover of the booklet containing the actor's part *(kakinuki*)*. (*See also* ACTORS.)

HAJIKI CHASEN. A wig with a "tea whisk" topknot *(chasen mage*)*, whose end flows down the back and which is worn with a forelock signifying the character's youth. (*See also* MAEGAMI KATSURA.) It is worn by strong-charactered young samurai such as Kokingo in *Yoshitsune Senbon Zakura** and Kijirō in *Kiichi Hōgen Sanryaku no Maki**.

HAKAMA. The formal, wide, culotte type of pleated trousers that are worn over kimono in traditional male Japanese dress. They are seen very frequently in Kabuki.

HAKATA KOJŌRŌ NAMI MAKURA. Chikamatsu Monzaemon*. Also called *Kezori, Koi Minato Hakata no Hitouchi*. English title: *The Adventures of the Hakata Damsel* (Miyamori); *The Girl From Hakata, or Love at Sea* (Keene). *Sewamono*. *Jōruri**. Three acts. October 1718. Takemoto-za, Osaka.

A work conceived in connection with the contemporary executions of smugglers. The first part of the play, including the scene on board the ship at Shimanoseki and the scene at the Okuda-ya teahouse, as well as the middle part, which takes place at Shinsei Machi, are still performed.

Soshichi, a Kyoto merchant who is traveling to Hakata, happens to be on board the pirate ship of Kezori Kuemon. He is thrown into the sea when he learns the ship's secret. Fortunately, he is saved, and he goes to visit his courtesan mistress, Kojorō, at the Okuda-ya. Here he once again meets the pirate Kezori. The latter forces him to join his gang of smugglers; the merchant does so in order not to lose the courtesan's love. When Soshichi's father learns of his son's having become a smuggler, he weepingly berates him. He gives Soshichi some money and makes him leave. Shortly afterwards, Soshichi is arrested, but commits suicide. The pirates are also captured, their ears and noses are cut off, and they are driven away.

The spectacle of the shipboard scene at the play's opening is striking; Kezori performs here with a great show of masculine bravado. The scene at the teahouse displays a marked contrast between strength and weakness: Soshichi is confronted by the pirate in Kojorō's presence. Another highlight derives from the lovers' show of affection for one another. The scene between Soshichi and his father portrays with great sensitivity the feelings of a parent for a wayward son.

HAKIMONO. *See* FOOTGEAR.

HAKONE REIGEN IZARI NO ADAUCHI. Shiba Shisō. Also called *Izari no Adauchi. Jidaimono**. *Jōruri**. Twelve acts. October 1801. Dōtonbori Higashi no Shibai, Osaka.

A play based on the true story of the successful revenge carried out by Iinuma Katsugorō on the murderer of his brother (1590). Act XI is still presented. The play is probably the puppet version of a play staged by the Kabuki in September of the same year at Kyoto's Kameya-za, with Arashi Sangorō and Nakamura Utaemon III*. The first Edo version was in 1808 at the Nakamura-za* with Bandō Hikosaburō III*, Segawa Kikunojō IV* (before he took that name), Segawa Kikunojō III, Ichikawa Omezō I, and Nakamura Utaemon III*.

Satō Kōzuke, who killed Mihira, brother of Iinuma Katsugorō, takes refuge in Hakone with Hōjō Ujimasa; he also changes his name to Takiguchi Ueno. In observance of the memorial services for Ujimasa's ancestor Tokimasa, the Hōjō family gives alms to beggars at Hakone's Amida Temple. Katsugorō, who has become a crippled beggar, is led there by his wife, Hatsuhana, who pulls him in a little cart. Infatuated with Hatsuhana, Kōzuke, seizes her mother, ridicules Katsugorō, and tries to seduce Hatsuhana. Hatsuhana flees from him and makes a prayer at the Tonozawa waterfalls; this leads miraculously to Katsugorō's being able once more to use his legs.

All are amazed when Mihira's servant runs in holding Hatsuhana's head and states that she was killed by Kōzuke. Ultimately, Kōzuke is slain, and the vendetta is successfully completed.

One of the strongest points about this play, which depicts a legendary miracle at Hakone's Gongen Shrine, is its effective contrasting of the three main characters: Katsugorō, a *nimaime** role; Hatsuhana, the *onnagata** lead; and Kōzuke, the *katakiyaku**.

HAMONO. A play or scene with an incomplete plot; the opposite of *dan mono**.

HANAMICHI. "Flower path," a raised passageway that joins the stage on the audience's left and passes straight through the auditorium. It is Kabuki's most characteristic stage element. It not only is used for entrances and exits, but actually forms an integral part of the stage; many important moments are acted here. A temporary *(kari*) hanamichi* may be set up on the audience's right, opposite the main *(hon*) hanamichi.* Tokyo's Kabuki-za* has a five-foot-wide *hanamichi;* the width of the temporary *hanamichi* is about two-thirds of this. The *hanamichi* is thought to have originally developed as a passageway on which members of the audience could give *hana* (gifts) to the actors. Then, it is believed, the performance functions fulfilled by the bridgeway *(hashigakari)* in the Nō theatre were added to it. At first, the *hanamichi* was located in the center of the stage, moving away from it on a diagonal. It came into use as an acting extension of the stage around the Kyōhō era (1716-35). The temporary *hanamichi* (then called the "eastern walkway," or *higashi no ayumi*)* came into use in the Anei era (1772-80). (*See also* THEATRE ARCHITECTURE.)

The word *hanamichi* is used in a different, but related, sense as well. In this usage it is a colloquial expression implying someone who has arranged all his affairs and retired from public life, much as a Kabuki actor playing the lead takes his exit on the *hanamichi* amidst the applause of his devoted fans.

HANA NO UENO HOMARE NO ISHIBUMI. Shiba Shisō, Tsutsui Hanbei, others. Also called *Tamiya Botarō; Shidodera* (or *Shidōji*). *Jidaimono**. *Jōruri**. Ten acts. August 1788. Hizen-za, Edo.

Based on a number of earlier treatments, this play combines two stories. One deals with Marugame no Tamiya Botarō, who, after his father was slain, became a student of swordsmanship under Yagyu Hida no Kami and slew the murderer; the other is that of the miracle performed by the seaman's god, Konpira. Act IV, *Shidodera,* is still performed. Kabuki produced its version rather late. Both Osaka and Edo first saw the play with live actors in 1812.

Young Tamiya Botarō has been entrusted to the care of the Shidō Temple. He has been instructed to behave as if deaf and dumb in order to throw his enemy off guard. Botarō's uncle, Tamiya Naiki, engages in a fencing match with Moriguchi Gentazaemon. This match provides proof that the latter was responsible for the death of Botarō's father, Gonpachi. Otsuji, the boy's nurse, prays on his behalf to Konpira and then commits suicide; as a result of her prayer, Botarō achieves mastery of the martial arts and leaves for Edo to carry out his revenge.

HANAYAGI RYŪ. A major school of Kabuki dance. It was founded by Hanayagi Jūsuke I. He became a student of Nishikawa Senzō IV at six years of age and a pupil of Ichikawa Danjūrō VII* at eight, but later returned to the former's classes, taking the name Nishikawa Yoshijirō. His great natural talents soon became apparent, and in 1849 he founded the Hanayagi school. From then until his death in 1903 he ruled the world of Kabuki choreography and that of classical dance. Among his representative works are *Dontsuku**, *Renjishi**, *Tsuchigumo**, *Tsuri Onna**, *Funa Benkei**, *Hagoromo**, and *Sannin Katawa**. The Hanayagi *ryū* excels in dances requiring sharp character transitions; their work always has sparkle and life. Jūsuke II succeeded to the name in 1918. He founded in 1923 the Hanayagi Association for the Study of Classical Dance (Hanayagi Buyō Kenkyū Kai), which was responsible for making great inroads in the study and performance of both classical and new works. The present leader of the school is Jūsuke III.

HANAYARI. The "flower spears" carried by police in certain dance dramas. Red and white cloth is wound in stripes around the handle, and cherry blossoms are attached to the tip.

HANAYOTEN. A costume worn by police in certain dance plays, this is a *yoten** decorated with a highly theatrical flower pattern. The characters wearing it are also known by the name. They carry "flower spears" *(hanayari*)* and flowering branches as weapons.

HANBEI. A Kabuki character whose name has come to mean "putting on an innocent face."

HANE NO KAMURO. Anonymous. *Shosagoto**. *Nagauta**. New Year's 1785. Kiri-za, Edo.

The original version of this work starred Segawa Kikunojō III* in a five-part "transformation piece*" *(henge mono)* entitled *Haru wa Mukashi Yukari no Hanabusa*. Only one section of this work remains.

In this piece we see a courtesan's young maidservant *(kamuro)* playing with a battledore before a shop in the pleasure quarters. Besides being bright and delightfully artless in flavor, the dance has a carefree atmosphere typical of old-style dances.

HANERU. An expression referring to the ending of the show and the emptying of the theatre. It also means that there is a "good house." A third meaning is "pocketing a kickback."

HANGI. A wood percussion instrument. (*See also* NARIMONO.)

HANGIRE. The *hakama**, or divided trousers, worn by noblemen in Nō plays. Kabuki *hangire* are similar to those of the Nō; they are worn with the short, wide-sleeved tunic called *uwagi*. *Hangire* are distinguished by superb fabric and embroidery.

HANJŌ. "Half-mat," the straw mats on which spectators used to sit and the man who rented them out. The *hanjō* renter was a jack-of-all-trades around the theatre, even playing small parts such as the legs of stage horses (*uma no ashi**) and palanquin bearers. Also drawn from the ranks of the *hanjō* were the barkers who stood in front of Edo period theatres and called out the day's attractions to passers-by. These men were called *hikkomi** or *kappa*. (*See also* KIDO GEISHA.)

HANJŌ O IRERU. "To throw *hanjō**"; the heckling and abuse of an actor or performance by the audience.

HANMARU. "Half-round"; a technique employed for trees, pillars, and similar objects whereby these elements—unlike cutouts and flats, which have two-dimensional surfaces—are built solidly on the side seen by the audience. Elements built in all three dimensions are called *honmaru* or *maru mono**. The latter would include garden rock arrangements, stones, and stumps placed on stage for the actor to sit on.

HAN MAWASHI. "Half-turn"; a partial revolution of the stage, which is used when a scene change is called for. The turn, about forty-five degrees, is normally used in scenes that shift from an interior setting to the exterior directly outside the scene's stage right entrance, as in *Naozamurai*, an act of *Kumo ni Magō Ueno no Hatsuhana**. (*See also* MAWARI BUTAI.)

HANNYA GUMA. A style of makeup created by Yamanaka Heikurō, an actor of *jitsuaku* villain roles (*see* KATAKIYAKU) during the Genroku era (1688-1703); it was later perfected by Onoe Kikugorō V*. This makeup, also called *Heikurō guma*, is formed by applying the *aiguma** style and then adding red to the eyes and mouth in a design suggesting the face of the jealous *hannya* spirit. This spirit is the subject of a renowned type of Nō theatre mask called the *hannya* and seen in such Nō plays as *Aoi no Ue.* Heikurō made himself up in this style for the role of an angry female demon in a 1705 play at the Ichimura-za*. According to legend, he got the idea from a true female demon whom he saw at his own home; seeing the scowling face of his wife (another version claims it was his maid), he supposedly fell down the steps and fainted.

HAORI. A type of half-jacket worn by many male characters.

HAPPI. Originally a Nō formal costume element, it is a sort of gold brocade jacket worn by the protagonist in the second half of plays derived from the Nō. The actor wears it over his outer kimono *(kitsuke*)* with *hangire**-style *hakama** below. Plays in which it is seen include *Tsuchigumo** and *Ibaraki**.

HARADASHI. Also called *nakauke,* this is a term for the minor villains *(hagataki*; see also* KATAKIYAKU) in *Shibaraku**. They wear red painted faces *(akattsura*),* wigs with stiff protruding side locks (the *ita bin**), and costumes with black lateral stripes on a white ground. Their name derives from the red "jutting belly" *(haradashi)* that they all display.

HARAGEI. "Internal art," a psychologically acute, restrained, and quiet type of acting, as opposed to the kind of acting in which the movement and emotions of the role are projected in an outwardly theatrical manner. It is a realistic rather than a stylized type of acting and was the specialty of Ichikawa Danjūrō IX*. Yuranosuke is usually acted in this fashion in the Act IV scene of castle evacuation in *Kanadehon Chūshingura**.

HARIKO. The property man's creative art of papier-mâché. Also called *haribote,* it is used to create substitute properties. Unbreakable plates and cups, religious statues, masks, and the like are all made of *hariko.* They are constructed by applying paper to a wood or plaster shape; this is covered with Japanese paper, which is smoothed over with an iron and painted with the appropriate color. For such objects as Buddha statues, a base of wood, wire, and bamboo may be made. Japanese paper is then applied and allowed to dry. Softened snake gourd *(hechima)* is next applied with glue, and the piece is then finished by being glazed with a hot iron, making what is called "snake gourd ware" *(hechima saiku*).* Many props formerly made the *hariko* way are now made of plastic. (*See also* PROPERTIES.)

HARIMONO. Wood-framed flats, about six feet in width by twelve feet in height, on which paper or cloth is pasted, as on opaque sliding doors *(fusuma),* and which are painted to represent scenic views or decorative patterns. Flats painted in this manner are called *kakiwari. Harimono* are constructed according to need and lashed together to form backgrounds and walls. Flats set up behind a stage entranceway to hide the area within from the audience's view are called *kagami**. They are painted in solid colors or with objects to match the scenic background. Flats and cutouts masking the wings to the left and right are known as *mikiri**. When flats used as walls and partitions are attached at right angles in the form of returns, they are called *tsuma. Tsuma* are normally two feet wide; to increase the depth of a room onstage an additional three-foot *tsuma* is attached. This is called *tashizuma. Aorigaeshi** is a *harimono* technique whereby the flat folds over from top to bottom or from one side to the other, revealing a new background. (*See also* SCENERY.)

HARI UCHI. A topknot worn by romantic males in history plays. Jurō in *Soga no Taimen** is a good example.

HARUSAME. "Spring rain"; when an actor sprays saliva on another actor as he delivers his lines onstage.

HASEGAWA KANBEI. A line of scenery specialists. (*See also* SCENERY.)

HASEGAWA SHIN. 1884-1963. A playwright, born in Yokohama and known as the novelist who wrote *Mabuta no Haha** (later dramatized). His real name was Shinjurō. Self-educated, he wrote popular novels from the late Taishō (1912-26) period on. He also wrote plays, among which are *Kurayami no Ushimatsu**, *Ippon Gatana Dohyō Iri**, and *Katsukake Tokijirō*. He became famous as the originator of plays about the lives of itinerant gamblers *(matatabi mono)*. Hasegawa, who himself had a life filled with troubles, often depicted the nobility of the townsman who must make a crucial decision between duty and personal feelings.

HASHI BAKO. "Chopstick box," a scenic device that involves a character who lies downward and makes his appearance through an opening in the scenery. A board on which the actor lies is pushed along in grooves, like the lid of a chopstick box. It is used mainly by ghosts for magical appearances.

HASHI BENKEI. Anonymous. Kineya Kangorō III (music). *Shosagoto**. *Nagauta**. Music composed in 1868.

A Kabuki version of the Nō play of the same title. The dance describes a tale of bravery in which occurs the famous battle between Ushiwakamaru (the young Yoshitsune) and Benkei (the warrior-priest) on Gojō Bridge.

There have been several versions of this work, each having a different type of musical background. The most famous example uses *nagauta* music. A briefer number, derived from *Hashi Benkei* and called *Gojō Bashi* (1902), is occasionally presented. (This is not to be confused with the *Gojō Bashi* scene in *Kiichi Hōgen Sanryaku no Maki*.)*

HASHIRI KOMI. The practice of extending stage platforms to make the actors' entrances and exits easier for them. The extension leads beyond the stage limits visible to the audience, to the sides and upstage. Its presence makes entrances from offstage areas appear more natural.

HASHIRU. "To run"; when dialogue is spoken at a rapid clip. Also used to refer to a performance that races along.

HATSU BUTAI. *See* DEBUT.

HATSUHARU KYŌGEN. *See* NEW YEAR'S PLAYS.

HAUTA. A type of music that has two main forms: the Kamigata *hauta*, which developed in the Kyoto and Osaka area, and the Edo *hauta*. The former is a branch of Kamigata *uta (jiuta*)*, which is an artistic manner of presenting folk and popular songs; many of the pieces are freely rendered *nagauta**. Edo *hauta* was a minor *shamisen** music popular in the late Edo period; it includes such pieces as *Harusame* and *Yarisabi*. The *utazawa* and *kouta** styles grew out of this type of music. It is a background music played in the *geza** and used to describe Kabuki characters and scenic backgrounds.

HAYAGAWARI. "Quick-change technique"; used when actors playing more than one role in the same scene make quick changes of costume and makeup from one role to another. Since the point is for the change to be made as fast as possible, the costumes are rigged in advance by such techniques as having the obi sash sewn on the kimono itself. Occasionally, a stand-in actor *(fukikae*)* is used as a means of heightening the stage effect. In this case, the stand-in usually will appear with his back to the audience while the main actor is actually offstage changing his costume. The quick-change idea first boomed in the early nineteenth century and was popularized in such pieces as *Osome Hisamatsu Ukina no Yomiuri** and *Tōkaidō Yotsuya Kaidan**. Quick-change techniques were especially popular in Kabuki dances. The technique has been seen in the Kamigata area quite often in recent years. (*See also* HIKINUKI; BUKKAERI; HAYA GESHŌ; TRANSFORMATION PIECES.)

HAYA GESHŌ. A quick makeup change. The rapid change of an actor's costume, makeup, and wig is called *hayagawari** (sometimes *haya goshirae*).

When there is no time to return to the dressing room for a change, the switch is made in the wings. A few plays allow the actor to perform his change while he is still on stage by using various trick techniques. In *Seki no To**, for example, the actor uses makeup materials concealed in a special ax, which also has a small mirror placed inside it.

HAYAGUKE. A trick costume used for quick-change techniques. It consists of a double costume, as the top and bottom of the outer kimono are sewn together to the under kimono at the waist; the device allows the outer costume to be removed in a moment, revealing the one underneath. (*See also* HAYAGAWARI; HIKINUKI.)

HAYAKANE. A makeup substance for quickly blackening the teeth. It is used primarily in quick-change scenes. *Hayakane* is made by mixing together crude wax, pine resin, lampblack, red coloring, rice honey, and lamp oil. Perfume is added as well. When it is to be used, the material is heated and softened over a flame. It comes off the teeth when rubbed strongly with a cloth.

HAYASHI. "Orchestra," Kabuki musicians who supply percussion and wind music. Basic are the four instruments adopted from the Nō: the flute *(fue)*, small drum *(kotsuzumi*)*, large drum *(ōtsuzumi*)*, and stick drum *(taiko*)*, though a number of other instruments are used as well. A broader usage of the term includes the playing of the *shamisen** and the use of vocal accompaniment. (*See also* GEZA; NARIMONO.)

HAYASHI BEYA. The "musician's room," a dressing room for the theatre's chanters and musicians. It is located to the rear of the *geza** enclosure. Since some musicians had been lower-ranking samurai before becoming performers, this room is said to have been equipped with a sword rack. The musicians' groups were called *ohayashi renchū*, the *o* in *ohayashi* signifying respect for their former status. Before the *hayashi beya* reached its present status, it faced the room provided for the lower rank of actors who were called *inari machi**; therefore, it was called the *hayashi machi* ("musicians' town").

HAYASHIGATA. *See* MUSICIANS.

HAZUSU. When the tone of the music or the pitch of a voice is erratic. Also when the actor's timing is off.

HEAD INSPECTION SCENES. *See* KUBI JIKKEN.

HEADS. *See* KUBI.

HECHIMA SAIKU. One of the creative crafts of the property man, it was invented in 1877. A three-dimensional object is made by building a base of wire, wood, and bamboo, over which Japanese paper is applied. This is dried, and then snake gourd is pasted on over the object. The snake gourd is glazed, a rough coat is added, and then paper is applied and painted. Buddha statues, horses, fish, and the like are produced by this technique, which allows for an emphasis on realism. Props made by this method have the advantages of being quick to produce, cheap, and lightweight. (*See also* HARIKO; PROPERTIES.)

HEIKE NYOGO NO SHIMA. Chikamatsu Monzaemon*. Also called *Shunkan*. English title: *Shunkan* (Leiter). *Jidaimono**. *Jōruri**. Five acts. August 1719. Takemoto-za, Osaka.

The story on which this play is based, the exile of Shunkan, is found in the epic entitled the *Heike Monogatari*. The play's first Kabuki version starred Anegawa Shinshirō at Osaka's Naka no Shibai in 1720. The role of Shunkan was given a definitive performance by Ichikawa Danzō III*, and subsequent actors have followed his methods to the present day.

Shunkan, Naritsune, and Yasuyori are exiled to Kikai Island for their attempt to overthrow the Heike clan. Because of the general amnesty granted as part of the celebrations following the birth of the Empress's daughter, the Imperial envoy, Senō Tarō, comes to the island with a pardon for the exiles. Shunkan's name, however, is not listed on the pardon; learning of the omission, he breaks down in tears. Fortunately, another envoy, Tanzaemon, bears a letter of pardon for Shunkan. When the exiles begin to board the boat to return to the capital, an island girl named Chidori, who is married to Naritsune, is not allowed to go with them. Shunkan, who has been informed of his wife's death, resolves to stay behind on the island so that Chidori can go with Naritsune. When Senō forbids this compromise, Shunkan fights with him and kills him. This deed forces him to remain behind on the island. As the ship departs for the capital, Shunkan pathetically waves to it.

Shunkan, who undergoes many striking emotional fluctuations, is depicted with deep humanity. The work is outstanding for the balanced variety of its dramatis personae. The final moment—as Shunkan looks out at the departing ship from the top of a protruding rock—is splendid in its dramatic poignancy.

HENGE MONO. *See* TRANSFORMATION PIECES.

HI AGARU. "To dry up"; when an actor's voice gets strained and he cannot say any more lines.

HIBARIYAMA HIME SUDEMATSU. Namiki Sōsuke*. Also called *Chūjō Hime*. *Jidaimono**. *Jōruri**. Five acts. February 1740. Toyotake-za, Osaka.

One of a number of plays based on the legend of Princess Chūjō. Kabuki's first version appears to be a play called *Chūjō Hime Taemae Enki*, written by Kawatake Shinshichi III*, and produced at Edo's Haruki-za in 1885. Suketakaya Kosuke and Ichikawa Kyuzō (later Ichikawa Danzō VII*) were in it.

Prince Toyonari's daughter, Princess Chūjō, is entrusted with an idol of "one-thousand-armed Kannon," the Goddess of Mercy. The idol is stolen by Chūjō's stepmother, Iwane Gozen, and the princess is accused of having lost it. Further, Iwane Gozen torments the princess in the snow as a punishment for losing it. With the aid of her maidservant Kirinoya, the princess takes refuge on Hibari Mountain. Toyonari is ordered to kill the princess; a maidservant named Senjū fails in her attempt to substitute herself for her mistress. Kirinoya also attempts to give her life in place of her mistress's, but her disguise is seen through. Finally, Iwane Gozen is killed by a lady-in-waiting, Sarashina. In repentance for the evil deeds of her stepmother, Chūjō becomes a nun; her servants, Kirinoya and Sarashina, follow her to take service at Taema Temple.

Scenes like the torture in the snow are fairly common in Kabuki. In these scenes, called *yukizeme* ("snow torture"; *see* TORTURE SCENES), a strange atmosphere is evoked by the stylized tormenting of a young girl amidst a stage setting white with snow.

HIDAKAGAWA IRIAI ZAKURA. Takeda Koizumo, Takemoto Saburobei, Kitamado Goichi, Chikamatsu Hanji*, others. *Jidaimono**. *Jōruri**. Five acts. February 1759. Takemoto-za, Osaka.

A wide-ranging play based on the famous legend of Dōjōji Temple and on the rebellion of Fujiwara no Sumitomo. Act IV, at Hidaka River, is still in the repertory. The earliest Kabuki version was at Osaka's Araki-za in 1764. Edo's Morita-za* produced it in 1770 with Iwai Hanshirō IV in the lead role of Kiyohime. The Kabuki version is often given as a one-act play titled *Jakago no Fuchi Hime no Adanami*.

Hindered from obtaining the Imperial throne, the crown prince Sakuragi disguises himself as Anchin, a monk, and meets with his mistress, Odamaki, at the home of Shōji. From here they flee to the Dōjōji Temple. Shōji's daughter Kiyohime has fallen in love with the prince and pursues him. However, the ferryman at the Hidakawa River refuses to ferry her across. The power of jealousy now turns her into a serpent, and in this form Kiyohime crosses the river.

Kiyohime is played in the manner of a puppet; this is the *ningyō buri** style, whereby the actor appears to be manipulated by puppet handlers, as in the puppet theatre. The technique is performed in a style approximating dance.

HIDEYAMA JŪSHU. A collection of plays with roles in which Nakamura Kichiemon I* specialized. (*See also* FAMILY ART.)

HIGASHI. "east"; a term referring to a place within the theatre. Since the Nakamura-za* and Ichimura-za* were located in Edo's Sakai-chō and Fukuya-chō, their stages were built facing south. The area in the theatre on the right side facing the stage was dubbed "east" as a result. Thereafter, "east" came to mean the right side of the house, no matter what direction the stage was facing. The name remains today. (*See also* NISHI.)

HIGASHI NO AYUMI. "The eastern walkway" or the temporary *(kari) hanamichi**.

HIIKI. A supporter or fan. In the Edo period, patrons formed associations and visited the theatre en masse; then they presented their favorite with gifts. Even today such fan clubs exist. In the Edo era, the famous backers' groups included Ichikawa Danjūrō's* Mimasu group, Nakamura Utaemon's* Ibishi group, and Bandō Hikosaburō's* Katsumi group. (*See also* AUDIENCES.)

HIIRI. A lighting effect representing the flame in a lantern, the lamp in a home seen in the distance at night, moonlight, and so on. It is quite effective when used for evening scenes in the Yoshiwara. *(See also* TŌMI.)

HIKAE YAGURA. "Alternate producers." There were times when, for one reason or another, an Edo period manager *(zamoto*)* was unable to produce plays at his theatre. At such times he would delegate his license to another man, who would use it to produce plays at another playhouse. This was the *hikae yagura* system (literally, "alternate drum tower" system). It first began when Kawarazaki Gonnosuke staged plays at the normally unlicensed Kawarazaki-za in 1735 as a substitute for the Morita-za*. The Miyako-za* was the Nakamura-za's* *hikae yagura,* while the Kiri-za served this function for the Ichimura-za*. (*See also* YAGURA; THEATRE MANAGEMENT.)

HIKIDAI. A small platform pushed forward from the rear of the stage with an actor on it. It is seen in *Kusazuri Biki**.

HIKI DŌGU. A scenic device seen when a setting is placed downstage. The set can be changed by being pulled off either to the left or to the right or even on a diagonal upstage. Movement is facilitated by building the set on wheels.

HIKI FUNE. Seats that were placed on an extension jutting out from the front of the rear galleries in Edo period playhouses. A line of dialogue in the play *Yoshitsune Senbon Zakura** refers to a distant sea battle that was supposedly being waged in this general locale. Some plays employed small property boats* *(fune)* that were pulled along *(hiki)* here by ropes; this practice gave rise to the term *hiki fune.*

HIKI MAKU. Kabuki's traveler curtain, pulled open and shut by a stage assistant *(kyōgen kata*)* who ran with the curtain from one side of the stage to the other. It is opposed to the *donchō* or drop curtain. (*See also* CURTAINS; JŌSHIKI MAKU.)

HIKINUKI. An exciting dramatic effect seen mostly in dance plays to reveal a character's true nature, to reflect a change in his personality, or simply to provide visual delight. It is a representative Kabuki costume trick; as the audience watches, the actor's costume is changed almost instantaneously. A kimono is worn under one that has been basted together; rounded buttons are strategically placed at the end of each thread (one at each cuff, one at the rear of the waist, one at the neckband, one at each underarm sleeve opening, and one at each sleeve's bag, making a total of ten). At the right moment the *kōken** stage assistant pulls the buttons and the upper kimono is whipped off. The technique is seen in *Musume Dōjōji**, *Fuji Musume**, *Sagi Musume**, *Honchō Nijūshikō**, and elsewhere.

The verb *hikinuku* is also used in the sense of a sudden change. (*See also* HAYAGAWARI; HAYAGUKE.)

HIKISEN. A technique whereby the curtain is hung from rings fixed in place by pegs; the latter are attached to a rope. When someone in the wings pulls the rope, the pegs fall out of the bamboo pole and the curtain drops swiftly. (*See* FURIDAKE; FURIKABUSE.)

HIKI WAKU. A specially built wood and metal frame that is mounted on wheels and used to carry scenery when the *hiki dōgu** scene change is employed.

HIKIWARI. A scenic technique by which the set divides to left and right and a trap lifts a new set into place at the rear.

HIKKAESHI. Also called *kaeshi,* these are moments when time must be filled between two acts, because the revolving stage is being prepared for a scene change. The curtain opens as soon as everything is ready. In order to distract the spectators from the delay, offstage music is played against a background provided by the rhythmic striking of the *hyōshigi** clappers. As the *shirase** beats are struck, the curtain opens.

HIKKOMI. Any important *hanamichi** exit. For example, after the cellar scene in *Meiboku Sendai Hagi**, Nikki Danjō exits impressively; he is left standing on the *hanamichi* after the curtain has closed, performs a *mie**, and moves off with great composure, as if walking on air. This kind of exit is called an "outside-the-curtain exit" *(maku soto no hikkomi).*

Also refers to barkers who stood outside Edo period theatres trying to lure customers inside. (*See also* HANJŌ; KIDO GEISHA.)

HIKKURI KAERU. When a program has been set and then is changed completely.

HIKOSAN GONGEN CHIKAI NO SUKEDACHI. Umeno Oroshi, Chikamatsu Yasuzō. Also called *Keyamura. Jidaimono**. *Jōruri**. Eleven acts. Fall 1786. Dōtonbori Higashi no Shibai, Osaka.

A dramatization of an actual revenge enacted by Keyamura Rokusuke in 1586. *Keyamura,* the ninth act, is performed today. Kabuki's first adaptation was staged in 1790 at Osaka's Naka no Shibai. Edo audiences saw the play in the summer of 1796 at the Miyako-za and in the fall at the Kawarazaki-za and Kiri-za. The theatres competed with rival productions.

Owing to a scheme hatched by the evil Kyogoku Takumi, a master fencer named Rokusuke is reduced to poverty. Osono, disguised as a mendicant priest while hunting for her father's murderer, accidentally meets up with Rokusuke at his home in Keya Village. He had been her late father's disciple in the art of fencing. Although he is her betrothed, this is their first meeting. Learning of Osono's vendetta plans, Rokusuke agrees, out of piety to her father's memory, to aid her. He soon realizes that the same man who killed Osono's father also tricked him into losing his respected position as a fencer. Seething with anger, he takes up the game and eventually carries out his and Osono's revenge.

Osono is an unusual part, combining feminity with great strength and martial prowess; she is a sort of female warrior or amazon. Her switch from a powerful fighter to a charming young housewife is a notable feature of the work.

HINADAN. The double-stepped platform, placed at the rear of the stage, on which the *nagauta** musicians perform. The *hinadan* is usually covered with red carpeting; as it resembles the stepped platform *(hinadan)* used for setting up dolls during Japan's annual Doll Festival, it has been given the same name. The onstage platform used by *gidayū**, *tokiwazu**, and *kiyomoto** musicians is the *yamadai*. It normally is of a single step; flats (called *kerikomi**) matching the scenic background are attached to the front.

The outside-the-curtain exit in *Ichinotani Futaba Gunki,* Kumagai, Matsumoto Kōshirō VIII*.

HINAWAURI. "Fuse cord seller," the man who sold fuse cords to pipe smokers in the Edo period theatres. He belonged to the ranks of the *tomeba**. His responsibilities included restraining the audience when they shouted out upon an actor's entrance on the *hanamichi**. The *hinawauri* also helped out onstage when needed.

HINOKI BUTAI. "Cypress-wood stage." In the past all major theatres had stages floored with cypress wood; to perform on such a stage was considered an act of distinction. The expression "to trod a cypress-wood stage" came to be used both for appearances on the stage of the major theatres and for any appearance at a ceremonial occasion.

HINOKORI. A term rarely heard nowadays, this used to refer to productions that were planned to open, but failed to do so because of managerial difficulties.

HIŌI. A sun blind attached to the front of the stage during Kabuki's early days, when it still was using a Nō type of stage. The *hiōi* awning included the stage and auditorium under one roof; eventually the gabled roof over the stage was removed and a picture-frame proscenium was installed. (*See* GAKUBUCHI). The sun blind's position was hidden from the audience by the stage frame and a suspended bridgeway installed in its place. This bridge was about two feet wide and was used for going from one side to another over the stage. Properties and lighting equipment were set here. Although the present version of this bridge is made of steel and can move up and down, it is still called by the old name, *hiōi.*

HIRA BUTAI. The flat stage floor, as contrasted to the *nijū* butai*, or platform stage, which is set upon it in many plays. Background and scenic elements are placed on the stage floor proper. Thus the scenic direction for *Kanadehon Chūshingura**s sixth act, "an eighteen-foot unit of straw thatch placed on the flat stage floor. . . ."

HIRAGANA SEISUIKI. Matsuda Bunkodō, Miyoshi Shōraku, Asada Kakai, Takeda Koizumo, others. Also called *Genta Kandō, Sakarō. Jidaimono**. *Jōruri**. Five acts. April 1739. Takemoto-za, Osaka.

Act II's *Genta Kandō* scene and Act III's *Ōtsu Hatago, Sasabiki,* and *Sakaro* scenes may still be seen.

In *Genta Kandō* the Kajiwara family maid, Chidori, is in love with the family's eldest son, Genta Kagesue. Kagesue's younger brother, Kagetaka, who harbors a secret passion for Chidori, rebukes Kagesue for not having been in the vanguard of the battle at Uji River. He wants his brother to atone for his disgrace by committing ritual suicide *(seppuku).* Their mother, Enjū, disinherits Kagesue, and he elopes with Chidori.

In Act II, Kiso Yoshinaka's mistress, Yamabuki Gozen, stops at an inn in Ōtsu. With her are her maid, Ofude (Chidori's sister); her father, Haito Kamada; and her son Komawakamaru. At the inn they are attacked by men seeking to assassinate the child. Yamabuki Gozen and Haito are slain. After battling hard, Ofude places Yamabuki Gozen's body in a bamboo cradle for burial. However, in the dark and confusion, Komawakamaru is mistakenly taken by Gonshirō, who, together with his daughter and grandson, has stopped at the inn while on a pilgrimage. The grandson, Tsuchimatsu, was killed in the melee. Gonshirō and his daughter, Oyoshi, now have the young lord in their possession.

In the scene at Gonshirō's home, his son-in-law, Matsuemon, is sought as a master of the naval art of *sakaro* (a method of rowing backwards) and ordered to serve as commander of Yoshitsune's boat. Ofude, having found Tsuchimatsu's traveling bag, comes searching for "Tsuchimatsu" and begs that the young lord be returned to her. Matsuemon—in reality Yoshinaka's faithful retainer, Higuchi Kanemitsu—now reveals his true identity and begs Gonshirō and Oyoshi to save the lad. The Kajiwara faction, having seen through Matsuemon's disguise, attempts to capture him out at sea, but is beaten off. Through the kindness of Hatakeyama Shigetada, the young lord is saved, but Matsuemon-Higuchi must surrender himself as the price.

The play is filled with such outstanding moments as the narrative tale *(monogatari*)* told by Kagesue in *Genta Kandō* concerning the events at Uji River; the display of female martial prowess in the *Sasabiki* scene; the change in the *Sakaro* scene of Matsuemon from boatman to samurai; and the fight scene toward the end of the play.

In the fourth act, called *Muken no Kane*, but rarely performed today, Chidori has become a courtesan, under the name of Umegae, and is supporting Genta. The latter is troubled by a 300-*ryō* debt incurred when he had departed for the front. Umegae thinks of a legendary bell that, when struck, provides riches, so Genta strikes a nearby stone water basin. From the floor above, where Genta's mother is standing, the needed money appears.

HISHI KAWA. "Boar bristles"; an effect whereby the side locks of a wig are made to stand on end like the bristles of a boar's fur. It is used on *aragoto** characters and other brave samurai, such as Otokonosuke in *Meiboku Sendai Hagi**, Mitsuhide in *Ehon Taikōki**, and Watonai in *Kokusenya Kassen**. A corruption of this term is *shishi kawa*.

HISTORY PLAYS. *See* JIDAIMONO.

HITOTSU BETTSUI. A wig that resembles a priest's shaven head. The character wearing it has left the priesthood only recently, and the side and back hair have not grown in evenly yet. A good example of a role in which it is worn is Oshō Kichiza in *Sannin Kichiza Kuruwa no Hatsugai**.

HITOTSUGANE. A metal percussion instrument. (*See* NARIMONO.)

HITOTSUYA. Kawatake Mokuami*. *Jidaimono**. Kabuki. One act. April 1890. Ichimura-za*, Tokyo.

A work based on the legend of Ubagaike Pond, as told in the chronicles of the miracles performed at Asakusa's Kannon Temple.

An old hag of Asajikehara in Musashi, Ibara, kills and robs travelers who stop at her home. One day, she puts up a child who is making a religious pilgrimage to the Kannon Temple. Her daughter Asaji is moved with compassion for the child, and she secretly lets him go. Ibara grows angry and is going to kill Asaji with a hatchet, but her whole body freezes and she is unable to move. It turns out that the child was really a manifestation of the Goddess Kannon; she appears riding on a purple cloud. Feeling remorse, Ibara throws herself into the Ubagaike Pond.

The plot derives from a dream that came to the author after seeing a painting by Kuniyoshi called *"Hitotsuya"* ("A House") hanging in the Kannon Temple. The play was a specialty of Onoe Kikugorō V* and Onoe Baikō VI* who were in its first production. It is included in the Onoe family play collection, *shinko engeki jūshu**.

HIZA KURIGE. Anonymous. Also called *Tōkaidōchū Hiza Kurige, Yaji Kita. Shosagoto*. Shinnai bushi**. 1848-53.

One of a number of Kabuki pieces based on Jippensha Ikku's (1766-1831) *Tōkaidōchū Hiza Kurige* (1802), a classic picaresque novel known in its English translation as *Shank's Mare.*

Kitahachi and Yajirobei are traveling companions. Yaji puts on a fox mask and threatens Kita. Kita is surprised, but soon realizes it is Yaji. While the two are traveling together, they imagine a child whom they see to be a goblin and strike him. The boy's father gets angry and Kita flees. Yaji, who is left behind, is severely taken to task and tied up; eventually he faints. His clothes and money are taken, and he is dressed in a hempen garment. Reviving from his faint and noticing his condition, he thinks he is dead. (*See also* HIZA KURIGE MONO.)

HIZA KURIGE MONO. A group of dances, plays, and films that are based on Jippensha Ikku's charming 1802 novel, *Tōkaidochū Hiza Kurige,* or *Shank's Mare,* as it is known in English (*See also* HIZA KURIGE). The subject of these works is the comic pair of Edoites, Yajirobei and Kitahachi, who are making a walking tour of the fifty-three stages of the Tōkaidō Highway, as they go from Edo to the Kamigata area. The first dramatization of the material was Tsuruya Nanboku IV's* *Hitori Tabi Gojūsan Eki,* which was soon followed by a number of other Kabuki versions, most of them in dance form. The first rather faithful adaptation was the 1928 *Tōkaidōchū*

Hiza Kurige staged at the Kabuki-za* that starred Ichikawa Ennosuke II (later Ichikawa En'o*) and Ōtani Tomoemon VI*.

HOME KOTOBA. Words of praise for the actors. In the Edo period it was the custom for a predetermined fan to rise during a pause in the acting and shout out a phrase of encouragement to an actor. Booklets in which such phrases were published also were known. This custom of shouting to the actors is dying out today. (*See also* AUDIENCES; KAKEGOE.)

HONAME. The use of real water to simulate rain. (*See also* AME.)

HON BUTAI. The stage proper, as opposed to the *hanamichi**. Old documents show that the *hon butai* originally was built according to the dimensions of the Nō stage; that is, it was about eighteen feet between the pillars at the front of the stage. This space grew wider in time, but even though the stage may have been wider than eighteen feet, stage directions in the playscripts continued to refer to an eighteen-foot stage width. The space between the *daijin bashira** on the stage of today's Kabuki-za* measures sixty feet. (*See also* THEATRE ARCHITECTURE.)

HONCHŌ (NIJŪSHIKŌ). Chikamatsu Hanji*, Miyoshi Shōraku, Takeda Inaba, Takemoto Saburobei, Takeda Hanbei. *Jidaimono**. *Jōruri**. Five acts. January 1766. Takemoto-za, Osaka.

The complex structure of this work revolves around the disputing Takeda and Uesugi (here called the Nagao) families. Act III, which takes place at Kansuke's home, and Act IV, called *Jūshikō* and *Kitsunebi*, are performed today. This work was almost immediately adapted by Kabuki and was staged the same year at Osaka's Dōtonbori Naka no Shibai, where Nakamura Utaemon I*, Yamashita Kinsaku, Arashi Yoshisaburō, Arashi Hinasuke, Mimasu Daigorō, and Bandō Tomisaburō appeared in it.

The Uesugi and Takeda families, though still involved in a feud, are searching for the criminal who shot the shogun and have maintained a truce for three years. When the murderer is not discovered, their respective children, Kagekatsu and Katsuyori, battle each other. A Takeda retainer, Itagaki Hyobu, had committed the treasonous act of exchanging his own young son, Minosaku, for Katsuyori many years ago, as the two looked much alike. Minosaku now dies in place of the true Katsuyori. Katsuyori, calling himself Minosaku, enters Uesugi's mansion and, with the help of Princess Yaegaki, whom he loves, obtains the prized helmet called Hosshō. Meanwhile, Yamamoto Kansuke's orphan sons Jihizō and Yokozō are each fighting for one or the other of the warring sides. The shogun's murderer, Saitō Dōsan, is discovered and commits suicide.

This is not a uniformly excellent work, but the *Jūshikō* scene, in which

Yaegaki figures prominently, is one of Kabuki's most outstanding. Yaegaki is one of the three most important Kabuki princess roles (*see also* AKAHIME; SANHIME).

HONCHŌSHI. The fundamental tuning used for the *shamisen**.

HON HANAMICHI. The "permanent" or "regular" *hanamichi**, as opposed to the temporary *(kari*) hanamichi.*

HON KYŌGEN. The main play on an Edo period program.

HONMAKU. A method of beating the *hyōshigi** clappers. (*See also* DARAMAKU.)

Also refers to a curtain used in the Kamigata area. It divides to the left and right at the center, in contrast to the Tokyo type, which is pulled across the stage from one end to the other. (*See also* CURTAINS; JŌSHIKI MAKU.)

HONMI. "Real blade"; the occasional use on stage of a real sword instead of one made of bamboo and painted to look like steel. (*See also* TAKEMI; KATANA.)

HONMIZU. The use of real water on stage. A water tank *(mizu bune)* may be set up on stage so that some of the acting may take place in it (in *Koitsukami*); water may be drawn from a well (in *Natsu Matsuri Naniwa Kagami*);* or a rain barrel is filled with water and an actor jumps into it (in *Sukeroku Yukari no Edo Zakura*).* (*See also* MIZUIRI; HON AME.)

HONTSURIGANE. A metal percussion instrument. (*See also* NARIMONO.)

HONYOMI. A ceremony held just prior to the start of rehearsals; the playwright reads the script of a new play to the whole company. The actors, playwrights, musicians, *gidayū** performers, and all other personnel connected with the production gather together for the occasion. As this is the first reading of the play and the actors learn which parts they will be playing, the event is an important one. The *honyomi* is a major duty of the playwright, who must be skilled at handling the occasional dissatisfactions that erupt at the reading. Nagawa Kamesuke* and Kawatake Mokuami* were known to be masters at this function. (*See also* REHEARSALS.)

HOREGŌRE. A metal percussion instrument. (*See also* NARIMONO.)

HORIKAWA NAMI NO TSUZUMI. Chikamatsu Monzaemon*. English title: *The Drum of the Waves of Horikawa* (Keene). *Sewamono*. Jōruri*.* Three acts. February 1707. Takemoto-za, Osaka.

A work based on a true vendetta carried out in 1706 by a man whose wife had committed adultery.

While her husband, the Inaba retainer Okura Hikokurō, is on duty in Edo, Otane is wooed by Isobe Shoemon. This is known by Miyagi Gen'emon, the drum teacher of Otane's son, Bunroku. In order to keep Gen'emon silent, Otane commits adultery with him. However, it is this affair that soon becomes common knowledge. Returning home, Hikokurō learns the facts from his sister, Yura, and kills his wife. Together with Bunroku and Yura, he raids Gen'emon's home and exacts his vengeance on the drum teacher.

This is one of Chikamatsu's three adultery plays. The others are *Daikyōji Mukashi Goyomi** and *Yari no Gonza Kasane Katabira**. The portrayal of Hikokurō, weeping and holding the corpse of his wife in his arms, is central. The drama depicts a contemporary family tragedy as well as a social tragedy. After a long period of neglect, the drama was revived at Tokyo's Masago-za in 1902.

HORIKOSHI NISŌJI. b.1721. A playwright who started out as an actor but turned to dramaturgy and became a chief playwright *(tate sakusha*)* in 1746. In 1751 he gained fame when he wrote *Honryō Hachi no Kizome.* He left for the Kamigata area the following year, but soon returned to Edo. Thereafter, he remained in Edo, and during the Meiwa and Anei eras (1764-80) he and Kanai Sanshō* were Edo's two foremost playwrights. He wrote about seventy plays. Nisōji's style, influenced by the rationality of the Kamigata drama, was rather realistic. He displayed a talent for adapting history plays into domestic plays and was the harbinger of the Edo style of domestic dramas. Also, he was the first to include a dance drama in the daily program. He created the new fashion of writing the titles and title notes *(tsunogaki*)* in the so-called Nayō calligraphic style; he also designed stage equipment. His major works include *Kuruwa Kurina Akinai Soga, Kamuri Kurabe Yatsu Kurumeshi, Yanagini Hina Shochō no Saezuri,* and *Sagi Musume**.

HOSHIGURI. A property used in history and dance plays when someone examines the stars in order to tell the future. Seven hemispheres of silver paper are suspended above a cloud board hanging over the stage. They hang from the flies by means of thin black threads *(jyari no ito*).* The acting in such scenes also is called *hoshiguri,* after the term for the silver balls.

HOTOTOGISU (KOJŌ NO RAKUGETSU). Tsubouchi Shōyō*. *Shin kabuki**. Three acts, ten scenes. Published September 1897; first performed May 1905. Kado-za, Osaka.

A tragedy about the fall of Osaka Castle; it takes the form of a sequel to the same writer's *Kiri Hitoha**.

On the night before the fall of Osaka Castle, Yodogimi, mother of Hideyori, learns that spies of Ieyasu (whose forces are attacking the castle) are attempting to rescue Princess Sen, who is Ieyasu's granddaughter and Hideyori's wife. This knowledge causes Yodogimi to become half-crazed. Meanwhile, Katagiri Katsumoto, who is quite ill, calls on Ieyasu and asks him to save the lives of Yodogimi and Hideyori. Princess Sen manages to escape amidst the confusion in the palace. Seeing the maddened condition of his mother, Hideyori attempts to kill her, but is stopped by others. Katsumoto comes running to the outside of the castle but the castle's interior is already being bombarded by artillery. The castle soon falls in flames.

The play depicts the tragedy of Yodogimi and Katsumoto. Yodogimi's mad scene *(Hoshi Igura no Ba)* is often performed as an independent play.

HYAKUNICHI. Also called *daibyaku,* this is a wig that gives the impression that the wearer has not shaved his pate for 100 days *(hyakunichi).* Long hair stands up bristle-like from the crown. The wig of Ishikawa Goemon in *Sanmon Gosan no Kiri** is a good example.

HYŌGO. A courtesan wig also called *date hyōgo* and *tate hyōgo.* It is rather showy and contains over twenty ornamental hairpins and decorative objects. The topknot is large and broad. A *habutae** is worn to beautify the hairline. Agemaki in *Sukeroku Yukari no Edo Zakura** is a famous role in which it is worn.

HYŌSHIGI. Also called *ki* and *tanniki,* these are wooden clappers struck together as a signal at such important points as the opening and closing of the curtain. They consist of two rectangular sticks that are about ten inches long and are beaten against each other. The sticks are made of oak, the best sound coming from those which have been cut from the same single block of wood. Square *hyōshigi* exist as well; however, the sides on these that are struck together are carved in a semicircular shape and only one spot is actually struck. The beating of the clappers is the job of the stage assistants who are known as *kyōgen kata**. (*See also* TSUKE.)

HYŌSHIMAKU. A method of striking the *hyōshigi** at the end of an act. A loud *kigashira**—*"chon!"*—is produced, followed by a low and rapid beating of the sticks. The sound gradually becomes louder and the tempo relaxes; then a *"chon chon chon"* is struck, and the curtain is pulled shut. As it stops, a single *"chon"* is beaten. This technique is used frequently in domestic plays.

I

IBARAKI. Kawatake Mokuami*. *Shosagoto*. *Nagauta*. April 1883. Shintomi-za, Tokyo.

Although this dance drama appears to have been derived from the Nō theatre, it is actually an original work; there is no *Ibaraki* in the Nō repertoire. It was first performed by Onoe Kikugorō V* and Ichikawa Sadanji I* and is included in the Kikugorō family play collection, the *shinko engeki jūshu*. It later became a staple in the repertoires of Onoe Baikō VI* and Onoe Kikugorō VI*.

Watanabe Tsuna, having cut off a demon's arm at the Rashomon gate, locks it in a Chinese chest and refuses to let anyone into his home. Tsuna's aunt, Mashiba, from the country comes to visit. At first he refuses to admit her; eventually, overcome by familial emotions, he permits her to enter. When she presses him to show her the arm, he complies; she then displays her true form, that of the demon, Ibaraki Dōji. Grasping her severed arm, she flies away. Afterwards, Ibaraki and Tsuna engage in a dance battle.

Highlights include the aunt's lamentation* *(kudoki)* in the play's first half, the transformation of the aunt into the demon, the battle in the latter part of the play, and, at the end, Tsuna's great *mie** with his tongue thrust out.

ICHIBANME MONO (or KYŌGEN). "Number one piece," the history play that formed the first part of an Edo period program. (*See also* JIDAIMONO.)

ICHIJŌDAI. A raised platform about the size of a *tatami* mat on which high-ranking characters sit in history plays.

ICHIKAWA CHŪSHA VII. (1860-1936). An actor who made the hereditary pen name *(haimyō*)* of the generations of Ichikawa Yaozō* into a stage name. He became a pupil of Ichikawa Danjūrō IX* and was active with him in supporting roles. From the Taishō period (1912-26) and into the Shōwa (1926-), he was known as an expert leading actor in history plays and was especially good in the role of Mitsuhide.

VIII. 1896-1971. Third son of Ichikawa Danshirō II*, he became Chūsha in 1953. His sober artistry made him an excellent supporting actor. Together with Matsumoto Kōshirō VIII* and others, he belonged to the Tōhō* troupe from 1961 on.

ICHIKAWA DANJŪRŌ I. 1660-1704. An actor who was said to be the son of a "street knight" *(otokodate)* called "Scarface" Juzō. He played the role of the superhuman Sakata Kintoki when he debuted at age thirteen (his name at the time was Ichikawa Ebizō) and is considered the founder of the Ichikawa family art* *(ie no gei)* of *aragoto**, Kabuki's exaggerated bravura style of acting. His supermanly style as the hero in such plays as *Fuwa* and *Shibaraku** was revered by the Edo townsmen. He was called by the *yago** Narita-ya, because of his belief in the god enshrined at Narita. He studied haiku poetry with Shiigamoto Saimarō and held the pen name of Saigyū (*see also* HAIMYŌ). Under the playwright's pen name of Mimasuya Hyōgo, he wrote many Kabuki plays. Danjūrō was stabbed to death by his fellow actor Ikushima Hanroku.

II. 1689-1758. Eldest son of Danjūrō I. Because of native talent and hard work, he became Edo's leading actor. In addition to *aragoto*, he possessed the technique of the soft, romantic Kamigata *wagoto** style that he displayed in *Sukeroku Yukari no Edo Zakura**, one of Kabuki's greatest creations. He was the first to perform in a majority of the plays later collected in the famous Ichikawa compilation, the *kabuki jūhachiban**, and laid a firm foundation for the later generations of Ichikawa actors.

III. 1721-1742. Died before he could attain greatness.

IV. 1712-1778. Was said to be the son of Danjūrō II. He was active from the Horeki (1751-63) and Meiwa (1764-71) periods on, and later he took the name of Matsumoto Kōshirō* II. He ran an actors' study group called the Engi Kenkyū Kai and became known for his employment of new production devices in Kabuki. He originated the manner in which Matsuomaru in *Sugawara Denju Tenarai Kagami** is still performed. In his last years he lived a secluded life at Kiba in the Fukagawa section of Edo, where he was known as "the boss of Kiba" *(Kiba no oyadama).*

V. 1741-1806. Son of Danjūrō IV, he became Danjūrō after being Matsumoto Kōshirō III*. He was the representative actor of the Kansei period (1789-1800), a talented *onnagata**, and a gifted writer. *Tomonashi Saru* is among his written works.

VI. 1778-1799. Like Danjūrō III, he died quite young.

VII. 1791-1859. Grandson of Danjūrō V. He acted from the start of the nineteenth century to the last days of the shogunate. His debut was at age four in *Shibaraku*, after which he went on to astonish the public with his talents, being able to handle every role type (*See also* KANERU YAKUSHA). In his later life he was punished for living too luxurious a life for an actor and was banished from Edo. During his exile he flourished in Kyoto and Osaka. It was his idea to establish the famous Ichikawa family play collection, the *kabuki jūhachiban.* This helped to guarantee the artistic authority of the Ichikawa family of actors. Danjūrō VII gained special attention with his creation of the Nō-derived play *Kanjinchō** because he chose to stage it in a manner quite like that of the original. (*See also* MATSUBAME MONO.)

VIII. 1823-1854. Eldest son of Danjūrō VII. His good looks helped make him the most popular actor during the last years of the shogunate. He was the first to play Yosaburō in *Yowa Nasake Ukina no Yogogushi** and was skillful not only in young lover *(nimaime*)* roles such as Yosaburō, but also in his family's *aragoto* art. During his father's exile from Edo he was honored for the discharge of his filial duties by receiving a reward from the city authorities; this helped his popularity climb even higher. In August 1854 he killed himself in Osaka. The grief over his death and the numerous "death pictures" *(shini e*)* of him that were published attest to his enormous popularity.

IX. 1839-1903. Fifth son of Danjūrō VII. He was adopted when young by the Kawarazaki family, managers of the Kawarazaki-za, but later succeeded to the name of Danjūrō IX. He excelled in all role types and was the representative actor of the Meiji era (1868-1912). He participated in the Meiji theatre reform movement, begun in the late 1870s, and was the first to act in living history plays* *(katsureki geki)* based on the depiction of actual historical facts. He established the *shin kabuki jūhachiban** collection, made up mainly of plays in which he had scored a triumph. His revisions of plays like *Kanjinchō* showed awareness of ancient customs and manners. He also explored the special boundaries of psychological acting, which he called *haragei** ("internal acting").

X. 1882-1956. Son-in-law and adopted son of Danjūrō IX. Though not from an acting family, he became an actor after Danjūrō IX's death, debuting in 1910. He was never recognized as a skilled performer, but he did make many important scholarly contributions to Kabuki. Known for most of his career as Ichikawa Sanshō, he was named Danjūrō X posthumously in 1956.

XI. 1909-1965. Eldest son of Matsumoto Kōshirō VII*. He was adopted in his early adulthood by the Ichikawa family; after becoming very popular as Ichikawa Ebizō, he took the name of Danjūrō in 1962. He first played the title role in *Sukeroku Yukari no Edo Zakura** in 1946, an event that signaled the advance toward success of the young postwar Kabuki stars. From then on, he gained popularity for his handsomeness and broadly based art. Thereafter, he was familiar to fans as Ebisama, an affectionate name given him as representative of Kabuki's young stars. Except for female impersonation, he acted in many kinds of roles and showed superb ability in *Genji Monogatari, Wakaki Hi no Nobunaga* (which he wrote), and other new works. His death, only three years after becoming Danjūrō XI, was a great blow to the world of Kabuki. His brothers are Matsumoto Kōshirō VIII* and Onoe Shōroku II*, two of Kabuki's foremost stars.

ICHIKAWA DANSHIRŌ I. 1651-1717. An actor and the eldest disciple of Ichikawa Danjūrō I*, he studied with both his master and Nakamura Denkurō I*. He flourished in the Edo theatre during the Genroku period (1688-1703) as an *aragoto** expert.

II. 1857-1922. There was a long hiatus between actors holding this name, but Ichikawa Ennosuke I, a pupil of Danjūrō IX*, eventually assumed the name of Danshirō II. He was outstanding in the part of Benkei in *Kanjinchō**.

III. 1913-1963. Eldest son of Ichikawa En'o I* and grandson of Danshirō II, he became Danshirō III in 1930. Along with his father, he was active as a Kabuki mainstay. His son is a popular star, Ichikawa Ennosuke III*.

IV, *yago** Omodaka-ya. 1946- . The second son of Danshirō III and younger brother of Ennosuke III, he was born in Tokyo. He debuted in 1957 and became Danshirō in May 1969. Together with his elder brother, he is active in the Haruaki Kai group. Danshirō is a fine actor and plays mainly male roles.

ICHIKAWA DANZŌ I. 1684-1740. A disciple of Ichikawa Danjūrō I*, he was good in *aragoto** and villain roles.

III. 1709-1772. A student of Danjūrō II*, he specialized in Kamigata plays, but also succeeded in *aragoto.*

IV. 1745-1808. Hailed from Kyoto, but moved to Edo in 1768. His short stature led him to create clever methods in his acting. Besides his quick-change techniques, he developed many other performance devices.

V. 1788-1845. Adopted son of Danzō IV, he was active from the Bunsei period (1818-30) to shortly before the end of the Edo era. His art was conservative, its chief characteristic being a superb spirit of realism.

VII. 1836-1911. Adopted son of Danzō VI and pupil of Danjūrō VII*. Although he stopped studying in 1868 and led a wandering life for about a decade, he returned to the Tokyo theatre world in 1879. He was involved in constant discord within his master's home and failed to receive his family's blessing when he appeared on the stage of a major theatre. Still, his acting was second only to that of the great Danjūrō IX*, Onoe Kikugorō V*, and Ichikawa Sadanji I* of his era. Many of Danzō's *kata** (formal acting patterns) still remain. He was without a peer in such villain's roles as Moronao in *Kanadehon Chūshingura** and Nikki in *Meiboku Sendai Hagi**.

VIII. 1882-1966. Second son of Danzō VII. After World War II the Kabuki world treasured his existence as a player of old men. However, his art was simple and inconspicuous. He retired in 1965 and went to Shikoku as a pilgrim. On his way back he drowned himself in the Inland Sea.

ICHIKAWA EBIZŌ X, *yago** Narita-ya. 1946- . Son of Danjūrō XI*, he was born in Tokyo, debuted as Ichikawa Natsuo in 1953, and became known as Ichikawa Shinnosuke in 1958. He, Kikunosuke (now Onoe Kikugorō VII*), and Onoe Tatsunosuke* were known cumulatively as the "three Sukes." He is one of Kabuki's brightest hopes for the future. He played *Sukeroku Yukari no Edo Zakura** and Togashi in *Kanjinchō** in January 1970 to celebrate his taking the name of Ebizō. By his serious and steadfast stage work he is devoting himself to being a worthy successor to the position that he holds as head of the Ichikawa family of actors. (*see also* SŌKE). There is no doubt that he will one day succeed to the name of Ichikawa Danjūrō XII.

ICHIKAWA ENNOSUKE III, *yago** Omodakaya. 1939- . An actor and the eldest son of Ichikawa Danshirō III*, he was born in Tokyo and debuted as Ichikawa Danko in 1946. From 1961 on, he devoted himself to school work at Keiō University and then returned to the stage after graduation, taking the name of Ennosuke in 1963. Since 1966 he has led the study group of actors known as the Haruaki Kai and continues to involve himself in exploring new territory. Because of his powerful voice, great versatility, boundless energy, and enthusiasm for experiment, he occupies the front line among today's young stars. He is a master at *keren** stage tricks and quick-change techniques.

ICHIKAWA EN'O I. 1888-1963. An actor and the eldest son of Ichikawa Ennosuke I (*see* ICHIKAWA DANSHIRŌ II). He made his debut as Ichikawa Danko in 1892, became Ennosuke II in 1910, and was active into the Shōwa era (1926-). In his youth he joined Ichikawa Sadanji II's* progressive Jiyū Gekijō ("Free Theatre") troupe, took part in the modern drama movement, and, in 1919, traveled abroad. His travels resulted in his influence extending to the "new dance" *(shin buyō; see also* DANCE) movement. He formed the Haruaki-za company in 1920 and produced many excellent new dance plays, including two representative works, *Mushi* and *Koma.* For a short time, he chaired the Gesai Kai troupe and performed Ibsen's *Wild Duck.* As a Kabuki actor he helped to develop Kabuki's contemporary reform movement. Following the deaths of Onoe Kikugorō VI* and Nakamura Kichiemon I* (just after World War II), he became known as Kabuki's senior actor, the president of the Actors' Association (Haiyū Kyōkai). In 1955 he became the first artistic envoy from Japan since the war and performed Kabuki in China. He took the name of En'o in 1963, giving his grandson Danko the name of Ennosuke III*.

ICHIKAWA JUKAI. Three generations of actors have borne this name. However, the first two were actually the pen names *(haimyō*)* of Ichikawa Danjūrō VII* and IX*.

III. 1886-1971. A disciple of Ichikawa Kodanji V*, he was later adopted by Ichikawa Sumizō V. He became Sumizō VI in 1907, joined Ichikawa Sadanji II's* troupe, and participated in the reform movement of the modern theatre. He also belonged to the Tōhō* troupe for about three years, beginning in 1935. Following the death of Sadanji II, he carried out experiments in New Kabuki *(shin kabuki*)* with Ichikawa Ennosuke II *(see also* ICHIKAWA EN'O). He moved to the Kansai area in 1946 and lived the life of a prima donna. He took the name of Jukai III in 1949. His youthful looks on stage and his pleasant voice never showed any signs of weakening, even in his old age.

ICHIKAWA KODANJI I. 1676-1736. An actor and the pupil of Ichikawa Danjūrō I*.

II. dates unknown. A pupil of Danjūrō IV*.

III. Dates unknown. A disciple of Danjūrō VII*.

IV. 1812-1866. The son of a seller of fuse cords *(hinawauri*)* at the Ichimuraza*. During the years that his master, Danjūrō VII, was banished from Edo, he was appreciated in Osaka for his quick-change technique and aerial stunts. He returned to Edo in 1847, and in 1854 he took part with Kawatake Mokuami* in producing a successful Kabuki play. He became the chief actor in Mokuami's specialty, "robber plays*" *(shiranami mono),* and was recognized as Edo's number-one actor following Danjūrō's death. He climbed from a low rank among contemporary actors to the position of troupe leader, or *zagashira**; this is a very rare success story in Kabuki annals. His son, who carried his father's artistic ability on through the Meiji era, was Ichikawa Sadanji I*.

V. 1850-1922. Son of Kodanji IV, he took the name in 1879. He acted mainly with Ichikawa Sadanji I.

ICHIKAWA KOMAZŌ X, *yago** Kōraiya. 1925- . An actor and the son of Bandō Shūchō III, he was born in Tokyo, debuted in 1927, and took the name of Komazō in 1954. He switched from the Shōchiku* to the Tōhō* company in 1961, along with Matsumoto Kōshirō VII* and others.

ICHIKAWA KYUZŌ V, *yago** Miyoshiya. 1910- . An actor born in Aichi prefecture, he debuted in 1914 and took his present name in 1954. According to Kabuki custom, he is considered the "namesake" son of Ichikawa Danzō VIII*. Kyuzō is the leader of the study group of actors called the Seihō Kai. He plays supporting roles as old men and also occasionally performs as an *onnagata**.

ICHIKAWA MONNOSUKE VII, *yago** Takinoya. 1929- . An actor born in Tokyo, he debuted in 1935 and became Ichikawa Shōchō in 1946, taking his present name in February 1962. Ever since the time of the first Monnosuke, who was a pupil of Ichikawa Danjūrō II*, this line has had a close relationship with the Danjūrō line. The present Monnosuke is active as a pure *onnagata**, performs together with Kabuki's younger stars, has judiciously developed his art, and has not lacked his share of training as a Kabuki hopeful.

ICHIKAWA NEDANJI II, *yago** Takajimaya. 1920- . Born in Tokyo, this actor made his debut in 1937 and became Nedanji in 1941. In 1954 he turned to television acting, but returned to Kabuki in 1963. He is a veteran supporting player.

ICHIKAWA RYŪ. A school of dance founded by the nineteenth-century star Ichikawa Danjūrō VII*. In the Meiji period Ichikawa Danjūrō IX* choreographed many dances now considered part of the Ichikawa school, such as *Momijigari**, *Kagamijishi**, and *Ninin Bakama.* The more successful of these were put in his collection, the *shin kabuki jūhachiban**. Danjūrō passed leadership of the school over to his daughter Suisen, an actress; after she died in 1944, Ichikawa Kōbai, an actress who specializes in the post-Kabuki style called Shinpa, succeeded to the name of Suisen III.

ICHIKAWA SADANJI I. 1842-1904. An actor; together with Ichikawa Danjūrō IX* and Onoe Kikugorō V* he belonged to great triumvirate of Meiji period stars popularly known as Dan-Kiku-Sa*. He was the pupil and then the adopted son of Ichikawa Kodanji IV*. After his father died, he received the support of Kawatake Mokuami*, the great playwright, and played the role of Marubashi Chūya in Mokuami's *Keian Taiheiki**. For this role he received great praise and wide public recognition. From 1893 on, he managed the Meiji-za*, where he continued to be active.

II. 1880-1940. The eldest son of Sadanji I, he was active from the late Meiji period through the Taishō (1912-26) and Shōwa (1926-) years. In 1909 he founded the Jiyū Gekijō ("Free Theatre") with Osanai Kaoru and earned special stature as a pioneer of the modern theatre movement. With the cooperation of the playwright Okamoto Kidō*, he performed one New Kabuki *(shin kabuki*)* play after another and began a new phase in Kabuki's history. Among the representative examples of these new plays are *Shūzenji Monogatari**, *Toribeyama Shinjū**, and *Banchō Sarayashiki**. In addition, he saw to the revival of such old *kabuki jūhachiban** plays as *Kenuki** and *Narukami**.

III. 1898-1964. Son of Ichikawa Monnosuke, he apprenticed himself to Onoe Kikugorō VI* and went from the name of Ichikawa Omezō to Ichikawa Sadanji III in 1952. He differed from the previous Sadanjis and specialized in the young lover type of role *(nimaime*)* and as an *onnagata**. After the death of Kikugorō VI, he brought the Kikugorō troupe together as its senior member and also worked as the president of the Actors' Association (Haiyū Kyōkai).

IV, *yago** Takinoya. 1940- . An actor and one of Kabuki's leading players of *aragoto** roles, he was born in Tokyo and debuted in May 1947. He changed his name from Ichikawa Otora to Omezō in 1962. His large size corresponds to his broad style. He succeeded to the name of Sadanji in February 1979.

ICHIKAWA SANSHŌ. *See* ICHIKAWA DANJŪRŌ X.

ICHIKAWA SOMEGORŌ VI, *yago** Kōraiya. 1942- . The eldest son of Matsumoto Kōshirō VIII*, this actor was born in Tokyo and debuted in May 1946, changing his name from Matsumoto Kinjirō to Somegorō in September 1949. He has cut a conspicuous figure in musical comedies such as *The King and I, Half a Sixpence*, and *Man of La Mancha*, in which he played after moving to the Tōhō* company in 1961. Somegorō also played *Man of La Mancha* in New York City for a season. He has not appeared in Kabuki very often since joining Tōhō, but, as the chief actor in the Kinome Kai group, he is grappling earnestly with Kabuki as well as more modern styles.

ICHIKAWA SUMIZŌ VII. *yago** Masudaya. 1902- . A veteran supporting actor, he was born in Tokyo, debuted in 1912, moved to Osaka in 1948, and took the name of Sumizō in 1949.

ICHIKAWA YAOZŌ IX, *yago** Tachibanaya. 1907- . A skillful actor of villain roles, he was born in Tokyo, debuted in January 1913, succeeded to the name of Matsumoto Komagorō in 1929, and became Yaozō in 1953.

ICHIMAKU MONO. In Kabuki's early period (the seventeenth century), these were plays of one act. (*See also* TSUZUKI KYŌGEN.)

ICHIMONJI. A black cloth border hung horizontally across the top of the stage. Stage machinery is placed so that the *ichimonji* hides it from the audience's view: at the same time, this cloth closes off the stage picture at the top. It is situated five to six feet upstage of the front stage curtain and depending on need, can consist of several layers and be made to go up and down.

ICHIMURA UZAEMON. This name began with the third manager of the Ichimura-za* in Edo. Uzaemon I began as the partner of Murata Kuroemon and became sole manager when Kuroeman died. Bearers of the name up to the fourteenth generation combined managerial work with acting. As actors, the foremost were Uzaemon XII (1812-1851) of the late Edo period, Uzaemon XIII (later Onoe Kikugorō V*), and Uzaemon XIV (1847-1893) of the Meiji era (later Bandō Kakitsu). The line has had no managerial authority since Uzaemon XV and has worked only as actors.

XV. 1874-1945. Adopted son of Uzaemon XIV, he became Uzaemon in 1903. Among modern actors he was one of the finest looking and most precise of speech; never in his whole career did he play the role of an old man. He was the perpetual actor of young lover roles *(nimaime*)*. Trusting to his looks and voice, he was not very strong in giving his roles psychological depth; still, he was always able to charm audiences with his lively and dashing appearance.

XVI. 1905-1952. Adopted son of Uzaemon XV. He was conspicuous as a player of young female roles, but he died young.

XVII, *yago** Tachibanaya. 1916- . The eldest son of Bandō Hikosaburō VI*, he was born in Tokyo, took the name of Bandō Kamesaburō in 1921 when he debuted, became Bandō Shinsui VII in 1935, and changed to Bandō Hikosaburō VII in 1942. He succeeded to the name of Ichimura Uzaemon in October 1955. Uzaemon lacks sparkle, but displays an appropriate rhythm when acting. He possesses an abundance of fundamental knowledge concerning Kabuki and presents a serious demeanor in his stage work.

ICHIMURA YOSHIGORŌ, *yago** Tachibanaya. 1918- . A good supporting actor and fine dancer, he was born in Tokyo, the son of Kataoka Nizaemon XII*. He was adopted by Ichimura Uzaemon XV* and debuted in 1922. He became Ichimura Matasaburō in 1941, Ichikawa Kakitsu XVI in 1946, and Yoshigorō in September 1967.

ICHIMURA-ZA. An Edo period theatre. The Ichimura-za's ancestor was the Murayama-za, built in March 1634 by Murayama Matasaburō, who had come to Edo from Kyoto. He erected the theatre midway between Negichō and Sakai-chō. After his death the theatre was managed by his son-in-law, Murata Kuroemon, but the latter died soon afterwards. Later, the license passed to the Ichimura family, and during the years 1663-67 the theatre was revived as the Ichimura-za. Thereafter, it was under the control of the generations of *zamoto** named Ichimura Uzaemon*, and it continued to be one of Edo's three great theatres along with the Nakamura-za* and the Morita-za* (*see also* EDO SANZA). It moved to Saruwaka-machi* in 1843. In 1872 Uzaemon XIV was forced by managerial difficulties to retire; actually, he changed his name to Murayama Matasaburō II and attempted to revive the theatre as the Murayama-za, thus ending the Ichimura-za's long tradition. Even after this managerial ploy the theatre failed to flourish, and its name was changed to the Miyamoto-za, the Satsuma-za, and finally, in 1878, back to the Ichimura-za. In 1882 the theatre moved to Shitaya Nichō-machi and, after 1908, was managed by Tamura Nariyoshi (1851-1920); its leading stars were Onoe Kikugorō VI* and Nakamura Kichiemon I*. The period of their reign was called the "Ichimura-za age" and was the beginning of a golden age of "young stars' Kabuki" *(wakate kabuki)*. The theatre burned down in 1932, and the Ichimura-za's name became nothing more than a memory. (*See also* THEATRE MANAGEMENT.)

ICHINICHI KAERI. The practice of two or more actors alternating in an important role from one day to the next. The event is usually of great interest to theatregoers, who have the chance to compare their favorites in talent and technique. The play most often used for this practice is *Kanadehon Chūshingura**.

ICHINOTANI (FUTABA GUNKI). Namiki Sōsuke*, Asada Itchō, Namioka Geiji, others. Also called *Kumagai Jinya*. English title: *Chronicle of the Battle of Ichinotani* (Brandon). *Jidaimono**. *Jōruri**. Five acts. December 1751. Toyotake-za, Osaka.

A dramatization of the *Heike Monogatari* tale of Kumagai and Atsumori at the battle of Ichinotani. Acts II and III are most frequently performed today. Because of its great popularity, the play was soon adapted for Kabuki actors, receiving its initial presentation in 1752 at two Edo theatres, the Nakamura-za* and the Morita-za*.

Yoshitsune had suggested to Kumagai that he show sympathy for the young Heike clan noble, Atsumori, so Kumagai substituted his own son Kojirō for Atsumori at the battle of Ichinotani. Back at the battle camp he provides Kojirō's head for the head inspection (*see* KUBI JIKKEN) by Yoshitsune, making it seem that he has killed Atsumori. A stone mason, Midaroku, charged with having erected a stone monument to Atsumori, is dragged onstage, but Yoshitsune recognizes him as Taira no Munekiyo, who saved his life in infancy. Yoshitsune thanks Munekiyo for his deed of benefaction and presents him with an armor case in which Atsumori is hidden. Kumagai achieves a state of enlightenment regarding the transience of the warrior's life, takes the tonsure, and becomes a priest; he then leaves for a pilgrimage through the country.

The best parts in the performance include the narrative speech *(monogatari*)* delivered by Kumagai, Kumagai's famous *mie** pose with a signboard, his exit down the *hanamichi** at the play's end after the curtain has closed, and the lamentation* *(kudoki)* of Kumagai's wife, Sagami. The role of Kumagai was given a definitive performance by Nakamura Utaemon III* (whose *haimyō** was Baigyoku). The Baigyoku *kata** were further developed by Ichikawa Danjūrō VII*, Ichikawa Danjūrō IX*, and Nakamura Kichiemon I*. Kumagai is one of several history play roles that are a touchstone of the Kabuki actor's art. Ranking with it are the roles of Matsuō and Genzō in the *Terakoya* scene of *Sugawara Denju Tenarai Kagami** and Yuranosuke in *Kanadehon Chūshingura**.

ICHIYAMA RYŪ. A school of Kabuki dance founded by the Osaka actor Ichiyama Shichijūrō. The Edo branch was started by Yamaguchi Shichijūrō, a disciple of Ichiyama Shichijūrō's son, the great actor named Segawa Kikunojō III*. Yamaguchi was originally a Kyōgen actor who became a Kabuki choreographer; in 1799 he took the name of Ichiyama and became choreographer at the Nakamura-za*, where he was very active in the early nineteenth century. He created the choreography for such dances as *Echigo Jishi**, *Matsukaze*, and *Tadanobu*. Ichiyama Shichijūrō II was quite active during the first third of the nineteenth century, and he maintained a spirited rivalry with the leaders of the other schools of Kabuki dance, such as the Fujima *ryū** and the Nishikawa *ryū**. The school did not continue to develop within the theatre world, but became the domain of female performers from the sphere of classical Japanese dance. (*See also* DANCE.)

ICHIYAZUKE KYŌGEN. A term for the making of Japanese pickles in one night; it refers to a play that has been written very quickly, or one staged very soon after some sensational event that it dramatizes, such as a double suicide. The word *kiwamono* has the same meaning. There are many such plays in Kabuki and the puppet theatre. As early as 1678 a play entitled *Yugiri Nagori no Shōgatsu* was performed in Osaka one month after the death of a Shinmachi district courtesan, Yugiri of the Ogi-ya brothel. Some years later (1703), Chikamatsu Monzaemon* fashioned *Sonezaki Shinjū** within three days after the double suicides of Ohatsu and Tokubei. (*See also* PLAYWRITING.)

ICHŌ. A wig whose topknot resembles a gingko nut *(ichō)*. It is a realistic piece worn by dashing men in the domestic plays. Megumi no Tatsugorō and Sakaya Sogorō are well-known roles using the *ichō*.

IDOKORO KAWARI. Scene changes that make no use of the revolving stage; when the *hyōshigi** are struck, the set is shifted through the use of the *seri** traps or the *dengakugaeshi**, *aorigaeshi**, or *hiki dōgu** techniques.

IEMOTO. The family line that founded a school of Japanese music, dance, Nō theatre, or Kabuki style. Japanese traditional arts maintain a succession system in which the leadership of a school is passed on from generation to generation. The leader of the school is known as the *iemoto* ("family founder"). When a school has a number of offshoots, the leader of the main branch is called *sōke**. (*See also* ACTORS.)

IE NO GEI. *See* FAMILY ART.

IGAGOE (DŌCHŪ SUGOROKU). Chikamatsu Hanji*, Chikamatsu Kasaku. *Jidaimono**. *Jōruri**. Ten acts. April 1783. Takemoto-za, Osaka.

Considered to be one of Japan's three great vendetta tales, this play deals with the revenge carried out by Araki Mataemon at Igagoe. The subject previously had been treated in a Kabuki play by Nagawa Kamesuke* in *Igagoe Norikake Kappa* (1777). In September 1783, only a few months after the play's puppet production, a Kabuki adaptation was produced at Osaka's Naka no Shibai. Edo's Ichimura-za* staged the play in January 1784. The numerous plays and films based on the play's subject matter are grouped as *Igagoe mono*.

A thrilling revenge is carried out by Wada Shizuma and his brother-in-law, Karaki Masaemon, following the death of Shizuma's father, Wada Yukie, at the hands of Sawai Matagorō. Act VI, the *Numazu* scene and Act VIII, *Okazaki*, are often staged.

Heisaku, a baggage carrier, puts up a traveler, Jūbei, for the night at Heisaku's own home on the Numazu highway. Heisaku's daughter Oyone steals Jūbei's medicine pouch, an act resulting in the discovery that Jūbei and Oyone are brother and sister and that Heisaku is Jūbei's father. Learning that the medicine pouch belongs to Matagorō, Heisaku follows after Jūbei to Senbonmatsubara. In order to get from Jūbei the information regarding the whereabouts of Matagorō, the old man stabs himself; this forces the son to divulge the information sought, although other obligations to Matagorō had restrained him until then. Though the old man dies, Oyone, who is hidden nearby, hears the information.

This scene is vastly interesting in its richly poetic sentiment and its theatrical use of the temporary *(kari) hanamichi**, which is used as part of the road traveled.

In the *Okazaki* scene Masaemon destroys the snow-covered barrier at Okazaki and saves his old teacher, Yamada Kobei. Masaemon's estranged wife, Otani, clutching her baby to her, finds her way to the gate and kills the baby as an act of vengeance.

IGAGURI. A priest's head covering that shows some hair sprouting from the shaved head.

II KOTOSHI. A "do-gooder"; the role of a male character who always appears just in the nick of time to help someone, to solve a problem, or to do some other deed of service.

IKASU. "To give life"; that is, to perform with spirit. Also, to make the most of or to restore a speech or scene previously cut.

IKEDA DAIGO. 1885-1942. A playwright born in Tokyo. *Saigō to Butahime** and *Meigetsu Hachiman Matsuri* are among the plays for which he is known. After graduating from Waseda University, he joined Tsubouchi Shōyō's* Literary Association (Bungei Kyōkai), later wrote plays for Ichikawa Sadanji II*, and in 1928 accompanied Sadanji to the Soviet Union as his stage manager. On his return to Japan he devoted himself to the study of Chinese dramatic literature. His real name was Ginjirō.

IKE KOROSHI. "Living and killing"; the strengthening or weakening of the background music according to the acting or other actions going on onstage. *Ike* means to give life to or to strengthen, while *koroshi* means the opposite. Used mainly for *shamisen** accompaniment, it may also refer to the delivery of dialogue.

IKITE IRU KOHEIJI. Suzuki Sensaburō. *Shin kabuki**. Three acts. June 1925. Shinbashi Enbujō*, Tokyo.

A modern work that reinterprets the ghost tale of Obata Koheiji, told by such earlier writers as Tsuruya Nanboku IV* and Kawatake Mokuami*. This masterpiece of the Taishō era (1912-26) was the author's last work.

Ochika, wife of the musician Daikurō, has been having an affair with a traveling actor, Obata Koheiji. When Koheiji lures Daikurō out fishing and then asks him to release Ochika, a quarrel ensues and Koheiji is thrown into the water. When Daikurō returns to his Edo home, Koheiji—whom Daikurō believed to have drowned—is there, trying to lure Ochika away. Enraged, Daikurō kills him. Along with Ochika he flees the city. Wherever they go, Koheiji's form appears and horrifies Daikurō; a traveler who resembles Koheiji follows after, as if to haunt them constantly.

IMAYŌ SATSUMA UTA. Oka Onitarō*. *Shin kabuki**. Two acts. October 1920. Shintomi-za, Tokyo.

A modern version of Namiki Gohei I's* *Godairiki Koi no Fūjime**. The use of *shinnai** music is old-fashioned, but the contents are new.

Sasa no Sangobei is having a love affair with Oman, a girl of the Chigusa-ya; both are disinherited by their parents. They place themselves in the custody of Sangobei's elder cousin, the boorish country samurai, Hishikawa

Gengobei. Gengobei, however, suddenly falls in love with Oman, separates the lovers, and tries to make Oman his own. Sangobei thus duels with and is killed by his cousin. Oman flees with her lover's sword. Knowing the strength of a woman's determination, Gengobei commits ritual suicide *(seppuku)*.

The role of this uncouth samurai, who gets drunk and unintentionally falls in love with his cousin's lover, was one of Ichikawa Sadanji II's* best.

IMOSEYAMA (ONNA TEIKIN). Chikamatsu Hanji*, Miyoshi Shōraku, Matsuda Baku, Chikamatsu Tonan, others. *Jidaimono**. *Jōruri**. Five acts. January 1771. Takemoto-za, Osaka.

Kabuki first presented this work in 1771, the year of its puppet theatre premiere, at Osaka's Kogawa-za. Edo did not see it until 1778. Various later versions of the play were staged, but the original has continued to be popular to the present day.

The story of Fujiwara Kamatori's defeat at the hands of Soga no Iruka and the legend of the pearl diver *(ama)* have been treated in a number of sources, including the Nō play *Ama* and Chikamatsu Monzaemon's *Taishokan* (1712). Therefore, *Imoseyama Onna Teikin* derives from a wide variety of legends and tales. It skillfully weaves the many threads together and provides a work whose grandiose conception, ingenious plot, and beautiful composition make it the representative play of the *ōdai mono** category. Its most frequently performed acts are Act II *(Yama no Dan* and *Yoshino no Dan)* and Act V, which contains the *Sugi Sakaya, Michiyuki,* and *Goten* scenes.

Because of the oppression of Soga no Iruka and the enmity between their parents, Daihanji's son (Koganosuke) and Sadaka's daughter (Hinadori), who are in love, have been separated from each other by the Yoshino River. An atmosphere as sad and beautiful as scattered flowers pervades the stage *(Yoshino no Dan)*.

Meanwhile, Kamatori's son, Tankai, disguises himself as Eboshiori Motome and is determined to kill Iruka; having fallen in love with Iruka's sister, Princess Tachibana, he attaches a spool to a thread of her kimono sleeve and follows her. Also in love with Motome is Omiwa, daughter of Sugi Sakaya; she too has depended on a thread and followed him. Arriving at the palace, she is sacrificed for the sake of Motome so that he can conquer Iruka; according to Imakuni, who kills her, her blood is required for a potion that is the only thing that can slay the otherwise charmed Iruka. She is pleased thus to be of service to Motome in the latter's vendetta *(Goten)*.

The magnificent Yoshino River scene, with the river dividing the stage in two, is a unique contribution by Hanji; the passage in which Hinadori's head is floated across the river with her dolls, as a token of marriage to Koganosuke, is the climax of this famous act. Further interest is provided by the use of two *hanamichis.** Other highlights include the *Goten* or palace scene in which Omiwa is mercilessly taunted by the palace maids.

IMPROVISATION. *See* KUCHIDATE; SUTE ZERIFU.

INAORU. "Resort to intimidation"; a term used when an actor puts pressure on a producer—for money or for other reasons—just before a production is scheduled to open.

INARI MACHI. An Edo period nickname for the lowest rank of actors. These players are also called *shita tachiyaku, wakaishū,* and *oshita* (*see also* ACTORS' RANKS). The term derives from the fact that their dressing room on the first floor was close to the backstage shrine of the fox god Inari, who was worshipped by actors as a tutelary deity. *Inari machi* literally means "Inaritown." The *inari machi* appear on stage in the roles of policemen *(torite),* passers-by, crowds, dogs, monkeys, cats, and the like and also as stage assistants *(kōken*).* They are kept busy with miscellaneous odd jobs as well. On the day of the annual Fox God Festival *(Hatsuuma),* the group's leader becomes a Shinto priest, and the *inari machi* conduct a private festival *(inari matsuri)* and hold a banquet by themselves.

INORI DASU. When a producer pays an extra sum of money in addition to the regular salary that his company is contracted for.

INTERMISSION. When the curtain closes at the end of an act or play and the house lights come up, this is known as *makuai.* The term does not apply to instances when the auditorium remains dim and music is played preparatory to the next scene; such intervals are called *tsunagi maku,* or "tie-together curtains" (*see* TSUNAGI). The *makuai* is used by actors and stagehands to prepare the following piece on the program; the audience uses the interval to relax. Today, a long intermission is thirty minutes; a brief one, five minutes. These intermissions used to be quite long, and the audience spent the time in the theatre teahouses. (*See also* SHIBAIJAYA; UNDŌBA.)

IORI. An Edo period billboard on which the names of the actors were written, set within their family crests (*see also* ACTORS' CRESTS). It was placed in front of the theatre during the annual *kaomise** ("face-showing") performances. It listed actors who were visiting from other cities, actors whose names were being changed, guest actors, and so on, and over it was placed a chevron-shaped roof of wood. This roof was the *iori kanban* ("hermitage billboard"), so named because of the little roof's resemblance to that on a Japanese hermitage. In the program, too, the names of these special actors were surmounted by a shape similar to the "hermitage billboard." (*See also* KANBAN: IORI KANBAN.)

IPPON GATANA DOHYŌ IRI. Hasegawa Shin*. *Shin kabuki**. Two acts, five scenes, July 1931. Tōkyō Gekijō, Tokyo.

A play depicting the conflict between duty and emotion among gamblers, it is representative of those which deal with the lives of wandering gamblers.

Losing the favor of his gang boss, a minor wrestler named Komakata Mobei returns penniless to Edo. Clutching his empty belly, he is on the verge of desperation when he is helped by Otsuta, a waitress at the Abiko-ya. Mobei vows to become a champion wrestler and departs. Ten years later Mobei, now a gambler, visits Otsuta just when she and her husband are in danger. He saves them, and they flee. Mobei calls out to their retreating figures that this was the least that he could do for them in gratitude for Otsuta's past kindness to him.

IPPON GUMA. "One-line *kuma**," a makeup style belonging to the *suji guma** class of *kumadori**. A thick line in black and red is applied from the temples to the cheeks. It is said to have been invented by Ichikawa Danjūrō II* and used in the *aragoto** plays of the Ichikawa family. Watonai in *Kokusenya Kassen** and the "belly-thrusting" soldiers *(haradashi*)* of *Shibaraku** are examples of characters who wear *ippon guma.*

IREKOMI. The admission of spectators to the theatre before the play begins; that is, the time between the opening of the theatre and the start of the show.

IRI. The number of spectators in the theatre. A good house is *ōiri**, a poor one, *fuiri**.

IRIKAKE. An expression used when the audience is so small that the production must be postponed until a later date.

IROE. A Kamigata term formerly used to refer to dancing, action, or gesture.

IROKO. Also called *butaiko, seigaiko, kagema, shinbeko, kabuki wakashu,* and *tayūko.* The rise of *wakashu kabuki,* or young men's Kabuki*, in the seventeenth century was concomitant with a rampant homosexuality. Young men's Kabuki was subsequently suppressed (1652). The actors were discriminated against as catamites and, if they appeared on stage, were called *iroko* ("color children"), a term denoting their sensual qualities. They performed in the roles of young men, children, or girls and were forced to obey the demands of their patrons and act as prostitutes. A good many actors hailed from their ranks. The *iroko* were employed at establishments that were the equivalent of brothels and made their assignations in the teahouses (*see also* SHIBAIJAYA). These were called *kagema* ("dark room") teahouses. (*See also* ACTORS.)

ISE ONDO (KOI NO NETABA). Chikamatsu Tokusō*. *Sewamono**. Kabuki. Four acts, seven scenes. July 1796. Kado no Shibai, Osaka.

A dramatization of a case of mass murder that occurred at the Abura-ya teahouse in Furuuchi, Ise, in May 1796. The original cast included Yamanaka Bunshichi as Mitsugi, Yoshizawa Iroha as Okon, and Yamanaka Bungorō as Manno.

Fukuoka Mitsugi of Ise is having difficulty in his search for a famous sword and its certificate, which belongs to his master's family. His lover, the Abura-ya courtesan Okon, knows that a guest from Awa has the certificate; in order to get it in her hands, she purposely alienates herself from Mitsugi. As a result of a quarrel with Manno, chief maid of the Abura-ya, Mitsugi kills Okon in a fit of insanity and then commits one murder after another.

Highlights of the play include the separation scene* *(enkiri)* between Mitsugi and Okon and the gruesome beauty of the blood-spattered murder scene. The incident on which the play is based sparked the creation of an earlier version, in May, very soon after the actual murders. In August, the star of this play, Arashi Sangorō, appeared in another version in Kyoto, almost immediately after the present play was produced in Osaka. *Ise Ondo Koi no Netaba* is said to have been written in three days, making it a classic example of an *ichiyazuke kyōgen** (a play seemingly written overnight). In Edo its main acting pattern was transmitted from Bandō Hikosaburō III*, who first presented it at the Kawarazaki-za in 1803 to Onoe Kikugorō III*, Onoe Kikugorō V*, and Ichimura Uzaemon XV*. This pattern is known as the Otowaya *kata**.

ISHŌ. *See* COSTUMES.

ISHŌ KATA. The man in charge of Kabuki costumes. (*See also* COSTUMES.)

ISUWARU. When an actor in one production remains to appear in the following production. The term literally means "staying in place."

ITA BIN. A wig with thickly pomaded and shiny side locks *(bin*)*; bamboo boardlike *(ita)* splints are inserted into the hair on each side. This extremely stylized wig is used exclusively in *aragoto** and history plays. Characters who wear it include Matsuomaru in the *Kuruma Biki* scene of *Sugawara Denju Tenarai Kagami** and the *haradashi** soldiers of *Shibaraku**.

ITADAKU. A word with many implications in everyday speech, it was formerly used in the theatre to refer to a failure of some sort or to something that was made poorly. Today, good acting is rewarded with the phrase *itadakeru*, "to be quite fine."

ITAGAESHI. "Board change"; a trick stage device that has been seen only rarely since the early Meiji era. When a character's head was decapitated, the actor would fall over. At the same moment the flooring in front of him would rotate so that a realistic head, affixed to the floor's underside, would come into view. It was used for scenes such as Senō's death in *Genpei Nunobiki no Taki**.

ITA NI KAKERU. "To run on the boards"; an expression meaning "to act."

ITATSUKI. "Fixed to the boards"; when the curtain opens and a character is discovered in position. Also called *kamaboko*. (*See also* KARA BUTA I.)

ITCHŪ BUSHI. A musical style founded by Miyakodayū Itchū (1650-1724) in the Kamigata area during the Kanbun era (1661-72). Originally performed at banquets and similar functions, it is said to have been first used on stage in 1707 for a recital of *Miyako Shinjū* at Kyoto's Kataoka Nizaemon-za*. Itchū I also performed in Edo at the Ichimura-za*. Later, this school of music seems to have taken hold in the latter city. Itchū I's son, Itchū II, was active in the Kamigata area, while Itchū I's foremost pupil, Miyako Kanetayū Sanchū, was active in Edo. Sanchū later succeeded to the name of Itchū III, but he saw the decline of *itchū bushi* in his last years. Itchū V (1780-1822) temporarily reversed the style's downward trend, reviving the form as an entertainment at banquets and parties. *Itchū bushi* is a refined narrative musical style with a dignified and elegant melodic line; it developed more as a private entertainment form than as a theatre music. Representative examples of its use are in such plays as *Shin Usuyuki Monogatari** and *Onoe no Kumo Shizuhata Obi*.

ITO KODAYŪ I. fl. 1661-1681. An actor who specialized in *onnagata** roles.

II. ?-1689. Quite a famous actor, he went to Edo in 1661 and was particularly noteworthy in courtesan roles *(keisei)*. His style of purple-dappled tie-dyed cloth became fashionable among Edo's women and was known as "Kodayū Kanoko" ("Kodayū's dappling"). It was called "Edo Kanoko" later, when the style caught on in the Kamigata area.

ITSUMO NO TOKORO. "In the usual place"; a term implying the placement of scenery or properties as fixed by tradition. The expression is often seen in the stage directions of plays.

ITTE KOI. "Let's go"; to move from one scene to another. Also said when returning to the setting for an earlier scene.

IWAI HANSHIRŌ I. 1652-1699. An actor who, next to Yamashita Hanzaemon* and Sakata Tōjūrō*, was one of the great stars of Osaka Kabuki in the 1680s. He became an actor-manager *(zamoto*)* in 1689 in Osaka. The line that he founded produced players who were mainstays of the Osaka theatre up to Hanshirō III; from Hanshirō IV on, the line prospered in Edo. Hanshirōs IV through VIII were representative *onnagata**.

IV. 1747-1800. From 1764 to 1800, he was evenly matched with Segawa Kikunojō III* as Edo's best *onnagata* and was noticed for opening up a new aspect in the acting of townswomen. He was called "Shirogane no Dayū" or "Megurō no Dayū" because he had a villa at Shirogane in Megurō (*dayū* means "master").

V. 1776-1847. Son of Hanshirō IV. During the Bunka-Bunsei era (1804-30) he, together with his eldest son Kumesaburō (later Hanshirō VI) and his second son Shijaku (later Hanshirō VII), were the chief Edo *onnagata* of the late Edo period. Because of his big, bright eyes he was called "the actor with the thousand-*ryō* eyes" *(senryō yakusha*)*. His good looks were rich in charm and sexual appeal. Like his father, he specialized in portraying townswomen, and he established the role type of the contemporary evil woman of his times *(akuba; see also* ONNAGATA). One of the great *onnagata* in Kabuki history.

VI. 1799-1836. Eldest son of Hanshirō V, he was first known as Kumesaburō II. Much was expected of him as an *onnagata*, but he died only four years after succeeding to the name of Hanshirō VI.

VII. 1804-1845. Second son of Hanshirō V, he was first known as Matsunosuke and then as Shijaku, taking the name of Hanshirō in 1844. Plagued by illness, he died a year later.

VIII. 1829-1882. Son of Hanshirō VII, he changed his name from Shijaku to Hanshirō in 1872. He was the most popular *onnagata* in Tokyo in the years surrounding the Meiji Restoration.

IX. 1882-1945. Son of Iwai Kumesaburō IV, he became Kumesaburō V in 1906 and went on to a highly active career at the Ichimura-za*. Later he switched to acting at the small theatres called *koshibai**. He received his name of Hanshirō IX posthumously.

X, *yago** Yamatoya. 1927- . A vigorous and versatile actor, he was born in Tokyo, debuted in 1935, became Ichikawa Shōen II in 1939, and took his present name in 1947. He was in the Tōhō* company for about six years, beginning in 1956, but later returned to Shōchiku*. His father was the dancer Hanayagi Toshitarō.

IYAJAHIME. "Princess No-No"; a reference to Princess Shirabe, who appears in the *Kuzu no Ha Kowakare* scene of *Ashiya Dōman Ōuchi Kagami**. Since she hates having come to the Eastern Provinces, she goes around shaking her head and muttering, "No, no" (*"iyaja, iyaja"*).

IZUMO NO OKUNI. fl. about 1605. This woman is considered to be the true founder of Kabuki, though the records of her life are varied and vague. The most common opinion holds that she was the daughter of a Matsue blacksmith, Nakamura Sanzaemon, and a priestess at the temple in Izumo. She organized a troupe of entertainers and in 1603 performed her version of a religious dance, the *nenbutsu odori*, in the dry bed of Kyoto's Kamo River. Gaining great popularity, she moved to Edo in 1607 and even danced for the shogun in Edo Castle. On the advice of her colleague, the Kyōgen comedian Sanjūrō, she presented vulgarized versions of Kyōgen farces and appeared as a man in such pieces as *Yayako Odori* and *Kaka Odori*. As her appearance was rather eccentric, she was called *kabuku* (a term implying "offbeat" or "avant-garde"), and her dances were termed *kabuki*. Later, the Chinese characters for song, dance, and skill—*ka-bu-ki*—were applied in writing the word. A legend states that there was an Okuni II and III, but the facts are unclear. The year of her death also is questionable. She may have died in Odawara in 1607 or in 1613, at the age of sixty-seven; or did she become a nun in her native village and die at eighty-seven, as another story holds? Courtesans all over Japan emulated her popularity and performed Kabuki dances. This phenomenon was called courtesan Kabuki* (*yūjo kabuki*) and women's Kabuki* (*onna kabuki*). The names of the Kabuki courtesan dancers Sadoshima Masakichi, Nakamura Sakon, Okamoto Tsunebu, Ono Kodayō, Dekishima Nagatomori, Sugiyama Tonomo, and Ikuma Tangomori remain from this period, but little more is known of them. (*See also* ACTORS.)

J

JANOME MAWASHI. Two revolving stages, one inside the other in concentric circles. The inner circle is called *naibon;* the outer, *gaibon.* Such stages can be made to turn independently of one another; they provide interesting effects when made to revolve in either the same or opposite directions. The *janome* ("bull's-eye") *mawashi* is said to have been invented by Hasegawa Kanbei in 1847 (*see also* SCENERY). However, Kabuki no longer uses such a stage device, although other theatres that produce elaborate shows still do. The Koma Gekijō in Tokyo's Shinjuku section has a triple stage, each part of which can revolve or can go up and down. (*See also* REVOLVING STAGE.)

JIDAI. A term derived from that for the history play genre *(jidaimono*).* It is used whenever a performance becomes exaggerated and bombastic.

JIDAIMONO. Also called *jidai kyogen,* this is the history play genre, as opposed to the *sewamono**, or domestic play. Up to the middle of the Edo period it was the Kamigata custom to present more than one play in a day; since the first play on the program was a history play, it also was called *ichibanme mono** or *ichibanme kyōgen* (literally, "first play of the day"). In general, *jidaimono* deal with materials based on the pre-Edo-era society of noble princes, monks, and samurai; plays known as *ōdai** or *ōcho mono,* dealing with lords of the Nara (696-794) and Heian (794-1185) periods, are central to the *jidaimono* repertoire. There is also a class of plays called *ōie kyōgen**, which treats the family disputes of Tokugawa *daimyō* and vassals. Thus, in a narrow sense, *jidaimono* are dramas treating historical material that derives from the time of the wars between the Genji and Heike clans to the downfall of Toyotomi, shortly before the establishment of the Tokugawa shogunate. As it was forbidden to dramatize events occurring to the warrior class of the Edo period, it was common to dress such events in the guise of earlier periods; a common device was to alter the names of the characters. (*See also* PLAY CATEGORIES.)

JIDAI-SEWAMONO. A play that mingles elements of the *jidaimono** genre with features from the *sewamono** genre. (*See also* PLAY CATEGORIES.)

JIGASURI. Also called *dorogire,* this is a cloth spread on the stage floor to suggest specific ground or floor effects. It may be gray, yellow, stone-colored, and so on. For an indoor scene it may depict a wood-grained floor. In snow scenes, an excellent effect is created by spreading a white cloth *(yuki nuno,* or "snow cloth") over the entire stage floor and *hanamichi**. There are also "wave cloths" *(nami nuno)* and "water cloths" *(mizu nuno)* to depict seas and rivers. In such cases, the stage assistants are dressed in costumes matching the floor. The wave costume is called *namiko* and the snow costume is *yukiko,* in order to distinguish them from the usual black costume, *kurogo**.

JIKATA. The seated singers, musicians, *shamisen** player, and so on, in contrast to the standing dancer *(tachikata).*

JI KYŌGEN (or SHIBAI). Plays associated with specific locales; a kind of amateur theatre performed by local laymen. Many *ji kyōgen* were performed for short periods of time at festivals such as the Bon, as rain prayers, or as ancestral memorial presentations. Village shrines often have a permanent stage for such purposes within the shrine compound. The zenith of such activity occurred during the second half of the nineteenth century, after which the *ji kyōgen* declined. They survive today only in certain rural and mountain villages.

JITSUKAWA ENJAKU I. 1831-1885. An actor, the adopted son of the proprietor of Osaka's Chikugo Shibai theatre in the Dōtonbori district. He became the pupil of Jitsukawa Enzaburō in 1841, but soon after was separated both from his adopted family and his teacher. He was called "Naked Enji" (Hadaka no Enji) and passed his days as a traveling player. He went to Edo in 1856, received training at the home of Nakamura Shikan IV*, returned to Osaka in 1861, and succeeded in having his skill recognized. He returned to his adopted family's home the following year, was reinstated under the roof of his master, and took the name of Enjaku. In 1868 he, Arashi Rikan IV, and Nakamura Sōjūrō I* were called Osaka's triumvirate of experts in the romantic style of *wagoto** acting.

II. 1877-1951. Eldest son of Enjaku I, he succeeded to the name in 1915. Together with Nakamura Ganjirō I*, he was one of the two representative actors of the Kamigata area during the first half of this century. He inherited his father's style and was best at *wagoto** roles, but was skilled in all types of parts, except female roles.

III, *yago** Kawauchiya. 1921- . One of Kabuki's major stars, he has an exceptional range. Born in Osaka, the son of Enjaku II, he debuted in 1927 and became Enjirō in 1934, taking his present name in March 1963. He is committed to performing the unique stage tricks *(keren*)* that he inherited from his predecessors as the specialty of his line; dancing is also one of his fortes. In addition, Enjaku is the unique possessor of what may be called a classic old-style Kabuki face.

JIUTA. When the *shamisen** was imported into Japan in the early 1560s, musicians were pleased by its lovely tones and employed it for a variety of musical uses, such as the accompaniment for ballads sung by blind minstrels in the Kamigata area. Yanagigawa Kengyō Kaganoichi first formally arranged this music in the early Edo period. The Edo style was called Edo *uta*, in contrast to the Kamigata *uta*, as there were regional differences in the styles; thus the term *jiuta* ("place song") arose to imply the regional quality of the music. Later, the *shamisen* was supplemented by the *koto** and then by the *kokyū** and the *shakuhachi* flute.

JIWA. The gradual murmuring of the audience when they become aware that the play they are attending is either a success or a failure.

JOBIRAKI. Part of the daily program in the Edo period. A day's performance schedule began with the ceremonial dance, *Sanbasō** followed by another ceremonial piece, the *waki kyōgen**, which was often derived from a Kyōgen theatre farce. Next came the *jobiraki*, a humorous one-acter lasting twenty to thirty minutes and having no relation to the plot of the main play on the program. It dealt with such events as the appearance of a spirit or a struggle for treasure. The *jobiraki* was considered a practice piece for apprentice playwrights and actors. The *futatateme** came after the *jobiraki*.

JOMAKU. On an Edo period program, this was the first act in which the plot of the main play began. It corresponded to the *mitateme** of the first play on the program (*see also* JIDAIMONO). The domestic section on the second half of the program was arranged as follows: *jomaku*, *nimakume* (Act II), *sanmakume* (Act III).

JŌRURI. A narrative-musical form accompanied by the *shamisen**. Around the middle of the Muromachi period (1392-1568), blind musicians recited tales to the musical accompaniment of a lutelike instrument *(biwa)* and a fan which was struck rhythmically on a block. One of these tales described the romance between Ushiwakamaru (the young Yoshitsune) and a wealthy man's daughter, Princess Jōruri. As this story grew very popular, such narrative recitals came to be called *jōruri.* The form developed more fully after Japan imported the *shamisen* and *jōruri* began to use it. When *jōruri* was incorporated shortly thereafter into the itinerant art of puppeteering, Japan's puppet theatre was complete. This took place during the late sixteenth century. It soon led to the birth of various schools of *jōruri* art. For example, there were Edo's *kinpira jōruri** and the Kamigata area's *harima bushi, kaga bushi, tosa bushi,* and other styles. During the late seventeenth century, Takemoto Gidayū (1651-1714) founded *gidayū bushi** in Osaka, and its popularity so overpowered the other schools that works based on the *gidayū* style occupied the leading position among all schools. Thus, the pre-*gidayū-bushi* forms are classed as "old," or *kojōruri**. A number of styles grew up in Edo beginning early in the eighteenth century. Among these were the *handayū bushi, katō bushi**, and *geki bushi**. New forms that had splintered from the *bungo bushi** style appeared in the mid-eighteenth century. These included the *shinnai bushi**, *tokiwazu bushi**, *tomimoto bushi**, *kiyomoto bushi**, and others. Many of the early *jōruri* plays were constructed in six acts, but five acts (three for domestic plays) later became the rule. These plays, in which the dramatic elements of epic poetry may often be found, occupy an extremely high position among Japan's old classical works. (*See also* PLAY CATEGORIES.)

JŌSHIKI. A thin straw matting that is spread over the stage. In special cases real *tatami* matting is used *(hontatami,* or "real *tatami*").

A different spelling of this term refers to any conventional theatre technique fixed by tradition—from settings, props, costumes, and wigs to acting, role types, and plays.

JŌSHIKI ANA. Standardized openings in the stage floor for the fitting of scenic elements; they allow even a house to be constructed on stage in a matter of minutes.

JŌSHIKI MAKU. The standardized Kabuki curtain, a show curtain used at the beginning and end of a performance. It is colored black, persimmon, and green, dyed in vertical stripes. It is said to have originated when Nakamura Kanzaburō I* used as a curtain the ship's sail that he was awarded for leading the sculling song when hauling the shogun's boat, Ataka Maru. (*See also* CURTAINS; HIKI MAKU.)

JŌSHIKI ŌDŌGU. The scenic elements of Kabuki settings that are fixed in style by long tradition. Also called *jōshiki mono.* Though standardized, they can be flexibly adapted to stage sets; they are either combined as is or partially reconstructed. The chief items included under this rubric are the levels *(ashi)* placed on the stage floor *(nijū*),* pillars, transom works, banisters, railings, stairs, sliding opaque doors, shoji screens, latticework, rain doors, fences, entranceways *(kido*)*, stone lanterns, wells, trees, shrubbery, tree stumps, folding stools, pilings, rain barrels, perspective backdrops, watchtowers, pine-board backdrops, the *furiotoshi** curtain, red-carpeted step units (*see also* HINADAN), *torii* gates, wash bowls, and shrine fences. These are scaled to the dimensions of the particular theatre's stage and can be used in any play; however, the lack of individuality in the set pieces may be considered a weakness. (*See also* JŌSHIKI; SCENERY.)

JŌSHIKI SEN. Also called *daijin dōri*, this represents an imaginary line joining the stage pillars *(daijin bashira*)* at either side of the stage. The line is used as the downstage limit of the setting.

JUN KABUKI. "Pure Kabuki," plays originally written for Kabuki and not for the puppet theatre. (*See also* PLAY CATEGORIES.)

JYARI NO ITO. A property term for props manipulated by long, thin strings that are meant to be invisible to the audience. Black silk or cotton thread is used for this purpose. Among *jyari no ito* props is the *unki**, which represents a cutout of clouds hung from above the stage, and the *suiki*, which gives the impression of a spout of water. The latter is a trick performed by attaching strips of silver paper to a flexible bamboo-like implement. The implement is tied so that the paper is bound at its base by a clasp; at the proper moment the clasp is loosed, and the mechanism springs up. (*See also* PROPERTIES.)

K

KABESU. A theatre person's slang for *kashi* (cakes), *bentō* (box lunches), and *sushi* (rice cakes with fish), the word being composed of the first syllables of each word. These have been the traditional foods eaten at the theatre. It also means those spectators who do not order Western foods.

KABUKI JŪHACHIBAN. "The Kabuki Eighteen," a collection of plays established by Ichikawa Danjūrō VII*; it stresses the special *aragoto** acting art of the Danjūrō line. In the Meiji period other acting families began to gather their most successful plays into similar collections. (*See also* FAMILY ART). Plays are listed here by their abbreviated titles.

PLAY	THEME	DATE OF FIRST PERFORMANCE	FIRST STAR	FIRST MAJOR REVIVAL DATE	REVIVING ACTOR
Fuwa	The crossing of scabbards by the love rivals, Fuwa and Nagoya.	1680	Danjūrō I*	1933	Danjūrō X*
*Narukami**	The angering of the impious priest Narukami by a beautiful princess, Kumo no Taema.	1684	Danjūrō I	1910	Ichikawa Sadanji II*
*Shibaraku**	The derring-do of a young warrior who saves the weak from danger.	1697	Danjūrō I		

PLAY	THEME	DATE OF FIRST PERFORMANCE	FIRST STAR	FIRST MAJOR REVIVAL DATE	REVIVING ACTOR
Fudō	A stage piece honoring the Ichikawa family's tutelary deity.	1697	Danjūrō II*	1912	Sadanji II
Uwanari	The madness of jealousy.	1699	Danjūrō I	1936	Danjūrō X
Zōhiki	A tug-of-war between Iruka and Gennaizaemon, who use an elephant instead of a rope.	1701	Danjūrō I	1913	Sadanji II
*Kanjinchō**	The feats of Benkei as he flees with Yoshitsune from the capital.	1702	Danjūrō I	1840	Danjūrō VII
*Sukeroku**	The dashing figure cut by Soga Gorō under the assumed name of Sukeroku.	1714	Danjūrō II		
*Oshimodoshi**	A performance in which a warrior repels an angry demon.	1714	Danjūrō II		
Uirōuri	The oratory of the seller of *uirō* medicine.	1718	Danjūrō II	1832	Danjūrō VII
*Yanone**	Sogo Gorō rushes off to aid his brother Jurō who is in danger.	1725	Danjūrō II	1882	Danjūrō IX*
Kanu	Kagekiyo does battle in the guise of a Chinese hero, Kanu.	1736	Danjūrō II	1929	Sadanji II
Kagekiyo	The breaking loose of Kagekiyo from prison.	1738	Danjūrō II	1908	Matsumoto Kōshirō VII*
Nanatsumen	The quick-change performance of Awazu Rokurō.	1739	Danjūrō II	1893	Danjūrō IX
*Kenuki**	The humor that comes from the enigma puzzling Kumodera Danjō.	1742	Danjūrō II	1909	Sadanji II
Gedatsu	Kagekiyo's *aragoto* acting of his malice and his religious salvation.	1760	Danjūrō IV*	1932	Danjūrō X

PLAY	THEME	DATE OF FIRST PER-FORM-ANCE	FIRST STAR	FIRST MAJOR REVIVAL DATE	REVIVING ACTOR
Jyayanagi	The jealousy of the angry ghost of Kiyo-hime who died of unrequited love.	1763	Danjūrō IV	1945	Danjūrō X
Kamahige	The dispute between the invulnerable Kagekiyo and Miho Tanishirō.	1774	Danjūrō IV	1910	Danshirō X

KABUKI-ZA. A famous playhouse first opened in Tokyo's Kyobashi district in Kobiki-chō (today called Chuō-ku, Ginza 4) in November 1889. It was managed by Fukuchi Ōchi* and financed by his partner, Chiba Katsugorō. The exterior was in Western style and the interior in pure Japanese style. In 1911 the exterior was reconstructed in Japanese style. A short circuit led to its destruction by fire in November 1921. Reconstruction was pushed forward, but, just before the building was completed, it burned down again, this time as a result of the great earthquake of 1923. It was rebuilt once more the following year and opened in January 1925. This four-story building had a steel frame and was made of concrete; its exterior was in Momoyama period (1568-1615) style. Aside from its left and right *sajiki** galleries, all seats were Western style. In May 1945, the Kabuki-za was destroyed in an air raid, and only the outer shell was left standing. Of course, it was rebuilt, opening its doors in January 1951. This is Tokyo's present Kabuki-za. Ever since 1889, this theatre palace has seen the performances of Japan's greatest Kabuki actors. It seats 2,600, has a stage width of eighty-seven feet, and is sixty-seven feet in length. (*See also* THEATRE MANAGEMENT; THEATRE ARCHITECTURE.)

KABUKI ZŌSHI. Illustrated booklets and scrolls depicting early Kabuki dances. A number of types were produced from the late sixteenth century through the early Edo period; many show the work of *Okuni kabuki* (*see also* IZUMO NO OKUNI) and *onna kabuki* (women's Kabuki*). They are an important source for understanding early Kabuki.

KABURITSUKI. Also called *amaochi** and *koichi*. The first row of spectators. The name is said to come from the fact that these seats seem to "bite at" *(kaburitsuku)* the stage. Another view holds that the term derives from the hats *(kaburimono)* polished with wood oil and worn by spectators in these seats. The seating here was thus "under the *kaburimono" (kaburimono tsuki no seki).*

KABURU. When the spectators suddenly "pour into" the theatre. Also used for the end of the performance. Another usage is when the actors get in front of each other and consequently cannot be seen by the audience; here the word means "to cover."

KABUSERU. When an actor cuts off another's lines or business before they have been completed.

KAERI JONICHI. "Return of opening day." The opening day of a run is called *shonichi* ("opening day*"). When a production has started its run, it is said that "opening day has begun" *(shonichi ga aku).* It occasionally happens that performances of a play that has already opened must be suspended; when the same play reopens later, it is called *kaeri jonichi**.

KAGAMI. "Mirror"; flats *(harimono*)* placed behind settings with entrances (sliding paper doors, shop curtains, shoji, and the like) to prevent the audience from seeing the back of the stage—that is, "masking." Black and gray are the conventional colors used in *kagami,* but in realistic plays scenic elements matching those in front provide masking. (*See also* MIKIRI; KERIKOMI.)

KAGAMIJISHI. Fukuchi Ōchi*. Also called *Shunkyō Kagamijishi. Shosagoto*. Nagauta**. One act. March 1893. Kabuki-za*, Tokyo.

There are many Kabuki *shakkyō mono** ("lion dances"); this one was created at the request of Ichikawa Danjūrō IX* and based on a previous number, *Makura Jishi* (1792). Thus, *Kagami jishi* is a revision of a work that, like itself, treats of a young lady's dancing with a lion hand puppet. In the original the lady is a courtesan, but here she is a lady-in-waiting.

As the court lady Yayoi dances at the New Year's celebrations with a lion puppet-head on her hand, the head takes possession of her soul and she begins to dance wildly. After an interval that is filled by the dancing of two butterflies, Yayoi returns to the stage in the guise of a lion and does a powerful dance.

The lion in the second half—whose vigorous dance is similar to that of Shakkyō, the lion in the Nō play of that name—contrasts vividly with the elegant court lady of the first half.

The play's highlights include the double fan dance of the first half, the moment when Yayoi is dragged down the *hanamichi** by the hand puppet,

Nakamura Tomijūrō V* as the lion in *Kagamijishi**.

and the wild dance of the second half during which the actor playing the lion swings a long white mane of hair around and around (*see also* KAMI ARAI). After Danjūrō's first performance of the play, it was not presented for a time. Onoe Kikugorō VI* revived it to great acclaim, and it has been seen frequently ever since. It is included in Danjūrō's play collection, the *shin kabuki jūhachiban**.

KAGAMIYAMA (KOKYŌ NO NISHIKIE). Yō Yodai. Also called *Onna Chūshingura. Jidaimono*. Jōruri**. Eleven acts. January 1782. Satsuma Geki-za, Edo.

This well-known play is based on an actual event that occurred in 1724 at the Edo palace of Lord Matsudaira of Suo: the maidservant Osatsu revenged her mistress, Omichi, by killing Sawano, who had insulted Omichi and caused her suicide. This event is woven together with events surrounding the family disputes *(oie mono*)* of the Kaga family. The parts most frequently performed today are the *Zōriuchi* scene of Act VI and the *Nagatsubone* and *Oku Niwa* scenes of Act VII. The many versions of this play's story are known collectively as *Kagamiyama mono*. Kabuki's first adaptation came in 1783 at Edo's Morita-za*.

The court lady Iwafuji has been plotting the usurpation of the shogunate for quite some time; her brother Danjō is in league with her. Because her secret message has been picked up accidentally by the court lady Onoe, Iwafuji plans to trap her when Onoe goes to the Tsurugaoka Temple for her mistress to place there an image of the Buddha. At the temple, Iwafuji beats Onoe with her sandal, an extreme form of disgrace for the recipient of the blows *(Zōriuchi)*.

Deeply mortified, Onoe returns to her room, writes a description of Iwafuji's evil deeds, and then commits suicide. Her maid Ohatsu, who has been sent on an errand, is uneasy when she hears the ill omen of a bird crying; she hurriedly returns, but Onoe is already breathing her last. Smearing the ill-used sandal with Onoe's blood, Ohatsu runs with it as if it were a dagger to the garden of Iwafuji *(Nagatsubone)*.

Appearing before Iwafuji, Ohatsu vents her spleen and finally kills Onoe's enemy. Iwafuji's coconspirators are found out, and Ohatsu is rewarded by being given the name of Onoe II *(Oku Niwa)*.

This play, which has almost an all-female cast, is a showcase for the skills of Kabuki's female impersonators. Onoe is a particularly great role for such an actor. The play used to be produced in the spring when the palace maids had some free time to themselves and went to the theatre in large numbers. There are many rewritten versions, of which Kawatake Mokuami's* *Kagamiyama Gonichi no Iwafuji* (known popularly as *Kotsuyose*, 1860) is most famous. (*See also* SPRING PLAYS.)

KAGEBARA. "Hidden stomach"; a dramatic situation wherein a major character, already having committed the act of ritual suicide *(seppuku)*, conceals his wound and enters the scene, enduring his suffering as he endeavors to solve a problem. Since Kabuki's early days various actors have created interesting stage business for such "hidden stomach" scenes. There is even an oral tradition to "try to have a chestnut burr against your abdomen when acting such scenes." An outstanding example occurs in the scene of "the three laughs" in *Shin Usuyuki Monogatari**.

KAGE HAYASHI. "Orchestra in the wings," the *geza** musicians when they play in the *geza* room at stage right, as opposed to when they appear on stage as the *debayashi**.

KAGE SHIBAI. "Shadow theatre"; during the late Edo era, groups who rowed up to people floating on pleasure barges down Edo's Sumida River and, for a fee, imitated the voices and manner of famous Kabuki actors upon request. (*See also* KOWAIRO.)

KAGEUCHI. The Kamigata technique of beating the *tsuke** clappers from the wings *(kage)*.

KAGOTSURUBE (SATO NO EIZAME). Kawatake Shinshichi III*. Also called *Sano Jirozaemon. Sewamono** Kabuki. Eight acts. May 1888. Chitose-za, Tokyo.

A dramatization of the tale of Sano Jirozaemon, a farmer said to have killed 100 men in the Yoshiwara pleasure quarters. Today the first half of the play, which revolves around the fate of Jirozaemon's father, is cut; the usual procedure is to begin with the scene in Yoshiwara's Nakanochō in which Jirozaemon falls in love at first sight. The first cast included Ichikawa Sadanji I* as Sano Jirozaemon, Nakamura Fukusuke (later Nakamura Utaemon V*) as Yatsuhashi, and Ichikawa Kodanji V* as Einojō.

Jirozaemon, an ugly, pockmarked farmer, falls madly in love with a spectacular courtesan, Yatsuhashi, while she is making a tour of the quarter. He visits her often until he finally decides to pay her bond and thus release her from her indenture. However, because of her present relationship with Einōjō, her lover, Yatsuhashi reviles Jirozaemon before a crowd of onlookers. The disgraced farmer restrains himself with an effort. Once he has returned to his country home and thought things over, he comes back to Yatsuhashi again and kills her with his magic sword.

The heart of the entire work is the scene in which the farmer is insulted. Also fascinating is the sequence in which the gorgeous courtesan makes her rounds of the flower-bedecked Yoshiwara and the foolish Jirozaemon falls headlong in love with her after only one glimpse of her smiling face.

The courtesan Yatsuhashi astonishes the country bumpkin Jirozaemon in *Kagotsurube Sato no Eizame**. Notice the elaborate obi, tied in front by the courtesan, and her clogs, which are so high that she must lean on the shoulder of a servant to support herself. Jirozaemon, Nakamura Kanzaburō XVII*; Yatsuhashi, Nakamura Utaemon VI*. *Courtesy of Waseda University Tsubouchi Engeki Hakubutsukan (Tsubouchi Memorial Theatre Museum).*

Shinshichi based his played on a number of earlier treatments dating back to the mid-eighteenth century. It is considered his representative *sewamono.* Sadanji was excellent as Jirozaemon, and his makeup as the pockmarked farmer is still used for the role. Sadanji, who was competing with the work of Ichikawa Danjūrō IX* and Onoe Kikugorō V* at other theatres, was at a disadvantage until he played this role. It put him on an equal standing with his rivals. Nakamura Kichiemon I* had a different interpretation of Jirozaemon, but he too made an enormous success of the role. One of the best players of the part today is Nakamura Kanzaburō XVII*.

KAHAKU. "Movement and dialogue"; a word composed of two characters that represent the essentials of acting. Plays based on these elements are called *kahakugeki* as opposed to *buyōgeki* (dance drama) or *ongakugeki* (music drama). Early Kabuki, in the first half of the seventeenth century, was principally dance drama. With the coming of *yarō kabuki*, or mature male Kabuki*, the emphasis switched to realistic acting *(monomane)* with a focus on representational movement and dialogue. Such plays flourished in the Genroku period (1688-1703); afterwards, many fine writers appeared and gave Kabuki hundreds of works in the manner of *kahakugeki.*

KAICHOBA. A scenic element used for the inclined plane representing mountain and hill paths. Its name comes from its resemblance to the special slope erected over the steps for the convenience of temple visitors when temples and shrines put a Buddhist image on public display *(kaichō).* The stage slope is placed on one side of a platform and joined to it, being fixed in place with a brace. (*See also* YAOYA KAZARI.)

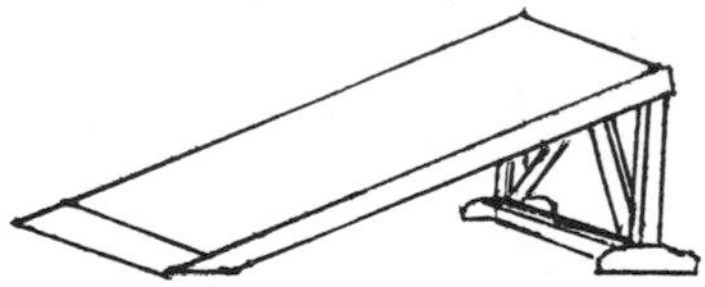

*Kaichoba**. After a drawing in Itō, *Butai Sōchi no Kenkyū.*

KAIDAN BOTAN DŌRŌ. Kawatake Shinshichi III*. Also called *Botan Dōrō. Sewamono**. Kabuki. Seven acts. July 1892. Kabuki-za*, Tokyo.

Otsuya—daughter of Hanto, a vassal of the shogun—dies of unrequited passion for Hagiwara Shinzaburō. Every night, her ghost leads her nurse, Okome, to Shinzaburō's home. Shinzaburō strings a charm around his house to protect him from the ghost, but the evil Tomozō receives money from the spirit and removes the charm. This leads to Shinzaburō's being haunted to death by the ghost.

The first performance of this play starred Onoe Kikugorō V*. Kikugorō VI* later perfected the performance style. There is a good deal of interest in the performance of the roles of Tomozō and the manservant Kosuke, whose characters are contrary to each other. The realism of Kikugorō's embodiment of Tomozō greatly increased the play's value.

KAIDAN MONO. *See* GHOST PLAYS.

KAIMAKU. "Opening of the curtain"; a term originating in Kabuki that has come to mean the opening of a festival or annual event.

KAISHAKU SURU. A term that originally meant "to assist at a ritual suicide," but has come to refer to anyone who offers help or assistance.

KAKEAI. When more than one musical style is used as background for a dance play. For instance, *Momijigari** uses *nagauta**, *gidayū**, and *tokiwazu** for its performance.

KAKEDASU. To speed up the tempo of the acting. Also, to cut into someone else's dialogue with one's own lines before the other actor has finished speaking.

KAKE ENSHIO. A type of property trick; it is a device for producing smoke just before the appearance of apparitions or some sort of magic. A famous example is when gunpowder is employed to make smoke appear for Nikki Danjō's entrance through the trap on the *hanamichi** in *Meiboku Sendai Hagi**. Because of the danger from fire, these devices are seen infrequently today. (*See also* FUKIBOYA.)

KAKEGOE. Words of praise shouted impromptu by the playgoers when stimulated by a fine piece of acting. Most commonly, spectators shout the actor's *yago** during a pause; they try not to miss the exact moment for a shout, for the timing is of great importance. Other shouts are of the actor's home address, his ordinal number, his pen name *(haimyō*)*, and so on. (*See also* HOME KOTOBA; AUDIENCES.)

KAKEMOCHI. When an actor or performer performs in more than one theatre in the same day.

KAKENAGASHI MONO. Something used on stage only once and then discarded. (*See also* KIEMONO.)

KAKERI. *See* GEZA: MUSICAL ACCOMPANIMENT CHART.

KAKIDASHI. An actor, usually a popular young star, whose name was written first in the Edo period programs and on the billboards; also called *shofude.* Contrasted with this was the name written last, called *tomefude.* (*See also* NAKAJIKU.)

KAKIGAE KYŌGEN. Plays with new plots, but with characters whose names were the same as those in already well-known plays. During the

Kyōhō era (1716-35) the dramatization of actual events relating to the samurai class was forbidden, so this method of disguising the events depicted was practiced widely. (*See also* SHUKŌ; SEKAI.)

KAKIMONO. "Written thing," the script for a new play. If a play is called a *kakimono* today, it means that it is being given its first production. Also, it refers to the use onstage of "writing props," such as deeds, letters, vows, and documents sealed in blood. These items are prepared by the men known as *kyōgen sakusha** (*see also* PLAYWRIGHTS' RANKS).

KAKINUKI. "Writing-removing"; an actor's part is extracted from the complete playscript and set down for his use in a separate booklet. It is the equivalent of what is known in Western theatre as "sides." Once the reading of the play to the actors is concluded, the cast settled on, and the *kakinuki* accepted by the players, tacit agreement exists that the play will be produced. According to custom, even actors with roles containing no lines are given *kakinuki*. It also is the custom to make up separate *kakinuki* booklets for each scene in which an actor appears if he is cast in more than one role. The month of the performance is printed on the upper right corner of the booklet's cover, the nature of the *kakinuki* enclosed is printed in the center of the cover, and the character's name and pen name (*haimyō**) are written on the left. In some cases a "congratulatory" name is put in the place of the character's name. The *kakinuki* is an item of great importance to an actor, and during his rehearsals he carries it wrapped in silken cloth. It is said that actors used to place it on the "god-shelf" (*butsudana*) in their homes.

KAKIOROSHI. A new play being performed for the first time. The word pertains particularly to new plays that in some sense, such as a memorial, apply to a certain actor. It also refers to a play written for a particular actor.

KAMAKURA SANDAIKI. Attributed to Chikamatsu Hanji*. Also called *Kamasan, Sandaiki*. *Jidaimono**. *Jōruri**. Ten acts. March 1781. Hizen-za, Edo.

A drama dealing with the fall of Osaka Castle, but placing the action, which really took place early in the seventeenth century, in the medieval Kamakura period (1185-1333). It hints that Tokimasa is Ieyasu, Takatsuna is Yukimura, Miuranosuke is Kimura Shigenari, and Princess Toki is Princess Sen. This substitution of fictional names for true historical ones is common in Kabuki (*see also* KAKIGAE KYŌGEN). For many years, only Act VII, the Kinugawa Village scene (commonly called *Miura Wakare*), is performed. Ki no Kaion* wrote a play with the same title as this, but his is a completely different work. Kabuki did not produce this work until 1818, when it was staged at Edo's Nakamura-za*.

Hearing that his mother is very ill, the seriously wounded Miuranosuke comes running to her bedside from the battlefield; his mother, however, rebukes her own son as a coward and refuses to have anything to do with him. Miuranosuke's betrothed is Princess Toki, the daughter of Tokimasa (her fiance's enemy in this battle;) she turns her back on her father and comes to the home of her future mother-in-law to nurse her. She rejoices at Miuranosuke's return, but, as he says he cannot marry the daughter of his enemy, she prepares to die. Miuranosuke tells her that he will marry her only if she kills her father. Faithful to Miuranosuke, the princess consents. Sasaki Takatsuna, who overhears this and is glad to learn of Princess Toki's gallantry, encourages Miuranosuke and gets him to return to the battlefield.

The theme of this play is the dilemma suffered by Princess Toki over the conflict between her love for both her father and her betrothed. Along with Princess Yaegaki and Princess Yuki, the role of Princess Toki is classed as one of Kabuki's three great princess roles (*see also* AKAHIME; SANHIME). It is a part demanding charm, dignity, and strength. Nakamura Utaemon V* excelled in the role, and its present exponent is Utaemon VI*.

KAMAWANU. A unique Kabuki design. There are many instances in Kabuki in which the colors, crests, and patterns associated with a family of actors are used to good effect. *Kamawanu,* traditional in the Ichikawa family of actors, is one of them. It is a pattern in which a sickle shape *(kama),* a circle shape *(wa),* and the syllabic character *nu* are combined to form the word *kamawanu* ("I don't care"). It was created by Ichikawa Danjūrō VII* when he performed Yoemon in *Kasane** during the first half of the nineteenth century. (*See also* YOKIKOTOGIKU.)

KAMI ARAI. "Hair washing"; a *kata** or acting pattern that appears in dances when the actor swings a long mane of hair hanging down before him from left to right and back again. The name comes from the movement's resemblance to the act of washing the hair. It is used by Kabuki lions when they frolic, for example, in the second part of *Renjishi** and *Kagamijishi**.

KAMIGATA KYŌGEN. Kabuki plays that are rich in the traditions of the old social conventions and emotional qualities of life in the Kyoto and Osaka area. Compared with Edo plays, they present certain distinct features. The main type of Kamigata play is the "courtesan" play called *keisei gai*; it is in these plays that *wagoto** acting flourishes. *Wagoto*'s soft, delicate style contrasts with the bolder and far more exaggerated Edo style called *aragoto**. *Keisei gai* plays depict the frequenters of the pleasure quarters in a realistic manner. Such plays include *Keisei Hotoke no Hara, Keisei Mibu Dainenbutsu,* and *Keisei Hangonkō**. The best remaining example of the style of acting in *keisei gai* is seen in the character of Fujiya Izaemon in *Kuruwa Bunshō**. (*See also* KAMIKO.)

KAMIKO. "Paper kimono." Originally a crude paper kimono, its Kabuki version, which purports to be made of paper, is actually made of beautiful crepe. The *kamiko* is worn by such characters as romantic young men of good families who find themselves in economic difficulties. Izaemon in *Kuruwa Bunshō** is the representative example.

KAMI NO MEGUMI WAGŌ NO TORIKUMI. Takeshiba Kisui*. Also called *Megumi no Kenka. Sewamono**. Kabuki. Four acts. August 1890. Shintomi-za, Tokyo.

The original cast for this play included Onoe Kikugorō V* as Megumi no Tatsugorō and Ichikawa Sadanji I* as Kisaburō. A real incident occurring in 1805 is dramatized in this play. Several earlier dramas were based on the incident, but the present one came closest to being a faithful representation of the facts. Also, unlike the others, it used the real names of the participants.

Put to shame by sumo wrestler Yotsuguruma at the Shimazakiro teahouse in Edo's Shinagawa pleasure district, Tatsugorō, a chief fireman of the Me company, unsuccessfully ambushes the wrestler at Yatsu Yamashita. Later, a fight breaks out in a theatre between some sumo wrestlers and a group of firemen. Tatsugorō, after secretly deciding to separate from his family for the honor of the firemen, departs for Shinmei in Edo. A great fight occurs here between the sumo wrestlers and the firemen, but Takida, a man of influence, and Kisaburō, a top official in Edo's fire service, negotiate a satisfactory settlement to the dispute.

The pantomime scene *(danmari*)* at Yatsu Yamashita is famous, as is the scene of Tatsugorō's sorrow, which is accompanied by a chanter and *shamisen** music. Among the play's delights is the scene of the quarrel among the large crowd of youthful partisans. The Kikugorō troupe makes a specialty of this work.

KAMISHIMO. "Top and bottom"; the formal attire of Edo period samurai. It consists of a *kataginu** jumper worn over the torso and *hakama** divided trousers worn below. Originally, the top and bottom were of an identical color. The costume has been freely adapted and stylized to suit the requirements of the various characters who wear it, and it has become one of the characteristic costume elements of Kabuki. In addition to the types of *kamishimo* worn offstage, such as the *asa kamishimo* (unlined and made of linen) and the *tsugi kamishimo* (the ordinary dress of samurai within their barracks), a number of other types appear in Kabuki. They vary in material, color, and design according to the role in which they are worn. For example, there are the brocade textiles of Kajiwara in *Miura no Ōsuke Kōbai Tazuna**,

A delicate young *wagotoshi* character, Izaemon, in the classic Kamigata kyōgen* *Kuruwa Bunshō**. Izaemon wears the *kamiko** kimono, said to be made of paper. Izaemon, Kataoka Takao I*. *Courtesy of Waseda University Tsubouchi Engeki Hakubutsukan (Tsubouchi Memorial Theatre Museum).*

Sanemori and Senō in *Genpei Nunobiki No Taki**, and Wada Hyoe in *Ōmi Genji Senjin Yakata**. Satin is worn by such gentle young samurai as Jūjirō in Act X of *Ehon Taikōki** and Katsuyori in *Honchō Nijūshikō**. Some romantic young samurai wear the exquisite embroidered and brightly dyed *irogamishimo*, worn with the long, trailing *hakama*; such an outfit is called *naga* ("long") *kamishimo*.

KAMISUKI. "Hair combing"; scenes that represent feelings of love and sorrow as a man's hair is being dressed and combed by his mistress, mother, or wife. The technique began with plays about the Soga brothers and was then adopted for numerous dramas. It is usual for the *meriyasu** style of music to provide an atmosphere of pathos in such scenes. *Kamisuki* moments are found in *Kumo ni Magō Ueno no Hatsuhana** and *Tōkaidō Yotsuya Kaidan**. The latter is a variation on the usual *kamisuki*; the participants here are mistress and servant, rather than lovers.

KAMITE. "Stage left," or the right side of the stage from the audience's point of view. The opposite side is called *shimote**.

KAMU. "To mesh"; said when two actors work well together in terms of timing.

KAN. "To die." Used in the onomatopoeic sense of a single tolling of a bell.

KANADEHON CHŪSHINGURA. Takeda Izumo II*, Miyoshi Shōraku, Namiki Sōsuke*. Also called *Chūshingura*. English title: *Chūshingura: The Treasury of Loyal Retainers* (Keene). *Jidaimono**. *Jōruri**. Eleven acts. August 1748. Takemoto-za, Osaka.

The famous revenge on their master's enemy by the forty-seven retainers of Akō (the "Akō vendetta") captured the imagination of the Japanese populace and was dramatized frequently by Kabuki and the puppet theatre. It also gave rise to a slew of "loyal retainer" plays *(gishi geki)*. This masterpiece holds the highest rank among such plays; *Chūshingura* and *Kanjinchō** are Kabuki's two most commonly produced works. Since its early days this play has been considered a cure for the theatre's doldrums and can always be expected to draw audiences when all else fails.

The play opens at the Tsurugaoka Shrine. Kono Moronao has summoned the wife of Enya Hangan, Lady Kaoyo, to identify a votive helmet. He makes improper advances to her, but is interrupted by Momonoi Wakasanosuke, whom he verbally abuses. Presented in a colorful old-fashioned style, this scene is beautiful to behold.

Act II is at the palace of Momonoi Wakasanosuke. The angry Wakasanosuke reveals his plan to slay Moronao to his old retainer, Kakogawa Honzō.

A love scene* *(nureba)* employing the technique of kamisuki* in *Kumo ni Magō Ueno no Hatsuhana**. Naozamurai (seated), Ichikawa Ebizō X*; Michitose, Bandō Tamasaburō V*. *Courtesy of Waseda University Tsubouchi Engeki Hakubutsukan (Tsubouchi Memorial Theatre Museum).*

Okaru meets her brother, Heiemon, in Act VII of *Kanadehon Chūshingura**. Okaru is played by Nakamura Senjaku II*, the son of the actor playing Heiemon, Nakamura Ganjirō II*. A *kurogo** supports the ladder from below. *Courtesy of Waseda University Tsubouchi Engeki Hakubutsukan (Tsubouchi Memorial Theatre Museum).*

Honzō does not remonstrate with him, but goes to Moronao immediately thereafter.

Act III contains the "present-giving" scene, the "quarrel" scene, and the "rear gate" scene. Moronao, who has become convivial after receiving a bribe from Honzō, offers an earnest apology for his behavior. Frustrated by his unrequited lust for Kaoyo, he takes out his resentment on Hangan. The hot-tempered Hangan slashes at Moronao. Sagisaka Bannai, a villainous clown character, has an outstanding moment in this scene. The "rear gate" scene is rarely performed; instead, the *kiyomoto** music known as *Ochiudo**, a later addition, is placed after the fourth act.

Act IV contains Hangan's ritual suicide *(seppuku)* and the evacuation from the castle. Following Hangan's death, his followers leave the castle. Highlights of the act include the pathetic suicide scene; Yuranosuke's hurried entrance at the last moment, just before his master dies; and the scene outside the gate of the palace, when Yuranosuke's strength of character is revealed as he decides to revenge his master's death.

Act V takes place on the Yamazaki highway. Yoichibei, Okaru's father, has obtained money for his son-in-law—Kanpei, a retainer of the late Hangan—by promising to sell his daughter into prostitution in Osaka's Gion district. Money in hand, he is returning home when he is killed and robbed by Ono Sadakurō. Then Kanpei, who is out hunting, mistakes Sadakurō for a wild boar and shoots him; he finds the purse and returns home.

Act VI presents Kanpei's suicide. The proprietress of the Ichiriki-ya brothel comes to Yoichibei's home to take Okaru back with her. Kanpei, hearing from her of the purse that she gave Yoichibei, realizes that the man whom he killed in the dark must have been his father-in-law. After Okaru leaves, he kills himself as an act of vindication. Highlights are the tragic scene of Okaru's being sold into prostitution and the acting of Kanpei.

Act VII is a complete change from the previous one, being set in the sumptuous surroundings of the Ichiriki-ya brothel. There Yuranosuke has been playing the profligate in order to deceive his enemy's spies. By chance, Okaru, who has become a prostitute there, meets her brother Heiemon. When Heiemon learns that Okaru—by looking into her pocket mirror from her seat on a second-story verandah—has peeked at a secret message being read by Yuranosuke, his reaction is spirited and exciting.

Act VIII is the *michiyuki**, or "travel dance," a common feature of many Kabuki plays. Honzō's wife, Tonase, and her daughter, Konami, travel to the home of Yuranosuke's son, Rikiya, for the wedding of the two young people.

Act IX takes place at the Yamashina retreat of Yuranosuke. Yuranosuke's wife, Oishi, treats Tonase and Konami coldly. She says that she wants to receive from her son the head of Honzō, who interceded when Hangan attacked Moronao. Honzō, standing at the gate disguised as an itinerant musician, reviles Oishi purposely in order to cause Rikiya to stab him. He then supplies Yuranosuke with a plan of Moronao's mansion and dies. Each role in this act is outstanding.

Act X depicts the loyalty of Amakawaya Gihei, and Act XI presents the successful raid on Moronao's mansion.

Kanadehon Chūshingura is one of the few Kabuki plays still to receive full-length productions* *(tōshi kyōgen)*, but Acts II, VIII, and X usually are omitted.

KANAI SANSHŌ. 1731-1797. An Edo playwright, he went from being the general manager *(chōmoto*)* of the Nakamura-za* to being a playwright and became a chief playwright *(tate sakusha*)* in the spring of 1759, when his *Eiga Sumidagawa* was staged at the Morita-za*. He was active from about 1751 to 1776. He and Horikoshi Nisōji* were considered Edo's two greatest contemporary playwrights. Of Sanshō's more than 100 plays the most characteristic were domestic dramas and dance plays. He also created new devices for the stage and is said to have originated the kind of curtain called *dōgu maku**, the background curtain *(kakiwari maku)*, and a sort of folding background scene. He wrote *Edo Murasaki Kongen Soga* (now known as *Sukeroku Yukari no Edo Zakura**; this was a revision of a play believed to have been created in 1713 by Tsuuchi Jihei II*), *Irojōgo Mitsugumi Soga, Kumo no Ito Azusa no Yumi Hari*, and others.

KANBAN. A "billboard" set out in front of the theatre; words and pictures on it advertised the production within. *Kanban* still grace the front of today's theatres, but not as they did in the past, when they were hung from the eaves in a row. During the early days of Kabuki, billboards hanging beneath the drum tower, or *yagura**, noted only the month and day that the performance began and the actors' names. Soon there appeared billboards on which the formal title of the play was written, as well as billboards that gave the titles of the acts, the cast lists, and so forth. Early billboards had words only, but illustrated versions began to be seen in the Genroku era (1688-1703). Later, a wide variety of billboard types came into use. Some of these are described below. By the first third of the nineteenth century most types were fixed; these conventions continued until the early Meiji period. In 1878, when the new Shintomi-za opened, all but the title billboard, the act title billboard, and the illustrated billboards were abolished; only the illustrated billboards remain today. Edo's illustrated billboards were of the Torii school (*see also* SHIBAI E), and the calligraphy was of the Kantei* school; Kyoto and Osaka used the Kamigata school of illustration and the Tōkichi* school of calligraphy. (*See also* THEATRE MANAGEMENT.)

danmari kanban. A "pantomime billboard." This billboard represented a picture of the *kaomise danmari* (*see also* DANMARI: KAOMISE DAN-

MARI), a type of pantomime performance. It was also called *sugomi no kanban.*

iori kanban. "Hermitage billboard." Having a chevron-shaped upper border, this billboard displayed the name and crest of an actor from the Kamigata area who had come to act in Edo or of an actor who was performing at a theatre only temporarily. (*See also* IORI.)

jōruri e kanban. Illustrated billboards depicting scenes from the *jōruri** (a dance with narrative accompaniment) on the program.

jōruri kanban. A billboard listing the title of the *jōruri* and its actors, chanters, and musicians.

konadai kanban. "Short-title billboards"; also called *yomai* ("four boards"). At one time Kabuki plays were written in four acts, each of which was briefly summed up on these billboards.

maneki. "Invitation." Also called *tsuri kanban,* these were billboards adorned with characters from dance dramas and other plays. The term also refers to the hanging of a "full-house poster" *(ōiri* no bira)* when there was a hit production.

mon kanban. A billboard on which were shown the actors' names, actors' crests* *(mon),* and role types.

ōnadai kanban. "Full-title billboard." The complete formal title* *(geidai)* was written on this billboard. Since it was a very long board, it stood up outside the theatre's entrance instead of being hung from above. In Kyoto and Osaka it was called the *geidai kanban.*

ōzume kanban. A billboard on which the climactic scene was pictured. (*See also* ŌZUME.)

sode kanban. A billboard that pictured the chief actor in *Shibaraku**, the play normally presented at *kaomise** performances.

waki kanban. A billboard giving the title of the *waki kyōgen**, a celebratory piece on the program.

yagurashita kanban. "Beneath-the-drum-tower billboard." Three boards (later five) hung beneath the *yagura**, or drum tower, listing the names of such persons as the *zamoto** and chief *(tate) onnagata**. These later developed into the illustrated billboards *(e kanban)* that depict the chief actors in group pictures—such as are still used today.

yakuwari kanban. "Cast-list billboard."

KANDA MATSURI. Mimasuya Nisōji III. Also called *Shimero Yare Iro no Kakegoe. Shosagoto*. Kiyomoto**. September 1839. Kawarazaki-za, Edo.

Edo's citizens took part in festivals with great enthusiasm; chief among Edo's festivals were the big three: the Kanda festival, the Sannō festival, and the Sanja festival. When these were held, the whole nation took pride in their magnificence. Dance plays presenting the festivities of these occasions are common in Kabuki, and this is one of the more popular examples.

The scene is before the sacred place of wine offering to the god of Kanda (a region of Edo). The piece depicts a variety of popular entertainments, concluding with a fireman's procession chant and conveying the gorgeousness and high spirits of the Edo festival.

KANEKO KICHIZAEMON. (?-1728). A comic actor active in the Kamigata area during the Genroku era (1688-1703). His short stature made him suitable for clown roles *(dōkegata*)* and his simple, light style is said to have been delightful. Kichizaemon also excelled in dance plays. Since his playwriting skills were notable, he gained a niche for himself in Kabuki history as a collaborator of the great Chikamatsu Monzaemon*; it is believed that his ideas strongly influenced Chikamatsu's dramaturgy. A work that has been translated into English as "Dust in the Ears" *(Nijinshu)* and is included in the book *The Actors' Analects* was written by this actor. Giving a true account of all the actors of his time, it is a precious historical record.

KANERU YAKUSHA. "All-around actor" or "actor of a thousand roles." Kabuki's complex dramatic qualities have resulted in certain actors' gaining skill in playing more than one narrow role type. A clear example of this is the actor who plays male and female roles with equal skill. The term used for playing roles outside of one's specialization is *kayaku**. Further, there have been actors capable of playing each and every role type in Kabuki. They are the *kaneru yakusha.* Naturally, such actors are truly outstanding and, historically, have been rather few. Among those deserving of the appellation are Nakamura Utaemon III* and IV* of the early nineteenth century, Ichikawa Danjūrō VII* and IX* of the middle and late nineteenth century, and Onoe Kikugorō VI* of the first half of the twentieth century. Many consider today's Ichikawa Ennosuke III* to be a *kaneru yakusha.* (*See also* ACTORS; ROLE TYPES.)

KANE ZUTSUMI. A stage property consisting of a packet of money that contains either small oblong coins *(koban)* or square, silver quarter-*ryō* *(ichibujin)* coins, a single package being worth 25 *ryō.* A package with 100 silver quarter-*ryō* coins is called *kiri mochi* ("sliced rice cake"), because it resembles a slice of *noshi mochi,* a kind of rice cake. The *koban* in a packet of such coins are really artificial, and the thickness is generally simulated by a spring device. When necessary, to make the packet easier to put in the actor's pocket, the actor can make the packet smaller by squeezing it.

KANJINCHŌ. Namiki Gohei III. English title: *Kanjinchō* (Scott; Brandon). *Shosagoto* Nagauta**. March 1840. Kawarazaki-za, Edo.

A work included in the famous play collection of the Ichikawa Danjūrō* line of actors, the *kabuki jūhachiban**. It is a Kabuki version of the Nō play *Ataka*, from which it borrows liberally. When *Kanjinchō* was created, the Nō theatre was still the province of the samurai class; for Kabuki to adapt one of its plays was a novel and bold concept, and considerable anxiety was caused by the event. What was especially unusual was Kabuki's attempt to adapt not only the play, but also the Nō style of performance, including similar costumes and props and a background that mirrored the setting of the Nō stage. It was the first Kabuki play to do so. (*See also* MATSUBAME MONO.) Danjūrō VII's production was a revision of a more traditional Kabuki play about the same subject by his ancestor, Danjūrō I*.

Suspected by his brother Yoritomo of being a dangerous rival, Yoshitsune is making his escape into the country. He is protected by Benkei and four retainers and, like them, is dressed as a *yamabushi* mountain priest (a sect of ascetic warrior-priests). When they approach the barrier at Ataka, they are stopped by the barrier guard, Togashi. Benkei improvises a story, claiming that a blank scroll that he holds is a subscription list *(kanjinchō)* and reads it aloud; then he skillfully answers a catechism concerning *yamabushi* matters. The party is about to pass through the barrier, but Yoshitsune's appearance as a baggage carrier raises someone's suspicions. Benkei, feeling great remorse but mindful that the deception must be carried through, beats his master. Togashi realizes Benkei's sincere devotion to Yoshitsune and lets them pass on.

The first half of the play contains abundant highlights such as the scroll reading, the catechism, a scuffle that ensues, and the beating of Yoshitsune; the second half features Togashi's warm-hearted actions, Yoshitsune's soft-spoken expression of gratitude, Benkei's *ennen no mai* dance, and his leaping *tobi roppō* (*see also* ROPPŌ) exit. The *nagauta* accompaniment is acclaimed for its many beautiful lines. These factors make *Kanjinchō* the highest-rated of all Kabuki dance dramas and, along with *Kanadehon Chūshingura**, one of Kabuki's two most frequently performed pieces.

Although Danjūrō VII originated the Nō style of performing the play, it was Danjūrō IX* whose revisions in the acting methods brought it great popularity. Danjūrō IX passed his approach on to Matsumoto Kōshirō VII*, who performed the play well over a thousand times in his career, Benkei being his favorite role.

KANJIN KANMON TEKUDA NO HAJIMARI. Namiki Gohei I*. Also called *Tōjin Goroshi*. *Jidaimono**. Kabuki. Four acts, twelve scenes. July 1789. Kado no Shibai, Osaka.

In 1764, Suzuki Denzō, the interpreter for a group of Korean envoys visiting Japan, was killed. Since Koreans were unusual in Japan at the time, this incident caused a sensation and was given several dramatizations.

Lord Izuminosuke of the Sagara family is acting as host to a reception for a group of Korean envoys in the Nagasaki pleasure quarters. Tenzō, the interpreter, is attracted to the courtesan Takao and requests that Totoki Denshichi, a Sagara retainer, act as intermediary for him with the girl. Knowing that Denshichi and Takao are lovers, Tenzō has the Sagaras at a disadvantage; unable to bear it any longer, Denshichi kills Tenzō.

Ichikawa Sadanji II* was responsible for reviving this play after it had been long unperformed. It is unique for the rich foreign atmosphere that it conveys.

KANJI SHITSU. An abbreviation of *butai kanji shitsu,* it means "supervisory room," a room which is located at the rear of the auditorium behind the spectators and from which the stage can be observed. The director, playwright, and stage designer gather here for the first few days of a production, but a full-time supervisor occupies this room throughout a run to maintain the stability of the performances. This post was created when the Kabuki-za* was reconstructed in 1925.

KANKYAKU. *See* AUDIENCES.

KANMURI SHITA. A wig worn with a kind of crown by such characters as the highly placed princes called *kuge.* Lord Ōkura wears it in *Kiichi Hōgen Sanryaku no Maki**, as does Kan Shōjō in *Sugawara Denju Tenarai Kagami**.

KANSHAKU GUMA. "Passion *kuma,*" a makeup style that depicts someone with a hot temper by stressing the blue veins of the face with *seitai** applied from the outer edge of the eyebrows to the temples. It is used frequently by the heroes of history plays, such as Mitsuhide in Act X of *Ehon Taikōki** (*See also* KUMADORI.)

KANTEI RYŪ. The distinctive calligraphic style in which Edo Kabuki's billboards, posters, and playscripts were written. A formalistic style of calligraphy using thick, rounded strokes, it is believed to have an "indoors" flavor aimed at enticing playgoers into the theatre. Edo's Okazakiya Kanroku, a teacher of his family's calligraphic art, did the *ōnadai kanban* (*see* KANBAN: ŌNADAI KANBAN) billboards at the Nakamura-za* in 1779 and was highly praised for his work, which he signed "Kantei." Soon his style came to be called the Kantei school *(ryū),* and work that resembled it, even earlier work, was regarded as belonging to this school. It appeared only on billboards at first, but was later used in programs and playscripts as well. Eventually it came to be considered Kabuki's characteristic calligraphic style, and today its influence extends even to the Kamigata area. (*See also* TŌKICHI RYŪ.)

KAOMISE KŌGYŌ. The "face-showing performance," the annual Edo period performance at which a theatre announced its newly engaged company of actors and they performed together for the first time. Actors were engaged from November to October of the following year, and it was the custom to belong to only one theatre at a time. The *kaomise* was held between November 11 and December 10. This contractual system originated in the Kamigata region and seems to have caught on in Edo during the Manji era (1658-61), where it continued until the late Edo era. The fixed order of putting on plays at the *kaomise* productions was settled on around 1750. The day's main play was chosen from one whose "world" (*sekai**) was represented by a historical tale such as the *Ise Monogatari, Hōgen-Heiji, Taiheiki,* or *Gikeiki.* The program began with a performance of a sacred dance, *Okina Watashi,* followed by another ceremonial dance, the *waki kyōgen**, which had strong ties to the playhouse. Then came the *jobiraki** and the *futatateme**. The prologue to the main play (*mitateme**) came next and then the main play itself. In Edo this latter was customarily *Shibaraku**, the popular *aragoto** play. It was adapted to conform to the "world" (*sekai**) determined by the playwrights. Occasionally, a special pantomime (*danmari**) was presented instead. The second half of the program (*nibanme kyōgen* or *yontateme**; *see also* SEWAMONO), usually occupied by a domestic play, was a narrative dance drama (*jōruri**) having no relation to the plot of the program's first half. Such works that are still performed include *Munekiyo, Seki no To**, *Modori Kago**, and *Yoshiwara Suzume.* Plays on the *kaomise* program were called *kaomise kyōgen.* A special *kaomise* program (*see* BANZUKE: KAOMISE BANZUKE) was published; on it were printed the names and likenesses of the company's actors. Even today the term *kaomise* remains, and many of the chief actors get together (November in Tokyo, December in Kyoto) and give a grand *kaomise* performance, although the original purpose no longer exists.

KAOSHI. "Face-master," a makeup* specialist. As the job requires a great deal of experience and craft, many *kaoshi* are recruited from the lower rank of actors called *nadai shita.* (*See also* ACTORS' RANKS; KUMADORI.)

KARA BUTAI. "Empty stage," moments when no actors are on stage, such as at the opening of the curtain or during the course of the play. The term *haki butai,* no longer used, means the same thing. (*See also* ITATSUKI.)

KARAI. "Pungent," the opposite of *amai**. Difficult, but high-caliber material.

KARAMI. "Grappler"; seen frequently in history and dance plays, these are policemen or soldiers who fight with the main character and thereby help to display his prowess. The main character's strength and ability are enhanced by the encounter. There are instances of a single *karami* as well as groups of them doing battle with the hero. Other terms with the same meaning are *torimaki* and *tottari.* The "flower warriors" (*see also* YOTEN) in

*Ochiudo** are an example of a group *karami.* A single *karami* appears in *Hikosan Gongen Chikai no Sukedachi**.

KARANI. In plays from the puppet theatre, the sound of "ton ton" played on the second string of the *shamisen** during quiet moments when there is no background recitation from the *gidayū* or the *shamisen** accompaniment.

KARASSEWA. Acting or a play that is even more realistic than a conventional *sewamono** or domestic play.

KARIGINU. A costume piece. Originally a hunting robe, this garment came to be worn by nobles of the Heian era (794-1185) as well as in the Edo period. A patterned *kariginu* was worn by the *dainagon* ("chief councillor of state") and other high officials and was the ceremonial dress of samurai from the fifth rank down. *Sashi nuki** (a type of *hakama**) were worn to cover the lower half of the body. This costume was adapted by Kabuki and was worn by characters holding high positions. Ashikaga Tadayoshi in the prologue to *Kanadehon Chūshingura** and Okina in *Sanbasō** wear it.

KARI HANAMICHI. "Temporary *hanamichi**." (*See also* HIGASHI NO AYUMI.)

KARUI. "Lightweight"; used when the acting is clever and facile, but also when it is shallow.

KASA. The straw hats that were widely used in the country and city and that are used in Kabuki both as an item of daily life and as a decorative element in dance dramas.

KASANE. Matsui Kozō II (words). Also called *Iro Moyō Chotto Karimame. Shosagoto**. *Kiyomoto**. June 1823. Morita-za*, Edo.

An independent version of the prologue to Act II (the Kinu Riverbank scene) in Tsuruya Nanboku IV's* *Kesakake Matsu Narita no Riken.* Following a long period in which the play was not produced, it was revived in 1920 by Ichimura Uzaemon XV* and Onoe Baikō VI* and was very well received. It since has become a staple of the repertory.

Arriving hand in hand at the side of the Kinu River, Yoemon and his mistress Kasane see a skull drift by. Yoemon had been the illicit lover of Kasane's mother and had killed her father, Suke, with a sickle. This sickle is embedded in the skull, which is Suke's. When Yoemon lifts the skull and extracts the sickle, Kasane's face immediately becomes disfigured. Soon after, Yoemon kills her with the sickle.

This dance drama is rich in dramatic power and has a uniquely eerie

The *kariginu** robe, worn by Naoyoshi in *Kanadehon Chūshingūra**. Naoyoshi, Nakamura Karoku*. *Courtesy of Waseda University Tsubouchi Engeki Hakubutsukan (Tsubouchi Memorial Theatre Museum).*

quality. The scene of lamentation* *(kudoki)* following Kasane's disfigurement is a high point.

KASUMERU. "To skim over," to soften the musical tone.

KASUMI MAKU. "Mist curtain," a curtain of pale blue stripes on a white background used to conceal the *yamadai* platform (*see also* HINADAN) on which the *jōruri** musicians often perform.

KASU O KUU. "To eat dregs"; cross words spoken when something fails.

KATA. "Form," the conventional methods used in the presentation of Kabuki plays. *Kata* essentially are fixed forms or patterns of performance and may be found in all production elements though the term most commonly refers to acting.

A *kata* may be said to have been born when an actor creates an appropriate interpretation of the spirit of a play and his role in it (in terms of movement, speech, appearance, and so on) and this interpretation is transmitted as a convention to the next generation of actors. For example, we speak of Ichikawa Danjūrō IX's* *kata* or those of the Otowaya family of actors. In such cases, either the entire *kata* or part of it is inherited; in the latter instance an actor adds new elements and interpretations of his own, keeping only a part of the original *kata.* When this happens, the new actor's *kata* may be handed on to posterity.

Kabuki derives its life strength as a modern theatre from the Edo period, which it preserves in its dramatic works. This period witnessed the creation of an infinite variety of performance techniques. Even though traditional *kata* existed during the Edo era, these were not accorded the importance that they acquired in modern times, because the individual actor's own creations and ideas were honored more highly. However, Kabuki became a "classical" art during the Meiji period; this led to the fixing of major performance techniques and a consequent stress on the importance of *kata.* Today's theatre, therefore, is heir to numerous *kata* associated with the great stars of the Meiji era: Danjūrō IX, Onoe Kikugorō V*, and Ichikawa Sadanji II*. (*See also* ACTORS; STYLIZATION.)

KATAGINU. A type of jumper worn with the *kamishimo** costume.

KATAHAZUSHI. A wig that gets its name from its "off-center" *(hazushi)* topknot. It is worn by various ladies of the palace in history plays. Plays with such characters even are called *katahazushi mono**. Well-known wearers of this wig include Masaoka in *Meiboku Sendai Hagi** and Onoe in *Kagamiyama Kokyō no Nishikie**.

KATAHAZUSHI MONO. Plays in which the *katahazushi** wig is worn.

KATAIRE. "Shoulder insert"; a costume symbolizing the poverty of its wearer by special cloths that are sewn to the shoulders and represent patches. The degree of pathos sounded is dependent on the specific pattern of the cloths used. Characters wearing this garment include Kanpei in Act VI of *Kanadehon Chūshingura**, Sodehagi in *Ōshū Adachigahara**, and Asagao in *Shō Utsushi Asagao Nikki**.

KATAKIUCHI TENGAJAYA MURA. Nagawa Kamesuke*, Nagawa Jusuke. Also called *Tengajaya(mura)*. *Jidaimono**. Kabuki. Six acts. December 1781. Kado no Shibai, Osaka.

This dramatization of a revenge incident that took place in Osaka's Tengajaya area is a representative work in the category of revenge plays* (*adauchi mono*). The first cast included Asai Tamejūrō, Mimasu Osazō, Arashi Yoshimatsu, Nakamura Jirōza, and Yamanaka Komesuke. Hayase Genjirō and his brother Irori are wandering in search of their late father's enemy and murderer, Tōma Saburoemon. Their servant, Adachi Motoemon, turns traitor when drunk and eventually leads Tōma to the brothers, who have become outcasts. As a result, Iori is slain. Genjirō's difficulties end when he successfully carries out his vendetta at Tengajaya.

Ōtani Tomoemon* was an outstanding player of Motoemon during the 1830s and 1840s. Since that time Motoemon has been the chief role for players of the category of roles called *sanmaime gataki* (comic villains). Highlights of the play include a humorous scene during which Motoemon sneaks through a skylight into the poor dwelling of the brothers and the interesting *mie** pose that Motoemon performs with his sword on his shoulder in the scene of Iori's death.

KATAKIYAKU. Actors who specialize in the roles of villains and the roles themselves. In terms of their social status, villain roles include evil princes (*kugeaku*), evil samurai (*jitsuaku*), and evil retainers (*hagataki**). Evil townsmen include the dishonest clerks and apprentices (*tedaigataki*). By age, villains may be seen as beautiful young men (*irogataki* and *iroaku*), middle-aged villains (*ojigataki*), and old villains (*oyajigataki**). *Kugeaku* roles include the princely villain in *Shibaraku** called Uke*, as well as Fujiwara Shihei in the *Kuruma Biki* scene of *Sugawara Denju Tenarai Kagami** and Iruka in *Imoseyama Onna Teikin**. All of these high-ranking villains wear the indigo-colored lines of the makeup called *kumadori**. (*See also* AIGUMA.) The *jitsuaku* is a samurai who is plotting to overthrow the house of his master; he is also called *kuni kuzushi* ("nation demolisher"). His face is painted white like a young lover's (*nimaime**); he wears an *ende** style of wig and is an imposing type whose function is to oppose the honest type of character known as *jitsugoto* (*see also* TACHIYAKU). Representative *jitsuaku* are Nikki Danjō in *Meiboku Sendai Hagi** and Moronao in *Kanadehon Chūshingura**. The *hiragataki* are the retainers of the *jitsuaku*. They paint their faces red (*see also* AKATTSURA). The *hagataki* are relatively unimportant villains who share qualities similar to those of the *hiragataki*. Among them there is the somewhat comical *handōgataki*, such as Bannai in *Kanadehon Chūshingura*, and the highly comic villain, the *charigataki*. The latter should more properly be included in the category of *dōkegata**, clown types. Evil clerks and apprentices who plan to destroy their master's family are the *bantōgataki* and *hagataki*. Many of these characters have humorous features; one is the clerk Zenroku in *Kore Wa Hyōban Ukina no Yomiuri**. The older villains (*ojigataki* or *oyajigataki*) often appear in history plays. Shihei in *Sugawara Denju Tenarai Kagami* is such a role, while the part of Junbei in *Shinrei Yaguchi no Watashi** is called a *jitsuaku*'s *oyajigataki* part. (*See also* ROLE TYPES.)

KATANA. *See* SWORDS.

KATAOKA GADŌ XIII, *yago** Matsushimaya. 1910- . A brother of Ichimura Yoshigorō* and Kataoka Roen VI* and the son of Kataoka Nizaemon XII*, he was born in Osaka. He made his debut in 1920, took the name of Roen in 1934, and became Gadō in 1938. He is a restrained, old-style *onnagata** and, though talented, is not presently favored with many roles.

KATAOKA GATŌ V, *yago** Matsushimaya. 1935- . A conservative actor who hails from Tokyo, he was born the son of Kataoka Nizaemon XIII* and debuted in 1940. Gatō plays an important role in such study groups as the Wakamatsu Kai. His eldest son, Shinnosuke, debuted at age four in 1971.

KATAOKA HIDETARŌ II, *yago** Matsushimaya. 1941- . An *onnagata** who often plays townsmen's daughters and princesses, he was born in Osaka, debuted in 1946, and became Hidetarō in 1956.

KATAOKA ICHIZŌ V, *yago** Matsushimaya. 1916- . Born in Tokyo, he is the son of Kataoka Ichizō IV. He debuted in 1922 and changed his name from Jūzō to Ichizō in 1934. Jūzō VI (1958-) and Kamezō IV (1961-) are his children.

KATAOKA JŪNISHŪ. A collection created by Kataoka Nizaemon XI* of the roles in which he specialized. (*See also* FAMILY ART.)

1. Sanshichi Nobutaka in *Umakiri*
2. Ishida no Tsubone in *Hade Kurabe Nishikawazome*

3. Akagaki Genzō in *Kanadehon Suzuri no Takashima*
4. Kiyoharu in *Kiyoharu Anshitsu*
5. Kankō in *Tenpaizan* (in *Sugawara Denju Tenari Kagami**)
6. Domo no Mata in *Keisei Hangonkō**
7. Lord Ōkura in *Kiichi Hōgen Sanryaku no Maki**
8. Hachirobei in *Sakuratsuba Urami no Samezaya**
9. Daimonjiya in *Kamiko Jitate Ryōmen Kagami*
10. Sarumawashi Yojibei in *Chikagoro Kawara no Tatehiki**
11. Omura in *Keppen Tori*
12. *Waki Kiyomaro Kawara no Wakare*

KATAOKA NIZAEMON. This illustrious family of Osaka actors has had, up to today, thirteen generations.

I. 1656-1715. The son of a popular Osaka *onnagata** named Tomishima Harunojō, he was originally a *shamisen** player, but switched to acting and eventually grew popular enough to become a troupe leader *(zagashira*)*. With his large build and piercing eyes he was thought to be the number one player of villain roles *(katakiyaku*)* in the Kamigata area during the Genroku era (1688-1703). He was active as an actor-manager *(zamoto*)* as well. Towards the end of his career he became a player of leading male roles *(tachiyaku*)*

II. fl. 1716. Son of Nizaemon I, he became Nizaemon II in 1716. At first he specialized as a player of young female roles, but later became a *tachiyaku;* he also worked as a *zamoto.* He died young.

III. fl. 1716-1735. Son-in-law of Nizaemon I. When Nizaemon II died, he took the name of Kataoka Shige'emon III, but did not take the name of Nizaemon—even though he considered himself third in the line. He was active through the Kyōhō era (1716-35), but little else is known of him.

IV. fl. 1716-1758. Supposedly the son of an Osaka draper, he was adopted by Fujikawa (Kataoka) Shige'emon and wrote plays under the pen name of Fujikawa Sakoku. He began his career as a player of young female roles in 1717 and later became popular as an actor of young men. In 1747 he changed his name from Fujikawa Hansaburō to Nizaemon IV, but quit acting in 1740 to devote himself to playwriting. However, in 1755 he returned to the stage.

V. fl. 1751-1772. An actor who was probably related to Nizaemon IV, but whose precise origins are unknown. His first name was Fujikawa Hansaburō III, and as such he became known as a leading *katakiyaku* in the Kamigata region. It is not known when he acceded to the name of Nizaemon V.

VI. An actor who called himself Nizaemon (his name had been Mioki Gizaemon) and thus is considered the sixth in the line.

VII. 1755-1837. An Osaka actor who succeeded to the name in 1787 after a period of time in which there was no Nizaemon. He was stout, but his well-balanced form and clear voice gave an impressive beauty to the stage.

He was most successful as a *katakiyaku* and flourished as a major Kamigata star in the early nineteenth century. He had been born the son of Asai Kunigorō in Kyoto and had begun acting as Nakamura Matsusuke, later taking his father's name as Kunigorō II. Although he specialized in villain roles, he was quite versatile and could also perform with skill and talent in *onnagata, jitsugoto, oyajigata,* and *shosagoto** roles. (*See also* TACHIYAKU.)

VIII. 1810-1863. Adopted son of Nizaemon VII, he changed his name from Arashi Kitsujirō to Kataoka Gatō and in 1837 changed it again, this time to his adopted father's pen name *(haimyō*)*, Gadō. He became Nizaemon VIII in 1857 at Edo's Nakamura-za*. Since his good looks resembled those of the immensely popular Ichikawa Danjūrō VIII*, he was almost as popular in Edo as he was in Kamigata. Most successful as a young lover *(nimaime** and *irotachiyaku)*, he expanded his skills in his later years by playing *jitsugoto* samurai, old men, villains, and *onnagata.*

IX. 1839-1871. Son of the artist, Nishikawa Kuniharu. He was adopted by Nizaemon VIII and became Kataoka Matsunosuke II in 1851, taking the name Kataoka Gatō in 1856. He received the name of Nizaemon posthumously in 1907.

X. 1851-1895. Third son of Nizaemon VIII. A popular child actor in Osaka, he took the name of Kataoka Gadō in 1872 and began to act at the major theatres. As his popularity grew, he got work at each of Tokyo's theatres and became Nizaemon X in Osaka in 1895. Distraught because his in-law Ichikawa Sadanji I* and his brother Kataoka Gatō refused to participate in the name-changing ceremony, he lost his mind and died the same year. He was only forty-four.

XI. 1857-1934. Fourth son of Nizaemon VIII, he became Nizaemon XI in 1907. In 1867 he moved from Kamigata to Edo, the city of his birth, and took the name of Kataoka Gatō. Thereafter he quickly developed his abilities and became very popular, along with his contemporary, Nakamura Ganjirō I*. Late in life he was respected as a doyen of Kabuki within the Tokyo Kabuki world. He excelled at many role types, but gained his greatest fame as a player of old men in classical and new plays, displaying an elegant simplicity in his style. Famous roles of his were Katagiri Katsumoto in *Kiri Hitoha** and the title role in *Meikō Kakiemon**.

XII. 1882-1946. The son of Nizaemon X, he was an *onnagata.* Born in Tokyo, he took the name of Nizaemon XII in 1936, having been Kataoka Gadō until then. After Onoe Baikō VI* died, he acted the roles of wife to the characters played by Ichimura Uzaemon XV*.

XIII, *yago** Matsushimaya. 1904- . A versatile mainstay of modern Kabuki, he was born in Tokyo, the son of Nizaemon XI. He debuted in 1905, became Gatō IV in 1929, and took his present name in 1951. In his youth he formed the Kataoka Chiyōnosuke Troupe (Chiyōnosuke is his name in private life and was his first stage name). In 1932 he organized the

Junior Kabuki at Tokyo's Shinjuku Daiichi Theatre. Later, he moved to Osaka and Kyoto and, aside from playing the *wagoto** style of that vicinity, often performed in history plays. He possesses a broad style and is valued for preserving the Kamigata style of Kabuki, along with Nakamura Ganjirō II*. He is considered a National Cultural Treasure.

KATAOKA ROEN VI, *yago** Matsushimaya. 1926- . The son of Kataoka Nizaemon XII*, he was born in Osaka, debuted as Kataoka Daisuke in 1934, and became Roen in 1959. He often appears in supporting roles.

KATAOKA TAKAO I, *yago** Matsushimaya. 1944- . One of Kabuki's most popular young stars, he was born in Osaka, the third son of Kataoka Nizaemon XIII*, and debuted in 1949. He is tall, has a powerful voice, and displays a superb temperament as hero and villain in history plays.

KATARI. An ornately written summary of the contents of a play; the *katari* was placed over the play's title on the theatre billboard and in the program. In the Kamigata area it was printed on the left and right of the title. The *katari* employed various technical literary devices such as *kakekotoba* ("pivot words") and *engo* ("linked words"). It was the responsibility of the functionaries called *kyōgen sakusha** to write it on the billboards, but by custom it was composed by the theatre's chief playwright *(tate sakusha*)*. (*See also* KANBAN; TSUNOGAKI.)

KATŌ BUSHI. Also known as *hizen bushi* and *handayū bushi*, this was a school of music founded in 1717 by Tenmanya Tōjūrō (1684-1725), the son of a fishmonger situated at Nihonbashi in Edo. He became the disciple of Edo Handayū and took the name of Edodayū Katō, the occasion being his performance of a new composition at the Ichimura-za*. From the succession of Katō II (d. 1754) to the name until the time of Katō VI (1727-1796), the style's popularity was at its apex. The intelligentsia and wealthy classes appreciated it as a genteel form of *shamisen** music. The music is performed today as the narrative accompaniment for *Sukeroku Yukari no Edo Zakura**.

KATŌGUCHI. A scenic element used as an entranceway; it is narrow at the top and broad at the bottom, has a flame shape, and is used in temple scenes. When a window has this shape, it is called *katōmado*.

KATSURAGAWA (RENRI NO SHIGARAMI). Suga Sensuke. Also called *Ohan Chōemon, Obiya. Sewamono*. Jōruri**. Two acts. October 1776. Kita Horie-za, Osaka.

Based on a real incident occurring sometime in the Kyōhō era (1716-35), this story was first dramatized in 1761. Several puppet and Kabuki works preceded and influenced the writing of the present play. Although many dance plays were later based on it, the first Kabuki drama to stem from this play was in 1777 at Osaka's Araki-za. It starred Yamanaka Bunshichi.

Obiya Chōemon, a merchant in his forties, meets his neighbor's daughter Ohan, who is young enough to be his daughter, at an inn in Ishibe; the two fall in love and pledge their troth. Learning of this , Chōemon's stepmother and stepbrother seek to have him turned out of the house and Gihei, the stepbrother, installed in his place. Despite these accusations, Chōemon's kind father, Hansai, and his wife, Okinu, give him comfort and support. Chōemon is grateful for their solicitude. However, Ohan is pregnant, and he has had no luck in recovering a famous sword for which he has been searching; he comes to the conclusion that life is not worth living. He hurries after Ohan, who has left a farewell note for him. The lovers rush to the Katsura River, where they will drown themselves.

Chōemon is acted in the *wagoto** style, but he has many of the qualities of the *shinbō tachiyaku** type of patient, suffering males. The parts of Ohan and Chōkichi, an apprentice who testifies that he is actually the father of Ohan's baby, are often played by the same actor.

KATSURA OBI. A headband tied like that used around the wigs worn in Nō plays (the *hachimaki**). It is tied at the rear and hangs down behind. Female roles wear it in Kabuki dances based on Nō style as well as in history plays, in which only upper-class women wear it: Among the characters on whom it may be seen are Shizuka in *Funa Benkei**, Sakae Gozen in *Meiboku Sendai Hagi**, and Fuji no Kata in the *Kumagai Jinya* scene of *Ichinotani Futaba Gunki**.

KATSUREKI GEKI. *See* LIVING HISTORY PLAYS.

KAWADŌRI. Also called *tsumiba;* one of the groups of people supporting Edo period actors. A group of tradesmen would form a backer's club for a specific theatre, go in a body to the play, present the actors with gifts, and give them moral and economic support. The supporters of the Nakamura-za* were the Arawaka, Shinbori, Hakazoki, Ōkawabate, Minato-chō, Saga-chō, Genyadana, Kuramae, and Reiganjima. Those at the Ichimura-za* were the Koami-chō, Kobune-chō, Edobashi, Kayaba-chō, Yoshi-chō, and Shinzaimoku-chō. Those at the Morita-za* were the Kobiki-chō, Konparu, and Uogashi. The name *kawadōri* ("by the river") arose because many of these groups were from sections of the city that were replete with rivers and canals. (*See also* HIIKI; DANTAI; AUDIENCES.)

KAWARA MONO. "Riverbed people" or *kawara kojiki* ("riverbed beggars") a term used during Japan's middle ages to refer to the crowds of poor people and outcasts who resided in dry riverbeds. Theatrical folk appeared among these lowly persons and, toward the end of the Muromachi era (1392-1568), miscellaneous entertainments were performed there. Kabuki's founder, Izumo no Okuni*, and her troupe performed in the dry bed of the Kamo River in Kyoto, and it was here that Kabuki drama was born. During the Edo period Kabuki actors were considered outside the four ranks of Confucian society (warrior, farmer, craftsman, merchant) and were placed among the outcasts. Because of the origins of their art, they were called derisively *kawara mono* or *kawara kojiki.* The Meiji period saw the end of the old social ranking system, but actors were still regarded as riverbed beggars. After the event that capped the theatre reform movement begun in the late 1870s—namely, the Kabuki performances played before the Emperor and his family in 1879—the status of Kabuki actors was raised and terms like *kawara mono* became a thing of the past. They disappeared entirely by the early Shōwa period (1926-). (*See also* ACTORS.)

KAWARAZAKI CHŌJŪRŌ IV, *yago** Yamazakiya. 1902- . An actor born in Tokyo and the son of the producer Kawarazaki Gonnosuke VIII. He received excellent training at the hands of Kataoka Nizaemon XI*, Ichikawa Sadanji II*, and Osanai Kaoru, the playwright. Hanayagi Jūsuke attended to his dance training. He debuted as Kawarazaki Toranosuke (his private name) when he participated at age three in the third annual memorial services for Ichikawa Danjūrō IX* on the stage of Tokyo's Kabuki-za*. His childhood years were spent with the Kataoka Youth Theatre (Kataoka Shōnen Geki), from which he graduated to a study of Kabuki's classical style in 1913. He took his present name in 1914, and in 1922 he joined Sadanji II's troupe. He was a founding member of the Zenshin-za* in 1931. Three years earlier he had accompanied Sadanji on a tour of the Soviet Union, during which he took the opportunity to study theatre there and in Germany and France. He later toured twice to the People's Republic of China. He has long been an outstanding player of male roles and has brought many progressive ideas to Kabuki through his work with the Zenshin-za.

KAWARAZAKI GONJŪRŌ III, *yago** Yamazakiya. 1918- . An outstanding veteran actor and the son of Gonjūrō II, born in Nagoya, he debuted as Kawarazaki Kaoru in 1935, became Gonzaburō III in April 1946, and took his present name in March 1956. At that time he held the rank of troupe leader or *zagashira** of the "young star Kabuki" *(wakate kabuki)* produced at Toyoko Hall, where he undertook the roles played by Ebizō (later Ichikawa Danjūrō XI*) at the Kabuki-za*. As he resembled Ebizō even in looks, he was called the "Shibuya Ebizō" (Toyoko Hall is in Tokyo's Shibuya section) and became quite popular. His style profits from his physical appearance, and he is best suited for villain roles. Gonjūrō is one of those actors who maintain the old customs.

KAWARAZAKI KUNITARŌ V, *yago** Yamazakiya. 1909- . The son of a well-known Western-style painter, Matsuyama Shōzō, he became the pupil of Ichikawa Ennosuke II (En'o*) in 1928 and debuted with the name of Ichikawa Shōya. In 1931 he joined in the creation of a new troupe, the Zenshin-za*, and as the *tate* (chief) *onnagata** of the company became a leading figure. He took the name Kunitarō in 1932. Kunitarō is excellent in all *onnagata** roles and exhibits an old-style quality in his roles of wicked women and wives in the domestic plays. His brothers Matsuyama Eitarō and Shōzō are very active as television actors.

KAWATAKE MOKUAMI. 1816-1893. An edo-born playwright, his true name was Yoshimura Shinshichi. At first, he was a pupil of Tsuruya Nanboku V. He called himself Kabu Genzō, Shiba Shinsuke, and, later, Kawatake Shinshichi II. He took the name Mokuami after he retired, although it is the name by which he is best known today. When his *Miyakodori Nagare no Shiranami* was produced in 1854, he took advantage of the occasion to team up with the actor Ichikawa Kodanji IV*, for whom he subsequently wrote plays of the *shiranami mono* ("robber play*") variety. He soon rose to the position of leader of the late Edo period theatre world. During the Meiji era he wrote history, domestic, and dance plays to display the prowess of Ichikawa Danjūrō IX*, Onoe Kikugorō V*, and Ichikawa Sadanji I*. In response to contemporary ideas he wrote in the genres called *katsureki mono* ("living history play*") *zangiri mono**, and *matsubame mono**. Mokuami practiced his profession for about fifty years and wrote over 360 dramas. He was best at domestic plays and expertly depicted the decadence of the late Edo period in rhythmic dialogue written in seven-five meter *(shichigochō)*. Numbered among his best plays are *Aotozōshi Hana no Nishikie**, *Keian Taiheiki**, *Sannin Kichiza Kuruwa no Hatsugai**, *Tsuta Momiji Utsunoya Tōge**, *Hachiman Matsuri Yomiya no Igiwai**, *Kumo ni Magō Ueno no Hatsuhana**, *Tsuyu Kosode Mukashi Hachijō**, *Renjishi**, *Tsuchigumo**, and *Momijigari**.

KAWATAKE SHINSHICHI I. 1747-1795. A chief playwright *(tate sakusha*)* of the mid-Edo period, he wrote many excellent puppet plays, including the famous *tokiwazu** dance piece entitled *Shinobu Uri.*

II. The name held by Kawatake Mokuami* before his retirement.

III. 1842-1901. The leading pupil of Mokuami. After his master's death he was the foremost active dramatist of the Meiji era. He worked at the Ichimura-za*, Kabuki-za*, and elsewhere and wrote about eighty dramas. Shinshichi III had a lighthearted and unconventional style, and most of his dramas are based on the tales of the traditional storytellers. These include *Kagotsurube Sato no Eizame**, *Kaidan Botan Dōrō**, *Hagoromo**, and *Shiobara Tasuke Ichidaiki**.

KAYAKU. The playing of roles outside one's specialty. For example, a proficient actor may play both male and female roles, a development that has caused the strict role-type system to break down. When an actor played a role outside his specialty, it was called either *kayaku* or *yonai**, and a special bonus was given him for doing so. (*See* YONAI KIN). Further, if he became a star and turned out to be versatile enough to play all role types, he was called an "all-around actor" *(kaneru yakusha*)*. (*See also* ACTORS.)

KEIAN TAIHEIKI. Kawatake Mokuami*. Also called *Kusu no Kiryū Hanami no Makubari, Marubashi Chūya, Hana Shōbu Keian Jikki. Jidaimono**. Kabuki. Eight acts. March 1870. Morita-za*, Tokyo.

A play dealing with the abortive revolt of Yui Shōsetsu (1651); the scenes most frequently revived are *Horibata* and the one dealing with Tadami's arrest *(Tadami Meshitori no Ba)*. Members of the first cast included Ichikawa Sadanji I*, Sawamura Tosshō (later Suketakaya Kōsuke IV), Nakamura Shikan IV*, and Nakamura Nakazō IV*. At the original performances the characters' names were fictional. When the work was revived in 1875, the historical names were used. Mokuami wrote the play for the twenty-nine-year-old Sadanji as a debt of gratitude to the actor's adoptive father, Ichikawa Kodanji IV*. As it was perfectly suited to Sadanji's talents and Mokuami guided him in the role, Sadanji's success was outstanding, making him an important actor. The costume Sadanji wore and his acting methods are still used for the role of Chūya.

Marubashi Chūya, pretending to be drunk, is actually taking a sounding of the depths of the moat surrounding Edo castle; his intentions are suspected and questioned by a supporter of the shogun, Matsudaira Izunokami, who has witnessed Chūya's actions. Later, Chūya's father-in-law, Tōshirō the bow maker, accuses Chūya of treason, and the would-be conspirator is forced to engage in a fierce battle for his life. He finally is bound and arrested.

The scene when Chūya attempts a sounding of the moat and is confronted by Izunokami, with whom he engages in a dialogue of subtle give-and-take, is a highlight of the play. The realism of the violent fight scene in which Chūya is arrested is said to have provided new ideas in the technique of Kabuki stage battles.

KEIGOTO. A Kamigata term for dances and dance dramas. The word means "scenic things." The word *keigoto* was coined to describe the many Kamigata dance pieces that were, up to the end of the Edo era, in the *michiyuki** ("travel dance") style; they normally revolved around a description of the scenery that the characters passed through *Keigoto* plays have frequent examples of sudden and complete scenic changes, which never fail to delight audiences. Act VIII of *Kanadehon Chūshingura** is a good example. (*See also* SHOSAGOTO; DANCE.)

KEIKO. *See* REHEARSALS.

KEISEI HANGONKŌ. Chikamatsu Monzaemon*. Also called *Domo no Mata. Jidaimono**. *Jōruri**. Three acts. 1708. Takemoto-za, Osaka.

This representative history play of Chikamatsu is a dramatization of the tale of Omitsu, daughter of Tosa Shogen, and her lover, Kamo Motonobu; within the play's structure are such subplots as Domo Matahei's miraculous painting and the rivalry between Fuwa Banzaemon and Nagoya Sanza. Only the scene at Tosa's home is still performed.

The Ōtsu artist Ukiyo Matahei is a born stutterer. He and his wife, Otoku, visit the master artist Tosa, who lives in seclusion. Another disciple, Shurinosuke, is given permission to use the Tosa name, but Matahei is refused the same privilege. He decides to kill himself, but first paints a picture on a stone water basin. When the picture penetrates the stone and appears on the other side, Shogen is impressed by the feat and grants Matahei permission to take the Tosa name.

Highlights of the play include the effective contrast between Matahei's stuttering and his wife's eloquence, the display of their love for one another, and the scene of the miraculous painting. Otoku, a role displaying strong-mindedness and pure love, is considered one of the three most difficult "wife" *(nyōbo)* roles.

KEISEI SETSUGEKKA. Kanezawa Ryūgyoku. Also called *Kari no Tayori. Sewamono**. Kabuki. One act. January 1830. Kado no Shibai, Osaka.

A simple-minded lord, Maeno Sajima—suspecting that his concubine, Tsukasa, is having an affair with the hairdresser, Goroshichi—sends a false love letter to him, which seems to have come from Tsukasa. Goroshichi falls into the trap and is beaten and reviled by Sajima, but the lord's retainer, Takaki Kuranoshin, sees to it that no harm is done. Tsukasa sends Goroschichi a letter of apology. Thinking it to be another trick, Goroshichi grows angry and goes to the lord. The lord becomes jealous on seeing Tsukasa's letter and is going to punish Goroshichi and Tsukasa, but he is killed by Kuranoshin. Moreover, it turns out that Goroshichi is Kuranoshin's nephew and that Tsukasa is his promised bride.

The humorous scene when Goroshichi goes into ecstasy after receiving the false love letter provides audiences with a genuine taste of the delicious and unique *wagoto** style of the Kamigata area. Entertaining songs are also interpolated into the text.

Among those in the play's first cast were Nakamura Utaemon III* (who wrote the play under his pen name) as Goroshichi and Nakamura Matsue as Tsukasa.

KENDAI. The reading stand for the text from which the *jōruri** singer delivers his performance in plays using a narrative musical accompaniment. The design of the stand differs according to the type of music used. That used for the *gidayū** style has two wooden legs fitted on a boxlike base with a reading board slanted toward the performer and placed atop the legs. Decorative tassels hang from either side. Gold or silver lacquer work covers the entire stand, and the artist's signature is inscribed as well. These stands are often the gifts of fans.

KENUKI. Tsuuchi Hanjūrō. Also called *Narukami Fudo Kitayama Zakura.* English title: *The Whisker Tweezers* (part of *Saint Narukami and the God Fudō* [Brandon]). *Jidaimono**. Kabuki. Five acts. January 1742. Sadoshima-za, Osaka. (*See also* NARUKAMI.)

A play in the Ichikawa family collection, the *kabuki jūhachiban**. After being performed by Danjūrō VII*, it fell into disuse until revived in 1909 by Ichikawa Sadanji II*.

As a result of a villain's secret plot to overthrow the Ono family, Princess Nishikie no Mae is suffering from a mysterious ailment that causes her hair to stand on end. Kumedera Danjō, who has come to the Ono castle as an emissary, sees his tweezers stand on end by themselves; this leads to his discovering a huge magnet in the ceiling and his killing of the enemy hiding there. The magnet was responsible for the princess's hair standing on end, because iron had been placed there secretly by her enemies.

Kenuki's "scientific" plot concerning a magnet was quite novel in its day, when magnets were unusual in Japan. Performed in the bravura style of *aragoto**, *Kenuki* has a number of exaggerated humorous touches typical of old-style Kabuki. Such moments include Danjō's use of giant tweezers for plucking his whiskers and the scene when Danjō flirts with and is scolded by a handsome youth. Among the various highlights are Danjō's striking *mie** poses, especially the five *mie* that he performs when he detects the magnet's influence, the *Genroku mie* (*see also* MIE: GENROKU MIE) that he strikes after thrusting his spear through the ceiling, and that struck outside the curtain as he makes his exit on the *hanamichi**.

KEREN. Performance techniques using acrobatics and other stage tricks. *Keren* aim to amuse on the least intellectual of levels. There are all sorts of scenic and property *keren* in addition to quick-changes and the kind of flying through the air known as *chūnori**. As Kabuki was a theatre of the common people, it was only natural that it develop a sideshow quality in certain respects; thus, some stage trickery was understandable. When reasonable limits were exceeded, however, there was always the danger of going astray. Actors who rely on such tricks for success used to be called *kerenshi* ("masters of trickery"), a word with pejorative overtones. The performance of *keren* is now coming back into favor, especially in the work of Ichikawa Ennosuke III* and Jitsukawa Enjaku III* (*See also* HAYAGAWARI.)

KERIKOMI. A type of scenic flat attached to the front of the platform used by onstage musicians; the painting on the flats matches that of the rest of the scenic background. (*See also* HINADAN; HARIMONO.)

KERU. "To kick"; to refuse a part that one is offered or to quit when one's conditions are not met.

KESHI MAKU. "Disappearance curtain," a convention whereby a stage assistant covers the body of a character who has died on stage with a red or black cloth or "curtain" so that his presence will not interfere with the acting that follows. The dead character frequently runs offstage with the curtain hiding his exit. The *keshi maku* also is used to hide actors as they make costume or makeup changes.

KESHI O TORU. To count the number of spectators in the theatre by consulting a seating plan. (*See also* ARAU.)

KESHŌ. "Makeup." (*See also* MAKEUP; KUMADORI.)

KESHŌGOE. "Makeup voice"; a kind of rhythmic choral shouting by a group of opponents who confront an *aragoto** hero. They shout *"aarya, kōrya,"* a conventional phrase used only under these circumstances. *Keshōgoe* is employed in *Shibaraku** as the hero Gongorō approaches the stage from the *hanamichi** and in the *Kuruma Biki* scene of *Sugawara Denju Tenarai Kagami** when Matsuomaru prepares to fight with his brothers.

KESU. "To disappear"; the gradual diminishing and then the ceasing of *geza** accompaniment music during an acted scene. Also, the clearing from the stage of any unnecessary objects by the *kurogo** stage assistants.

KICHIREI. Festive annual Kabuki customs. One such is the use of the word *kotobuki* ("celebration") as the first word in the title of plays produced at New Year's time. An example is *Kotobuki (Soga no Taimen*).*

KIDO. Entrance to the theatre. The theatre entranceway was quite low during early Kabuki; because one had to bend over to enter, it became customary to call the entrance a "mouse entrance" *(nezumi kido*)*. The low entrance was thought helpful in preventing people from entering free.

KIDO GEISHA. Employees of Edo period playhouses who stood on platforms by the entrance *(kido*)* to the theatre prior to opening day and read aloud the name of the play and the cast (a procedure called *yomitate*); mimicking the actors' voices *(kowairo*)*, they drummed up business for the theatre. It usually was their job to arrange rendezvous between the actors and playgoers. Though called *geisha*, they were men.

KIDO GUCHI. "Entrance mouth"; a gateway type of stage element used as the entrance and exit from a house. Variations include the *sewakido*, used for townsmen's homes; the *niwakido*, used to mark off the boundaries of a garden; and the *yamakido*, used for homes in the mountains or fields. In certain plays, the stage assistants pick up and remove the gateway when it no longer is required by the actors. (*See also* KESU.)

KIEMONO. Properties used up during each stage performance. They are the responsibility of the property man *(kodōgu kata)* and include dishes and bowls that are smashed, letters that are torn, oil for lanterns, charcoal for tobacco trays, and so forth. (*See also* KAKENAGASHI MONO.)

KIERU. "Disappearance," a word used when people leave in the midst of an event, without waiting for it to end. It comes from the sudden disappearance of ghosts in Kabuki plays.

KIGANE. A wood percussion instrument. (*See also* NARIMONO.)

KIGASHIRA. The first sharp beat of the *hyōshigi** clappers heard toward the end of an act when a climactic piece of dialogue or movement is concluded. For example, at the end of the brothel scene in *Gotaiheiki Shiraishi Banashi**, Daikokiya Sōroku speaks a line of dialogue and strikes his pipe's ashes into a bamboo receptacle. At this precise moment the *kigashira* beat is heard, followed by a rapid beating of the sticks as the curtain closes.

KIICHI HŌGEN SANRYAKU NO MAKI. Matsuda Bunkodō, Hasegawa Senshi. Also called *Kikubatake, Ōkura Ichijō Kikubatake. Jidaimono*. Jōruri**. Five acts. September 1731. Takemoto-za, Osaka.

A play that derives its materials from the chronicle called the *Gikeiki* and the Nō play entitled *Kurama Tengu*. It dramatizes the life of Ushiwakamaru (the young Yoshitsune) from his early days up to his meeting with Benkei, the warrior-priest, at Gojō Bridge. Act III, *Kikubatake*, and Act IV, *Ōkura Kyō*, are performed most often today. Kabuki first staged this play in 1732 at Kyoto's Koroku-za and soon after at Osaka's Kado no Shibai.

In the chrysanthemum garden scene *(Kikubatake),* we learn that Ushiwakamaru and his retainer, Kisanta, having changed their names to Torazō and Chienai, have come to live as servants in the castle of Kiichi Hogen in order to steal his three-volume *Book of Tactics.* Kiichi sees through Torazō's disguise and recognizes him as Ushiwakamaru. He grants the *Book of Tactics* to the boy—whom his daughter, Princess Minazuru, loves—prays for the revival of the Genji clan, and kills himself.

In the *Ōkura Kyō* scene Tokiwa Gozen, Ushiwakamaru's mother (whose second husband is Lord Ōkura), has been practicing archery while secretly cursing the Heike clan. Yatsuragi Kageyu learns of this and plans to tell Kiyomori, Tokiwa Gozen's hated Heike enemy, whose concubine she has become. Lord Ōkura, whom everyone believes to be feeble-minded, reveals that his behavior has been a ruse; he kills Kageyu and tells Tokiwa Gozen, Yoshioka Kijirō, and Kijirō's wife, Okyo—all of whom seek the revival of the Genji—that he wants to help their cause. The needs of the moment, however, demand that he immediately revert to his seeming madness. He does so, amusing himself by doing a Kyōgen dance.

The play's highlights include the effective contrasts among the various characters who figure in the *Kikubatake* scene and the sham madness of Ōkura in the following scene.

KIKKAKE. A "cue" indicating that there will be a transition in the action of the play. The cue may involve the acting, the set, the music, or the lighting. The term comes from the word *keiki,* "a chance or opportunity." Theatre people say, for example, "the stage will revolve at the actor's *kikkake* of throwing himself down in tears."

KIKU-KICHI. An abbreviated term for Onoe Kikugorō VI* and Nakamura Kichiemon I*, the two most popular stars of their day. These actors played together at Tokyo's Ichimura-za* beginning in November 1909 under the management of Tamura Nariyoshi (1851-1920). So popular were they that the period of their "rivalry" was called the "Ichimura-za period." From the first, their artistic temperaments varied; this clash gave their work together a peculiar charm, acknowledged by their joint nickname, Kiku-Kichi. They were responsible for creating a golden age of young stars. Following the dissolution of this combination, their fans constantly called for them to appear again together, which they frequently did until their deaths at mid-century.

KIMIAI. The manner of expressing, through facial and body movement, the feelings of two or more characters who confront and "feel out" one another in a scene. In a sense, *kimiai* is like the *mie* pose*, although there is no accentuation from the wooden clappers. There is frequent recourse to such mimelike acting; it forms a basic foundation of the Kabuki actor's artistic skill.

KIN. A metal percussion instrument. (*See also* NARIMONO.)

KINCHAN. "Mr. Money"; a slang term for the audience.

KI NO KAION. 1663-1742. A puppet-theatre playwright. Born in Osaka, he rivaled Chikamatsu Monzaemon*, the chief writer for the Takemoto-za, and was the chief playwright *(tate sakusha*)* at the Toyotake-za, where he wrote for the chanter Toyotake Wakadayū. About fifty of his plays exist, including the representative works *Wankyū Sue no Matsuyama, Shinjū Futatsu Harobi,* and *Keisei Muken no Kane.* His style shows skillful construction with an excellent variety of effects.

KINPIRA JŌRURI. A popular puppet-play form during the Manji and Kanbun eras (1658-72). It originated in Kyoto and was brought to Edo, where it became a great hit by Sugiyama Shichirozaemon and Satsumadayū. A fictional character known as one of the Shitennō, or "Big Four," Kinpira was the son of Sakata Kintoki, a great superman of legend. *Kinpira jōruri* music was designed to provide a spirited background for the superhuman exploits of this valiant warrior. The form became quite popular, as it suited the vigorous temperament of the newly established capital of Edo. This musical style accompanied the vivid movements of the ranbunctious puppets that are said to have been the main influence on Edo Kabuki's *aragoto** style.

KINSHU. A financial backer of Kabuki productions during the Edo period; in Western parlance, an "angel." He was called *shuchi** or *oshuchi* in the Kamigata area. Another Edo name for him was *kinkata.* Though the manager or *zamoto** had the license to produce plays, his reliance on a *kinshu* for funds gave the latter a good deal of influence. The *kinshu* of the Nakamura-za* during the Bunka-Bunsei era (1804-30) was Ōkubo Kinsuke; he was called Kyōbashi-sama, since he resided in Kyōbashi. Similarly, Chiba Katsugorō, the famous Meiji era backer, was called Gorobei-chō-sama after the street on which he lived. (*See also* THEATRE MANAGEMENT.)

KIOIJISHI (KABUKI NO HANAKAGO). Segawa Jokō III*. *Shosagoto*. Tokiwazu**. April 1851. Nakamura-za*, Edo.

One of the annual Edo theatrical events was the Soga Festival (called the Sanno Festival after 1867). This dance play concerns that festival; the entire company puts on a lively display of their various talents. A wide variety of dances, like the *te no mai,* clown dances, and lion dances *(shakkyō mono*),* plus recitals of the tale known as the *Soga Monogatari*, chants by processions of firemen, and a number of other entertainments are presented before the sacred place of wine offering. The various pieces overflow with the spirit of old Edo. A "mad lion dance" constitutes the highpoint in the performance. Ichikawa Kodanji IV* and Bandō Takesaburō (later Bandō Hikosaburō V*) were the first stars of the piece.

KIPPU. "Tickets." Paper tickets first came into use when the Teikoku Gekijō* adopted them in 1911. Prior to that, a wooden check *(kido fuda)* was used. Playgoers buying a *kido fuda* at the entrance were generally from a lower economic stratum. The upper classes reserved their seats at the theatre teahouses (*see also* SHIBAIJAYA), entered the theatre from these resorts, and sat in a better class of seats. Reserved seating under the ticket system first appeared at the Teikoku Gekijō. (*See also* THEATRE MANAGEMENT.)

KIREMONO. The payment of a special bonus.

KIRERU. The ending of a scene.

KIRIANA. A "hole" or "trap" cut out from the stage floor. This trap, which is usually closed over, is used when a character appears from below the stage (the *naraku** area), when someone dives into a well or pond, when a ghost appears and vanishes, and so forth. It is prepared as occasion demands. The *kiriana* on the *hanamichi** is called the *suppon**. (*See also* SERI.)

KIRIDASHI. Scenic cutouts of flat or board construction used to depict mountains, trees, remote villages, stone lanterns, and the like. They are held in place to the stage floor with a long stage brace. (*See also* HARIMONO.)

KIRI HITOHA. Tsubouchi Shōyō*. *Shin kabuki**. Seven acts. March 1904. Tōkyō-za, Tokyo.

The first *shin kabuki* history play written by Tsubouchi, who felt that the contemporary *katsureki* plays (living history) plays* that were then in fashion were deficient in appeal and weak in content. He published the play serially, beginning in 1904, in the journal *Waseda Bungaku.* This famous play was written using the techniques of Kabuki's traditional history plays, but taking its motif from the history plays of Shakespeare. *Kiri Hitoha* breathed fresh life into Kabuki, which at the time was suffering from the stagnation that had set in following the deaths of Onoe Kikugorō V*, Ichikawa Danjūrō IX*, and Ichikawa Sadanji I*.

The scene is in the besieged Osaka Castle. The fortunes of the Toyotomi family have declined markedly, and the winter army of the Tokugawas is just outside. Toyotomi Hideyori's faithful retainer, Katagiri Katsumoto, wracks his brains to find a way of dealing with the various unreasonable demands made by the Tokugawas. However, because of the schemes of a group surrounding Hideyori as well as the rashness of Ishikawa Izunokami, all comes to naught. Katsumoto can do nothing but entrust his affairs to his loyal ally, Kimura Shigenari, and retire to his castle at Ibaraki.

The sad story of the pathetic young Kogerō, who resembles Ophelia, and the simple-minded youth named Ginnojō is woven into the plot. *Kiri Hitoha* is a tragedy of grand events; the character depiction is superb, and an atmosphere of composure and dignity is created. Nakamura Utaemon V* established the role of Yodogimi as it is still played. The sequel, which treats of the summer battle, is *Hototogisu Kojō no Rakugetsu**.

KIRI KABU. "Tree stumps"; a property built to look like a tree stump and used as a seat in outdoor scenes, such as the *Kuruma Biki* scene of *Sugawara Denju Tenarai Kagami**.

KIRI KYŌGEN. A closing dance piece on an Edo period program. (*See also* ŌGIRI.)

KIRIMAKU. The functionary who operates the *agemaku** room at the end of the *hanamichi**.

KIRINAMI SENJU. fl. 1688-1703. An actor of young women's roles during the latter part of the seventeenth century. He was active mainly in Kyoto, where he made a career out of playing the courtesan in *Butsu Momoyasan Kaichō* at the Miyako Mandayū-za.

KIRIOTOSHI. A crowded section on an Edo period theatre's ground floor level, which was not divided up into boxes. The word, meaning "to cut off," was chosen either because part of the stage was "cut off" for these seats or because the section was a "cut" lower than all the others. It existed in the mid-eighteenth century, but later, after the creation of the partitioned boxes *(masu*)*, remained only at the rear of the *hanamichi**. In the early nineteenth century this section disappeared entirely. (*See also* THEATRE ARCHITECTURE.)

KIRI TSUGI. A costume worn by beggars, outcasts, exiles, and the like. It has patches and pieces of loose material hanging from it to show its wearer's poverty. Shunkan in *Heike Nyogo no Shima** is such a character.

KIRI WARA. A topknot whose end looks as though it were a bunch of straw sliced clean through; it is part of a wig worn by samurai who display their courage. Examples are Tsuna in *Ibaraki**, Matsuomaru in the *Ga no Iwai* scene of *Sugawara Denju Tenarai Kagami**, and Wada Hyoe in the *Moritsuna Jinya* scene of *Ōmi Genji Senjin Yakata**.

KITSUKE. The outermost garment or kimono of a Kabuki costume. It is the most basic costume for actors of both male and female roles. *Kitsuke* are worn over undergarments *(shitagi)* and are tied with an obi; over the *kitsuke* male roles wear the *suō* robe and females wear the *uchikake**. Garments worn with the *kitsuke* are selected on the basis of character type and their visual relation to the *kitsuke*. Since the *kitsuke* provides the major color tone of the costume, it is an extremely important garment.

KITTO NARU. "To become sharp"; when an actor reacts to another by accentuating and sharply defining his emotional response. One sometimes hears the expression *kitto mie* (*see also* MIE), referring to a pose that acts as a visual climax to an emotional moment.

KIWAMETSUKI BANZUI CHŌBEI. Kawatake Mokuami*. Also called *Yudono no Chōbei. Sewamono**. Kabuki. Four acts. October 1881. Haruki-za, Tokyo.

There are many plays about the so-called street knights *(otokodate)* of the Edo period; the *otokodate* Banzui Chōbei often is the subject of such plays. Plays abut Chōbei's life usually depict the consequences of the antagonism between the *otokodate* and the *hatamoto*, or lower-ranking vassals of the shogun. Chōbei's heroic last moments are a common conclusion. When this play is performed today, it is customary to produce *Kinpira Hōmon Arasoi* by Kawatake Shinshichi III* as the play-within-a-play in the scene of the quarrel at the Murayama-za. In the first production Ichikawa Danjūrō IX* played Chōbei and Ichikawa Gonjūrō played Jūrozaemon and Gorozō.

A follower of Mizune Jūrozaemon, leader of the Shirae group of *hatamoto*, creates a disturbance at the Murayama-za, but is chastised by Chōbei. Since Mizuno no Gorozō had thought previously of killing Chōbei, he uses this opportunity to invite Chōbei to his home. The latter, steeled for death, bids his wife and children farewell. Entrusting his affairs to Token Gonbei, a devoted friend, he enters his enemy's home alone. At the play's conclusion he is stabbed by Mizune's spear while bathing.

The outstanding moments in this play occur during Chōbei's farewell scene with his family and later in a scene just prior to his being slain, when he displays his exhilarating charm as an *otokodate*. In the scene of Chōbei's murder, Danjūrō IX is said to have imitated the cries of his late stepfather, Kawarazaki Gonnosuke, when the latter was murdered by a thief who broke into his home. Of the various great actors who have specialized in the role since Danjūrō, Nakamura Kichiemon I* most closely followed Danjūrō's methods. During his career he played the role in twenty-nine revivals.

KIYOMOTO BUSHI. A school of musical narrative recital with *shamisen** accompaniment that takes its name from Kiyomoto Enjudayū (1777-1825), who founded it in 1814. Enjudayū split off from the *tomimoto bushi** school and established this style, which captures the feeling of Edo culture at its fullest. It encompassed within its framework the popular contemporary schools of *hauta**, *zokuyō*, and *utazawa* music, giving it a splendidly distinctive character. It has profound ties with Kabuki and has wide application both as dance play music and as a musical accompaniment for straight plays. Representative works using *kiyomoto* are the *Naozamurai* part of *Kumo ni Magō Ueno no Hatsuhana**, *Sanja Matsuri**, *Ochiudo**, and *Yasuna**.

KIZAMI. The beating of the *hyōshigi** clappers, like a rapid drumroll, when the curtain opens or closes. When the curtain is about to open, two loud beats are struck; while it is opening, the beating gradually increases in speed. After the *kigashira** is struck at the end of an act, the clappers beat rapidly as the curtain is pulled closed.

KIZEWAMONO. Also called *kizewa kyōgen* and *masewamono*, these are plays that realistically depict the lower stratum of city life during the Edo era. The origins of the genre can be found in the work of Namiki Gohei I* early in the Kansei period (1789-1800). It was perfected in the Bunka-Bunsei period (1804-30) by Tsuruya Nanboku IV* and, during the last years of the Edo period, by Segawa Jokō III* and Kawatake Mokuami*. Even though the genre appears realistic, the performances are, to a great degree, stylized and use rhythmic speech and movement. Since the style depends on music provided from the *geza** room, it is hard to call it pure realism. It lacks neither Kabuki's essential musical accentuation nor its underlying theatricalism. Thus, we must use the word *realism* here only in a relative sense. Still, compared to most other true Kabuki genres, this might be said to approximate most closely what is known in the modern theatre as realism, or even naturalism. (*See also* PLAY CATEGORIES.)

KOBAYASHI ICHIZŌ. 1873-1957. Founder of the Tōhō* producing company.

KŌDAN YOMIYA NO AME. Uno Nobuo*. *Shin kabuki**. Two acts, eight scenes. September 1935. Kabuki-za*, Tokyo.

Ryūtatsu, former priest of Myōren Temple and uncle of Tajū, is "freeloading" at the home of Tajū (also known as Asobinin or "Playboy" Taju), located in the Kuroechō section of Fukagawa in Edo. Ryūtatsu's daughter Otora had lived here formerly, but when Tajū's wife, Oichi, learned that her husband had tried to make advances toward the girl, she removed Otora from the house by forcing her to become someone's mistress. One summer night, Ryūtatsu has Tajū fetch a hundred *ryō* that he had hidden in the temple. Tajū complies in the hope of getting a rich reward, but receives only a two-*ryō* tip. Disappointed, he murders the old man with rat poison. Then, he puts the corpse in a wicker basket and dumps it in the river. Ryūtatsu returns as a ghost and kills Oichi. Hearing that Otora has drowned herself, Tajū goes out to Maruta Bridge, but sees the ghost of Ryūtatsu; shocked by the sight, he falls off the bridge into the river and drowns.

This is one of Uno's best *sewamono** plays, it offered superb opportunities to Onoe Kikugorō VI*, who starred in its first production. In one of its best scenes, Kikugorō acted out the avariciousness of the old man by showing Ryūtatsu going to bed, clutching the hundred *ryō*. The ghost scenes also were acted with verve. There is a humorous flavor mixed with a human warmth that provides the piece with excellent points. The characters are vividly drawn against the gloomy background of old Edo.

KODŌGU. *See* PROPERTIES.

KODŌGU BEYA. The "property room." It is located for convenience's sake in a corner on stage right. The prop master *(kodōgu kata; see also* PROPERTIES) prepares the props according to a list drawn up for each play *(kodōgu tsukechō)*. Hand props are delivered to each leading actor in his dressing room. Lesser actors must go to the prop room to get their props and return them when no longer needed.

KOGIRE. A term for those borderline items that may be treated both as costumes or properties. It originally referred to "small things"—gloves, headbands, hoods, footwear, drawers, and leggings—but has come to include such objects as tobacco, paper (for snow and letters), and other such *kiemono** or "one-time-only" props. Moreover, in the Kamigata area, the word refers to armor, swords, fans, tobacco pouches, wallets, and similar properties. Today, those items considered costume pieces are handled by the *ishō kata* or costumer (*see also* COSTUMES), those which are used up at each performance by the stagehands, and things like pouches by the prop masters *(kodōgu kata)*. However, the distinctions are complex, and special customs are followed. The man in charge of *kogire* is a specialist employed by a specific theatre. (*See also* PROPERTIES.)

KOI NYŌBŌ SOMEWAKE TAZUNA. Yoshida Kanshi, Miyoshi Shōraku. Also called *Shigenoi Kowakare. Jidaeimono**. *Jōruri**. Ten acts. February 1751. Takemoto-za, Osaka.

A revision of Chikamatsu Monzaemon's* play *Tanba no Yosaku Matsuyo no Komurobushi*. Act X, *Dōchū Sugoroku Shigenoi Kowakare*, is performed often. The play's first Kabuki version was at the Naka no Shibai in Osaka in October of the same year. Onoe Kikujirō played Onoe.

Princess Shirabe, young daughter of the Yurugi family, has been betrothed to the scion of the Iruma family, but resents having to go to them in the Eastern Province, which is unknown to her. The child pack-horse driver Jinenjō no Sankichi arrives, shows her a game of *dōchū sugoroku* (a popular children's game played on a map; one variant is still played in Japan), and puts the girl in the mood to travel. The girl's nurse, Shigenoi, brings a reward of sweets for the boy. When she reveals her name, Sankichi tells her that she is his long-lost mother. For proof, he shows her an amulet case. He asks her if they may not live together now, but Shigenoi, through her tears, tells him that her present position in life makes it impossible for her to comply. At this point, the princess's departure is announced. It is suggested that the boy sing a pack-horse driver's song to celebrate the princess's departure; he does so with tears in his eyes, as Shigenoi bravely struggles not to weep.

Sankichi's role, lying at the heart of the play, is a great one for a child actor. Shigenoi is a role that must demonstrate a psychological complexity made up of strength and sorrow.

KŌJŌ. A verbal greeting to the audience from the stage. During the Genroku period (1688-1703), there was a special actor's role—the *kōjō yaku*—for delivering the *kōjō*; then, the *kōjō* was valued as a kind of acting. Later, it became a special theatre event, and the troupe's representative actor performed a distinctive ceremony when he recited it. For example, a *kōjō* was performed on the occasion of an actor's taking a new name, the promotion of an actor to *nadai* status (*see also* TITLES), a Buddhist service, a memorial performance for a dead actor, and so forth. The play would be stopped temporarily and an announcement delivered to the audience.

Occasionally, a separate act is performed for the *kōjō*; in this, the chief actors of the company line up in formal dress on stage before gold-painted screens. Besides the usual *kōjō* there is the *jōrurifure*, in which *nadai* actors perform the *kōjō* before a *jōruri** scenic background. The *kiri kōjō* is performed at the end of a play. The action will suddenly cease, and an actor will turn and bow to the audience, saying, "That's all for today," and thus mark the end of the performance. This is sometimes done when a program is running late and must conclude. Also, in Edo times there was an *onagori* or "farewell" *kōjō* performed when an actor left Edo for the Kamigata area and when an actor from that area was to return. A singular example of a *kōjō* is seen when a full-length performance* *(tōshi kyōgen)* of *Kanadehon Chūshingura** is produced. Before the curtain opens for the first act, a puppet appears, dressed in formal robes, and tells the audience the whole cast of the play. This is the *kōjō ningyō* ("*kōjō* puppet"). The puppet theatre presents its *kōjō* by having a man robed in black appear and stand outside the curtain while introducing the play's main title, chanter, *shamisen** player, and puppet manipulators.

KOJŌRURI. "Old *jōruri**," Takemoto Gidayū (1651-1714) established the *gidayū bushi** style of *jōruri* when he created the Takemoto-za in 1684; all earlier schools of *jōruri* thereafter came to be called "old," or *kojōruri.* Belonging under this rubric are the schools of Uji Kaganojō, Okamoto Bunya, Yamamoto Kakudayū, and Inoue Harimanojō, as well as the Edo schools of *kinpira jōruri**, *hizen bushi, tosa bushi,* and others. The materials of *kojōruri* were generally derived from old dances and fairy tales. They are juvenile, flat, and prosaic; the scripts are simple, and their most marked quality is their lack of realism.

KOKAJI. Kimura Tomiko. *Shosagoto**. *Nagauta**. September 1939. Meiji-za*, Tokyo.

A Kabuki version of the Nō play entitled *Kokaji.* Its first stars were Ichikawa Ennosuke II (Ichikawa En'o*) and Kataoka Nizaemon XII*.

Kokaji Munechika, swordsmith of Sanjō, has received an order to forge a sword for the Emperor Ichijō, but he has not been able to comply and is worried. When he goes to pray to Inari Myōjin, fox god of the harvest, he meets a young boy who tells him to put his trust in the sword and then vanishes. When Munechika is about to forge his sword, Inari Myōjin appears and helps him to meet the Imperial request. During the interval between the play's two halves, villagers enter and perform dances to a *nagauta* accompaniment.

The role of the boy is played by the same actor who appears as the god, the latter performing an exciting dance in the second part of the play. He performs to the rhythmical beating of the hammer as the sword is forged.

KŌKEN. "Behind-seeing"; the man who stations himself behind an actor on stage, adjusts his costume, hands him hand props and takes them away, and prompts him. Many *kōken* are pupils of the actors whom they assist. In cases in which they wear a black costume and a black hood they are called *kurogo** or *kuronbo.* When a dance drama is performed, they appear in formal crested kimonos and divided skirt-trousers *(hakama*)* and with their faces exposed; they may also wear *kamishimo** formal wear and wigs. If an accident befalls the performer in a dance, the *kōken* must be prepared to take over the performance immediately. To be a worthy *kōken* the individual must be familiar with every facet of performance. (*See also* KYŌGEN KATA.)

Wearing formal *kamishimo** with Ichikawa crest, *kōken** sits quietly on stage. After a drawing in Toita, *Waga Kabuki.*

KOKERA OTOSHI. The opening of a theatre after it has been newly built or renovated. The term's derivation is vague although it is thought to have come from the sweeping away of the wood chips *(kokera)* of a newly completed wooden roof as a sign of welcoming. It was an established custom to perform the celebratory dance *Sanbasō** as the theatre's opening presentation.

KOKERU. When the actors' timing is off.

KOKUMOCHI. A small-sleeved, solid- or almost solid-colored kimono with three to five circular, appliquéd white crests. This is one of the conventional costumes worn by particular role types: farmers in history plays and wives in domestic plays. Examples of roles in which it is seen are Okaru in Act VI of *Kanadehon Chūshingura**, Jihizo in *Honchō Nijūshikō**, and Tonami in the *Terakoya* scene of *Sugawara Denju Tenarai Kagami**. These are roles of sincere, simple, and diligent people. The color of the kimono is usually purple, tinged with yellow and red *(kuri ume)* or light blue *(asagi)*.

KOKURITSU GEKIJŌ. *See* NATIONAL THEATRE OF JAPAN.

KOKUSENYA KASSEN. Chikamatsu Monzaemon*. English title: *The Battles of Coxinga* (Keene). *Jidaimono**. *Jōruri**. Five acts. November 1715. Takemoto-za, Osaka.

A play based on the exploits of the true historical figure known to the West as Coxinga. He was a powerful pirate of mixed Chinese and Japanese blood who supported the Ming dynasty of China during its final days of sovereignty before succumbing to the Manchus. The work received a successful seventeen-month continuous run when it was first performed. Also, the play took excellent advantage of the puppet theatre's capabilities, making it one of that form's true masterpieces; its grand scale and the curiosity aroused by its depiction of a foreign country were of great popular interest.

Kokusenya Kassen is also noteworthy in the annals of Japanese puppet theatre because it was the first work to discard the comic performance by a stupid puppet character that was traditionally held between the acts of a puppet play. Kabuki was quick to adapt the play, producing it at Kyoto's Miyako Mandayū-za in 1716 with productions at two Osaka theatres a year later. Edo also saw competitive productions in 1717, one at the Nakamura-za*, the other at the Ichimura-za*. The many Japanese plays on Kokusenya are grouped as the *Kokusenya mono*.

Rōikkan (Tei Shiryū) has been exiled to Japan from Ming China. When he learns that the Ming dynasty has been overthrown by the Tartars, he sets sail for the great Asian continent with his son, Watonai (Coxinga), and his Japanese wife. Once there, he enlists the aid of Kanki, husband of Kinshōjō, his daughter by a previous marriage. Kanki finds that it goes against his conscience to acquiesce merely because of his affection for his wife. He plans to kill his wife, for Kinshōjō's death would sever their marital bond so he could become Rōikkan's ally, but his mother-in-law prevents him. Kinshōjō kills herself to free her husband of his ties. Watonai changes his name to Kokusenya, musters his strength, and goes into battle for the restoration of the Ming dynasty.

In Kabuki, the main feature of the production is the *aragoto** style of performance used for Watonai.

KOKYŪ. A Chinese fiddle used in Kabuki music.

KOMOCHI YAMANBA. Chikamatsu Monzaemon*. Also called *Shaberi Yamanba, Yaegiri Kuruwa Banashi. Jidaimono*. Jōruri**. Five acts. July 1712. Takemoto-za, Osaka.

Act II is performed today; it is called *Yaegiri Kuruwa Banashi* or *Shaberi Yamanba.* The name of Yaegiri comes from that of a famous *onnagata**, Ogino Yaegiri I*, upon whose style the playwright based the role.

Tabakoya ("Tobacco Dealer") Genshichi, who is really Sakada Tokiyuki, is invited to the palace of Kanefuyu to cheer up the latter's daughter, Princess Omodaka, by singing a ballad *(kouta*)* to her. This visit brings about a fated meeting between Genshichi and Yaegiri, his ex-mistress. On the pretext of telling a tale of the pleasure quarters, she reviles him for having failed to kill his father's enemy; soon after, he dies from shame. Genshichi's spirit then enters Yaegiri's womb; she gains the power of a demon, routs the forces of the enemy, and flies off to parts unknown. Presently, she turns into a mountain witch *(yamanba)* and gives birth to a superhero, Kintoki.

A chief feature of the piece is the artful speech *(shaberi)* delivered by Yaegiri.

KOMORI. Nasuyama Kinpachi (lyrics for *kiyomoto** accompaniment), Tsuuchi Jihei (lyrics for *tokiwazu** accompaniment). Also called *Yamatogana Tamuke no Itsumoji. Shosagoto*. Kiyomoto* version: March 1823; Morita-za*, Edo. *Tokiwazu* version: September 1829; Kawarazaki-za, Edo.

The *kiyomoto* version is one part of a five-part "transformation piece*" *(henge mono),* the full title of which is given above. Its first star was Iwai Hanshirō VII*.

A nurse from Echigo Mountain runs after a bird that has snatched her fried bean curd *(tōfu)* and does a number of entertaining things, such as performing songs and dances.

The *tokiwazu* version, created for Segawa Kikunjō V*, is called *Hana Ichō Magaki no Ukareme* or *Mitsu Men Komori.* In order to amuse a baby, the nurse dances with three masks, using one after the other. The masks represent a fat-faced women *(okame),* a god *(Ebisu),* and a mask known as *gedō.*

KORE WA HYŌBAN UKINA NO YOMIURI. Sakurada Jisuke III*. Also called *Osome Hisamatsu Choinose no Zenroku. Sewamono**. Kabuki. Three acts. May 1862. Morita-za*, Edo.

Among the plays in which Osome and Hisamatsu are the leading figures is a comedy concerning the unrequited love of the clerk Zenroku for Osome. Today, the third act and the *Kuramae* scene, taken from an older work named *Some Moyō Imose no Kadomatsu*, are still performed.

Osome of the Abura-ya, a pawnshop, and the apprentice Hisamatsu are lovers. She is worried, though, that she will have to marry Yamagaya Seibei. The clerk Zenroku takes advantage of the lovers' relationship by reading Hisamatsu's love letter to Osome; he then tries to trap Hisamatsu. As part of his plan, he sends a letter to Osome. However, Yamagaya Seibei switches another one for it. When it is read aloud, Zenroku is silenced.

The *Kuramae* scene is acted by Zenroku in a manner that imitates the movement of a puppet; this is the *ningyō buri** style. The play's alternate title comes from the highly comic scene in which Seibei "lightly places" *(choito noseru)* an *utazaimon* (a kind of popular religious hymn written on a scroll) on Zenroku's head.

The cast of the first production included Ichikawa Kodanji IV* as Zenroku, Nakamura Fukusuke as Hisamatsu, and Ichikawa Fukutarō (later Ichikawa Sadanji I*) as Osome.

KOROSHIBA. *See* MURDER SCENES.

KOSHIBAI. "Small theatres," third-class theatres of the Edo period, in contrast to such first-class playhouses as the three licensed theatres of Edo (*see also* EDO SANZA). These theatres were known by a variety of names: *miyachi shibai**, *hyakunichi shibai, odedeko shibai,* and *donchō shibai* (*see also* DONCHŌ YAKUSHA). They were not allowed to use such elements as a revolving stage, a traveler curtain, or a *hanamichi**. Such small-scale theatres continued into the Meiji era, but reform measures abolished the distinction between large and small theatres in 1900. However, the *koshibai* tradition continued to exist for a number of years. By the end of World War II most of these playhouses had disappeared.

KOSHIRAE. "Preparation," the actor's job of putting on his makeup, costume, and wig as he gets ready to appear on stage.

KOSODE SOGA AZAMI NO IRONUI. Kawatake Mokuami*. Also called *Izayoi Seishin, Satomoyō Asami no Ironui.* English title: *The Love of Izayoi and Seishin* (Motofuji). *Sewamono**. Kabuki. Six acts. February 1859. Ichimura-za*, Edo.

A "robber play*" *(shiranami mono)*, a type quite popular at the time, that treats the sensational contemporary event of a break-in at a money storehouse. It does so within the context of a storyteller's tale *(kōshaku)* of a priest-turned-thief, Oni Bōzu Seikichi, who was executed in the Bunka period (1804-18). It was written especially for the talents of Ichikawa Kodanji IV* and Iwai Kumesaburō (later Iwai Hanshirō VIII*). The scenes shown today begin with the *michiyuki**, or "traveling scene," of Izayoi and Seishin and go so far as Seishin's change of mind and the blackmail scene at Hakuren's home.

Seishin, a priest expelled from his temple because of his illicit love for a woman, throws himself into the waters of the Inase River with his mistress, Izayoi. Izayoi is saved by the poet, Hakuren, and Seishin, unable to drown, pulls himself up onto land. Neither knows of the other's fate. Seishin attends to the convulsions of a temple page, Motome, who happens to be passing by; noticing the purse worn by the sick page, his heart makes an about-face, and he murders the boy. From then on, he follows a path of evil. Later, he takes the name of Oni ("Demon") Asami no Seikichi, he meets Izayoi by chance (she is now a nun), and the two go off to blackmail Hakuren. The latter, however, is really Odera Shōhei, the thief. It also turns out that he is Seishin's brother.

The play's major visual and aural moments include the famous *kiyomoto** song *Ume Yanagi Naka Yoi Zuki*, performed as Izayoi and Seishin mime their romantic relationship under the moon shining on the river bank; the charm of the sequential dialogue *(watari zerifu*)* enacted in the Seishin-Motome scene; and the give-and-take among Izayoi, Seishin, and Hakuren when the lovers attempt to blackmail the poet-thief. Outstanding proponents of Seishin have been Onoe Kikugorō V* and VI*, Ichikawa Danzō VII*, and Ichimura Uzaemon XV*.

KOTO. The Japanese "harp," a thirteen-stringed instrument played with two hands and placed on the ground before the musician. Next to the *shamisen**, it is probably the most widely known Japanese stringed instrument in the West.

KOTOBUKI KŌGYŌ. "Congratulatory productions." The formal or congratulatory plays traditional to each of the three great Edo theatres—the Nakamura-za*, Ichimura-za*, and Morita-za*—were called *kotobuki kyōgen*. Because these theatres held a hereditary license from the shogunate allowing them to produce plays, each had a deep-rooted history. Their respect for formalities and conventions led them to treat those plays which had been great successes at their theatres in the early days with great reverence as "memorial plays" *(kinen geki)*. Among the *kotobuki kyōgen* or *ie kyōgen* ("family plays") were the Nakamura-za's *Saruwaka*, *Shinbochi Daiko*, and

Kadomatsu; the Ichimura-za's *Kaidō Sagari;* and the Morita-za's *Busshari.* They were presented at special memorial performances called *kotobuki kōgyō.* At the Nakamura-za this meant that the play was produced at the annual "first calendar sign" *(kinoene)* performance; at the Ichimura-za it was given on the occasion of the 100th and 150th anniversaries of the theatre; and at the Morita-za on the 150th anniversary.

KOTSUZUMI. A small drum that figures prominently in Kabuki music. It is held in the hand by ropes girdling its frame; the player strikes the skin with his other hand. (*See also* GEZA: MUSICAL ACCOMPANIMENT CHART.)

KOUTA. "Small song," a type of music that was popular in Edo and developed from *hauta**. Since it has a rapid tempo, it is also called *hayama uta* ("quick song"). A solo performer sings it in a simple and chaste tone, accompanied by a *shamisen** player who continues to perform the melody when the singing has ended.

KOWAIRO. The act of imitating the voices of famous actors, a popular pastime in old Japan. (*See also* ŌMUSEKI; KAGE SHIBAI.)

KOWAIRO O TSUKAU. A mock *kōjō** ceremony held by an important actor's students and servants; the master is imitated, but the ideas expressed are the performers'.

KOYAKU. *See* CHILDREN'S ROLES.

KUBI. Also called *kiri kubi,* these are decapitated heads—an important stage property. They may be either heads made to look realistic or patently artificial ones called *dakubi,* which are made of cloth and connected together on a string. The latter are seen in exaggerated plays—*Shibaraku** or *Gohiiki Kanjinchō**, for example—when a powerful warrior chops off the heads of a large number of assailants with a single blow. When there are scenes of head inspection *(kubi jikken*)*, the head is placed in a box called the *kubioke.* The box is of pawlonia wood and is cylindrical in shape, being a foot in diameter and just over an inch in thickness. The head is placed in the box, which is covered by a lid. Occasionally, the actual head of a character appears on a stand under which a hole has been opened. This is called *hon kubi,* or "real head."

KUBI JIKKEN. "Scenes of head inspection," a conventional type of scene found in history plays. A head inspector is appointed to examine the head of an enemy. As the inspector sits down before the head, the formal nature

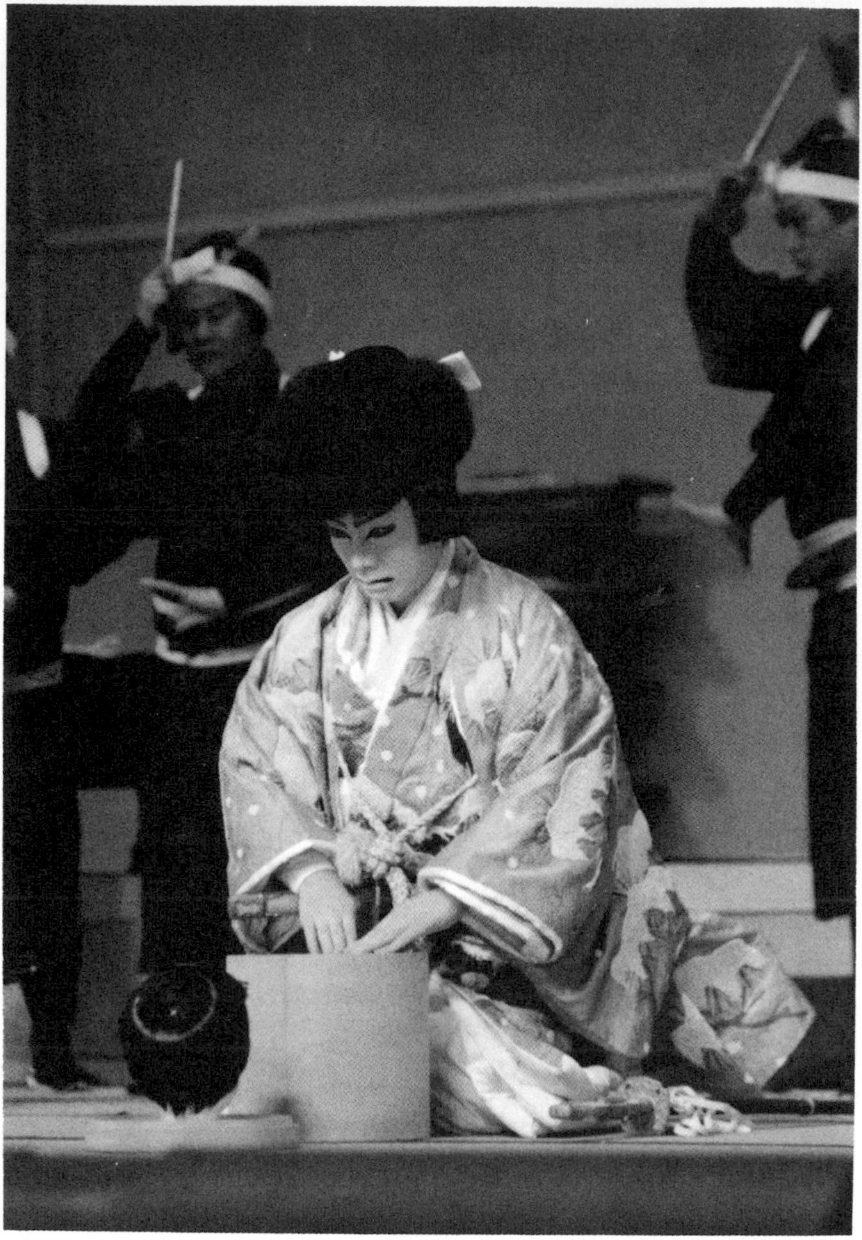

The head inspection scene *(kubi jikken*)* in the *Terakoya* scene of *Sugawara Denju Tenarai Kagami**. Matsuomaru, Onoe Tatsunosuke I*. *Courtesy of Kokuritsu Gekijō.*

A scene from *Suzugamori** showing Banzui Chōbei wearing the *kubi nuki** robe. Shirai Gonpachi, Ichikawa Ebizō X*; Chōbei, Kawarazaki Gonjūrō III*. *Courtesy of Waseda University Tsubouchi Engeki Hakubutsukan (Tsubouchi Memorial Theatre Museum).*

of the inspection ceremony is theatrical in itself; dramatic interest is further increased by the irony usually injected into the plot. The head is commonly that of someone with a deep personal relationship to the inspector. The inspector is the only one who is aware of the relationship. All other observers are ready to take the inspector at his word. The audience watches with relish the performance of the inspector, who must convey his pain at seeing the head of a loved one, but who, for various reasons must not betray his emotions to those at the ceremony. He must claim that the head belongs to someone else. Even more difficult than the acting during the moments of inspection is the very first movement as the actor prepares to and then lifts the lid, revealing the head. The inspector never knows for sure that the head in the box is the one that he suspects it to be; he must subtly portray his trepidation at the action that he is about to take. His expressions—when he does lift the lid, first views the head, and realizes whose it is—often require acting genius to execute well. Famous examples of *kubi jikken* are found in the *Terakoya* scene of *Sugawara Denju Tenarai Kagami** and the *Kumagai Jinya* scene of *Ichinotani Futaba Gunki**.

KUBI NUKI. A costume design consisting of a bold pattern running from the breast of the kimono over the shoulders and to the back. It is seen on Asahina in *Kusazuri Biki** and Chōbei in *Suzugamori**.

KUBOTA MANTARŌ. 1889-1963. A playwright and novelist. Born in Tokyo, he wrote richly poetic books and plays that captured the flavor of downtown Tokyo in the old days. His plays include *Kokorogokoro, Mijikayo,* and *Ōdera Gakkō.* Also a director and actor, Kubota was a Keiō University graduate and belonged to the Japan Art Academy (Nihon Geijutsuin). Further, he chaired the Japan Theatre Association (Nihon Engeki Kyōkai).

KUCHIBAN. Also called *gakuya kuchiban,* he is a functionary who prevents uninvited persons from entering the backstage* area. He also takes care of the actors' footwear and sees to the needs of whoever enters the *gakuya* (backstage*) area. His Western counterpart is the stage-door watchman.

KUCHIDATE. An improvised performance based on a plot established by the leading actor *(zagashira*)*; all dialogue is made up by the performers. This improvisational style was used in early Kabuki as well as in other forms of theatre in Japan. It still is used by groups of strolling players who may not have a script at hand.

KUDARI YAKUSHA. "Going-down actors," actors who came to perform in Edo theatres from Osaka or Kyoto. Much of this cultural interchange took place in the November hiring period and was given special mention in the programs and on the billboards for the annual *kaomise** or "face-showing" performances. (*See also* NORIKOMI.)

KUDOKI. *See* LAMENTATION SCENES.

KUITSUKU. "To bite at"; a term used when good attendance is the result of putting on a good production.

KUMA. An abbreviation of *kumadori**, Kabuki's unique makeup style.

KUMADORI. Also called *kuma**, Kabuki's most distinctive makeup technique. It is a nonrealistic makeup that emphasizes the movement of the facial muscles. *Kumadori* resembles Chinese opera's face painting, which some scholars feel had a strong influence on its origins. In China the highly exaggerated face painting used for the general class of roles called *l'ien pu* tends to obliterate the actor's own facial expression. Kabuki's *kumadori*, however, emphasizes the facial expressions growing out of the character's personality. As is true of *l'ien pu*, *kumadori* styles may be said to be fixed for the roles that wear it.

Kumadori is said have been first used in 1673 when its prototype was created by the thirteen year-old Ichikawa Danjūrō I* at the Nakamura-za*. The legend has it that he received critical acclaim for his unique makeup of red and black patterns. *Kumadori* became the special province of the Ichikawa line of actors and was imitated by others. It developed as one of the chief stage elements of Edo Kabuki. The growing stylization of Kabuki performance witnessed a perfection of *kumadori* technique in the hands of Danjūrō VII* in the early 1850s.

Kuma's three basic colors are red, black, and blue, although red ochre, purple, and gold are employed on occasion, too. There are at least 100 varieties of this makeup, but the major ones are *beni guma**, which is chiefly of red lines, and *aiguma**, consisting of blue lines. *Ippon guma** and *nihon guma** are representative of the *suji guma** subcategory of *beni guma*, while *saru guma**, *mukimi guma**, and *kaen guma* are other subcategories of this type. The red color signifies righteousness, superhuman strength, and passion; blue indicates the negative qualities of fear and evil. The main *aiguma* is the *hannya guma** seen on the *kugeaku* (evil prince) characters in *Sugawara Denju Tenarai Kagami** and *Shibaraku**. This makeup symbolizes a feeling of deep enmity. Other *aiguma* types include the *Fudō guma*, based on the features of the deity Fudō. There also are special *kuma* for supernatural characters like the earth spider in *Tsuchigumo** (which uses the color brown) and the various gods, buddhas, and devils.

KUMO MAKU. "Cloud curtain," a scenic element used for depicting clouds. (*See also* DŌGU MAKU.)

KUMO NI MAGŌ UENO NO HATSUHANA. Kawatake Mokuami*. Also called *Kochiyama to Naozamurai, Kochiyama Michitose to Naozamurai.* English title: *Naozamurai* (Leiter). *Sewamono**. Kabuki. Seven acts, sixteen scenes. March 1881. Shintomi-za, Tokyo.

Kawatake Mokuami, dramatizer of the exploits of daring bandits (robber plays*), based this work on a storyteller's tale *(kōdan)* by Matsubayashi Hakuen, popularly known as Dorobo ("Thief") Hakuen. The title of the tale was *Tenpō Rokkasen.* Since 1910 this play usually has been divided into two parts and played separately as *Kochiyama* and *Naozamurai* (a fuller title for the latter is *Yuki no Yube Iriya no Azemichi*).

The play was first produced in 1874 at the Kawarazaki-za, but only a part of the full-length work was performed. Its title was *Kumo no Ueno Sane no Sakumae.* This play's plot was incorporated in the *Kochiyama* section of the later full-length version. In 1881 the *Naozamurai* section was added, and the play took the form that is now familiar. Onoe Kikugorō V* played Naojirō and Iwai Hanshirō was Michitose. Others in the cast included Ichikawa Danjūrō IX, Ichikawa Sadanji I*, Nakamura Sōjūrō I*, and Ichikawa Kodanji V*.

In order to rescue the daughter of a townsman from the clutches of an evil nobleman, Lord Matsue, Kochiyama boldly enters the lord's castle disguised as a priestly messenger from a temple at Ueno. Having arranged for the girl's return to her father, he is on the point of leaving when Kitamura Daizen, a retainer of Matsue, recognizes him as Kochiyama the outlaw. Kochiyama, however, switches from his priestly manner and hurls a speech of defiance at his accusers; he then exits with great composure. All breathe a sigh of relief, as Kochiyama had threatened to reveal Daizen's past to the police if anyone there dared to arrest him.

In the second part, Naojirō (Naozamurai), pursued by the law, decides to flee Edo; caught in a snowstorm, he goes to an inn in Iriya to visit his lovesick mistress, the courtesan Michitose, before departing from the city. His fellow gang member Ushimatsu, however, secretly reveals Naojirō's whereabouts to the police, and the fugitive is soon surrounded.

The major part of the *Kochiyama* scene comes when Kochiyama delivers his famous diatribe using the colloquial Edo language of the time; *Naozamurai* is noted for its lovely *kiyomoto** musical accompaniment and a moving lamentation scene* *(kudoki)* that is performed in dance-mime by Naozamurai and Michitose.

KURAI BŌSHI. A name for the eyebrow style in nobleman roles; other names are the *bōbō mayu, tenjo mayu* and *takamayu.* The natural eyebrows are obliterated, and false eyebrows are drawn on above them, on the forehead. These are applied thickly in the center with the edges shaded off. When Sekibei in *Seki no To** becomes Ōtomo Kuronushi, he puts on this eyebrow style.

KURAIRI. "Warehousing"; when business is good, an investor's money is returned, and more is borrowed for further financing.

KURA ISHŌ. "Warehouse costumes"; a former system of costume storage. As a rule, Edo period actors had to supply their own stage costumes out of their salaries. However, subordinate actors found this too heavy a financial burden. The *zamoto** created the *kura ishō* system for these actors, who borrowed a predetermined list of items when needed. Among such costumes were those of nobles, *daimyō*, court ladies, police officers, soldiers, and the like. These often crude costumes were kept in a theatre warehouse. As the producer now supplies all the actors' costumes, the *kura ishō* system has ceased to exist. (*See also* COSTUMES.)

KURAI ZUKE. "Ranking." An annual critical report on the actors, the *yakusha hyōbanki**, was published beginning in the early Edo period; and from about 1688 on, it applied a ranking to each actor. This ranking or rating was placed before the name, and the actor's crest was placed above it. A rank of "best" *(jō)* or "middle" *(chū)* was placed in the upper portion of the rating entry. At first the ranks were limited to *jōjōkichi* ("best-best-excellent"), *jōjō* ("best-best"), *chū no jō* ("middle-best"), and *chū* ("middle"). Gradually, however, these terms grew more complex, and above *jōjōkichi* there were *kyoku* ("extremely good"), *taikyoku* ("marvelous"), and *murai* ("peerless"), the last being the highest rank attainable.

KURAYAMI NO USHIMATSU. Hasegawa Shin*. *Shin kabuki**. Three acts. June 1934. Tōkyō Gekijō, Tokyo.

Okome, the wife of Ushimatsu, a cook who has killed a man in a brief outburst of passion, travels to the home of her brother Shirobei and his wife to seek succor at their hands. A year later, driven by his love for Okome, the fugitive Ushimatsu returns to visit her. Stopping at a brothel near Itabashi, he discovers that she has become a prostitute. Okome has been disgraced by having been sold into prostitution by her brother, but Ushimatsu mistakes her position as an act of treachery. His refusal to listen to her excuses results in her hanging herself that night. Later, learning the facts, Ushimatsu hurries straight to Shirobei's home. Shirobei has gone to the bathhouse, but his wife is home. Hoping to save herself and her spouse, she offers herself to him. Disgusted by this dishonorable behavior, he slays her and then kills Shirobei at the baths. Ushimatsu then manages to escape.

The entire piece is pervaded by the pathos of a man who toys with a gloomy destiny, and it has a striking effect on the hearts of most audiences. Onoe Kikugorō VI* was outstanding in the title role.

KURI. The shape of the hairline. Kabuki wigs are created by first making a copper head plate *(daigane*)* and then fitting to it the actor's head. After the actor makes his suggestions, the wig making commences. The most important factor at this point is how the hairline looks since it can be a crucial element visually in the presentation of a role. It is likely to be the deciding factor in whether or not the wig is well matched with the actor's face. Since it is a delicate business, it must be handled with great sensitivity. (*See also* WIGS.)

KURIAGE. A term referring to the climactic part of a dispute or argument when both parties say, *"saa, saa, saa"* (an expletive meaning something like "well, well, well,") simultaneously. Similar phrases included under this rubric are *nani nani shōka, saa sore wa,* and *nan to hensho wa dodo dōda.* There is a good example of it in the Hamamatsu-ya scene of *Aotozōshi Hana no Nishikie*.*

KUROFUDA. Also called *kyūyōfuda,* this is a system used when an emergency arose and an audience member had to be contacted immediately. The playgoer's name was written on a board (the *kurofuda*) in chalk and posted on the downstage right pillar *(daijin bashira*).* When someone was paged orally, the job of paging fell to the backstage manager *(tōdori*).* Also, lower-rank actors were used for making announcements of this sort.

KUROGO. Also called *kuronbo.* The stage assistant who helps an actor onstage during a performance; also his costume. Since *kuro* ("black") means "nothingness" in Kabuki terms, he wears a black cotton robe and black gauze hood, suggesting invisibility. In most cases the *kōken** type of stage assistant also wears black. (*See also* KYŌGEN KATA.)

KURO MAKU. "Black curtain," a special Kabuki curtain that covers most of the upstage area of the set to represent darkness.

KUROZUKA. Kimura Tomiko. *Shosagoto*. Nagauta*.* November 1939. Tōkyō Gekijō, Tokyo.

A work based on the Nō play of the same name (called *Adachigahara* by the Kanze school of Nō actors). The first star of the play, Ichikawa Ennosuke II (En'o I*), provided the original conception that the play should end tragically with the demon's unsuccessful attempt at achieving salvation.

A small party of priests stops overnight at the home of an old lady, Iwate, in Adachigahara. Iwate, who is really a demon in disguise, asks them not to

Genta Kagesue describes the battle at the Uji River in *Hiragana Seisuiki's** *Genta Kandō* scene. Observe the black-robed and black-masked stage assistants *(kurogo*)* crouching behind Genta and the character at his left. Genta, Morita Kanya XIV*. *Courtesy of Waseda University Tsubouchi Engeki Hakubutsukan (Tsubouchi Memorial Theatre Museum).*

look into her bedroom. One of them disregards this advice, however, and peeps in, only to view the horrid sight of human carrion on which someone has been feeding. It is clear now that the woman is a demon. Repenting her evil deeds, the old lady places her faith in Buddha to save her soul for the next world. She soon realizes that her secret has been discovered and, angered by human inconstancy, angrily confronts the party. Ultimately, she is weakened by the priest's prayers and, before dawn, vanishes.

Among the three parts into which the work is divided, the first is in Nō style, the second in "new dance" style *(shinbuyōfu)*, and the last in pure Kabuki dance style. A highlight is when the demon dances joyfully and looks up at the moon to request that she achieve Nirvana, a moment that En'o is said to have borrowed from the Russian ballet that he viewed while on a foreign tour. This style has been inherited by Ennosuke III*.

KURU. "Going over"; the act of repeating one's lines to oneself in the wings while waiting to make an entrance.

KURUMA BIN. A wig that has had several tufts of hair pulled out in bunches on each side lock; these bunches are pomaded with oil until they are hard. A style of wig worn by the hero in *Shibaraku** and Gorō in *Yanone**, it resembles a number of carriage *(kuruma)* wheel spokes sticking out from the head. Its exaggerated appearance makes it suitable for the *aragoto** style. The most famous example, which captures Kabuki's quintessential formalized beauty, is the five-spoke wig in *Shibaraku*. A less exaggerated version is used occasionally in domestic plays and may be seen on such characters as Banzui Chōbei in *Suzugamori** and Gosho no Gorozō in *Soga Moyō Tateshi no Goshozome**.

KURUWA BUNSHŌ. Chikamatsu Monzaemon*. Also called *Yoshidaya Yūgiri Izaemon, Yūgiri Izaemon*. English title: *Love Letter from the Licensed Quarter* (Brandon). *Sewamono**. Kabuki. One act, two scenes. Current version, October 1808. Nakamura-za*, Edo.

One of many plays written about the famed Osaka courtesan Yūgiri. The first was Chikamatsu's *Yūgiri Nagori no Shōgatsu* (1679), written for Sakata Tōjūrō I*. Chikamatsu's 1712 puppet play, *Yūgiri Awa no Naruto*, was presented in adapted form in 1780 and 1793, but the first Kabuki play based on these materials and titled *Kuruwa Bunshō* was not staged until 1808. In its cast were Bandō Hikosaburō III* as Izaemon and Segawa Kikunojō III* (then called Senjō) as Yūgiri.

Fujiya Izaemon, who has been disinherited by his family, is the lover of the Shinmachi district courtesan Yūgiri. One day, toward the end of the year, he comes to the Yoshida-ya brothel wearing a paper kimono *(kamiko*)*. Although he has no money, he is welcomed and treated warmly by Kizaemon, the proprietor; however, when he hears that Yūgiri is occupied with a wealthy patron from Awa, he grows distraught. When the courtesan appears, he rebukes her for her inconstancy, but soon recognizes her sincerity; they take each other's hands. Just then Izaemon's disinheritance is reversed, and the ransom money allowing him to redeem Yūgiri from indenture to the brothel is delivered.

The essence of the Kamigata area *wagoto** style is captured by the sight of *kamiko*-clad Izaemon, whose reduced straits have ended his previous liberality, and of Yūgiri, whose lovesickness is signified by the purple band *(hachimaki*)* that she wears around her head. The stage picture abounds in the spirit of the New Year in its delightfully colorful decor. *Kuruwa Bunshō* is performed today with a musical background made up of a collaboration between *gidayū**, *tokiwazu**, and *kiyomoto** schools, a method that has been used for this play since the Meiji era. It is performed in a manner closer to dance than to straight acting.

KUSAI. "Foul-smelling"; unnecessarily exaggerated acting.

KUSAZURI BIKI. Anonymous. Also called *Shofudatsuki Kongen Kusazuri. Shosagoto**. *Nagauta**. January 1814. Morita-za*, Edo.

A play presenting in dance form an event described in the *Soga Monogatari*, an old narrative.

Soga no Gorō, to save his brother Jurō from danger, grapples with Kobayashi no Asahina over the treasured suit of armor with which Asahina has absconded. Asahina then calms down the hot-tempered youth.

This subject has given rise to many Kabuki works, but only a few remain. Plays such as *Kikuju no Kusazuri* and *Kongen Kusazuri Biki* substitute a courtesan for Asahina. This particular piece is acted in the bravura *aragoto** style and is in keeping with the sense of humor prevalent during the early nineteenth century. It is an enchantingly bright and colorful dance.

KUSUGURI. "Titillation," clever acting that makes the audience laugh.

KUU. "To eat"; the cutting of dialogue or business from a scene. Also, acting that overshadows that by one's stage partners, as in the expression "to eat one's partner" *(aite o kuu)*. It also may be used when an actor cuts off the dialogue of another with his own lines; here, the expression is "to eat dialogue" *(serifu o kuu)*.

KUWAEME. "Teeth-grip eyes"; this is a device similar to the *kuwaemen**. During a fight scene, when a comic character is gripped at the nape of the neck by a powerful opponent, he may put this device on his face (it is gripped between the teeth by a tongue-like protrusion) to give the effect of his eyeballs popping out of his head. It is seen in *Suzugamori**.

KUWAEMEN. A stage property. It is a trick mask with a protrusion on its inner face so that it may be held in place by the teeth. A well-known version is the *sogimen**.

KYAKUSHOKU. "Dramatization," the making of a play out of a story, novel, or legendary tale. In Edo days, though adaptations from other sources were made for the stage, the word referred to the writing of all scripts. *Shigumi** is the word that formerly meant what *kyakushoku* represents today.

KYŌGEN KATA. Playwrights occupying the fourth and fifth ranks among the resident dramatists at an Edo period theatre. Today, their chief duties have to do with miscellaneous aspects of performance and stage management. They attend rehearsals and handle the actors' problems. The *kyōgen kata*—or *kyōgen sakusha**, as he also is known—appears on stage dressed in a black costume *(kurogo*)* and has the important job of prompting the actors; his skill often enhances the actor's art. When Ichikawa Danjūrō VII* was to give the premiere performance of *Kanjinchō**, the young Kawatake Mokuami* filled the position of *kurogo*; he learned the entire script by heart and prompted Danjūrō without holding a book. The *kyōgen kata* also beats the *hyōshigi** clappers when the curtain opens and closes and when the set is being changed. A man with many responsibilities, he supervises the progress of the entire performance. (*See also* PLAYWRIGHTS' RANKS.)

KYŌGEN MAWASHI. "Play-revolving"; a role that figures importantly in the plot of a play. Also, someone who gets things done in a self-effacing manner.

KYŌGEN O KAKU. "To write a play"; when someone thinks up a clever story and uses it skillfully to deceive another person.

KYŌGEN SAKUSHA. Formerly a low-ranking playwright, this now refers to a man who acts in the capacity of a stage assistant. (*See also* KYŌGEN KATA; KUROGO; PLAYWRIGHTS' RANKS.)

KYŌKA GIKYOKU JŪSHU. A collection of plays created by Ichikawa Sadanji II* from his biggest successes, most of them being the work of Okamoto Kidō*. They are all in the New Kabuki *(shin kabuki*)* genre. The total does not amount to ten plays *(jūshu)*. (*See also* FAMILY ART*.)

PLAY	DATE	AUTHOR
*Shuzenji Monogatari**	1909	Okamoto Kidō
Sasaki Takaoka	1914	Okamoto Kidō
*Toribeyama Shinjū**	1915	Okamoto Kidō
*Banchō Sarayashiki**	1916	Okamoto Kidō
Onoe Itahachi	1918	Okamoto Kidō
*Imayō Satsuma Uta**	1920	Oka Onitarō*
Bunkaku	1924	Matsui Shōyō
Shinyado Yobanashi	1927	Okamoto Kidō

KYŌRAN MONO. *See* MADNESS PIECES.

L

LAMENTATION SCENES. The Japanese term, *kudoki,* formerly referred to Heian period (794-1185) *biwa* (a lutelike instrument) and Nō theatre melodies that evoked a feeling of sorrow and nostalgia. Such melodies were incorporated into puppet theatre music and *nagauta** music (Kabuki's major musical style), where they became a central feature. The term has come to mean dramatic scenes in which the heroine sorrowfully gives vent to her deepest feelings. It is a major type of accompaniment music and is thoroughly complemented by the actor's mime. (*See also* SHŪTANBA.)

LION DANCES. *See* SHAKKYŌ MONO.

LIVING HISTORY PLAYS. Called *katsureki geki* (or *mono*), this style of history play *(jidaimono*)* was originated by Ichikawa Danjūrō IX* during the Meiji era. *Katsureki* plays show a reverence for historical accuracy and an attention to ancient martial and court customs. Although other Edo period history plays were based on the old historical chronicles and narratives, Danjūrō held in contempt their many stage inaccuracies and absurdities and intended to reform the drama in line with Western ideas then infiltrating Japanese culture. The seed for this attempt was sown in his simple realistic performance of *Sanada Kōmura* in 1871. From about 1877 to 1887, he was aided by the progressive producer Morita Kanya XII*, as well as by reform-minded government officials and scholars. At the same time, Kawatake Mokuami* was entrusted with the task of writing new plays based on historical fact. Performances were staged with strict attention to the accurate rendition of classical speech, behavior, and character depiction based on research; this led to a new method of Kabuki staging. In 1878, when Mokuami's *Nichō no Yumi Chigusa no Shigedō* was performed, the critic Kanagaki Rōbun (1829-1894) originated the word *katsureki* ("living history") as a sarcastic jibe at such plays. The *katsureki* movement was supported by contemporary scholars and the intellectual elite. It was, dramatically, an uninteresting genre, and it was sustained only by Danjūrō's brilliant acting. The general public found these plays to be dull, but *katsureki* drama was maintained up to 1881 on the strength of Danjūrō's will. Ultimately, it could not resist public opinion, suffered setbacks, and was replaced by a more moderate sort of production. However, *katsureki* plays provided the stimulus for the later birth of historically accurate dramas under the banner of New Kabuki *(shin kabuki*)*. Representative *katsureki* plays include *Takatoki**, *Sakai no Taiko*, and *Momoyama Monogatari*. (*See also* PLAY CATEGORIES.)

LOVER ROLES. *See* NIMAIME.

LOVE SCENES. A simple love scene between a man and a woman is called *iromoyō*, whereas *nureba* are more ardent scenes of love; the latter word refers to scenes of sensuality and their performance. During the Genroku period (1688-1703) plays were performed in which there were scenes of quarreling and embracing between courtesan and client; *nureba* are the scenes that developed from these early examples. The distinctive sensuality and alluring beauty brought to the stage by the *onnagata** allowed for a great expansion of such scenes. *Nureba* are performed with an extremely formalized type of stage beauty. In general, the acting conventions stress the woman's aggressiveness and the man's passivity. Of course, the passion of the characters is conveyed more through suggestion than actual representation. Examples are the *sushi* shop scene between Osato and Yasuke in *Yoshitsune Senbon Zakura** and the scene between Princess Yaegaki and Katsuyori in *Honchō Nijūshikō**. A realistic and decadent appeal was added to these scenes during the last years of the Edo period, as seen in the Susaki embankment scene in *Kozaru Shichinosuke* and the clandestine meeting of Otomi and Yosa in *Yowa Nasake Ukina no Yokogushi**. Another classic example occurs between Naozamurai and Michitose in *Kumo ni Magō Ueno no Hatsuhana**. These scenes are rather frank in content.

M

MA. *See* PAUSES.

MABUTA NO HAHA. Hasegawa Shin*. *Shin kabuki**. Two acts, four scenes. March 1931. Meiji-za*, Tokyo.

After much searching, Banba no Chūtarō finds his mother, from whom he was separated when a child. His mother, Ohama, who runs a profitable business, is overcome with anxiety for her daughter's welfare when the ragged-looking Chūtarō presses his claims on her. Therefore, she coldly chases her son away. The neighborhood leech, Sumekura no Kantarō, who hangs around Ohama's household, learns about the Chūtarō affair and chases after him. The two men fight at the embankment of the Ara River, and Chūtarō kills his antagonist. Ohama has second thoughts about her treatment of Chūtarō and, fearing for his safety, runs out in search of him. She calls his name, but Chūtarō, resenting the cold treatment that she originally gave him, ignores her calls and, for the sake of his sister's happiness, departs.

MACHI MAWARI. "Around the town"; an old custom of having a troupe of actors parade around a town before beginning their performance. (*See also* NORIKOMI.)

MACHINEE. A "matinee" or afternoon performance. Originally, these were modeled after the European plan, one or two being given each week for the benefit of students and the poorer classes. At such matinees these theatregoers could see, for cheaper prices, a production featuring the younger stars of the day. The system began in Japan in 1912 when the Teikoku Gekijō* began to produce monthly programs that ran for twenty-five days, including eight matinees. Today, when the monthly run is made up of two different programs, one in the afternoon and one in the evening, the afternoon program is called the matinee. (*See also* NIBUSEI.)

MADNESS PIECES. *Kyōran mono* is the term for a type of dance play whose major theme is insanity *(kyōran).* They were inspired by a similar class of Nō plays. By the second half of the seventeenth century many such works were to be found in the repertoire. The two varieties of *kyōran mono* feature either a male or female dancer; the female-centered works *(kyōjo mono)* include *Shuzuhata Obi, Sumidagawa**, *Oshichi Kyōran,* and the modern *Onatsu Kyōran**. Male dances include *Wankyū, Yasuna**, and *Nakazō Kyōran.*

MADOBUTA. Rain shutters, which were called *akari mado* ("light windows") during the Edo period. They were located in the upper part of the side galleries *(sajiki*)* in the old theatres. Translucent sliding screens were fitted into the *akari mado,* and light coming into the theatre's interior could be regulated according to how far these windows were opened. When darkness was required, they were closed. Such effects often were used in ghost plays and pantomimes *(danmari*).* The man in charge of these windows was the *madoban;* he also was responsible for guarding the entrance to the backstage area (*see also* KUCHIBAN), but combined this function with his gallery duties.

MAEGAMI KATSURA. The wig of a youth whose forelock *(maegami)* still has not been cut off. There are a variety of names for the shapes of the forelock. Those split down the center into two parts are the *hachiware,* those stiffened with pomade are the *aburakomi,* those fashioned like a pompom are the *tsukamitate**, and so on.

MAE JASEN. A topknot style that is the opposite of the *hajiki chasen** (which points to the rear); its top portion lies low on the front of the pate. Characters wearing it are amorous *nimaime** in the history plays as well as policemen. Sakuramaru in the *Ga no Iwai* scene of *Sugawara Denju Tenarai Kagami**, Koganosuke in *Imoseyama Onna Teikin**, and Jūjirō in Act X of *Ehon Taikōki** are representative examples.

MAGE. *See* TOPKNOTS.

MAI. A type of dancing that originally featured a circular or rotational style of movement; Nō theatre dancing was a strong factor in its development. It is opposed to the type of dance style called *odori**, although nowadays both words commonly refer to classical Japanese dance. The word *buyō,* a term of recent coinage, is written with the characters for *mai* and *odori* and stands for all Kabuki dance. (*See also* DANCE.)

MAKEUP. One of the most striking visual elements of Kabuki performance. Kabuki makeup, or *keshō*, is highly conventionalized, as each role type has a fixed style established by long tradition. There are numerous conventional eye-line styles, lip styles, eyebrow styles, and so forth. According to the role, the base makeup may go from stark white to red to natural-looking flesh tones; a white base *(oshiroi*)* is most familiar to audiences, since so many characters use it. Kabuki's most distinctive makeup style is the *kumadori**, a system of lines painted on the face (and often on the arms and legs as well) to symbolize the fundamental nature of the character.

For purposes of classification, *kumadori* makeup styles are often referred to by character type: "good" characters, "evil" ones, spirits, and gods. Bold lines are applied to the face to harmonize with the *aragoto** acting style.

Makeup materials include *abura beni**, *taihaku, edo beni,* and *oshiroi**, among others. Since only men appear in Kabuki, actors who have to appear as women tie a special silk cloth tightly around their heads to raise their eyes and increase their attractiveness; it is a very uncomfortable technique, but looks quite effective from the audience. (*See also* HABUTAE.)

MAKU. *See* CURTAINS. The word *maku* is also used as an abbreviation of *daramaku**, a method of striking the *hyōshigi** clappers.

MAKUAI. *See* INTERMISSION.

MAKU DAMARI. "Curtain gathering," the place where the gathered traveler

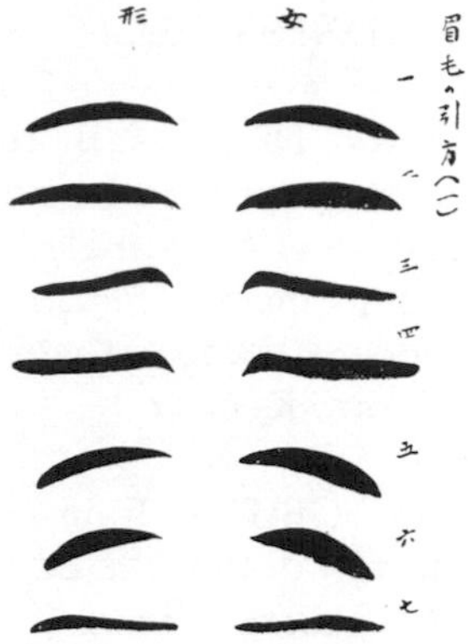

Eyebrow styles for *onnagata** roles. From Kojima, ed., *Kao no Tsukurikata.*

Male-role eyebrow styles. From Kojima, ed., *Kao no Tsukurikata.*

Lip styles. On the left are male styles; on the right, female. From Kojima, ed., *Kao no Tsukurikata.*

The *Genroku mie* (see MIE) in *Shibaraku**. Kamakura Gongorō no Kagemasa, Ichikawa Ebizō X*. Gongorō's sleeves are being held up by two stage assistants, hidden behind them. He wears a *kuruma bin** wig and *nihon suji* makeup to denote his *aragoto** character. *Courtesy of Waseda University Tsubouchi Engeki Hakubutsukan (Tsubouchi Memorial Theatre Museum).*

curtain *(hiki maku** or *jōshiki maku**) is kept after it has been pulled open. It is called *maku doya* in the Kamigata area. During the Edo period a rope hanging there was used to tie the gathered curtain. (*See also* CURTAINS.)

MAKU GIRE. The closing of the curtain at the end of a play. Kabuki heightens the moment by employing music, the beating of the *tsuke** and the *hyōshigi**, and even the way in which the actors disport themselves.

MAKU MAWARI. The man who takes care of all the scenic curtains. He is in charge of such items as the wave curtain, ground cloths, snow cloths, and shop curtains (*noren; see also* NORENGUCHI). He works in a room called the *Kogireya.* (*See also* CURTAINS.)

MAKU NI KAKERU. "Put up the curtain"; to stage a certain play. A separate meaning applies when an actor is dissatisfied with his salary and refuses to perform, thus canceling the production.

MAKU NO UCHI. The box lunches *(bentō)* bought at the theatre and eaten between the acts *(maku no uchi)*. Formerly, they held rice balls of about one and one-half inches in diameter. These were boiled thoroughly, garnished, and placed in small bamboo boxes that were stacked up in the theatre teahouses *(see also* SHIBAIJAYA). Today's theatre restaurants sell *bentō*, but their contents are more varied than those of the old days; usually, a mound of rice sprinkled with black sesame is included with other common delicacies. Everything is attractively arranged in compartmentalized boxes. (*See also* KABESU.)

MAKU O SHIBORU. "To squeeze the curtain"; holding back the stage-right lower corner of the curtain as a character makes an exit on the *hanamichi** after the curtain has closed. The curtain is held back so the *geza** musicians can watch the actor until he is out of sight. (*See also* HIKKOMI.)

MAKURU. "To roll up the sleeves"; when an actor speaks so fast that his words can not be understood.

MAKU UCHI. "Within the curtain"; a general term for whatever and whoever is engaged in production work behind the curtain. The term includes the actors, property men, costumers, wig makers, musicians, and so on. (*See also* URA KATA.)

MAKU ZURI. "Curtain-hanging"; when a long and narrow cloth hangs down within both sides of the proscenium frame and marks off the stage area in the fashion of a tormentor or false proscenium. The cloth is called the *genji* curtain *(genji maku). Maku zuri* refers to the space delineated by the inner edges of the *genji* curtains. When the *genji* curtains are not used, the *maku zuri* becomes that space delineated by the proscenium opening. (*See also* GAKUBUCHI.)

MALE ROLES. *See* TACHIYAKU.

MANAGERS. *See* ZAMOTO; NADAI; THEATRE MANAGEMENT.

MARUGUKE. A rounded, cotton-padded, ropelike cord, used as an obi or as the cord tied on the obi *(obijime).* Coming in various colors and forms, the *maruguke* is widely used among actors of male and female roles. It is especially effective in *aragoto**, in which a very thick and exaggerated *maruguke* is used.

MARU MONO. Also *honmaru,* these are stage properties, such as trees, pillars, and the like built in the round. (*See also* HANMARU.)

MASAKADO. Takarada Jusuke. Also called *Shinobi Yoru Koi wa Kusemono. Shosagoto*. Tokiwazu**. July 1836. Ichimura-za*, Edo.

Ichimura Uzaemon XII and Ichikawa Kuzō starred in this work's first production.

Ōyaketarō Mitsukuni, hearing a rumor that a ghost has appeared at Taira Masakado's old castle, arrives there to investigate. A beautiful courtesan, Kisaragi, appears before him. When he relates to her the circumstances of Masakado's death in battle, she reveals her true being as Takiyasha, Masakado's daughter. Failing in her attempt to win Mitsukuni over to her side, she uses the magic powers of a huge toad and engages in a battle with him.

The main features of this work are Takiyasha's seduction and Mitsukuni's tale of battle as well as the spectacular fight scene, during which the entire palace setting is mechanically collapsed.

MASAKARI. A topknot resembling a broadax *(masakari).* It is worn at formal announcement ceremonies *(kōjō*)* by the Ichikawa family of actors and is seen on the *haradashi** soldiers of *Shibaraku** and the firemen in *Mekura Nagaya Ume ga Kagatobi**.

MASSUGU. "Straight"; the opposite of cross or displeased *(okanmuri)*; cheerful.

MASU. Also called *shikkake masu* and *kirimasu,* these are the square, wood-partitioned boxes in the pit *(doma*)* of old Kabuki theatres. In April 1766, the Nakamura-za* began to reserve seats by stretching a rope across the *doma* as a partitioning device. When the new Ichimura-za* and Nakamura-za were built in August 1772, they used wood partitions called *masu* to set up box seating. The original measurements were four feet eight inches by five feet, and one box could seat seven people. Later, the *masu* gradually were reduced in size. Finally, they were down to three feet square and could seat four persons. After the great earthquake of 1923 all theatres were built with Western-style seating, and the *masu* were abolished. (*See also* THEATRE ARCHITECTURE.)

MATSUBAME MONO (or KYŌGEN). A dance play performed on a stage modeled after that of the Nō theatre, which has a pine tree painted on the panels at the rear, an *agemaku** or "lift-curtain" for entrances from stage right, and an *okubyō guchi** or "coward's door" on stage left. The word *matsubame* is used to refer to the back and side walls of these sets.

The content of a *matsubame mono* also derives primarily from Nō or Kyōgen plays. Another name for these works is *nō torimono* ("plays taken from the Nō"). The first of such works was performed by Ichikawa Danjūrō VII* in March 1840; it was the still very popular *Kanjinchō**. (*See also* PLAY CATEGORIES.)

MATSUMOTO KŌSHIRŌ I. 1674-1730. A star actor in Edo along with Ichikawa Danjūrō II* during the late seventeenth and early eighteenth centuries. He excelled in *aragoto**, the bravura style. Danjūrō IV* and V* held the names of Kōshirō II and III, respectively, before taking the former names.

IV. 1737-1802. Born in Kyoto, he became a pupil of Danjūrō IV* in 1757 and took the name of Kōshirō IV in 1772. He was an excellent player of the soft, romantic, *wagoto** style and also excelled in *jitsugoto* (*see also* TACHIYAKU) roles.

V. 1764-1838. Son of Kōshirō IV. After becoming Kōshirō V in 1801, he starred in Japan's three great cities (Edo, Kyoto, and Osaka) for a third of a century. His piercing eyes and high-bridged nose suited him for villain roles of the *jitsuaku* (*see also* KATAKIYAKU) variety. His performance techniques are still preserved in the *kata**, or formal acting patterns, that he left behind. He was nicknamed Hanataka ("High Nose") Kōshirō.

VI. 1812-1849. Son of Kōshirō V. Considered little more than mediocre, this actor took his name in 1844. He died young.

VII. 1870-1949. Adopted son of the Fujima Kan'emon dance family, (*see also* FUJIMA RYŪ), he later became a disciple of Ichikawa Danjūrō IX* and, in 1911, went from the name of Ichikawa Komazō to Kōshirō VII. He had distinguished himself by this time and was a popular favorite. Kōshirō VII was a worthy successor of Danjūrō's style and brought a quality of composure and dignity to his acting of leading male roles. He also was superb as a dancer, especially in the role of Benkei in *Kanjinchō**, which he performed over sixteen hundred times during his career. He had a progressive spirit, and he enacted the opera *Roei no Yume* in 1905, formed the New Kabuki Study Association (Shin Kabuki Kenkyū Kai), and attempted performances of new plays and translations. His eldest son was Danjūrō XI*, and his second son succeeded to the name of Kōshirō VIII. His third son is the popular star named Onoe Shōroku II*.

VIII, *yago** Kōraiya. 1910- . He debuted in January 1926 as Matsumoto Junzō and, beginning in 1929, studied with Nakamura Kichiemon I*, whose influence on him was great. In 1931 he took the name of Ichikawa Somegorō V and achieved his present name in 1949. In 1961 he took his family and followers with him and switched from the Shōchiku* production company to the Tōhō*, forming the Tōhō Kabuki troupe, one of the most controversial events in postwar Kabuki. Offering a steady and dignified style, Kōshirō is splendid in the roles of honest merchants in domestic dramas and leading men in the history plays, as was Kichiemon. He also shows a profound understanding in his acting of new plays. Ichikawa Somegorō VI* is his eldest son, and his second son is the well-known Nakamura Kichiemon II*.

MATSUMOTO RYŪ. A school of Japanese dance in which the acting family of Matsumoto Kōshirō* specializes. There have been eight generations of actors with this name. The line has had close connections with the Ichikawa Danjūrō family, as Kōshirō II and III later became Danjūrō IV* and V*, respectively. Also Kōshirō VII was a disciple of Danjūrō IX* and fathered the actor who became Danjūrō XI. Kōshirō VII also headed the Fujima* school of dance and was a master dancer. Establishing the traditions of the Matsumoto family style as a school with himself as the leader, he passed these traditions on to his son Junjirō, who later became Kōshirō VIII*.

MATURE MALE KABUKI. Known as *yarō kabuki*, this was the form that survived when *wakashu kabuki* (young men's Kabuki*) was prohibited in 1652. All actors had to shave their attractive forelocks and rely more on acting talent than on sex appeal to earn a living. Plays and acting became more complex and realistic as a result. The name comes from the shaved-head style *(yarō atama)* that actors were forced to wear. (*See also* MURASAKI BŌSHI.)

MAWARI. The striking of the *hyōshigi** clappers before a play begins as a warning to the actors and stagehands to get ready. The *kyōgen kata** first strikes the *hyōshigi* twice in front of the backstage manager's room (*see also* TODORI) and then walks around the stage area, striking the clappers in single beats. The word means "going around."

MAWARI BUTAI. *See* REVOLVING STAGE.

MAYAMA SEIKA. 1878-1948. A modern playwright who, at first, studied under Oguri Fūyō and was recognized as a naturalistic novelist. Later, as a dramatist of history plays in the *shin kabuki** ("New Kabuki") style, he wrote such plays as *Genroku Chūshingura**, *Shōgun Edo o Saru**, and other dignified and serious works that constitute profound psychological character studies. He became leader of the modern literary and theatrical world on the strength of these creations. He was a respected scholar of the Genroku period (1688-1703) novelist named Ibara Saikaku (1642-1693). Akira was his private name.

MAYU TSUBUSHI. "Eyebrow remover," a material to obliterate the eyebrows *(mayu)* so that makeup can be applied over them. *Taihaku**, a compressed oil with refined sugar in it, is kneaded together, producing a flesh color that is applied to the eyebrows. *Oshiroi** (the white makeup used as a base for most roles) is put on over this. Then, eyebrows appropriate to the role are drawn on.

MEBARI. "Eye line"; the manner of emphasizing the size of the eyes by drawing an eye line to make them bigger and more attractive. Male-role actors normally draw the eye line with black ink or a mixture of black and red. Female impersonators used red and beautify the eyes by drawing a line from the inner corners to the outer.

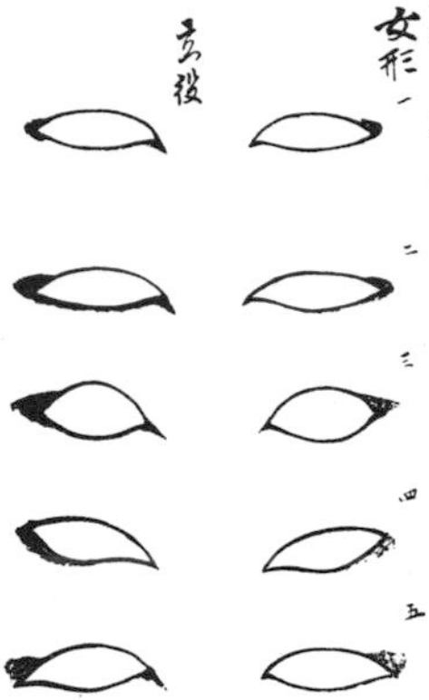

*Mebari**, or eye-line, styles. Those on the left are male styles; those on the right are female. From Kojima, ed., *Kao no Tsukurikata*.

MEGANE. "Spectacles"; a wig whose topknot is rolled into two circles, resembling a pair of eyeglasses. It is used by clerks and clownish characters in the domestic plays. Tohachi in *Yowa Nasake Ukina no Yokogushi** is an example.

MEIBOKU SENDAI HAGI. Nagawa Kamesuke* (Kabuki version). Also called *Sendai Hagi, Jidaimono**. Kabuki and *jōruri**. Five acts. First Kabuki performance: April 1777; Naka no Shibai, Osaka. First puppet performance: January 1785; Yuki-za, Edo. *Date Kurabe Okuni Kabuki* was first performed in July 1778; Nakamura-za*, Edo.

There are similarly titled plays in both Kabuki and the puppet theatre depicting the quarrels of the Date clan. The work performed today consists of scenes from these plays and from Sakurada Jisuke I's* *Date Kurabe Okuni Kabuki*, arranged as follows: *Hanamizu Bashi, Take no Ma, Goten, Yukashita, Taiketsu,* and *Ninjō*. Actors in the first production were Nakamura

Utaemon I*, Yamanaka Bunshichi, Asai Tamejūrō, Nakamura Jirōsō, Kiriwara Monji, Sawamura Sōjūrō III*, Matsumoto Jirosō, Yamanaka Tōsuke, and others. Nikki Danjō and his allies are plotting the overthrow of the Date clan, and a scheme is laid to ensnare Masaoka, the nurse of the young lord Tsurikyō. Masaoka, afraid that her young charge's food will be poisoned, says that he is ill and confined to bed; she prepares his food with her own hands and feeds it to him. Sakae Gozen, wife of the governor-general of Kamakura (who is a conspirator of Nikki), arrives as an envoy; together with Yashio Gozen, Nikki's sister, she pays a visit to the "sick" child and presents him with a box of cakes from the governor-general. Masaoka's son Senmatsu dashes in and eats one of the cakes. Yashio, seeing the poison go to work, kills him with her dagger. Because Masaoka has remained unflinching at the last moments of her own son, Sakae Gozen believes that Masaoka has switched the children around and thinks that the nurse can now be trusted; she gives her a list of the conspirators and reveals the evil plot to her. After the party has left, Masaoka embraces the dead child and weeps. She is attacked by Yashio, who was secretly lurking in the room. Although she kills Yashio, a huge rat appears and, grabbing the list of conspirators in his teeth, escapes. The retainer Arajishi Otokonosuke, hiding in the cellar, inflicts a blow of his iron fan upon the rat's brow. Using magic, the rat takes the form of Nikki Danjō and vanishes.

Because of a charge by Watanabe Geki, a loyal samurai, Geki and Nikki become the litigants in a court trial. Nikki's friend, the judge Yamana Sōzen, puts Geki's side at a disadvantage, but another judge, Hosokawa Katsumoto, appears and reveals Nikki's misdeeds; the scene ends in victory for Geki and his allies. The malicious Nikki stabs Geki, but eventually is killed.

The Bamboo Room scene *(Take no Ma)* and the palace scene *(Goten)* are performed in a style based on the puppet theatre. Masaoka's suffering, especially her heroic fortitude when her son dies before her eyes, and the mourning over his death when her motherly love overwhelms her are masterfully drawn. The part represents a true test of the female impersonator's skill. The cellar scene *(Yukashita)* is presented in Kabuki's *aragoto** style; Otokonosuke wears *kumadori** stylized makeup, and there is a splendid contrast between his dynamic movements and the restrained movements of Nikki Danjō, the *jitsuaku* role (*see also* KATAKIYAKU).

MEIDO NO HIKYAKU. Chikamatsu Monzaemon*. Also called *Koi Bikyaku Yamato Orai, Umegawa Chūbei*. English title: *The Courier for Hell* (Keene). *Sewamono**. *Jōruri**. Three acts. March 1711. Takemoto-za, Osaka.

Chūbei, adopted son of the proprietor of the Kame-ya courier service, is in love with a Shinmachi district courtesan, Umegawa. He has used money that he borrowed from his friend Hachiemon to make payment toward the price of redeeming the courtesan from her bond. Hachiemon purposely speaks ill of Chūbei, hoping to make him stop coming to the pleasure quarters. Unable to bear Hachiemon's abusive language any longer, Chūbei breaks the seal on a packet of exchange money with which he has been entrusted, redeems Umegawa, and returns with her to his native village. There, at Ninokuchi, the two meet surreptitiously with his father, Magoemon, and run away again. Ultimately, they are captured.

The climax occurs in the second act, when the seal on the packet is broken. This act is often performed in Kabuki in a version called *Koi Bikyaku Yamato Orai*, in which Hachiemon is depicted as an evil and antagonistic character. Critics consider Chikamatsu's original characters to have been superficial.

MEIJI-ZA. A theatre located at Chūo-ku, Nihonbashi, Hama-chō, Tokyo. Its ancestor was the Koshō-za, opened in Hisamatsu-chō in the same district in April 1873. It later was renamed the Hisamatsu-za and the Chitose-za after fires and other vicissitudes. It took its present name in November 1893 after being rebuilt and opened anew. Ichikawa Sadanji I* and his son Sadanji II* became its leaders and raised it to a position rivaling the Kabuki-za*. In 1912 a Shinpa actor (Shinpa is a modern form of theatre that evolved from Kabuki in the late nineteenth century), Ii Yōhō (1871-1932), took over the management, but the theatre fell into the hands of the Shōchiku* conglomerate in 1919. It has passed through earthquake and war. In November 1950 it became an independent theatre and opened as the Meiji-za Joint Stock Company. It burned down in 1957, but was rebuilt by the following March and soon was back in business. (*See also* THEATRE MANAGEMENT.)

MEIKŌ KAKIEMON. Enomoto Torahiko*. *Shin kabuki**. Three acts. October 1912. Kabuki-za*, Tokyo.

The Arita potter Kakiemon has labored hard to produce a red-patterned type of pottery. The pottery seller Aritaya Gohei exploits Kakiemon and saves a fortune by doing so. His son Heisaburō is in love with the potter's elder daughter, Ōtsu, who returns his affections. Gohei, in order to further his own prestige, refuses to allow his son to marry the girl, who dies of heartbreak. Kakiemon cuts off all his contacts with Gohei. This results in his being persecuted in every way; however, with the cooperation of his younger daughter, Otane, and his pupil, Kurisaku, he is successful in the manufacture of red-patterned pottery. Heisaburō is deeply grieved by his father's behavior. When a conflagration breaks out, he kills himself. On the basis of his success, Kakiemon pays off his old score against Gohei.

The work shows the power of money and the unbendable character of a determined man. It is an adaptation of Samuel Smiles's *Self-Help*, though it succeeds as an original piece of theatre.

MEKURA NAGAYA UME GA KAGATOBI. Kawatake Mokuami*. Also called *Kagatobi*. *Sewamono**. Kabuki. Seven acts. March 1886. Chitose-za, Tokyo.

Against the background of a quarrel between the firemen of a samurai lord *(daimyō)* and those of the town, the play tells the story of the masseur Dōgen. The plot concerning the masseur is the part mainly performed today. Included in the first cast were Onoe Kikugorō V*, Ichikawa Kuzō (later Danzō VII*), and Bandō Kakitsu.

Dōgen kills and robs the farmer Tajiemon on an embankment near Ochanomizu. Tajiemon's sister, Osetsu, is married to Dōgen and lives with him and their daughter, Oasa. Seeing Dōgen treat her mother poorly, Oasa shows Dōgen the five *ryō* that she has received from her employer, Iseya. This gives the conniving Dōgen an idea for extorting money from Iseya. During the blackmail attempt at Iseya's shop, the fireman Matsuzō appears. Suspecting Dōgen of having killed Tajiemon, he produces a tobacco pouch that Dōgen dropped at Ochanomizu. The sight of this frightens Dōgen, and he gives up his scheme and returns empty-handed. Soon after, a dog digs up a blood-stained kimono from under Dōgen's house; this provides undeniable proof of his guilt. He is captured before the Red Gate of Hongo.

The chastisement of Oasa in Dogen's home, the blackmail, and the capture are well written and are handled in the playwright's superb flowing emotional rhythm. There are two pantomime, or *danmari**, scenes in the play—the murder at Ochanomizu and the capture before the Red Gate.

MEN O TSUKAMU. "To grasp a face"; meaning a face-to-face confrontation. Also called *tsura o tsukamu.*

MERI. Short for *meriyasu**, a type of *geza** music. Used in the sense of a quiet, melancholy attitude.

MERIHARI. A Kabuki vocal technique for producing power and flexibility of tone. *Meri* refers to the relaxed low tones and *hari* to the higher tones. Kabuki speech is produced from an alternation of *meri* and *hari.*

MERIYASU. A brief piece of *nagauta** music performed in the *geza** room during scenes with no dialogue, it accentuates the scene's emotional mood. Most *meriyasu* tunes are steeped in tranquility and sung by a single person accompanied by a *shamisen**. On rare instances two voices may be heard. When dialogue is spoken, the *shamisen* alone accompanies the spoken portion, followed by the continuation of the *meriyasu* singing. *Meriyasu* is used in love scenes, scenes of hair-combing *(kamisuki*)* scenes in which farewell notes are written, and scenes of melancholy, sorrow, and suicide.

The word's derivation is unclear. Some hold that it derives from the name of a Kyoto samurai, Meri Yasuji, while others claim that it comes from an expression for the feeling of melancholy or gloom: *meiiriyasui.* Still others say that the word is taken from the name of a knit fabric worn as tights in Kabuki. Since this *meriyasu* material is flexible, the argument goes, the word could easily mean a musical performance that also was flexible.

MICHIYUKI MONO. "Road-going"; a kind of dance, also called *keigoto**. Many *michiyuki* pieces present a pair of lovers on their way to the place where they will commit or attempt to commit double suicide *(shinjū)*; while going to their destination, they describe the beauty of the scenery in a way that produces a feeling of great pathos. The word *michiyuki* comes from a dramatic technique in the Nō plays, in which the term describes a conventionalized journey. After the *michiyuki* was given a new form in Chikamatsu Monzaemon's* puppet play *Sonezaki Shinjū**, it became obligatory to include such a scene in later puppet plays. The scene on Mount Yoshino in *Yoshitsune Senbon Zakura** and Act VIII in *Kanadehon Chūshingura** are good examples, although the double suicide scene is altered in these works to encompass different situations. Kabuki adopted such scenes for its original plays, too, beginning with those accompanied by the musical styles of *itchū bushi** and *tosa bushi* in the Genroku era (1688-1703); many later examples are backed by *tokiwazu**, *kiyomoto**, and *tomimoto** music. These scenes formed an important part of a day's performance. (*See also* SHOSAGOTO; DANCE.)

MIDORI. The practice of arranging a program made up of separate scenes and acts from long plays along with short plays. The opposite is a program consisting of a full-length play* *(tōshi kyōgen)*.

MIE. A picturesque and striking pose taken by an actor at a climactic moment in a play in order to make a powerful impression on the audience. The movements made in assuming the pose culminate in a rhythmic snapping of the head, as the actor produces a glaring expression with his eyes. Normally, wooden clappers *(tsuke*)* are struck and music is played as the actor makes his pose. These rhythmic devices act to strengthen the pose's effect.

The *mie* seen in the *aragoto** style of play and in the history play are on a grand scale, but those in the relatively realistic domestic play are fewer and more restrained. There may be one, two, or more actors performing *mie* simultaneously, and there is a great variety of types.

emen no mie. "Picture *mie*," an emphatic pose of picturesque beauty. A number of characters strike an impressive tableau as the curtain closes or as they rise on a stage trap.

Fudō no mie. A *mie* modeled after Lord Fudō, the Buddhist deity who stands guard at the gates of Hell. The actor stands or sits erect, holding a sword at his side with the point directed straight upwards. In his other hand he grasps a Buddhist rosary.

Genroku mie. Named for a period in Japanese history (1688-1703), this is a pose that displays great power and is used in *aragoto* plays. The actor takes an impressive step with his left foot, grabs his sword with his left hand, and holds his right hand behind and above him in a fist. It is used by Umeomaru

The *hashira maki no mie in Narukami**. Narukami, Onoe Shōroku II*. *Courtesy of Waseda University Tsubouchi Engeki Hakubutsukan (Tsubouchi Memorial Theatre Museum).*

in the *Kuruma Biki* scene of *Sugawara Denju Tenarai Kagami** and by Gongorō in *Shibaraku**.

hashira maki no mie. A "pillar-wrapping *mie*" that occurs in such works as *aragoto* plays and *danmari** pantomimes. Both of the actor's hands grasp a pillar or tree while one foot is wrapped around it. According to the convention, only the chief actor can perform such a *mie*. Priest Narukami in *Narukami** performs this exciting pose.

hippari no mie. A "pulling *mie*"; two characters pose as if pulling at each other with their eyes. It resembles the *emen no mie*. Its essential spirit is to represent the hostile feeling between two characters. Sometimes it is merely a tableau *mie* in which the actors involved have different focus points for their eyes, as in the final moments of *Terakoya* (an act of *Sugawara Denju Tenarai Kagami*).

ishinage no mie. The "stone-throwing *mie*"; with the legs slightly apart, the body is turned somewhat to the side and the right hand held high as if throwing a stone. A famous example is enacted by Benkei in *Kanjinchō**.

soku mie. Here the feet touch at the heels, and the actor stands erect. Also called *soku ni tatsu mie*.

tenchijin no mie. Three characters pose in a *mie*, one in a high position, one in a middle position, and one in a low position; thus the term, which means "heaven, earth, and man." In *Kanjinchō*, Benkei, Togashi, and Yoshitsune strike this *mie* just before the reading of the subscription list.

tenchi no mie. The "heaven and earth *mie*"; two actors pose, one in an elevated position, as on a platform, and the other in a lower position. Hisayoshi and Goemon in *Sanmon Gosan no Kiri** perform this *mie*.

MIGAWARI MONO. Plays in which character substitutions are enacted as plot ingredients. Such substitutions usually require one character to die in place of another, the intent being to deceive an enemy about the victim's identity. Often the climax is in the form of a head inspection scene *(kubi jikken*)*. Examples are *Ichinotani Futaba Gunki** and *Sugawara Denju Tenarai Kagami**.

MIGAWARI ZAZEN. Okamura Shikō*. English title: *The Zen Substitute* (Brandon); *Migawari Zazen* (Richie and Watanabe). *Shosagoto**. *Tokiwazu** and *nagauta**. March 1910. Ichimura-za*, Tokyo.

A Kabuki dance version of the Kyōgen play called *Hanako*, done in *matsubame mono** style.

In order to visit his paramour, Hanako, Lord Yamakage Ukyō attempts to deceive his shrewish wife, Tamanoi. Saying that he is going to perform Zen meditation, he puts Tarō Kaja, a servant, in his place and leaves. During his absence, Tamanoi discovers the ruse and, covering her head and shoulders, takes the servant's place in the Zen position. Ukyō returns home in high

An example of a *hippari no mie* pose in *Ōmi Genji Senjin Yakata**. Notice how effectively the long, trailing *hakama** trousers contribute to the composition of the pose. Wada Hyoe (left), Onoe Shōroku II*; Moritsuna, Matsumoto Kōshirō VIII*. *Courtesy of Waseda University Tsubouchi Engeki Hakubutsukan (Tsubouchi Memorial Theatre Museum).*

Benkei performs the *ishinage no mie* in *Kanjinchō**. Benkei, Matsumoto Kōshirō VIII*. *Courtesy of Waseda University Tsubouchi Engeki Hakubutsukan (Tsubouchi Memorial Theatre Museum).*

spirits. He drunkenly recounts the tale of his pleasures to Tamanoi, thinking she is Tarō. Tamanoi, no longer able to contain her anger, explodes.

The humor of the piece really begins with Ukyō's second entrance, when he fails to recognize his wife. *Migawari Zazen* rose to fame as a dance play when it was performed by the actors Onoe Kikugorō VI* and Bandō Mitsugorō VII*.

MIHAKARAI. "On one's own judgment." When no special requests are made pertaining to costumes, wigs, or props, the men in charge arrange such items according to their own discretion. (*See also* ATSURAE.)

MIKIRI. Flats and cutouts *(kiridashi*)* placed at the rear and sides of the stage to mask the areas behind from the audience's view. When the audience can see past the scenery to the backstage areas, it is called *mikirareru* ("to be able to see all"). (*See also* KAGAMI; HARIMONO.)

MIMASUYA HYŌGO. 1660-1704. The pen name of Ichikawa Danjūrō I*, the representative actor of Edo Kabuki who is known as the founder of the bravura acting style called *aragoto**; he also wrote more than fifty plays in which he himself performed. He wrote the first versions of the *kabuki jūhachiban** plays entitled *Fuwa, Narukami**, and *Shibaraku**. Sixteen of his plays are extant, representative works including *Sankai Nagoya, Tsuwamono Kongen Soga, Genbei Kaminari Denki, Isshin Gokai no Tama, Keisei Ōshōkun,* and *Hoshiai jūnidan.* His distinctive style was based on *aragoto*'s vivid theatrics and dreamlike atmosphere; the works also have a strong sense of the tragic about them.

MINAMI-ZA. A theatre located at Higashiyama-ku, Shijō, Kyoto. It was one of the seven theatres in its district that were given permisson to produce plays in the Genma era (1615-23). The Shōchiku* company purchased it in 1906, it was rebuilt in 1919 and is standing today. It is a concrete structure with a steel frame and a gabled roof; the exterior is seasoned with the Momoyama period (1568-1615) style of architecture. It is Kyoto's one and only Kabuki theatre; every December the popularly termed *miyako no kaomise* ("capital city face-showing performance"—Kyoto was once Japan's capital) is held here. (*See also* THEATRE MANAGEMENT.)

MINARAI SAKUSHA. A playwright-in-training during the Edo era; his duties were to aid the main playwrights at rehearsals. He copied out the *kakinuki**, or actors' parts, for the actors and brought the proper props and costumes to their homes. Among his opening-day duties was taking notes on each actor's variations. He was kept busy learning everything that a playwright should know about theatrical production. When no performances were scheduled, he did odd jobs for the chief playwright *(tate sakusha*)* and second-rank playwright *(nimaime sakusha*)*. (*See also* PLAYWRIGHTS' RANKS.)

MINO. Short for *minoge*, the hairline. It is made by plaiting hair like a straw raincoat *(mino)* and then attaching it to the copper base *(diagane)*. The top layer of hair and the hairline, called *keshō mino*, are arranged from hair that is finely and beautifully bound together. It is used in the older, more stylized history plays like *Shibaraku** and the *Kuruma Biki* scene of *Sugawara Denju Tenarai Kagami**, as well as for the role of Kuzu no Ha in *Ashiya Dōman Ōuchi Kagami**. The use of *habutae** silk is a more realistic method of depicting the hairline and has replaced the *mino* in most plays. In the case of *habutae* wigs, the hairs are sewn individually onto the *habutae* as if they grew there, creating a more realistic effect. (*See also* WIGS.)

MINOWA NO SHINJŪ. Okamoto Kidō*. *Shin kabuki**. September 1911. Meiji-za*, Tokyo.

Because Fujieda Geki spends too much time with the Yoshiwara district courtesan Ayae, he is dismissed from his position and finds himself pressed for money. Ayae steals out of the pleasure quarters and hides in the Minowa home of Geki's nurse. There is a rigorous inquiry made after her. When Geki's uncle urges his death, the two lovers are driven into a corner. Finally, they commit suicide on the day of the Bon Festival (July 13).

Geki's principle of living for love made a great impression on contemporary youths, who praised the work highly.

MISONO-ZA. A theatre located in Nagoya's Naka-ku district; its ancestor, the Nagoya Gekijō, was built on the same site in May 1897. The theatre was renovated in 1935, but was destroyed during the war in March 1945. Rebuilt in October 1947, it was renamed the Misono-za. The building has two basement floors and eight above-ground floors; the first through fifth stories contain a theatre, but other stories have a bowling alley, a hall for general rentals, parking facilities, and the like. The Misono-za is traditionally the focal point of Nagoya's theatrical culture. (*See also* THEATRE MANAGEMENT.)

MISUUCHI. "Within the enclosure"; the playing of music from within the *geza** room, as opposed to the onstage appearance of the musicians. *(See also* DEGATARI; DEBAYASHI).

MITATEME. Also called *mitsume* and *mitatsume*, this is the third piece on a daily Edo period program; it followed the *futatateme**. The *mitateme* was the first act of the main play. It corresponded in Edo to what was called later the *jomaku**, or "curtain raiser." In Kamigata it equaled the *kuchiake*. *Mitateme* were written by the lower-ranking playwrights called *sanmaime** (not to be confused with the class of actors called by the same term; *see also* PLAYWRIGHTS' RANKS).

MITSU NINGYŌ. Sakurada Jisuke III*. Also called *Sono Sugata Hana no Utsushie*. *Shosagoto**. *Tokiwazu**. September 1819. Kawarazaki-za, Edo.

A dance piece set in Yoshiwara's Nakanochō Street. It shows a bold samurai dancing a tale of the licensed quarters, a footman *(yakko)* demonstrating in dance the characteristic *yakko* style of movements, and a geisha who mimes a lamentation* *(kudoki)*.

The work is devised to present the respective talents and looks of three actors evenly matched in skill and popularity. Its first three stars were Bandō Mitsugorō III*, Nakamura Utaemon III*, and Iwai Hanshirō V*.

MIURA NO ŌSUKE KŌBAI TAZUNA. Hasegawa Senshi, Matsuda Bunkodō. Also called *Kajiwara Heizā Homare no Ishikiri, Ishikiri Kajiwara. Jidaimono**. *Jōruri**. Five acts. February 1730. Takemoto-za, Osaka.

This work, set against the background of Yoritomo's raising of troops, depicts such historical personages as Miura Ōsuke, Hatakeyama Shigetada, and Kajiwara Kagetoko. Kabuki produced its version in August 1730 at Kado no Shibai. Edo's first production was much later, at the Kiri-za in 1795.

In order to procure 300 *ryō* in war funds, Manata Bunzō asks his betrothed, Kozue, to become a courtesan. Kozue's father, Rokurōdayū, comes to the temple to sell a famous sword in his possession to the Heike clan's samurai Ōba Saburō. Ōba asks Kajiwara, whom he encounters just then, for his opinion of the sword; it is proposed that two prisoners be lain one on top of the other and executed at one blow by Kajiwara with the sword, to test its power. Only one prisoner, however, is available. Rokurōdayū offers to substitute himself for the missing prisoner. Kajiwara recognizes the sword's value, and not wishing Ōba to buy it, purposely slays only the prisoner. Since only one body is sliced through, Ōba sneers derisively and leaves. Afterwards, Kajiwara reveals to the father and daughter that he secretly sides with the Genji clan and, cutting through the stone water basin before the shrine, proves the authenticity of the famous sword and asks to buy it.

The play's three main passages occur when Kajiwara first looks at the sword and realizes that it is famous, when the sword is tried on the two living bodies, and when the sword cuts through the stone basin. Kajiwara is considered one of the more gallant of Kabuki heroes. The villanous roles of the Ōba brothers, the "young lady" *(wakaonnagata)* role of Kozue, the "old-man" *(oyajigata*)* role of Rokurōdayū, and the comical prisoner supply the play with abundant variety.

Kajiwara prepares to test his blade in *Miura no Ōsuke Kōbai Tazuna**. Kajiwara, Nakamura Kanzaburō XVII*.

MIYACHI SHIBAI. Small theatres *(koshibai*)* that received special permission to produce plays for a brief period on the grounds of shrines and temples. In 1661 five *koshibai* were permitted to play on booth stages *(koya)* for 100 days, an event called a "100-day performance" *(hyaku nichi shibai).* These small theatres possessed no drum tower *(yagura*)* like the large government-licensed theatres nor were they allowed to use the Kabuki traveler curtain *(hiki maku*).* Instead, they used a drop curtain *(donchō; see also* DONCHŌ YAKUSHA*); thus, *koshibai* came to be called *donchō shibai* (the word *shibai* can mean "theatre" or "play" or may be used generically to refer to the Kabuki).

MIYAKO-ZA. A theatre that operated as an alternative *(hikae yagura*)* for the Nakamura-za* in the Edo period.

MIYORI. A topknot often worn in samurai roles. Also called *ōichō.* It is seen on Yuranosuke in *Kanadehon Chūshingura**, Mitsugi in the Futami Beach scene of *Ise Ondo Koi no Netaba**, and Geki in *Meiboku Sendai Hagi**.

MIZUGOROMO. A costume originally used in the Nō theatre for priests, fishermen, and woodcutters and used for similar characters in Kabuki. It has broad sleeves, is solid-colored or striped, and is either black or brown. Benkei in *Funa Benkei** wears it.

MIZUHIKI. A long, narrow, horizontal border cloth hung above the stage at its downstage edge. Its sole purpose is to hide the scenic contrivance behind it. Another name for it is the *mizuhiki maku.* (*See also* ICHIMONJI.)

MIZUIRI. "In the water"; the immersion of a character in real water on stage. For example, there is a scene in *Sukeroku Yukari no Edo Zakura** in which Sukeroku conceals himself in a full barrel of water; even if performed in the winter, it is customary to use only cold water in this scene. There is a special wig called the *mizuiri* as well; it takes its name from the fact that its disheveled locks and lacquered sheen give it the appearance of having been soaked in water. Such a wig is worn by Sōshichi in *Hakata Kojorō Nami Makura**.

MIZU JŌSHI. "Watery tone"; when an actor's performance is very low-key. Also, when the *shamisen** music is played in low tones.

MIZUKI TATSUNOSUKE. 1673-1745. An actor of female roles during the Genroku period (1688-1703). In 1691, his role of Arima no Fuji in *Musume Oya no Katakiuchi,* performed at Kyoto's Miyako Mandayū-za, was a big success. The year 1695 saw him travel to Edo, where he played the same role in his farewell performance play, *Mizuki Tatsunosuke Tachiburu Mai.* His Edo debut, in which he performed a spear dance and a cat dance, gained him great popularity there. His return to Kyoto in 1697 was marked by his immense success in a dance piece requiring seven quick changes. This is said to be the origin of the later craze for quick-change dances. Dance was his specialty, and, as such, he was the representative *onnagata** of his time. Mizuki's popularity brought about a fashion in hats that was named after him. He founded a school of dance still in existence, the *Mizuki ryū.*

MIZU KYŌGEN. Plays employing real water on stage; they usually were performed during the summer months. (*See also* SUMMER PLAYS.)

MOCHIYAKU. "Possessed role," the role that one has been assigned in a play. Also, a role with which an actor is associated in the public's mind. For example, if *Honchō Nijūshikō** is going to be performed with Nakamura Utaemon VI*, his role will be that of Princess Yaegaki.

MODORI. "Return," a dramatic device by which a good person acts in a villainous way, but later in the play reveals his true nature, circumstances having forced him to behave as he has up to this point. Also, when a truly evil person experiences a complete change of heart and becomes good. Sakanaya no Gonta in *Yoshitsune Senbon Zakura** and Senō Jūrō in *Genpei Nunobiki no Taki** are good examples.

MODORI BASHI. Kawatake Mokuami*. Also called *Modori Kage Koi no Tsuno Moji. Shosagoto*. Tokiwazu**. October 1890. Kabuki-za*, Tokyo.

A play based on the Nō play of the same name; it deals with the legend of Watanabe no Tsuna, who cut off the arm of a female demon. *Ibaraki** is the dance play in which the demon is shown returning to retrieve her arm.

At Modori Bridge in Ichijō, Watanabe no Tsuna is asked by Oyuri, the daughter of a fan-paper folder, to accompany her to Gojō. Seeing her reflection in the water, he begins to doubt her. When he presses her with questions, she instantly reveals herself as a demon. Tsuna battles with the demon and manages to cut off its arm.

This dance drama, in which a woman changes into a demon and performs a spectacular battle, is full of highlights. It is included in the *shinko engeki jūshu** collection of Onoe family specialties. Onoe Kikugorō V* played the demon, and Ichikawa Sadanji I* played Tsuna in the premiere production. In contrast to other such Meiji dance plays, like *Ibaraki**, it is performed not in Nō style, but in pure Kabuki style, including a strong quality of the "living history*" *(katsureki)* technique.

MODORI KAGO. Sakurada Jisuke I*. Also called *Modori Kago Iro ni Aikata. Shosagoto*. Tokiwazu*.* November 1788. Nakamura-za*, Edo.

The palanquin bearers Nanpa no Jirosaku and Azuma no Yōshirō, who are bearing a palanquin with a courtesan's young handmaiden in it, stop to rest at Kyoto's Murasakino, and each dances his regional dance. Then they call the girl, who does a dance showing the visitors to the two famous pleasure quarters, Yoshiwara and Shimabara. The two men recognize each other as Ishikawa Goemon and Masashiba Hisayoshi, sworn enemies, and engage in a fight.

This number is the only remaining section of an annual "faceshowing" *(kaomise*)* work with a plot based on the medieval chronicle called the *Taikōki.* The full-length piece was called *Kara Sumō Hanaeda no Kata.* It is one of the most famous of *tokiwazu* pieces and preserves the old-style Kabuki flavor. Nakamura Nakazō I* played Jirosaku and Matsumoto Kōshirō IV* was Yoshirō in the first production. The handmaiden was Matsumoto Komesaburō.

MOGIRI. The inspection of admission tickets, the person in charge of this function, and the theatre entrance are all called by this term. It derives from the word for tearing a ticket in half *(mogiru).*

MOJIBARI. A scenic element consisting of flats, shoji, and sliding paper doors *(fusuma)* constructed of linen cloth, which the audience can see through. The shoji screens in the *Jūsshukō* scene of *Honchō Nijūshikō**, situated on stage left and right, are made in this way.

MOKKIN. A bamboo percussion instrument. (*See also* NARIMONO.)

MOKUGYŌ. A wooden percussion instrument. (*See also* NARIMONO; GEZA; MUSICAL ACCOMPANIMENT CHART.)

MOMIJIGARI. Kawatake Mokuami*. *Shosagoto*. Nagauta*, tokiwazu*,* and *gidayū**. October 1887. Shintomi-za, Tokyo.

A Kabuki dance version of the Nō play of the same name. It is included in the collection devised by Ichikawa Danjūrō IX*, the *shin kabuki jūhachiban**.

Taira Koremochi's party, out hunting deer on Mount Togakushi, encounters Princess Sarashina, who is giving a banquet in the heart of the mountains while on a maple-viewing expedition *(momijigari).* Koremochi is invited to join the feast; he drinks sake and falls asleep. The god of the mountain appears and warns him of imminent danger. Princess Sarashina manifests herself as a vicious demon and attacks Koremochi and his retainer, but Koremochi battles back and vanquishes her.

The trio of musical styles used—*nagauta, tokiwazu,* and *gidayū*—achieves grand scale for this piece. A dance by the mountain god is inserted in the work even though it is not found in the Nō. Other dances performed include the double fan dance by Sarashina (during the play's first half) and the choreographed battle of the second part. Each of the characters on stage has something to perform. *Momijigari* is representative of Meiji period dance plays. Written for Danjūrō IX (the demon), Ichikawa Sadanji I* (Koremochi), and Nakamura Shikan IV* (the god), it is rich in details influenced by the current mode of "living history*" plays.

MOMOHIKI. An undergarment worn by men.

MON. "Crests." (*See also* ACTORS' CRESTS.)

MONOGATARI. A narrative speech in which the hero recounts past events and his attitude toward them while acting out his words in mime. The technique is seen chiefly in history plays taken from the puppet theatre; the character who is speaking usually occupies a seat at center stage and, using a fan, accompanies his tale with dramatic movements. Such scenes make a powerful impression on audiences. The *monogatari* of Kumagai in the *Kumagai Jinya* scene of *Ichinotani Futaba Gunki** and of Sanemori in *Genpei Nunobiki no Taki** are well known; they display formalistic movements as the dialogue and music intertwine with one another. The battle report of the *gochūshin** is also a form of *monogatari.* (*See also* SERIFU.)

MONOLOGUE. Known as *dokuhaku.*

MORITA KANYA. A line of theatre managers *(zamoto*)* and actors. Kanya I (?-1679), the adopted son of the founder of Edo's Morita-za*, Morita Tarobei, became a theatre manager in 1661. Actors in the line included Kanya II (?-1734), who excelled at dance; Kanya III (?-1722), a player of leading male roles; Kanya IV (?-1743); Kanya VI (1724-1780), an *onnagata**; Kanya VIII (1759-1814), an actor of leading men roles; Kanya IX (?-1838); Kanya XI (Bandō Mitsugorō IV*), active in the late Edo period; Kanya XIII of the Taishō era (1912-26); and Kanya XIV, who was the last holder of the name. Kanya XII was known as the number-one person in the Meiji theatre world because of his innovative managerial policies.

XII. 1846-1897. In 1872 he took the decisive step of moving the Morita-za* from the theatre street (Saruwaka-machi*), in which it long had been located, to a spot in the heart of Tokyo. At the same time, he began the reform of theatre architecture and of the audience system; he created his new theatre in conformity with the new times, Japan being in the throes of an infatuation with the newly introduced culture of the West. In 1875 he renamed the

Kumagai enacts a vivid tale, using the technique called *monogatari**, in *Ichinotani Futaba Gunki**. Kumagai, Nakamura Kichiemon II.* *Courtesy of Waseda University Tsubouchi Engeki Hakubutsukan (Tsubouchi Memorial Theatre Museum).*

theatre the Shintomi-za and, with the first-class actors in his employ, established a golden epoch of Kabuki. During this time, he mixed with government officials, literary men, and scholars, exhibited all sorts of reform measures, and exerted himself in the advancement of the actor's status. The management of the Shintomi-za ran into difficulties around 1882, and Kanya broke with the theatre completely in 1894; he had had little luck during his last years. Besides being a producer, he was a pupil of Kawatake Mokuami* in playwriting and wrote plays under the name of Furukawa Shinsui.

XIII. 1885-1932. Third son of Kanya XII, he succeeded to the name in 1907. He specialized in the romantic acting of *wagoto** roles and willfully came to grips with new plays and translations. From 1914 to 1923, he took part in the new theatre movement as part of the experimental group known as the Bungei-za. He possessed old-fashioned looks and an excellent spirit of inquiry as well as abundant comprehension, making his a unique talent.

XIV. 1907-1975. He was adopted by Kanya XIII and debuted as Bandō Tamasaburō in 1914. In January 1926 he became Bandō Shūka, and he took the name of Kanya in July 1935. In 1932 he was active in "junior Kabuki," which he played a role in organizing. He acted mainly in young lover *(nimaime*)* roles, but had a broad range and could act all types of parts. Kanya was well versed in the styles of Kabuki movement and speech and was a precious asset. Tamasaburō V* is his adopted son, as is Shūka IV.

MORITA-ZA. A theatre founded in Edo's Kobiki-chō section in 1660 by Morita Tarobei. A year later the managership was shifted to Morita Kanya I*. Because of financial difficulties, the theatre developed an alternating management system *(hikae yagura*)* with the Kawarazaki-za in 1734 and maintained it until the Meiji era. Like other Edo playhouses, it was forced to move to Saruwaka-machi in 1843 as part of the government's reform measures. In 1856 the spelling of Morita was changed, with the character for "forest" *(mori)* replacing that for "keeper." When the Meiji period began, the great theatre manager *(zamoto*)* Morita Kanya XII* immediately decided to take advantage of the new liberal attitudes and move his theatre from the city's outskirts back into its heart, a move his competitors soon followed. His new playhouse opened in October 1872 in Shintomi-chō. Business problems, however, forced him to turn the theatre into a joint-stock corporation in 1875; the Morita-za was renamed the Shintomi-za. It burned down in 1876, but he had it rebuilt immediately with a sturdier method of construction and reopened it in April 1877. He soon made the theatre a showplace of Meiji Kabuki, presenting the best actors and productions of the day. The era was even called the Shintomi-za period. However, in August 1894 Kanya's financial problems caused him to withdraw from management. In 1909 the Shōchiku* corporation acquired the Shintomi-za. The theatre was destroyed in the earthquake of 1923 and was never rebuilt.

Ⓐ AKARI MADO
Ⓑ SAJIKI
Ⓒ HANAMICHI
Ⓓ GEZA
Ⓔ DOMA
Ⓕ OKURI MAKU
Ⓖ MASU
Ⓗ TSUKEUCHI
Ⓘ YUKA
Ⓙ KARI HANAMICHI
Ⓚ TAKA DOMA
Ⓛ SHIN TAKADOMA
Ⓜ SAJIKI

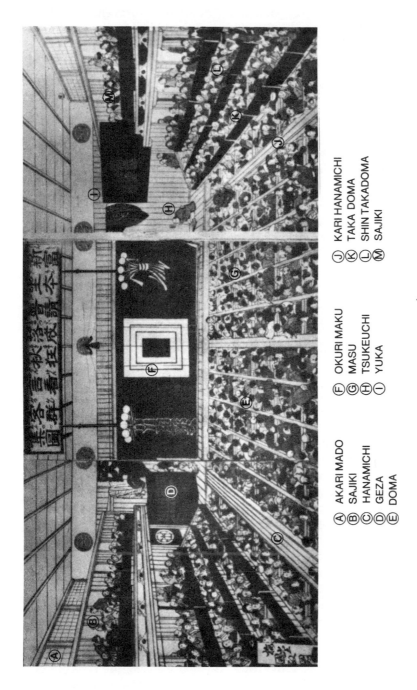

The interior of the Shintomi-za after its reconstruction in 1878. The size and proportions of the stage reveal Western influence. On the curtain are printed the *mon* or crest (*see also* ACTORS' CRESTS) and name of Ichikawa Danjūrō*. *Courtesy of Waseda University Tsubouchi Engeki Hakubutsukan (Tsubouchi Memorial Theatre Museum).*

MUKIMI GUMA. "Trough-shell *kuma*." Said to have been created by Ichikawa Danjūrō II*, this is a *kumadori** applied by drawing a softened line from below the inside corner of the eye, past the eye and upward at the eye's outer corner, continuing to the outer edge of the eyebrow. Its name presumably comes from its similarity to the shape of a shucked trough shell *(bakagai no mukimi)*. Characters wearing it include Sukeroku in *Sukeroku Yukari no Edo Zakura**, Gorō in *Soga no Taimen**, and Sakuramaru in the *Kuruma Biki* scene of *Sugawara Denju Tenarai Kagami**.

MUKŌ. "Yonder"; the curtained entranceway *(agemaku*)* at the end of the *hanamichi**, as viewed from the stage.

MURASAKI BŌSHI. An accessory worn on the occasion of an actor's taking a new name. It is a purple crepe band worn on the wig by the *onnagata**, who, in the past, always wore the *murasaki bōshi* on their foreheads when participating in ceremonial occasions. When young actors were forced to shave their foreheads as a prerequisite for Kabuki's survival—in the period of *yarō*, or mature male Kabuki*—they put a fashionable man's silk band *(yarō bōshi)* on their heads in order to continue looking sexually attractive. In later years the practice of wearing wigs made the *yarō bōshi* unnecessary, but the custom of wearing a purple piece of silk on the forelock continued on special occasions. (*See also* WIGS.)

MURDER SCENES. Scenes of murder and the style in which they are performed are called *koroshiba*. Their performance has developed in a distinctive way. A kind of scene called *teoi goto* ("wounded scene") was originated during the Genroku era (1688-1703); in these the actor would perform as if seriously wounded. Such scenes were transmitted through the history plays dealing with revenge* *(adauchi kyōgen)* and samurai family disputes *(oie kyōgen*)*. For example, in the scene in *Katakiuchi Tengajaya Mura** in which the would-be avenger is killed, the acting stresses the villain's cruelty as he carries out a gruesome and pathetic murder. Many murder scenes occur in the domestic plays. They often revolve around acts of vengeance following an *enkiri* scene of forced separation*, as in *Godairiki Koi no Fūjime**, *Ise Ondo Koi no Netaba**, and *Kagotsurube Sato no Eizame**. During the early nineteenth century, realistic elements were added to these scenes, and slimy stage blood and real water came into use. Despite the increased sense of brutality, the performance as a whole did not lose its stylized Kabuki quality nor was the use of music and heightened acting ignored.

MUSHIRI. A wig that has bear fur on the crown, signifying that the character has been letting his hair grow there. It is worn by masterless samurai and romantic scoundrels such as Yosa in *Yowa Nasake Ukina no Yogogushi**, Gonta in *Yoshitsune Senbon Zakura**, and Yoemon in *Kasane**.

MUSIC. Underlying almost all Kabuki performance is a musical background of one sort or another. The acting depends on this background to achieve its effects of rhythm and form. There are several distinct styles of Kabuki music, each aiding the actor in its own way. Offstage "effect music" produces both literal and stylized sound effects as well as background mood music. This music comes from behind a screened window, downstage right. The room behind the window is called the *geza**, and music originating here is called *geza ongaku ("geza* music"). *Geza* music utilizes a wide assortment of percussion instruments and several string and wind instruments, occasionally combined with singing, choral or solo. (*See also* AIKATA; AINOTE.)

Other musical forms are dependent on vocal and string accompaniment, the principal instrument being the *shamisen**. These musical types normally provide a narrative accompaniment to the action and are collectively known as *jōruri**. The four major types are *nagauta**, *tokiwazu**, *kiyomoto**, and *tomimoto**. *Jōruri* musicians frequently appear on stage, formally seated in rows on long platforms, dressed in the formal samurai style of garb called *kamishimo**. (*See also* DEGATARI; DEBAYASHI; NARIMONO.)

Borrowed and adapted from the puppet theatre is the unique form of chanted accompaniment called *gidayū bushi**; it also is simply called *jōruri*, although this usage implies both its function as narrative music and its derivation in puppet-theatre performance. (*See also* CHOBO; YUKA.)

MUSICIANS. Called *hayashigata* or *narimonoshi*. Each theatre usually has its own company of musicians. They belong to a number of schools, such as the Umeya, the Tanaka, the Mochizuki, the Fukahara, and so on.

MUSUBU. "To tie together or link"; a term meaning the same as *doron**—that is, the disappearance of an actor in the midst of a production. It derives from the sorcerer's trick of making himself invisible by linking the fingers of both hands in a shape resembling the Chinese character for the number nine.

MUSUKO. Osanai Kaoru. *Shin kabuki**. One act. March 1923. Teikoku Gekijō*, Tokyo.

This is an adaptation of Harold Chapin's *Augustus in Search of a Father*, but the piece is, for all intents and purposes, an original creation, having beautifully assimilated the Chapin story.

Some time past midnight, during a heavy snowfall, a police officer comes to the hut of the old fire watcher for a chat. Passing him as he leaves is the old man's son, Kinjirō, who had run away from home nine years earlier after committing a crime. He has come to visit his father. The father does not recognize the son. Firmly believing his son to have led an admirable life, he tells his life story to the visitor. The policeman returns and Kinjirō runs out into the snow, but the officer knows who the visitor is and chases after him. Kinjirō, fleeing the policeman, faces the fire watcher's hut, cries out, "Papa!" and then departs.

This modern one-act masterpiece thrillingly depicts the strange momentary encounter of a father and his son against the background of night and snow.

MUSUME DŌJŌJI. Fujimoto Tōbun. Also called *Kyōganoko Musume Dōjōji*. English version: *Musume Dōjōji* (Richie and Watanabe). *Shosagoto**. *Nagauta**. March 1753. Nakamura-za*, Edo.

A representative example of the many Kabuki dances based on the Nō play *Dōjōji*.

On the day of the dedication services for the new hanging temple bell of Dōjō Temple, the angry spirit of Princess Kiyo arrives at the temple in the guise of a temple dancer *(shirabyōshi)*; while she is dancing, she leaps onto the huge bell. When the power of the priests' prayers lift the bell into the air, she turns into a serpent.

This piece exhausts all of the colorful techniques of the Kabuki female impersonator's dancing. A magnificently heightened atmosphere provides great spirit to the performance. There is an abundant variety of movement, colorful costumes, and music.

The featured dancer performs a number of dances, including a *michiyuki** or "travel dance"; a dance with a flower-decked hat; one with small bell drums; and so forth. The play also includes the role of an *oshimodoshi** ("queller of demons"), who appears at the end and performs in the bravura *aragoto** style; he successfully subdues the demon. Other versions of this work include *Futari Dōjōji*, in which there are two main dancers, and *Yakko Dōjōji*, which includes a character who dances with three masks. (*See also* DŌJŌJI MONO.)

MUSUME GONOMI UKINA NO YOKOGUSHI. Kawatake Mokuami*. Also called *Kirare Otomi. Sewamono**. Kabuki. Three acts, nine scenes. July 1864. Morita-za*, Edo.

Mokuami revised his popular *Yowa Nasake Ukina no Yokogushi** by making the lead role a female so that Sawamura Tanosuke III could play it.

Akama Genzaemon's mistress, Otomi, is discovered in a secret rendezvous with her lover, Izutsu Yosaburō. Thinking he has killed her, Genzaemon puts her in a large wicker basket, which he discards. Komori ("Bat") Yasu, who takes an interest in her, saves her and keeps her whereabouts secret. Later, Otomi takes to operating a teashop with Yasu and Satta Tōge; it is here that she again meets Yosaburō. Yosaburō has her go to Genzaemon, who has been running a brothel in Fuchū, so that she can extort 200 *ryō* from him. On the way, she quarrels with Yasu and kills him.

The play reflects the decline of Japan during the late Edo era as the Tokugawa regime began to fall apart. Its action stresses scenes of torture, murder, and extortion. It also brings the role type of the "rough woman" *(akuba)* vividly to life.

N

NAANAA. "You know? You know?" When two actors whisper into each other's ears and behave as if concocting some plan, saying *"naanaa"* as they do so; the expression, therefore, is used to imply the planning of something in advance.

NADAI. The name under which Kamigata theatrical producers reported to and were registered at the office of a shogunate administrator. Since the nominal person reporting in Edo was the *zamoto**, the *zamoto* and the *nadai* were identical. In the Kamigata area, though, the nominal person was thought to be the chief actor of a company, a practice beginning in the mid-eighteenth century. Although this person was called the *zamoto* (using a different Chinese character to spell *"moto"* than that employed in Edo), the person actually holding the license to produce was someone else. (Note: This word is spelled with different characters than *nadai,* the word for "title." *See* TITLES.)

NADE TSUKE. A wig with long hair growing at the rear and combed down smoothly. It is worn by mountain priests *(yamabushi),* mountain ascetics, military strategists, and fortune tellers. Ikkyu in *Sukeroku Yukari no Edo Zakura** and Kiichi in *Kiichi Hōgen Sanryaku no Maki** wear it.

NAGAUTA. "Long song," a school of narrative music *(jōruri*).* One of the types of music sung by blind Kamigata priests to a *shamisen** accompaniment during the late seventeenth century was a long work called *nagauta.* Known as Kamigata *nagauta,* the style traveled to Edo where it was performed in Kabuki, becoming Edo *nagauta.* Looking with contempt on the Edo version, which was used as theatre music, the practitioners of Kamigata *nagauta* soon came to call their art *jiuta** or Kamigata *uta;* thus, when we now say *nagauta,* we mean Edo *nagauta.* This type developed as a form of music from the end of the Genroku era (1688-1703) to the early Kyōhō (1716-35). During the Hōreki and Meiwa years (1751-71), superb singers and *shamisen* players appeared, and *nagauta* was soon perfected. Pieces dating from this time include *Musume Dōjōji**, *Shūjaku Jishi**, and *Sagi Musume**. *Nagauta* flourished in the Anei and Tenmei eras (1772-88) and achieved its golden age during the first half of the nineteenth century when transformation pieces* (quick-change dances, or *henge mono*) were popular. *Nagauta* intermixed with the other narrative schools, such as *tokiwazu** and *kiyomoto**; when *ōsatsuma** music was adopted by *nagauta*, a rousing musical style was born. With the Meiji era and the consequent adaptation to Kabuki dance of Nō and Kyōgen plays, *nagauta* works were strongly influenced by the style of Nō chanting.

Generally a refined musical style, *nagauta* is suitable for home enjoyment. It contains many musical forms and has abundant instrumental musical elements. Because of this, *nagauta* is widely admired not only as a singing style, but also as a theatrical and dance music, being used to portray the emotions and background of the dramatic events. *Nagauta* performance is flexible and may range from one *shamisen* player to a full orchestra of twenty musicians with ten singers and ten *shamisen* players, in addition to flute and drum players. (*See also* GEZA.)

NAGAWA KAMESUKE. fl. 1764-1788. A playwright who was a disciple of Namiki Shōzō* and was active in the Kamigata area. He perfected the dramatization of popular tales *(kōdan)* and the four-act history play technique. Among his works are such plays as *Meiboku Sendai Hagi**, *Katakiuchi Tengajaya Mura**, *Hade Kurabe Ise Monogatari**, and *Igagoe Norikake Kappa.*

NAGE NINGYŌ. "Throwing puppet." Also called *dō ningyō*, this is a life-sized dummy with a costume put on over its bamboo torso. The dummy is substituted for an actor when a character is supposedly carried and then thrown into the air during a fight. An example occurs at the end of *Narukami** when Narukami, in a rage, grabs one of the priests around him and flings him high overhead.

NAGOYA SANZABURŌ. d. 1603. Nagoya is a character who, legend states, was the cofounder of Kabuki with Izumo no Okuni*. As a youth he was an excellent lance thrower in the service of Goma Ujisato and achieved such success in his first battle that he was sung of in a popular song. He became a masterless samurai after Goma died and seems to have joined up with a group of traveling entertainers. As Nagoya died on April 10, 1603, it is doubtful that he ever had any connecton with Okuni. According to the stories written about Okuni, her former lover Sanzaburō appeared to her as a ghost and, yearning for the old days, performed a dance with her. It is thought that Okuni merely cashed in on the popularity of the romantic Sanzaburō. If we examine all the written evidence, it seems possible that

Sanjurō, an actor who is said to have married Okuni, has been confused with Sanzaburō.

NAIMAZE. "Mixture," a new play created by combining two or more entirely different plots. Kabuki plays usually were restricted with regard to the "worlds" *(sekai*)* that they could depict. This led to an abundance of plays using the same characters and worlds (*see also* KAKIGAE KYŌGEN). In the years following the turn of the nineteenth century, a kind of complex play *(naimaze)* was devised that mixed two or more worlds. An example would be the combination of *Meiboku Sendai Hagi** and *Kasane** into *Date Kurabe Okuni Kabuki*. (*See also* PLAYWRITING.)

NAIYOMI. A "private reading." When the chief playwright *(tate sakusha*)* completed a new play, he first read it at the home of the manager *(zamoto*)* and then at the home of the leading actor *(zagashira*)*. As it was imperative that there be no leaks to other companies of the plot and dramatic novelties, the *tate sakusha* normally went out unaccompanied and everyone was cleared out of their homes so that no one else could hear the play as it was read. It was during the *naiyomi* that casting decisions and script revisions were made.

NAKAJIKU. "Central axis." Also called *nakafude*, those actors who compare favorably with the *zagashira** in skill and family standing. When the *nakajiku*'s name appeared on an Edo period program, it was placed in the center of the cast list. Often there were two or three actors deserving *nakajiku* rank in a company. Only one, however, could have his name in the central position. Such an actor was called the *ippon no nakajiku* and was the ranking actor of *nakajiku* status. When a *nakajiku* played several roles on a program, his name was not listed next to each of his roles. Instead, all the roles he played were listed along with the central listing of his name.

NAKAMAKU. "Between the acts." Originally, it was customary to have a single title for both of the plays on a day's program (the history play *[ichibanme mono*]* and the domestic play *[nibanme mono*]*; *see also* JIDAIMONO; SEWAMONO). In 1796, however, a separate title was provided for the domestic play. Thus, the program was thought of as a "double feature." Further, toward the end of the Edo period a separate dance drama, the *nakamaku*, was inserted between the two halves. It is said that the word *nakamaku* first was used in 1840 when Ichikawa Danjūrō VII* produced the dance play *Kanjinchō**. The *nakamaku* system has continued into the Shōwa era (1926-). Today, instead of using the terms *ichibanme, nakamaku,* and *nibanme,* the procedure is to call the order of the plays simply "first" *(daiichi)*, "second" *(daini)*, and so on. The Kamigata equivalent of *nakamaku* is *naka kyōgen*. (*See also* KAKIDASHI.)

NAKAMURA BAIGYOKU I. The pen name *(haimyō*)* of Nakamura Utaemon III*.

II. 1840-1921. An actor, born in Kyoto, who held several names, including Nakamura Fukusuke III, before acquiring the name of Baigyoku. He was active with Jitsukawa Enjaku I* in the Kamigata area, but soon began to appear frequently in Tokyo with Ichikawa Danjūrō IX* and Onoe Kikugorō V*. He costarred with Nakamura Ganjirō I* in his later years and became a leader in the world of Kamigata Kabuki. He was quite versatile, excelling in both history and domestic plays, as well as in both leading male and female roles.

III. 1880-1948. Adopted son of Baigyoku II. He held the name of Fukusuke IV before becoming Baigyoku III in 1935. He appeared as an *onnagata** opposite Ganjirō I for many years, often appearing as the wife of Ganjirō's male roles. He excelled in history and domestic plays, being especially good in plays taken from the puppet theatre. He became one of Kabuki's prized possessions as his art matured during his last years.

NAKAMURA DENKURŌ I. 1662-1713. An actor who, along with Ichikawa Danjūrō I*, exemplified *aragoto** acting during the Genroku period (1688-1703). He took the name of Denkurō in 1684, after managing the Nakamura-za* as Nakamura Kanzaburō IV*. He was unrivaled in his acting of Asahina in *Yakko Tanzen* (1686) and *Oiso ga Yoi* (1688) both performed at the Nakamura-za. Asahina is a popular role found in several plays that are still performed. Denkurō created such elements of the character's costume as the *ita bin** style of wig, the sickle-shaped beard, the *saruguma** makeup, the circular crane-shaped crest design, and other features that are still used for the part. He also specialized in the swaggering walking style called *tanzen* (*see also* ROPPŌ).

II. 1719-1777. Adopted son of Denkurō I. Besides inheriting Denkurō's style, he specialized in the roles of brave samurai in the history plays. He was active mainly during the mid-eighteenth century.

NAKAMURA FUKUSUKE VIII, *yago** Narikomaya. 1946- . An actor and the adopted son of Nakamura Utaemon VI*, he was born in Tokyo, debuted in 1951 as Kagaya Fukunosuke, and became Fukusuke in 1967. As an *onnagata** and player of young male roles *(wakashugata*)*, he is one of those shouldering the burden of the coming generation of Kabuki stars.

NAKAMURA GAN'EMON III, *yago** Narikomaya. 1901- . An actor and the son of Gan'emon I, he was born in Tokyo, debuted in 1905 as Nakamura Umemaru, became a pupil of Utaemon V* in 1911. He took the name of Nakamura Umenosuke, then succeeded to his present name in 1920. He organized the Kabuki experimental group—the Tomodachi-za—in 1925, founded a troupe in 1930 with Ichikawa Yaozō (later Ichikawa Chūsha VII*), and propelled a reform movement in Kabuki. In May 1931 he established the Zenshin-za* troupe along with Kawarazaki Chōjūrō IV* and became its leading figure. From 1952 to 1955 he traveled incognito in China. His powers of comprehension are outstanding, and his deep psychological penetration as an actor is well known. He acts with a fidelity to life and has a youthful charm, appearing not only in the classics, but also in new plays and translations. The title role in *Heike Nyogo no Shima** is one of his greatest Kabuki successes.

NAKAMURA GANJIRŌ I. 1860-1935. An actor and the son of the popular early Meiji Osaka star, Nakamura Ganjaku. After being separated from his parents at an early age, he became the pupil of Jitsukawa Enjaku I*; his life of traveling on the road meant one difficulty after another. When he at last achieved popularity in 1877, he was reunited with his father, and during the following year he took the name of Ganjirō I. With his restrained style and looks he excelled in the romantic acting of *wagoto** roles, showing his characteristic qualities especially well as the heroes in Chikamatsu's domestic plays, in which he was peerless. His best roles included Kamiya Jihei in *Shinjū Ten no Amijima**, Chūbei in *Meido no Hikyaku**, and Izaemon in *Kuruwa Bunshō**. Besides these, he was outstanding in history plays, especially as Moritsuna in *Ōmi Genji Senjin Yakata** and Yuranosuke in *Kanadehon Chūshingura**.

II, *yago** Narikomaya. 1902- . The son of Ganjirō I, this actor is among today's finest veteran *onnagata** and players of young male roles, despite his advanced age. Born in Osaka, he debuted in 1907 under his actual name (Hayashi Yoshio), later became Nakamura Senjaku I, changed this to Nakamura Shijaku in 1941, and took the name of Ganjirō in January 1946. He is the top Kabuki actor of Osaka. When he was fourteen, during his Senjaku period, he was leader of a children's troupe; later, at eighteen, he served as troupe leader or *zagashira** of the "junior Kabuki" and played leading *onnagata* roles under his father's wing. He became a motion picture actor in 1955, but returned to Kabuki rather quickly. Ganjirō's acting is always sparkling and brilliant. He is one of the best at the Kamigata *wagoto** style, yet he also displays great ability in each of his history play roles. Jihei in *Katakiuchi Tengajaya Mura**, Minakata Jujibei in *Futatsu Chōchō Kuruwa Nikki**, Tokubei in *Sonezaki Shinjū**, and Yashio in *Meiboku Sendai Hagi** are among the parts that he frequently portrays.

NAKAMURA JAKUEMON IV, *yago** Kyoya. 1920- . A popular and versatile *onnagata**, he was born in Tokyo, the son of Ōtani Tomoemon VI*. He debuted as Ōtani Hirojirō in 1927, took his father's name in 1948, and in September 1964 became Jakuemon. As a child he was thought to be a prodigy. His conversion to *onnagata* specialization following his postwar demobilization and his brilliance in this endeavor were frequent topics of conversation several years ago. He understands new works as well and is the most outstanding representative of the new *onnagata*. His eldest son is Ōtani Tomoemon VIII*, and his next son is Nakamura Shibajaku VII.

NAKAMURA KAMON II, *yago** Komamuraya. 1913- . An actor and the son of a well-known storyteller in the *rakugo** tradition, he debuted in 1925 as the pupil of Nakamura Utaemon V* and later became a pupil of Ichikawa Ennosuke II (En'o I*). He joined the Zenshin-za* troupe in 1933 and took the name Ichikawa Kikunosuke. In 1955 he took his present name. He resigned from the Zenshin-za in 1965 and, a year later, joined Utaemon VI's* company. He specializes in young lover and villain roles and is valued as a supporting actor.

NAKAMURA KANZABURŌ. This line of actors and managers descends from the managerial family that ran Edo's Nakamura-za*. Kanzaburō I and II were also actors. Thereafter, until Kanzaburō XIII—aside from Kanzaburō IV (1662-1713), who gave up managing and became an actor (*see also* NAKAMURA DENKURŌ I)—all were strictly managers. The fifteenth (1873-1940) and sixteenth did not publicly assume the name, and the seventeenth (the present Kanzaburō) took the name as the third son of Nakamura Karoku III*. He took it, of course, not as a manager's, but as an actor's name.

I. 1598-1658. He left Kyoto for Edo and in 1624 opened a theatre on the Nakabashi thoroughfare. Excelling in the comic role of Saruwaka, he called the theatre the Saruwaka-za as an advertisement for his performance. The theatre was the predecessor of one of Edo's great playhouses, the Nakamura-za.

II. 1647-1674. Second son of Kanzaburō I. He was outstanding in dance plays as a player of young male roles *(wakashugata*)*. In addition, he was active as a *zamoto**, or manager, for many years.

XVII, *yago** Nakamuraya. 1909- . One of the century's greatest stars, he was born in Tokyo, the third son of Nakamura Karoku. His brothers were the late Nakamura Tokizō III* and Nakamura Kichiemon I*. He debuted as Nakamura Yonekichi in November 1916, became Nakamura Moshio in October 1929, and took his present name in January 1960. During his Moshio days he joined the Tōhō* company and acted in new plays and translations, but he later returned to Shōchiku*. He idolized his adopted father, Onoe Kikugorō VI*. Though profoundly influenced by Kikugorō's style, he also possesses the style of his brother Kichiemon, so the breadth of his acting is wide. In this sense he has inherited the traditions of Taishō (1912-26) and Shōwa (1926-) Kabuki and may be said to be in the front line of today's stars. His daughter is the actress Namino Kuriko, a star of the Shinpa theatre. His adopted son-in-law is Sawamura Tōjūrō II*, and his eldest son is Nakamura Kankurō (1955-). As a young Kabuki actor, Kankurō is receiving a rigid training from his father, and his future looks bright.

NAKAMURA KAROKU I. 1779-1859. A pupil of Nakamura Utaemon III*, he took the name of Nakamura Moshio and changed it in 1804 to Karoku. From the 1830s to the 1850s he was active in Kyoto and Osaka. Extremely handsome, he excelled at *onnagata** roles, especially those of courtesans. He even became known as Keisei ("Courtesan") Karoku. His second son became Karoku II in 1873.

III. 1849-1919. Third son of Karoku I, he took the name in 1878. Though he was in Ichikawa Danjūrō IX's* company, he did not share Danjūrō's ideas on production. He left the company to develop his own style at another theatre, where he became popular. His eldest son was Nakamura Kichiemon I*; his next son was Nakamura Tokizō III*; and his third son was Nakamura Kanzaburō XVII*.

NAKAMURA KICHIEMON I. 1886-1954. An actor and the eldest son of Nakamura Karoku III*. He debuted in 1897, appearing in May in the "Children's Theatre" at Tokyo's Asakusa-za. Soon after, he became a *zagashira**, or troupe leader, and gained renown. Guided by the theatre manager Tamura Nariyoshi (1851-1920), he appeared in 1905 at the Ichimura-za* with Onoe Kikugorō VI* and was a huge success, bringing about the brief "golden age" known as the "Ichimura-za period." The void left by the deaths of the Meiji stars Ichikawa Danjūrō IX* and Onoe Kikugorō V* was satisfactorily filled by the rivalry between Kikugorō VI and Kichiemon. Kichiemon withdrew from the Ichimura-za in 1921, developed an independent style, and entered the second quarter of the twentieth century with an added quality of maturity. In 1943 he organized the Nakamura Kichiemon Troupe. He inherited the style of Danjūrō IX, as evidenced by his displaying authentic old customs in the acting of history plays. The depth of his presentation and the quality of his tone were first-class. We may safely say that Shōwa period (1926-) Kabuki rested on the shoulders of Kichiemon and Kikugorō.

II, *yago** Harimaya. 1944- . The son of Matsumoto Kōshirō VIII*; his brother is Ichikawa Somegorō VI*. He was born in Tokyo and debuted as Nakamura Mannosuke in 1948. In 1961 he switched to Tōhō* from the Shōchiku* company, along with his brother and father, and took his grandfather Kichiemon's name in October 1966. After his crossover to Tōhō, audiences were not often blessed with his work in Kabuki, but he and his brother make efforts to perform Kabuki with the Kinome study group.

NAKAMURA KICHIJŪRO II, *yago** Harimaya. 1907- . The son of Kichijūrō I, he debuted in 1923 and received his present name in 1945. In 1961 he and a group of actors led by Matsumoto Kōshirō VIII* left the Shōchiku* company for Tōhō*, where he now plays supporting roles.

NAKAMURA MATAGORŌ II, *yago** Harimaya. 1914- . Revered as one of Kabuki's finest acting teachers, Matagorō was born in Tokyo, the son of Matagorō I, and made his debut in 1921. In 1961 he took part in the crossover from Shōchiku* to Tōhō* led by Matsumoto Kōshirō VIII*. He has a broad range, playing both male and female roles, and a thorough knowledge of the many varieties of movement and speech called for in Kabuki dramas.

NAKAMURA MATSUE V, *yago** Kagaya. 1948- . With Nakamura Fukusuke VIII*, this actor is an adopted son of Nakamura Utaemon VI*. He debuted as Kagaya Hashinosuke in 1956 and became Matsue in April 1967. It is expected that he will be one of the leading *onnagata** of the coming generation.

NAKAMURA NAKAZŌ I. 1736-1790. An actor supported by Ichikawa Danjūrō IV*, he was acknowledged during the 1760s as an excellent player of villain's roles. When he performed the role of Sadakurō in *Kanadehon Chūshingura** at the Ichimura-za* in 1766, he revised the role's traditional style of appearing in the garb of a mountain priest; instead, he wore a black kimono tucked up at the back and his hair half grown in on top, and he carried a torn umbrella bearing a bull's-eye pattern. So acclaimed were these innovations that the Nakazō style is still the basis for this role's performance. Although it was only a minor role before he revised its stage business, Sadakurō is now played by Kabuki's first-quality actors. Nakazō put various other new performance techniques into use, and many remain today. They are known as *Hidetsuru kata*, Hidetsuru having been Nakazō's haiku-writing pen name *(haimyō*)*. He studied the Shigayama* school of dance and was responsible for the revival of interest shown in it. Such dances as *Shigayama Sanbasō* and *Kotobuki Yotsugi Sanbasō* extended his fame even into court circles. Nakazō's autobiography is extant in two volumes, *Settsugekka Nemonogatari* and *Hidetsuru Nikki*.

II. 1759-1796. A pupil of Ōtani Hiroji III, he held several names before assuming the name of Nakazō II in 1794. Unfortunately, he died two years later.

III. 1800-1886. Son of Shigayama Sei XI, a female dancer of the Shigayama school. After receiving great praise for his performance of Komori ("Bat") Yasu in *Yowa Nasake Ukina no Yokogushi**, staged in March 1853 at the Nakamura-za*, he made a career out of playing the role. He was a weighty figure because of his seniority early in the Meiji era, and Ichikawa Danjūrō IX* and Onoe Kikugorō V*, among others, are said to have learned from him. Since he was not good-looking, having a rather large mouth, he specialized in the roles of older male villains and was especially famous as a player of the *jitsuaku* category of evil men (*see also* KATAKIYAKU). His literary works include his autobiographies, *Temae Miso* and *Zekku Chō.*

IV. 1885-1916. Born in Edo, he studied under Nakamura Kanzaburō XIII. He held the names of Nakamura Ginnosuke and Nakamura Kangorō before becoming Nakazō in 1915. A year later he died. He specialized in villain and old men roles and was quite an expert in the realm of old theatrical customs.

NAKAMURA NARITARŌ II, *yago** Shinkomaya. 1900- . A Kamigata veteran who rarely performs today, he was adopted by Nakamura Kaisha and made his debut in 1911. In 1921 he changed his name from Nakamura Tarō to Naritarō.

NAKAMURA RYŪ. A school of Japanese dance. The Shikan *ha*, or branch, was founded in the late Edo period by the great Nakamura Utaemon III*. He rivaled the other major Kabuki dancer-actor of his day—Bandō Mitsugorō III*—in quick-change dances, such as *Hama Matsukaze, Tadanobu,* and *Shigayama Sanbasō.* Utaemon IV* excelled in dances such as *Utsubo Zaru**, *Sanja Matsuri**, and *Rokkasen**. His son, the popular Nakamura Shikan IV*, was a Meiji star who broadened the scope of pure Kabuki dance. Utaemon V* reigned over Kabuki dance during the first third of this century. His eldest son inherited his dancing talent and displayed it from an early age; this was Nakamura Fukusuke V. At the time of the "new dance" movement (*shin buyō; see also* DANCE) during the Taishō era (1912-26) the Hagoromo Association was founded and study of classical and new works was begun. Fukusuke founded a study group for his apprentices and called it the Suzumenari Association; unfortunately, he died not long after. The present *iemoto** is Nakamura Fukusuke VII*.

Another subschool is the Toraji *ha*, founded in the third quarter of the eighteenth century by Nakamura Yahachi, a Kabuki flute player and choreographer. His major works were *Matsukaze Murasame, Asahina,* and *Tsuri Kitsune.* The second in the line was his daughter Toraji; all male *iemoto* in the line were named Yahachi and all females Toraji. Today Toraji V leads the school.

The main branch was founded in the mid-eighteenth century by Nakamura Tomijūrō I*, third son of Yoshizawa Ayame I*, who was perhaps the greatest female impersonator in Kabuki history; Nakamura Shingorō adopted Tomijūrō, though. He created the greatest dance plays of his time, such as *Shakkyō* (*see also* SHAKKYŌ MONO), *Musume Dōjōji**, and *Asama.* The name has passed down to the present in a convoluted sequence of successions.

NAKAMURA SENJAKU II, *yago** Narikomaya. 1931- . One of today's leading *onnagata**, he was born in Tokyo, the son of Nakamura Ganjirō II*.

He debuted in 1941 under the name that he still holds, later went into film acting, but returned to the stage in August 1955. From 1950 on, he was under the guidance of the director-critic Takechi Tetsuji and, together with Bandō Tsurunosuke (Nakamura Tomijūrō V*), was a mainstay of "Takechi Kabuki." The popularity of these actors during their "Sen-Tsuru" period formed the basis for a revival of interest in Kabuki in the Kamigata area. Aside from the refreshing performance that he gives in the role of Ohatsu the courtesan—in Chikamatsu Monzaemon's* *Sonezaki Shinjū**, which he plays with his father in the role opposite him—he displays beautiful acting in other Chikamatsu works and in new plays as well.

NAKAMURA SHICHISABURŌ I. 1662-1708. A famous actor of the late seventeenth century, specializing in romantic *wagoto** roles. He lived in Edo. Ichikawa Danjūrō I's* *aragoto** style was the most popular Edo form at the time, but Shichisaburō managed to gain fame and fortune with his realistic methods. In 1698 he went to Kyoto and played Tomoenojō in *Keisei Asamagatake*, surprising the famous Kyoto star Sakata Tōjūrō* by the depth of his art.

There were five generations of the line, but the only famous one other than the first was Shichisaburō II (fl. 1764-1772).

NAKAMURA SHIKAKU II, *yago** Shinkomaya. 1900- . A veteran *onnagata**, born in Tokyo, he is the son of Nakamura Denkurō V. He debuted in 1905 and became Shikaku in 1919. Shikaku joined the Tōhō* company in the famous crossover of 1961. He is well versed in the old customs for female impersonators but, since moving to Osaka, has performed with taste in new plays as well.

NAKAMURA SHIKAN. The name taken by the actor Nakamura Utaemon III* during the last years of his career. Shikan II was the name held by Utaemon IV* before taking the latter name. Shikan III was active during the first half of the nineteenth century in Osaka. Shikan V and VI were better known as Utaemon V* and VI*, respectively.

IV. 1830-1899. Adopted son of Utaemon IV, he went to Edo in 1838, took the name of Nakamura Fukusuke I, and performed as an actor of young leading roles. He suffered from epilepsy and was estranged from his adopted family, but in 1852 he was reinstated and appeared onstage, gaining great popularity. He became Shikan IV in 1860 and thereafter made a name as one of the representative actors of the first half of the Meiji era. Possessing a dignified personality, he specialized in the leading roles of history plays, playing both heroes and villains. Dancing was one of his specialties.

VII, *yago** Narikomaya. 1928- . The son of Nakamura Fukusuke V, he debuted in November 1933 as Nakamura Kotarō and, after 1940, was under the supervision of Onoe Kikugorō VI*, from whose hands he received priceless training. In October 1941 he became Fukusuke VII and took his present name in April 1967. Along with Onoe Baikō VII* and his uncle, Utaemon VI, Shikan is in the front line of *onnagata** stars. His training advanced rather slowly for a time, but, as soon as he took his present name, it instantly proceeded at a run. His technique is orthodox in its approach to female impersonation.

NAKAMURA SŌJŪRŌ I. 1835-1889. Intended to be an actor from childhood, he became the pupil of a country actor and acted on provincial tours. Sōjūrō was discovered while performing in a Nagoya theatre and became the pupil of Nakamura Shijaku II. He took the name of Nakamura Sōjūrō in 1865 and acted frequently at the Chikugo Shibai in Osaka. As he could not tolerate the theatre reforms of the Meiji period, he retired and opened up a dry goods store. Immediately, theatre people began to request his return to the stage; eventually, he acceded. For five years, from 1877 to 1882, he was in Tokyo, where he rivaled Ichikawa Danjūrō IX* in popularity. In the Kamigata area he exceeded Jitsukawa Enjaku I* in public favor. He specialized in the delicate roles of the *wagoto** style, had deep concerns about the new theatre reforms, and brought about a new style of acting.

NAKAMURA TOKIZŌ. A line of actors. Tokizō I was the name held by Nakamura Karoku III* before he took the latter name. Tokizō II, who died young, was his adopted son.

III. 1895-1959. Second son of Karoku III. He changed his name from Nakamura Yonekichi to Tokizō III in 1916. An *onnagata**, he played wife roles *(nyōbo)* to his brother, Nakamura Kichiemon I*. In his last years he reached the limits of perfection. He was best in the roles of wives in the domestic plays. Tokizō was well known as the father of a large family.

IV. 1926-1962. Second son of Tokizō III. He changed his name from Nakamura Shijaku to Tokizō IV in 1960. He was a beautiful *onnagata* and, along with inheriting his father's art, possessed a flashy side. Much was expected of him, but he died young.

NAKAMURA TOMIJŪRŌ I. 1719-1786. Third son of the great *onnagata** Yoshizawa Ayame I*, he was a famous *onnagata* of the mid to late eighteenth century. He received great praise for his performance of *Shakkyō* (*see also* SHAKKYŌ MONO) in Osaka in 1736 and later played in Kyoto and Edo. In 1779 he attained the highest ranking in the contemporary critical annuals *(yakusha hyōbanki*)*. Loved in all types of female roles—from proper young ladies to courtesans, to samurai wives, to townsmen's wives, to amazons—he excelled in dance as well. When *Musume Dōjōji** was first brought to Edo in 1753, Tomijūrō rivaled the great Segawa Kikunojō I* in the popularity of his dancing. (*See also* NAKAMURA RYŪ.)

II. 1786-1855. This actor became Tomijūrō II in 1833 and was the top *onnagata* of his day in Kyoto and Osaka. Since he lived in Osaka's Naniwa district, he was called "Naniwa no Dayū."

III. 1859-1901. An *onnagata* who began his career in Osaka, but later moved to Tokyo, where he became Tomijūrō III in 1891. He appeared mainly in history plays in the roles of women of the samurai class.

IV. 1908-1960. In 1930 he took the name of Bandō Tsurunosuke and was active in "junior Kabuki" as an *onnagata.* He received the name of Tomijūrō in 1945. After the war he moved to the Kamigata area and became famous there. He also took an active part in the experimental theatre group, the Yagurama-za, of which he was chairman.

V, *yago** Kikuya. 1929- . A superb dancer-actor, playing male and female roles with equal facility, he was born the son of Nakamura Tomijūrō IV and Azuma Tokuho of the Azuma school of dance. He debuted as Bandō Tsurunosuke in 1943 and became Ichimura Takenojō in 1964. During his Tsurunosuke period he performed together with Nakamura Senjaku II* in experimental Kabuki productions directed by Takechi Tetsuji. This experience helped him cultivate his dynamic acting powers and deep understanding of his roles. He and Senjaku gave rise to what is sometimes called the "Sen-Tsuru" era. Tomijūrō has crystal-clear speech and fascinates with his overflowing enthusiasm onstage. Even in new plays the depth of his penetration is far above average.

NAKAMURA TŌZŌ, *yago** Kagaya. 1938- . Son of a well-known doctor, Tōzō became a pupil of Nakamura Utaemon VI* in 1961 and debuted as Nakamura Tamatarō, receiving his present name in April 1967. He specializes in *onnagata** roles, but plays other types as well. A talented dancer, he is the brother of the actress Katsuma Murasaki.

NAKAMURA UMENOSUKE III, *yago** Narikomaya. 1930- . A mainstay of the Zenshin-za* company, he was born the son of Nakamura Gan'emon III* and debuted in March 1939. Umenosuke has been an able successor of his father's art and is capable of playing not only the classics, but a broad range of other plays as well.

NAKAMURA UTAEMON I. 1714-1791. An actor active through most of the eighteenth century. Born the second son of a doctor in Kaga Province, he loved the theatre from childhood and went to Kyoto to become an actor. In 1742 he took the name of Nakamura Utaemon and appeared in a major theatre; then he went to Edo in 1757, where he became popular and grew friendly with Ichikawa Danjūrō IV*. He returned to Osaka in 1761 and thereafter was active in the Kamigata area, gaining fame for his portrayals of *jitsugoto* roles (*see also* TACHIYAKU).

II. 1752-1798. A pupil of Utaemon I. He became Utaemon II in 1782, like his master gaining renown as a player of *jitsugoto* parts. Later in his career he assumed the name of Nakamura Tōzō.

III. 1778-1838. Son of Utaemon I. He succeeded to the name in 1791. In 1809 he went to Edo, gained fame, and rivaled Bandō Mitsugorō III* and Matsumoto Kōshirō V* in popularity. Though not blessed with good looks or fine speech, he was superb at creating new performance ideas and bequeathed his manner of playing *(kata*)* Umeomaru in *Sugawara Denju Tenarai Kagami** to future actors. His rivalry with the expert dancer Mitsugorō caused frequent quarrels. As a playwright he wrote under the name of Kanezawa Ryūgoku. Several of his works are extant.

IV. 1798-1852. A pupil of Utaemon III. He went to the Kamigata area on the heels of his master, returned to Edo in 1827, and rivaled Mitsugorō IV* in fame. He became the fourth in the line in 1836 and thereafter surpassed Mitsugorō in popularity. Though superb in dance, he played all types of roles, receiving the revered title of *kaneru yakusha**, or "all-around actor." Nakamura Shikan IV*, famous early Meiji star, was his son.

V. 1866-1940. Adopted son of Nakamura Shikan IV. In 1901 he changed his name from Nakamura Fukusuke IV to Shikan V and became Utaemon in 1903. A highly popular player of young female roles during his Fukusuke period, he became a representative Kabuki star during the Taishō (1912-26) and into the Shōwa (1926-) periods. After the deaths of Ichikawa Danjūrō IX*, Onoe Kikugorō V*, and Ichikawa Sadanji I* in the early years of this century, he was Kabuki's leading light. As Yodogimi in Tsubouchi Shōyō's *Kiri Hitoha** and *Hototogisu Kojō no Rakugetsu** he advanced into new territory and became known as an *onnagata** who combined good looks with dignity.

VI, *yago** Narikomaya. 1917- . One of Kabuki's two leading *onnagata*, he was born in Tokyo, the second son of Utaemon V. He debuted in 1922 as Nakamura Kotarō, became Nakamura Fukusuke VI in 1933, Nakamura Shikan VI in 1941, and took his present name in April 1951. His style is often compared with that of Onoe Baikō VII* (his chief rival), but Utaemon possesses an old-fashioned quality that emerges from his traditional attitude toward the *onnagata*'s life. His position derives from both his good looks and his total determination as an artist. He also attempts "experimental" performances, an expression of which was his formation in March 1955 of the Tsubomi Kai, a study group. In addition, his roles in New Kabuki *(shin kabuki*)* plays and the results of his revivals of old classics speak well of his inquiring spirit.

NAKAMURA-ZA. A theatre first opened in March 1624 by Nakamura (Saruwaka) Kanzaburō I*, who had come to Edo from Yamashirō. It was situated in the Nakabashi district, where Nihonbashi-dōri, 2-chome is today. The Saruwaka-za was its first name, but this was later changed to the Nakamura-za. In May 1632 the theatre was forced to move to Go-machi and then had to move to Sakai-chō in May 1651. Because of management problems plaguing the theatre from the fall of 1793 to October 1797, the Miyako-za* put on plays in its stead (as a *hikae yagura**, or alternative theatre). Aside from this period the theatre continued to be managed by the generations of *zamoto** named Kanzaburō until the early years of Meiji. In 1875, Kanzaburō XIII retired and the position of *zamoto* fell to another. The theatre's name thereafter was changed frequently, usually after being damaged by a fire. In 1884 it moved to Asakusa's Shin Torikoe area and in 1892 was known as the Torikoe-za. In January 1893 a fire put an end to the traditions of Edo's oldest theatre. (*See also* THEATRE MANAGEMENT.)

NAKA-ZA. A theatre in Osaka's Dōtonbori district. It was founded as the Naka no Shibai in 1652 by Shioya Kuroemon. The Shōchiku* company took over its management in 1920, rebuilt it, and called it the Naka-za. It was the first major Osaka Kabuki theatre used by such modern actors as the late Nakamura Ganjirō I*. It was destroyed in an air raid in 1945, but was rebuilt and reopened in January 1948. Nowadays, Shōchiku's new comedies are played here, as Kabuki only rarely graces its stage.

NAKU. "To weep"; used during trying conditions when nothing seems to go right.

NAMAJIME. A topknot style worn by such *tachiyaku** role rypes as the *jitsugoto, aragoto**, and *sabaki yaku*. Characters wearing it include Sukeroku in *Sukeroku Yukari no Edo Zakura**, Sanemori in *Genpei Nunobiki Taki**, and Kajiwara in *Miura no Ōsuke Kōbai Tazuna**.

NAMAKO. A scenic element consisting of a pine log of five to six inches in diameter, split in two and placed in the ground to mark the border of a river or pond. Small holes are bored in the top and artificial flowers and grass inserted in them.

NAME-TAKING CEREMONY. *See* SHŪMEI; KŌJŌ.

NAMI ITA. "Wave boards," a relatively symbolic scenic element consisting of boards cut to three feet in length by about a foot in height, rounded off on the left and right, and painted with waves. Brackets are attached to their rear to fix them to the stage; they are placed to represent the water's edge in a waterside scene. When the sea is depicted in the background, waves of up to six feet in height are painted on oblong flats (*harimono**) that are placed at the rear of the stage; these are called *nami tesuri*. Occasionally, the effect of making the waves grow higher is achieved by placing two or three boards at intervals one behind the other.

NAMIKI GOHEI I. 1747-1808. A playwright born in Osaka. He was the pupil of Namiki Shōzō* and became chief playwright *(tate sakusha*)* at Kyoto's Hayakumo-za in 1775. A major figure in Kamigata theatre during the Tenmei era (1781-88), Gohei moved to Edo in 1794 with the actor Sawamura Sōjūrō III*. In Edo he wrote plays for Sōjūrō and a number of other famous stars, such as Matsumoto Kōshirō V*, Ichikawa Danzō IV*, and Sōjūrō V*. His works number more than 110. Expert at both history and domestic plays containing many realistic and rationalistic qualities, he injected many strong points of Kamigata dramaturgy into Edo theatre. In 1795, when his Edo version of his own *Godairiki Koi no Fūjime** was staged, he introduced the Kamigata method for composing a theatre's offerings. The Kamigata area had long been accustomed to producing two plays a day at each theatre; the first play *(ichibanme mono*)* was a history play and the second *(nibanme mono*)* a domestic play. In Edo, on the other hand, it had been customary to produce one play with both the history play style and the domestic play style scenes under a single title. Thus, a play like *Sukeroku Yukari no Edo Zakura** presented its hero, Sukeroku, as the domestic style equivalent of a previously introduced character, the historical Soga Gorō. As a consequence, many Edo plays followed the *jitsu wa* ("in reality") convention whereby the playwright would first introduce a historical character and then his domestic style counterpart. At a crucial moment, the latter would reveal that "in reality" he was the former, but he had assumed a disguise for reasons related to the specific plot. In 1781 Sakurada Jisuke I* had made inroads into breaking up this convention by making the history and domestic characters unrelated, but it took Gohei to bring about the presentation of two separate plays on the same program rather than on one long one. Further, Gohei performed a great service in establishing such playwright customs as the gathering of the entire company at the home of the *tate sakusha* for a conference prior to the annual *kaomise** program. He also helped raise the status of dramatists. His outstanding works include *Kanjin Kanmon Tekuda no Hajimari**, *Sanmon Gosan no Kiri**, and *Godairiki Koi no Fūjime**.

Less successful were Namiki Gohei II (1768-1819) and Gohei III (1790-1855). The former is remembered mainly for having written the words to the *kiyomoto** dance *Yasuna**, while the latter's dance drama *Kanjinchō** assures him a place in Japan's theatre history.

NAMIKI SHŌZŌ. 1730-1773. A puppet-theatre playwright, he was the son of a theatre teahouse proprietor in Osaka's Dōtonbori district. He studied under Namiki Sōsuke* and was a playwright for the puppets at the Toyotake-za. After his master's death, he became a Kabuki writer. He was the chief figure in the Kamigata theatre world of the Hōreki-Anei eras (1751-80) and wrote about 100 plays. Shōzō excelled at history plays and conceived his works on a grand scale; his complex plots wandered down many trails. He was adept at transferring the techniques of writing puppet plays to Kabuki. This writer also was famous for the new stage equipment and machinery that he devised, his greatest accomplishment being the perfection, in 1758, of the revolving stage* *(mawari butai)*; in addition, he was behind the creation of such devices as the *hiki dōgu** (a kind of wagon stage) and the large and small stage traps *(seri*)*. His best works as a playwright include *Yadonashi Danshichi Shigure no Karakasa**, *Osanago no Adauchi*, *Keisei Ama no Hagoromo*, *Sanjikkoku Yofune no Hajimari*, *Kiritarō Tengu no Sakamori*, and *Kuwanaya Tokuzō Irifune Monogatari*.

NAMIKI SŌSUKE. 1695-1751. A puppet-theatre playwright who was also called Matsuya Sōsuke. Born in Osaka, he first belonged to the Toyotake-za, but later switched to the Takemoto-za and took the name Namiki Senryū. He collaborated on such masterpieces as the immortal *Sugawara Denju Tenarai Kagami** and *Yoshitsune Senbon Zakura** and, together with the renowned puppet manipulator Yoshida Bunzaburō (d. 1760), brought the puppet theatre to its golden era. In his last years he returned to the Toyotake-za.

NAMI NUNO. A ground cloth representing waves. (*See also* JIGASURI.)

NAMU SAN. "Good heavens!" An expression used in the sense of something being done randomly or haphazardly.

NANBAN. A walking style in which the normal process of swinging the right hand and shoulder to the rear while stepping forward on the right foot and vice-versa for the left side is reversed; thus the hand and shoulder move forward at the same time as the foot on that side of the body. It is often used in the Shigayama* school of dance.

NANBANTETSU GOTŌ NO MENUKI. Namiki Sōsuke*. Also called *Gotō no Sanbasō; Yoshitsune Koshigoejō*. *Jidaimono**. *Jōruri**. Five acts. February 1735. Toyotake-za, Osaka.

A work based on the fall of Osaka Castle. Act III, *Yoshitsune Koshigoejō*, is still performed.

Yoshitsune shuns the fawning Nishikidō brothers, who are addicted to a life of pleasure. Izumi no Saburō wants to use Gotohei as a strategist for Yoshitsune. Gotohei's drunkenness angers his wife, Seki-Jō. However, Saburō, who has confidence in Gotohei, tests his character by firing a gun near him while he is sleeping off the effects of too much drink. When the shot is fired, he jumps up immediately, in full possession of his senses, ready to repulse any enemy. With this proof of his ability, Saburō invites him to enter Yoshitsune's military service as his strategist.

The actor playing Gotohei has some outstanding moments on stage, especially when he is urged by the Nishikidō brothers to drink sake, does so, gets drunk, and performs a *Sanbasō** dance. Another highlight comes when Saburō fires the gun near the sleeping Gotohei, who rises instantly to display his true character, a total change from the way that he had behaved before.

NANORIDAI. "Name-saying platform," a platform about six feet square set up in the midst of the spectators in the pit during the Edo era. Actors stepped onto the *nanoridai* from the *hanamichi** and performed acting bits, such as informing the audience of their character's name, reciting special speeches, and so forth. It was the only interesting stage device created during the Genbun era (1736-40), but it no longer exists. (*See also* THEATRE ARCHITECTURE.)

NARABI DAIMYŌ. Rows of formally dressed *daimyō* who appear in various history plays and provide an impressive background to the action. The term has been adopted as a general expression to refer to any group of individuals who sit in formal rows without saying or doing anything. Similar terms refer to rows of courtesans *(narabi keisei)* and rows of ladies-in-waiting *(narabi koshimoto)*.

NARAKU. "Hell." The area beneath the stage and *hanamichi**. Its existence came about when the revolving stage* and elevator traps (*see* SERI) made it necessary for the theatre to have a cellar area. It was quite dark there in the early days, so the term *naraku* was coined to describe the area. Today, the area houses the electric mechanism for the traps and revolve, the heating and air conditioning systems, and some dressing rooms. The term *naraku* is now used to apply to the underground passageway running beneath the *hanamichi* from the stage to the *agemaku** room.

NARIMONO. A general term for *geza** musical instruments other than the *shamisen**. The performance of these instruments or the music performed is called *narimono*, a word used interchangeably with *hayashi**. The musicians* performing *narimono* are the *hayashigata* or *narimonoshi.* When they appear on stage and sit on the bottom step of the stepped and red-carpeted musicians' platform *(hinadan*)*, they are termed *shita kata* ("lower people"). The main *narimono* instruments are the *ōtsuzumi** and *kotsuzumi** drums, the *taiko* drum, the flute (*fue*, the Nō theatre version; another flute

Important musical instruments played in the *geza**. (A) *Chappa, matsumushi, rei, atarigane**; (B) *kin, mokugyō*; (C) *dora*; (D) *hontsurigane*; (E) *soroban*; (F) *ōdaiko*; (G) *kotsuzumi**; (H) *taiko*; and (I) *okedō*. *Courtesy of Waseda University Tsubouchi Engeki Hakubutsukan (Tsubouchi Memorial Theatre Museum).*

is the bamboo *shinobue*), the *ōdaiko* drum, and the numerous accessory instruments called the *daibyōshi, okidō, gaku taiko, e daiko, uchiwa taiko, mame taiko* (all drums); *hontsurigane, dora, sōban, hitotsugane, matsumushi, horegōre, atarigane**, *chappa, ekiro, kin* (metal instruments and bells); *mokugyō, kigane, hyōshigi**, *hangi, binzasara* (wooden instruments); and *yotsu take* and *mokkin* (bamboo instruments), among others.

NARUKAMI. Tsuuchi Hanjūrō, Yasuda Abun, Nakada Mansuke. English title: *Saint Narukami*, part of *Narukami and Lord Fudo* (Brandon); *Narukami* (Watanabe). *Jidaimono**. Kabuki. One act. January 1742. Ōnishi Shibai, Osaka.

This play belongs to the Ichikawa family play collecton, the *kabuki jūhachiban**. It is an independent play, but was originally the fourth act of *Narukami Fudō Kitayama Sakura*, which also includes two other *jūhachiban* plays, *Kenuki** and *Fudō*. The plot of this play is a classic one in Japan; it has its antecedents in ancient Indian and Chinese legends. A famous Nō play, *Ikkaku Sennin*, tells much the same tale. Ichikawa Danjūrō I* performed several times in a work treating the same story. His son, Danjūrō II*, also appeared in an earlier version before achieving great success in 1742 with *Narukami Fudō Kitayama Sakura*, which combined the Narukami play with other familiar plots, such as that of *Kenuki** and *Fudō*. *Narukami, Kenuki*, and *Fudō* were revived often as one-act plays by actors in the Danjūrō line.

The priest Narukami, who holds a grudge against the Emperor, cages up the dragon god of rain in a cave beneath a waterfall and confines himself to a stone hut. As a result, a drought afflicts Japan; in order to save the suffering farmers, the Imperial court dispatches the beautiful Princess Kumo no Taema. She seduces the priest into depravity and releases the rain god from his cave. The god mounts to heaven, and a cloudburst occurs. The priest grows violently angry when he learns that he has been duped and runs after the princess.

Narukami is a well-constructed work that vividly portrays the human feelings of the fiery priest. Great moments include the seduction scene of the first half of the play, during which the princess urges the priest to drink sake and arouses him sensually; another comes in the second half's closing moments when the angry priest, acting in the bravura *aragoto** style, wraps his hands and feet around a pillar and performs a "pillar wrapping" pose called *hashira maki no mie* (*see also* MIE). This work was revived by Ichikawa Sadanji II* in 1910 after a long period of neglect. His rewritten version was by Oka Onitarō*.

NATIONAL THEATRE OF JAPAN. Known as the Kokuritsu Gekijō, it is located in Tokyo's Hayabusa-chō in Chiyoda-ku. The National Theatre opened in November 1966 and was created as a place for the presentation of

Japan's traditional performing arts. It also serves as a research center, theatrical archives, training center for young classical performers, and so on. It is the first theatre in Japan to have been built under national sponsorship. The National Theatre possesses a large and a small playhouse, and its exterior is modeled after the appearance of an ancient Japanese log cabin *(azekura)*. The large theatre holds 1,746 spectators and is chiefly for Kabuki. In the little theatre public performances of Bunraku, Nō, Japanese dance, folk performances *(minzoku geinō)*, and the like are held. It holds 630 spectators.

NATORI GUSA HEIKE MONOGATARI. Kawatake Mokuami*. Also called *Shigemori Kangen. Jidaimono**. Kabuki. Three acts. May 1876. Nakamura-za*, Tokyo.

A dramatization in *katsureki geki* ("living history*") style of several tales from the *Heike Monogatari*, one of Japan's famous medieval chronicles. Today only the *Shigemori Kangen* scene is played. Shigemori hastens to Kiyomori, who wants to close in on the Imperial Palace. Shigemori advises Kiyomori against acting with a weak plan. Since Kiyomori refuses to listen, Shigemori gathers all his troops together. In the face of this, Kiyomori finally agrees to Shigemori's ideas.

Shigemori was one of Ichikawa Danjūrō IX's* best roles, so this scene was included in his collection of favorites, the *shin kabuki jūhachiban**.

NATSU KYŌGEN. *See* SUMMER PLAYS.

NATSU MATSURI (NANIWA KAGAMI). Namiki Sōsuke*, Miyoshi Shōraku, Takeda Koizumo. *Sewamono**. *Jōrūri**. Nine acts. July 1745. Takemoto-za, Osaka.

In August 1745 Kyoto's Miyako Mandayū-za and Hoteiya-za competed with a Kabuki version of this play which deals with materials similar to those used in *Yadonashi Danshichi Shigure no Karakasa** by Namiki Shōzō*. In 1747 Edo's first production was staged. The play depicts a rivalry between "street knights" *(otokodate)*. The scenes performed today are Act III's *Sumiyoshi Torii Mae*, Act VI's *Sabu Uchi*, and Act VII's *Nagamachi Ura*.

Danshichi Kurobei has been put in prison for wounding one of Ōtora Sagaemon's retainers, but he is released through the good offices of Tamashima Heitayū. Danshichi gets into a fight with Issun Tokubei, a bodyguard of Sagaemon, before the Sumiyoshi Shrine, but they make peace when they realize that they both are really supporters of Isonojō and his father, Heitayū, and enemies of Sagaemon. They swear blood brotherhood to each other *(Sumiyoshi Torii Mae)*.

Heitayū's son Isonojō is in love with the courtesan Kotoura. She is seeking to escape the clutches of Sagaemon, who desires her, so the two take refuge at the home of Tokubei's father-in-law, Tsurifune no Sabu. Since Isonojō has been recently involved in a scandal concerning stolen money, it is necessary for him to leave town for a while. Tokubei's wife, Otatsu, arrives and undertakes to accompany Isonojō back to his home in the country. Since there is some doubt about the propriety of Isonojō's traveling with a woman as strikingly beautiful as Otatsu, she sacrifices her beauty by taking red hot tongs and pressing them to her face, disfiguring it. Because of a matter having to do with some money, Danshichi's father-in-law, Giheiji, tricks Kotoura and takes her away with him *(Sabu Uchi).*

Danshichi has promised to look after the girl's welfare, so he pursues Giheiji and Kotoura. He overtakes them in a back street off the Nagamachi and pleads with Giheiji to return the girl, but the selfish old man mercilessly reviles him and, to make matters worse, refuses to comply. Danshichi eventually kills him and, concealing himself in the noisy festival procession passing just then, flees the scene. *(Nagamachi Ura).*

Highlights of the first scene include Danshichi's change from the look of a prisoner to that of a dashing *otokodate* (following a shave and a haircut) and the fight scene between Danshichi and Tokubei. The scene in Sabu's home features the acting of the *onnagata** playing Otatsu, who must make a memorable show of gallant behavior. The back-street scene in which the villainous Giheiji is murdered is performed with real water and mud and presents Danshichi in a beautiful pattern of movement as he dominates the stage wearing only a loincloth, which reveals a body almost completely covered with tattoos. This macabre, yet visually exciting, murder scene vividly conveys the spirit of the summer season.

NEBIKI NO KADOMATSU. Chikamatsu Monzaemon*. English title: *The Uprooted Pine* (Keene). *Sewamono*. Jōruri*.* Three acts. January 1718. Takemoto-za, Osaka.

The protagonists of the play are a couple famous in folksong, Yamazaki Yojibei and his courtesan mistress Azuma.

Naniwa Yohei, who has come down in the world, is madly in love with a Shinmachi district courtesan, Fujiya Azuma, but he has no money with which to frequent the pleasure quarters. Azuma, struck by his feelings, confides his dilemma to Yojibei, who gives Yohei ten *ryō* so that he can at least be a brothel guest. Yohei, deeply impressed by Azuma's spirit and Yojibei's gallantry, leaves for Edo with the money so that he can get a job and earn a living. Before leaving, however, he is involved in an incident during which he inflicts a wound upon Yojibei's love rival, Haya Sansuke. Out of a sense of duty, Yojibei assumes responsibility for the crime and is confined to the home of Jōkan, his father. Azuma comes to visit him, and with the sympathy of Yojibei's wife (Okiku) and Jōkan the couple run away together. Later, Yojibei wanders about in a state of madness while Azuma cares for him. Having earned a lot of money, Yohei returns from Edo, redeems Azuma, and has the lovers married. Yojibei recovers his sanity.

The heart of the piece occurs in the scene in Jōkan's home. Here we see the expression of human emotions by a shopkeeper and by a samurai when Jōkan and Jibuemon, Okiku's father, draw near their children. Other highly emotional moments include the presentation of Azuma and Yojibei's deep feelings as they prepare to run away.

NEHON. A special term used in the Kamigata area for Kabuki scripts. It is also an abbreviation for the published illustrated scripts called *eiri nehon.* They were rice-paper books in script form composed of dialogue and stage directions. They usually came in six or seven volumes, and each volume had several illustrations, the pictures resembling the faces of contemporary actors. The practice began in the Anei period (1772-80) and reached its apex in the first third of the nineteenth century. (*See also* SHŌHON.)

NEMURU GA RAKUDA MONOGATARI. Oka Onitarō*. *Shin kabuki**. Three acts. March 1929. Hongo-za, Tokyo.

A comedy based on a story told in the traditional *rakugo** style.

Rakuda no Uma, disliked by the people of his neighborhood, has died after eating blowfish *(fugu).* Everyone rejoices at the news. Soon, Hanji, a friend of the dead man's whom he had treated as his younger brother, comes along and entices "Paper Collector" Kyuroku, who is hesitant at first, to bring Uma's corpse with him to the tenement proprietor's residence. There they make the corpse do a comical dance. They are treated to sake and tidbits, and Hanji and Kyuroku start to feast. The latter, who was reticent at first, now becomes animated and starts to quarrel with Hanji. Then, news arrives that Hanji's mother has died, and the tone softens.

This short piece is often staged as an entr'acte, and it expresses well a side of lower-class life in Edo, depicting the changes and vicissitudes of the human mind.

NEOI. An actor who is a true-born son of a vicinity where the generations of his ancestors have lived. For example, it is common to refer to one of the Ichikawa Danjūrō* line as an Edo-*neoi* actor.

NETA. The word *tane* ("seed") with the syllables reversed. It means the source from which a play's subject derives.

NEW KABUKI. *See* SHIN KABUKI.

NEW YEAR'S PLAYS. An Edo period seasonal programming event called *hatsuharu kyōgen* or *hatsu shibai.* In the Kamigata area, where it was the second production of the season (following the November *kaomise** performances), it was termed *ni no kawari.* At first, the custom was to open on the second day of the new year, but during the Ansei era (1854-59) the practice of starting on the fifteenth day was established. It was an old custom in Edo for the New Year's plays to deal with the story of the Soga brothers' vendetta; thus, the final scene of the program's history-play half was the popular *Soga no Taimen**. This custom continued up to 1868. (*See also* THEATRE MANAGEMENT.)

NEZUMI KABE. "Rat wall," the scenic element of a wall used in the shabby stage houses of poor people and farmers. It is seen, for example, in Act VI of *Kanadehon Chūshingura** and in the Fuku River scene of *Tōkaidō Yotsuya Kaidan**.

NEZUMI KIDO. The "rat entrance"; a name given to the entranceway to theatres during the Edo period. The name was taken from the doorway's resemblance to a rodent hole, as it was so low that spectators had to bend over in order to go in and out through it. In eighteenth-century theatres it was situated just under the *yagura** drum tower at the theatre's front. The *nezumi kido* was created as a measure to prevent spectators from rushing inside without paying for their admission. (*See also* THEATRE ARCHITECTURE.)

NIBANME MONO. The second half of an Edo period program. The Kamigata custom was to have two plays on a program, the first being a history play *(ichibanme mono*)*, the second a domestic play. The *nibanme mono* was a domestic play. (*See also* JIDAIMONO; SEWAMONO.) The custom was introduced to Edo in 1795 by Namiki Gohei I*.

NIBUSEI. The production method by which two programs are presented in one day. Separate day and evening programs first began to be produced in the Kamigata area during the Meiji period. The system was adopted in Tokyo by the little theatres *(koshibai*)*, but was not followed by the big theatres *(ōshibai*)* until after the Teikoku Gekijō* adopted it in May 1923. This system is common today, except at the National Theatre of Japan*. Although it is quite profitable for the producers, it has been criticized as overworking the actors. Some theatres, such as the Kabuki-za*, present different plays on each program. Others repeat the same plays at each performance. The National Theatre repeats the same play at each performance, but it presents its two programs per day only on Sundays, offering only matinees (*see also* MACHINEE) on Wednesdays and holidays.

NICHŌ. The backstage warning signal given to ensure that the stage properties are ready and to hasten the actor's preparations. It is struck about ten minutes before the curtain is opened. The term derives from the two beats *(nichō)* of the *hyōshigi** given in front of the backstage manager's room *(tōdoriza; see also* TŌDORI). Hearing it, the actors begin to put on their wigs. Many theatres now use a bell for this function, but even this is rung twice.

NIDAN. A platform for a *mie** in dance plays, usually by a ghost at the final tableau. This "two-step" *(nidan)* playform is used by leading *onnagata** in contrast to the *sandan**, or "three-step," variety used by *tachiyaku**.

NIGATSUDŌ (RŌBEN SUGI NO YURAI). Kako Chikajo(?), Toyozawa Danpei. *Jidaimono**. *Jōruri**. Three acts. February 1887. Hikoroku-za, Osaka.

The young son of Nagisa no Kata—wife of Minase, a Suga family samurai—is snatched away by an eagle while he is watching the picking of tea. His mother, having become mad, wanders throughout the country, searching for her son. Thirty years later, having just recovered her senses, she arrives in Nara. One day, when the famous Tōdaiji Temple priest Rōben pays a visit to Nigatsu Hall, he discovers a notice posted on the great cryptomeria tree in the compound. It reads: "I am searching for the whereabouts of my son, snatched away from me thirty years ago." He finds the writer of the notice and confronts her; she is little more than a beggar. During her tale, he realizes that they are mother and son, and with great joy he returns with his mother, having her ride in a splendid palanquin.

This play, which is quite uncomplicated for a Meiji period work, is rich in dramatic effect, despite its simplicity.

NIHON BUYŌ. Classical Japanese dance. (*See also* DANCE.)

NIHON GUMA. Also called the *Matsuō no guma*, this "two-line *kuma*" is a makeup style worn by Matsuō in the *Kuruma Biki* scene of *Sugawara Denju Tenarai Kagami**. The makeup consists of two oblique lines rising from the eyebrows and paralleled by two others, one on either side of the eyes. It has come to be called *nihon guma* in recent years to contrast it with *ippon* ("one-line") *guma**. This style is said to have been created by Ichikawa Danjūrō IV*. It is almost the same as that called *Shikan suji* (named for an actor).

NIJŌJŌ NO KIYOMASA. Yoshida Gensaburō. *Shin kabuki**. Two acts. October 1933. Tōkyō Gekijō, Tokyo.

A drama featuring the role of the loyal retainer Katō Kiyomasa; it is based on the historical meeting in 1611 at Nijō Castle between Tokugawa Ieyasu (1542-1616) and Toyotomi Hideyori (1593-1615). The part of Kiyomasa was written for Nakamura Kichiemon I*.

Expecting danger, Kiyomasa, though ill, undertakes to protect his young lord, Hideyori, when he is summoned to meet with Ieyasu at Nijō Castle. He manifests his usual sincerity during the meeting. On the return trip, in the interior of the boat taking them down the Yodo River, Hideyori sincerely thanks Kiyomasa. Thinking of the young lord's present low estate, the latter weeps.

The acting of Kiyomasa, when he has resolved to stab Ieyasu with the dagger hidden at his bosom, and the exchange of affection between master and servant, as they look up at the tower of Osaka Castle from their boat, are rich in the flavor of *shin kabuki*. The role of Kiyomasa, one of Kichiemon I's best, is included in his collection, *hideyama jūshū** (*see also* FAMILY ART).

NIJŪ. Also called *nijū butai*, these are scenic platforms built on a higher level than the stage floor. Such platform sets depict house interiors, embankments, hills, and so forth. A flooring about five inches thick, the *hiradai*, is attached to a platform of standard height (called the *okuashi*, *hakama*, or *sashiashi*). Painted flats *(kekkomi)* conceal the front face. The stage platforms are classed according to their height as the *shakudaka* (one foot), *tsune ashi* (one foot five inches), *chūashi* (two feet three inches), and *takaashi* (two feet ten inches). Ordinary people's homes are on *tsune ashi*, while *takaashi* is used for palaces and temples. When a verandah extension is built onto the front or sides of a *nijū* setting, a wooden platform called the *hon'en*, measuring two or three feet in depth by three to nine feet in length, is employed. (*See also* SCENERY.)

NIKU JUBAN. Also called *niku* ("flesh"), this is a tight-fitting flesh-colored undergarment worn to signify nakedness after the outer costume has been removed. Gallant commoner characters also wear it as a base for tattoos that are painted on it. From the audience, the *niku juban* painted with tattoos looks like the actor's own skin, especially since the actor normally wears white body makeup matching the white color of the tattooed garment. It is seen on Danshichi in *Natsu Matsuri Naniwa Kagami** and Benten Kozō in *Aotozōshi Hana no Nishikie**. Actors dressed as huge characters such as sumo wrestlers wear a thick padded *niku*. Among those who wear it are the wrestlers in *Kami no Megumi Wagō no Torikumi**.

NIMAIME. Young, handsome lover roles; also, the actor who plays such roles. The word comes from the practice, during the Edo era, of writing these actors' names on the second of the eight billboards *(kanban*)* hanging in front of the playhouses. *Nimaime* means "second flat thing." The *nimaime*'s onstage costume and makeup are generally fixed by tradition; he wears white face makeup and behaves like a gentle, delicate young man. An important *nimaime* type is the *iro wakashu*, a beautiful youth who has just reached adult status and who is the love interest in a play. He is performed in the *wagoto** style, a Kamigata method that emphasizes the foolishness of a young man who is blindly in love. *Nimaime* roles often are played with a rather comical aspect in such situations, it being said that "the *nimaime* must act with the heart of a *sanmaime*" (a clownlike role; *see also* DŌKEGATA). Since he is a lover, he also is called the *irogotoshi* or the *nuregotoshi*, terms denoting a romantic character. Such characters also include the *wakadanna*, whose femininity and flaccid physical features gave rise to another term by which he may be known—*tsukkorobashi* ("pushover"). And there are those *nimaime* called *pintokona* who were formerly samurai and have a rather haughty mien.

A popular type of scene is the *yatsushi* ("disguise"), which shows a young lord whose family has been destroyed by the machinations of evil men; he has changed his lordly status for that of a commoner and visits the brothel where his former lover, now a courtesan, is employed. The former samurai displays ardor and refinement despite his lowly guise. *Yatsushi* also refers to the important class of *nimaime* role types that feature such characters. Another type of *nimaime* is the noble young lord in *Shibaraku** who is designated a *tachishita* ("under the sword") role type; just as he is about to be killed by the villains, the *aragoto** hero of the play shouts, "Wait a minute!" *(shibaraku)* and appears on the *hanamichi** to save him. The *tachishita* is a weakling who shudders beneath the villain's sword and has a different name in order to identify him from all other *nimaime* types. (*See also* TACHI-YAKU.)

NIMAIME SAKUSHA. The playwright who was next in importance to the *tate sakusha** in an Edo period theatre. He was the *tate sakusha*'s adviser in everything. His playwriting duties involved the writing of the fourth piece *(yontateme*)* on the *kaomise** program. This was a dance performed to a *jōruri** narrative accompaniment. He also prepared the *sewamono** portion of the *kaomise* production, and was responsible for writing a suitable act suggested by the *tate sakusha* for any other new plays being created at the theatre. If the chief playwright was ill, he wrote from his superior's dictation, a practice called *fude tori* ("taking the brush"). He also ran the preliminary reading of the play, the first company reading *(honyomi*)*, and helped those actors who had problems with their roles. (*See also* PLAYWRIGHTS' RANKS.)

NIN. "Person"; used in expressions such as "his person is fine" *(nin ga ii)* or "his person is appropriate" *(nin ga kanau)*, when an actor is well suited to his role.

NINGEN BANJI KANE YO NO NAKA. Kawatake Mokuami*. *Sewamono**. Kabuki. Three acts. February 1879. Shintomi-za, Tokyo.

An adaptation from *Money*, a novel by the English writer Bulwer-Lytton, this play's value lies in its being one of the *zangiri mono** ("cropped-hair plays"), which show the new customs introduced into Japan from the West during the early Meiji period. Members of the first cast were Onoe Kikugorō V* as Rinnosuke, Ichikawa Sadanji I* as Utsuzō, Nakamura Nakazō III* as Seizaemon, and Iwai Hanshirō VIII* as Okura.

When his father's business fails, Efu Rinnosuke is put in the care of his uncle from Yokohama, Henmi Seizaemon. Seizaemon is a stingy deputy and treats Rinnosuke coldly. However, when a certain relative dies, a large share of his inheritance is left to Rinnosuke. Seizaemon quickly begins to treat Rinnosuke as if he were important and asks him to marry his daughter Ohin. To test Seizaemon's sincerity, the youth says that he has used the money to pay off his father's old debts. Hearing this, Seizaemon reverts to his original attitude. Presently, Rinnosuke revives his father's shop and marries Okura, Seizaemon's niece, who, as a maidservant at Seizaemon's house, had been treated as poorly as he.

Ningen Banji Kane Yo no Naka was the first Kabuki adaptation from another nation's literature and was applauded for its satirization of contemporary manners.

NINGYŌ BURI. A scene from a puppet play or part of a scene that is acted by the characters in puppet fashion; a puppet manipulator seems to move the actors from behind. The movements are jerky, like those of puppets. Characters who use the technique include Yaegaki in *Honchō Nijūshikō**, Oshichi in *Hade Sugata Onna Maiginu**, Ofune in *Shinrei Yaguchi no Watashi**, and Iwanaga in *Dan no Ura Kabuto Gunki**.

NINJŌ BANASHI BUNSHICHI MOTOYUI. Sanyūtei Enchō (verbal narrative), Enokido Kenji (dramatic adaptation). Also called *Bunshichi Motoyui. Sewamono**. Kabuki. Three acts. September 1902. Kabuki-za*, Tokyo.

On his way home, Chōbei the plasterer, having obtained 100 *ryō* by the efforts of his faithful daughter, saves a young clerk from throwing himself into the river. Named Bunshichi, he says that he was going to die because he lost his master's money. Chōbei gives him the 100 *ryō*. This leads to Chōbei's wife quarreling with him. However, Bunshichi and his master come to Chōbei's home and explain that the money thought to be lost was actually never paid by a customer, and they apologize profusely. The master, aware of Chōbei's public spirit, suggests that he ransom Chōbei's daughter Ohisa from her position as a courtesan and have her marry Bunshichi. Bunshichi contrives a new paper cord for tying up his hair, leaves the shop with Ohisa, and gains a reputation as "Bunshichi of the paper cord" (Bunshichi Motoyui).

The play depicts people of good intentions, and the performance, based on the style inherited by Onoe Kikugorō VI* from Kikugorō V*, has made

The technique of *ningyō buri**, whereby a character is manipulated as if a puppet. A scene from *Hidakagawa Iriai Zakura**. Kiyohime, Onoe Baikō VI*. *Courtesy of Waseda University Tsubouchi Engeki Hakubutsukan (Tsubouchi Memorial Theatre Museum).*

the work a choice item among modern *sewamono*. Others in the original cast were the actors who eventually became Ichimura Uzaemon XV* and Onoe Baikō VI*.

NISHI. "West," the audience's left as they face the stage. (*See also* HIGASHI.)

NISHIKAWA RYŪ. A school of Japanese dance, founded by Nishikawa Senzō in 1698. He had been a Nō musician, became a Kabuki musician, and finally turned to choreography. Senzō II was an outstanding choreographer (*furitsukeshi; see also* FURITSUKE) at Edo's three theatres during the late eighteenth and early nineteenth centuries, leaving such works behind as *Sagi Musume**, *Yoshiwara Suzume, Yosaku, Ataka no Matsu,* and *Seki no To**. Senzō IV was an outstanding figure in the line's history and did the original choreography for *Kanjinchō**, as well as creating highly praised choreography for *Utsubo Zaru**, *Rokkasen**, and *Tomoyakko*. Senzō V was responsible for devising the dances for such famous works as *Noriai-bune**, *Ayatsuri Sanbasō* (*see* SANBASŌ) and *Kyō Ningyō*. The leadership of the school was passed down through the years to several other dancers, including some females, and is now in the hands of Senzō X. There are two subschools, the Nagoya Nishikawa *ryū* and the Seiha Nishikawa *ryū*.

NOBORI. Banners given by a backer to a theatre, producer, or actor. They were arranged in a line near the entrance to the theatre in the old days.

NONKO. A large, thick topknot with a high base; it is worn by "street knights" (*otokodate*) and gang bosses (*oyabun*). Characters on whom it may be seen include Banzui Chōbei (in several plays), Tsurifune no Sabu in *Natsu Matsuri Naniwa Kagami**, Kyō in *Harusamegasa*, and others. The *kabuse nonko* belongs to the same class and is a topknot worn by young *otokodate*, such as Gosho no Gorozō and Kurotegumi Sukeroku. The *iro nonko* is seen on romantic footmen, such as Chienai in *Kiichi Hōgen Sanryaku no Maki** and Tsumahei in *Shin Usuyuki Monogatari**.

NORENGUCHI. An entranceway seen in sets representing house interiors. It is about six feet high by two to four feet in width and has split curtains (*noren*) hanging from its top, giving it its name. According to the scene, the pattern on the curtains might be of waves, bracken, flowing water, jute leaves, and so on. The design usually is white on a pale blue, navy, or gray background.

NORI. Acting and speaking in time to the rhythm of the *shamisen**. Also called *ito ni noru* ("riding the strings") and *chobo ni noru* ("riding the *chobo**").

It is used frequently in scenes of *monogatari**, *gochūshin**, and lamentation* *(kudoki)*. The musical accompaniment usually stops about halfway through the actor's lines, and he returns to more normal speech, a technique called *hanareru*. An example is Kanpei's speech in *Ochiudo**, in which the *nori* is performed beginning with the words *"umi no shujin no . . . "* and normal speech resumes at *"saa korekara wa."*

NORIAIBUNE. Sakurada Jisuke III*. Also called *Kashiragaki Ise Monogatari, Kioi Uta Soga no Hanadashi, Noriaibune Eho Manzai*. *Shosagoto**. *Tokiwazu**. January 1843. Ichimura-za*, Edo.

This number is all that is left of a longer piece known by the alternate titles given above.

Noriaibune introduces a variety of characters gathered in early spring at the Sumida River ferry; they include two comic dancers, a carpenter, a white-wine seller, a priestess, a man-about-town, a female mariner, and the like, all of whom display their particular occupation in dance.

The dance effectively depicts the customs of city people in early spring. At its heart is the dance of Manzai and Saizō. It is often presented as a New Year's performance*. Ichimura Uzaemon XII danced six roles in the original production, and was supported by Nakamura Utaemon IV*, Ichikawa Kuzō, Seki Sanjūrō III, Onoe Kikujirō, and Bandō Shūka. Kabuki productions of this play lagged until 1896, when an excellent revival was staged at Tokyo's Haruki-za by Ichikawa Ennosuke I and Nakamura Kangorō. This production brought the work back to popularity.

NORIBENI. Stage blood. It is prepared by mixing and cooking several ingredients—industrial-grade cinnabar, wheat flour, glue, salt, and lye—into a sort of paste. This is rolled into a small ball and wrapped in paper. When needed for use, it is smeared on the body. In some cases the *noribeni* is boiled until it is of a thin consistency. This may be splashed on the actor or placed in the shell of an egg, which is crushed so that the blood seems to pour forth naturally. *Fukumi ko* is the term for the effect of blood oozing from the mouth; a preparation is made of red coloring, cinnabar, and unrefined sugar and then placed in a small pellet. When the actor bites this, the blood flow out. A famous example of its use is by Sadakurō in Act V of *Kanadehon Chūshingura**. *Abura beni**, an oil-based red makeup, is used to represent wounds in such places as the forehead; it is kept ready in the palm of the hand and applied when the actor puts his hand to his head.

NORIKOMI. When actors from the Kamigata area performed in Edo, they were called *kudari yakusha** ("going-down actors"); the opposite term was *agari yakusha* ("going-up actors"). The ceremony enacted when such actors arrived at the place where they were to perform was called *norikomi* ("embarkation"). Popular actors from Edo who were to play in Osaka boarded an ornately decked boat and entered the theatre from the Dōtonbori canal. This was called *fune* ("boat") *norikomi.* When the actor entered the theatre, he was welcomed onstage by the chief local actors, and a drinking bout ensued. In the case of provincial tours, the whole company would march all around the town as a publicity stunt and then enter the playhouse. This was called *machi mawari** ("around the town"). On occasion, a performance would be put on as soon as the actors arrived. This was termed *norikomi shonichi* or *noriuchi.* (*See also* ACTORS.)

NOSHIME. A kimono worn under formal *kamishimo** dress by samurai in the Edo period. Made of solid-colored silk, only the waist and lower portion of the sleeves have a pattern. Originally a Nō costume, it is used in Kabuki as a *kitsuke** for *daimyō* and other high-ranking samurai. Hangan in *Kanadehon Chūshingura** is a good example. Jūjirō in Act X of *Ehon Taikōki** and Katsuyori in *Honchō Nijūshikō** are instances of young samurai who wear *noshime* bearing exquisite designs.

NUIGURUMI. Special property costumes worn by actors impersonating animals. They were formerly under the charge of the costume masters, but are now taken care of by the prop personnel. There are *nuigurumi* costumes that cover the entire body, others worn only from the neck down, and others worn from the hips upward. The horse is the largest example and is worn by two men in leggings resembling a horse's limbs. For a boar, the hind legs are obviously human, and the *nuigurumi* is worn on the back. The wide variety of Kabuki animals includes bears, foxes, badgers, sheep, elephants, lions, dogs, cats, rats, and monkeys. (*See also* UMA NO ASHI.)

Actor wearing *nuigurumi** representing a boar. After a drawing in Fujinami, *Kabuki no Kodōgu.*

NUREBA. *See* LOVE SCENES.

NUREGOTO. The style of acting used in love scenes*.

NYŪJŌ RYŌ. "Admission fees." As a rule, the most expensive seats at Edo Kabuki performances were those in the *sajiki** galleries on the left and right of the theatre, followed by those in the box seating in the pit (*doma**). After this came the seating in the *kiriotoshi** seats, where the masses sat huddled together. In addition, there were the seats at the rear of the stage called the *yoshino** and *rakan** sections as well as the rear seating on the second story, which constituted the lowest category of seats. Until 1868 the usual number of persons in a box *(masu*)* was seven. Thereafter, five persons could occupy these places. Chair seating appeared on a partial basis in the mid-Meiji era, while a complete system of chair seating did not appear until the Teikoku Gekijō* opened in 1911. (*See also* THEATRE ARCHITECTURE; THEATRE MANAGEMENT.)

O

OBENTŌ O TSUKERU. "To add a box lunch"; when an actor adds lines or business not called for in the original script.

ŌBEYA. The communal dressing room on the third floor of the Edo period playhouses. It was used by the lesser ranks of actors, from the *nadai shita* (*see also* ACTORS' RANKS) downward. The *ōbeya* was a large wood-floored room located amidst the leading actors' dressing rooms and near the entrance to the third floor. Theatre gatherings were held here, such as the dress rehearsal *(sōzarai),* the first company meeting before the staging of a new play, the musical rehearsal *(tsuketate),* and so on (*see also* REHEARSALS). The actors using this room were called the *ōbeya* or *ōbeyasan* and the *sangai** ("third floor"). However, since the lower-ranking *onnagata** were housed in a large second-floor room, the term *ōbeya* referred only to players of male roles. (*See also* CHŪ NIKAI; BACKSTAGE.)

OCHIIRI. The death of a wounded stage character. The verb *ochiiru* ("to lapse or fall into," that is, "to pass away") also is common. There are many scenes of *ochiiri,* one being Act VI in *Kanadehon Chūshingura**: Kanpei, after stabbing himself, delivers a lengthy account of his recollections and then dies.

OCHIUDO. Mimasuya Nisōji. Also called *Michiyuki Tabiji no Hanamuke. Shosagoto**. *Kiyomoto**. March 1833. Kawarazaki-za, Edo.

A musical work based on the "rear gate" *(Uramon)* scene of Act III in *Kanadehon Chūshingura**. The setting is taken from the play's eighth act and the words are borrowed from the *Ninokuchi Mura* scene. Since the musical setting is excellent and quite popular, the inclusion of this scene in full-length productions* *(tōshi kyōgen)* of *Kanadehon Chūshingura* is usual.

While Kanpei is hurrying with Okaru to her home in the country, they come to a place in the mountains near Totsuka. Kanpei blames himself for disloyalty to his master, not having been at his side when his master committed the infraction that led to his death by ritual suicide. Kanpei wants to kill himself, but Okaru stops him; he will wait for a better opportunity. A comical villain named Sagisaka Bannai, a retainer of the evil Moronao, arrives with the intention of taking Okaru for himself, but Kanpei drives him away and then heads for Yamazaki.

This is a beautiful scene showing the two young lovers traveling through the Totsuka Mountains in spring, Mount Fuji towering in the background. It is a good example of a *michiyuki mono**.

ŌDACHI. An exaggeratedly long sword used by *aragoto** characters. (*See also* SWORDS.)

ŌDAIKO. A large stick drum. (*See also* NARIMONO; GEZA: MUSICAL ACCOMPANIMENT CHART.)

ŌDAI MONO. Also called *ōcho mono*, these are plays that deal with Imperial society during the Nara (696-794) and Heian (794-1185) periods of Japan's middle ages. However, although Emperors, princes, and other members of the Imperial family freely appear onstage, the sets, costumes, ideas, and so on are all distinctly of the Edo period. These plays include *Sugawara Denju Tenarai Kagami** and *Imoseyama Onna Teikin** (*See also* JIDAIMONO; PLAY CATEGORIES.)

ŌDATEMONO. Also called *tatemono;* a term for the leading actors in a troupe, the *zagashira** and *tate onnagata**. It is used also to refer to the highest-ranking people in society.

ŌDŌGU. *See* SCENERY.

ODORI. "Dance." Originally, the word implied a type of dancing employing leaps and jumps, as opposed to the more stately style of Nō theatre dance *(mai*)*. It refers now to most Kabuki dance. (*See also* DANCE.)

OGIE BUSHI. A musical style founded sometime during the Hōreki and Meiwa eras (1751-71) by Ogie Royū (d. 1767), a *nagauta** musician. It was handed down as an entertainment for private parties in the Yoshiwara pleasure quarters. This school of music has a delicate and charming flavor.

OGINO SAWANOJŌ. 1656-1704. An *onnagata** of the last years of the seventeenth century, he gained fame in Osaka, went to Edo in 1692, and was active playing opposite Ichikawa Danjūrō I*. He was thought of as the best contemporary player of young female roles *(wakaonnagata)* in Kyoto, Edo, and Osaka. Roles in which he specialized were those of wives and courtesans in both history and domestic plays.

OGINO YAEGIRI I. d. 1736. The most famous actor in his line. He appeared mainly as a player of young female roles *(wakaonnagata)* in Osaka, went to Edo in 1705, and became popular there. After returning to Osaka in 1708, he became an actor-manager *(zamoto*)* and was the most popular of Osaka's *wakaonnagata.* Yaegiri, the heroine of Chikamatsu Monzaemon's* *Komochi Yamanba** was given this actor's name in order to cash in on its appeal.

The next two generations of actors in the line failed to achieve comparable fame.

ŌGIRI. The ending of a domestic play, the second play on an Edo period program. In it the hero and heroine performed a *michiyuki** ("travel dance") or *shosagoto** (dance drama) related to the plot; such pieces are called *ōgiri kyōgen.* During the last days of the Edo era the *ōgiri* was performed as an independent dance play having no relation to the play preceding it. It was staged in order to provide a bright and lively aura to the day's performance. Another term meaning the same thing is *kiri kyōgen.* (*See also* ŌZUME.)

ŌGURUWA. Scenes using a spectacular set, a complex plot, and a lively crowd of characters, that is, scenes in which everything is on a grand scale. The Daitoku Temple incense offering scene in *Hisago Gunki* and the Yoshino River scene in *Imoseyama Onna Teikin** are examples.

OHAKO. An acting family's artistic forte and its special plays and roles (*see also* FAMILY ART). Thus, since the Ichikawa family's specialty is the collection of plays called the *kabuki jūhachiban**, the word *jūhachiban*—when written—may be read *ohako.* The word *ohako* is said to derive from the idea of placing one's important art in a box *(hako).*

OIE KYŌGEN (or MONO). Also called *sodo mono,* these are plays dealing with the quarrels within an Edo period family over the right to succession or treating the theme of revenge. *Daimyō* and their vassals are the main characters. Evil retainers and their henchmen plot the overthrow of a family; because of these wicked machinations loyal samurai are forced to undergo various hardships. The evil ones ultimately are killed, and peace comes to the family. Such plays flourished greatly in the Genroku era (1688-1703) and were normally played at the annual *kaomise** ("face-showing") and *ni no kawari* performances in the Kamigata area; the plays invariably included the same role types and dramatic elements. For example, there was the weak-minded young lord; his mistress, the courtesan; the evil, plotting regent; the downfall of the noble samurai, and so forth. Later, real family quarrels occurring during the Tokugawa regime were dramatized, but since there was a ban against use of the real names of the participants, most of the dramas were placed in periods prior to that of the Tokugawa, making them "history plays" *(jidaimono*).* Famous *oie mono* include *Adachi Sodo, Kaga Sodo,* and *Yanagizawa Sodo.* (*See also* PLAY CATEGORIES.)

OIKOMI. "Driven into a corner"; an abbreviation of *oikomiba,* seating in which the spectators were crammed together as closely as possible. Also called *ōiriba.* This area was located to the rear of the crosswalk *(ayumi*)* connecting the theatre's two *hanamichi**; the *kiriotoshi** or unpartitioned seating in the *doma** was also *oikomi*-style. When the number of *masu** boxes gradually increased toward the end of the Edo period, all that remained of the *oikomi* seating was a portion at the rear of the first and second floors and at the rear of the *hanamichi.* These seats were extremely inexpensive. (*See also* THEATRE ARCHITECTURE.)

ŌIRI. "Full house," a term used when a successful play performs to packed houses. When such occasions arise, the producer presents all concerned with a small red-paper package on which the word *ōiri* is written in white. The package contains a congratulatory bonus and is called *ōiri fukuro* or simply *ōiri.* When the opposite occurs and a play fails, *fuiri** ("poor house") is the term applied. *(See also* ATARU; FŪFŪ.)

ŌJI. A distinctive wig with long hair trailing down the back. It is worn by villains in history plays. Iruka in *Imoseyama Onna Teikin** is an example.

ŌJIDAI. "Grand period"; acting and production in old history plays employing fantastic situations and highly exaggerated and stylized performance elements.

OJIGI O SURU. "To bow humbly"; when an actor skillfully declines a role for which he does not care.

OJISAN. "Pop," a familiar term used in reference to an actor who is old enough to be one's father.

OKAMOTO KIDŌ. 1872-1939. A playwright, born in Tokyo and best known for his plays *Shūzenji Monogatari*, Toribeyama Shinjū**, and *Banchō Sarayashiki**, as well as for a popular novel, *Hanshichi Torimono Chō.* At first he was a dramatic critic for a newspaper, but took up writing plays for Ichikawa Sadanji II*. His style is unconventional, restrained, and brimming with seasonal associations and poetic sentiments. As the representative writer of New Kabuki *(shin kabuki*),* he was successful enough for there to have been a time called the "golden age of Kidō drama." His private name was Keiji.

OKAMURA SHIKŌ. 1881-1925. A playwright born in Kōchi, he specialized in writing new plays based on Kyōgen farces; these include *Bōshibari**, *Migawari Zazen**, and *Tachi Nusubito**. His charming and gentle style in such plays as *Wankyū Sue no Matsuyama* was highly appreciated, too. He first gained recognition as a playwright and later became both playwright and manager at the Ichimura-za*. His private name was Kyūjuji.

OKA ONITARŌ. 1872-1943. A playwright born in Tokyo, he is known as having been a scathing and witty critic. He aided Ichikawa Sadanji II* in his late Meiji period reforms at the Meiji-za* and wrote many plays for this actor. His masterpieces include *Gozonji Azuma Otoko* and *Imayō Satsuma Uta**, works that are rich in feeling. His private name was Katorō.

OKKAKE. "Pursuit," a performance technique for scenes in which a villain is being pursued through the streets. The movement is rhythmically exaggerated to the accompaniment of lively music, giving the scene a comic quality. The pursuit in the *Ainoyama* scene of *Ise Ondo Koi no Netaba** is a famous example.

OKOTSUKU. A movement to restore balance when a character seems to stumble or fall while moving or dancing. It often is seen in hurried exits on the *hanamichi** and in dance dramas.

OKUBYŌ GUCHI. The so-called coward's door, a small entranceway found on sets modeled after the Nō stage. Placed on the stage-left side, it is four feet three and one-half inches high and two feet six inches wide. (*See also* MATSUBAME MONO.)

ŌKUCHI. Short for *ōkuchi hakama*, a costume deriving from the Nō theatre. It consists of divided culotte pants *(hakama*)* with a very wide cuff and with stiff cloth extending to the left and right at the rear of the hips. It is worn in dance plays taken from the Nō, such as *Kanjinchō**, in which it may be seen on Benkei.

OKUMI. Also called *ōkubi*, this is a part of the seating that remained on both sides of the *hanamichi** during the period when the *hanamichi* met the stage at an oblique angle and the first floor seating was being partitioned into square boxes *(masu*)*. *Okumi* was a lower class of seats. (*See also* THEATRE ARCHITECTURE.)

OKUNI KABUKI. The type of performance given by the founder of Kabuki early in the seventeenth century. (*See also* IZUMO NO OKUNI.)

OKURA. "Warehouse," a word used when a production scheduled to open is canceled. It implies that the production will be placed in the warehouse until ready.

OKURI MAKU. "Gift curtain," a Kabuki traveler curtain presented by the audience to a particular actor, usually in recognition of a special commemorative performance. Although the design differs from one actor to another, the usual *okuri maku* has the phrase "To [such and such an actor] from [such and such a donor]" written on it. A stylized painting of a strip of folded, dried abalone *(noshi)* normally appears on the stage-left side of the curtain. (*See also* CURTAINS.)

OKU YAKU. The word *oku* ("within") signifies the dressing rooms or the backstage* area *(gakuya)*. Thus, the *oku yaku* was a functionary who was concerned with all matters related to these areas. Though under the direct control of the *zamoto** or manager, he saw to the employment of actors and negotiations concerning their salaries and roles; he also controlled the negotiations held with the playwrights, scenery and property personnel, and musicians. In addition, he was an arbitrator of disputes that occasionally broke out among members of the company. In today's terms his job approached that of the *seisakusha* ("producer"). Leading actors also were called *oku yaku* when they performed managerial duties. (*See also* THEATRE MANAGEMENT.)

OMIE O KIRU. "To cut a *mie**"; said when someone speaks in an exaggerated fashion or displays great generosity.

ŌMI GENJI (SENJIN YAKATA). Chikamatsu Hanji*, Miyoshi Shōraku, Takemoto Saburobei, others. Also called *Moritsuna Jinya, Kinpachi. Jidaimono**. *Jōruri**. Nine acts. December 1769. Takemoto-za, Osaka.

This play traces the tragic demise of the historical Toyotomi family, but places the action in the Kamakura period (1185-1333), several hundred years before the actual events. Examples of historical characters whose names are changed are Tokimasa for Ieyasu, Moritsuna for Sanada Nobuyori, and Takatsuna for Sando Yukimura. Only the eighth act, *Moritsuna Jinya*, is still regularly performed. The original puppet play was very popular; Kabuki's own version followed soon after and opened in 1770 at Osaka's Nishi no Shibai.

The brothers Sasaki Moritsuna and Sasaki Takatsuna have been battling on opposite sides, one for Tokimasa and the other for Yorie. Takatsuna deliberately causes Moritsuna's son Kojirō to capture his own son Koshirō alive and makes it seem that he, Takatsuna, has been killed in battle. Tokimasa, who has brought what is presumed to be Takatsuna's head, orders Moritsuna to inspect it and verify its identity (*See also* KUBI JIKKEN). Moritsuna sees at a glance that the head is false, but Koshirō, shouting "Father!" at the sight of the head, commits suicide; moved by the boy's gallantry, Moritsuna decides to lie and testifies that the head is Takatsuna's.

The play's highlight is Moritsuna's troublesome predicament concerning his complex choice between personal feelings and duty. As he inspects the head, Moritsuna must register surprise that the head is a substitute, suspicion toward the death of Koshirō, sudden awareness of the boy's motives, a feeling of satisfaction, and the need to deceive his superiors—a range of transitions requiring great psychological subtlety in performance. Moritsuna's mother, Mimyō, is also a very difficult role, one of the three most difficult "old women" characters in Kabuki. (*See also* SANBABĀ.)

OMIGOROMO. A robe worn as civilian dress by lords, nobles, and generals in history plays. It is worn over the topmost kimono and is a *haori** jacket-like robe with a high standing collar. A thick cord decorates the chest. Yoshitsune wears it in *Yoshitsune Senbon Zakura**, as does Harunaga in *Toki wa Ima Kikkyō no Hataage**.

OMOI. "Heavy"; used when the acting is composed and dignified, but also used in the opposite sense to suggest that the acting is rough. Further, the word may be used to describe a dull audience, as in the expression "today's audience is heavy" *(kyō no kyaku wa omoi)*.

OMOIIRE. The physical representation of a role apart from the speaking of dialogue; the actor's mime. Scripts often have the direction "free expression" *(jutsunaki omoiire)*, thus giving the actor the freedom to display the role's psychological nuances through his own devices.

ŌMORI HIKOSHICHI. Fukuchi Ōchi*. *Shosagoto**. *Gidayū** and *tokiwazu**. October 1897. Meiji-za*, Tokyo.

Taking the chronicle called the *Taiheiki* as its source, this is a *katsureki* ("living history*") dance drama and one of the *shin kabuki jūhachiban** collection established by Ichikawa Danjūrō IX*, who starred in its first production.

In the mountains of Matsuyama in Iyo Province, Ōmori Hikoshichi rescues Princess Chihaya, daughter of Kusunoki Masashige, when she is challenged by Dodo Saemon. Alone with Hikoshichi, she watches him carefully for a sign of carelessness, puts on a demon *(hannya)* mask, and tries to attack him, since he is her father's enemy. However, he wards off her attack and then describes her father's last moments to her, clearing up

Yoshitsune in *Yoshitsune Senbon Zakura**, wearing the *omigoromo** robe. Yoshitsune, Onoe Kikugorō VII*. *Courtesy of Waseda University Tsubouchi Engeki Hakubutsukan (Tsubouchi Memorial Theatre Museum).*

her misconceptions about his death. To prove his sincerity, he presents her with her family's ceremonial sword and leaves. He later deceives Saemon about his no longer having the sword by feigning madness.

The major features of the work are the tale of Kusunoki's death *(monogatari*)* and the use of a horse during Hikoshichi's display of madness.

OMOTE KATA. "Front men," a general term for all those who are engaged in duties involving theatre management*. The opposite term, *ura kata** or "rear men," refers to those who work backstage.

ŌMU. Taking its name from the mimicry of parrots *(omū),* this word describes a kind of humorous performance in which, following a telling piece of acting, a clownish character *(dōkegata*)* mimics the actor, making the audience laugh. Examples are the separation scene* in *Soga Moyō Tateshi no Goshozome**, in which Gorozō is mimicked by Gosuke, and the scene between Chokūrō and Hokaibō in *Sumidagawa Gonichi no Omokage**. Perhaps the most famous example is the scene between Yodarekuri and Sansuke following the touching acting of Chiyo and Tonami in the *Terakoya* scene of *Sugawara Denju Tenarai Kagami**.

ŌMUKŌ. "Great beyond"; a general term for seats in the rear balcony. The word refers mainly to those *oikomi** members of the audience who watched the play from the rear of the second story's *sajiki** galleries. These seats later were called *tachimi** ("stand and see") and remain today in only one theatre. From the old days on, many of the people seated here were connoisseurs and severe critics of the stage. The expression *ōmukō o unaraseru* ("to bring down the gallery") thus refers to exceptional acting and stage effects that please these discerning theatregoers. Similarly, the expression *ōmukō kara koe ga kakaru* ("the gallery shouts out its approval") is proof to an actor that his work has been appreciated. (*See also* THEATRE ARCHITECTURE.)

ŌMUSEKI. A booklet in which extracts from famous Kabuki speeches are published. Convenient for learning to imitate the voice and manner of the actors, they were already being published in the mid-seventeenth century. They were rice-paper books usually two to five pages long, and in later years they included an actor's likeness as part of their contents. Modern books of this sort printed from movable type are known by the same term and also are called *meizerifushū*. (*See also* KOWAIRO.)

ŌNADAI. The leading actors. *Ōdatemono** has the same meaning. In addition, it refers to the full title of a play given a full-length production* *(tōshi kyōgen)* and the writing of this title on the billboard. (*See also* KANBAN: ŌNADAI KANBAN.)

ONAMI NI YARU. "To play it raw"; said when an actor performs his part just as it is written without embellishing dialogue or business. Also, used pejoratively when an actor performs without applying any discernible skill, playing his role as his own self.

ONATSU KYŌRAN. Tsubouchi Shōyō*. *Shosagoto**. *Tokiwazu** and *nagauta**. September 1914. Teikoku Gekijō*, Tokyo.

Tsubouchi published his theoretical work on the new musical theatre, *Shingaku Geki Ron (Argument for a New Musical Drama)*, in 1914. It heralded the beginning of the reform movement in Japanese dance. Putting his ideas into practice himself, Tsubouchi wrote many new dance dramas, such as *Shinkyoku Urashima*. *Onatsu Kyōran* is the most frequently performed and representative work among his dance plays. It is based on the sad tale of Onatsu and Seijūrō in Ibara Saikaku's novel *Koshoku Gonnin Onna* (1686). Its first performance, by Onoe Baikō VI* and Matsumoto Kōshirō VII*, was a great success. Onatsu was Baikō's greatest role.

This is a deeply touching work that shows, with abundant poetic sentiment, the forlorn figure of Onatsu, who, mad as the result of a reckless love affair with Seijūrō, wanders aimlessly on a country road on an autumn evening. Also depicted in the play are village children, a drunken packhorse driver, and an old couple making a pilgrimage.

ONNAGATA. The class of actors who play female roles; also, a general term for the female roles themselves. After the prohibition of *onna kabuki* (women's Kabuki*) in 1629 (*see also* IZUMO NO OKUNI), Kabuki was fated to have its male actors play female parts. In addition to raising the quality of Kabuki's dramatic materials, these actors perfected the art of representing women on stage realistically. Thus, female impersonation became one of Kabuki's distinguishing characteristics. *Onnagata* also are called *oyama*, the latter term possibly deriving from the fact that courtesans were called by that term. It is said that as courtesan roles were quite common in early Kabuki, the word came to be used for those who performed these roles. Another theory holds that the term derives from the name of an expert manipulator of female puppets, Oyama Jirosaburō.

In the early period, *onnagata* were divided into two large groups: *wakaonnagata* and *kashagata*. The former portrayed young ladies, princesses, courtesans, and other such youthful women; the actors in such roles were themselves youthful. The syllable *kasha* in *kashagata* signifies a middle-aged waitress and is used in the sense of any middle-aged woman; the type is called *kakagata* and *fuke oyama* as well. Among *kashagata* roles is the *onna budō* ("female warrior"), a samurai's wife who is herself skilled in martial arts and who effectively deals with men in stage fights. On the other hand, there is the townsman's wife who faithfully serves her husband and who manages household affairs; she is the *sewa nyōbo*. There are also the rough women known as *akuba* who have appeared in Kabuki since the early nineteenth century. Often, these women have arms and shoulders covered with tattooing.

The ranking *onnagata* in a troupe is the *tate onnagata** or *tate oyama*; following him in rank are the leading *onnagata* of *nadai* rank (*see also* TITLES), who were given their own personal dressing room on the second floor in the Edo era. There are also the lower ranks of *onnagata*, consisting of such subdivisions as the *jochū*, *nakai*, *koshimoto*, and *kanjo*. Since they used the large second floor dressing room *(chū nikai*)* communally, they were nicknamed *chū nikai*. (*See also* ACTORS' RANKS; ACTORS.)

ONNA GOROSHI ABURA NO JIGYOKU. Chikamatsu Monzaemon*. Also called *Abura no Jigyoku*. English title: *The Woman Killer and the Hell of Oil* (Keene). *Sewamono** *Jōruri**. Three acts. July 1721. Takemoto-za, Osaka.

This play appears to be a dramatization of a true contemporary event. It was adapted for Kabuki the same year at Osaka's Naka-za*.

Kawachiya Yohei of the Tenman oil shop takes advantage of the generosity of the shop's chief clerk, his stepfather Tokubei, and leads a dissipated life; he becomes hopelessly debauched and is punished by his mother, Osawa, by being disinherited. Yohei is at a loss as to how to pay back money that he has borrowed under false pretenses. He requests money from Okichi, wife of the Toshimaya oil shop owner; he robs and kills her when she refuses, and then flees. When, on the first anniversary of her death, he shows up looking as innocent as he can, he is arrested, because evidence has been obtained against him.

The scene when Tokubei and Osawa, fearing for their son, come separately to leave money with Okichi for Yohei and thus show their affection for him is outstanding. Another highlight is the gruesome murder scene. The playwright imbues Yohei with modern touches that are novelties for a Chikamatsu character.

ONNA KABUKI. *See* WOMEN'S KABUKI.

ONOE BAIKŌ. This name was originally the *haiku*-writing pen name *(haimyō*)* of Onoe Kikugorō I*, but eventually came to be used as a stage name. Besides its temporary stage use by Kikugorō IV*, it was used by Baikō VI and VII.

VI. 1870-1934. Adopted son of Kikugorō V*. He became Eizaburō V in 1891 after being Einosuke and was highly popular as a player of young female roles *(wakaonnagata)*. He played opposite his adopted father and became Baikō VI in 1903. When the Teikoku Gekijō* opened in 1911, he became its artistic director and joined up in an acting combination with

Ichimura Uzaemon XV*, with whom he played many roles as a leading *onnagata**. He inherited his adopted father's *onnagata* style and displayed his abilities in new plays and dances as well.

VII, *yago** Otowaya. 1915- . With Nakamura Utaemon VI*, he was one of Kabuki's "matchless pair" of *onnagata*. He was born in Tokyo, the illegitimate son of Kikugorō VI*, and debuted in May 1921. He changed his name from Ushinosuke to Kikunosuke III in 1935 and took his present name in 1947. From his Kikunosuke period on, he played opposite his famous father and received a strict artistic training. A gentle, graceful, though somewhat stout *onnagata*, he is one of the few first-class *onnagata* who bolster today's Kabuki.

ONOE KIKUGORŌ I. 1717-1783. A star of the Hōreki period (1751-63), he was a student of Onoe Samon in Kyoto. He later left for Edo, where he achieved great success. He specialized in *onnagata** roles, but also had a successful career as a player of male roles, particularly in the play *Kanadehon Chūshingura**.

II. 1769-1787. The son of Kikugorō I, he died young, though he showed promise of becoming a major actor.

III. 1784-1849. Was adopted by the top student of Kikugorō I, Onoe Shōroku I (Onoe Matsusuke I*), and, after a period as Matsusuke II, became Kikugorō III in 1815; thirty years had passed since there had been a Kikugorō. His acting reflected the sadness and gloom of the townsman's life, and he was especially brilliant in the type of play known as *kizewamono**, which concentrated on the *demimonde*. He also was noteworthy in ghost plays* *(kaidan mono)*. Tsuruya Nanboku IV*, an outstanding playwright of the time, wrote many of his vehicles. Kikugorō was one of Kabuki's most versatile actors, being lauded as a *kaneru yakusha** or "all-around actor." Many of his *kata** still are used by modern actors.

IV. 1808-1860. An extremely popular player of female roles. As Nakamura Kacho, he had been the pupil of Nakamura Karoku. He became Onoe Kikueda following his 1831 marriage to Kikugorō III's daughter. That same year he changed his name to Onoe Eisaburō and was adopted by his father-in-law, as is the Japanese custom. Kikugorō IV was the only pure *onnagata* in the line. His features and physique fitted him more for the classic middle-aged women of the history plays than for younger types. He became Onoe Baikō in 1846 and received the name of Kikugorō in 1856.

V. 1844-1903. Grandson of Kikugorō III. Toward the end of the Edo era he became the manager *(zamoto*)* of the Ichimura-za* and took the name of Ichimura Uzaemon XIII. At eighteen, he played the part of Benten Kozō in the first performance of *Aotozōshi Hana no Nishikie**. During the Meiji era he was one of the great triumvirate of stars including Ichikawa Danjūrō IX* and Ichikawa Sadanji I*. He collected the ten best plays from the Onoe family's successes in the *shinko engeki jūshu** collection. Domestic dramas were his forte. He often played *onnagata* and ghostly roles handed down from his grandfather. The next generation of Kabuki actors was greatly influenced by this star.

VI. 1885-1949. Eldest son of Kikugorō V. He received his training at the hands of Danjūrō IX, under whom his natural talent was increasingly refined. In his youth he was rivaled in popularity at the Ichimura-za by Nakamura Kichiemon I*; for a time, there was a Kiku-Kichi* or "Ichimura-za period" that excited contemporary theatregoers. He founded the Japan Actor's School in 1930 to give instruction to the younger generation. In addition to being a *kaneru yakusha*—having inherited his father's artistry in domestic plays and received an education under Danjūrō—he also had great creative power with which he forged new elements in Kabuki acting. He was a pioneer in the development of the so-called modern or New Kabuki *(shin kabuki*)*, and his acting showed genius in its grasp of character and psychology in the new plays. He was also a marvelous dancer and displayed his superb ability in old and new dances.

VII, *yago** Otowaya. 1942- . Born in Tokyo, the son of Onoe Baikō VII*, he debuted in 1948. In May 1965 he changed his name from Ushinosuke to Kikunosuke IV. As a young *onnagata** star he is in the front rank, along with such *tachiyaku** as Ichikawa Ebizō X* and Onoe Tatsunosuke I*. His popularity reached great proportions when he starred in the NHK television series *Minamoto Genji.* He acts all types of romantic roles, but is mainly an *onnagata*, like his father. He took his present name in 1975.

ONOE KIKUJIRŌ IV, *yago** Otowaya. 1904- . A respected veteran *onnagata**, he was born in Tokyo, debuted in 1909, became Bandō Tatesaburō IV in 1919, and took his present name in 1935. He was in Kikugorō VI's* troupe from the Taishō era (1912-26) to 1939 and played opposite Kikugorō as his partner. Later, he changed to Ichikawa En'o I's* troupe and in 1949 switched to Osaka. His brother was Nakamura Tomijūrō IV*.

ONOE KIKUZŌ VI, *yago** Otowaya. 1923- . A fine *onnagata**, he was born the son of Onoe Taganojō III*, debuted in 1935, and took the name of Kikuzō in 1946.

ONOE KUROEMON II, *yago** Otowaya. Born in Tokyo, the son of Onoe Kikugorō VI*, Kuroemon is the only Kabuki actor to have left Japan to take up extended residence in America. He is on the staff of the Loeb Drama Center at Harvard University and has staged several Kabuki plays in the United States, using student actors. At one time he studied at the Pasadena Playhouse. He debuted at the Ichimura-za* in 1926 as Onoe Sakin and took his present name in 1940, when he played Gorō in *Soga no Taimen**

at the Kabuki-za*. Following a stroke that he suffered while rehearsing at the Teikoku Gekijō*, he decided to spend most of his time as an instructor in American colleges and universities.

ONOE MATSUSUKE I. 1744-1815. An actor, born in Osaka. He left for Edo in 1755 and became a pupil of Onoe Kikugorō I*, taking the name Onoe Matsusuke. In 1804 he used quick-change techniques to play the three roles of Ōhimaru, Tokubei, and Zatō Tokuichi in *Tenjiku Tokubei Ikoku Banashi**, a feat that garnered him much admiration. Later, he was a hit in a succession of plays written by Tsuruya Nanboku IV* and came to be considered the founder of ghost play* *(kaidan mono)* acting. In 1809 he changed his name to Onoe Shōroku I. He had a great influence on later production technique because of his original artistry in making quick costume and makeup changes.

II. Adopted son of the first Matsusuke. He later became Onoe Kikugorō III*.

III. 1805-1851. Son of the third Kikugorō. Born in Edo, he changed his name from Onoe Eizaburō II to Matsusuke III in 1815.

IV. 1843-1928. Born the son of a servant attached to Matsumoto Kōshirō V*. He became a pupil of Onoe Kikugorō V* and, in 1871, was praised for his acting as the blind masseur, Joga, to his master's Naozamurai in *Kumo ni Magō Ueno no Hatsuhana**. This type of role became his career specialty. He succeeded to the name of Matsusuke during the same year. He was unrivaled in supporting roles in the domestic plays and provided never failing support to Kikugorōs V and VI*. His outstanding roles included Kōmori ("Bat") Yasu in *Yowa Nasake Ukina no Yokogushi**, Tauetsu in *Tōkaidō Yotsuya Kaidan**, and Chōbei in *Tsuyu Kosode Mukashi Hachijō**.

V. 1887-1937. Born in Tokyo, he was a disciple of Kikugorō V. After being known as Onoe Kikumatsu and Onoe Isaburō, he became Matsusuke in 1935. He was recognized as an outstanding supporting actor during the period of Kikugorō VI's stardom at the Ichimura-za*.

ONOE SHŌROKU II, *yago** Otowaya. 1913- . One of the greats of modern Kabuki, he is the son of Matsumoto Kōshirō VII* and the brother of Kōshirō VIII* and the late Ichikawa Danjūrō XI*. He debuted in 1918 and changed his name from Matsumoto Toyo to Onoe Shōroku in March 1935. He was a pupil of Onoe Kikugorō VI* and, as a central figure in his master's troupe, inherited his style. Shōroku displays Kikugorō VI's art in domestic plays and his father's style in history plays, where his acting is quite rich. He is also one of Kabuki's leading dancers and choreographers (*see also* FUJIMA RYŪ). Further, he avidly presents new works and Western plays; *Cyrano de Bergerac* and *Othello* are examples.

ONOE TAGANOJŌ III. 1887-1979. Born in Tokyo, he debuted in 1890, and changed his name from Ichikawa Kizaburō to Ichikawa Onimaru in

1905. In 1921 the great Onoe Kikugorō VI* engaged him for his troupe at the Ichimura-za*, where he was admired for his *onnagata** performances opposite the master. In June 1927 he succeeded to the name of Taganojō III. Even in his old age he displayed sparkling work on stage.

ONOE TATSUNOSUKE I, *yago** Otowaya. 1946- . An extremely popular and able young star, this eldest son of Onoe Shōroku II* was born in Tokyo, debuted in 1952, and took the name of Tatsunosuke in May 1965. He resembles his father in face and speech and is a diligent student of his father's style. Like his father, he displays great versatility as both an actor and dancer. He is one of the trio of young stars known in the 1960s as the "three Sukes"—Tatsunosuke, Shinnosuke (the present Ebizō*), and Kikunosuke (the present Kikugorō*).

ONRYŌ. "Angry ghost"; to press someone for money that has been borrowed. The term suggests the tenacity of a ghost, which will not rest until it has carried out its revenge.

ONZOSHI. The sons of star actors. Originally, it was the title of a court noble's son who had not yet taken over his father's position and is the title held by Lord Genji's son in the *Genji Monogatari*. It has come to mean children who are capable of succeeding their fathers and becoming leaders themselves.

ŌOTOSHI. The climactic moment in a tragic scene when a character's emotions overwhelm him and he bursts forth in tears. The term originally was used in the puppet theatre to refer to the skills of the narrator and *shamisen** player when performing a particularly difficult passage. Famous *ōotoshi* are performed by Mitsuhide in *Ehon Taikōki** and Matsuomaru in the *Terakoya* scene of *Sugawara Denju Tenarai Kagami**.

OPENING DAY. The first day of a run is known as *shonichi*. This day used to be celebrated in Kabuki by having the company and crew repair to the leading actor's home, where a congratulatory address would be read. The chief actor usually invited his pupils to his home for a banquet, too. Among the various opening days the most revered was that of the New Year's play* *(hatsuharu)*, when a *shizome** ceremonial program would be enacted. The second day was called opening day at New Year's time. However, from the late Edo period on, a number of factors, mainly financial, often militated against the program's opening even on the second day. Even in such cases, however, the old conventions were observed, if somewhat surreptitiously. A placard reading "The play opens on the second" was hung by the theatre's front office; on that date the placard was removed and another one, which said "You may see the new plays on [such and such a date]," was put up instead, thus prolonging the opening. At length, the night before the actual opening, long rectangular paper lanterns were hung outside the theatre; they read "The play opens tomorrow." These were called the *myōnichi andon* ("tomorrow lanterns"). (*See also* THEATRE MANAGEMENT.)

ŌRANMA. The black-painted beam running across the top of the stage between the stage right and left pillars *(daijin bashira*)* or the transom work placed in front of this beam. The beam can be raised or lowered according to need.

ORIRU. "To descend"; to refuse a part.

ŌSAKAZUKI (SHUSEN NO TSUWAMONO). Kawatake Mokuami*. *Jidaimono**. Kabuki. One act. May 1881. Saruwaka-za*, Tokyo.

This is the dramatization of a tale concerning Baba Saburobei, a retainer of the Lord of Echigo, who is said to have drunk at one draught the entire contents of a seven-*gō* capacity (nearly one-and-one-half-quart) sake bowl in the company of his drinking companion, the Lord of Tōdō.

A masterless samurai, Baba Saburobei of Takeda becomes a footman in the service of Lord Naitō Kii and drinks only sake. At a flower-viewing party Saburobei is summoned to be drinking partner to Ii Kanimori, a heavy drinker. He is questioned about an old scar on his brow, and, being drunk, he replies by describing a battle in which he received the scar. He is now recognized by Lord Kanimori, with whom he had fought in the summer battle for Osaka Castle. Lord Kanimori, wishing to make Saburobei his vassal, rehires him for the house of Naitō at an increased salary of 1500 *koku* (almost 68,000 gallons) of rice.

This is a delightful drama about a man and his sake; its plot is woven around the central incident of Saburobei's narrative recital. It was written for the unique talents of Ichikawa Sadanji I*. This role and his performance in *Keian Taiheiki** were his two greatest successes.

OSAMARU. To agree to or to be content with something. Also, when the props and scenery for a play are well disposed and all goes well with the entrances, exits, and placement of the characters.

OSAN JITSU. "The three days": opening day, the fifteenth day, and the twenty-eighth day of a run. It used to be the custom for apprentice actors to visit the homes of their masters on these days.

ŌSATSUMA BUSHI. A narrative musical style *(jōruri*)* founded by Ōsatsuma Shusendayū I (1695-1759) early in the Kyohō era (1716-35). It is a delightful style created to suit the *aragoto** acting in which the Ichikawa Danjūrō* line of actors has specialized for over two and one-half centuries. However, with a growing taste for greater stage realism at the end of the eighteenth century, *aragoto* declined in favor, thus causing a falling off in *ōsatsuma bushi*'s popularity. As there were no later successors to the leadership of this school, it was absorbed by the *nagauta** school. Today, *nagauta* musicians perform in the *ōsatsuma* style when accompanying an *aragoto* piece. *Ōsatsuma*'s distinctive quality is the intense nature of the narrative and *shamisen** accompaniment.

OSHA. "Members of the tribe," a term of respect for newspaper writers and theatre critics.

ŌSHIBAI. The "major" theatres, as opposed to the "small theatres" *(koshibai*)* that once flourished. (*See also* DONCHŌ YAKUSHA.)

OSHIDASHI. "Pushing out"; a word used to signify that an actor's stage appearance is both grand and impressive. It is used in such expressions as "his *oshidashi* is superb" *(oshidashi ga rippa).* A close English equivalent is *presence.* Another usage refers to moving the stage set from the rear of the stage to the front. Wagon stages *(hiki dōgu*)* are used for this purpose. An example is in *Kagamijishi**, when the platform on which the butterflies have been placed is pushed forward from its position near the musicians' platform *(hinadan*).*

OSHIGUMA. "Pressed-face *kuma*"; the practice by actors of placing a paper or silk cloth over their *kumadori** makeup so that an impression is taken from the face. It is done at the request of patrons who make the *oshiguma* into hanging scrolls or decorative folding screens.

OSHIMODOSHI. "Queller of demons," a type of *aragoto** performance and the role type that performs it. The character of the *oshimodoshi* wears a formalized costume emphasizing his valor; he enters holding a thick, young bamboo stalk in one hand. His activity is chiefly to repel some raging demon or apparition. The *oshimodoshi* is included in plays such as *Musume Dōjōji** and *Narukami**. There is no fixed character for him. He may be called such names as Ōdate Sabagorō or Takenuki Gorō.

OSHIROI. The ground-flour base used for the heavy white makeup worn in many roles.

ŌSHŪ ADACHIGAHARA. Chikamatsu Hanji*, Takemoto Saburobei, others. Also called *Sodehagi Saimon, Adasan. Jidaimono*. Jōruri**. Five acts. September 1762. Takemoto-za, Osaka.

This play combines the provincial legends of *Adachigahara* (or *Kurozuka**)

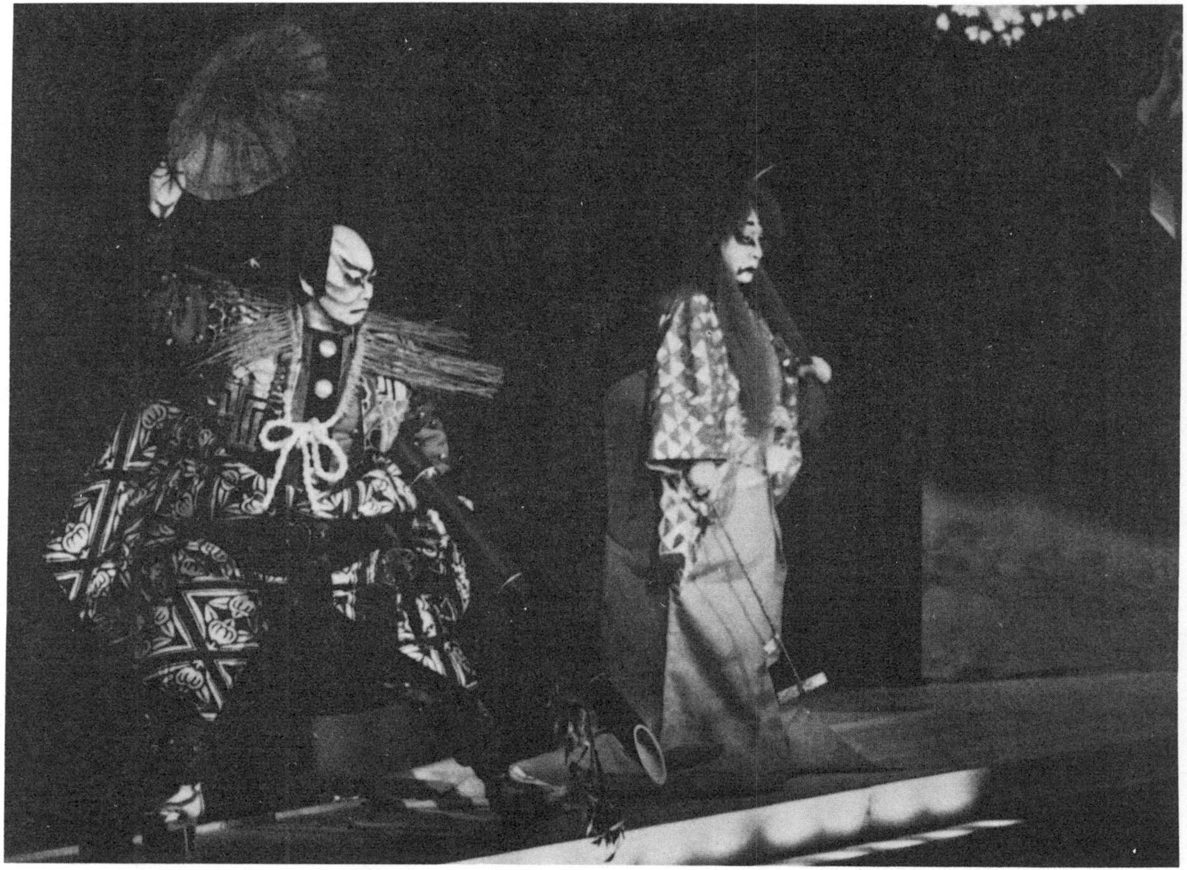

At the end of *Musume Dōjōji** the demon battles on the *hanamichi** with the "queller of demons" (*oshimodoshi**). Oshimodoshi, Ichimura Uzaemon XVII*; demon, Kiyohime Onoe Baikō VII*. *Courtesy of Waseda University Tsubouchi Engeki Hakubutsukan (Tsubouchi Memorial Theatre Museum).*

and *Utō*—told in Nō plays with these titles—with a plot concerning the Abe brothers, Sadatō and Munetō. They are planning to restore their family power, having been defeated in war nine years earlier. Only Act III, which occurs at the palace of Tamakino Miya, is still produced. The first Kabuki production was in 1763 at Edo's Morita-za*.

Sodehagi, daughter of Minamoto no Yoshie's father-in-law, Kenjō Naokata, is disinherited because of her love affair with Sadatō. Following her husband's defeat in battle, she has become a blind, wandering beggar. With her young daughter, Okimi, clutching her hand, she comes to visit her father; he has been sentenced to death for an offense that he committed at Tamakino's palace. When her obstinate father refuses to see her, she pleads outside the gate on the pretext of chanting a prayer. Sadatō enters, disguised as Chūnagon, an Imperial messenger whose task is to verify Naotaka's death. There follows an unexpected reunion of husband and wife. This is followed by a reunion of brother and brother when Munetō appears, dressed as a prisoner. Naokata commits ritual suicide *(seppuku).* Sodehagi soon kills herself as well. Yoshie, enemy of the brothers, sees through their disguises, but allows them to depart, promising to meet up with them again on the battlefield.

Sodehagi's baleful entreaty to the gods, which she recites while playing the *shamisen**, is the play's main feature. Sodehagi and Sadatō usually are played by the same actor.

OSOME HISAMATSU UKINA NO YOMIURI. Tsuruya Nanboku IV*. Also called *Osome no Nanayaku. Sewamono**. Kabuki. Three acts. March 1813. Morita-za*, Edo.

A drama revolving around the young lovers Osome and Hisamatsu and an evil pair—Oroku, a wicked maid, and Kihei, a thief.

The Abura-ya pawnshop apprentice Hisamatsu, son of Ishizu, and his sister, the court lady Takekawa, are engaged in discovering the whereabouts of their family's heirloom sword. The sword has been pawned by Kihei at the Abura-ya. Meanwhile, Kihei's mistress, Oroku, has been trying hard to raise money from Takekawa, her former mistress. Hearing by chance of a quarrel between clerks of the Abura-ya, the evil couple carry the corpse of one of the clerks to the Abura-ya, in hopes of extorting some money. However, Osome's betrothed, Yamagaya Seibei, cleverly foils their wicked plans. Kihei is killed by Hisamatsu. Hisamatsu and Osome soon go to the Sumida River to commit double suicide, but they are saved and the sword ultimately is returned to its rightful owners.

The central interest of the play is in the rapid changes required of the one actor who plays Osome, Hisamatsu, the geisha Koito, Takekawa, Osome's mother (Teisho), the country girl Omitsu, Oroku, and Osome's fiance. The work was first performed by the famous female impersonator Iwai

Hanshirō V*, who received great acclaim for his acting, especially as Oroku. Others in the cast were Matsumoto Kōshirō V* and Ichikawa Danjūrō VII*. Highlights include the comic extortion scene, the gloomy murder of Kihei, and the extremely rapid costume changes.

OSOME NO MICHIYUKI. Tsuruya Nanboku IV*. Also called *Michiyuki Ukina no Tomodori. Shosagoto*. Kiyomoto*.* November 1825. Nakamura-za*, Edo.

Both Kabuki and the puppet theatre successfully dramatized the love story of Osome and Hisamatsu. The present work is totally in the Edo dance style. Its first performers were Iwai Shikajaku (Osome), Iwai Kumesaburō II (Hisamatsu), and Ichikawa Danjūrō VII* (monkey trainer).

Osome and Hisamatsu, despairing of ever finding happiness in this world, decide to commit double suicide. They slip away from home and come to an embankment on the Sumida River. A monkey trainer happens along and guesses their intentions. He offers a musical prayer, although his "prayer" really contains various pieces of advice for the lovers, who then decide to live.

The play features a lamentation* *(kudoki)* by Osome and the clever use by the monkey trainer of four bamboo sticks while he makes his remonstrances.

ŌTANI TAKEJIRŌ. 1877-1969. One of the founders of the Shōchiku* theatrical conglomerate.

ŌTANI TOMOEMON I. 1744-1781. An actor, born in Osaka, and the pupil of Ōtani Hiroji. He moved to Edo in 1769 and was highly regarded there as a player of villain's roles. Thereafter, Tomoemon II (1769-1830), III (1763-1839), and IV also specialized in such roles.

IV. 1791-1861. Son of the Osaka playwright, Dekishima Sensuke, and student of Tomoemon II. He moved to Edo in 1832 and took the name of Tomoemon IV. There were two Tomoemons during the decade from 1832 to 1842, for Arashi Shagan had become Tomoemon III in 1831. Tomoemon IV was an enormous success as Adachi Genzaemon in *Katakiuchi Tengajaya Mura** at Edo's Nakamura-za* in 1835. His portrayal led to this role's becoming one of Kabuki's most important. In general, he was outstanding in the roles of petty thieves and crooks, since he did not have the looks or flair for leading villain roles.

V. 1833-1873. Son of Tomoemon IV. He was born in Edo and took the name of Tomoemon V in 1865. Active as a *tachiyaku** in Edo, Osaka, and Kyoto, he was admired especially for his work in history plays. He changed his name to Ōtani Hirōji in 1870.

VI. 1886-1943. Son of Nakamura Sagisuke, he was a disciple of Nakamura Utaemon V* and passed through a series of five names before becoming Tomoemon VI in 1920, a half-century after the name had fallen into disuse.

He was an important supporting actor and played old men's roles in the company of Onoe Kikugorō VI* and Ichikawa En'o I*.

VII. The present Nakamura Jakuemon IV*.

VIII. 1945- . Eldest son of Nakamura Jakuemon IV. He became Tomoemon in 1964. He is a skilled and popular player of young men and women.

OTOKOSHŪ. "Manservant," an employee who serves the actors and is employed in backstage activities. He greets backstage visitors, cleans the rooms, aids in the preparation of meals and baths, arranges costumes and properties, and does other odd jobs. When he has put in long service, he may go so far as to assume a part in discussions of the actors' salaries and supervision of their students. An actor's manservant may have considerable influence over him, adding managerial duties to those which he already fulfills.

OTOWA JIROSABURŌ. d. 1732. An actor, he gained fame in Osaka and Kyoto as a player of mature, manly roles *(jitsugoto; see also* TACHIYAKU). He possessed literary talent and performed in his own plays toward the end of his career.

ŌTSUZUMI. A waist drum that figures importantly in *geza** music.

OYAJIGATA. Important older male roles played by veteran supporting actors. Heisaku in *Igagoe Dōchū Sugoroku** and Shiradayū in *Sugawara Denju Tenarai Kagami** are examples. (*See also* TACHIYAKU.)

OYAJIGATAKI. A type of elderly villain role. (*See also* KATAKIYAKU.)

OYASU. To have the orchestra play at a lively pace.

ŌZUME. "Grand conclusion," the final act in a multiact play, in which all complications are resolved. During the Edo period when a daily program was divided into two halves, the first being a history play and the second a domestic play, the word referred to the last act of the history play. (*See also* ŌGIRI.)

P

PANTOMIME. *See* DANMARI.

PAUSES. The Japanese word, *ma,* originally referred to the interval between one word of dialogue and the next, but it changed to mean those places in an actor's performance where he stops momentarily and there is a pause until he resumes again. *Ma* are employed during an actor's speeches as well as during his movement and gestures. The word often is used loosely to refer to that entire area of performance known as timing. When the actor's timing is off, such expressions are used as "his *ma* was poor" *(ma ga warui)* or "he missed his *ma*" *(ma ga nukeru).*

PEI PEI. The lowest class of actors (*See also* ACTORS' RANKS.)

PEN NAMES. *See* HAIMYŌ.

PIKAICHI. The top stars or leading lights of a theatre company.

PLAY CATEGORIES. Several varieties of Kabuki drama exist today. These include the classical "pure" Kabuki *(jun kabuki*)*—that is, plays originally written for the Kabuki theatre and not for any other form—and *gidayū kyōgen**, plays first written for puppet performance. There is also *shin kabuki** or New Kabuki. Dance dramas are a category unto themselves *(shosagoto*).* Among *jun kabuki* plays are those in the famous collection called the *kabuki jūhachiban** and the writings of dramatists like Sakurada Jisuke*, Namiki Gohei*, Tsuruya Nanboku*, and Kawatake Mokuami*. These works were written for and first performed by the artists of the Kabuki theatre. *Gidayū,* or puppet plays adapted for Kabuki presentation, include works by Chikamatsu Monzaemon*, Namiki Sōsuke*, Takeda Izumo*, Chikamatsu Hanji*, and many others. *Gidayū* plays are called by such other names as *jōruri*, maruhon mono, denden mono**, and, more recently, *maruhon kabuki.*

Classification according to content yields two main dramatic categories (each has a number of subcategories): *jidaimono** and *sewamono**. Briefly, *jidaimono* (history plays) deal with the Japanese historical periods known as the Kamakura and Muromachi eras (eleventh through sixteenth centuries); the leading characters are of heroic stature. *Sewamono* (domestic plays or dramas of the middle class) treat urban society of the Edo era; the chief characters are ordinary citizens. Subdivisions of *jidaimono* include *ōdai mono**, *oie mono**, *jidai-sewamono**, and *katsureki geki* (living history plays*). *Sewamono* subcategories are *kizewamono** and *zangiri mono**.

The works known as New Kabuki are written by such dramatists of modern tendencies as Tsubouchi Shōyō* and Okamoto Kidō*; generally, these are literary men with no permanent theatrical connections. They contrast with Kabuki's earlier playwrights, who normally were attached to specific theatres.

Shosagoto or *buyōgeki*, Kabuki's dance dramas, include such subgenres as *michiyuki mono** and *kyōgen jōruri* (dances accompanied by one or another of the musical styles called *kiyomoto**, *nagauta**, or *tokiwazu**); in addition, there are independent works classed as *henge mono* (transformation pieces*) and *matsubame mono**; "new dance" dramas *(shin buyōgeki)* may be added to this. Just as the spoken drama may be broken into two main categories—*sewamono* and *jidaimono*—so may dance plays be similarly divided into *shosagoto* (literally, "pose pieces") and *shosageki* (literally, "pose dramas"). All other subgenres may be subsumed under these. (*See also* DANCE.)

The number of Kabuki plays written since its beginnings in the early seventeenth century easily exceeds ten thousand; most of these have disappeared. About two hundred classic works are still performed. Many were first written for the puppet theatre. These display a clear structure and consistent plotting. On the other hand, pieces written originally for the Kabuki often demand that they be appreciated for other qualities, because they are frequently inconsistent and illogical in style and form.

PLAY COLLECTIONS. *See* FAMILY ART.

PLAYWRIGHTS' RANKS. Playwrights were called *kabuki sakusha* or *kyōgen tsukuri* (the latter being the older term) and were employed by specific theatres.

Up to approximately the Kanbun and Enpō periods (1661-81) most contemporary actors possessed a modicum of literary talent and could get by in improvised performances *(kuchidate*)*. Following the development of independent plays *(hanare kyōgen)* and complex multiact plays, however, it became necessary to have someone who specialized in writing scripts.

The first Kabuki playwrights were also actors. In 1680 came the first public acknowledgment of the existence of an independent Kabuki dramatist: the name of Tominaga Heibei* was printed in the *kaomise** production program, giving him credit as playwright. A few years later, the position of the playwright was strengthened by the appearance of the great Chikamatsu Monzaemon*. By the Hōreki era (1751-63), Kabuki's distinctive playwright system was firmly established. The head dramatist was the *tate sakusha**; he was followed (in descending order of importance) by the *nimaime sakusha**, *sanmaime sakusha**, *kyōgen kata**, and *minarai sakusha**. They wrote plays in the "playwright's room" (*sakusha beya**), where they prepared the year's repertory for their troupe.

As it was a basic principle to revise anew all plays being revived, the plays were freely rewritten with primary consideration being given to the actors who would now appear in them. Scripts were by no means sacred and could be altered at will. (*See also* PLAYWRITING.)

The Meiji period saw the performance of plays written by scholars and literary men who were not employed by the theatres, a practice that led to the gradual disappearance of the playwright system. From the Shōwa period 1926-) on, the chief duties of the *kyōgen sakusha* have been concerned with problems of production and stage management. (*See also* KYŌGEN KATA.)

PLAYWRITING. From the beginning, Kabuki plays have been written with the actor at their core, the chief point being to show off the actor's art and his charm to best advantage. Thus, in the scripts used in rehearsal the name of the actor playing the role is printed before his dialogue, not the character's name, as is true of published plays. Kabuki plays normally were created or revised to suit the requirements of specific actors. Consequently, they have undergone alteration whenever presented. For such a system to work, the actors had to contribute a great deal. There are a good many works called masterpieces today that were created precisely at that moment when the playwright and actor were in perfect accord in ability and will.

All playwrights were attached formally to the various theatres and plays usually were written as collaborative efforts with anywhere from two or three to twelve or thirteen writers working on a script. The playwright's creed was to please the producer, the actor, and the audience; many of the plays, therefore, are merely workmanlike, being sparse artistically. Moreover, as there was a regular system of plotting and dramatic "worlds" (*sekai**) to draw upon, it was only natural that earlier works be imitated and rewritten (*see also* KAKIGAE KYŌGEN). Nevertheless, some gifted dramatists wrote plays with a fair share of such qualities as novelty and wit—though not to be measured on the same scale as modern drama. (*See also* PLAYWRIGHTS' RANKS.)

POSES. *See* MIE.

POTTO. A side-lock wig that, with its hair standing slightly on end, suggests an honest country character. An example is Yasaku in *Yasaku no Kamabara*.

PRINCESS ROLES. *See* AKAHIME; SANHIME.

PRODUCER. *See* ZAMOTO; NADAI.

PROGRAM BOOKS. *See* BANZUKE.

PROMPTER. *See* KŌKEN; KYŌGEN KATA; KUROGO; TSUBUZUKE.

PROPERTIES. Objects used onstage by the actor were called *kodōgu.* These include those which he carries with him as well as things like household implements, birds, animals, drawings, writings, and food. The *kodōgu kata* ("prop master") makes and looks after the *kodōgu. Kodōgu* are grouped in several classifications: (1) *mochidōgu,* hand props; (2) *dedōgu,* scenic props; (3) *kiemono**, props used up at each performance; (4) *nuigurumi**, animal costumes worn by the actors; (5) *hakimono,* footgear*, including *geta* (clogs), *zōri* and *waraji* (types of straw sandals), and shoes.

In former days each actor was responsible for his own props, but with Kabuki's growth in realism and complexity it became common for the theatres to have permanent props. In 1885 a man named Fujinami Yohei* (1829-1906) single-handedly undertook the responsibility for the props at all Kabuki theatres and began a property retail business that continues today under Yohei IV.

When a play is chosen for production, a property notebook *(kodōgu tsukechō)* is prepared for each act's scenic props and each actor's hand props. The necessary items are then assembled according to this list. Kabuki theatres have property rooms in which the scenic props are stored and from which the hand props are distributed to the actors. This room is the *kodōgu beya**. The prop master sees to the collection, arrangement, and mechanisms of the scenic props. He also is responsible for such sound effects as falling rain, insects and birds, thunder, waves, wind, and the like.

There is a great diversity of large-scale props which are handled in cooperation with the *ōdōgu**, the major scenic elements. These props include the *toitagaeshi**, a "rain door" that provides unusual effects in *Tōkaidō Yotsuya Kaidan**.

Among the interesting props handled by the prop master are the *sukumidō**, the *sogimen** or *nashiwari,* the *kuwaeme**, the *fukiboya**, the *chisuji no ito** or *kumo no suso,* and those props which are manipulated by the *jyari no ito** technique.

PUBLICITY. *See* BANZUKE; KANBAN; KATARI; KIDO GEISHA.

PUPPET THEATRE. *See* GIDAYŪ KYŌGEN; JŌRURI; KINPIRA JŌRURI.

PURE KABUKI. *See* PLAY CATEGORIES; JUN KABUKI.

Q

QUICK-CHANGE TECHNIQUES. *See* HAYAGAWARI; HAYA GESHŌ; TRANSFORMATION PIECES; BUKKAERI; HIKINUKI; ŌDŌGU; KEREN; HAYAGUKE.

R

RAIJO. *See* GEZA: MUSICAL ACCOMPANIMENT CHART.

RAIN. *See* AME; HON AME.

RAKAN (DAI). "Buddha's six hundred disciples' platform"; an inexpensive seating position in old theatres. (*see also* YOSHINO.)

RAKU. An abbreviation for *senshūraku**, the closing day of a production.

RAKUGO. A popular form of storytelling, usually presented as part of the variety show called *yose. Rakugo* generally are comic stories told by a narrator who sits on a platform called the *kōza* during the length of the narration. Many Kabuki plays originated in *rakugo* stories.

REHEARSALS. The word *keiko* refers to the period of time during which actors and other theatre personnel prepare for the production of a play, that is, the rehearsal period. When a play is selected for production, the actors and the other production people gather together to hear the play read *(honyomi*)* by the *kyōgen sakusha**. Rehearsals begin after the actors' parts *(kakinuki*)* are given out. In the past there was a great difference between the amount of time devoted to rehearsals for an old play and a new one, but today about a week of rehearsals, including a day or two of actual performance, is usual for all plays. It takes about two days to read the play for corrections *(yomiawase)* as the actor reads his part and the *kyōgen sakusha* reads the stage directions and narrative speeches. During this process the actor gets to understand the thrust of the dialogue and the progress of the action. Then the actors get on their feet and work out the acting in two days of "standing rehearsals" *(tachi keiko)*, everything up to now being termed "sitting rehearsals" *(hira keiko)*. After this, a day is given over to a technical rehearsal with music, sound effects, and so on (the *tsuketate* rehearsal), followed by one day of the *sōzarai* or "partial dress rehearsal." In the latter, most of the elements of production are included; the actors may only wear part of their costumes or appear without makeup, depending on circumstances. Frequently performed plays do without the *tsuketate* and *sōzarai* rehearsals; such cases are called *tsukesō*. Since the late Meiji days there has been a kind of full-dress rehearsal in which the set is dressed and the actors perform in full makeup and costume; it is called *butai keiko* ("stage rehearsal"). When new plays are staged, adjustments continue to be made even after opening day. It may require a week or more until the presentation is perfected.

RENGE BUTAI. "Lotus stage," scenic methods such as the *hiki dōgu**, *wari dōgu**, and *aorigaeshi**, in which one set is placed behind another in order to be revealed when the forepart is removed.

RENJISHI. Kawatake Mokuami*. *Shosagoto**. *Nagauta**. July 1872, Murayama-za, Tokyo.

A Kabuki dance derived from the Nō play *Shakkyō (see also* SHAKKYŌ MONO). Mokuami's first version was staged in 1861. Another adaptation was produced in 1901.

On a stage decorated with peony blossoms, the lively spirits of a father and son lion appear. First, two Kyōgen actors appear holding lion hand masks; the father lion kicks his son into the valley to harden him, and the son climbs back up. In the latter half of the play, the actors appear costumed and made up as father and son lions, and they gambol among the peonies, waving their long manes around in a whirl of joy. In the section separating the two halves there is a performance of a humorous passage taken from the Kyōgen farce *Shuron*. Sawamura Tosshō and Bandō Hikosaburō were the play's first stars.

RENJŪ. Also called *kenren, kumi,* and *kumiken,* all of which mean a clique or group of some sort. These were organized bodies of spectators who supported the various actors. Osaka had its *danna renjū* or "gentlemen's cliques," such as the Ōte, Sasase, Sakura, Fujiishi, and Dōjima, whereas Edo claimed its large *koen dantai* ("supporters' organizations"), such as the Kawadōri, Uogashi, and Yoshiwara groups. There were also connoisseur groups such as the Rokuji club and the Suigyo club. The criticism of such groups carried authority. (*See also* AUDIENCES; HIIKI.)

RENRIBIKI. An acting technique used in ghost plays*. The ghost makes eerie gestures as if controlling the movements of a character who is attempting to flee. The fleeing person mimes as though he were being pulled backwards by the hair. He struggles to get free but to no avail. The acting of the character caught by the ghost is called *renribiki* ("entwined pulling"). To

The bloodthirsty ghost of Hōkaibō (above) uses its ghostly powers to prevent Shinza from escaping in *Sumidagawa Gonichi no Omokage**. The photo illustrates the *renribiki** technique. *Courtesy of Waseda University Tsubouchi Engeki Hakubutsukan (Tsubouchi Memorial Theatre Museum).*

accent the weirdness of the scene, a big drum is beaten ominously offstage. Famous examples are in *Kasane** and *Tōkaidō Yotsuya Kaidan**.

REVENGE PLAYS. Called *adauchi kyōgen*, or *katakiuchi mono*. The number of such plays in Kabuki and the puppet theatre reflects the high esteem in which samurai vendettas were held during the Edo era. Beginning in the Kansei era (1789-1800, these dramas stressed the villain's dreadful nature. There was a marked tendency toward the presentation of murder scenes and the killing of the would-be avenger by the intended victim. Also popular were plots in which a decent person was oppressed. Representative plays of this genre include *Youchi Soga Kariba no Akebono**, *Kanadehon Chūshingura**, *Igagoe Dōchū Sugoroku**, *Katakiuchi Tengajaya Mura**, *Konpira Megumi no Ki*, *Kameyama no Katakiuchi*, and *Gotaiheiki Shiraishi Banashi**. (*See also* PLAY CATEGORIES.)

REVOLVING STAGE. Known as *mawari butai*. Consisting of a large circle set in the stage floor on which two or three sets, front and rear, are placed, it effects smooth changes of scenery by revolving on its base. A Japanese invented such stages before they were used in Western theatre. The revolving stage began to be used in the Kyōhō era (1716-35), when the playwright Nakamura Denshichi devised the *bun mawashi* method. This was a platform that was mounted on wheels and could be revolved by pushing it; the stage was called the *mawari dōgu*. In 1758 a revolving stage of a different sort was used for Namiki Shōzō's* play *Yobune no Hajimari*. It consisted of an extra stage placed on top of a wheeled circular platform. This platform had an axle that turned it at its center. The axle ran through the stage floor to the basement *(naraku*)*, where it was received by a bearing that made the stage circle revolve. Later, a method was devised whereby a circle was cut in the stage floor and wheels were attached to its underside; these were received by a framework under the stage. An axle ran from the center of the circle to the ground beneath the stage. Whereas old-time stages were operated manually by teams of workers under the stage, today's revolving stages are operated by electricity. When the stage revolves while the stage lights are on, the technique is called *akaten*. *Kuraten* is revolving the stage in the dark. These terms are used for scene changes even when the stage is not revolved, though the former means "lighted revolve" and the latter "darkened revolve." (*See also* THEATRE ARCHITECTURE; SCENERY.)

RIEN. "The pear garden"; a word deriving from the tradition that Emperor Ming Huang of ancient China trained musicians and entertainers in a pear tree garden. The word has come to mean the "theatre world." An Edo period sinologue applied this term, which originated in the Chinese theatre, to Kabuki.

ROBBER PLAYS. *Shiranami mono*, a subgrouping of plays within the category of plays called *kizewamono**, are called "robber plays" because of their robber heroes. The word *shiranami* (literally, "white waves") is based on a Chinese word for robbers that is written with the same characters. The main works of this subgrouping were written by Kawatake Mokuami* for the talents of Ichikawa Kodanji IV*. Famous examples are *Sannin Kichiza Kuruwa no Hatsugai** and *Aotozōshi Hana no Nishikie**, the latter having been written for Ichimura Uzaemon XIII (Onoe Kikugorō V*).

ROKKASEN (SUGATA NO IRODORI). Matsui Kōji. *Shosagoto**. *Nagauta** and *kiyomoto**. March 1831. Nakamura-za*, Edo.

Six of the most famous *waka* poets of the Heian period (794-1185) are shown in a humorous, Edo-style, five-part transformation piece* *(henge mono)*. Nakamura Utaemon IV* and Iwai Hanshirō VI* were featured in the original cast.

Following the elegant dance *(nagauta)* of Sōjō Henjō the priest, is a dance *(kiyomoto)* by Bunya Yasuhide, who is accompanied by court ladies. This dance conveys the flavor of the Yoshiwara pleasure district. Then there is a romantic dance *(nagauta)* depicting the love between the handsome Ariwara no Narihira and Ono no Komachi, succeeded by a complete change to a dance by Kisen, who performs as a mendicant priest, banging two drums and singing a parody of the scriptures, while accompanied by a tea-serving maid. Finally there is a dance about Kuronishi and Komachi, taken from the Nō play *Sōshi Arai*.

This work about the five unsuccessful lovers of Japan's most famous *femme fatale*, Ono no Komachi, is fascinating and reflects the mood of the late Edo era. The dances of Kisen, Bunya, and so on often are given as independent pieces, although *Rokkasen* is one of the few *henge mono* still to be given complete performances.

ROLE TYPES. Kabuki characters have been categorized according to sex, age, and personality. The Japanese word for role types is *yakugara*. It was prescribed once that actors specialize in those parts best suited to their particular talents. For instance, actors who specialized in playing female roles belonged to the *onnagata** class, while those whose forte was evil man belonged to the *katakiyaku** category. The major divisions (which still exist) were between male and female roles *(tachiyaku** or *tateyaku* and *onnagata)*. Among male roles the three main classifications are good men *(tachiyaku)*, evil men *(katakiyaku)*, and comic men *(dōkegata** or *sanmaime**)*. *Onnagata* classifications contain the roles of youthful women *(wakaonnagata)*, middle-aged women *(kashagata)*, and old women *(fuke oyama)*.

In 1652 *wakashu kabuki** or young men's Kabuki*, was banned. One of the conditions of Kabuki's revival was the incorporation of dramatic content on a higher plane than had been the case in the past. The increased emphasis on drama soon led to a division of the actors into male- and female-role specialists. Such specialization became an established convention and was the beginning of the "role-type" system. Kabuki plays became increasingly more complex, and roles were classed according to their differing qualities of good or evil, strength or weakness. Later, regulation of the system deteriorated, and versatile actors came to play several different role types. Talented performers were accorded the esteemed title of *kaneru yakusha** ("all-around actor"), which was a recognition of their versatility. The role-type system also regulated the characters of Kabuki plays, and playwrights spent a good deal of effort creating a role in terms of its unique features. The growth of the *onnagata*'s art, in particular, profited from this development. (*See also* ACTORS' RANKS.)

ROPPŌ. A stylized *hanamichi** exit. As the character walks or bounds off, he makes exaggerated movements with his feet and arms, which are seemingly extended in all directions (*roppō* means "six directions"). The technique began during the early Edo period when actors copied the flashy movements of the dashing young men about town *(otokodate)*. At first, it was primarily a method used for *hanamichi* entrances *(deba*)*, but later became an art of exiting (*see also* HIKKOMI). There are many varieties of *roppō*, most of them being in the bravura style of *aragoto**. Chief among these is the *tobi roppō*, or "flying roppō," in which the actor bounds off using one foot after the other (Umeomaru in the *Kuruma Biki* scene of *Sugawara Denju Tenarai Kagami**); the *katate* ("one-handed") *roppō*, in which the exit is made with one hand holding an object while the other is free to gesticulate (as in *Tenjiku Tokubei Ikoku Banashi** and *Ibaraki**); the *kitsune* ("fox") *roppō*, in which both hands are curled over like fox paws while the actor's movements suggest those of a fox (Tadanobu, the fox spirit in *Yoshitsune Senbon Zakura**); the *keisei* ("courtesan") *roppō*, in which both hands swing in all directions and the feet spell out a series of Japanese figure eights (seen in *Miyajima Danmari*); and others, such as the *tanzen* ("before the bathhouse") *roppō*, the *yūrei* ("ghost") *roppō*, and the *oyogi* ("swimming") *roppō*.

"ROUGH BUSINESS." *See* ARAGOTO.

RUNWAY. *See* HANAMICHI.

RYŌKAN TO KOMORI. Tsubouchi Shōyō*. *Shosagoto**. *Tokiwazu**. June 1929. Teikoku Gekijō*, Tokyo.

The *hanamichi** exit known as the *keisei roppō*, seen in the pantomime *(danmari*)*, *Miyajima no Danmari*. Nakamura Jakuemon IV*.

Ryōkan, returning from begging for alms, happens to pass by a group of village children at play. He joins in their games, but notices that he has forgotten his begging bowl. He grieves at having forgotten something so important, but the children cheer him up with a game of handball. Meanwhile, a game of blindman's bluff is begun; Ryōkan is blindfolded and made to look for the children. Catching hold of someone, he looks to see who it is. It is a farmer who, unbeknownst to the old beggar, has brought his bowl back to him. Ryōkan is overjoyed and respectfully presses his hands together.

This modern dance, in which the old beggar becomes like a child and takes pleasure in playing with children, is performed often.

RYŪJIN MAKI. A fanciful *suō* robe on which the right sleeve is removed and placed to the rear, where it is folded in a traditional manner resembling a strip of dried abalone. The left sleeve is stretched in a stiff rectangle with bamboo splints; this sleeve has a large crest on it. The *hakama** trousers are worn tucked up at the thighs. The *ryūjin maki* is worn by envoys and other such officials in history plays derived from the puppet theatre. Among those wearing this costume are Terukuni, the magistrate in the *Domyōji* scene of *Sugawara Denju Tenarai Kagami**, Shundō Genba in *Terakoya* (an act of the same play), and Genta in *Hiragana Seisuiki**.

Senō, the envoy, ridicules Shunkan in *Heike Nyogo no Shima**. Senō wears the *ryūjin maki** costume. Shunkan (left), Nakamura Kichiemon II*; Senō, Ichikawa Sadanji IV. *Courtesy of Waseda University Tsubouchi Engeki Hakubutsukan (Tsubouchi Memorial Theatre Museum).*

S

SABAKI. A wig with untidy hair. There are many occasions—a fight scene, a murder scene, a suicide scene—when the actor will cut the cord holding his topknot in place so that the hair tumbles down in *sabaki* fashion. This provides one of Kabuki's characteristically beautiful effects. The topknot cord is rigged beforehand with a button type of device that is painted black so that the audience cannot see it. When this is pulled, the topknot falls apart and the hair tumbles in disarray. A character who performs this rather common technique is Gonta in *Yoshitsune Senbon Zakura**. There are two main varieties of *sabaki* for female roles. One, simply called *sabaki*, uses a wig whose topknot comes undone; its forelock, side locks, and back pouch, however, stay in place. Ofune in *Shinrei Yaguchi no Watashi** uses it. The other, called *fusa* ("tuft") *sabaki*, allows all the hair to fall down. A character using it is Lady Tamate in *Sesshū Gappō ga Tsuji**.

SAGARI. A free ticket for those connected with the theatre.

SAGEGAMI. "Hanging hair," a wig on which hair that should be tied up in a topknot is allowed to flow freely down the back. It is worn in history plays by female characters like Kaoyo in *Kanadehon Chūshingura**, Kasuga in *Kasuga no Tsubone*, and Yodogimi in *Kiri Hitoha**. The *kasshiki* is a variety of *sagegami* that has the front hair parted and falling down behind. Shizuka in *Funa Benkei** and Lady Sakae in *Meiboku Sendai Hagi** wear it.

SAGI MUSUME. Horikoshi Nisōji*. Also called *Yanagi ni Hina Shochō no Saezuri. Shosagoto**. *Nagauta**. March 1762. Ichimura-za*, Edo.

A one-scene dance play in which a single actor makes four different costume changes. Edo's first revolving stage is believed to have been used when this work premiered. After being unproduced for a long time, a fine revival starring Ichikawa Danjūrō IX* was staged in 1886.

Today, the featured dancer appears by entering from the shadows of the willows on a device knowns as the *shamoji**, a board which is mounted on wheels and on which the actor stands upright. The dancer displays various quick-change techniques by which he changes from a snow heron to a city girl. The *hiki nuki** trick, whereby the loosely basted threads of an outer kimono are pulled out by a stage assistant to reveal the kimono underneath, is seen. Also employed is the *bukkaeri**, a partial version of *hiki nuki.* Other changes involve wig tricks—for example, when both sides of the carefully dressed hair are made to fall in disarray.

SAIGŌ TO BUTAHIME. Ikeda Daigo*. *Shin kabuki**. One act. May 1917. Yuraku-za, Tokyo.

Otama, a waitress at the Kyoto brothel known as the Sanbonki, is a rather large woman and is nicknamed Butahime ("Princess Pig"). She is in love with the fat Satsuma samurai Saigō Yoshinosuke, who is busy plotting the overthrow of the shogunate. Saigō, being pursued by the shogun's agents, pays a visit to Otama after a long absence. He knows that she has resolved to die for him, and he, despite his previous intentions, resolves to die with her. However, Okubō Toshiyuki and Nakamura Hanjirō arrive to see him. They announce that their clan chief's intention is to reestablish Imperial rule in Japan. Saigō takes heart and departs for Edo on a secret mission.

The play conveys a certain pathos and humor that arises from the vision of the pair of heavyset lovers. Also notable is the play's human treatment of the historical figure Saigō.

SAJIKI. The galleries, which were considered a better class of seating in Edo theatres. There were *sajiki* used for viewing festivals as far back as the Heian period (794-1185); such galleries were used exclusively by the nobility. *Sajiki* were erected during the Kamakura and Muromachi periods (twelfth through sixteenth centuries) for viewing subscription performances *(kanjin)* of *dengaku* and Nō. Early Kabuki theatres had roofed *sajiki* on both sides of the auditorium with bamboo screens hiding the spectators behind them from sight. These were considered the best grade of seats for upper-class spectators. When completely roofed-in Kabuki theatres were erected, *sajiki* were set up on either side of the auditorium in two levels. The best seats were thought to be those nearest the stage in the second story *(nikai) sajiki.* The lower-level *sajiki* was called the *uzura**. (*See also* THEATRE ARCHITECTURE.)

SAKAGUMA. "Upturned bear"; a wig presenting an unshaved pate on which hair has been growing. Bear fur is applied to this spot to simulate human hair. The wig worn by masterless samurai and villainous characters is called *mushiri**, *sakaguma*, or *nakaguma*, depending on the length of hair grown in. A major role in which it is worn is Sadakurō in *Kanadehon Chūshingura**.

SAKATA TŌJŪRŌ. 1647-1709. The representative Kamigata actor during the late seventeenth century. From 1673 to 1681 he was active in Kyoto and Osaka, but he first began to garner fame in February 1678 with his portrayal of Izaemon in *Yūgiri Nagori no Shōgatsu*, a play about the death of a famous geisha, Yūgiri of Osaka's Shinmachi district. He played the role of Yūgiri's lover Izaemon four times that year and eighteen times during his career. His style, like that of Izaemon, was pure "young lover" *(nimaime*)*. It is said that he was perfectly suited to portray the kind of characters who had brought their own ruin upon themselves, roles which were called *yatsushi* (*see also* NIMAIME). He was a big hit in 1693 in Chikamatsu Monzaemon's* *Butsu Momoyasan Kaichō* as Kamon and thereafter was the top *yatsushi* actor in Chikamatsu's *keisei* ("courtesan") plays (*see also* KAMIGATA KYŌGEN). His art has often been compared to that of Edo's Ichikawa Danjūrō I*, his contemporary. Whereas Danjūrō reflected the atmosphere of the newly established city of Edo and was the representative actor of his time in the *aragoto** style, Tōjūrō expounded the literary and realistic art of *wagoto**, of which he was the major performer., Aside from his role of Izaemon, Tōjūrō's outstanding successes were as Umenaga Bunzō in *Keisei Hotoke no Hara*, Takatō Tamiya in *Keisei Mibu Danenbutsu*, and other parts in which he acted the role of a young lover who suffers tragically.

There were three generations of actors bearing the name of Sakata Tōjūrō, but only the first was an important star.

SAKAZAKI DEWA NO KAMI. Yamamoto Yuzō. English title: *Sakazaki, Lord Dewa* (Shaw). *Shin kabuki**. Four acts. September 1921. Ichimura-za*, Tokyo.

At the battle of Osaka Castle, Lord Sakazaki Dewa manages to rescue Princess Sen (wife of Hideyori) from the flames, despite a serious facial wound that he has suffered. Ieyasu promises him that, if possible, he can become her husband. However, Princess Sen has given her heart to the handsome Honda Heihachiro, and Ieyasu is unable to keep his promise. Princess Sen ultimately marries Honda, but Lord Dewa intrudes upon the wedding procession with the intent of kidnapping her. Failing in his attempt, he commits ritual suicide *(seppuku)*.

The work beautifully depicts the psychological transitions in Dewa's character as he suffers from unrequited love.• The play is considered the dramatist's masterpiece. Onoe Kikugorō VI* received acclaim for his realistic portrayal of Lord Dewa when the play first was produced.

SAKURADA JISUKE I. 1734-1806. An Edo-born playwright who became a pupil of Horikoshi Nisōji*, was promoted to *nimaime sakusha** in 1758, and later was employed at a Kyoto theatre, where for more than three years he practiced the Kamigata style of writing. He later returned to Edo and became chief playwright *(tate sakusha*)* at the Morita-za* in 1767. He had a big hit with *Edo no Hana Wakayagi Soga* at the Ichimura-za's* spring performances of 1769. This work brought him into prominence, and for the next forty-odd years he occupied a leading position among Edo playwrights. He was the main supplier of plays for Ichikawa Danjūrō III* and V* and Matsumoto Kōshirō V*. A prolific writer, he created over 120 plays and 100 dance dramas. His work was influenced by Nisōji and Kanai Sanshō*, and he was a force in the infusion of jokes, wit, and satire into Edo domestic plays. His dance plays were known widely as "Sakurada's *jōruri*" (*jōruri** meaning a narrative dance piece in this context). His best works include *Gohiiki Kanjinchō**, *Date Kurabe Okuni Kabuki* (*see also* MEIBOKU SENDAI HAGI), *Suzugamori**, *Banzui Chōbei Shōjin no Manaita**; his dance plays are represented by *Modori Kago**, *Migawari Oshun*, *Yoshiwara Suzume*, and *Kumo Hyōshi Mai*, among others.

II. 1768-1829. An Edo playwright who was a disciple of Jisuke I and took the name of Jisuke II in 1808. In 1817 he became a *tate sakusha*. He excelled at dance dramas, his works including *Sarashime**, *Ohan, Tobae**, *Kugutsu Shi*, *Shiokumi**, *Shitadashi Sanbasō* (*see also* SANBASŌ), and *Asatsuma Bune*.

III. 1802-1877. An Edo playwright, he later called himself Kyōgenjō Sakō and Sakurado Sakō. The pupil of Jisuke II, he became Jisuke III in 1833. He was promoted to *tate sakusha* in 1838 and was active through the 1850s, but he yielded his position as the leading playwright when Kawatake Mokuami* rose to fame at mid-century. He was weak in invention and relied mainly on adaptations for his success. Numbered among his works are *Akegarasu Hana no Nureginu**, *Kore Wa Hyōban Ukina no Yomiuri**, *Mitsu Ningyō**, *Noriaibune**, and *Dontsuku**.

SAKURA FUBUKI. Hasegawa Shigure. *Shin kabuki**. Five scenes. February 1911. Kabuki-za*, Tokyo.

Sakuma Shichirozaemon has been placed in the custody of Saito Dōsan, lord of the Inabe Castle in Mino Province. Shichirozaemon is a villain who killed Suda Yahachi and then fled. Both Yahachi's wife, Katsuko, and his mistress, Sayuri, seek Yahachi's revenge. Sayuri becomes a nun, but Katsuko steals into the castle as a maid and kills her enemy. Afraid that she will cause trouble to others, Katsuko entrusts her affairs to Sayuri, when the latter comes to visit her, and then kills herself.

The idea of having a man's wife and mistress seek his revenge is a novelty in Kabuki.

SAKURA GIMINDEN. Segawa Jokō III*. Also called *Higashiyama Sakura Sōshi, Sakura Sogō*. *Sewamono**. Kabuki. Seven acts. August 1851. Nakamura-za*, Edo.

A dramatization of the actual event in which Sakura no Kiuchi Sogorō of Shimōsa made a direct appeal to the shogun on behalf of the farmers of his district, who were suffering under extremely heavy taxation. As can be seen in one of the alternate titles, the historical period has been changed from the Edo period to the Higashiyama period (late fifteenth century). The script for today's performances dates from 1861 when Kawatake Mokuami* revised the play for Ichikawa Kodanji IV* at Edo's Morita-za*. The present title, *Sakura Giminden*, was first used in 1894 for a production at Tokyo's Shintomi-za.

Sōgō, aware of the fruitlessness of previous entreaties in Edo, decides to make a direct appeal to the shogun. On his way to say farewell to his family in his home town, he comes to the ferry at Inba Lake. The ferry has been chained up at the order of the local *daimyō*, but Jinbei the ferryman, knowing of Sōgō's resolve, cuts the fetters and departs with Sōgō in the ferry. Sōgō bids his wife and children farewell and soon arrives in Edo. On a day when the shogun is visiting a temple in Toyeizan (in Edo), Sōgō breaks the law and presents his appeal. Lord Matsudaira Izu receives the appeal unofficially, but has Sōgō arrested.

This drama contains many scenes in which a feeling of pathos prevails, but few contain much color and depth in performance. It is one of the only examples of what might be called social-protest drama in the Kabuki canon.

SAKURAMARU. A term taken from the name of one of the triplets in *Sugawara Denju Tenarai Kagami**. Sakuramaru commits ritual suicide (*seppuku*, spelled with characters meaning "cut belly"), so the name is used when someone spends his own money on something (*jibara o kiru*, "to spend one's own money" or "to cut one's own purse strings" is spelled with characters that mean "to cut one's own belly.")

SAKURA SHIGURE. Takaya Gekkō. *Shin kabuki**. Two acts, four scenes. December 1906. Minami-za*, Kyoto.

Saburobei, disinherited by his father, Shōyū, ransoms the courtesan Yoshino from bondage to the brothel and, renouncing the world, lives a life of elegance with her. One day, Shōyū, who has been caught in the late afternoon rain, takes shelter at his son's home, though he does not know to whom the house belongs. He is struck by the refinement of the lady of the house. On his way home he learns that the lady is Yoshino. Ultimately he reverses his son's disinheritance.

The play skillfully uses Kabuki techniques and is filled with color. Also, it depicts with great clarity the human love of elegance, the feelings between parent and child, and the love of a man and woman for each other. It is Gekkō's representative work.

SAKURATSUBA URAMI NO SAMEZAYA. Anonymous. Also called *Otsuma Hachirobei, Unagidani. Sewamono*. Jōruri**. October 1774, Toyotake-za, Osaka.

Hachirobei, a dealer in secondhand goods, is having trouble raising the money that he needs to help his master's daughter. His wife, Otsuma, who knows of his difficulties, devises a plan with her mother by which Otsuma gives herself to the evil Yohei to raise the money. Against her wishes she must castigate Hachirobei, whom she really loves. Taking her remarks for the truth, Hachirobei kills both Otsuma and her mother. Later, when he learns the true facts, he commits ritual suicide *(seppuku)*.

Hachirobei learns the truth about Otsuma from his young daughter Ohan, to whom Otsuma has told everything. The child's role is thus very important in the play. The present performance style is based on that originated by Kataoka Nizaemon XI*.

SAKUSHA BEYA. The "playwrights' room," a room in which the house writers discharge various duties. It is located near the backstage entrance adjacent to the *tōdori*'s* room. The literary staff prepares the actor's parts *(kakinuki*)* and scripts here. The room is used as a waiting room or lounge by the literary staff and by those *kyōgen kata** who act as stage assistants during the running of a show.

SAMISEN. *See* SHAMISEN.

SANBABĀ. "Three grandmas," the three most difficult and important old lady roles in history plays: Kansuke's mother, Koshiji, in *Honchō Nijūshikō**; Mimyō in *Ōmi Genji Senjin Yakata**; and Kakuju in *Sugawara Denju Tenarai Kagami**. Some critics include Koshiji in *Shinshū Kawanakajima Kassen** instead of Koshiji in *Honchō Nijūshikō**. Another character often substituted for one of the above is Enju in *Hiragana Seisuiki**.

SANBAI KAZARI. A scenic term, also pronounced *sanbō kazari.* The placement of three sets on the revolving stage* *(mawari butai)* to facilitate quick scene changes. Back-to-back sets on the revolve are called *nippai kazari* or *nibō kazari.*

SANBASŌ. *Shosagoto**.

It is not known when Kabuki began to produce *Sanbasō* (*Sanba* for short) plays; though their existence during the Okuni Kabuki* period is not definite, it is believed that Nakamura Kanzaburō I* staged a piece called *Rankyoku Sanbasō.* A publication of 1678 lists a *Shiki Sanbasō.* Before long, it became customary to produce an adaptation of the Nō play *Okina* at annual theatre

Mimyō, one of the three great old lady roles of the history play genre. The play is *Ōmi Genji Senjin Yakata**, and the actor is Onoe Taganojō III*. *Courtesy of Waseda University Tsubouchi Engeki Hakubutsukan (Tsubouchi Memorial Theatre Museum).*

events, such as the *kaomise** and New Year's performances, as well as at the opening ceremonies for new theatres. The adaptation was called *Okina Watashi*; the manager played the role of Okina; his son acted Senzai; and the leading actor *(zagashira*)* or choreographer *(furitsukeshi)* performed the role of Sanbasō. Kyoto's Asai Tamejūrō became the first *onnagata** to dance Sanbasō when he did so at a 1728 *kaomise* performance. Eventually, each theatre produced its own version of a Sanbasō dance early in the morning when the theatre opened for business. It was a daily ritual, regardless of the plays on the rest of the program, and was performed by the lowest-ranking actors. The practice, called *bantachi**, died out in the early Meiji period.

Many dance plays came to be based on the Sanbasō characters, each piece having its own special treatment of the traditional materials. Some of those that are still popular are described below.

Shitadashi Sanbasō. Sakurada Jisuke II*. Also called *Mata Kuru Haru Suzuna no Tanemaki, Tanemaki Sanbasō. Kiyomoto** and *tokiwazu**. September 1812. Nakamura-za*, Edo.

A dance of Senzai and Sanbasō, in which Sanbasō has the affable appearance of a clown. The work delights with its clever music and dancing.

Ayatsuri Sanbasō. Minekoto Hachijurō. Also called *Yanagi no Ito Hikuya Gohiiki. Nagauta**. August 1852. Chikugo Shibai, Osaka.

There was, until the Meiji period, a dance in which Senzai and Okina performed as clockwork puppets while Sanbasō danced in imitation of them as a string-operated puppet. In today's version, Sanbasō is pulled out of a puppet's box, and there is a sequence of mime as the stage assistant *(kōken*)* acts out the untangling of his strings.

Kotobuki Shiki Sanbasō. *Jōruri**. January 1859. Nakamura-za*, Edo. This piece is based on puppet-theatre style. It is performed by both the puppets and Kabuki. Two Sanbasō appear, and there is a great liveliness in the presentation of their dancing rivalry.

Shiki Sanbasō. Shiun Iori. *Kiyomoto.* Traditionally held to have been composed in 1838. This was originally a celebratory number. It was a musical piece accompanying Okina's oral reading of the names of four-season flowering plants.

SANDAN. A standardized, stepped platform, three feet wide with risers each about nine inches high and treads of nine to twelve inches in depth. It is used with the stage platform arrangement called *takaashi no nijū* (*see also* NIJŪ). Further, in dance plays it also is covered with a red carpet and brought out to center stage at the end of an act so that the chief actor may mount and cut a *mie** pose on it. Female impersonators use a two-stepped platform, the *nidan**.

SANGAI. "Third floor"; a term describing actors who occupied the large dressing room *(ōbeya*)* on the third floor of old theatres. Such actors are among the lowest-ranking in a troupe. (*See also* ACTORS' RANKS.)

SANGESANGE. A musical accompaniment played when Yosa enters on the *hanamichi** in the *Genyadana* scene of *Yowa Nasake Ukina no Yokogushi**. The term has come to be used colloquially when one is going to solicit something from someone else, as in *sangesange o suru* ("to put the squeeze on somebody").

SANHIME. "Three princesses," the three most important and difficult princess roles in Kabuki: Yaegaki in *Honchō Nijūshikō**, Princess Yuki in the *Kinkakuji* scene of *Gion Sairei Shinkōki**, and Princess Toki in *Kamakura Sandaiki**.

SANJA MATSURI. Segawa Jokō II. Also called *Yayoi no Hana Asakusa Matsuri. Shosagoto*. Kiyomoto**. March 1832. Nakamura-za*, Edo.

A dance version of a type of puppet performance given at the Sanja Festival in Asakusa. The part remaining today, which has changed from the original puppet version, deals with fishermen at the Miyato River. Bandō Mitsugorō IV* and Nakamura Shikan II were the original performers.

The plot concerns two fishermen who, while drawing in their net, display through dance a good soul and an evil soul, which have crept into their hearts.

The moral philosophy *(shingaku)* popular at the time and the clever style of the performance, which uses masks, infuse this work with originality and interest.

SANJŪSAN GENDŌ MUNAGI NO YURAI. Wakatake Fuemi, Nakamura Akei. Also called *Gion Nyogo Koko no Enishika Yanagi. Jidaimono*. Jōruri**. Five acts. December 1760. Toyotake-za, Osaka.

A dramatization of the history of the Sanjūsan Gendō Temple in Kyoto. A number of earlier versions of the story preceded this play.

The tonsured Emperor Shirakawa is ill. It is learned that his illness is caused by a dead ancestor who is buried underneath a certain willow tree. Thus, this willow is cut down and is going to be made into a ridgepole for the temple. Once before, when this willow was to be felled, it was saved from destruction by Osone Heita. The willow's spirit, in the form of a young woman named Oryū, married Heita and had a son by him, Midorimaru. Still, the willow ultimately is cut down and dragged away. Oryū's regret, however, causes the tree to stop en route so that it can not be budged. Midorimaru is summoned; when he sings a workman's song, the big tree's filial emotions are touched and it begins to move along easily.

This work depicts the marriage of a human to the soul of a willow tree. The acting of Oryū, as we hear the sound of the ax cutting down the tree, and the glowing form that appears to Heita and Midorimaru when Oryū vanishes suddenly do "play to the gallery," but they are, nevertheless, at the heart of this play's appeal.

SANMAIME. A type of humorous character. The word also is used to refer to stupid people in general. (*See also* DŌKEGATA.)

SANMAIME SAKUSHA. The third-ranking playwright in an Edo period theatre, he had similar duties to the *nimaime sakusha** and originally was responsible for the *mitateme** (third scene on the program) and the opening act *(jomaku*)* of the day's domestic play. He wrote whichever scenes were his forte at the direction of the chief playwright *(tate sakusha*)*. As a rule, he always was present at the theatre when the plays were being performed. (*See also* PLAYWRIGHTS' RANKS.)

SANMON (GOSAN NO KIRI). Namiki Gohei I*. Also called *Kinmon Gosan no Kiri*. Kabuki. Five acts. April 1778. Naka no Shibai, Osaka.

Only a part of Act II is performed today. In the original production, the actors included Arashi Hinasuke as Ishikawa Goemon and Onoe Kikugorō I* as Hisayoshi.

Ishikawa Goemon was a famed outlaw who is said to have been executed with his son by being boiled in oil. Many legends about his life arose, and they often found their way into songs, stories, and plays. This play was the first Kabuki version.

While the bandit chief Ishikawa Goemon is admiring the view of flowers from his vantage point at the top of the main gate of Kyoto's Nanzen Temple, a hawk appears in the air. From the note attached to the hawk's feet, Goemon learns that his own father, dead at the hands of Hisayoshi, was Sō Sekai, who was planning to overthrow Japan in the name of the Ming dynasty of China. Because of Hisayoshi, however, the plot is now known. Just then, Hisayoshi, disguised as a pilgrim, appears, and the two men face each other in rivalry—Goemon on the high verandah, Hisayoshi on the ground.

The plot is simple and the act brief. However, there is great pleasure in viewing the magnificent set as well as the bold figures cut by the actors. It also is a delightful piece musically. A temple gate that rises on a huge stage lift *(seri*)* occupies the entire stage. Goemon is fitted out with a huge padded gown and an immense wig signifying that he has gone for 100 days without shaving his crown (*see also* HYAKUNICHI).

SANNIN KATAWA. Takeshiba Kisui*. *Shosagoto**. *Kiyomoto** and *tokiwazu**. October 1898. Meiji-za*, Tokyo.

A Kabuki version of a Kyōgen farce with the same title.

A sham blind man (Hannojō), a sham cripple (Tarosuke), and a sham deaf-mute (Omaki) are hired by a samurai whose sake they drink while he is away. When the lord returns, the three are drunk. They become confused and go back to their original sham behavior, but the blind man pretends to be a deaf-mute, the cripple, a blind man; and the deaf-mute, a cripple. The lord chases them out.

The acting of the pretended disabilities is highly comic, and the music is quite lively. Stars of the first production were Ichikawa Sumizō, Ichikawa Kodanji V*, Sawamura Tanosuke IV*, and Ichikawa Sadanji I*.

SANNIN KICHIZA (KURUWA NO HATSUGAI). Kawatake Mokuami*. *Sewamono**. Kabuki. Seven acts. January 1860. Ichimura-za*, Edo.

Modern performances of this work begin midway through Act II, when the three thieves swear to blood brotherhood, and continue to the detection of their crimes and their deaths. This material makes up a complete five-act presentation. Performing in the original version were Ichikawa Kodanji IV*, Iwai Kumesaburō (later Hanshirō IV*), Seki Sanjūrō III, Kawarazaki Gonjūrō (later Ichikawa Danjūrō IX*), Ichimura Uzaemon XIII (later Onoe Kikugorō V*), Azuma Ichinojō, and others.

The prostitute Otose has picked up a 100-*ryō* purse dropped by Jūzaburō, her lover, and runs with it to the bank of the O River. A woman's figure appears. It is actually the disguised Ojō Kichiza, who throws Otose into the river and seizes her money. Obō Kichiza, who is passing by, struggles with Ojō for the money, but Oshō Kichiza enters and arbitrates the matter. The three join up with each other as sworn brothers. Oshō Kichiza takes charge of the 100 *ryō*. Otose, saved by Yaoya Kyūbei, learns that Denkichi, to whose house she has been brought, is her father and that Jūzaburō, her lover, is her twin brother. The 100 *ryō* that changes hands so often is given to Denkichi by Oshō Kichiza, who is also his son, but the old man is killed by Obō Kichiza soon after. Obō does not know the relationship between Denkichi and Oshō. Obō has left some evidence, a small knife that dropped at the murder scene. Otose and Jūzaburō come with it to Oshō at the Kichijoin Temple to ask their brother to revenge their father's death. Oshō learns from them that they plan to kill themselves to expiate their sin of incest. He persuades them that their deaths can be turned to good account if he uses their heads to fool the police into thinking they are the heads of his confederates. The police are not fooled for long, though, and eventually they surround the three thieves. Rather than be taken, the trio stab each other and die.

The first scene of the play, at the river bank, is very picturesque in visual terms and in the rhythmical speech *(tsurane*)* delivered by the three men. Other interesting features include the passing of the 100 *ryō* from one hand to another, the complex web of human relationships, and the pathetic scene of the old man's murder. It is a good example of the *kizewamono** genre, depicting conditions at the end of the Edo period, during the years of the shogunate's decline.

SANRIATE. A costume element, similar to knee pads, seen on stylized male characters in certain history and dance plays when they wear their *hakama** trousers hitched up at the thighs. Such characters tie one beneath each knee at the so-called *sanri* spot. The pad consists of a small triangular or rounded piece of material. The color is red or canary yellow, and it provides a nice accent to the character's appearance. The solo dancer in *Tomoyakko* wears it, as do Tsumahei in *Shin Usuyuki Monogatari** and Genba in the *Terakoya* scene of *Sugawara Denju Tenarai Kagami**.

SANZESŌ (NISHIKI BUNSHŌ). Sakurada Jisuke III*. *Sewamono**/*shosagoto**. Six acts. July 1857. Nakamura-za*, Edo.

An unusual work that uses *tokiwazu** narrative accompaniment throughout its six acts. The first five acts are half danced and half acted, while Act VI, set at the Sanja Festival, is entirely in dance style. Its lengthy use of *tokiwazu* accompaniment puts this work in a class by itself. In the first production the cast included Kataoka Gatō II, Ichikawa Enzaburō, Arashi Koroku, Seki Utasuke, and Sawamura Tosshō.

The piece tells of the courtesan Osono, who has killed her evil brother Chōan and runs away with her lover, Rokusaburō, to commit double suicide at the Susaki Riverbank. They become ghosts and visit Enma, king of the underworld. After various vicissitudes, everything that has occurred during the first five acts turns out to be a dream, only the final act taking place in reality.

The piece was revived in 1957 by Nakamura Kanzaburō XVII* and Nakamura Utaemon VI* at the Shinbashi Enbujō*.

SARASHIME. Sakurada Jisuke II*. Also called *Mata Koko ni Sugata Hakkei, Omi no Okane. Shosagoto**. *Nagauta**. June 1813. Morita-za*, Edo.

A one-scene piece in which the actor dances while making costume changes. It was written for Ichikawa Danjūrō VII*.

The play begins with a scene in which Okane, a powerful girl, restrains a horse. Among other things, it contains the girl's stylized fight with a group of male opponents, whom she handles in a firm but feminine fashion, a Bon dance, and a showy display with a bleaching cloth.

SARAU. To receive praise from a spectator for one's acting. The word also means "to practice."

SARU GUMA. "Monkey *kuma,*" a makeup style invented by Nakamura Denkurō I*, it is the oldest extant *kumadori**. Denkurō made his face up in this style when playing the role of Asahina in 1690 at the Nakamura-za*. It also is called the *Asahina no guma.* Three lines are drawn horizontally across the monkey-like forehead, and then a curve is drawn downward and up again past the eyes to the cheeks. Before becoming an actor, Denkurō was a theatre manager under the name of Saruwaka Kanzaburō IV, so the style is called *Saruwaka no saruguma* as well.

SARUWAKA-MACHI. A street on which Edo's theatres were located from 1842 to 1872. As part of the Tenpō period (1830-43) reforms of 1841, the theatres—which up to then had been in the heart of Edo—were ordered to move to the Seiten-chō area in Asakusa; this place on the outskirts of the city was renamed Saruwaka-machi after the name of a seventeenth-century actor (*see also* NAKAMURA KANZABURŌ I). In 1842 the Nakamura-za* moved to 1-chome, Saruwaka-machi, while the Ichimura-za* moved to 2-chome. In May of the following year the Kawarazaki-za (Morita-za*) moved to 3-chome. Furthermore, all theatre personnel had to make their homes in this desolate neighborhood. In 1872 the Morita-za, led by the progressive Morita Kanya XII*, moved to Tokyo's Shintomi district, located in the midst of the city. The Nakamura-za moved to Tokyo's center in 1884 and was followed in 1892 by the Ichimura-za, depriving the Saruwaka-machi theatre street of its *raison d'être.* (*See also* THEATRE STREET.)

SARUWAKA-ZA. The first official theatre opened in Edo. *See also* NAKAMURA-ZA.

SASAKI TAKATSUNA. Okamoto Kidō*. *Shin kabuki**. One act. October 1914. Shintomi-za, Tokyo.

Sasaki Takatsuna, at the battle of Ishibashiyama, performed the valorous act of slaying a pack-horse driver, seizing his horse, and rescuing his master, General Yoritomo. However, since Yoritomo did not reward him sufficiently, Takatsuna has been passing his days in discontent. He now has in his service the son and daughter of the pack-horse driver whom he killed; they perform a memorial service for their father on the anniversary of his death and atone for his sins. Just then, Takatsuna refuses to greet Yoritomo, who is proceeding to the capital; instead, he becomes the disciple of the priest Chisan, who chances to be passing by. Takatsuna takes the tonsure and heads for Takano.

Takatsuna's nihilistic character was appreciated when the work was first produced. It was one of Ichikawa Sadanji II's* great roles, and the piece was included in his collection of favorites, the *kyōka gikyoku jūshu**.

SASHIDASHI. "Thrust-forth"; a conventional type of lighting device. The lighting in the old theatres was not sufficient; so when a leading actor entered, a lit candle on a small square stand attached to a long, red-painted handle would be held before and behind him by stage assistants, thus lighting his face. The technique is used nowadays only in certain old classics. The candle serves the purpose of a facial spotlight, so the device has come to be known as *tsura akari* ("face light") as well.

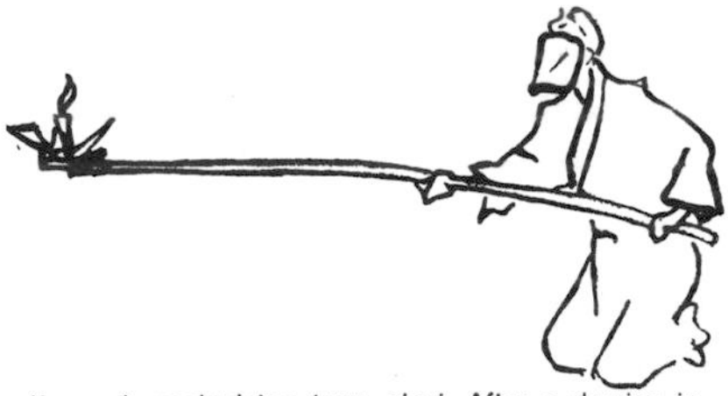

*Kurogo** manipulates *tsura akari*. After a drawing in Toita, *Waga Kabuki*.

SASHIGANE. "Thrust-metal"; a property term. When birds, butterflies, or other flying creatures appear on stage, they are simulated by models resembling them that are attached to a short, black-lacquered flexible pole *(sashigane)* manipulated by a stage assistant. The artificial animals are attached by a whale hair or by piano wire to the pole. When a ghost appears, a flaming *sashigane* (the *shōchōbi*) is used. A cloth or wire is steeped in a mixture of boric acid and alcohol, lit, and allowed to flicker on the pole. In the dance piece *Tobae**, a kind of *sashigane* is used when a pestle sprouts wings and begins to fly. Similarly, Danjō's tweezers in *Kenuki** move around at the end of a *sashigane*.

SASHI ISHŌ. "Rented costumes." Nowadays, the costumer *(ishōya)* is responsible for a theatre's costumes. He rents and buys what is needed, according to a special costume book. However, if the contracted costume house cannot provide the costumes on time or if the greater part of the costumes are already owned by the theatre troupe, a few may be rented from an outside concern. (*See also* COSTUMES.)

SASHI NUKI. A *hakama** trouser garment worn beneath a *kariginu** or *nōshi* robe (a kind of court gentleman's robe). A cord is run through the cuff, and when the *hakama* is put on, the cord is pulled—gathering the material—and tied just above the ankles. A typical character wearing the *sashi nuki hakama* is Okina in *Sanbasō**.

SATSUKI KYŌGEN. Plays performed during the Edo period in the fifth month. The formula was to perform these plays beginning with the annual fifth-month, fifth-day festival for a twenty-day period. *Satsuki kyōgen* were chiefly sequels to the Soga brother stories of the New Year's plays* *(hatsuharu kyōgen)* or revenge plays* with other characters. Ghost plays* and plays with many stage tricks *(keren*)* later became popular at these performances. (*See also* THEATRE MANAGEMENT.)

SAWAMURA GENNOSUKE IV. 1859-1936. An actor, he first achieved success in 1881 as a substitute for Iwai Hanshirō VIII*. The following year he took his master's name, becoming the fourth Gennosuke. For about the next ten years he worked as a supporting player to Ichikawa Danjūrō IX* and Onoe Kikugorō V*, two of the greatest stars of the Meiji era. From about 1903 on, he worked at the small theatres known as *koshibai**. He gained great success and popularity with his roles of evil women of decadent nineteenth-century Edo. Gennosuke lived in Tanbo at Asakusa and was called "Tanbo no Dayū." This actor was one of the last to possess the quality of the Edo period *onnagata**. His representative role was Kirare Otomi in the play called *Musume Gonomi Ukina no Yokogushi**.

V, *yago** Kinokuniya. 1907- . The son of dramatist Kimura Watabana, this contemporary *onnagata* debuted in 1913 and took his present name in 1936. He brings an especially elegant flavor to his work in domestic plays in the roles of townsmen's wives and the tarnished women of the rear tenements.

SAWAMURA SŌJŪRŌ I. 1685-1756. Third son of the samurai Miki Wakasa, he became an actor in Osaka after joining Sawamura Chōjūrō as a pupil. In 1718 he went to Edo and in 1720 took the name of Sōjūrō. In 1747 he was a hit as Okishi Miyauchi in *Ōya Su Yonjū Shichi Hon.* This character was based on the leading figure in the Akō vendetta of the forty-seven faithful samurai. When the story was given its definitive dramatization a year later in *Kanadehon Chūshingura**, the puppet portraying Oboshi Yuranosuke is said to have reflected Sōjūrō's appearance in the earlier version. Later, this actor took the name of Suketakaya Kōsuke I and gained popularity alongside Ichikawa Danjūrō II*. As a playwright he wrote several works for the stage.

II. 1713-1770. Was noticed by Sōjūrō I and became his adopted son. He showed talent as a player of the kinds of villains called *jitsuaku* (*see also* KATAKIYAKU) during the Hōreki era (1751-63).

III. 1753-1801. Second son of Sōjūrō II, he stood out beginning with his work as a child actor. During the Kansei era (1789-1800) he was active as a master at love scenes* *(nureba).* He is said to have been the best actor ever to have played Oboshi Yuranosuke in *Kanadehon Chūshingura.*

IV. 1784-1812. Eldest son of Sōjūrō III. During the late Kansei period he was known as one of the era's three top young stars, along with Onoe Kikugorō III* and Ichikawa Danjūrō VII*. Unfortunately, he died at a young age.

V. 1802-1853. Received the patronage of Matsumoto Kōshirō V* and went from a lower rank to the name of Sōjūrō V. From the Tenpō era (1830-

43) through the Kaei (1848-53) he demonstrated the Sawamura line's artistic specialty of quiet ease in such plays as *Karukaya Dōshin Tsukushi no Iezuto*. A rare example of an actor who achieved fame on the basis of talent alone, having no family background in the theatre, he was very handsome and stood out in the type of male role called *wajitsu**. He also displayed ability as a dancer and an *onnagata**. In his later years he changed his name to Sawamura Chōjūrō V and then Suketakaya Kōsuke III.

VI. 1838-1886. Eldest son of Sōjūrō V. After changing his name on two occasions, he took the name of Suketakaya Kōsuke IV in 1879. Outstanding in *wajitsu* roles, he was considered a peer of Ichikawa Danjūrō IX* and Onoe Kikugorō V*. He never took the name of Sōjūrō, but the Sawamura family considers him to have been entitled to the position of sixth in the line.

VII. 1875-1949. Adopted son of Suketakaya Kōsuke IV, he took the name of Sōjūrō in 1908. When Japan's first Western-style theatre—the Teikoku Gekijō*—opened in 1911, he was a member of its first company, along with Onoe Baikō VI* and the future Matsumoto Kōshirō VII*. He is considered the last person to have possessed the true Edo style of *wagoto** acting. His eldest son became Suketakaya Kōsuke V, and his second son took the name of Sawamura Tanosuke V*.

VIII. 1908- . Third son of Sōjūrō VII. He was adopted by Ichikawa Sadanji II* in 1929, taking the name of Ichikawa Shōen, but he left Sadanji's family and returned to his own in 1933 reassuming his earlier name of Tosshō in 1935. He was active for a number of years as a leading *onnagata* at the Shinjuku section of Tokyo's Shinkabuki-za, and he took the name of Sōjūrō VIII in 1953. Illness forced him to leave the stage in his later years.

IX, *yago** Kinokuniya. 1933- . Son of Sōjūrō VIII, he debuted as Sawamura Genpei in 1941 and became Sawamura Tosshō in 1953. He bears the style of his grandfather, Sōjūrō VII, and is an excellent player of *onnagata* and young male roles *(nimaime*)*, being well-versed in the *wagoto* style of acting. He is the brother of Sawamura Tōjūrō II*. He took his present name in 1976 at the Kabuki-za*.

SAWAMURA TANOSUKE I. A name held by the actor Sawamura Sōjūrō III* before he took the latter name.

II. 1788-1817. Third son of Sawamura Sōjūrō III. He debuted in Edo in 1793. He moved to Kyoto in 1801 and a year later took the name of Tanosuke II. With Kamigata as his home area, he gained fame in Edo as well and became known as one of the more promising *wakaonnagata* (*see also* ONNAGATA) during the first part of the nineteenth century. He died young, however, and did not fulfill his promise. Good-looking and gifted as a dancer, he invited comparison with his great contemporary, Segawa Kikunojō IV*. Though an *onnagata*, he also achieved success in male roles.

III. 1854-1878. Second son of Sawamura Sōjūrō V*, he was a child prodigy and, at fifteen, became the leading *onnagata* at the Morita-za*. His name was quite popular in connection with certain female fashions of the times: the "Tanosuke topknot," the "Tanosuke collar," and the "Tanosuke clogs." He became ill with gangrene in 1865. Two years later a foreign doctor named Hepburn had to amputate his leg. His acting, though, did not come to an end. Eventually, he went insane and died in 1878. His excellent looks and sex appeal gave him great support in his portrayals of evil and cunning women.

IV. 1857-1899. Adopted son of Tanosuke III. He took the name of Tanosuke in 1881 and became a leading *onnagata*. Illness plagued him, and he was relatively young when he died.

V. 1902-1968. Second son of Sōjūrō VII*. He took the name of Tanosuke V in 1920. He retired in 1964.

VI, *yago** Kinokuniya. 1932- . A fine contemporary *onnagata**, he is rather stout, but graceful and effective nonetheless. He debuted as Sawamura Tajirō and took the name of Tanosuke in 1964.

SAWAMURA TŌJŪRŌ II, *yago** Kinokuniya. 1943- . A beautiful *onnagata**, he is the son of Sawamura Sōjūrō VIII*. He debuted in January 1957 and, for about six years beginning in 1958, was active in films, but returned to the Shōchiku* organization in 1963. He changed his name from Sawamura Kiyoshirō I to Tōjūrō in 1976. He is the brother of Sōjūrō IX*.

SAWARI. A highlighted passage in a *gidayū bushi** narrative recital; a speech is sung to a *shamisen** accompaniment with deep feeling and beauty of tone. Originally, *sawari* referred to portions of musical narrative in a variety of styles, not only *gidayū bushi*. Today, the term is interchangeable with *kudoki* for scenes of lamentation* in plays taken from the puppet theatre *(gidayū kyogen*)*. In daily conversation, *sawari* refers to the punch line of a joke.

SCENERY. Kabuki settings generally are called *ōdōgu*, a term deriving from the title *ōdōgu kata* ("scenic person"), a theatre functionary responsible for constructing scenery. *Odōgu* is contrasted with *kodōgu* ("properties*") and includes within its scope whatever scenic properties the actors cannot carry onstage themselves: the revolving stage*, the traps, the hanging decorations, the curtains*, and the like.

The *ōdōgu kata*'s responsibilities involve building and setting up scenery (which is done according to a scenery notebook, the *ōdōguchō*), opening and closing the curtain, beating the wood clappers, and so forth. Hasegawa Kanbei I (d. 1659) and his successors were famous *ōdōgu* specialists; the first in the line is said to have become involved with Kabuki in the mid-seventeenth century, and up to eleven generations of scenic artists succeeded

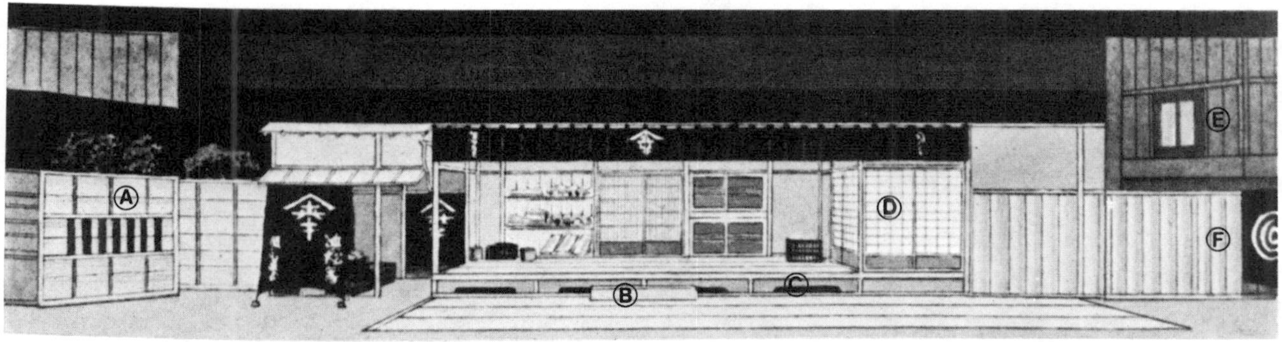

Ⓐ GEZA
Ⓑ BYAKUROKU
Ⓒ TSUNE ASHI NO NIJŌ
Ⓓ SHOJI YATAI
Ⓔ YUKA
Ⓕ STAGE LEFT AGEMAKU

Stage setting for *Aotozōshi Hana no Nishikie**, the *Hamamatsu-ya* scene. *Courtesy of Tanaka Ryō, from his* Kabuki Jōshiki Butai Zushū.

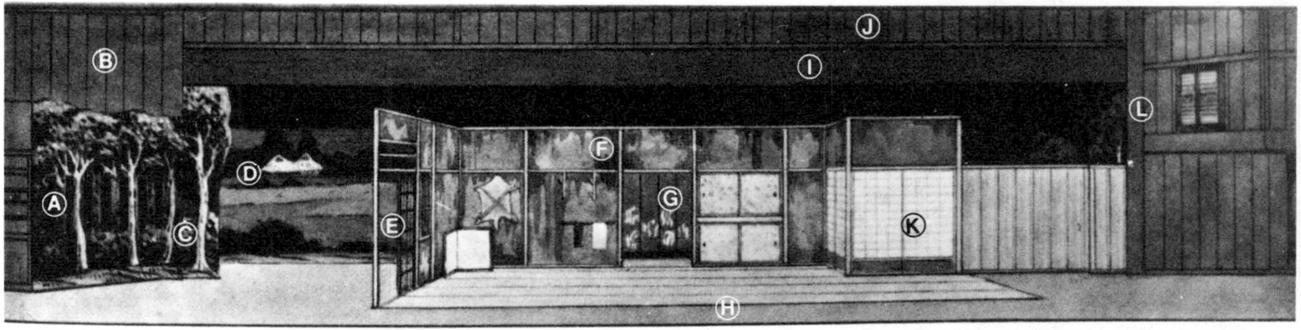

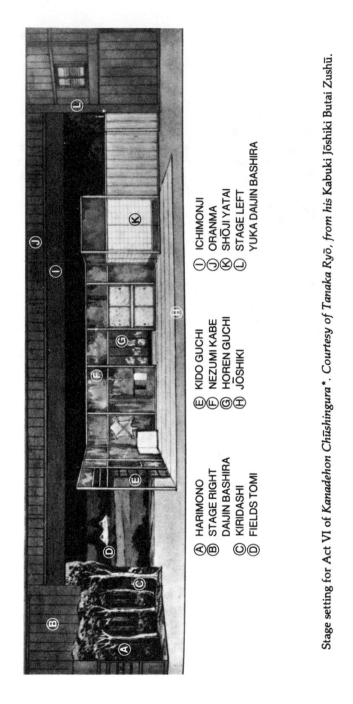

Ⓐ HARIMONO
Ⓑ STAGE RIGHT DAIJIN BASHIRA
Ⓒ KIRIDASHI
Ⓓ FIELDS TOMI
Ⓔ KIDO GUCHI
Ⓕ NEZUMI KABE
Ⓖ HOREN GUCHI
Ⓗ JŌSHIKI
Ⓘ ICHIMONJI
Ⓙ ORANMA
Ⓚ SHŌJI YATAI
Ⓛ STAGE LEFT YUKA DAIJIN BASHIRA

Stage setting for Act VI of *Kanadehon Chūshingura**. *Courtesy of Tanaka Ryō, from his* Kabuki Jōshiki Butai Zushū.

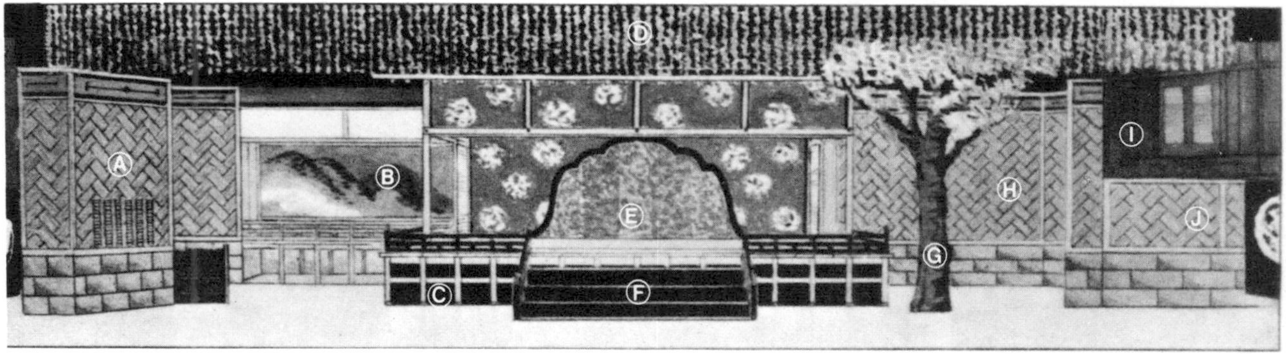

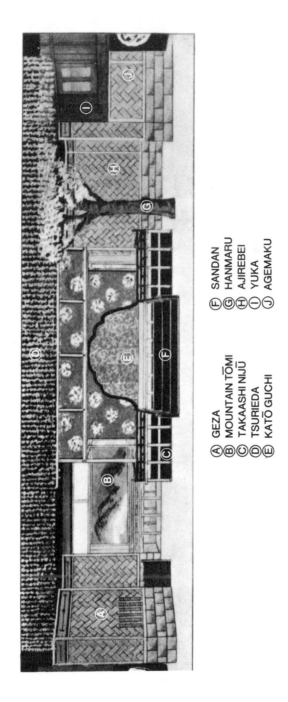

Ⓐ GEZA
Ⓑ MOUNTAIN TŌMI
Ⓒ TAKAASHI NIJŪ
Ⓓ TSURIEDA
Ⓔ KATŌ GUCHI
Ⓕ SANDAN
Ⓖ HANMARU
Ⓗ AJIREBEI
Ⓘ YUKA
Ⓙ AGEMAKU

Stage setting for the *Shi no Kiri,* or Kawazura mansion, scene in *Yoshitsune Senbon Zakura*. Courtesy of Tanaka Ryō, from his* Kabuki Jōshiki Butai Zushū.

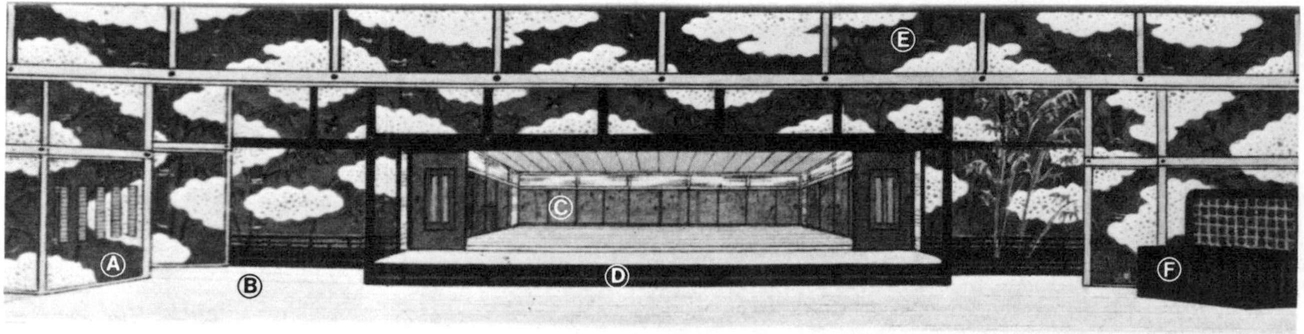

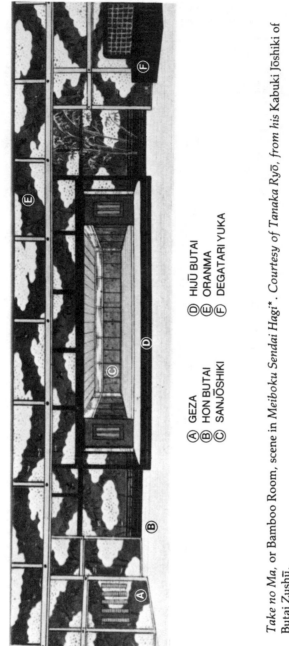

Ⓐ GEZA
Ⓑ HON BUTAI
Ⓒ SANJŌSHIKI
Ⓓ HIJŪ BUTAI
Ⓔ ORANMA
Ⓕ DEGATARI YUKA

Take no Ma, or Bamboo Room, scene in *Meiboku Sendai Hagi**. *Courtesy of Tanaka Ryō, from his* Kabuki Jōshiki of Butai Zushū.

Setting for typical *matsubame mono** type of play, such as *Kanjinchō**. *Courtesy of Tanaka Ryō, from his* Kabuki Jōshiki Butai Zushū.

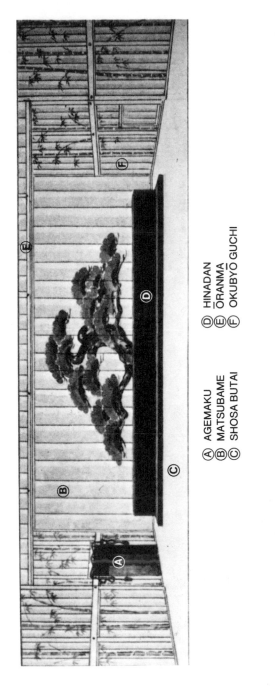

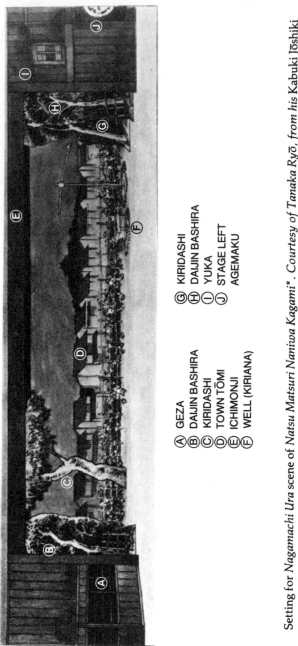

Ⓐ GEZA
Ⓑ DAIJIN BASHIRA
Ⓒ KIRIDASHI
Ⓓ TOWN TŌMI
Ⓔ ICHIMONJI
Ⓕ WELL (KIRIANA)
Ⓖ KIRIDASHI
Ⓗ DAIJIN BASHIRA
Ⓘ YUKA
Ⓙ STAGE LEFT AGEMAKU

Setting for *Nagamachi Ura* scene of *Natsu Matsuri Naniwa Kagami**. *Courtesy of Tanaka Ryō, from his* Kabuki Jōshiki Butai Zushū.

him through the late nineteenth century. Almost all of the complex variety of stage mechanisms and sets were perfected by these men.

Kabuki sets are fixed according to height, length, and width, as well as the thickness of pillars and the coloring of walls and sliding screens. For this reason, almost all scenic elements in Kabuki may be called "standardized scenery" or "scenery by formula" *(jōshiki ōdōgu**).

Kabuki theatres usually have a revolving state* *(mawari butai)*, which is used for multiple-scene plays. A separate setting is constructed on each half of the stage, front and rear; by revolving the stage 180 degrees, one can change the scene. This method is called *nippai kazari*. In contrast to this "double decor" is *ippai kazari* ("single decor"), when only one scene is set, and *sanpai kazari* ("triple decor"), when three scenes are set.

In constructing such scenic elements as a house, one places the setting upstage from an imaginary line *(jōshiki sen** or *daijin dōri)* joining the stage pillars *(daijin bashira**) at either side of the stage; that is to say, the line itself or a point slightly upstage is used as the downstage limit of the set.

Kabuki is famous for the variety and ingenuity of its stage effects. The greatest trick effects are those of scenic destruction, when castles or homes are destroyed by fires and earthquakes, for example. Roofs dangle from the flies, pillars sink into the holes in the stage floor, and stage traps drop at the same moment.

Unusual scenic devices include the *gandōgaeshi**, the *hikiwari**, the *hiki dōgu**, the *aorigaeshi**, the *wari dōgu**, the *dengakugaeshi**, the *butsudan gaeshi**, the *hashi bako**, and the *shamoji**. Curtain techniques include the *furiotoshi**, *furikabuse**, and *hikisen**.

SCRIPTS. *See* SHŌHON; KAKINUKI; NEHON.

SEASONAL PROGRAMMING. *See* SUMMER PLAYS; SATSUKI KYOGEN; SPRING PLAYS; BON KYŌGEN; NEW YEAR'S PLAYS; AUTUMN PLAYS; KAOMISE KOGYŌ; THEATRE MANAGEMENT.

SEGAWA JOKŌ III. 1806-1881. A playwright born in Edo. He studied under Tsuruya Nanboku IV* and became chief playwright *(tate sakusha**) at the Nakamura-za* in 1848. He often collaborated with the actor Ichikawa Kodanji IV* during the late Edo era. Soon after, though, he was left in the shadow of Kawatake Mokuami's* success and spent his last years in obscurity. He specialized in *oiemono** dramas and in domestic plays. His overly detailed and conscientiously rendered plots were often tedious. Representative works are *Kioijishi Kabuki no Hanakago**, *Sakura Giminden**, and *Yowa Nasake Ukina no Yokogushi**.

SEGAWA KIKUNOJŌ. There have been six generations of actors bearing this appellation. The first to the fifth were *onnagata** and acted during the Edo era. Every one of them was lauded as an outstanding player.

I. 1693-1749. Gained fame first in February 1728 when he acted the courtesan Kinzan in *Keisei Makura Kagami*; another hit of that year was *Muken no Kane.* He went to Edo in 1730 and was successful there in such dance plays as *Shakkyō* (*see also* SHAKKYŌ MONO) and *Furyū Aioi Jishi.* In 1744 he received an extremely high rating in the contemporary critiques (*yakusha hyōbanki**) and was the number-one *onnagata* in each of Japan's three greatest cities. His personal practice of living his daily life as a woman gave vividness to his art. A sign of the degree of his popularity was the fashion of wearing a kind of headgear, the "Segawa hat," to the theatre. His ideas on acting are written down in the *Onnagata Hiden* as a reference for future female impersonators.

II. 1741-1773. Adopted son of Kikunojō I. In January 1756 he danced *Momo Chidori Musume Dōjōji* to great praise at Edo's Ichimura-za* and instantly became a favorite of local audiences. His popularity was such that a number of contemporary fashions were named for him. While still in his teens, he became a *tate onnagata** and soon led the field among female impersonators born in Edo. He was a mere thirty-two when he died.

III. 1751-1810. Second son of the Osaka choreographer (*furitsuke**) Ichiyama Shichijūrō. He debuted in Osaka at fifteen, moved to Edo in 1774, and joined the Segawa family, changing his name from Ichiyama Tomisaburō. In 1782 he became Kikunojō III in accordance with the will of the late Kikunojō II. He surpassed all the actors of his time in both female and male roles, but especially in the former, and achieved tremendous public acclaim and a huge salary. In 1790 he appeared at both Edo's Ichimura-za and Nakamura-za*, earning an immense yearly income of 1,850 *ryō.* His *yago**, or "shop-name," was Hamamuraya, and he was often referred to with awe as "Hamamuraya Daimyōjin" (*daimyōjin* is a Shinto god's title). In 1801 he changed his name to Segawa Rokō and in 1807 to Segawa Senjō. He excelled in ingenue and courtesan roles, his greatest successes being in *Shakkyō, Muken no Kane, Seki no To**, and *Musume Dōjōji**. His nickname was Senjō Rokō.

IV. 1782-1812. Son-in-law of Kikunojō III. He was called Enya Rokō because his mother was the daughter of a theatre teahouse proprietor named Enya. Active in the early years of the nineteenth century, he was second in popularity only to the great *onnagata* Iwai Hanshirō V*, but his death at thirty ended a promising career. He had taken the name of Kikunojō IV in 1807.

V. 1802-1832. Adopted son of Kikunojō IV, he was a popular *onnagata,* although an early death cut short a flourishing career. He had debuted as Segawa Tamon at age four and gained fame as an excellent child actor. He took the name of Kikunojō in 1815 when he was thirteen. Like others in his line, he had a well-known nickname: Tamon Rokō (Rokō was the line's *haimyō**, or pen name).

VI, *yago* Hamamuraya. 1907- . Born in Tokyo, he was adopted by the future Iwai Kumesaburō V in 1918 in hopes that he would revive the fortunes of the dormant Segawa family. He joined the Zenshin-za* troupe in 1932 and took his present name a year later.

SEITAI. A blue cosmetic used to depict the shaven part of the head in male roles. It is used for the blue color in certain *kumadori** makeups as well.

SEKAI. The backgrounds or "worlds" of fixed periods and characters used for the creation of Kabuki plays. Playwrights commonly composed their works like a tapestry with the *sekai* as the woof and the plot as the warp. The number of *sekai* was fixed, being derived for history plays from such historical narratives as the *Ise Monogatari, Masakadoki, Hōgen Heiji, Gikeiki, Taiheiki, Heike Monogatari,* and others. Their well-known characters and situations were borrowed by many playwrights. In the case of domestic plays, the worlds were generally chosen from famous incidents for which conventional characters' names were combined with the plot. "Worlds" gradually developed and increased as Kabuki was infiltrated by famous puppet-play characters. (*See also* PLAYWRITING; SEKAI SADAME.)

SEKAI SADAME, "World decision," a planning council held on the twelfth day of the ninth month, according to the old calendar. The council decided what the background or "world" *(sekai*)* would be for the November *kaomise** performance. They also chose the nature of the play's theme. The *tate sakusha*, zamoto*, zagashira**, and *tate onnagata** made up the council.

SEKI NO TO. Takarada Jurai. Also called *Tsumoru Koi Yuki Seki no To. Shosagoto*. Tokiwazu**. October 1784. Kiri-za, Edo.

Yoshimine Munesada, guardian of the barrier at Osaka Pass, happens to meet Princess Komachi, his mistress, there by chance. Munesada, suspecting the barrier guard Sekibei, sends Komachi off to the home of an ally as a precaution. Sekibei is actually Omoto no Kuronushi, a great villain who aims at control of the nation. Kuronushi, wishing to effect a ritual that will put a curse on the Emperor, goes to chop down a nearby cherry tree, but the spirit of the tree appears in the form of the courtesan Somezome; while she recites a tale of the licensed quarters, Kuronushi's true character is revealed.

The work was performed for the annual "face showing" *(kaomise*)* performances, in which a company of actors was introduced to the public. Since only the portion described is extant, it is difficult to discern a clear plot. However, as a dance it displays the old style. The love story of Munesada and Komachi, the tale of the licensed quarters told in the second half, and the half-drunken dance of Kuronushi are highlights. The *tokiwazu* accompaniment is among the greatest in the dance repertory. At the first production, Kuronushi was danced by Nakamura Nakazō I*, Komachi by Segawa Kikunojō III*, and Munesada by Ichikawa Monnosuke II.

SEMEBA. *See* TORTURE SCENES.

SENRYŌ YAKUSHA. "Thousand-*ryō* actor"; a term applied to actors who earned 1,000 or more *ryō* per season during the Edo era. The sum was first achieved during the early years of the eighteenth century. It was an uncommon salary, which only a few superlative actors received. Therefore, the appellation of *senryō yakusha* designated an outstanding actor of unusual skill and character. Early representatives included Yoshizawa Ayame I* and Ichikawa Danjūrō II*.

SENSHŪRAKU. The closing day of a production, it was called *raku* for short. It is theorized that the term comes from the final piece in a *gagaku* (an ancient type of ceremonial court music) performance, where this term also is employed, or that it derives from the line *senshūraku tami no nade* ("A thousand autumns rejoice the people's hearts") at the close of the Nō play *Takasago*. However, it is likely that the element *shū* ("autumn") means termination (*shū* is the Chinese pronunciation of the character used to write the Japanese word *owaru*, "to conclude") and that *raku* is charged with the sense of conclusion found in the word *otosu* ("to end a story"); the Chinese pronunciation of the latter is *raku*.

SEPARATION SCENES. Known as *enkiri*, these are a feature of domestic dramas. Many plays contain situations in which a woman, because of her feelings of duty, unwillingly reviles her lover and forces a separation, angering him so that he ultimately kills her. The scene in which the woman verbally abuses the man is called *aisozukashi*. Examples of plays using the convention are *Godairiki Koi no Fūjime**, *Ise Ondo Koi no Netaba**, and *Soga Moyō Tateshi no Goshozome**.

SERI. The stage traps. A trap consists of a mechanism that can go up or down and is fitted into a space cut from part of the stage floor. *Seri* are large and small and vary in size from theatre to theatre. Generally, however, there is one *seri* downstage of the *jōshiki sen** line, which passes through the lower lip of the stage and another one upstage. The downstage one is about four to five feet wide and three to four feet deep. Characters may go up or down on it, depending on need. The large *seri* is eighteen to thirty feet in width and six to twelve in depth; it is used to raise and lower actors and large pieces of scenery. The *seri* on the *hanamichi** is the *suppon**. When a *seri* is used to bring actors or sets upward, the words *seridashi* or *seriage* are used to describe the technique. *Serisage* or *serioroshi* refer to the reverse process. Higuchi Han'emon is said to have invented this mechanism in the Hōei period (1704-10), but it was Namiki Shōzō's* creation that was used on a truly large scale, from 1753 on. Today, a superb effect is achieved when a magnificent temple gate occupying almost the entire stage rises in *Sanmon Gosan no Kiri** or when the Temple of the Golden Pavilion does likewise in *Gion Sairei Shinkōki**.

SERIFU. The art of stage speech. The etymology of the word is vague, but it is believed to derive from the meaning of the word *seriau*—"to compete for," in the sense that one must use words to reply to one's rival or partner. As Kabuki is a formalistic theatre, characters not only must have suitable visual representation, but also must speak in a musical fashion, showing flexibility in their voices, to provide proper intonation and pitch variations. It used to be said that an actor's "voice was first, gestures second, and looks third." Such a saying demonstrates clearly the importance placed in Kabuki on good stage speech. There are many special speech conventions in Kabuki, including *kudoki* (lamentation*), *kuriage**, *monogatari**, *nori**, *sute zerifu**, *tsurane**, *wari zerifu**, *watari zerifu**, and *yakubarai**.

SERIFU O KAMU. "To bite one's speech"; said when an actor's words get twisted up and he has difficulty straightening them out. Same as *zekku*.

SERIFUZUKUSHI. Booklets in which the best stage speeches of popular actors were published. The front cover carried a picture of the actor, the month and year of the performance from which the passages were taken, and the contents of the booklet. These two- and three-leaf booklets are of inestimable value as research source material. (*See also* ŌMUSEKI.)

SESSHŪ GAPPŌ GA TSUJI. Suga Sensuke, Wakatake Fuemi. Also called *Gappō*. English title: *Gappo and His Daughter* (Bowers). *Jidaimono**. *Jōruri**. Two acts. February 1773. Kita Horei-za, Osaka.

The scene at Gappō's house in the second part is still performed.

Tamate is the daughter of Gappō, a hermit living at the west gate of the Tennō Temple. She becomes the second wife of Michitoshi Takayasu and the stepmother of Jiromaru and Shuntokumaru. Jiromaru, together with his accomplices, plans to trap his half-brother, Shuntokumaru, and seize the leadership of the family. Tamate seduces her stepson Shuntokumaru and causes him to drink poisoned sake, which gives him a form of leprosy. She appears to have done this because of jealousy over his love for Princess Asaka. He flees his wicked stepmother's clutches and, together with Princess

Asaka, takes refuge at Gappō's home. Tamate arrives there in pursuit of him, but Gappō angrily stabs her. As she dies, she confesses that she made Shuntokumaru drink the poison in order to save his life following her discovery of Jiromaru's evil plot. Out of the same vessel that contained the poison, Shuntokumaru must drink the blood of a woman born precisely at the hour, day, and month of the Year of the Tiger. Then his leprosy will be cured. The vessel is produced, and Tamate's lifeblood is given the youth to drink. He recovers, and peace is restored to his family.

Tamate is one of the greatest roles for a Kabuki female impersonator. When she makes her first appearance—her sleeve torn, the evening approaching—she must demonstrate the passion of a mature woman. This role provides an abundance of emotional transitions to enact.

Kabuki's first version of this puppet play was at Tokyo's Kiri-za in 1885. Bandō Shūchō II, Nakamura Utaemon V*, and Nakamura Baigyoku II* and III* were outstanding exemplars of Tamate in this century.

SEWA. The opposite of *jidai**; acting that is natural and colloquial in tone.

SEWAMONO. Also *sewakyōgen*, this term is used in contrast to *jidaimono**, the history play category. These "domestic plays" take their materials from the life of the townsmen and deal chiefly with the atmosphere of life among the populace, the conflict between duty *(giri)* and emotion *(ninjō)*, problems of love affairs, and so forth. The word *sewa* is used in the sense of "gossip," "chitchat" *(sekenbanashi)*, or "worldly tales" *(segatari)*. What is implied is the regular inclusion of realistic elements of a contemporary nature. Thus, *sewamono* may be said to be the "drama of contemporary life." It is thus essential that such plays be basically realistic in performance. The origins of the genre can be seen in the *keisei gai* ("courtesan plays") (*see also* KAMIGATA KYŌGEN) of Kabuki's early days. Courtesan plays achieved their crowning success when acted by Sakata Tōjūrō* during the Genroku era (1688-1703). *Sewamono perse* first were produced in the puppet theatre, beginning with Chikamatsu Monzaemon's* *Sonezaki Shinjū** (1703). Following its success, a series of plays based on contemporary events occuring to city dwellers were produced (double suicide—*shinjū*—was the most popular theme). It was their distinctive feature that there was barely any difference between the characters presented onstage and those seated in the audience. Tsuuchi Jihei* and Horikoshi Saiyō were prolific Edo dramatists in this vein, but Edo's characteristic style was developed in the emotional works of a later writer, Sakurada Jisuke I*. Namiki Gohei I* came to Edo from the Kamigata area and deepened the realistic elements. Tsuruya Nanboku IV* then appeared in the early nineteenth century and Kawatake Mokuami* at mid-century. They gave birth to the increasingly realistic *kizewamono** or *masewamono* style. (*See also* PLAY CATEGORIES.)

SHAKKYŌ MONO. A play grouping made up of dance pieces based on the Nō lion play called *Shakkyō*. Since Kabuki's early years saw *onnagata** occupying the major dance positions, lion dances were feminized: The dancer appeared in the first half as a beauty, usually a courtesan, dancing with a hand mask of a lion; she reappeared in the second half with the same basic physical look, but with an air of wildness or lunacy added, to suggest the presence of the lion's spirit. A large number of lion dances were produced in this fashion, including *Fūryū Aioi Jishi* and *Shūjaku Jishi**. When male-role actors later began to dominate Kabuki dance, they presented the lion by appearing in stylized *kumadori** makeup, as in *Kagamijishi**, *Renjishi**, *Sannin Shakkyō*, and *Shin Shakkyō*.

SHAMISEN. Sometimes spelled *samisen*. Also called *sangen*, this is Japan's representative stringed instrument and the major musical instrument accompanying Kabuki and puppet-play performances. The *shamisen* came to Japan from China or the Ryukyus during the Eiroku era (1558-69). The original import's body was covered by snakeskin, but this was changed to dog or cat skin to suit it better to Japanese performance. The plectrum and bridge were further improved. It was first used to accompany the *jōruri** narrative recitals, which usage helped bring about *jōruri*'s perfection. The *shamisen* eventually was adopted by Kabuki. There are three main types of *shamisen*: (1) the thick-necked and thick-bodied kind for *gidayū bushi**; (2) the middle-sized type for *kiyomoto** and *tokiwazu**; and (3) the smallest one for *nagauta**. Of course, each produces a different sound. (*See also* GEZA; NARIMONO.)

SHAMOJI. "Ladle"; a trick device that allows an actor to make an eerie appearance as if sliding on air. The actor stands on a small platform on wheels; the platform is attached to a long tongue that pushes the device into position. It is used in *Tōkaidō Yotsuya Kaidan**.

SHARIN. "Wheels"; a word meaning to "overact."

SHIBAI E. "Theatre pictures," or original pictures of Kabuki scenes, actors, theatrical customs, billboards, programs, and the like. Their inception goes back to the Kabuki of Izumo no Okuni*, Kabuki*s founder, in the early seventeenth century. One can see illustrations of Kabuki theatres in contemporary folding screens and illustrated scrolls. Chiefly a response to the requests of noblemen and the wealthy classes, these were painted by contemporary masters.

Early in the seventeenth century, pictures showing the life of the common people came to be popular. Such subjects had not previously been stressed in Japanese art. These pictures became the art form known as *ukiyoe*, or "pictures of the floating world." Production of these inexpensive pictures expanded during the seventeenth century, and the wood-block print was soon developed to meet the public demand. The townsman's greatest objects of pleasure—Kabuki and the great pleasure quarters—were taken as primary subjects of the *ukiyoe* wood-block prints. Later, with the growth of travel, scenery became the chief subject of such works.

The early years of theatrical wood-block prints were pioneered by Hishikawa Moronobu (d. 1695?), whose work led to the prevalence of the Moronobu school. Torii Kiyonobu (1664-1729) and Torii Kiyomasu (1694-1716?) appeared in the Genroku era (1688-1703) and depicted the top actors of their time in wood-block prints. These pictures are known separately from the other Torii works as the *yakusha e* or "actors' pictures." Kabuki has a profound relationship with the Torii line of artists; from the Genroku period to today, the Torii school has provided the main artists for Kabuki billboards and programs. The Torii style's outstanding feature is its thick, bold, curved lines, which made it particularly suitable for Edo Kabuki.

The early wood-block prints were simple black-and-white pictures with the figures outlined in India ink. Then came a process by which color was applied to the picture with a brush; these were the "red pictures" *(tane)* and "lacquered pictures" *(urushie).* This method gradually evolved into one of printing the picture with two or three colors, a technique achieved in the Meiwa era (1764-71) when Suzuki Harunobu (1725-1770) accomplished great reforms. He created realistic multicolored prints of great beauty. These are the *nishikie*, or "wood-block color prints." Because of artists like Katsukawa Shunshō (1726-1792)—who began to depict the actor in his role realistically, so that the face actually resembled that of the particular actor—theatrical wood-block color prints boomed. Among these prints appeared the theatre interior prints of Utagawa Toyoharu (1735-1814), the folio-sized prints *(ōnishiki)* of Torii Kiyonaga (1752-1815) (fourth in the line of Torii artists), and the works of Tōshūsai Sharaku (fl. 1794-1795), whose distinctive style of actor portraiture, based on the realism of Shunshō, is well known. After these artists there appeared Utagawa Toyokuni I (1769-1825). He and his many disciples left an enormous number of theatre prints to posterity. Following him, theatrical prints were mainly based on the Utagawa style. His most outstanding pupils were Kunisada (1786-1864; later Toyokuni III), Kuniyoshi (1798-1861), Kuniyasu (1804-1832), and Kunimaru (d. 1820s). Kunisada was the leading practitioner of theatrical prints during the first half of the nineteenth century and left many works behind. His pupil, Toyoharu Kunichika, produced actors' pictures until the late 1890s. We may look upon his work as the swan song of Edo-style theatrical prints. The great quantity of theatre prints extant from Kabuki's early period are a highly useful source of data for understanding the Kabuki of the past. As the wood-block prints were an especially popular theatrical souvenir, their manufacture flourished and picture-book shops did a bustling business. (*See also* SHINI E.)

SHIBAIJAYA. "Theatre teahouses," a kind of theatrical facility found in the environs of playhouses from the Edo period through the Taishō (1912-26). At first, they were places where playgoers could check their packages and order a cup of tea while waiting for someone. Beginning in the eighteenth century, however, they became a place where actors and their guests could fraternize, seats for the *sajiki** or *masu** sections could be secured, and the playgoer could repair for refreshments during the long intermissions.

There are said to have been sixteen teahouses in Edo's Kobiki-chō theatre street and fifty in Sakai-chō and Fukiya-chō in 1714. It was in this year that the Lady Ejima-Ikushima Shingorō scandal occurred: Ejima and her actor friend held a secret rendezvous at the Yamamura-za* *shibaijaya* (*See also* EJIMA-IKUSHIMA INCIDENT). Because of this scandal, teahouses were prohibited from renting out their private rooms to guests. The practice flourished again, however, at a later date. Civic officials were not lazy about overseeing the theatres in order to prevent such an event from recurring. Actors and their guests now had to carry on their meetings at these teahouses in a perfectly proper manner.

Patrons occupying the theatre's *sajiki* and *masu* sections reserved their seats through the teahouse. On going to the theatre, they first went to the teahouse. After a brief rest there, they changed into white-thonged "good luck" slippers and were led into the theatre. As the intermissions were lengthy, they would return for a rest to the teahouse, where they would eat dinner. Thus, a playgoer needed adequate dining funds in addition to the price of admission to the theatre.

The Teikoku Gekijō*, a theatre opened in 1911, adopted a new system of theatregoing and did without the teahouses. Soon after, there was an outcry to get rid of the old-fashioned teahouses. This was accomplished following the great earthquake of 1923.

In 1788, Osaka's Dōtonbori theatre district had a teahouse for every syllable of the Japanese syllabary (forty-eight), and the number reached over sixty by the late Edo period. These places were called *maejaya* ("front teahouses"). The number was reduced to about twenty by the Shōwa period, and by 1933 none were left. The teahouses with the foremost standing as restaurants were called *ōjaya* or *hyōjaya.* Those on a small scale were the *kojaya,* while those which sold food and drink within the theatres proper were the *mizujaya.* Each had its respective standards of excellence.

SHIBAI MACHI. *See* THEATRE STREET.

SHIBARAKU. Mimasuya Hyōgo*. *Jidaimono**. Kabuki. One act. 1697. Nakamura-za*, Edo.

This play is one of the famous Ichikawa family collection, the *kabuki jūhachiban**. Danjūrō I* staged his own play, *Daifukuchō Asahina Hyaku no Monogatari*, which contained the seed of the piece that came to be known as *Shibaraku.* A performance style closer to that which became familiar to generations of Kabuki theatregoers was created for the 1697 *Sankai Nagoya,* written by Danjūrō I (under the pen name of Mimasuya Hyōgo) with himself in the leading role. The piece has an unusual title since it is taken from a shout, "*Shibaraku!*" ("Wait a moment!"), delivered from offstage by the hero just before he enters on the *hanamichi**. For many years, the chief character had a different name whenever the play was revived. In recent times he has been known mainly as Kamakura Gongorō Kagemasa. *Shibaraku* was customarily performed as part of the annual November *kaomise** productions, by which a company of actors was introduced to the public. It is a classic example of the *aragoto** style of performance.

At a shrine precinct the evil Lord Uke commands his attendants (called *haradashi**, or "belly thrusters," because of their huge, bright red, padded abdomens) to behead Yoshitsune and Katsura-no-Mae, innocent characters who will not bow to his will. At this point a great shout is heard—"Wait a moment!"—and the hero appears on the *hanamichi.* He speaks there at great length about his name (the *tsurane** convention), comes up to the main stage, cuts off the heads of a group of soldiers with one blow of his huge *ōdachi* sword (*see also* SWORDS), saves the threatened characters, and retires down the *hanamichi* with great authority.

Among the work's famous visual effects is the striking contrast between the makeup of Uke and Gongorō. The former wears stylized *aiguma** makeup of blue lines painted over a white base, while the hero wears red lines on white in the style called *suji guma**. He also wears the bizarre *kuruma bin** wig and a huge, persimmon *suō,* or outer robe bearing the Ichikawa family crest: three rice measures, one inside the other. Gongorō's *tsurane* speech, his grand *Genroku mie* (*see also* MIE: GENROKU MIE), and his splendid bounding exit (*roppō**) on the *hanamichi* fully exemplify the *aragoto* style. A female version of the play also exists—*Onna Shibaraku.*

SHIBIRE HIME. "Paralyzed princess," princesses who appear onstage, but merely sit there, neither speaking nor moving. Princess Omodaka in *Komochi Yamanba** is an example.

SHICHISAN. "Seven-three," a spot on the *hanamichi** where bits of acting are performed. (*See also* SUPPON; DEBA.)

Gongorō cuts a *mie** as he prepares to make a *roppō** exit in *Shibaraku**. Gongorō, Onoe Shōroku II*.

SHIDASHI. A "walk-on" or "utility" role. Walk-ons have no lines and appear only to lend atmosphere to the picture. They are played by members of the subordinate class of actors called *shitamawari*. (*See also* ACTORS' RANKS.)

SHIGAYAMA RYŪ. A school of Japanese dance. It was founded by the Edo choreographer Shigayama Mansaku and is considered to be the oldest traditional school of Kabuki dance. The line has produced nine successive male *iemoto** connected with the theatre; *iemoto* subsequent to the ninth have been female, and the school has lost its close ties with the theatre. The present *iemoto* is the fifteenth. At one time the acting line of Nakamura Nakazō* exemplified the Shigayama school in Kabuki.

SHIGUMI. A word that formerly meant the adaptation of nontheatrical literature for the stage. (*See also* KYAKUSHOKU.)

SHIGUSA. The physical side of acting, that is, movement and gesture. (*See also* FURI.)

SHIITAKE. A male wig whose topknot tip is big, wide, and shaped like a dry mushroom *(shiitake)*. It is worn by footmen and couriers.

SHIITAKE TABO. "Dry-mushroom back-hair"; The back-hair of wigs worn by certain court ladies. The *tabo*, or back-hair, is stiffened by pomade and highly polished. Masaoka in *Meiboku Sendai Hagi**, Onoe in *Kagamiyama Kokyō no Nishikie**, and Iwafuji in the same play wear it.

SHIKE. The loose strands of hair hanging by the ears on male and female wigs. The style of the *shike* provides subtle hints about the degree of the character's amorousness, anxiety, or fearsomeness. The *bojike* worn by male-role actors is a pomade-thickened strand of hair hanging down from behind the ear and suggests the character's gentle, romantic nature. It is seen on Jirō in *Soga no Taimen** and Sakuramaru in the *Kuruma Biki* scene of *Sugawara Denju Tenarai Kagami**. The *itojike* has threads mingled with the hairs and hangs down in long strands. It is worn by powerful villains like Daizen in the *Kinkakuji* scene of *Gion Sairei Shinkōki**.

SHIKI. Also *shingi;* a stage brace used to fasten scenery to the stage floor. Usually, it is a wooden pole with metal hooks at either end, but some are made entirely of metal. Such braces are found only in Japan.

SHIKIRIBA. A room in which the theatre's affairs were handled from the Edo period through the mid-Meiji. It was called the *kanjōba* in the Kami-

Sukeroku stands at the *shichisan** on the *hanamichi** after entering in *Sukeroku Yukari no Edo Zakura**. Sukeroku, Ichikawa Ebizō X*. *Courtesy of Waseda University Tsubouchi Engeki Hakubutsukan (Tsubouchi Memorial Theatre Museum).*

gata area. The *shikiriba* was situated slightly to the left of the theatre's front entrance and was used mainly for business matters. It corresponds to today's "theatre office" *(gekijō jimūsho).*

SHIMACHIDORI (TSUKI NO SHIRANAMI). Kawatake Mokuami*. *Sewamono**. Kabuki. Five acts. November 1881. Shintomi-za, Tokyo.

This masterpiece was written to commemorate the playwright's decision to retire from the ranks of the so-called *shiranami mono* ("robber play*") dramatists. The chief characters are all thieves, and the plot concerns the ultimate reformation of the entire gang. The play is also famous for its generous depiction of the Western customs that were being introduced to Japan at the time. Thus, the play is considered a *zangiri mono** ("cropped-hair play") as well. Performances usually begin with Act IV, in which Shimazō is seen running his sake shop, and conclude with the final scene, set at the Shōkan Shrine. The first production starred Onoe Kikugorō V* as Shimazō and Ichikawa Sadanji I* as Senta. Others in the cast were Iwai Hanshirō VIII*, and the future Nakamura Utaemon V*.

Soon after Shimazō and Senta had burglarized the Fukushima pawnshop, Shimazō decided to reform and opened a sake shop at Kagurasaka. Senta ascertains that his former girlfriend, Oteru, has become the mistress of Mochizuki Kagayaki. When he plans to break into her home, he invites Shimazō to come along. At the risk of his life, the latter meets with Senta before the Shōkan Shrine to persuade his friend to reform. They quarrel, but Senta ultimately is persuaded and the two decide to surrender to the police.

SHIMADA. A female wig generally worn by unmarried female characters. One version, the *takashimada,* has a topknot tied high on the head. A contrasting style is the *tsubushi shimada,* which has a low topknot. As its usage is broad, it is worn by servants, townsmen's daughters, geisha, and so on. Benten Kozō usually makes his entrance in the *Hamamatsu-ya* scene of *Aotozōshi Hana no Nishikie** wearing the *takashimada* (Benten is disguised as a young woman from a good family).

SHIMOTE. "Stage right." (*See also* KAMITE.)

SHIN. "Heart," the very center of the revolving stage. (*See also* REVOLVING STAGE.)

SHINA. The actor's use of his entire body to suggest sex appeal.

SHINBASHI ENBUJŌ. A theatre located at Chuō-ku, Ginza 6-chome, Tokyo. It opened in April 1925 with an announcement that its aim was to elevate the art of the Shinbashi-area geisha entertainers. In addition to staging productions of the geisha's *Azuma Odori* dances, the theatre also was rented to the Shōchiku* company for their productions. After being destroyed in World War II, the theatre was rebuilt and reopened in March 1945. Its main feature is Shinpa productions, but Kabuki and other forms of entertainment are performed here, too.

SHINBŌ TACHIYAKU. Also called *shinbōyaku*, these are certain leading male roles that are seen infrequently in Kabuki. The character acts with restrained facial and physical expression and must project psychological depth. He is a quietly suffering character who undergoes greater inner torment than more obviously active characters, and he must be portrayed with a high degree of skill. Enya Hangan in Act IV of *Kanadehon Chūshingura** is an example. (*See also* ROLE TYPES.)

SHINI E. "Death pictures," a class of actors' pictures *(yakusha e; see also SHIBAI E)*. When an actor dies, a picture of him is published, carrying his Buddhist name, his age at death, and the month and day on which he died. Of course, this practice is limited to the more popular actors and is a response to the wishes of the late actor's fans. An enormous number of different varieties of *shini e* were published for Ichikawa Danjūrō VIII* and Bandō Shūka I*, actors of the late Edo era.

SHINJŪ TEN NO AMIJIMA. Chikamatsu Monzaemon*. Also called *Ten no Amijima, Kamiya Jihei Kamiji.* English title: *The Love Suicide at Amijima* (Shively); *The Love Suicides at Amijima* (Keene). *Sewamono**. *Jōruri**. Three acts. December 1720. Takemoto-za, Osaka.

Kamiya Jihei, a husband and father, has been having an affair with the Sonezaki courtesan Koharu. Jihei's brother Magoemon visits Koharu, disguised as a samurai, and listens as she discusses her true feelings. Eavesdropping, Jihei hears her say that she has no intention of committing suicide with him. He thereupon angrily tries to stab her, but is prevented from doing so and admonished by his brother. He cuts off his relationship with the courtesan. Later, learning that Tahei, his love rival, is going to ransom Koharu from bondage to her brothel, Jihei grows ashamed of himself. Hearing of this, his wife, Osan, reveals that Koharu has given her husband up at her request. She fears that Koharu will kill herself after Tahei redeems her. Jihei wracks his brains for a means to procure the money to redeem Koharu, but Osan's father, Gozaemon, turns his back upon the young man and forcibly takes Osan away with him. As expected, after Tahei redeems her, Koharu commits double suicide with Jihei.

Kabuki frequently produces revisions of this play titled *Shinjū Kamiya Jihei* and *Ten no Amijima Shigure no Kotatsu.* Outstanding features of the work are the emotional qualities displayed by Osan and the gentle, romantic Kamigata style of acting called *wagoto** in which Jihei is performed.

SHINJŪ YOI GŌSHIN. Chikamatsu Monzaemon*. *Sewamono*. *Jōruri*. Three acts. April 1722. Takemoto-za, Osaka.

Chikamatsu's last *sewamono*, the play is based, like many others, on a true story. A play with the same subject by Ki no Kaion was produced the very same month at the Toyotake-za.

Hanbei of the Yao-ya is an adopted son. While traveling to his original family home to perform a memorial service for his real father, his adopted mother expels his wife, Ochiyo, from their home, sending her back to her parents. On his homeward journey to Osaka, Hanbei calls at the home of Ochiyo's parents and learns what has occurred. Realizing the risk involved, he takes charge of Ochiyo and returns with her to Osaka. However, as he is unable to change his adopted mother's mind, he gives Ochiyo secret instructions and then divorces her in front of the old lady. Soon, the couple plot together and leave the house to commit double suicide.

SHIN KABUKI. "New Kabuki," new works written for Kabuki since the Meiji era by scholars and literary men who were not attached formally to the theatres. These works are written according to modern European dramatic standards, but are staged with Kabuki's production apparatus. *Shin kabuki*'s origins can be seen in the late-nineteenth-century reforms instituted by Ichikawa Danjūrō IX* with his *katsureki*, or "living history" plays*, and their new style of realistic presentation. However, Tsubouchi Shōyō's* *Kiri Hitoha** (1884) usually is considered the first work in the genre. Shōyō was followed by Mori Ōgai, Matsui Shyō, and Takayasu Gekkō, among others, who produced many such plays. The genre was firmly established by Okamoto Kidō's* *Shūzenji Monogatari** (1911) and the subsequent performance of all the plays that he wrote for Ichikawa Sadanji II*. (*See also* PLAY CATEGORIES.)

SHIN KABUKI JŪHACHIBAN. The "new Kabuki eighteen," a collection established by Ichikawa Danjūrō IX*; only two successes of an earlier Danjūrō (Danjūrō VII*) are included. The word *jūhachiban*, meaning "number eighteen," does not mean "eighteen plays," but signifies an acting family's artistic forte. (*See also* KABUKI JŪHACHIBAN; FAMILY ART.) Many of these works are in the *katsureki* ("living history*") genre founded by Danjūrō IX.

PLAY	NOTE	DATE OF FIRST PRODUCTION
Tora no Maki	*Kiichi Hōgen Sanryaku no Maki's* Oku Niwa* scene. First performed by Danjūrō VII.	1850
Renshō Monogatari	Part of *Ichinotani Gaikako Yōkoku*. First performed by Danjūrō VII.	1852

PLAY	NOTE	DATE OF FIRST PRODUCTION
Jishin Gatō	Actual title: *Zōho Momoyama Monogatari**.	1869
Sanada Harinuki Tsutsu	A *katsureki* work written by Mokuami*.	1871
Koshigoejō	Part of *Yoshitsune Koshigoejō.* (a revision of a scene in *Nanbantetsu Gotō no Menuki**)	1872
Sakai no Taiko	Actual title: *Taiko no Oto Chu Sanryaku.*	1873
Shikigawa Mondo	Part of *Youchi no Soga Kariba no Akebono**	1874
Kibi Daijin	Actual title: *Kibi Daijin Shina Banashi.*	1875
Sanemori Kangen	Actual title: *Natori Gusa Heike Monogatari**.	1876
Egara Mondo	Part of *Hoshizukiyo Kenmon.*	1880
Tsuri Kitsune	A dance drama derived from a Kyōgen farce.	1882
Nakamitsu	Actual title: *Nidai Genji Homare Migawari.*	1884
*Takatoki**	Part of *Hōjō Kudai Meika Isaoshi;* the dance of Takotoki with the *tengu* goblins.	1884
*Funa Benkei**	A dance drama derived from the Nō.	1885
Yamabushi Setsumatsu	Part of *Senzai Soga Genji Ishizue.*	1885
Seiji Gakumai	Part of *Senzai Soga Genji Ishizue.*	1885
Ise no Saburō	Actual title: *Mibae Genji Michinoku Nikki.*	1886
*Momijigari**	A dance drama derived from the Nō.	1887
Tako no Tametomo	Actual title: *Nani Ōshima Homare no Tsuyuyumi.*	1888
Bunkaku Kanjinchō	Part of *Nachi Taki Kisei Bunkaku.*	1889
Hidari Shotō	The classical dance *Meisaku Hidari Shotō.*	1890
Takano Monogurui	A dance drama derived from the Nō.	1891
Nakakuni	A dance drama version of a Nō play, *Tōgō.*	1891
*Suō Otoshi**	A dance play derived from a Kyōgen farce.	1892
Onna Kusunoki	Part of *Motomezuka Migawari Shinda.*	1892
*Kagamijishi**	A revision of the classical dance *Makura Jishi*	1893
Shin Nanatsumen	A revision of *Nanatsumen.*	1893
Ninin Bakama	A dance piece derived from a Kyōgen farce.	1894
Mukai Shōkan	A new work by Kawatake Shinshichi III*.	1895
Fukitori Tsuma	A dance piece derived from a Kyōgen farce.	1896
Tokihira no Shichi Warai	Part of *Tenmangū Natane no Gokū.*	1897
*Ōmori Hikoshichi**	A new dance piece by Fukuchi Ōchi*.	1897

SHINKABUKI-ZA. A theatre in Osaka's Naniwa section. It opened in October 1958, intended as a successor to the Osaka Kabuki-za, which produced plays from 1932 to 1958. The theatre is managed by the Sentochi Theatrical Joint Stock Corporation. Osaka's equivalent to Tokyo's Kabuki-za*, the playhouse is situated within a five-story building with an exterior of Momoyama period (1568-1615) style.

SHINKO ENGEKI JŪSHU. A collection of ten favorite plays of the Onoe family, which contrasts with the *kabuki jūhachiban** and *shin kabuki jūhachiban** collections of the Ichikawa family. The collection was established by Onoe Kikugorō V*, and additional numbers were added by Kikugorō VI* and Onoe Baikō VI*. (*See also* FAMILY ART.)

PLAY	NOTE	DATE OF FIRST PRODUCTION
Rakan	Matsusuke I* received great praise for his performance of the role of Rakan, a wizard. The role was developed as a specialty of the Onoe family.	1808
Kodera no Neko	A cat's apparition, specialized in by Matsusuke I.	1808
*Tsuchigumo**	Taken from the Nō play of the same name, it deals with the battle between the spirit of a monstrous spider and the retainers of Lord Raiko.	1873
*Ibaraki**	The arrival of a demon to regain its arm, cut off by Watanabe no Tsuna, and the battle that ensues.	1883
*Hitotsuya**	The miracle of the goddess Kannon, which causes a change of heart in a wicked old hag.	1890
*Modori Bashi**	Watanabe no Tsuna's discovering that a beautiful girl is really a demon and his cutting off of its arm.	1890
Kiku Jidō	A dance by the legendary character Jidō, who has lived 700 years.	1892
*Hagoromo**	Derived from the Nō play of the same name, this features an angel's flying off.	1898
Osakabe Hime	The battle between the apparition of Princess Osakabe and Minamoto Musashi on the castle tower at Himeji Castle.	1900
*Migawari Zazen**	Derived from *Hanako*, a Kyōgen farce. The humor comes from Yamakage Ukyō's drunkenness.	1910

SHINNAI BUSHI. A school of music born in Edo during the Anei and Tenmei periods (1772-88). It was descended from the *bungo bushi** style of

Miyakoji Bungo (1660?-1740). After *bungo bushi* was prohibited (because it was said to have inspired too many love suicides), Bungo's disciples—Tsuruga Wakasanojō (1717-1786) and Tsuruga Shinnai (1747-1810)—became very popular with their own type of narrative *(jōruri*)* music. This style differed from the other schools in its *kudoki* ("lamentation*") passages by infusing a strongly suggestive tone into the sorrowful music running through the scene. The mingling of this music with Kabuki during its early period was considerable. Remaining today are *Akegarasu Hana no Nureginu**, *Wakagi no Adanagusa**, and other works.

SHINOBUE. A type of flute. (*See also* NARIMONO.)

SHI NO KIRI. "Fourth conclusion"; originally the last part of a puppet-play's fourth act, the term now is reserved for the Kawazura mansion scene in Act IV of *Yoshitsune Senbon Zakura**.

SHINOZUKA RYŪ. A school of Japanese dance founded by Shinozuka Bunsaburō (d. 1845) in the Kamigata area. It was the major school of dance in Kyoto for a number of years, but eventually died out.

SHINPAN UTAZAEMON. Chikamatsu Hanji*. Also called *Osome Hisamatsu, Nozaki Mura. Sewamono**. *Jōruri**. Two acts. September 1780. Takemoto-za, Osaka.

The most famous of the various dramatizations of the love story of Osome and Hisamatsu.

Hisamatsu is the son of a samurai family, but for the good of the family he was entrusted to the Nozaki Village farmer Kyusaku, the brother of his wet nurse. He left Nozaki Village and went to Osaka, where he began service at the Abura-ya, a pawnshop. He has fallen in love with Osome, daughter of his employer, but Osome is obligated to marry into the Yamaieya family. Having stolen money that he had collected for his employer, Hisamatsu returns to the home of Kyusaku. Kyusaku wishes to use this opportunity to wed Hisamatsu to his own daughter, Omitsu, who cheerfully undertakes the preparations. Osome arrives there, having come on the pretext of paying a visit to the village shrine. Kyusaku advises her indirectly, explaining why Osome and Hisamatsu cannot be united. However, the pair secretly decide to commit double suicide. Omitsu learns of this and cuts off her hair, signifying that she will become a nun, in order to bring about the lovers' union. Otsune, widow of the Abura-ya, arrives to take Osome back with her. Because of her debt of obligation to Omitsu, she sends the lovers home separately, Hisamatsu by palanquin and Osome by boat.

The play is very effective in presenting Omitsu's overflowing joy and girlish innocence as she prepares the wedding meal, followed by her tragic reversal. Osome's qualities of the selfish, city-bred girl are contrasted with Omitsu's selfless qualities. The final scene, in which Omitsu gazes intently and emotionally at the parting of the lovers, is quite modern in treatment.

SHINREI YAGUCHI NO WATASHI. Fukuuchi Kigai. Also called *Yaguchi no Watashi. Jidaimono**. *Jōruri**. Five acts. January 1770. Geki-za, Edo.

Edo's Kiri-za produced the first Kabuki version of this puppet play in 1794, but Ichikawa Danjūrō VII's* performance as Tonbei in 1831 at the Kawarazaki-za made the role far more important than in earlier versions. It helped make the play very popular, and it has remained so through the years. Only Act V is performed today.

Nitta Yoshimine and his mistress, Utena, arrive at the home of Tonbei, the ferryman, to ask for a night's lodging. Tonbei wishes to slay Yoshimine, but his daughter, Ofune, has fallen in love with the samurai and she lets him escape with Utena. She puts herself in Yoshimine's place and is stabbed by Tonbei. Terribly angry, Tonbei fires the signal to the surrounding troops and takes off in pursuit of Yoshimine. Even though she has been mortally wounded, Ofune beats the great drum, a signal to raise the siege. Tonbei, who is rowing on the river, dies after being struck in the throat by an arrow.

The character of the incredibly greedy Tonbei, who—though he has killed his daughter—still lusts after the reward for killing Yoshimine, is well contrasted with that of the lovely Ofune, who dies wretchedly. Rokuzō, a servant who is in love with Ofune, is a clown type of role and gives the play a touch of variety. The scene in which Ofune decides to save Yoshimine often is performed as if Ofune were a puppet (*ningyō buri** style). Her acting when she bangs the drum although mortally wounded is an outstanding moment for the actor of young female roles and is called *teoi goto* ("wounded acting"). Sawamura Sōjūrō VII* was one of the greatest players of the role.

SHIN SARAYASHIKI TSUKI NO AMAGASA. Kawatake Mokuami*. Also called *Sakanaya Sogorō. Sewamono**. Kabuki. Three acts. May 1883. Ichimura-za*, Tokyo.

Otsuta, younger sister of the fishmonger Sogorō, has been chosen by Isobe Kazuenosuke to be his concubine. Kazuenosuke's evil retainer, Iwagamidayū Tenzō, is looking for an opportunity to seize his master's power. Thus, he lies that Otsuta is having an affair with Monzaburō, son of an old retainer. Kazuenosuke accepts this as the truth and murders the girl. Sogorō hears of his sister's pathetic last moments from her friend Onagi. He then gets wildly drunk on sake, although he has long abstained from drink. With his strength and courage fortified by the alcohol, he breaks into Kazuenosuke's mansion. However, the old retainer, Urado Juzaemon, sees to it that a disaster is averted. Kazuenosuke, repenting of his hot temper, gives condolence money to Sogorō. The latter, having sobered up, returns home.

The play's acting highlight occurs in Act II at Sogorō's home, when he becomes inebriated. Juzaemon was first played by Arashi Rikan IV, Kazuenosuke by Kataoka Gadō III, Ohama by Kawarazaki Kunitarō III, Onagi by Iwai Matsunosuke IV, Otsuta, Otsuta's ghost, and Sogorō by Onoe Kikugoro V*, Tenzō by Onoe Matsusuke IV, with other roles played by Ichikawa Sumizō V and Sawamura Tosshi VII. The play is the outstanding work of Mokuami's later years. Kikugorō was brilliant as Sogorō, and he handed his approach on to his son, Kikugorō VI*, who played it often.

SHINSHŌ. "A fortune"; one's wages.

SHINSHŪ KAWANAKAJIMA KASSEN. Chikamatsu Monzaemon*. Also called *Terutora Haizen*. *Jidaimono**. *Jōruri**. Five acts. August 1721. Takemoto-za, Osaka.

A dramatization of the battle between Uesugi Kenshin and Takeda Nobuharu at Kawanakajima. Only Act III is still performed.

Naoe Yamashiro no Kami, respected retainer of Nagao Terutora (Kenshin) invites Horiji, mother of the Takeda strategist named Kansuke, to dinner at Terutora's mansion. The intent is to see if Kansuke can be weaned away from Takeda to Terutora. Realizing this, Horiji becomes furious and kicks over her dinner stand. Terutora, enraged, is ready to slay her on the spot, but Okatsu, Kansuke's wife, intercedes. As she is prevented from speaking by a serious stammer, she communicates her feelings by playing the *koto**, asking through the music for Terutora to take her life in place of the old lady's. The *daimyō* is appeased and returns his sword to its sheath.

Horiji is often considered to be one of the three most important old lady's roles in Kabuki (*see also* SANBABĀ).

SHIN TAKADOMA. "New high pit," the foremost elevated tier of seats in the pit *(doma*)*. Arranged in boxes and running along the sides of the theatre, the seats were installed in the enlarged theatres of the early period. (*See also* THEATRE ARCHITECTURE.)

SHINUKI. A sequence in a dance drama when one or two characters step forth in turn from a crowd of people and perform a segment of the dance. At the end everyone dances. It often is seen in such dances as *Noriaibune** and *Dontsuku**, which portray the customs and manners of the townspeople. *Shinuki* also refers to the individual moments in fighting scenes *(tachimawari*)* when the hero is assaulted by one, two, or three men at a time.

SHIN USUYUKI MONOGATARI. Matsuda Bunkodō, Miyoshi Shōraku, Kogawa Hanbei, Takeda Koizumo. *Jidaimono**. *Jōruri**. Three acts. May 1741. Takemoto-za, Osaka.

A dramatization of the story *Usuyuki Monogatari*, which concerns the famous swordsmiths Munemasa, Kuniyuki, and Kunitoshi. The entire play is still performed. Though originally a puppet play, it was strongly influenced by two earlier Kabuki plays on the same subject. Kabuki's adaptation of the play was staged at Kyoto's Hayakumo-za three months after its puppet theatre premiere.

Sonobe Hyoe's son, Saemon, goes to the Kiyomizu Temple to perform a dedication service for a sword. He loves and is loved by Lord Sasaki Iga's daughter, Usuyuki. On orders given by the evil Akizuki Daizen, Masamune's son, Dankurō, inscribes a curse on the sword that Saemon had dedicated to the shogun. Saemon is suspected of being responsible for the curse and is placed in the charge of Iga, while Usuyuki is put in the charge of Hyoe. The two fathers let their charges go free and commit ritual suicide *(seppuku)* in apology. Seeing that they unexpectedly had come to the same decision in order to help the young couple, Hyoe, Lord Iga, and Hyoe's wife (Ume no Kata) laugh with satisfaction, the men doing so through the pain of their self-inflicted wounds. Later, Dankurō is wounded in the arm when he attempts to steal his father's secrets; he repents of his crimes and acknowledges Daizen's evil deeds. Masamune hands his secrets over to Rai Kunitoshi.

The scene of flower viewing at Kiyomizu Temple and the later one in which the young couple falls in love have become classics. Events of love and evil unfold against a gorgeous background. Act I's balletic fight scene *(tachimawari*)*, featuring the manservant Tsumahei, is of special interest. The scene of the "three laughs" at Sonobe Hyoe's home is one of Kabuki's most famous scenes. The actors in the scene have a difficult task in accurately portraying people who must laugh while enduring great pain, both physical and emotional. Another famous scene occurs in Masamune's home when, after his change of heart, the wounded Dankurō fights off his attackers with one arm. Obviously, *Shin Usuyuki Monogatari* is a masterpiece full of surprises and dramatic conflict.

SHIOBARA TASUKE ICHIDAIKI. Kawatake Shinshichi III* (aided by Kawatake Mokuami* and Takeshiba Kisui*.) *Sewamono**. Kabuki. Six acts. January 1892. Kabuki-za*, Tokyo.

A dramatization of a "human nature" story by Sanyūtei Enchō (1838-1900), a *rakugo** storyteller. In the original company were Onoe Kikugorō V* as Tasuke, Ichikawa Chūsha VII* (then known as Yaozō) as Kadoemon, Onoe Matsusuke IV and Bandō Shūchō II. Kikugorō's outstanding methods as Tasuke were adopted by his son, Kikugorō VI*, who made the role one of his great successes.

Tasuke has been adopted by Kadoemon, a farmer of Jōshū. Following Kadoemon's death, his stepmother (Okame) and her daughter (Oei), his own wife, begin to treat him cruelly. Seeing that his very life is in danger, he leaves for Edo on his beloved horse. However, as he is penniless and jobless, he intends to drown himself. He is saved by Yamaguchiya Seneimon, goes into service at this man's house, and works with wholehearted zeal. He receives approval, marries Ohana of the Fujino-ya, and becomes independent. He is successful selling charcoal, and his store becomes quite prosperous. Soon after, he again meets Okame, who is now a beggar, and he takes her back. His stepmother repents her sins and returns to a life of virtue.

The scene in which Tasuke takes leave with his horse, Ao, on the night of the full moon is well known. Another famous scene is the one in which Ohana cuts off her long sleeves with a hatchet and resolves to marry Tasuke.

SHIOKUMI. Sakurada Jisuke II*. Also called *Shichimai Tsuzuki Hana no Sugatae*. *Shosagoto**. *Nagauta**. March 1811. Ichimura-za*, Edo.

One scene from a seven-change dance drama, it is based on the Nō play *Matsukaze*. Many Kabuki dance plays have used the same subject, beginning with *Ura Chidori Mirume no Shiokumi* in 1762. The present work first starred Bandō Mitsugorō III*. This first production used both *nagauta* and *tokiwazu** music, but since the 1823 Morita-za* revival only *nagauta* has been employed.

The fishergirl Matsukaze dances while wearing the robe and cap of her former lover, Ariwara Narihira, who left them for her as keepsakes.

Though Matsukaze is a fishergirl, she has the looks and charm of a princess. Other Matsukaze dances include *Mirume no Shiokumi*, *Hanshirō no Shiokumi*, and *Hama Matsukaze*.

SHIRAI MATSUJIRŌ. 1877-1951. A cofounder of the Shōchiku* theatrical conglomerate.

SHIRANAMI MONO. *See* ROBBER PLAYS.

SHIRASE. "Warning," a signal made with the *hyōshigi** clappers by the *kyōgen kata**. It is a double beat heard when the stage revolves, when the scenery is changed, or when the pace of the narrative accompaniment is accelerated.

SHIRIPPANE. A hit production, one that continues to draw crowds after the middle of its month-long run.

SHISENRYŌ (KOBAN NO UMENOHA). Kawatake Mokuami*. *Sewamono**. Kabuki. Six acts. November 1885. Chitose-za, Tokyo.

This play draws its materials from a true-life Ansei era (1854-59) incident in which the money warehouse at Edo Castle was broken into. Onoe Kikugorō V*, Ichikawa Kuzō (later Ichikawa Danzō VII*), Bandō Kakitsu, Onoe

Matsusuke, Kawarazaki Kunitarō III, and Iwai Matsunosuke were in the first cast. In this century the outstanding combination of Kikugorō VI* and Nakamura Kichiemon I* made a specialty of this play. The language and manners of the prisoners are quite close to actuality, making the play very unusual for its day.

Fujioka Tōjūrō, a masterless samurai, and the homeless Tomizo conspire together and successfully steal 4,000 *ryō* from the treasury at Edo Castle. They temporarily bury the money under the verandah of Tōjūrō's house. Following the great Ansei period earthquake, Tōjūrō realizes a great profit in lumber and begins to operate as a money lender. Having taken his share of the stolen money from Tōjūrō, Tomizō has been freely spending it, but, fearful of being discovered by the law, he leaves for his mother's home in Kaga. On the way he meets his wife, a noodle seller, and her father at Kumagaya and saves them from a predicament in which they are embroiled. Eventually, Tōjūrō is arrested in Edo and Tomizō is seized at Kaga. On his way back to Edo, Tomizō meets his wife in Kumagaya, and they drink a farewell cup together. The two men, put in Denbamachi Prison, are soon marched out and executed for their crime.

The encounter of Tōjūrō and Tomizō outside the Yotsuya Palace gate, the scene of the disposal of the money at Tōjūrō's home, and the farewell from the Kumagaya noodle shop are excellently conceived. A special attraction of the play is the realistically produced prison scene.

SHIZOME. An event at the New Year's* *(hatsuharu)* performance of Edo period Kabuki. It was performed from New Year's Day to the third day of the new year and included a piece, *Okina Watashi*, modeled on the Nō play *Okina*. The role of Okina was played by the *zamoto**, or manager; his son, the *wakadayū**, played the role of Senzai; and the company chief actor or choreographer played Sanbasō. *Andon* (Japanese paper-covered lanterns) were hung from the pillars *(daijin bashira*)* on either side of the stage. These lamps were called *Okina andon* for the occasion. When the piece was over, the *makibure* was performed. This involved placing a scroll on a stand, after which the scroll was taken off and read; its contents included the complete title *(nadai*)* of the New Year's play, the names of each act, and the cast list. Following this, there was a dance (the *odori hatsume)* by a child actor. A special version of this ceremony was performed by the Ichikawa Danjūrō* line of actors. The current Danjūrō, being the leading actor of his troupe, would tell his audience, "In accord with time-honored custom *(kichirei*)*, I will now glare for you." He would then hold

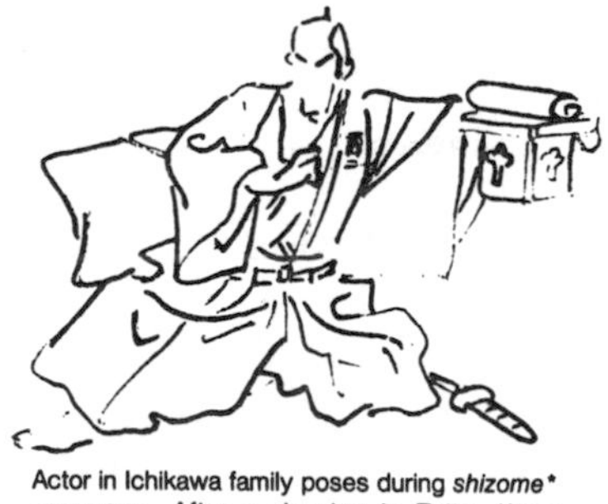

Actor in Ichikawa family poses during *shizome** ceremony. After a drawing in Toita, *Waga Kabuki.*

the stand with its scroll in a special pose as he performed a *mie**. This pose still may be seen when an actor takes a new name in the Ichikawa family. *Shizome* or *shizomeshiki* was the collective term given to these ceremonies.

SHIZU. A gift of money, to which a banner was attached; given by a fan to an actor.

SHŌCHIKU. The abbreviated name for a theatrical producing company, the Shōchiku Kabushiki Gaisha (Shōchiku Joint Stock Corporation). Together with the Tōhō* Kabushiki Gaisha, it is one of the two wealthiest and most powerful theatrical organizations in Japan. It was founded in 1902 in Kyoto by the twin brothers Shirai Matsujirō (1877-1951) and Ōtani Takejirō (1877-1969). The word Shōchiku is formed by the Chinese readings of the elements *matsu* ("pine") and *take* ("bamboo") in their names. At first the company was called the Shōchiku Gomegaisha ("Shōchiku and Co.") and was involved mainly in the Kamigata area. In 1910, Ōtani went to Tokyo, where he acquired the Shintomi-za (*see also* MORITA-ZA). In 1914 he achieved the chief managerial position at the Kabuki-za*. Just before the great earthquake of 1923, the two brothers, Ōtani in Tokyo and Shirai in the Kamigata area, were in control of almost all of Japan's Kabuki and Shinpa theatres, and they ruled the Japanese theatre world. Later, they entered the motion picture business as well as the world of Japanese variety entertainment. In 1936 they became the Shōchiku Kabushiki Gaisha, their present name. After World War II they endeavored to rehabilitate the bombed and burned-out theatres. Their rational approach to theatrical producing led the brothers to accomplish many meritorious deeds for Japanese theatre. Today, the motion picture industry is in a decline, and from a managerial viewpoint there seems to be little that can be done. In addition to its theatrical work, Shōchiku is entering the so-called leisure industry. (*See also* THEATRE MANAGEMENT.)

SHŌGUN EDO O SARU. Mayama Seika*. *Shin kabuki**. Four acts. Third part of a three-part work, *Edo Shirō Sozeme*. January 1934. Tōkyō Gekijō, Tokyo.

Katsu Awa, a supporter of the shogun, pays a visit to Saigō, who is planning to attack the shogunate, at the Satsuma clan's mansion in Edo. He promises to surrender Edo Castle to Saigō. The shogunate vassal Yamaoka Tetsutarō visits the shogun, Tokugawa Keiki, who, amidst the stern vigilance of Akiyoshi troops, has confined himself in the Daijiin Temple in Ueno. Yamaoka explains to the shogun the great principles of Imperialism. Keiki finally comes to a decision. Imperial rule is restored and, although regretted by the people of Edo, Keiki leaves town in the direction of Mito.

At the heart of the play is the speech by Yamaoka on Imperial rule. The actor playing the role must be a skillful orator. The final scene, which takes place at dawn at the approach to the bridge at Senjū and features the shogun looking back at the city of Edo, is filled with Seika's special sentimental quality.

SHŌHON. A word with several meanings. First, a Kabuki playscript. Also called *daihon, daichō, kyakuhon,* and, in the Kamigata area, *nehon**. *Daichō* and *daihon* have the sense of a notebook or book forming the foundation of a performance (the character for *dai* suggests a stand or support). The term does not include books printed with movable type, but is limited to books transcribed by brush writing on Japanese paper.

Two varieties exist. One is the "horizontal" *(yokohon)* book, and the other is the "vertical" *(tatehon)*. The former, created in the late Edo period, was written by the playwright on rice paper folded horizontally in two. It was read by the chief actor *(zagashira*)* and manager *(zamoto*)*, who added their corrections. When a clean copy of this script was written on rice paper and folded in half vertically, it usually was called the *shōhon* ("correct book"). Each act was placed in a separate book with a cover bearing the month of the performance, the play's title, the scene, and the actors who were to appear in it.

As a rule, these books have thirteen lines to a page and are written in the calligraphic style called *kantei**. Originally, there was some freedom regarding the number of lines to a page and the size of the characters; there was also no restriction on which calligraphic styles could be used. Beginning in the late Edo period, however, the style came to be fixed by convention. The speeches are listed not by characters' names, but by actors' names, according to the Edo period custom. *Shōhon* have become an invaluable reference about the time of performance, the nature of the production, and the acting of plays produced in the past. The year and era, the month, a good luck phrase, the number of pages, the playwright's name (or, sometimes, that of the theatre proprietor), and, finally, a prayer for longevity were written on the rear cover. The oldest extant playscript is one of the play *Shinjū Kimon Kado*, performed in 1710 at Osaka's Ogino Yaegiri-za.

Second, *Shōhon* refers to wood-block printed books that contained all kinds of narrative poetry *(jōruri*)* and prose set to music. The term refers here to the fact that the phrases and musical settings were correct according to the original chanter's script. The first use of the term in the puppet theatre was in reference to the 1634 *Hanaya*, which was the "Correct Script of the Peerless Satsuma Dayū." This sort of *shōhon* was arranged in the Kyōhō era (1716-35) in the fashion of Uji Kaganojō's (1635-1711) type script: eight lines to a page. Later, a seven-line script became quite popular, following the use of scripts with ten, six, nine, eleven, and twelve lines.

Third, *shōhon* for works performed in such musical styles as *katō bushi**, *itchū bushi**, *tokiwazu**, *tomimoto**, and *kiyomoto** had the picture of the chief actors drawn on the cover along with the names of the musicians. Later, such scripts became even simpler; the play's title alone was printed on a green cover. These are called *usumono* or *usumono shōhon* ("thin scripts").

SHŌJI YATAI. A roomlike construction with sliding shoji screens that is used when the script has a direction like "a curtained entry upstage, a six-foot shoji room on stage left." There are *yatai* constructions in palace scenes, shrines, temples, castles, and battle camps as well as those generically called *sewa yatai,* which are found in mercantile houses, teahouses, farmers' houses, and the like. The *yatai* are included among the standardized scenic elements *(jōshiki ōdōgu*)*. Standard *yatai* are sixteen feet wide. When a bigger *yatai* is required, three feet are added to both sides of the standard version, a practice called *tsuke* ("added on") *yatai.*

SHŌMEN O KIRU. "Playing up front"; those times when the actor explicitly performs ("cuts") a *mie** for the delight of the spectators. Since the convention is a prerogative of star actors only, novices rarely get to do it.

SHŌNEBA. An important moment in a scene during which the essential nature *(shone)* of the hero is revealed. It provides the actor with a highlight of his performance. Many *shōneba* are placed in the heart of the action, as is the case with the head inspection scenes (*see also* KUBI JIKKEN) of *Terakoya* in *Sugawara Denju Tenarai Kagami** and *Kumagai Jinya* in *Ichinotani Futaba Gunki**.

SHONICHI. *See* OPENING DAY.

SHOSA BUTAI. "Pose stage." Also called *oki butai* and *shiki butai,* this is a low set of *nijū** platforms placed on the stage for dance plays and certain highly theatrical plays, such as those in *aragoto** style, to aid the actors' sliding step movements and to produce a reverberating sound when stamped on. Both the stage proper and the *hanamichi** are covered with these platforms when they are called for.

SHOSAGOTO. Dance dramas (literally, "pose pieces"). Also called *buyōgeki, furigoto**, *hyōshigoto*, and *keigoto**. *Shosa* originally meant "behavior" or "conduct" and was used for all the elements of acting. Gradually, it came to mean "dancelike acting." Dance drama, which developed along with the growth of *tokiwazu**, *kiyomoto**, and *nagauta** music during the Tenmei, Bunka, and Bunsei eras (1780-1830), came to be called *shosagoto,* Actually, it is customary to call works accompanied by *nagauta* music by this term, while *kiyomoto* and *tokiwazu* pieces are *jōruri** or *jōruri shosagoto*.

SHŌ UTSUSHI ASAGAO NIKKI. Yamada Anzanshi. Also called *Asagao Nikki, Shō Utsushi Asagao Banashi. Jidai-sewamono**. *Jōruri**. Five acts. January 1832. Takemoto Mokumokudayū-za, Osaka.

This play has an interesting history. Around 1806, Chikamatsu Tokusō dramatized a *kōshoku* story called *Asagao*, but no one was able to obtain a suitable actor for the role of Miyuki, so the script went unproduced. Four or five years later an illustrated book called *Asagao Nikki* was published and widely read. In 1812, a play called *Shō Utsushi Asagao Nikki* was produced in Osaka. This was not Tokusō's play (he had died two years earlier), but was the work of Dekishima Sensuke, and it was not a success. In 1814, the actor Sawamura Tanosuke returned to Osaka from Edo and appeared in a new version of Tokusō's play, adapted by Nagawa Harusuke. It had eight acts and twelve scenes and was called *Keisei Tsukushi Tsumagoto*. In the production, at the Kado no Shibai, Arashi Yoshisaburō acted Asajirō and Tanosuke played Miyuki. This play was then turned into a puppet play; its authorship was attributed to Yamada Anzanshi (a posthumous name for Tokusō). Akimatsu Enshūjin made final revisions on the script. The script now used in Kabuki is an adaptation of the puppet play, made around 1850.

While firefly hunting on the Oji River, Miyuki, daughter of the Akizuki family, falls in love at first sight with Miyagi Asajirō. Asajirō is ordered to go to Kamakura, and the lovers are forced to part. Later, someone named Komazawa Jirozaemon is to be married to Miyuki, but, unable to forget Asajirō, she runs away. She goes blind from constant weeping over her sad fate, calls herself Asagao ("Morning Glory"), and wanders as a beggar to the vicinity of Hamatsu. At an inn in Shimada she plays the *koto** for Komazawa at his request. Indeed, Komazawa is actually Asajirō. Because of his companion, he does not reveal who he is. He leaves, sending her medicine for her eyes, money, and the fan on which he had written a poem about the morning glory to her at their first meeting. Miyuki, learning that Komazawa was her lover of former days, rushes after him. A rainstorm forces her to stop at the Oi River. She is going to kill herself in despair, but her father's servant, Sekisuke, and the landlord of the inn (a former servant of her family) arrive in time. When she drinks the medicine, her eyes open again.

There is a classical beauty to the firefly-hunting scene, during which the two young people fall in love at first sight. The scene at the inn with the hateful Iwashirō, Asajirō's companion, and the playing of the *koto* are indebted to a famous Kabuki scene known as *Akoya no Kotozeme* in the play *Dan no Ura Kabuto Gunki**. There is also a good fight scene between Sekisuke and the ferrymen at the Oi River.

SHUCHI. A Kamigata term for the *kinshu**, or financial backer, of Edo period theatres.

SHŪJAKU JISHI. Anonymous. Also called *Hanabusa Shūjaku Jishi. Shosagoto**. *Nagauta**. March 1754. Nakamura-za*, Edo.

This lively dance piece is based on the Nō play *Shakkyō* (*see also* SHAKKYŌ MONO). It was first performed by Nakamura Tomijūrō I*.

Shūjaku Jishi shows a courtesan dancing with a hand-held lion mask; she becomes mad with the spirit of the lion and dances with a fan to which are attached peony flowers and which she uses as a hat.

One of the lion dances *(shakkyō mono* or *shishi mono)* performed by Kabuki's female impersonators, this is a strong reminder of the time when dance was their special sphere. Other such dances include *Kagamijishi**, *Aioi Jishi*, and *Makura Jishi.*

SHUKŌ. The "horizontal" line of a Kabuki play's plot, as opposed to the "vertical" line of the play's dramatic "world" *(sekai*)*. Once the playwright had decided on the gist of the plot and the characters who would appear, he displayed his talent by taking these materials and making something novel and unusual from them. The so-called *kakigae kyogen** were a by-product of this writing method. (*See also* PLAYWRITING.)

SHŪMEI. The ceremonial succession by the son or pupil of a well-known family to the name of his father, elder brother, master, or some ancestral relation. If the actor has become the adopted son of another family, he also may inherit that family's name(s). The actor taking a new name is recognized as having attained a certain level of proficiency signified by the name. An eminent actor's son passes through any number of name levels from childhood on, and many achieve their family's highest name. The actor progresses from one level to the next according to his age and the growth of his skill. Fans, towels, and similar items with his name printed on them are given to his backers and relatives at the *shūmei.* He also makes salutations to them from the stage. When the *shūmei* ceremony is done on a large scale, one act of a program is given over to the recital of a special announcement *(kōjō*)* of his new name. He greets the audience from the stage while his family and actors closely related to him are lined up onstage in formal cos-

*Onnagata** addresses audience during *shūmei** ceremony. His costume is *kamishimo**. On forehead is *murasaki bōshi**.

tume. This is called the *shūmei hiro* ("announcement ceremony for the taking of a new name"). In addition, a play with deep family associations is selected for production, and the actor taking the new name plays the leading role. This play is called the *shūmei hiro kyōgen.* The actors' patrons celebrate the name taking and offer him enthusiastic support. He is given gifts, and blessings are bestowed on his future prospects. Along with this system of handing on a family's names goes the transmission of the family art* to a new generation, the latter being the true purpose of the *shūmei.* Encouraged by the *shūmei* to develop his art even more, the actor exerts himself so as not to disgrace the family name.

SHURABA. Scenes of violent battle in history plays.

SHURO BUSE. A stage set representing an embankment is usually shown by painting grass on flats placed against the front of a *nijū** platform. In more realistic cases, actual hempen *(shuro)* leaves are supplied so that it looks as if real grass were growing. This is called *shuro buse.* In such cases, boards measuring three to four feet by five to six inches and having rounded edges are painted like the embankment and set up where needed. They are called "embankment boards" *(dote ita).* Holes are drilled in the upper part, and flowers are inserted in them.

SHŪTANBA. "Scenes of lamentation," tragic scenes in which the characters—forced by evil circumstances to separate from each other (parents and children, husbands and wives, masters and retainers)—openly express their grief at parting. (*See also* LAMENTATION SCENES.)

SHŪZENJI MONOGATARI. Okamoto Kidō*. *Shin kabuki**. One act, three scenes, May 1909. Meiji-za*, Tokyo.

One of the plays written for Kabuki in the Meiji era by playwrights who were outside the Kabuki playwright's world. It already has come to be performed as one of Kabuki's classical works.

Yashyō, the mask maker of Itō, is a famous man whose work is greatly revered. He is ordered to make a mask of Minamoto Yoriie, an important lord who has been shunned by the Hōjō clan and confined in Itō. However, no matter how often he tries, the shadow of death appears on the mask, and Yashyō cannot make a mask with which he is satisfied. Nevertheless, Yoriie, who comes to demand the mask, is content and takes it with him. Then, Yashyō's daughter Katsura, requesting service with a samurai, obtains a position as Yoriie's concubine. That night, the mansion is attacked and Yoriie dies. Katsura puts on the mask made by her father and fights bravely, barely escaping with her life, and returns to her father's home.The appearance of the shadow of death on the mask, which predicted Yoriie's death, gives Yashyō great satisfaction in the power of his art. Further, in order to make a model for a mask depicting a maiden on the brink of death, he draws a picture of the shadow of death as seen on his own daughter's face.

Besides giving one view of Yoriie's death, this play also vividly portrays the famous Yashyō. Matched with him is the noble Katsura; Kaede, her gentle younger sister; and an apprentice, Haruhiko. The relations among all of these characters are well drawn. In the middle of the play there is placed a moonlit scene at the approach to the Torakiyo Bridge over the Katsura River; in it, the fleeting love of Yoriie and Katsura is revealed.

SIDELOCKS. *See* BIN.

SODE. "Sleeves," the flats placed between the proscenium arch and the stage pillars *(daijin bashira*)* at either side of the stage, in order to mask the backstage area from the audience. (*See also* MIKIRI; KAGAMI.) Also, the area near these flats is called *sode*.

SOGA MATSURI. The "Soga festival," an annual Edo theatre event. It was a convention of seasonal programming to stage a play dealing with the Soga brothers at the New Year's performance* *(hatsuharu kyōgen)*. When the production was a hit and had a long run, it was celebrated for several days at the end of May. Paper lanterns were hung in the theatre and its dressing rooms, and various events took place as part of the festivities, including a dance in which the entire company took part.

SOGA MOYŌ TATESHI NO GOSHOZOME. Kawatake Mokuami*. Also called *Gosho no Gorozō. Hototogisu Tateshi no Goshozome. Sewamono**. Kabuki. Six acts, twelve scenes. February 1864. Ichimura-za*, Edo.

A drama based on Ryutei Tanehiko's (1783-1842) novel, *Asamagatake Omokage Sōshi*. The first half of this play, in which Yuri no Kata, the wife of Asama Tomoenojō, beats his concubine, Hototogisu, to death is rarely performed. In the cast of the first production were Ichikawa Kodanji IV* as Gorozō, Onoe Kikujirō as Satsuki, Seki Sanjūrō III as Doemon, and Onoe Kikugorō V* (known then as Ichimura Kakitsu).

Gorozō was originally a samurai in the employ of the Asama family, but he was expelled from the house because of his love affair with a lady-in-waiting, Satsuki. He became an *otokodate*, or "street knight," and Satsuki became a courtesan. Tomoenojō, present head of the Asama family, falls in love at first sight with Oshū, a courtesan who resembles his dead concubine (she is actually her elder sister). He would like to redeem her from prostitution, but has no money. Gorozō occupies himself with attempts to raise money for his old master. His courtesan-wife Satsuki receives 100 *ryō* from her guest Hoshikage Doemon, who happens to be the enemy of Oshū's and Hototogisu's father. She is heartlessly reviled by Gorozō. He gets angry without knowing her true motives and is going to kill her, but ends up killing his master's loved one, Oshū, instead. Oshū has dressed exactly like Satsuki in order to sacrifice herself for Gorozō's wife.

The scene of the meeting between Gorozō and Doemon at the Nakanochō in Yoshiwara offers beautiful poetic dialogue in the exchange between the two principals. There is also an extremely picturesque quality to the setting. Nowadays, the production style emphasizes Gorozō's dashing manners more than the tragic elements in the story.

SOGA NO TAIMEN. Anonymous. Also called *Kotobuki Soga no Taimen, Kichirei Soga no Taimen, Soga Ryōsha no Tamamono, Taimen. Jidaimono**. One act. New Year's 1676, Nakamura-za*, Edo.

It was an Edo period custom to produce every New Year's a play in which the Soga brothers figured. The conclusion of these productions was invariably the confrontation scene presented in *Soga no Taimen*. It is thought that this custom was based on a desire to ensure good luck for the coming year. Thus, even more important than the dramatic tension that one might expect from a confrontation between the Soga brothers and their mortal enemy, Kudō, was the stress placed on the ceremonial and theatrical qualities of the presentation. This can be observed, for example, in the customary interpretation of Kudō as a leading male role rather than as a villain, which would have been the playwright's original intention. It was traditional, in fact, for the part to be played by the company's leading actor *(zagashira*)*. Everything about the highly formalized, colorful production style suggests symbolic, ceremonial overtones.

The Soga brothers' revenge on the murderer of their father is one of the three most prominent and often dramatized revenge stories of the Edo period, along with the tale of the vendetta of the forty-seven faithful samurai and that of Araki Mataemon's 1634 revenge on the murderer of his father-in-law (*see also* KANADEHON CHŪSHINGURA; IGAGOE DŌCHŪ SUGOROKU). The Soga brothers lost their father when they were children; they had to wait until they reached maturity before they could carry out their revenge. It was accomplished during a hunting party held on Mount Fuji in 1193. Both brothers were slain in punishment, but their deed of filial loyalty lived on in the imagination of the Japanese people for many centuries, kept alive by such narratives as the *Soga Monogatari*. There had been Soga plays even before *Soga no Taimen*, but this play's 1676 performance by Ichikawa Danjūrō I* gave it the stature to survive and join the permanent repertory. All aspects of this performance have undergone extensive change and revision over the years, but the original substructure remains.

Through the intercession of their friend Kobayashi no Asahina, the Soga brothers, Jūrō and Gorō, receive an audience from Lord Kudō no Suketsune during his New Year's celebrations. Seeing his father's slayer face to face, the impetuous young Gorō can barely restrain his anger and dashes the cup of sake offered to him by Kudō to the ground. However, he is restrained from doing further harm by his brother and Asahina. The brothers declare their intention to avenge their father's death, but the contemptuous Kudō scoffs at them and offers to give them their opportunity at a hunt that he has planned for the springtime. Promising to be there, the brothers depart.

The performance of this classic always shows Jūrō as a *wagoto** type of role, a tradition begun by the seventeenth-century actor Nakamura Shichisaburō I*, while Gorō is acted in *aragoto** style. Asahina is played in a somewhat humorous *aragoto* style created by Nakamura Denkurō I*.

SOGIMEN. A trick mask worn in humorous fight scenes. Also called *nashiwari.* When the actor wearing the mask is sliced at by an opponent's sword, a clasp at the top of the mask is loosened. The front part of the mask falls forward, revealing what is supposed to represent the inside of the actor's head, although it is comically stylized. (*See also* KUWAEMEN.)

Character in fight scene wearing *sogimen** mask. After an old print.

SŌKE. A family that originated an artistic tradition that has come to be considered a school. This concept exists within the spheres of both the entertainment arts and the arts of tea ceremony and flower arrangement. In dance and flower arrangement the master of the particular school is called the *iemoto**. The *sōke* are the families that laid the foundation of the schools of which these *iemoto* are the leaders. In Kabuki the title of *sōke* applies to the Ichikawa Danjūrō* family. The acting patterns *(kata*)* of each family of disciples bearing the Ichikawa surname have reigned supreme in the theatre world since the early period.

SŌKEN. "All-see"; when a group of actor's fans go en masse to the theatre. In the Edo period they often went wearing the same clothing, making a bright display of their presence. (*See also* AUDIENCES; DANTAI.)

SOKU NI TATSU. A stance taken with the legs straight and the heels together.

SOKUTAI. The clothing worn for government business at the Imperial Court beginning with the Heian period (794-1185). It is used in Kabuki as the formal costume for high-ranking nobles *(kuge)*. Characters wearing it include Lord Ōkura in *Kiichi Hōgen Sanryaku no Maki**, Sadatō in Act III of *Ōshū Adachigahara**, and Ōtomo Kuronushi in *Rokkasen**.

SONEZAKI SHINJŪ. Chikamatsu Monzaemon* (present version by Uno Nobuo*). English title: *The Love Suicides at Sonezaki* (Keene). *Shin kabuki**. One act, three scenes, August 1953. Shinbashi Enbūjō*, Tokyo.

The original version of this play, the first *sewamono** in the puppet repertory, originally was presented with great success at Osaka's Takemoto-za in May 1703. It is said to have been based on a true story. The present play is a relatively faithful rendering of the original. The incident of the discovery of Kuheiji's misdeed is based on an adaptation of the story called *Ohatsu Tenshinki*.

In a teahouse in the compound of the Ikutama Shrine, Tokubei presses his friend Kuheiji for the money that he has loaned him. Kuheiji insists that the seal on the promissory note is a forgery. He and his friends beat Tokubei, who is deeply shamed by the affair. That night, Tokubei visits Ohatsu at the Tenma-ya. She quietly hides him under the skirt of her kimono, and he conceals himself beneath the verandah. Kuheiji, who has come to carouse, speaks insultingly of Tokubei. Hearing him, the lovers manage to signal each other that they are resolved to die. Late at night, they steal out of the shop and go to Sonezaki to commit double suicide. Later, Kuheiji's crime is discovered, and he is arrested.

SONOHACHI BUSHI. Also called *miyasono bushi*, this is a musical style founded in Kyoto by the foremost disciple of Miyakoji Bungonojō (*see also* BUNGO BUSHI), Miyakoji Sonohachi (fl. 1735). It was perfected by Sonohachi II (da. 1785), in the Hōreki era (1751-63). Performed in Kyoto and Osaka theatres in the early nineteenth century, it sank rapidly in favor after 1811. The music is heard in many "lovers' suicide" plays *(shinjū mono)* and has a quality of romantic pathos. It is maintained today as an old type of music. Plays in which it is employed include *Meido no Hikyaku** and *Toribeyama Shinjū**.

SOSORI. An old tradition whereby on the last day of the run the cast of a play would switch roles, an *onnagata** taking a *tachiyaku** part and vice versa. Sometimes a minor actor would play a major role, and the leading actors would take the small parts. The event was meant in fun and always provided much merriment.

SPEECH. *See* SERIFU.

SPRING PLAYS. *Yayoi kyōgen*, the annual spring productions, were performed in the third month of the year during the Edo period. Called *san no* *kawari,* or "third program change," in the Kamigata area. In Edo until the late eighteenth century the *yayoi kyōgen* were basically an extension of the New Year's play* *(hatsuharu kyōgen)* about the Soga brothers. However, in the nineteenth century the dramatist Namiki Gohei I* moved to Edo and established a system whereby the domestic play on the second half of the New Year's program was given a separate title from that formerly given to the day's performances as a whole. Also, the New Year's production was ended in the second month, and a completely new play was produced beginning on the first day of the annual third-month festival. Because this was the month that palace maids went home for a vacation, such plays as *Kagamiyama Kokyō no Nishikie** and *Meiboku Sendai Hagi** were performed. These depicted the lives of ladies-in-waiting, maidservants, and other females employed in the service of *daimyō. Sukeroku Yukari no Edo Zakura** was also a popular play on these spring programs.

STAGE. *See* THEATRE ARCHITECTURE.

STAGE ASSISTANTS. *See* KŌKEN; KUROGO; KYŌGEN KATA.

STYLIZATION. To speak of Kabuki performance is to refer not only to the acting, but to all those elements which make up a stage presentation—costumes, wigs, makeup, sets, properties, and music, that is, the entire apparatus of production.

Since Kabuki has been an actor-centered theatre since its inception, it was the custom for the leading actor of a troupe to arrange the production so that each actor's personal approach could be communicated, while retaining some sense of an ensemble. This method is fundamentally different from that of modern Western theatre, in which all of the actors are subordinated to the individualistic schemes of a director.

Kabuki's visual beauty is one of its best-loved qualities. This is a theatre in which great value is placed on precise forms *(kata*)*. There is, thus, a heavy emphasis on stylization in performance. The ideas conveyed by the word *stylization (yoshikisei)* are complex, implying the influence made on Kabuki by earlier performance arts as well as the unceasing evolutionary process of shedding old conventions while creating new ones.

Pure Kabuki produced the characteristic acting styles of *aragoto** (the bravura style) and *wagoto** (the gentle, romantic style), in addition to *danmari**. (the art of pantomime). On the other hand, the narrative plays adapted from the puppet theatre, although based on the puppet style of performance and using the narrative accompaniment of chanter and *shamisen** player, also took shape as a unique type of Kabuki performance. Moreover, distinctive performance styles evolved for each of the various classifications of Kabuki drama, so there is a different style for history plays and domestic plays and even for subclassifications of these genres. These diverse performance styles have existed side by side and have mutually influenced each other. Though complex, the various styles have been transmitted from generation to generation.

SUAMI. A net shirt worn to represent chain mail. The *suami*, which mainly is seen on valiant warriors, is worn under the outer kimono *(kitsuke*)*. Some characters who wear it are Shirasuga Rokurō in *Honchō Nijūshikō**, Nikki Danjō in *Meiboku Sendai Hagi**, and Mitsuhide in *Toki wa Ima Kikkyō no Hataage**.

SU DE AKERU. "To open simply"; the opening of the curtain without the conventional accompaniment of *geza** music or the beating of the *hyōshigi**.

SUGAWARA (DENJU TENARAI KAGAMI). Takeda Izumo II*, Miyoshi Shōraku, Namiki Sōsuke*. English title: *Sugawara's Secrets of Calligraphy* (contains *Kurama Biki [Pulling the Carriage Apart]* and *Terakoya [The Village School]*) (Leiter); *The House of Sugawara* (Ernst). *Jidaimono**. *Jōruri**. Five acts. August 1746. Takemoto-za, Osaka.

The basis of this work, which ranges from the exile of Sugawara Michizane to his deification as the god Tenshin, is the tale of the triplet brothers Matsuomaru (Matsuō), Sakuramaru (Sakura), and Umeomaru (Umeō). The plays' three authors have depicted, in three distinctive styles, the tale of the separation of these brothers from their father. *Sugawara Denju Tenarai Kagami* is known as one of the three greatest puppet plays, along with *Kanadehon Chūshingura** and *Yoshitsune Senbon Zakura**, all by the same authors. Still performed frequently in Kabuki are Act I's *Hippo Denju* scene, Act II*s *Domyō Temple* scene, Act III's *Kuruma Biki* and *Ga no Iwai* scenes, and Act IV's *Tenpai Mountain* and *Terakoya* scenes. Kabuki first presented this play in October 1746 at Kyoto's Asao Gengorō-za. Slightly less than a year later, Osaka's Naka no Shibai produced it, while Edo saw the play in May of that year (1747), in rival productions at the Ichimura-za* and Nakamura-za*.

Kan Shōjō (Sugawara) hands over the secrets of his calligraphic art to Takebe Genzō, whom he has recalled from banishment. At this point, Kan Shōjō is summoned by the Imperial Court; his respected position is taken from him, and he is accused of plotting treason. All of this is the work of Fujiwara Shihei's evil plan. Shōjō is exiled to distant Kyūshū. Genzō and his wife, Tonami, helped by Umeomaru, take Shōjō's son Kan Shūsai away with them in order to protect him *(Hippo Denju)*.

On his journey toward Kyūshū, Shōjō visits the home of his aunt, Kakuju, near Domyō Temple. Sukune Tarō and Haji Hyoe, arriving as false envoys take Shōjō with them, planning to kill him, but he manages to substitute for himself a wooden image that he has carved. He bids his daughter, Princess Kariya, farewell *(Domyōji)*.

Umeomaru and Sakuramaru lie in waiting for Shihei while he is returning from a visit to a shrine. They attack his carriage, but are overwhelmed by his authority and power and fail to achieve anything *(Kuruma Biki).*

The triplets and their wives gather at the home of their father, Shiradayū, for the old man's seventieth birthday celebration. Blaming himself for Shōjō's downfall, Sakuramaru commits ritual suicide *(seppuku),* and Shiradayū sets out for Shōjō's place of exile in Kyūshū *(Ga no Iwai).*

Washizuka Heima, who planned to attack Shōjō, is captured with the aid of Umeomaru. Shōjō learns of Shihei's treachery from Umeomaru and angrily kills Heima. He becomes a thunder god and flies off in the direction of the capital *(Tenpaizan).*

Genzō and Tonami open a village school *(terakoya)* and give refuge to Kan Shūsai. Ultimately, he is discovered, and his head has to be cut off. The head of another boy, Kotarō, is used as a substitute, and Matsuomaru, who comes to inspect the head, says that it is the real head of Kan Shūsai. Returning to the school later, Matsuomaru and his wife reveal that Kotarō is their own child and tell of their true feelings in having made this act of sacrifice for Shōjō *(Terakoya).*

The scenes of *Domyōji, Ga no Iwai,* and *Terakoya* all present the separation of a father from his child. The most frequently produced scenes are *Kuruma Biki* and *Terakoya,* the former being acted in the *aragoto** style. Matsuomaru in the *Terakoya* scene is considered to be one of the weightiest of all male Kabuki roles.

SUITENGŪ MEGUMI NO FUKAGAWA. Kawatake Mokuami*. Also called *Fudeya Kōbei. Sewamono**. Three acts. February 1885. Chitose-za, Tokyo.

A play written for the opening of the Chitose-za, located in Tokyo's Hamamachi district, to gain the divine favor of the nearby god of the Suitengū Shrine. Kōbei was first acted by Onoe Kikugorō V*, and Sangorō by Ichikawa Sadanji I*. The play presents the plight of the early Meiji period samurai, deprived of their traditional stipend by the new government, and reduced to straitened circumstances.

The wife of Funatsu Kōbei, a descendant of samurais, has died, and he is left with two young daughters and an infant son; he can barely make a living by selling brushes. However, the evil usurer Kinbei demands that Kōbei pay him back the money that he has loaned him. He then takes all of Kōbei's possessions, even the kimono that his infant son received in kindness from the wife of the fencing master Ogihara. These events drive Kōbei mad. Holding a charm that he bought from the Suitengū Shrine, he walks insanely to the Fuka River and throws himself in. He is saved from death, however, by the rickshaw man Sangorō, an omen of Suitengū's benificence. In addition, his madness is cured. Because of a newspaper report, "sympathy" money is contributed, and with Ogihara's help Kōbei rehabilitates himself.

Besides depicting one phrase of the poverty of samurai descendants during the Meiji era, the play also shows the customs of the new era, presents scenes of downtown Tokyo, and has a good deal of human warmth. It is one of the few *zangiri mono**, or "cropped-hair plays," still in the repertory.

SUJI GUMA. "Line *kuma,*" a makeup created by Ichikawa Danjūrō II*. It is the representative *beni guma** makeup. To put it on, one draws lines from the inner ends of the eyebrows to the forehead, from the temples to the cheeks, and from the nostrils to the cheeks. Examples of characters wearing it are Gongorō in *Shibaraku** and Umeomaru in the *Kuruma Biki* scene of *Sugawara Denju Tenarai Kagami**. (*See also* KUMADORI.)

SUJI O URU. "To sell the plot"; to act in such a way that one indirectly lets the audience in on what is going to happen later in the play.

SUKASU. "To make transparent"; flat, lifeless dialogue.

SUKEROKU (YUKARI NO EDO ZAKURA). Tsuuchi Jihei II*. English title: *Sukeroku: Flower of Edo* (Brandon); *Sukeroku* (Bowers). *Sewamono**. Kabuki. One act. March 1713. Yamamura-za*, Edo.

A play belonging to the famous collection of the Ichikawa family, the *kabuki jūhachiban**. The first Sukeroku was Ichikawa Danjūrō II*, for whom the play was created. The subject matter had been familiar to Kabuki audiences for at least three decades before this work was produced. Sukeroku and Agemaki may have been actual lovers who committed double suicide, though the date of their deaths is unclear. The present work neglects the suicide aspect of the story and concentrates on Sukeroku's scheme to retrieve his family's heirloom sword.

Sukeroku, actually Soga no Gorō, is searching for his family's treasured sword, Tomokirimaru, so he spends his time in the Yoshiwara pleasure quarters, where he provokes quarrels, causing men to draw their swords. Ultimately, he learns that the bearded Ikyu, who frequents the establishment of his courtesan mistress, Agemaki, possesses the sword that he seeks. He kills Ikyu and retrieves the sword.

This plot may be simple, but the play is packed with variety—from Sukeroku's excellent speeches to the *katō bushi** style of music that accompanies his dancelike entrance *(deha*)* on the *hanamichi**. Such interesting characters as Ikyu, his followers Kanpera Monbei and Asagao Senbei, who is a country samurai, and other brothel visitors provide humorous elements. Other notable features are the gentle, delicate *wagoto** acting of Sukeroku's brother Shinbei and the dignified portrayal of the courtesan Agemaki. Sukeroku himself is played in a style combining the bravura *aragoto** method with the more elegant *wagoto**. His costume—with its two front kimono flaps pressed back to show the lining, pawlonia wood clogs, purple headband, and bull's-eye-patterned umbrella—is quite dashing and manly. Further, the splendor of the courtesans is magnificently portrayed in vividly colored costumes and elaborately coiffured wigs. When this popular piece was performed in the old days, it was patronized by the Yoshiwara and the Uogashi groups of actors' patrons. Thus, in a certain sense, the work can be seen as a drama of the townsmen. There is a *Sukeroku Kuruwa no Momo Yogusa*, acted by the Onoe family, in contrast to the present Ichikawa version.

SUKETAKAYA KODENJI II, *yago** Suketakaya. 1909- . An actor who has been a conscientious player of old-man roles since his youth. He is the adopted son of Sawamura Tosshi, debuted in 1913, and changed his name from Sawamura Harunosuke to the present one in 1927.

SUKUMIDŌ. "Shrinking body," a trick technique used in comic fight scenes to make it look as if the actor's head were hit so hard that it was driven into his torso. A frame of bamboo and rattan is erected and dressed in a costume. The actor gets inside it. As soon as he is hit on the head, he raises the frame. The effect is of his head disappearing into his body.

SUMA NO MIYAKO GENPEI TSUTSUJI. Hasegawa Senshi, Matsuda Bunkodō. Also called *Ōgiya Kumagai, Genpei Sakikage Tsuzushi. Jidaimono**. *Jōruri**. November 1730. Takemoto-za, Osaka.

The first Kabuki version of this puppet play was staged in 1736 at Osaka's Mimasu Daigorō-za. The play was supplemented by the popular Ogiya scene for the 1832 revival at Osaka's Kado no Shibai. It starred Iwai Hanshirō VII*, Nakamura Utaemon III* and was so successful that it became a featured part of subsequent revivals. Only the *Ogiya Kumagai* scene is performed today.

Taira Atsumori, who calls himself Kohagi and is disguised as a woman, has taken refuge at the home of a retainer, Ogiya Kazusa, in Gojō. He is discovered, however, and Aniwa no Heiji comes to arrest him. Kumagai Naozane happens to appear and saves Atsumori. Kazusa's daughter Katsurako, who is in love with Atsumori, is substituted for him. At Kyoto's Gojō Bridge, Atsumori confronts Kumagai and promises to meet him again on the battlefield.

There are no other love scenes in Kabuki like the one between Katsura and Atsumori, dressed as Kohagi, and this is the highlight of the play's first half. Aniwa wears the humorous *kumadori** type makeup called *kani guma* ("crab face") and, together with his retainer Kinuzumi Chuta, provides the piece with comic villainry. There is a funny scene in which they examine

Kohagi's breasts. The scene of Gojō Bridge, added later, resembles the famous meeting of Benkei and Ushiwakamaru (dramatized in *Gojō Bashi* [*see also* HASHI BENKEI]). This scene's quick changes, with Kohagi becoming Atsumori and Kumagai changing to a display of armor, make it quite pleasing visually.

SUMIDAGAWA. Yamazaki Shikō. *Shosagoto**. *Kiyomoto**. October 1919. Kabuki-za*, Tokyo.

A work deriving from the Nō play of the same name and having a musical score that is strongly modern in feeling.

A madwoman, searching for her child, comes to the ferry at the Sumida River. The boatman shows her a grave at the riverside. He tells her that a young lad in the company of slave dealers had taken ill, died, and been buried there. Learning of her child's ill fortune, she madly follows the child's apparition.

SUMIDAGAWA GONICHI NO OMOKAGE. Nagawa Shimesuke. Also called *Hokaibō, Futa Omote. Sewamono** Kabuki. Four acts. May 1784. Kado no Shibai, Osaka.

One of the richest of Kabuki plays in comic spirit. The dishonorable priest Hokaibō is humanly and amusingly portrayed as a petty crook and lecher. The final act, known as *Futa Omote*, is a dance performed to *tokiwazu** accompaniment. Ichikawa Danzō IV was the original player of Hokaibō.

As a result of his search for a family treasure (a scroll painting of a carp), the young samurai Yoshida Matsuwaka has taken service at the Eiraku-ya, under the name of Yosuke. Okumi, the daughter of the house, falls in love with him and agrees to marry Ōsakaya Gen'emon to obtain the scroll. In a room at the Saishichi, a restaurant in Mukoshima, Yosuke and Okumi are so involved in discussing the fact that Yosuke has obtained the scroll that they fail to notice Hokaibō, who comes in and replaces it with his subscription list for a temple bell. Further, Hokaibō picks up a love letter written by Yosuke to Okumi and, by means of this letter, tries to trap Yosuke. However, Jinza, a curio dealer and friend of Yosuke, is aware of Hokaibō's machinations. He manages to make a switch and reads aloud, instead, a letter that Hokaibō had written to Okumi. As a result, Hokaibō is severely chastised.

Chōkurō, a clerk at the Eiraku-ya, also tries to make Okumi his own. He ties her up and confines her in a palanquin before the Shirahige Shrine, but she is seized by Hokaibō, who hides her in a large wicker basket. Yosuke and Gen'emon appear and begin to fight with each other; Hokaibō hastily conceals himself. Yosuke kills Gen'emon. Then Jinza appears and attempts to hide the dead body in the wicker basket. He finds Okumi inside, puts the dead body inside in her place, and helps Okumi and Yosuke disguise themselves and escape. Princess Nowaki, Yosuke's betrothed from his home town, arrives in search of him; Hokaibō tries to force his attentions on her. He tells her of Yosuke's affair with Okumi. When she rejects him, he kills her; she dies in a rage of jealousy. Jinza appears again and fights with Hokaibō, whom he eventually slays. Okumi and Yosuke arrive at the Sumida River ferry, but they are plagued by the ghost of Hokaibō, who appears looking exactly like Okumi. However, the ferryman's wife, Ozushi, quells the ghost by holding up an image of the goddess Kannon.

There is a good deal of humor in the constantly changing whereabouts of the precious scroll, just as there is much interest in the suspenseful scene in which the characters struggle for Okumi before the shrine. The acting in the *Futa Omote* scene, when the ghost mimics each speech by Okumi (a technique called *ōmu** or "parroting"), is also highly effective. *Futa Omote* retains elements of the old dance style and is often performed as an independent piece.

SUMMER PLAYS. When the dog days of summer came around, it was the Edo custom to close the theatres and renovate them. Taking advantage of this period, the young actors gave performances at special reduced prices. These performances were known as *natsu kyōgen* and *doyō shibai* ("dog days theatre"). At first, most of the plays performed were from the classical puppet repertoire, but, beginning in the late eighteenth century, the majority were domestic plays closely related to the season; such, for instance, were the *mizu kyōgen**, in which real water was used, and the ghost plays*, which were said to give warm theatregoers the "chills." (*See also* BON KYŌGEN; THEATRE MANAGEMENT.)

SUNOKO. "Drainboard." The ceiling or upper part of the stage is a grid that resembles a drainboard in its construction. The Kamigata area *sunoko* is made of wood and bamboo and is called *budōdana* ("grape shelf").

SUŌ OTOSHI. Fukuchi Ōchi*. Also called *Suō Otoshi Nasu no Katari*, *Shosagoto**. *Nagauta** and *gidayū**. October 1892. Kabuki-za*, Tokyo.

A Kabuki version of a Kyōgen farce by the same name. At its first performance Ichikawa Danjūrō IX* played Tarō Kaja and Nakamura Fukusuke (later Nakamura Utaemon V*) was the uncle's daughter. Others in the cast were Ichikawa Somegorō (later Matsumoto Kōshirō VII*) and Ichikawa Shinzō.

When his master is about to leave on a pilgrimage to the Grand Shrine at Ise, Tarō Kaja, a servant, is ordered to go to his master's uncle's house and to invite the uncle along. The uncle is out just then, but his daughter appears and serves Tarō sake. After doing a dance with his fan, Tarō receives a robe *(suō)* as a going-away gift. Having returned home, he tries valiantly to hide the garment so that his master and Jirō Kaja, a rival servant, will not take it. In his drunken state, however, he lets it slip, and a struggle for it ensues.

Tarō's dance in the first half is quite delightful, as are his humorous efforts in the second half to hide the garment wherever he can, even under his arm and in his crotch.

SUPPON. "Snapping-turtle," a stage trap located at the place on the *hanamichi** called *shichisan**. It is used for the entrances of ghosts, sorcerers, and other unusual characters. It is about two feet eight inches in width and four to five feet in length and is mechanized so that the floor can go up and down. Three theories attempt to explain the derivation of the term. One claims that it comes from the resemblance of the actor's head—when it is seen rising from below—to that of a turtle in its shell. Another holds that since the corners of the trap are slightly rounded, it resembles a tortoise shell. The third theory states that the name comes from the snapping-turtle-like sound made when the trap rises fully to the level of the *hanamichi* floor.

SUPPORI. A wig built on a *daigane**, or copper head-frame, which includes a piece for the crown. Silk or paper covers the crown portion, over which *seitai**, or blue makeup, is applied. This is finished off by a coating of wax. Characters wearing it include Danshichi in *Natsu Matsuri Naniwa Kagami**, Hayami no Tōta in the Mount Yoshino scene of *Yoshitsune Senbon Zakura**, and Bannai in *Kanadehon Chūshingura**. A type with silver coating on the pate is called the *gindai no suppori* or *gin atama.*

SUTE ISHI. "Rubble mound," a scenic element of canvas-covered stones that actors sit on during conversations in certain outdoors scenes.

SUTE ZERIFU. "Throw-away speech," dialogue ad-libbed during a scene. The scene's emotional tone is retained but the actors provide their own improvised dialogue in certain "open" sections. The technique is much more frequent in domestic plays than in history plays. In many cases, improvisational dialogue has been retained and made a part of the regular script to be handed down as *kata** to future generations. (*See also* SERIFU.)

SUZUGAMORI. Tsuruya Nanboku IV*. Also called *Ukiyozuka Hyoku no Inazuma. Sewamono**. Six acts. March 1823. Ichimura-za*, Edo.

Originally played by Ichikawa Danjūrō VII* (as Chōbei) and Iwai Hanshirō VI* (as Gonpachi), this work depicts a legendary encounter between the famed *otokodate*, or "street knight," Banzui Chōbei and Shirai Gonpachi. Only Act II is still performed.

A gang of evil palanquin bearers are stationed near the Suzugamori execution grounds, where they lay in wait to rob travelers passing through. Gonpachi, who killed a man in his home province, is being sought by the police. He is fleeing to Edo when the bearers attack him in hopes of claiming a reward. He beats them off with great skill. Banzui Chōbei, who is being carried by in a palanquin, sees the attack, admires Gonpachi's ability, and promises to aid him if he is going to Edo.

Among the play's highlights are the scene of the youthful Gonpachi's often comic fight with his attackers, the famous pose taken when Gonpachi examines his blade by the light of the palanquin's paper lantern, the moment when Chōbei's voice can be heard introducing himself, and the sparkling dialogue between the two men.

SWORDS. *Katana,* an important property. It is difficult to imagine a Kabuki work about the Edo or pre-Edo periods in which swords are not essential; thus, there is a great variety of stage swords. In special cases a real sword (*see also* HONMI) is used, but normally the swords are made of lacquered oak or bamboo covered with metallic foil (*see also* TAKEMI). Metal and Duralumin are also used in fashioning stage swords. Special examples of stage swords include the *ōdachi**, a huge sword used in *aragoto** acting; the trick *nari tsuba,* whose sword guard is made so that it will ring loudly during battles; the *kabe zuru,* which is built so that the blade slides down into its central portion, but appears to have pierced a character's body; and the *oremi,* which seems to break during a battle. The blade of the long *ōdachi* used in *aragoto* plays is finished in black lacquer; scarlet coloring, called *chi nagashi* or "flowing blood" is inserted in the sword ridge. A sword that has no sword guard *(tsuba)* or sheath and is covered in silver paper is called *sanma.*

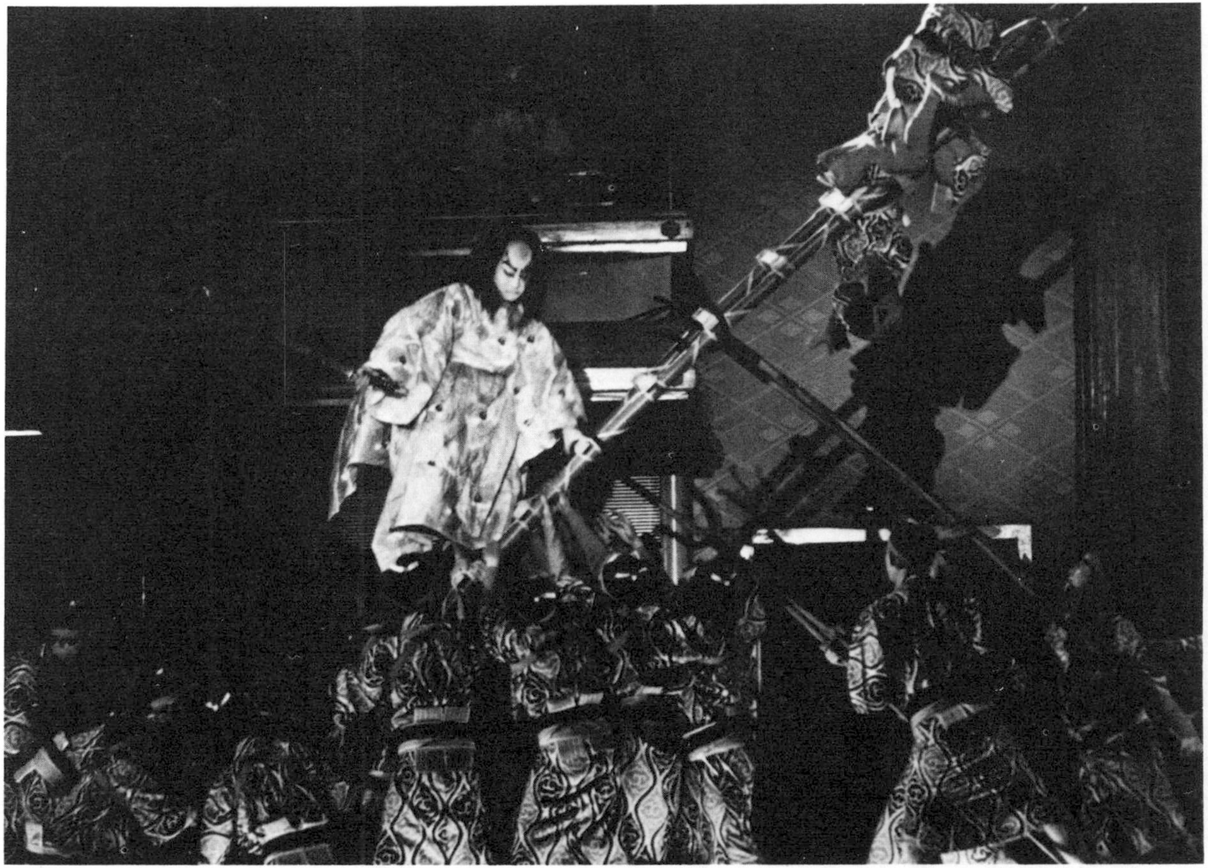

An exciting moment in *Yamatogana Ariwara Keizu** during a spectacular fight scene *(tachimawari*)*. This scene occurs amid the audience on the *hanamichi** runway. Ranpei, Bandō Minosuke VII*. *Courtesy of Waseda University Tsubouchi Engeki Hakubutsukan (Tsubouchi Memorial Theatre Museum).*

T

TABI MAWARI. "Going around in socks"; a troupe that plays only on tours.

TABO. The pouchlike arrangement of back-hair found on many wigs. (*See also* WIGS.)

TACHIMAWARI. Also called *tate,* these are the formalistic fighting methods used in such scenes of violence as military battles, murders, arrests, and quarrels. The fighting movements are intertwined with *mie** poses and have a dancelike quality. *Tachimawari* emphasize beautiful forms and have many spectacular elements. Music and the beating of clappers usually accompany classical *tachimawari,* but neither is incorporated in the fight scenes of "living history" plays* *(katsureki)* or in *shin kabuki**. Ordinarily, weapons such as swords, spears, and a small hand weapon called the *jitte* are selected, but bare-handed fighting also is seen at times. The forms *(kata*)* of *tachimawari* are choreographed and taught to the actors by a specialist called the *tateshi**. There are scores of such *kata* that may be combined in a performance.

chidori. "Plover," a technique used when a mob attacks the hero; he parries their blows one by one as they pass by him to the left and right.

ebizori. "Prawn shape," a pose taken when the hero is attacked by a crowd of opponents. He steps forward exaggeratedly, and everyone else falls over backward in a backbend position resembling the shape of a prawn.

giba. When the performer signifies his being thrashed by jumping as high as he can and landing on his buttocks with legs apart. There are several kinds of *giba:* the *mune* ("chest"), *hara ("stomach"),* and *soko* ("side") *giba.*

jakago. "Gabion," a *kata* in which a group of men holds the hero by the waist.

koshi ni tsuku. "Grabbing the waist"; a technique by which each man in the group grabs the waist of the person in front of him, forming a chain. It is seen often in *danmari** pantomimes.

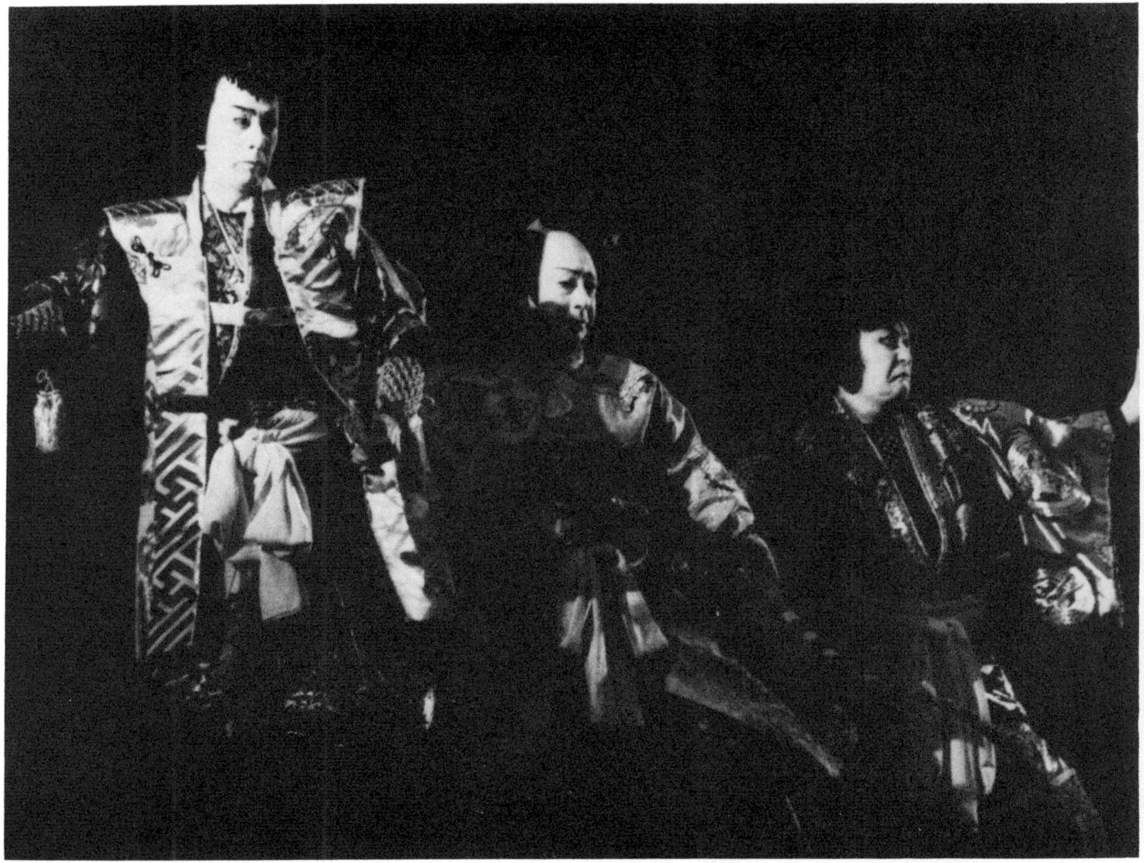

The *koshi ni tsuku* technique in the *danmari** pantomime scene of *Jiraiya*. Left to right, Ichikawa Danjūrō XI*, Onoe Baikō VII*, and Bandō Mitsugorō VIII*. *Courtesy of Waseda University Tsubouchi Engeki Hakubutsukan (Tsubouchi Memorial Theatre Museum).*

shosadate. "Pose fight," a fight scene during a dance play. It is even more formalized than other *tachimawari*. One such scene occurs between Kanpei and the flower-bearing warriors *(hanayoten; see also* YOTEN) in *Ochiudo**.

tenchi. "Heaven and earth," a technique seen during sword or spear fights when the weapons are crossed above and then below.

tonbo. Short for *tonbogaeri*, "somersaults"; also called *tonbo o kiru* ("to cut a somersault") and *kaeru* ("return"). The most important movement in stage fighting, it occurs when the actors perform somersaults at the moment of being struck or slashed at. It is said that one-third of the varieties of *tonbo* no longer exist, having been forgotten over the years. The following are still known, though: the *santoku*, in which only one foot is thrust forward onstage after a forward flip, while both hands are behind; the *atogaeri*, a back flip (as performed, for example, by the rat in the cellar scene of *Meiboku Sendai Hagi**); the *nise chū*, often seen in dances, in which one leg is thrust out on the stage as if a flip has been performed even though it has not; and the *heimagaeri*, a back flip from a kneeling position (performed by Senō in *Genpei Nunobiki no Taki**).

yamagata. The "crossing of swords." Each of two assailants swings his sword downward from overhead, first to the left of his enemy and then to the right. The term means "mountain shape."

yanagi. The "willow," an oblique parry during a fight with swords or sticks. One fighter parries a blow from behind over one shoulder without turning around.

TACHIMI. "Stand-see." Also called *hito makumi*, or "seeing one act," this means going to the theatre to see only one act of a play. This system remains only at Tokyo's Kabuki-za*. The seats sold for this purpose, *tachimi seki*, were formerly those most to the rear on the mezzanine level. Today they are in the last section of the third balcony. One reaches them from a separate entrance with its own box office. Because there is a barrier in front of the *tachimi*, the occupants of these seats are called, humorously, "bears" *(kuma)*.

TACHI NUSUBITO. Okamura Shikō*. *Shosagoto**. *Nagauta**. September 1917. Ichimura-za*, Tokyo.

A Kabuki version of the Kyōgen farce entitled *Tachibai*. Its first cast included Onoe Kikugorō VI*, Bandō Mitsugorō VI*, and Bandō Hikosaburō VI*.

A thief is accused by an official of trying to steal a country man's sword. The thief apes the country man when questioned about the sword's history, but he is found out and runs away.

The thief's acting when he mimics the country man's actions falls little by little behind the country man's tempo, providing a very amusing touch.

The wounded Senō prepares to do an acrobatic flip *(heimagaeri)* in *Genpei Nunobiki Taki**. Senō, Bandō Mitsugorō VIII*. *Courtesy of Waseda University Tsubouchi Engeki Hakubutsukan (Tsubouchi Memorial Theatre Museum).*

TACHIYAKU. Also called *tateyaku,* these are leading male roles. Originally, the word referred to the "standing" *(tachi)* actor, performing opposite the "seated" musicians. The word was used to differentiate the actors of all the male roles from those playing female or children's roles. Moreover, the word came to mean those male characters who were upright, honest, prudent, and discreet, in contrast to the types known as *oyajigata** (old men), *katakiyaku** (villains), and *dōkegata** (clowns). The classification of *tachiyaku* includes such roles as those of the superhuman warrior *(aragotoshi; see also* ARAGOTO), the weak-spirited young lover *(wagotoshi* [*see also* WAGOTO] or *nimaime*), men of judgment who clear up difficult problems *(sabaki yaku),* and men who bear up with patience under a heavy load *(shinbōyaku* or *shinbō tachiyaku*), as well as the *jitsugoto* category of mature and capable men of dignified bearing. All are important role types and play opposite the *onnagata* as leading man roles. As a rule, the leading actor of a troupe, the *zagashira**, is chosen from among the *tachiyaku.* Another term, *otokogata,* is used to distinguish all male-role actors—no matter what role type—from players of female roles.

TAIHAKU. A compressed oil used in obliterating the eyebrows. (*See also* MAYU TSUBUSHI.)

TAIKO. A stick drum. (*See also* GEZA: MUSICAL ACCOMPANIMENT CHART.)

TAIKO NO OTO CHŪ NO SANRYAKU. Kawatake Mokuami*. Also called *Sakai no Taiko, Jidaimono**. Kabuki. Four acts. March 1873. Murayama-za, Tokyo.

One of the plays in the *shin kabuki jūhachiban** collection. In its first cast were Ichikawa Danjūrō IX* and Onoe Kikugorō V*.

The castle at Hamamatsu is surrounded day and night by the enemy forces, which constantly threaten to attack. Sakai Sa'emon contrives a plan to save his master, Ieyasu, from certain death. He opens the gates of the castle and lights a watchfire within. His intention is to bring on a confrontation with the enemy. The tension mounts, but Sakai, after drinking sake, falls asleep. The shogun's tea server climbs the watchtower to strike the hour on the great drum. Seeing the castle threatened by imminent attack, he becomes panic-stricken. Sakai suddenly springs to his feet, climbs the tower, and beats the drum with great force. Hearing the sound of this drum, the enemy grows frightened of the castle's reserve strength. It raises the siege and withdraws.

TAKABA. "High place," a raised place situated on the ground-floor level of Edo period theatres in a corner behind the *oikomi** seating in the pit *(doma*).*

A theatre functionary was stationed here, holding a plan of the theatre, allocating seats, and overseeing the auditorium.

TAKADOMA. "High pit"; box seats arranged before and alongside the *sajiki** galleries on both sides of the auditorium in Edo period theatres. They were situated slightly higher than the pit *(doma*)* itself. (*See also* THEATRE ARCHITECTURE.)

TAKATOKI. Kawatake Mokuami*. Also called *Hōjō Kudai Meika no Isaoshi. Jidaimono**. Kabuki. One act. November 1884. Saruwaka-za*, Tokyo.

This play, of which only the act entitled *Takatoki* remains, is an example of the "living history" play* *(katsureki geki)* and is included in the Ichikawa Danjūrō IX* collection, the *shin kabuki jūhachiban**. Danjūrō IX was the first Takatoki, in a cast that included Nakamura Utaemon V* and Ichikawa Gonjurō.

Adachi Saburō, a masterless samurai, has killed Shogun Takatoki's pet dog. The high-handed Takatoki is furious and intends to have Saburō executed. This is prevented through the intervention of the priest Shironosuke. Takatoki is having a drinking party with his concubine, Kinugasa, when the lights are extinguished suddenly and a large number of long-nosed goblins *(tengu)* appear. They ridicule the shogun, forcing him to dance until he faints. Recovering his senses, Takatoki glares in vexation at the mocking *tengu* voices that he hears in the air.

Highlights include the unusual *tengu* dance and the striking pose taken by Takatoki as, spear by his side, he stares into the air.

TAKATSUKI. Hisamatsu Hitokeo. *Shosagoto*. Nagauta**. September 1933. Tōkyō Gekijō, Tokyo.

A work created by Onoe Kikugorō VI*, who incorporated tap dancing, popular at the time, into its structure.

A *daimyō* has gone flower viewing. As there are no serving tables for the wine cups, he sends his servant, Jirō Kaja, for them. Jirō is duped into buying high clogs *(geta)* instead. Moreover, he drinks a gourd of sake together with the clog seller, puts on the clogs, and begins to dance. Seeing this, the lord gets furious and runs after the servant.

This is a charming dance in Kyōgen farce style, the highlight being the rhythmic stamping of the clogs during Jirō's dancing.

TAKEDA IZUMO I. d. 1747. A puppet-theatre playwright who, in November 1705, convinced Takemoto Gidayū (1651-1714), the famous chanter and founder of the Takemoto-za, not to retire (*see also* GIDAYŪ BUSHI). He became the theatre's manager, for which he won fame.

II. 1691-1756. Son of Izumo I, he inherited the theatre's management from his father. He took the playwright's pen name of Senzenken and collaborated in writing such major works as *Ashiya Dōman Ōuchi Kagami**, *Sugawara Denju Tenarai Kagami**, *Yoshitsune Senbon Zakura**, and *Kanadehon Chūshingura**. His endeavors during the golden age of puppet drama were outstanding.

TAKEMI. The bamboo swords wielded by Kabuki actors. They are designed to look like real swords, which are used only on special occasions. It is said that real swords have been prohibited for stage use since 1704, when Ichikawa Danjūrō I* was slain during a performance by another actor. (*See also* HONMI; SWORDS.)

TAKEMOTO GIDAYŪ. 1651-1714. Founder of the *gidayū bushi** style of narrative recital.

TAKESHIBA KISUI. 1847-1923. A playwright born in Edo, he studied with Sakurada Jisuke III* and later became the pupil of Kawatake Mokuami*. He wrote such plays as *Bunkaku Kanjinchō* for Ichikawa Danjūrō IX* while chief playwright *(tate sakusha*)* at the Shintomi-za (*see also* MORITA-ZA) and Kabuki-za*. His *Kami no Megumi Wagō no Torikumi** and *Ueno Senjō* were written for Onoe Kikugorō V*, while *Matsuda no Kenka* and *Tōyama Sakura* were created for Ichikawa Sadanji I*. His output includes over seventy plays.

TAMAMONO MAE (ASAHI NO TAMOTO). Chikamatsu Baishiken, Sagawa Totarō. Also called *Tamasan, Michiharu Yakata. Jidaimono**. *Jōruri**. Five acts. March 1806. Mitama Keidai Shibai, Osaka.

Baishiken and Tōtarō's play is actually a revision of a 1751 work by Namioka Kippei and others. The play dramatizes the legend of a magical fox. Only Act III, set at Michiharu's palace, is still performed.

Washizuka Kintōji comes to the palace of Michiharu, Minister of the Right, on orders from Prince Usuyuki. Kintōji's task is to receive the sword called Shishio ("King of the Beasts"), which is supposedly in the possession of Michiharu's wife, Haginokata. However, as the sword has been lost, Michiharu's two daughters, Katsura and Hatsunoha, are made to play a game of *sugoroku* (a board game). The loser's head is to be taken back in lieu of the missing sword. Princess Katsura wins, yet Kintōji deliberately kills her. It turns out that Katsura is Kintōji's own daughter, whom he had abandoned years before, and that he had stolen the sword himself.

This has roughly the same plot as the *Benkei Jōshi* scene of *Goshō Zakura Horikawa Youchi**. Haginokata's display of affection for Katsura, whom she has raised as her own, and the reversal of Kintōji's evil character at the end are the work's main features.

TAMERU. To take plenty of time in performing one's speech or action.

TAPPA. The height of the proscenium from floor to lower edge. The term is used also to speak of the height of the stage scenery and platforms. It was originally an architectural term referring to the height of buildings such as houses.

TASUKERU. "To help out." When an actor has to appear onstage so often that he has no time to get into costume and makeup for one of his roles; he will get another actor to play the role for him and will not appear in the part at all. When this happens, it is described by the term *tasukeru.*

TATE GATAKI. A major villain's role. (*See also* KATAKIYAKU.) Minor villains are *hagataki**.

TATE ONNAGATA. "Chief female impersonator." Known also as *tate oyama,* this is the highest-ranking *onnagata** in a troupe or at a theatre. He holds the rank following the *zagashira**, or troupe leader, and is in charge of the *onnagata* of the company. Although it has been rare, some *tate onnagata* also held the rank of *zagashira* simultaneously. (*See also* ACTORS' RANKS.)

TATE SAKUSHA. "Chief playwright," who is also called *tate tsukuri* and *rissakusha.* The *tate sakusha* was at the head of a playhouse's literary staff. He was responsible for the dramatic values of the production and held a very important troupe position. He devised the play's overall plot, drew up a plan of its structure, and, in consultation with the manager and leading actor, decided on the company's repertory. When a new play was to be written, he devised a scenario and divided the writing duties between the *nimaime sakusha** and the *sanmaime sakusha**. He then read and corrected the results. He also had the job of writing the most important act of the play. According to Kawatake Mokuami's* *Kyōgen Sakusha no Kokoroe (A Rule Book for Playwrights)* the *tate sakusha*'s responsibility, in the case of major plays and *kaomise** works, was to write the pantomimes *(danmari*),* denouement *(ōzume*),* and domestic play scenes. Accompanied by the *nimaime sakusha,* he read the uniformly revised script to the manager and leading actor, corrected it according to their ideas, discussed the casting, and made up a clean copy. Later, he read the play *(honyomi*)* to a gathering of all those involved with the production just prior to the start of formal rehearsals. It was also his responsibility to see to matters ranging from the designs for the billboards and programs to the layout and design of the sets. If he had artistic skill, he made a sketch of the set himself; if not, he guided someone else in designing it. As Mokuami was an expert at drawing, he designed his own sets. His beautiful pictures have been left to posterity. The *tate sakusha* attended rehearsals, watched the entire play, corrected the dialogue, and made cuts in the script. Many of his duties were those associated with the modern director. (*See also* PLAYWRIGHTS' RANKS.)

TATESHI. "Fight scene master," a specialist attached to a theatre who devises all the fight scenes *(tachimawari*)* involving battling with long swords, judo, and the like. He discusses things with the leading actor and arranges everything beforehand with a subordinate actor as a partner. Then, with music and wooden clappers *(tsuke*)*, he substitutes for the chief actor, demonstrates the movements, and sets them. In the old days, this was the job of the chief of the lower grade of actors, which was called the *ōbeya**.

TATE WAKARE. The division of *shamisen** players and singers into two groupings when a *nagauta** performance requires at least two lead performers for each. An example occurs in *Imoseyama Onna Teikin**.

TATSUOKA MANSAKU. 1742-1809. A playwright and son of the actor Tatsuoka Mankiku. Originally an actor, he studied playwriting under Namiki Gohei I* and Nagawa Kamesuke*. Along with Gohei and Chikamatsu Tokusō*, he was a leading Kamigata dramatist of the Tenmei period (1781-88). History plays were his forte, as were revisions of old plays. Mansaku's works include *Keisei Haru no Tori, Anuimoto Date no Okidō,* and *Hade Kurabe Ishikawa Some.*

TATTSUKE. A kind of *hakama** whose lower part dovetails into tight leggings; they were worn originally by travelers. The *tattsuke* are worn by characters like Kakubei in *Echigo Jishi**. In Edo period Kabuki, theatre ushers *(dekata*)* wore a solid blue version of these pants.

TAYŪ. One meaning is "master," the highest position that an *onnagata** can hold. Since the term originally was given to the highest-ranking courtesans, the actresses in Kabuki's early form, *yujō kabuki* or courtesan Kabuki*, were *tayū* and the leader and producer was the *tayūmoto*. The *onnagata* period followed later, and it is thought that the term simply remained. Further, many of the heroines in the early plays were courtesans. Since the leading *onnagata* played these roles, they also came to be called *tayū*. Moreover, the word was used to designate musicians of *gidayū** and *jōruri** music, as many of the persons who supervised public entertainments and ceremonies from ancient times were of noble rank. Such persons were called *tayū*, so the term seems to have been a conventional reference to people connected with public entertainments.

Also refers to the man responsible for putting on plays at a theatre. This usage probably stems from the practice of calling early procurers by this name. Since Edo theatre proprietors were frequently engaged in the brothel business as well, *tayūmoto* became an alternate term for *zamoto**.

TEAHOUSES. *See* SHIBAIJAYA.

TEIKOKU GEKIJŌ. The "Imperial Theatre," located in Yuraku-chō, Chiyoda-ku, Tokyo. It opened in March 1911 as Japan's first purely Western-style theatre. Its accoutrements and management were totally modern, and its exterior was in Renaissance style. Western seats were used throughout the interior, a reserved-seat ticket system was established, there were usherettes and restaurants, and so on. It was rebuilt after the 1923 earthquake and continued to produce plays until after World War II. In January 1964 the theatre was closed while it was demolished and rebuilt. It reopened, totally new, in September 1966. This large and well-appointed playhouse belongs to the Tōhō* company's network of theatres. (*See also* THEATRE MANAGEMENT.)

TENBENI. "Heavenly red"; courtesans' letters. The name derives from the red part at the top of the letter. *Mino*-type paper, or drawing silk that is backed by paper, is the material used for such missives.

TENJIKU TOKUBEI (IKOKU BANASHI). Tsuruya Nanboku IV*. Also called *Oto ni Kiku Tenjiku Tokubei. Jidaimono**. Kabuki. Five acts. July 1804. Kawarazaki-za, Edo.

A drama largely based on the *Tenjiku Tokubei Monogatari*, a verbatim record ascribed to the Edo merchant marine Tenjiku, who had been to India. There are a number of earlier and later plays dealing with this material; they are known collectively as "Tenjiku Tokubei plays" *(tenjiku tokubei mono)*. Onoe Matsusuke I* was the first star of the present play.

Yoshieka Sōkan in reality is the Korean warrior Moku Sōkan. In order to accomplish his goal of overthrowing the Japanese government, he teaches his son, Ōhimaru (Tokubei), how to practice sorcery. He then kills himself. Tokubei uses his magic skills to appear and disappear, but his magic is foiled at the Higashiyama Palace by the lifeblood of a woman born in the hour, day, and year of the Serpent.

Highlights include the quick costume changes and acrobatic acting. At one point Tokubei appears as a huge toad. There is an unusual underwater quick change that is especially noteworthy.

TENTEN. A word taken from the name of the music played in Act III of *Kanadehon Chūshingura** when Momoi Wakasanosuke enters in a rage. It now implies a state of indignation or anger.

TEODORI. "Hand dance"; expressive movements of the hands while dancing, but without using any hand props such as towels or fans.

TEREKO. The playwriting practice of taking two completely different plots and combining them into a single plot; each plot has sufficient connection with the other to help develop the action. The word has come to have the meaning of "to put things in the wrong place." (*See also* PLAYWRITING.)

TEUCHI. When a theatre troupe agrees to bear all expenses for a production, including the rental of the theatre. The normal procedure is to work on a percentage agreement and not to carry the entire load. (*See also* THEATRE MANAGEMENT.)

Another meaning is the celebratory hand-clapping of a group of backers at the ceremonial parts of a *kaomise** production in the Edo period.

Finally, *teuchi* refers to the ceremonial hand-clapping—striking the palms together for three claps, three times in succession—on cementing an agreement. It is done at a company's first rehearsal at the close of the ceremonial preliminaries.

THEATRE ARCHITECTURE.

theatre buildings. When the *onna kabuki,* or women's Kabuki* troupe of Izumo no Okuni* performed its dances in the dry bed of the Kamo River in Kyoto during the Keichō era (1596-1614), it employed a stage modeled after that used in the special public performances of Nō theatre *(kanjin nō),* by which money was raised for some charitable cause. The gable-roofed stage was a square measuring twelve feet (later, eighteen) in each direction. It was equipped with a bridgeway *(hashigakari)* and backstage* dressing room *(gakuya).* The audience arrangement consisted of a *doma**, or pit area, in front of the stage and raised galleries, called *sajiki**, to the left and right of the stage. The *sajiki* were considered the best seats. As there was no roof over the

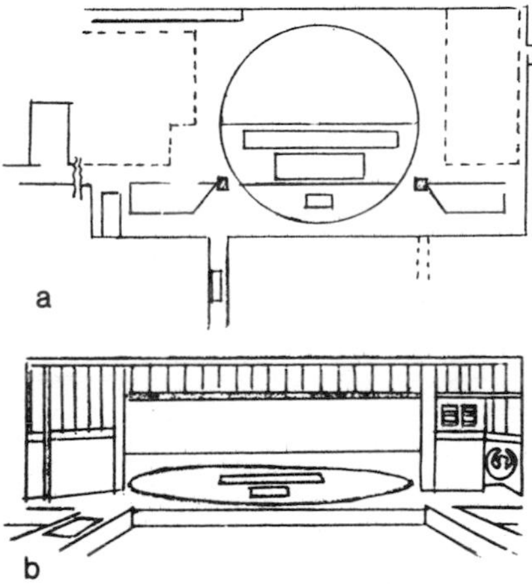

(a) Plan of Kabuki-za* stage. (b) Front view of Kabuki-za stage.

pit, it was inevitable that something be built to protect the people there from the elements. It was customary for the walls surrounding the theatre to be in the fashion of a bamboo palisade, and a tower *(yagura*)* was erected at the front. Below the *yagura* was a small entrance door *(nezumi kido*)*. The spectators had to bend over to pass through. A single billboard *(kanban*)* was hung just beneath the tower.

There was a gradual development of theatre architecture as Kabuki passed from women's Kabuki to *wakashu kabuki*, or young men's Kabuki*, and then to *yarō kabuki*, or mature male Kabuki*. With the advent of the Kanbun era (1661-72), a traveler curtain *(hikimaku** or *jōshiki maku*)* and stage sets came into use, the old Nō style bridgeway was shortened, and a forestage *(tsuke butai)* was created. Further, it is conjectured that the *hanamichi**, Kabuki's own bridgeway, was erected so that gifts *(hana)* could be presented to the actors. During the Genroku era (1688-1703) the scale of the theatres increased, Edo's Nakamura-za* growing to a width of 66 feet, a length of 90 feet, and a stage width of 30 feet. Kyoto's Minamigawa Shibai was far larger than those in Edo, having dimensions of 96 feet by 180 feet. It was in this period that illustrated billboards (*see also* KANBAN: E KANBAN) began to appear at the front of the theatres. During the Kyōhō era (1716-35) a wooden roof was added, the forestage grew increasingly wider, the *hanamichi* came to be used as an extension of the stage's acting area, and a three-storied backstage area was constructed. In the Genbun era (1736-40), a "name-saying platform" *(nanoridai*)* held a temporary position at the side of the *hanamichi*, midway down its length. The pit of the Nakamura-za of this period supposedly was capable of seating 800 spectators. During the Hōreki (1751-63) and the Meiwa (1764-71) years, the revolving stage* *(mawari butai)*, the *seri** traps, the *gandōgaeshi** technique (whereby a whole set is turned over on an axis to reveal its underside, consisting of another set), the *hikiwari** setting (in which a set is rolled off to left and right, revealing another set behind), and other scenic techniques were invented. (*See also* SCENERY.) In the Anei era (1772-80) a temporary *(kari) hanamichi* was set up on the right side of the auditorium. It faced the regular *(hon) hanamichi* on the audience's left. The gabled roof over the stage was removed during the Kansei era (1789-1800), making the Kabuki stage completely free of the Nō theatre's architecture.

As later years saw no conspicuous stage inventions, we may say that the Kabuki stage reached a stage of perfection during the Bunka-Bunsei period (1804-30). In 1872, however, the newly build Morita-za* (later called the Shintomi-za) had a frontage of 108 feet and a depth of 139 feet. These dimensions put it on a much grander scale than the Edo theatres that had preceded it. It was constructed with a tin roof, as a fire precaution. There was no forestage, a picture-frame stage was employed, and a number of other reforms were incorporated. In 1911, the Teikoku Gekijō* was built in

Western style throughout. It had a great influence on the building of many Japanese theatres thereafter.

theatre interiors. On entering a Kabuki theatre, one comes upon a broad lobby filled with information booths, shops, checkrooms, smoking parlors, dining rooms, and so forth. These modern innovations began with the Teikoku Gekijō's construction in 1911. Passing through the lobby, the spectator arrives at the doors to the auditorium. Nowadays, almost all seating is Western style, but there may be some *tatami* mat seating in the *sajiki* areas on the sides of the theatre.

A newcomer to a Kabuki theatre is invariably struck by the sight of the *hanamichi*, a raised passageway on the audience's left that passes through the auditorium from the rear to the stage proper and is considered an extension of the acting area. When the small curtain *(agemaku*)* at the audience's rear is pulled aside for an actor's *hanamichi* appearance, the interior room from which the actor appears is revealed. This room is the *toya.* At Tokyo's Kabuki-za*, directly opposite the *toya*—at the rear of the auditorium on the right—is the *kanji shitsu** ("supervisor's booth"), a room where those in charge of the production sit to watch the performance. In the case of the Kokuritsu Gekijō (National Theatre of Japan*) this room is just to the right of the *hanamichi.*

A proscenium arch separates the audience from the stage. A curtain, either pulled in traveler fashion or flown, is situated here. Within the stage area, to the rear and sides, are the dressing rooms and backstage areas *(gakuya).*

THEATRE MANAGEMENT. *Kanjin* ("subscription") is a word originally used to refer to the acts of accepting admission fees and presenting performances. The dances of Kabuki's legendary founder Izumo no Okuni*—in the dry bed of Kyoto's Kamo River—were a type of *kanjin.* Soon, imitators of Okuni sprang up, and the promoter (called *seisakusha* today, but originally known as the *kanjinmoto*) came into existence to bring about a more efficient means of gathering income from performances. Thus began the business end of producing Kabuki.

In February 1624, Nakamura (Saruwaka) Kanzaburō I* built Edo's first theatre, at Nakabashi. Seven theatres were licensed in Kyoto during the Genma period (1615-23). In Osaka it was during the Keian era (1648-52) that Araki Yojibei* was first given permission to open a theatre. Thus, by the mid-seventeenth century, Kabuki had received governmental recognition and the business of putting on plays had begun.

Authority to produce plays was absolute. The man holding the franchise to do was the *zamoto** (also called the *tayūmoto* [*see also* TAYŪ] and, in Osaka, the *nadai**), and great weight was placed on the hereditary nature of the position. Along with the growth of Kabuki production the one-man *zamoto* system occasionally gave way to a partnership operation with each of several financial backers *(kinshu*)* contributing his share to the production of plays. When his theatre hit a slump, the *zamoto* would sometimes enter into a collaborative relationship with another *zamoto* and produce plays in alternation with him. (*See also* HIKAE YAGURA; YAGURA.)

Because of the limited lighting equipment at theatres, Edo period performances generally were held from 6 A.M. to 6 P.M. (from dawn to dusk). This custom continued till the Meiji era. In 1878 the Shintomi-za (*see also* MORITA-ZA) began the performance of evening programs. Afterwards, when electric lighting was installed, evening performances became common. In April 1912, the Teikoku Gekijō added eight matinees to their monthly schedule. Sometime later, the production system was changed to a two-part daily bill. A run lasted about twenty-five days with a new program every month. This system still holds true at a number of theatres. (*See also* NIBUSEI.)

During the Edo era there were regular annual theatre events following a prescribed format, year after year. In November, after the theatre had engaged a new line-up of players, the *kaomise** or "face-showing" performances were given, the purpose being to introduce the new faces to the public. Then there was the New Year's performance*, called the *hatsuharu kyōgen* or *ni no kawari.* Following it was the *san no kawari* or *yayoi* program ("spring plays*"), usually held in March. Then came May's *satsuki kyōgen**, the *bon** and *natsu kyōgen* ("summer plays*") of summer, the *aki kyōgen* ("autumn plays*"), and finally the *mochitsuki shibai,* an end-of-the-year program put on by second-class actors during the break between the *kaomise* closing of December 10 and the opening of the New Year's program. Scarcely any of these annual events are observed today. Other unique events included special performances commemorating the year of a theatre's founding *(kotobuki kōgyō*)* or the death of a great star *(tsuizen kōgyō).*

THEATRE STREET. Called *shibai machi,* which also referred to a residential district for theatre people. During the Edo period, theatres were permitted to produce plays only in specific locations. The intent was to make government supervision easier and also to provide a preventive measure against conflagration. Theatres could not produce plays and theatre personnel could not live in any other area. Early Edo theatre streets were Sakai-chō, Fukuya-chō, and Kobiki-chō. After 1842 and until the Meiji Restoration of 1868, the theatre street was Saruwaka-machi* in Edo's Asakusa section, located on the outskirts of town. Osaka's theatre street was Dōtonbori, and Kyoto's was Shijō.

TITLES. *Nadai* or *geidai* is the title of a Kabuki play. The convention of writing Kabuki titles using an odd number of Chinese characters (three, five, or seven) began in the late seventeenth century. To offset the restricted choices to which this convention led, the Japanese syllabary *(kana)* was employed. The syllabary was printed in small figures alongside the Chinese characters so that the title could present a different reading than the one offered by a strict adherence to the Chinese characters. Puppet plays in particular were given titles whose Chinese characters often had no relation to the actual words with which the title was read. This is one reason that it is almost impossible to translate meaningfully many Kabuki titles into English. The Japanese themselves are frequently at a loss when it comes to understanding the meaning of formal titles.

The word *nadai* also refers to the leading class of actors, those whose names appeared on the billboards and in the programs. (*See also* ACTORS' RANKS.)

TOBAE. Sakurada Jisuke II*. Also called *Ōnnagori Oshie no Mazebari. Shosagoto*. Kiyomoto*.* September 1819. Nakamura-za*, Edo.

A dance that captures the humorous flavor of the cartoon-like comic pictures called *tobae,* first created by Toba Sōjō in the middle ages. The present work is all that remains of a nine-change *henge mono,* or "transformation piece*."

The comic manservant Masuroku chases after a mouse with a measuring box while wearing his nightclothes, a pestle sprouts wings, and other funny things happen during this lighthearted dance.

First created by Nakamura Utaemon III*, this piece was a specialty of Onoe Kikugorō VI* as well.

TOCHIRU. "To fumble"; when an actor makes a mistake in his dialogue or business or when something goes wrong because of a stagehand's error. It was the convention for the one who was at fault to apologize by serving noodles *(soba)* to everyone backstage. This gives us the expression *tochiri soba,* which is something like "to eat humble pie."

TŌDORI. The person who supervises everything that goes on backstage, that is, the "backstage manager." The first Nakamura Kanzaburō* selected one of his senior pupils for this position, and thereafter the job fell to senior actors with thorough knowledge of backstage and general theatre affairs. It was thus a position of authority. The *tōdori* sat in a room (the *tōdori za*) backstage near the dressing room entrance. The room was built a step higher than the floor proper. Aside from the *tōdori* himself, no one but the producer or his son could enter the *tōdori za,* and the actors had to bow before it when passing. The *tōdori* checked the company attendance before the theatre opened. Then he had to negotiate with the front office for the day's payment allocations, select substitute actors, make notifications of their substitution, attend to paging duties, manage all backstage notices, mediate in quarrels, and take care of a variety of other things, as well as seeing to the formal announcement called *kiri kōjō* (*see also* KŌJŌ) made at the end of the performance. Only his title still remains, the job having become little more than the management of miscellaneous backstage duties. Even the *tōdori za*, once so highly respected a place, is referred to today as a mere "stage office" *(butai jimushō)*.

TŌHŌ. The short way of referring to the Tōhō Kabushiki Gaisha (Tōhō Joint Stock Corporation). It and Shōchiku* are today's most powerful Japanese theatrical combines. The company was founded in August 1932 by Kobayashi Ichizō (1873-1957). Coming into the possession of a Tokyo theatre that housed a girls' opera company, he inaugurated his company as the Joint Stock Company of the Tokyo Takarazuka Gekijō. In 1934 he erected the Tokyo Takarazuka Gekijō in the city's Hibiya section. A year later he built the Yuraku-za, which put on plays with the Tōhō theatre troupe. The year 1943 saw the merger of the Tōhō Joint Stock Motion Picture Company (Tōhō Eiga Kabushiki Gaisha), which was renamed the Tōhō Joint Stock Company. However, a great blow was struck by a 1945 movie lot strike, which dragged on for about five years. The once purged Kobayashi was reinstated as company president, and the company's fortunes were revived. Today, Tōhō's theatre empire includes the Takarazuka girls' company, musicals, movies, drama, and so forth. Centered in Tokyo's Yurakuchō district are the Tokyo Takarazuka Gekijō, the Nihon Gekijō, the Teikoku Gekijō*, the Geijitsu-za, and others, all actively producing a variety of theatrical entertainments. Tōhō Kabuki, as it is called, which features the work of Hasegawa Kazuo and Yamada Isuzō, was founded with the aim of competing with the classical Kabuki staged by Shōchiku* by offering new plays. In 1961 several Shōchiku Kabuki stars, including Matsumoto Kōshirō VIII*, Nakamura Matagorō II*, Ichikawa Chūsha VIII*, and others were lured to Tōhō, which from that time has endeavored to produce classical Kabuki along with its other types of drama. (*See also* THEATRE MANAGEMENT.)

TOITAGAESHI. The "rain-door switch," a special effect used in *Tōkaidō Yotsuya Kaidan**. The character of Oiwa is murdered, and her corpse is lashed to a rain door. This door is constructed with a head-size hole, where the corpse's head is placed. Lashed to the other side of the door is the body of Kōhei, the servant, who has also been slain. The bodies of Oiwa and Kōhei are represented by headless dummies. When the door is leaned against a riverside embankment, an actor puts his head through the hole to suggest the character seen by the audience. The actor is hidden behind the door in a secret compartment within the embankment. By means of a rapid makeup change, the same actor can appear as Kōhei and Oiwa. (*See also* SCENERY.)

TŌJŪRŌ NO KOI. Kikuchi Kan. English title: *Tōjūrō's Love* (Shaw). *Shin kabuki**. One act, three scenes, October 1919. Roka-za, Osaka.

A drama based on anecdotes concerning the famous late-seventeenth-century actor Sakata Tōjūrō*. Tōjūrō is to play the role of Mippu in the premiere of a new Chikamatsu Monzaemon* play and is worried over the proper approach to his part. He seduces Okaji, wife of the owner of the Munekiyo teahouse. She is unfamiliar with the play and accepts his wooing; he dodges her and leaves. He receives great praise for his performance, which he has modeled after his experience with Okaji, whose heart he has so carelessly trampled on. After first hinting to the actor that she will do so, Okaji commits suicide backstage. Nevertheless, Tōjūrō will not allow a woman's death to influence his art. Looking indifferently at her corpse, he leaves it to make his appearance on stage.

In a way, this is a play about "art": It depicts the character of a famous artist who will not permit even the sacrifice of a human life to hinder the progress of his work.

TŌKAIDŌ YOTSUYA KAIDAN. Tsuruya Nanboku IV*. Also called *Yotsuya Kaidan. Sewamono**. Kabuki. Five acts. July 1825. Nakamura-za*, Edo.

Onoe Kikugorō III* was a big success in the first production; he played the three roles of Oiwa, Kōhei, and Yomoshichi, using quick-change techniques*. Ie'mon was played by Ichikawa Danjūrō IX* with Iwai Hanshirō VI* and Matsumoto Kōshirō V* in other roles. The play is one of Kabuki's greatest ghost stories, by the master of the genre.

Tamiya Ie'mon, a masterless samurai of the Enya (Akō) clan, has been living a dissolute life since the demise of his master. After being urged by Yotsuya Samon—father of his common-law wife, Oiwa—to separate from the girl, he kills the old man in an Asakusa rice field. At the same time Naosuke Gonbei, a hawker of medicine, bears a jealous grudge toward Osōde, Oiwa's sister. He kills the samurai Okuda Shozaburō, his former master, mistaking him for Sato Yomoshichi, Osōde's lover. Deceived by Ie'mon and Naosuke into believing that they will be revenged for the deaths of Samon and Yomoshichi, Oiwa pairs up again with Ie'mon and Osōde is linked to Naosuke in a common-law marriage (Act I).

Ie'mon, who has grown weary of his wife following her difficult postnatal convalescence, agrees to marry Oume, the daughter of the neighboring Itō family. The Ito family gives Oiwa what they say is a medicine; it is really a poison. When she drinks it, her face becomes horribly disfigured. Oiwa learns of her husband's true feelings and dies bearing great hatred for him. Ie'mon kills Osaragi Kōhei, a servant who tries to steal a miracle drug in Ie'mon's possession, and he nails Oiwa and Kōhei to the sides of a large rain door that he sets adrift on the river (*see also* TOITAGAESHI). Later, the malice of his dead wife's spirit forces him to kill both Itō and his daughter, who have come to his house (Act II).

While fishing at the Onbō Canal, Ie'mon throws Itō's wife and her maid (who have come there as beggars) into the river, where they drown. However, the ghosts of Oiwa and Kōhei, whose bodies float by on the rain door, begin to haunt him (Act III).

Naosuke and his common-law wife, Osōde, are living at the Sankaku mansion at the Fuku River. Naosuke learns of Oiwa's death from the sight of her comb, which has been retrieved from the canal. Desiring to avenge the deaths of Samon, Oiwa, and Yomoshichi, Naosuke and Osōde pledge their troth as man and wife, but Yomoshichi, whom they believed dead, now appears. In order to atone to Yomoshichi for her life of adultery with Naosuke, Osōde causes Naosuke to kill her. From her farewell note Naosuke learns that she was, in actuality, his own younger sister. The man whom Naosuke had killed was not Yomoshichi, but his own former master. In expiation he commits suicide (Act IV).

Ie'mon, who has taken refuge on Mount Hebi, is haunted by ghosts and is finally killed by Yomoshichi (Act V).

Act II presents a skillful fusion of the real and the unreal in the brutality of Ie'mon and the gloomy death of Oiwa. Other outstanding features are the use of mechanical tricks to make the ghosts appear in Acts III and V and the clever plotting of cause and effect in Act IV. This is no simple ghost story; its callous depiction of society and human emotions offer ample reason for its durability, even on today's stage. The use of masterless samurai from the Akō clan (the clan that figures in the famous vendetta dramatized in *Kanadehon Chūshingura**) and the reciprocal relation of certain points in the play to *Kanadehon Chūshingura* were primary factors in this drama's success when it was first produced.

TŌKICHI RYŪ. A style of calligraphy seen on programs and billboards in the Kamigata area during the Edo period. This method features sharp, angular strokes, as opposed to the rounded style of Edo's Kantei* school. It was founded by Nan'oken Tōkichi, a clerk in the cashier's office at the Osaka Kaku no Shibai (a theatre).

TOKI WA IMA KIKKYŌ NO HATAAGE. Tsuruya Nanboku IV*. Also called *Badarai no Mitsuhide, Tokimo Kikkyō Shusse no Ukejō. Jidaimono**. Kabuki. Five acts. July 1808. Ichimura-za*, Edo.

A work that depicts the problems involved in the rebellion carried out by Akechi Mitsuhide. It is based on such puppet theatre works as *Mikka Taiheiki* (1767) and *Ehon Taikōki**. Matsumoto Kōshirō V* was the first Mitsuhide, and Sawamura Sōjūrō IV* played Harunaga. The two main acting traditions for Mitsuhide are those originated by Kōshirō and Ichikawa Danjūrō IX*. The former invests the role with a quality of the villain *(katakiyaku*)* style developed by the Ichikawa Danzō* line, but the latter stresses the role's straightforward qualities as a *tachiyaku** hero.

Mitsuhide has been ordered to prepare a banquet for the Imperial messenger, but his lord, Oda Harunaga, claims that Misuhide's behavior is treasonous. He orders Mori Ranmaru to strike Mitsuhide on the forehead with an iron fan and then has Mitsuhide put in domiciliary confinement. Through the offices of Ranmaru, Mitsuhide is forced to drink sake from a tub used to wash horses' feet *(badarai)*. He also is given the bobbed hair of his wife, Satsuki, who had sold it during Mitsuhide's period of wandering as a masterless samurai. These insulting acts disgrace Mitsuhide before the assembled company. He returns to an inn on Mount Atago where Shōha, engaged with him in a game of linked verse, urges him to rebel against Harunaga, whom Mitsuhide now hates. Mitsuhide kills Shōha, though. Messengers come from Harunaga and report that Misuhide's property is to be confiscated. Mitsuhide kills them and now resolves to rebel.

Nanboku's most original treatment of his materials is actually in a part of the play that is no longer presented, the first half of Act I. Instead, audiences are shown Mitsuhide's rather modern temperament, which is displayed in the psychological movement toward his eventual decision to rebel.

TOKIWAZU BUSHI. A musical narrative *(jōruri*)* form created by Miyakoji (later Tokiwazu) Mojidayū (1709-1781), following the 1739 prohibition against the *bungo bushi** music of his master, Miyakoji Bungonojō (1660?-1740), for having a harmful effect on the citizenry. From its inception, *tokiwazu* was considered a style for use in Kabuki musical narration and came to play an important part both as a narrative style and as a dance-drama music. Representative works include *Seki no To**, *Modori Kago**, *Utsubo Zaru**, and *Noriaibune**.

TOKOYAMA. The man who receives the wig from the wig maker *(katsuraya)* and specializes in its handling. After the wig maker has attached the hair to the copper base *(daigane*)* and painted the crown blue or attached hair to it, thus completing its basic construction, the *tokoyama* combs and dresses it according to the role in which it will be worn. He then brings it to the actor, takes care of it during the run, keeps all the wigs in order, and is in charge of all matters related to the wigs. He occupies a special room backstage (the *tokoyama beya*). In the Edo period the *tokoyama* in charge of male wigs worked in a third-floor room, near the male-role actors, while those handling the female wigs used a second-floor room near the *onnagata**. (*See also* WIGS.)

TOMEBA. An Edo period functionary who prevented people from entering the theatre for free and from quarreling inside the theatre. The *tomeba* gathered closely together at a place near the left side of the theatre's entrance. From among them were chosen the guards who sat on stage left to suppress undue activity in the audience (they also were called *butai ban**) and the guards (called *nanakuchi*) who kept watch at each of the theatre's entrances and exits. Later, they were included among the *dekata** ushers.

TŌMI. "Distant view," a background showing a scenic vista. Those with mountains painted on them are *yama tōmi*, those with seas are *umi tōmi*, those with a row of houses are *chōya tōmi*, those with garden landscapes are *niwa tōmi*, those with fields are *yahata tōmi*, and so on. Vistas that allow the light from lamps or the moon to shine through from the background, thus representing an evening scene, are called "light-entering vistas" *(tōiri no tōmi)*.

TOMIMOTO BUSHI. A musical narrative *(jōruri*)* style created in 1747 by Tomimoto Toyoshidayū (1716-1764), who splintered off from the *tokiwazu bushi** school and changed his name to Tomimoto Buzennojō I. His son Buzennojō II (1754-1822) brought about the "golden age" of *tomimoto* music. With the advent of *kiyomoto** music this style declined, and by the Meiji period there was no traditional leader *(iemoto*)* of the school. *Kurama Jishi* is a well-known *kiyomoto* piece in which *tomimoto* passages may be heard as a part of the accompaniment.

TOMINAGA HEIBEI. fl. 1673-1697. A playwright who began his career as an actor, but switched to playwriting during the Enpō era (1673-80) and was active in the Kamigata area until around 1697. When he was given the playwright's credit in the November 1680 *kaomise** performance program, it was a first for Kabuki dramatists. He opened the door for playwrights to occupy an independent position in Kabuki. Eight plays signed by his hand have come down to the present day; all are of the *oie mono** genre. Their plots revolve around revenge themes and the plays combine intellectuality and cleverness. Examples are *Kashima no Kanameishi* and *Tanba no Yosaku Tazuna Obi*.

TOPKNOTS. The topknot arrangements at the top and rear of most wigs are called *mage*. Many wigs are known by the name of their topknots. Distinctive male topknots include the *hari uchi** and *hari tsuba*, which have been cut at the end to resemble a rank of sewing needles; the *kiri wara**, which has been cut at the tip to look like a sheaf of straw; the *namajime**, which has been hardened with pomade to look like a stick; and the *happoware*, which has a large tip separated to the left and right. (*See also* WIGS.)

TORIBEYAMA SHINJŪ. Okamoto Kidō*. *Shin kabuki*. One act, two scenes. September 1915. Hongō-za, Tokyo.

A work based on the story of the lovers' suicides of Osome and Hankurō. Originally treated in a puppet-theatre play, it was rewritten for Ichikawa Sadanji II*.

Kikuchi Hankurō, an attendant of the shogun who has proceeded in his company to the capital, falls in love with a Gion courtesan, Osome. He frequents her often. When he has to return to Edo, he discusses with his friend Sakata Ichinosuke whether he should sell him his heirloom sword in order to raise money to buy the girl's freedom. Ichinosuke. a man of the world, laughs at this idea and pays it no heed. Genzaburō, Ichinosuke's brother, comes to call for him. He criticizes his brother for his dissipation. Hankurō, who is fond of his friend, is unable to sit by idly during this. A duel develops, during which Hankurō kills Genzaburō in the dry bed of the Shijō River. Resolved to die, Hankurō leaves with Osome, whose hopes are now crushed, to commit double suicide on Toribe Mountain.

The love between the obstinate Edo samurai and the Kyoto courtesan is handled in typical Kabuki fashion, the play having been a perfect vehicle for Sadanji II's talents. He included it in his collection of favorite plays, the *kyōka gikyoku jūshu**, and it has since become a *shin kabuki* staple.

TORTURE SCENES. Those scenes in which a character is subjected to torture by any one of a number of means are known as *semeba*. The cruelty in these scenes is emphasized to gain sympathy for the beautiful young men or women who are usually the victims. Torture methods include the "snow torture" *(yukizeme)* of *Hibariyama Hime Sudematsu**, the "*koto* torture" *(kotozeme)* of *Dan no Ura Kabuto Gunki**, the "snake torture" *(hebizeme)* of *Kaga Sōdō*, and the "third degree" *(gōmon)* of *Sakura Giminden**. The feeling of brutality in these scenes was increased in the early nineteenth century. Many *semeba* are incorporated within the ghost plays* written during that period.

TOSAKA. A female forelock style. It is cut and combed to either side and is seen on the wigs worn by Princess Takiyasha in *Masakado** and by Otomi in *Musume Gonomi Ukina no Yokogushi**.

TŌSHI KYŌGEN. *See* FULL-LENGTH PRODUCTIONS.

TOYA NI TSUKU. "Go to roost"; when a company meets difficulties while touring and is forced to sleep backstage. Also, the term has come to mean being confined indoors when ill.

TRANSFORMATION PIECES. *Henge mono,* a type of Kabuki dance play. They are composed of several brief dances; for each, the leading dancer must make a change of costume and a change of role type. Originally, the term meant a piece in which a ghostly apparition took various forms. In the Genroku period (1688-1703) the *onnagata** Mizuki Tatsunosuke* produced a seven-change piece, but the genre reached its apex in the Bunka-Bunsei period (1804-30), when there were produced works ranging from three changes to as many as twelve. The themes of these transformation pieces usually revolve around the four seasons, the five great festivals, the twelve months, and so forth. In addition to the role types based on distinctions of age and sex, the variety of professions and occupations engaged in by people during the Edo period were represented as well. The dances are peopled by such Edoites as shop boys, valets, footmen, peddlers, boatmen, geisha, townsmen's daughters, baby-sitters, and wandering minstrels. All classes of society are represented. Quick costume changes before the audience's eyes—such as the *hiki nuki** technique—are used, and music is provided by *nagauta**, *tokiwazu**, or *kiyomoto** styles. Aside from *Rokkasen**, however, few of these works survive today, though parts of many of them do remain and are given as independent dances. Representative works include *Shiokumi**, *Echigo Jishi**, *Sagi Musume**, *Fuji Musume**, *Tobae**, *Tama Usagi*, *Kisen*, and *Sanja Matsuri**. (*See also* HAYAGAWARI.)

TRAVEL DANCE. *See* MICHIYUKI MONO.

TRICK TECHNIQUES. *See* KEREN.

TROUPE LEADER. *See* ZAGASHIRA.

TSUBOORI. Originally a way of wearing the female small-sleeved kimono *(kosode)* of the early feudal era, this became the manner of wearing the noblewoman's costume called the *karaori*—a beautifully woven kimono with designs of flowers and birds—in Nō plays. The collar is folded back at the lapels and kept wide open at the breast. It is called *tsuboori* ("jar-fold") since the waist is pulled up and tucked in around the obi, giving the impression of a jar. Kabuki's version is a wide-sleeved brocade garment resembling a long *haori** jacket. Female characters in Nō-style Kabuki plays wear *karaori* in this fashion. Shizuka in *Funa Benkei** and Mashiba in *Ibaraki** are examples.

TSUBOSAKA (REIGENKI). Toyotake Ōsumidayu, Toyozawa Danpei. *Sewamono**. *Jōruri**. One act. February 1887. Hikoroku-za, Osaka.

A rewritten version of a piece by the puppet theatre composer Danpei and his wife, Kako Chikajō, for an 1883 (some sources give 1879) production at Osaka's *Ōebashi no Do*. This, in turn, had been based on an earlier work

Mashiba in *Ibaraki**, wearing the *tsuboori** robe. Mashiba, Nakamura Utaemon VI*. *Courtesy of Waseda University Tsubouchi Engeki Hakubutsukan (Tsubouchi Memorial Theatre Museum).*

by an anonymous author. Kabuki's premiere version came in 1888 at Kyoto's Shijō Shibai; it featured Bandō Minosuke.

Sawaichi, a blind masseur who lives in the vicinity of Tsubosaka Temple, wonders whether his lovely wife, Osato, who has been slipping out of the house every night, has a lover. However, Osato has been going to the temple to pray to the goddess Kannon that her husband's eyesight be restored. Learning of this, he expresses his gratitude for her real motives, and they go together to the temple. Resigned to the incurability of his blindness, Sawaichi throws himself into the valley after his wife has returned home. When Osato discovers what he has done, she throws herself after him. But Kannon performs a miracle, and the couple is saved. In addition, Sawaichi's eyes are cured.

Osato's lamentation* *(kudoki)* is famous and provides an outstanding example of the *onnagata*'s* art. Another major moment is when Osato seems about to lose her mind after learning that her husband has jumped into the valley.

TSUBOUCHI SHŌYŌ. 1859-1935. Playwright, novelist, and man of letters. Born in Mino, Shōyō (real name Yūzō) was the prophet of a new theory of literature for Japan. He reformed the history and dance dramas of Kabuki, took part in the development of Japan's modern theatre *(shingeki)*, and translated the works of Shakespeare into Japanese, among other great accomplishments. A supremely enlightened scholar, he was the leading light of the Japanese literary and theatrical world from the Meiji period through the Taishō (1912-26) and Shōwa (1926-). A graduate of Tokyo University, he held the degree of Doctor of Literature. In 1928 he was honored for his meritorious service by the founding of a theatre museum named after him at Waseda University. Shōyō's plays include such works as *Ryōkan to Komori**, *Onatsu Kyōran**, *Kiri Hitoha**, and *Hototogisu Kojō no Rakugetsu**.

TSUBU. "Grain"; in the phrase *tsubu o tateru*, it means bringing greater clarity and life to the acting and production.

TSUBUZUKE. When an actor is unsure of his lines and a stage assistant crouching behind him feeds them to him word by word. Also called *bōzuke* and *betatsuke*.

TSUCHIGUMO. Kawatake Mokuami*. English title: *The Monstrous Spider* (Bowers). *Shosagoto**. *Nagauta**. June 1881. Shintomi-za, Tokyo.

The Nō play *Tsuchigumo* provided the source of this work; it is included in the Onoe family collection, the *shinkō engeki jūshu**. Onoe Kikugorō V*, Bandō Kakitsu, and Ichikawa Sadanji I* were in the first production.

Minamoto Raiko is confined to quarters by a strange illness, and the priest Chichū comes to pray for him. When Raiko's swordbearer becomes suspicious of the priest, the latter's true character as the evil earth spider *(tsuchigumo)* manifests itself and it throws its web over Raiko. Raiko draws his famous sword, Hizakitamaru, and forces the beast to retreat. Then he sends his four chief retainers in pursuit of the spider. They do battle and defeat it at its mountain lair.

This dance play is filled with variety, from the relatively static first half—at the end of which the spider throws his thousand strands at Raiko (*see also* CHISUJI NO ITO)—to a second half containing violent action, during which the warriors battle with the spider, played in *aragoto** fashion.

TSUGIASHI. A method employed to make the actor look bigger than he is. Something is placed in the *tabi* socks to elevate the heels. When the long, trailing *hakama** trousers called *nagabakama* are worn, the actor wears high *zōri* sandals. The technique is used for such roles as wrestlers, giants, and other large individuals.

TSUKAI MAWASHI. "Use around"; when the same props, scenery, or costumes are seen in different scenes.

TSUKAMARU. "To hold fast"; when one's part requires one to perform onstage until the very end of the play. Also, when one must perform in a play even though one's role is secondary.

TSUKAMIKOMI. "To grab up"; when whatever happens to be at hand is used onstage as a prop. Similarly, the term applies when costumes and wigs are used in touring productions even though they are not appropriate for the specific actor or play.

TSUKAMITATE. A pompon-shaped forelock worn on the wigs of upstanding young samurai. Examples are Umeomaru in the *Kuruma Biki* scene of *Sugawara Denju Tenarai Kagami** and Matano in *Miura no Ōsuke Kōbai Tazuna**.

TSUKE. The beating of the clappers on a square wooden board placed on the floor at stage left. Timed to the movement of the actors, the beats serve to emphasize the sounds of fighting and running and also to accentuate the actors' *mie** poses. The board struck is the *tsukeita,* and the person doing the striking is the *tsukeuchi.* Among the methods of striking the *tsuke* are the *batabata**, when someone runs on or off; *idaten,* when characters such

*Kyōgen kata** strikes *tsuke** while watching performance. After a drawing in Toita, *Waga Kabuki.*

as couriers run in a stylized manner; *battari**, for the usual *mie* at final curtains; and *sawariuchi*, a technique used in combination with the chanter and *shamisen** player (*See also* CHOBO) in plays adapted from the puppet theatre. There are also special Kamigata area techniques such as the *kageuchi**, so called because the beater does his job from the wings *(kage)*. A *kyōgen kata** is the functionary normally assigned to the job of beating the *tsuke*. (*See also* HYŌSHIGI.)

TSUKECHŌ. A sort of promptbook, which lists all the necessary wigs, props, sets, costumes, and so forth for each act of a play.

TSUKE MAWASHI. "To trail after"; a technique used when two or more characters cautiously circle one another. This formalized method of creating tension is enacted by Chōbei and Gonpachi in *Suzugamori**.

TSUKIKAE. To change a play scheduled for performance.

TSUKKOMU. "To plunge into"; when one enjoys acting and puts one's all into it.

TSUMEYORI. "To draw near"; a method frequently seen in history plays: two opposing individuals or groups confront each other with hostility and draw near to do battle while moving with a stylized shuffle-like step. Examples are the confrontation between Yoshitsune and Midaroku in the *Kumagai Jinya* scene of *Ichinotani Futaba Gunki** and Togashi and Benkei and his four retainers in *Kanjinchō**.

TSUMIMONO. "Piled goods," a production gimmick. Merchandise contributed as gifts by the organized groups of actor or theatre supporters was piled up at the front of the playhouse in a decorative manner. There are no specific backer groups today (*see also* DANTAI; RENJŪ; HIIKI), but in order to advertise their wares, commercial companies pile up their products in front of theatres at the time of special performances, such as the *shūmei** ceremony (when an actor takes a new name) or the *kaomise** program.

TSUNAGI. "Tie-together"; a term used when a stage set is being changed. The curtain is closed for a brief interlude and opened soon after. During the interval, the *tsuke** are beaten lightly in strokes of two beats each. This is called *tsunagi* or *tsunagi noki*. When music is used to fill the interval, the *tsuke* are not employed. (*See also* INTERMISSION.)

TSUNAMOTO. The fly gallery; where the ropes for hoisting and lowering scenery and lighting equipment are gathered. The *tsunamoto* are usually in the wings to the left and right of the stage.

A dramatic confrontation between Benkei, on the left, and Togashi in *Kanjinchō**. The characters move using a sliding step called *tsumeyori**. Benkei, Nakamura Kichiemon I*; Togashi, Ichikawa Ebizō X*. *Courtesy of Waseda University Tsubouchi Engeki Hakubutsukan (Tsubouchi Memorial Theatre Museum).*

TSUNBO SAJIKI. "Deaf man's gallery." Also called *hyaku sajiki* ("hundred gallery"), these are the seats in the rear part of the second-story *sajiki**. The name was coined because when the house was full, it was almost impossible for people seated here to hear the dialogue.

TSUNOGAKI. "Horn writing." Also called *ryaku shite tsuno* ("abbreviated horns") and *warigaki* ("divided writing"), this was a simple two-line statement that hinted at the theme and contents of a play. It was printed above the billboard titles of Kabuki and puppet-theatre plays in the Edo era. An older term for it is *kogaki* ("small writing"). Old examples include the phrase, "His father was Chinese, his mother Japanese," written over the title for *Kokusenya Kassen**, and "Black *kosode* garment, light blue morning kimono" for *Tsuwamono Kongen Soga.* (*See also* KANBAN.)

TSURAHARI. "Face display," the first entrance in a play.

TSURANE. Certain interesting long speeches, delivered by *aragoto** heroes, in which they state in sonorous tones an account of their intentions, origins, and virtues. It is a kind of heroic speech said to have been influenced by recitations used in the religious *ennen* performances. It appears frequently as a characteristic Kabuki device. Representative *tsurane* include the *hanamichi** speech by Gongorō in *Shibaraku**. It was once part of the Ichikawa family tradition to have each actor write his own *tsurane* in this play, but the task eventually fell to the playwrights employed by the theatres. The *iitate,* a technique whereby a list of items is read aloud, and the *nanori zerifu,* which represents a spoken history of a name, are types of *tsurane.* Other variant techniques include *wari zerifu**, *watari zerifu**, and *yakubarai**. (*See also* SERIFU.)

TSURIEDA. Decorative borders hanging over the stage. They are often made of artificial flowers, thus giving rise to the term *tsurieda* ("hanging branches"). In *Sukeroku Yukari no Edo Zakura** they are cherry blossoms, while in *Momijigari** they are maple leaves.

TSURIMONO. "Hanging things," scenic elements hung from the flies, including large tree branches, roofs, and scenic backgrounds.

TSURI ONNA. Kawatake Mokuami*. Also called *Ebisu Mōde Koi no Tsuribari. Shosagoto*. Tokiwazu*.* Published December 1883. First performed July 1904. Tōkyō-za, Tokyo.

A dance dramatization of the Kyōgen farce entitled *Tsuri Onna.* Ichikawa

Ennosuke (later, Ichikawa En'o I*), Nakamura Kangorō, and Ichikawa Sumizō were its first stars.

In order to fish for a wife, a feudal lord and his servant Tarō Kaja pay a visit to the Ebisu Shrine at Nishinomiya. Although the lord fishes up a beautiful girl, Tarō's catch is homely. Tarō is disgusted, but the girl pursues him as he flees hither, thither, and yon.

The play's chief point derives from the humor of the foolish attempts by the ugly girl to woo Tarō Kaja.

TSURUYA NANBOKU IV. 1755-1829. A playwright, born at Nihonbashi in Edo, and the son of a dyer. He became the son-in-law of Nanboku III, a name representing several generations of actors. He started writing as an apprentice playwright (*see also* PLAYWRIGHTS' RANKS; MINARAI SAKUSHA) in 1776 and took the name Sakurada Heizō and then Sawa Heizō. In 1782 he changed his name again, and then in 1812 he took the name that he subsequently made famous: Nanboku IV. He passed in twenty years from the lowest strata of playwrights to the position of *tate sakusha**, or chief playwright (1801). In 1804 he rose to prominence with a play that he wrote for Onoe Matsusuke I*, *Tenjiku Tokubei Ikoku Banashi**. After this, he wrote 120 plays in a period of twenty-five years and published 25 picture books under the name of Uba Jōsuke. Nanboku was best at domestic plays, skillfully capturing the decadence of the Bunka-Bunsei period (1804-30). He comprehended the need of the masses for bizarre theatrical excitement and combined the qualities of cruelty, indecency, and humor in the intense and realistic plays that he gave to the world. In particular, his many ghost plays* *(kaidan mono)* are masterpieces. Among his works in this vein are *Iroeiri Otogi Zōshi, Onoe Shōroku Sentaku Banashi,* and *Akuni Gozen Keshō Kagami,* all of which were written for Onoe Matsusuke. Matsusuke specialized in ghost plays packed with quick changes *(hayagawari*)* and stage trickery *(keren*)*. Another star, Matsumoto Kōshirō V*, fully displayed his acting of cold-blooded badmen in such plays as Nanboku's *Tokiwa Ima Kikkyo no Hataage*, Reigen Soga no Kamigaki, Ehon Gappō ga Tsuji*,* and *Reigen Kameyama Hoko.* Kōshirō's *kizewa* acting style (a style suited to the realistic plays of lower-class life, *kizewamono*)* was perfected in his performances of Nanboku's *Kokoro no Nazo Toketa Iroito, Nazo no Obi Chotto Tokubei,* and *Kachizumō Ukina no Hanabure.* Plays such as *Kakitsubata Iromoe Dozome* and *Sakurahime Azuma Bunshō* were vehicles for the charms and good looks of Iwai Hanshirō V* of the "thousand-*ryō* eyes." Using quick changes, Hanshirō would play several roles in these plays. Nanboku also wrote such major ghost plays as *Tōkaidō Yotsuya Kaidan** and *Ukiyo Tsuka Hikiyo Inazuma* for the acting art of Matsusuke's son,

Onoe Kikugorō III*, who excelled at such works, being expert in quick-change techniques and in the portrayal of both male and female roles.

TSUTA MOMIJI UTSUNOYA TŌGE. Kawatake Mokuami*. Also called *Bunya Goroshi, Utsunoya Tōge. Sewamono**. Kabuki. Five acts, eleven scenes. September 1856. Ichimura-za*, Edo.

The stars of the first production were Ichikawa Kodanji IV* as Bunya and Nisa, and Bandō Kamezō as Jūbei. This was the first of many plays Mokuami wrote for the skills of Kodanji; it was excellently suited to the actor's talents with its abundance of special tricks *(keren*)* and quick-change techniques*. A modern team that made a specialty of the play was Onoe Kikugorō VI* and Nakamura Kichiemon I*.

Bunya, with the 100 *ryō* that he has obtained from the sale of his sister to a brothel, wishes to become leader of a group of Kyoto masseurs. He is watched carefully at an inn in Mariko by the crook, Daiba no Nisa. Jūbei, who is staying at the same inn, rescues Bunya from danger; the latter leaves early the next morning for Utsunoya Pass. Since Jūbei has followed Bunya because he has to procure 100 *ryō* for his master, he asks Bunya to lend him the money. When Bunya refuses, Jūbei kills and robs him. Bunya's ghost, filled with hatred, possesses Jūbei's wife; when she reviles him for his evil deed, he kills her, too. However, Nisa, who witnessed Bunya's murder, comes to Jūbei to extort the money from him. Jūbei lures Nisa to the Suzugamori fields, where he slays him. Laden with crimes, Jūbei is finally arrested.

The play excellently depicts the various types of people staying at the inn in Mariko. Central to the entire piece is the scene at Utsunoya Pass, where Bunya and Nisa—two roles of contrasting virtue—are played by the same actor, who keeps making quick costume changes. The gloomy murder is also a highlight of the work. The scene at Jūbei's house when Bunya's ghost appears and reappears is fascinating. This is a *sewamono* masterpiece of Mokuami's mature period.

TSUUCHI JIHEI II. 1679-1760. A playwright, the son of Tsugawa (also read Tsuyama) Heiji, and a player of old men's roles during the last part of the seventeenth century, he later turned to playwriting. He went to Edo with his father in 1700, and in 1710 his *Isshin Nibyakudō* was produced successfully. Thereafter, he was associated with all the Edo theatres, and it is said that he wrote about 200 plays during his career. He created the Edo "four-act play" and wrote plays that mixed history and domestic styles. This mixture *(jidai-sewamono*)* remained a dramaturgic custom in his posterity's work. A playwright who gave dignity and authority to his profession, Jihei is admired as the man who brought a resurgence to the world of Edo dramaturgy. His representative plays include *Yorimasa Goba Matsu, Shikirei Yawaragi Soga* (in which Ichikawa Danjūrō II* first played the popular role of Sukeroku [*see also* SUKEROKU YUKARI NO EDO ZAKURA]), and *Arigataya Rinzei Genji.*

TSUYU KOSODE MUKASHI HACHIJŌ. Kawatake Mokuami*. Also called *Mukashi Orihōnba Hachijō, Kamiyui Shinza. Sewamono**. Kabuki. Four acts. June 1873. Ichimura-za*, Tokyo.

A dramatization of Shunkintei Ryūkyō's human nature story entitled *Shirakoya Seidan.* Onoe Kikugorō V* played Shinza in the first production, with a supporting cast including Nakamura Nakazō IV*, Bandō Kakitsu, and Iwai Hanshirō VIII*.

Shirakoya's daughter, Okuma, and the shop assistant named Chūshichi are in love with each other. However, the Shirakoya family fortunes are sinking, and Okuma decides to flee with her dowry money and the husband of her choice. Hearing of this, the barber Shinza encourages the couple to elope, but he interrupts them on their way, abducts the girl, and takes her to his own home. Yatagorō Genshichi tries to negotiate for her with Shinza; he receives nothing for his troubles but insults. Shinza is, however, argued down by his clever landlord, Chōbei, who gets the barber to return the girl and, in addition, takes with him half of the kidnap ransom money obtained by Shinza. Later, Shinza is killed by Genshichi at the Enmado Bridge over the Fuku River.

The dialogue spoken by Shinza and Chōbei in their scene at Shinza's home is very well written. Chōbei berates the rascally Shinza to the point at which he even beats him with a slice of *bonito*, a kind of dried fish. This gives a very realistic impression of the manners of contemporary Edo townsmen.

TSUZUKI KYŌGEN. "Continuous-act plays," plays written subsequent to the establishment of *yarō kabuki*, or mature male Kabuki*, in 1653: The need to develop Kabuki artistry led to the creation of multiple-act plays with complex plots, in contrast to the simple one-act, mainly dance-oriented pieces of earlier years. (*See also* PLAYWRITING.)

The *Take no Ma* scene from *Meiboku Sendai Hagi**. The standing characters wear *uchikake** robes. Yashio (left), Nakamura Ganjirō II*; Masaoka, Nakamura Utaemon VI*. *Courtesy of Waseda University Tsubouchi Engeki Hakubutsukan (Tsubouchi Memorial Theatre Museum).*

U

UCHIKAKE. Also called *shikake, kake,* and *kaidori.* Originally a type of kimono (the *kosode*) worn by upper-class samurai wives over their topmost kimono, it was used as well in the Edo period by wealthy townswomen and courtesans. As an overgarment worn by female characters, it has a broad scope and is seen on samurai wives, palace ladies, and other upper-class women, as well as on courtesans. The cloth, colors, patterns, and embroidery display an elaborate beauty.

UCHIWA TAIKO. A type of hand drum. (*See also* NARIMONO.)

UKAMERU. To say one's lines halfheartedly, without emotion. Also, to make a sudden change and to begin acting grandly.

UKE. A special term reserved for the role of the evil prince in *Shibaraku**. It is thought to derive from the point in the play at which the *uke* character, confronted by the protagonist, calls the word out. It literally means "receive." Very popular in the Edo period for its symbolic representation of the forces of good overcoming those of a repressive government, as embodied by the evil prince, this play was performed annually, but almost always with new names for the characters. On a number of occasions, the *uke* role was called Kiyohara Takehira.

UKERU. "To accept"; when a production or the acting get good reviews.

UKON GENZAEMON. fl. 1652. An *onnagata** during the days of *wakashu kabuki,* or young men's Kabuki*, he is said to have founded the Kabuki art of female impersonation. He moved to Edo in 1652 and gained acclaim for his *Kaido Kudari* dance. His master was Nippon Densuke, a Kyōgen actor. It is unclear whether this Densuke is the same as the one who performed in Izumo no Okuni's* troupe. After young men's Kabuki was banned and all actors were forced to shave their boyish forelocks, which increased their sex appeal, Genzaemon devised a cloth covering *(murasaki bōshi*)* for the shaved spot, producing a new item of interest. (*See also* ACTORS.)

Other representative actors of the period from the young men's Kabuki to the early days of the mature male Kabuki* *(yarō kabuki)* were Sagendai, Kogendai, Nakamura Kanzaburō I*, Tamagawa Sakumi, Tamagawa Sennojō I, Nakamura Sakon, Nakamura Kazuma I, Tamagawa Sen'ya, Takii Sanzaburō, Dekishima Kozarashi, Tamagawa Kichiya, and Tamon Shōzaemon.

UMA. "Horses." The property horses used in Kabuki either resemble real horses or are a patently artificial kind called *honiharu.* The latter consists of a tubular frame resembling the front half of a horse and covers the wearer from head to waist with a head and forefeet like those of a horse; the rear feet are those of the wearer himself. More usual is the stage horse that looks like the genuine article. This frequently seen property, made by the *kodōgu kata*,* is worn by two men who act as the front and rear of the animal. Horses ridden by samurai are covered in velvet, while pack horses have a cotton covering. (*See also* NUIGURUMI; UMA NO ASHI.)

Kabuki horse. After a drawing in Toita, *Waga Kabuki.*

UMA NO ASHI. "Legs of the horse," one of the roles that fall to the lowest rank of actors. Two men dress in a property horse and perform as the front and rear legs. It was once said of the actor Furukawa Yanagi that "when the 'horse's legs' was promoted, his head was cut off" and that "The 'horse's legs' didn't show his face at the face-showing *[kaomise*]* production." The sense of the first sentence is that Yanagi was promoted and became a stage policeman *(torite)*; in that role he was killed onstage and decapitated. The latter sentence means that the entire face of the leading actor was depicted in a painting and also in the program, but there was no mention of the actor playing the horse's legs. This is always the lot of the low-ranking actors. (*See also* UMA.)

UMA NO SHIPPO. "Pony tail," a wig worn by country girls and women. It is dressed in a style that resembles the tail of a horse. Characters such as Chidori in *Heike Nyogo no Shima** wear it.

UMATATE. A vacant storage space in the wings, out of the spectators' sight. Scenic elements such as flats *(harimono*)* are piled there. The word *umatate* ("hitching post") is thought to come from its resemblance to a place where one might hitch his steed. In order for the set pieces to be removed as smoothly as possible, they are carefully stacked in order of their use.

UMEMOTO RYŪ. A school of dance founded in Osaka in the early Meiji period by Umemoto Sensei. Now under its third *iemoto**, it is active in creating new dances and is a leading school in the world of Kamigata area dance.

UMERU. "To fill in"; said when something goes wrong during a performance and a gap opens; a common expression is "fill the gap" *(ana o umeru) (see also* ANA GA AKU). The word also has the sense of filling up a poor house, that is, "papering the house" by distributing free seats.

UMIJI. An actor's habit of prefacing his dialogue with interjections such as "aa," "uu," "ee," as a momentum-producing method to help make what follows clearer and more interesting.

UNDŌBA. "Movement place," a promenade area. Edo period theatres had no lounges. When the Shintomi-za (*See also* MORITA-ZA) was built in 1878, a promenade was constructed to the rear of the *sajiki** galleries on either side of the theatre for use during intermissions. This was called the *undōba.* The word still applies to theatre lounges and lobbies.

UNKI. A prop representing a cutout of clouds. It hangs from above the stage by means of nearly invisible wires. (*See also* JYARI NO ITO.)

UNO NOBUO. 1904- . A playwright born in Tokyo, he is today's foremost writer of *shin kabuki** plays. After graduating from Keiō University and publishing his first work, *Fubuki Tōge,* he was acknowledged to be an up-and-coming dramatist. He wrote many plays, such as *Kōdan Yomiya no Ame** and *Haru no Yukige,* which were given life by the skillful realism of Onoe Kikugorō VI*. Nobuo captured the life of the Edo townsman in modern terms and in a style brimming with emotion.

URA KATA. "Rear people," a general term for all personnel who work behind the scenes. The name is directly contrasted with that for workers "out front": *omote kata**. Among the *ura kata* are those who work on the sets, costumes, wigs, props, and even the scripts. *Ura kata* are those in charge of the performance, as opposed to those who deal with the theatre's management.

USHIRO O TSUKERU. "To stay behind"; when an actor is so shaky in his lines that an assistant, dressed in black, must hide behind a property or crouch behind the actor's back and prompt him. During the Edo period, such prompting lasted from the first to the third day of a run. Since today's rehearsal periods are much shorter, the prompter may have to stay for a longer period of time. (*See also* TSUBUZUKE; KYŌGEN KATA; KUROGO; KŌKEN.)

USUDORO. A light beating of the drums in *dorodoro** fashion to evoke a feeling of eeriness when a ghost enters.

USUI. "Thin"; the sparse areas of the theatre when attendance is poor.

UTAU. "To sing"; when an actor delivers his lines in a melodic fashion, as if singing them. Also, when one is overwhelmed by some obstacle and "cries uncle."

UTSU. "To put on a play." The day of performance is *uchibi,* the mid-month performance is the *nakabi,* and the closing day is *uchi osame* or *senshūraku**.

UTSUBO ZARU. Nakamura Jūsuke. Also called *Hana Butai Kasumi no Saru Hiki. Shosagoto*. Tokiwazu**. November 1838. Ichimura-za*, Edo.

A Kabuki version of the Kyōgen farce of the same name. Nakamura Utaemon IV*, Ichikawa Kyuzō, and Ichimura Uzaemon XII were in the first production.

The scene takes place at the extremely colorful Narutaki Hachiman Shrine, adorned with a row of blossoming plum trees and with hanging branches *(tsurieda*)* of plum blossoms framing the action. A female *daimyō* comes to the shrine and sees a charming little monkey there; she asks its handler if she can make a quiver from its skin. When refused, she takes aim to shoot the creature, but the handler pleads for its life and persuades the *daimyō* to let it live. This leads to a delightful dance of thanksgiving. The piece has numerous amusing and touching moments.

UWAOKI. "Upper place"; the top stars in a company. *(See also* ODATE-MONO.)

UZURA. "Quail," the ground-floor seats running parallel to the *hanamichi** on both sides of the theatre during the Edo period. The term arose because these seats were behind a system of wooden crossbars resembling a quail's cage *(uzura kago).* Although crossbars are gone, some theatres still retain this area for those who wish to watch the play in traditional fashion, seated on cushions placed on *tatami* mat flooring. (*See also* THEATRE ARCHITECTURE.)

V

VILLAINS. *See* KATAKIYAKU.

W

WAGOTO. "Gentle style," the delicate style of acting used by certain male characters in love scenes. Speech and movement are performed in a very soft and refined manner. It is considered a basically realistic style, especially when compared to the bombastic *aragoto** style. *Wagoto* was founded in the *keisei gai* or "courtesan plays" (*see also* KAMIGATA KYŌGEN) of the late seventeenth century by the great Kamigata romantic actor Sakata Tōjūrō*. This style came to be regarded as a tradition of Kamigata area domestic plays, but the art spread to history plays and even to *aragoto.* Thus, the popular character of Sukeroku in *Sukeroku Yukari no Edo Zakura** is played as a mixture of *wagoto* and *aragoto.* Normally, the *wagoto* role must be that of a fine young man. Many of these characters have a decidedly humorous quality about them. Famous examples include Izaemon in *Kuruwa Bunshō**, Jihei in *Shinjū Ten no Amijima**, and Jūrō in *Soga no Taimen**. (*See also* NIMAIME.)

WAJITSU. A role type possessing elements of both the *wagoto** and *jitsugoto* (*see also* TACHIYAKU) types. When the quality of Kabuki plays began to improve in the late seventeenth century, character depiction grew more complex and some characters were created by combining the fixed qualities of two separate role types. This was the case with the *wajitsu* type. Ranpei in *Yamatogana Ariwara Keizu** is close to being such a type. (*See also* ROLE TYPES.)

WAKADAYŪ. A young producer; also, the son of the producer or *tayū**. It was the custom during the Edo period for *Ōkina Watashi* to be produced at the annual "face-showing," or *kaomise**, performances and on the opening day of the spring season (*see also* SPRING PLAYS). The producer would play the part of Okina, and the *wakadayū* would play Senzai. In addition, he occasionally acted the parts of high-ranking people such as Lord Ashikaga Tadayoshi in the prologue of *Kanadehon Chūshingura**.

WAKAGI NO ADANAGUSA. Kiyomizu Senkatsu. Also called *Ranchō*. *Sewamono**. Kabuki. Five acts. May 1855. Chikugo Shibai, Osaka.

A dramatic version of a *shinnai bushi** musical number, *Ranchō*.

An Ishiyama clan samurai, Agehachō Zaburō, changes his name to Ranchō and, in this guise, carries out a search for his lord's missing heirloom tea canister. While frequenting the Yoshiwara pleasure quarters, he falls in love with Konoito. His mistress, Omiya, begs Konoito to break off with Ranchō. Konoito is moved by Omiya's feelings and, obeying her request, rebukes Ranchō. The latter, enraged, kills her. However, as Konoito resembles a princess of the Ishiyama family, her body is used as a substitute for the Ishiyama girl. Further, Ranchō obtains the canister and is allowed to rejoin his master's service.

The heart of this play is contained in the lovers' quarrel when Ranchō visits the brothel (*see also* SEPARATION SCENES), the lamentation* *(kudoki)* of Omiya when she confronts Konoito, and the Yoshiwara atmosphere conveyed by the *shinnai bushi* accompaniment. The play was a specialty of Sawamura Gennosuke IV* and Sawamura Sōjūrō VII*.

WAKASHUGATA. Actors who play the parts of young men and the roles themselves. During the Edo era, the *washugata* was the handsome young man appearing opposite the pretty young lady *(wakaonnagata)*. Today, however, it is considered one of the role types subsumed by the *nimaime** category. In the early period of Kabuki many plays dealt with homosexual themes, and the *wakashugata* played a major role in such plays. There are still some roles that show the traces of this background—for example, Rikiya in *Kanadehon Chūshingura** and Koganosuke in *Imoseyama Onna Teikin**. (*See also* IROKO; ROLE TYPES.)

WAKASHU KABUKI. *See* YOUNG MEN'S KABUKI.

WAKAYAGI RYŪ. A school of Japanese dance founded in 1893 by Hanayagi Yoshimatsu, a disciple of Hanayagi Jūsuke (*see also* HANAYAGI RYŪ).

WAKI BASHIRA. A pillar supporting a raised platform area on stage left. (*See also* DAIJIN BASHIRA.)

WAKI KYŌGEN. A celebratory piece often performed on Edo period programs.

WARI DŌGU. "Divided scenery," scenery that can be pulled apart on rollers and slid offstage, revealing other scenery behind it.

WARI ZERIFU. "Divided dialogue," a technique occurring when two characters deliver related long speeches, speaking antiphonally. Also called *kakeai zerifu.* Like the *watari zerifu,* the final line is spoken in unison. The fire-tower scene in *Sannin Kichiza Kuruwa no Hatsugai**, in which Obō Kichiza and Ojō Kichiza address each other on the two *hanamichi**, is an example. (*See also* SERIFU; TSURANE.)

WARUMI. Said of a comic male character when the gestures used are excessively effeminate. Instances are Tōhachi in *Yowa Nasake Ukina no Yokogushi** and Chōkurō in *Sumidagawa Gonichi no Omokage**. Dance examples include Kisen in *Rokkasen** and Asahina in *Kusazuri Biki**.

WATARI ZERIFU. "Pass-along dialogue"; when a group of characters deliver a single speech by dividing the lines up among them, the last line being spoken in unison. When lines in seven-five meter are read in this way, the effect is quite musical. The "mustering scene" *(Seizoroi no Ba)* in *Aotozōshi Hana no Nishikie**, when the five thieves recite their *tsurane** speeches, and the scene in *Soga Moyō Tateshi no Goshozome** in which the two *hanamichi** are employed are famous examples. (*See also* SERIFU; WARI ZERIFU; TSURANE.)

WATASU. To pick up one's cues.

WATER EFFECTS. *See* MIZUIRI; MIZU KYŌGEN.

WIGS. One of Kabuki's most important visual elements, they are known as *katsura.* Wigs are worn in the Nō theatre by female characters and spirits. In Kyōgen a kind of symbolic wig, the *katsura bōshi,* is worn. This is actually a kind of cloth headgear with long strips of material hanging down on both sides of the face. Kabuki adopted this *katsura bōshi* in its early days. In 1629, however, females were forbidden from acting in Kabuki, and young men became the main performers. In 1652 a law was passed prohibiting their performance as well. The young men were followed by the mature male Kabuki,* which saw a change from the *katsura bōshi* when the actors were ordered to shave off their attractive forelocks. It became necessary for them to wear false hair, that is, wigs. The first wigs

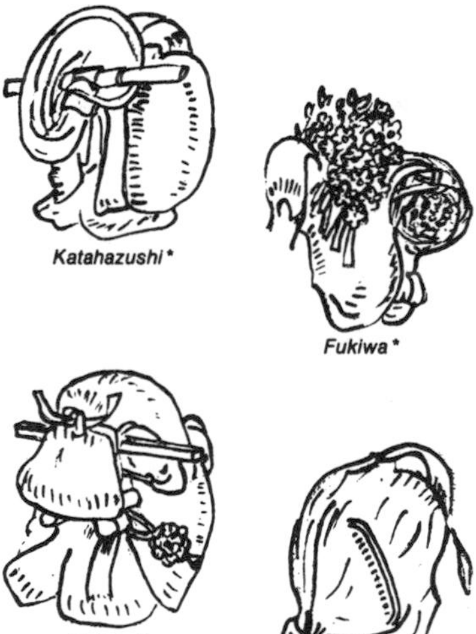

WIGS

were called *zukin, wata bōshi,* and *oki tenugui.* These were merely unrealistic head adornments. When Kabuki's dramatic qualities began to develop in depth, however, it became requisite that actors in female roles look like real women. Thus, soon after the mid-seventeenth century, female wigs came into general use. This was followed by gradual use of wigs for male roles, as the variety of roles and role types began to expand.

Today's wigs are made by constructing a copper base *(daigane*)* to fit the actor's head and applying a special silk cloth *(habutae*)* to the copper. The hairs are sewn individually onto the cloth. The great advance in the art of wig making occurred early in the eighteenth century. With the appearance of exquisite wigs it became important that each role have a beautiful wig accurately capturing the personality of the character.

The man who makes the *atama* (the basic wig with copper base and hair) is the *katsuraya.* He works according to the preferences of the actors and from a wig-list book. He measures the base to fit the actor's head and attaches the hair to the base. The *tokoyama** is the craftsman who dresses the wig in the correct style. He is employed by the theatre, where he sees to the care and maintenance of the wigs.

Wig names are a complex matter, the major categories being (1) those named after the role in which they are worn, (2) those named according to the shape of their topknot *(mage*),* (3) those named after the shape of their side locks *(bin*),* (4) those named after the shape of their forelock *(maegami*)* (5) those named after the shape of the rear part, (6) those with a name peculiar to themselves, (8) those with a combination of several of the

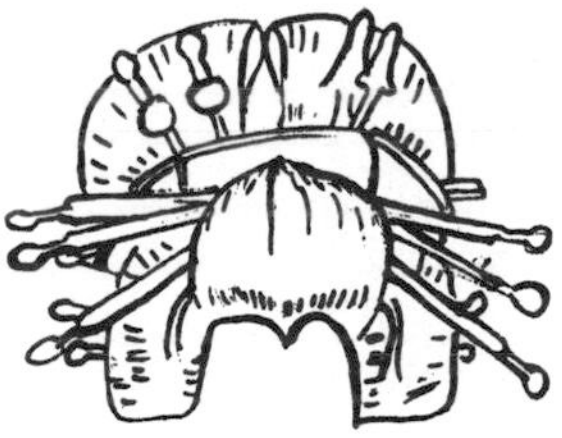
*Hyōgo**

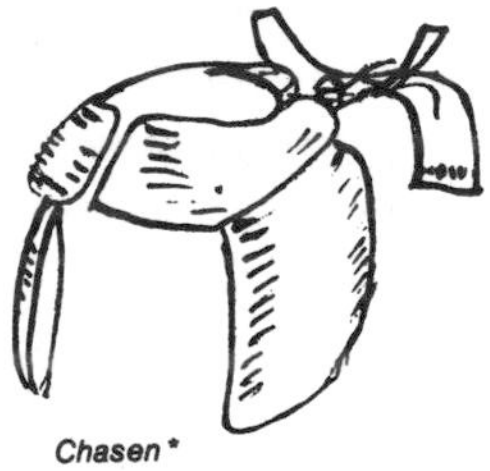
*Chasen**

*Futatsu ori** with *fukoro tsuki**

*Wakashu**

*Hishi kawa**

*Tsukamitate**

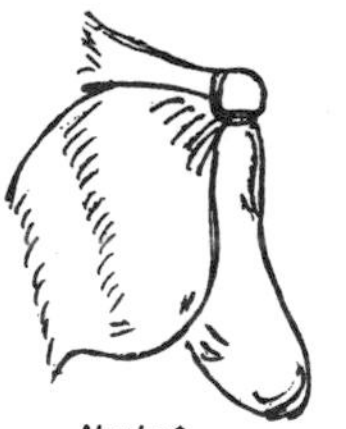
*Nonko**

*Ita bin**

WIGS

above. At all events, every wig has a characteristic name by which it is known.

Wigs known because of their topknots are the *futatsu ori**, the *ōichō*, the *chasen**, and the *megane**, all being for male roles. Female wigs in this category include the *marumage*, the *fukiwa**, and the *katahazushi**. Those male wigs which consist of a copper shell surrounding the head on the sides and rear, but which are open on top and front, where the head was shaved, are known as *kōramono*. They include wigs such as the *sakaguma**, which gives the appearance of a head which has not been shaved on top; the *fukige*; the *rashabari*, which has a sheet of black wool on top; the *gin atama*, which is painted silver; and so forth. Side-lock wigs *(bin mono)* include the *kuruma bin** and the *hachimai bin*. Male wigs known by their rear parts are placed in two basic categories, the *fukoro tsuki** (wigs with the back hair in a pouch arrangement) and the *abura tsuki** (wigs with the back hair pomaded and pressed flat against the head). The pouch styles are arranged realistically. The pomaded types are prepared by applying *bintsuke abura**, a kind of compressed cosmetic oil, to the back hair. Female wigs known by their back-hair arrangements *(tabo)** are of two main types: the *jitabo*, a realistic style, and the *maru tabo*, a somewhat stylized fashion worn chiefly in the history plays.

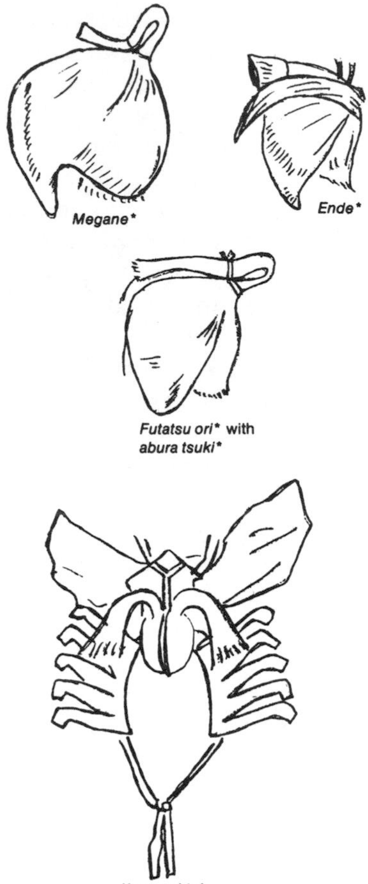

*Megane** *Ende**

*Futatsu ori** with *abura tsuki**

*Kuruma bin**

WIGS

WOMEN'S KABUKI. Called *onna kabuki*, it was one of the first forms of Kabuki, founded by Izumo no Okuni* early in the seventeenth century.

WOOD-BLOCK PRINTS. *See* SHIBAI E; SHINI E.

WOODEN CLAPPERS. *See* TSUKE; HYŌSHIGI.

Y

YABU DATAMI. A scenic element consisting of thickets made by attaching bamboo leaves to bundles of branches held in place by a wooden frame. The whole structure is three to four feet high and about four to five feet wide. It supposedly represents a thick growth of bamboo grass brush.

YADONASHI DANSHICHI (SHIGURE NO KARAKASA). Namiki Shōzō*. *Sewamono**. Kabuki. Three acts. September 1767 (some sources give 1768). Shijō Kitagawa Shibai, Kyoto.

One of the *Yadonashi Danshichi* plays, which have been given many performances since the eighteenth century. There is a legend that this play was written in one night. (*See* ICHIYAZUKE KYŌGEN.) Actors in the first production included Takeda Uhachi, Nakamura Matsushirō, Takeda Isematsu, Nakayama Ryuzō, Takeda Tokizō, and Takeda Manroku.

Danshichi, who has become a fishmonger because he lost a precious sword entrusted to him, is taken care of at the home of Otsugi in Sakai. Otsugi's acquaintance Risuke, owner of the Iwai bathhouse in Osaka, has chanced to obtain the sword. Then Danshichi is aided by Risuke in his search for the sword's accompanying certificate. Danshichi learns that his rival Kazuemon has the certificate. Risuke plans to use Danshichi to obtain the certificate from Kazuemon; he persuades the geisha Otomi, Danshichi's mistress, to pretend being won over by Kazuemon and to rebuke Danshichi. Danshichi, at the home of the playwright Shōzō, hears a discussion of a new play, in which a woman gets killed. The words have been spoken to rouse his manhood. He resolves to turn murderer and, not realizing Risuke's true intentions, slays Otomi.

This is a Kamigata style of play, acted in the romantic fashion of that region. The concept of showing the private life of an actual playwright on the stage is quite unusual.

YAGO. "Shop name." Kabuki actors of the early Edo period were considered too lowly to be allowed surnames. Many, therefore, used a name derived from a sideline business in which they were involved. This became known as their *yago*. The *yago* could be the name of a place with which the family had a deep connection, the name of a place from which the actor hailed, the name of an ancestor's occupation, and so on. Among the earliest *yago* were Yoshizawa Ayame I's* Tachibanaya and Ichikawa Danjūrō I's* Naritaya, revealing that the custom began during the Genroku era (1688-1703). The Danjūrō line's *yago* was selected because of the family's connection with the shrine of Fudō at Narita. Since Otowaya Hanshichi was the father of Onoe Kikugorō I*, the Kikugorō line's *yago* is Otowaya. The *yago* is a kind of nickname and is used by the audience as a word of encouragement that is shouted out to the actor during a performance. (*See also* HOME KOTOBA; KAKEGOE.)

YAGURA. A tower construction shaped like a *kotatsu* (a sunken charcoal brazier set in the floor of many Japanese homes) and erected in front of Kabuki theatres. The word originally referred to the roof construction of the outer gate leading to a samurai's mansion and to the observation post or command post set up in a strategic point at a castle. The meaning later referred to the tower erected over the entrance to theatre buildings. This tower was a symbol of the license granted to the theatre to produce plays. Set up on the tower were five feathered spears in imitation of the five spears symbolizing the shogun's authority. *Bonten** were placed on the *yagura*, curtains bearing the crest of the producer surrounded it, and a drum (the *yagura taiko*) within it was beaten to announce the opening and closing of a day's performance. In this way the *yagura* bore the stamp of government approval and was regarded as a sacred symbol of the theatre. The producer was often called the *yagura nushi*, the beginning of a performance was expressed by "the *yagura* is beginning" *(yagura o ageru)*, and the authority to produce was called *yagura ken*. Permission to produce was a special hereditary privilege that was proclaimed on a large billboard hung beneath the *yagura*. This was the *yagurashita kanban* ("billboard beneath the *yagura*"; *see also* KANBAN: YAGURASHITA KANBAN). In the puppet theatre the representative performer of a troupe had his name placed on a large billboard hung in front of the theatre. He was called the *yagurashita*. Today, the *yagura* is erected only for special performances. (*See also* THEATRE MANAGEMENT.)

YAHAZU BIN. "Arrow-feather side locks," a wig whose side locks are stiffened with pomade and made to jut out like the feathers of an arrow. Like the *ita bin**, it is a stylized wig and is worn by villains such as Genba in the *Terakoya* scene of *Sugawara Denju Tenarai Kagami** and Iwanaga in *Dan no Ura Kabuto Gunki**.

YAKUBARAI. Also *yakuharai,* this is an "exorcism speech." An ornate musical style of dialogue with many plays on words, spoken by the leading figure in domestic plays. The term comes from the resemblance of the words to those used in the ritual exorcism of winter. An earlier term meaning the same thing is *keiyō zerifu.* Tsuruya Nanboku IV* uses it in his plays, but it is most common in the works of Segawa Jokō III* and Kawatake Mokuami*. (*See also* TSURANE; SERIFU.)

YAKUGARA. *See* ROLE TYPES.

YAKUNIN GAENA. The cast list of a production.

YAKUSHA HYŌBANKI. "Actors' critiques," published works modeled after the early Edo period courtesan critiques, the *yūjo hyōbanki.* The oldest actors' critique extant is the *Yarōmushi* of 1659. *Hyōbanki* critiques were published every year thereafter. By 1877, when the practice ceased, over 200 years of critiques had been published.

In the early days the actors' looks and sex appeal were given more importance than their talents. Contemporary Kabuki was more dependent on the charm of its performers than on its dramatic qualities; it was simply a medium for "show business." The late seventeenth century saw the emphasis shift to criticism of the actor's performance.

With the publication in 1699 of the *Yakushaguchi Shamisen,* the contents of the *hyōbanki* were set formally, and from then on the same basic format was used. The contents consisted of various ideas regarding critical matters contained in dialogue form. The preface was a piece in literary style, setting forth the critical yardsticks to be followed. Three books were published annually, one each for Kyoto, Edo, and Osaka. They were printed in *yokohon,* or "horizontal book," form. This was altered in the late Edo period, since the actors' rankings had become increasingly complex. When the Meiji period opened, a new type of critique was produced as a joint effort by the Rokuji, a group of theatre connoisseurs. Although they called their work *yakusha hyōbanki,* they spelled the word *yakusha* with the characters used for the word *haiyū,* which also means "actor." This was a "horizontal book" printed with movable type. Later, newspaper criticism appeared, and the *yakusha hyōbanki,* which had such a long tradition behind it, faded away. Thus, the actors' critiques lasted for many years. Every year, each actor's skill was reevaluated. From these records we may learn many facts about Kabuki performance, trends among actors, movement of actors from city to city, their artistic styles, and so forth. The *hyōbanki,* thus, are priceless sources for students of Kabuki. *(See also* KURAI ZUKE; CRITICISM.)

YAMAGUMI. "Mountain group," a stylized stage unit representing a small hillock. It consists of a high *nijū** *(takanijū)* platform covered by *kerikomi** flats. A three-dimensional effect is achieved by the use of pawlonia logs covered with mesh wire. An example is seen in *Narukami**.

YAMAI HACHIMAKI. "Illness headband," a headband tied around a character's head to signify illness. One of the stylized conventions of history and dance plays it is seen in the puppet theatre too. The headband is made of purple crepe or taffeta for youthful roles, while old people use black pongee. A knot usually is tied at the left with the strands hanging down alongside the face. Matsuomaru in the *Terakoya* scene of *Sugawara Denju Tenarai Kagami**, Yugiri in *Kuruwa Bunshō**, Yasuna* in the dance play of that name, and Sukeroku in *Sukeroku Yukari no Edo Zakura** are famous examples of roles that wear this headband. (*See also* HACHIMAKI.)

YAMAMURA RYŪ. A school of dance founded around 1840 by the Kamigata actor Yamamura Matagorō I.

YAMAMURA-ZA. A theatre founded by Yamamura Kobei in Edo's Kobikichō in 1642. Along with the Nakamura-za*, the Ichimura-za*, and the Morita-za*, it was one of the four great Edo theatres for over a half century. However, after it became the focal point of the 1714 Ejima-Ikushima incident*, it was ordered closed. Many of the theatre's personnel were banished, the theatre's assets were auctioned off, and the place was permanently abolished. (*See also* THEATRE MANAGEMENT.)

YAMANBA. Mimasuya Nisōji. Also called *Takigi Ō Yukima no Ichikawa. Shosagoto**. *Tokiwazu**. November 1848. Ichimura-za*, Edo.

Yamanba is a dance version of a part of Act IV of Chikamatsu Monzaemon's* *Komochi Yamanba**. Ichikawa Danjūrō VII*, Bandō Hikosaburō IV*, and Ichikawa Kodanji IV* were in the first production.

Sakata Kurodo's wife has become a mountain hag on Ashigara Mountain, where she has raised the orphan, Kaidōmaru. Sata no Tsukao, a retainer of Yoshimitsu, comes there, notices the child's unusual strength, calls him Sakata Kintoki, and returns with him to the capital.

The best part of the number is when the mountain hag dances her trip through the mountains. Each character's personality is skillfully matched against the others'. Also, the play delights because it contains an abundance of old-fashioned Kabuki atmosphere.

YAMASHITA HANZAEMON. 1652-1717. Along with Sakata Tōjūrō*, a representative Kamigata actor of male roles during the Genroku era (1688-1703). After Tōjūrō's death he became the most popular player of leading male roles in the region. He had good looks, bearing, and speech, the actor's three important prerequisites; and he specialized in the roles of warriors, in the romantic type of acting called *yatsushi* (*see also* NIMAIME), and in gloomy roles *(ureigoto)*. In later life he changed his name to Kyōemon.

YAMATOGANA ARIWARA KEIZU. Asada Itchō, Namioka Kujiko, Namiki Soryū, Toyotake Jinroku, and others. Also called *Ranpei Monogurui*. *Jidaimono**. Five acts. December 1752. Toyotake-za, Osaka.

A work based on the love story of the sisters Matsukaze and Murasame and on a famous historical dispute over the succession to the Imperial throne. Kabuki's first production of the play was in 1753 at Kyoto's Yamashita-za, with Fujioka Ōyoshi and Arashi Ugenta. Edo's premiere Kabuki production was in 1760 at the Nakamura-za*, starring Nakamura Sukegorō, Nakamura Shichisaburō, and Segawa Kikunojō II*. Today, only Act IV is performed.

In order to cheer up his master, Ariwara no Yukihira, the footman Ranpei has the teahouse waitress Orin pass herself off as Matsukaze, the girl for whom Yukihira pines. Ranpei has Orin's husband, Yomosaku, pretend to be Matsukaze's brother, and he accompanies them to his lord's presence. Yukihira is delighted by the visit. Ranpei's son, Shigezō, pursues an escaping criminal, and Ranpei is much disturbed by fears for his son's well-being. He even neglects Yukihira's orders, causing the lord to grow furious and to draw his sword. Ranpei is seized by temporary insanity brought on by viewing the glint of a blade. Yomosaku, actually Oe no Otondo, a vassal of Yukihira, suspects Ranpei and sounds him out. He learns that Ranpei had stolen Yukihira's genealogy under pretense of madness. This leads to Ranpei's being surrounded by Yukihira's men and engaged in a great fight. Finding himself facing his own son in battle, he loses heart. Taking Shigezō's hand, he gives the youth the genealogy, making the feat of obtaining it seem to be Shigezō's.

The play's chief highlights are Ranpei's behavior when he feigns madness and the great battle in the palace's rear garden.

YANONE. Murase Genzaburō; revised by Fujimoto Tōbun. *Jidaimono**. Kabuki. One act. January 1719. Nakamura-za*, Edo.

Yanone is one of the plays in the famous Ichikawa family collection, the *kabuki jūhachiban**. Ichikawa Danjūrō II* was the star of the first production.

Soga Gorō is polishing arrows when Ōsatsuma Shuzendayū comes to wish him a happy new year. When Gorō later sleeps on his friend's gift, a picture of a treasure ship, his brother Jūrō appears to him in his dream and tells him that he is in danger. Gorō awakens, borrows a horse loaded with radishes from a passing radish seller, and, using a huge radish as a whip, heads for the palace of the evil Kudō.

Yanone had great popularity with the masses at the time of its premiere.

Its abundance of corny jokes, the sharpening of the arrows, the novelty of riding an unsaddled horse with a huge radish as a whip, its depiction of Gorō in the bravura *aragoto** style of costume and makeup, its pictorial beauty, its blending of the musical background with the play's rougher qualities—all these factors transmit the essence of the old-style Kabuki.

YAOYA KAZARI. "Greengrocer decor"; a scenic element in perspective, giving the viewer a feeling of distance. The representative example is the "1000-mat room" *(senjōshiki)* seen in scenes set in the grand hall of palaces. The *yaoya* is a ramp built on an inclined plane, lowest near the audience, highest on its upstage end. It gets its name from its resemblance to the fruit and vegetable display boxes found in front of greengrocer shops. In the Kamigata area these ramps are called *kaichōba**.

YARIBUSUMA. "Shower of spears"; entrances and exits in which a character is surrounded by spears before, behind, and to either side of him. Wada Hyōe's exit in *Ōmi Genji Senjin Yakata** is an example. Similarly, there are scenes in which someone is besieged by men holding bows and arrows *(yabusuma)*. Fukashichi is the center of such an exit in the palace scene of *Imoseyama Onna Teikin**.

YARI NO GONZA (KASANE KATABIRA). Chikamatsu Monzaemon*. English title: *Gonza the Lancer.* (Keene). *Sewamono**. *Jōruri**. Two acts. August 1717. Temeoto-za, Osaka.

A dramatization of an event that occurred in Osaka one month before the play was written.

Sasano Gonza, young page to the lord of Matsue in Unshū, is a master in the use of spears and the number-one pupil of the tea-ceremony master named Saka Ichinoshin. Because his master is in Edo, he asks the master's wife, Osai, to show him the secrets of the tea ceremony so that he may perform a celebratory tea ceremony for his young lord. Osai, who is in love with Gonza, agrees on the condition that he marry her eldest daughter. That night he receives the secret instructions, but Kawazura Bannojō—who had been in love with Osai himself and who bears a grudge against her—falsely accuses the pair of adultery. Taken by surprise, the pair nevertheless intend to allow Ichinoshin to perform his manly duty and kill them. Taking each other's hands, they run off together. Ichinoshin returns, and together with Jinpei, Osai's brother, who has slain Bannojō, he kills the pair at Fushin in Kyoto.

Osai's immorality is shown to be the result of accident more than passion. Thus, her sad fate is strongly underlined by her essential innocence.

YARŌ KABUKI. *See* MATURE MALE KABUKI.

YASUNA. Shinoda Kinji. Also called *Miyama no Hana Todokanu Edaburi. Shosagoto*. Kiyomoto**. March 1818. Miyako-za*, Edo.

A dance dramatization of the second act of *Kosode Monogurui.*

Sakaki no Mae, beloved of Abe no Yasuna, has died; he wanders about madly, carrying her kimono as a reminder of her.

Originally a work presenting the four seasons in a seven-change dance, only the "spring" section is still performed. It was revived by Ichikawa Danjūrō IX*, and after it was performed by Onoe Kikugorō VI* with a psychological interpretation, his method came to be required for the piece.

YATAI. A roomlike construction found in many sets. (*See also* SHŌJI YATAI.)

YATAI KUZUSHI. "Scenic destruction," a trick method used in earthquake scenes to make houses onstage collapse. It is seen in *Zōhō Momoyama Monogatari**.

YAYOI KYŌGEN. *See* SPRING PLAYS.

YOBAN TSUZUKI. "Four acts in a row"; an Edo playwriting method of writing a four-act play to be performed on a day-long program. Act I *(ichibanme*)* presented the introduction; Act II *(nibanme*)*, the inciting incidents; Act III *(sanbanme)*, the development and foreshadowing of the conclusion; and Act IV, the finale.

YODARE. "Drivel"; said when an actor gets old and has trouble saying his lines clearly. The term implies senility.

YOKIKOTOGIKU. A costume pattern. Like the Ichikawa Danjūrō* line's *kamawanu** design, it has strong associations with a family of actors, the Onoe. It combines the picture of a hatchet *(yoki)*, the character for a harp *(koto)*, and a picture of a chrysanthemum *(kiku)*. Onoe Kikugorō II* originated it.

YONAI. Playing a role other than one's specialty. (*See also* KAYAKU.)

YONAI KIN. A bonus payment made to an actor in addition to his regular salary. Originally, it was paid to a *tachiyaku** actor when he played a role outside his specialty, such as an *onnagata** or old person's role (*see* KAYAKU), but later it came to be paid as an increment for the purchase of makeup and costumes. Even now actors get *yonai kin* as a measure to keep them happy.

YONTATEME. In the Edo period, the "fourth piece" on the program. It was the same as the second act of the *nibanme mono** or second half of the program.

YORIZOME. "Gathering together"; one of the events related to the *kaomise** productions of the Edo period. The *kaomise* plays would be prepared and their cast lists distributed to the company about the tenth of October. On the seventeenth, the new company would get together for the first time. This was the *yorizome.* The actual scripts would be given out, and the rehearsals would begin.

YOROI. *See* ARMOR.

YOROSHIKU. "As you see fit"; an expression often found in playscripts when a playwright gives the actor freedom to do as he deems best with no special instructions on what is required.

YOSHINO. Also called *tsūten,* this is an audience area found in pre-Shintomi-za (1878; *see also* MORITA-ZA) theatres. It was a space located on both sides of the stage into which the spectators crammed themselves; part of the seating was behind the curtain. There were also some seats on the stage left area itself. These were the lowest class of seats in the theatre. There were two levels, the upper being called *yoshino* and the lower known as *rakan dai**. The upper section was called *yoshino* (the name of a mountain famed for its cherry trees) because of the excellent view afforded there of the hanging artificial flowers *(tsurieda*)* that decorate the front of the stage picture. The term *rakandai* came about because the audience seated there resembled Buddha's 500 disciples *(rakan).* (*See also* THEATRE ARCHITECTURE.)

YOSHITSUNE SENBON ZAKURA. Takeda Izumo II*, Namiki Sōsuke*, Miyoshi Shōraku. Also called *Senbon Zakura. Jidaimono*. Jōruri*.* Five acts. November 1747. Takemoto-za, Osaka.

A dramatization of the legend of Yoshitsune, the great medieval general. It takes place following the downfall of the Heike clan's regime. When a full-length production* *(tōshi kyōgen)* is offered, it is usual to present Act II's *Fushimi Inari* and *Daimotsu Ura* scenes, Act III's *Moku no Jitsu* and *Sushiya* scenes, and Act IV's *Yoshinoyama Michiyuki* and *Kawazura Yakata* scenes.

Before the Inari Shrine in Fushimi, Yoshitsune gives his mistress, Shizuka Gozen, a drum named Hatsune as a keepsake. He presents his own armor to his retainer, Tadanobu, and entrusts Shizuka to this noble samurai during his absence. Wishing to sail to Kyūshū, Yoshitsune's party comes to Ginpei, the shipping agent. Ginpei is really the Heike general Tomomori, and his wife and child are Suke no Tsubone and Antoku Tennō, Child Emperor of Japan. Tomomori feigns being a vengeful ghost and attacks Yoshitsune's group, which, however, sees through his ruse. Defeated, Tomomori ties the rope of a huge anchor around his body and sinks into the sea. His wife embraces the Child Emperor and throws herself into the sea after him.

The fox, or *kitsune roppō*, in *Yoshitsune Senbon Zakura**, Kitsune-Tadanobu, Onoe Shōroku II*.

Koremori's wife, Wakaba no Naishi, and their son—having been entrusted to the retainer Kokingo—are surrounded by their pursuers, and Kokingo is killed. The *sushi*-shop proprietor Yazaemon, happening by, returns with Kokingo's head, hoping to substitute it for that of Taira no Koremori, whom he has been concealing. He is taking the risk because he feels indebted for past favors to the Taira clan. Koremori, having assumed the guise of an apprentice at the *sushi* shop (*sushi* is a food made with rice and fish), has taken the name of Yasuke, and is betrothed to Yazaemon's daughter, Osato. Gonta, Yazaemon's ne'er-do-well son, comes to the shop, deceitfully obtains money from his mother, and hides it in an empty *sushi* tub. Yazaemon returns with Kokingo's head and hides it in another tub, near that in which Gonta placed the money. Koremori's wife and child come to the shop. Koremori learns from them of their recent experiences. Osato, overhearing, realizes she can never be Koremori's bride. Learning that the enemy general, Kajiwara Kagetoki, is coming to inspect the head of "Koremori," Koremori and his family leave to find safer quarters. Gonta leaves right afterwards, grabbing the tub with Kokingo's head as he goes, and leaving the one with the money. Soon, Gonta returns, bearing the tub with Kokingo's head and dragging with him the bound-and-gagged persons of a woman and child, whom he claims are the wife and son of Koremori. Kagetoki accepts the head as Koremori's, and rewards Gonta with a battle robe of the great lord Yoritomo. He then leads the prisoners away. Afterward, Yazaemon, incensed at Gonta's behavior, stabs him. Gonta reveals that he had been inspired by his father's act of loyalty. The woman and child that he presented as Naishi and her son were actually his own wife and child, and the head taken away by Kajiwara was the false one. Gonta's true character is now apparent. Koremori and his family appear and give thanks for Gonta's deed. A Buddhist rosary and a priest's robe are found within the robe left by Kajiwara, and they realize that Yoritomo wished to save Koremori by making him a priest. Koremori shaves his head and betakes himself to Takano.

During the travel dance *(michiyuki*)* of Shizuka and Tadanobu on Yoshino Mountain, Tadanobu describes in dance the tale of the death of his brother, Tsugunobu, in battle. Tadanobu then comes to Kawazura Hōgen's mansion, where Yoshitsune is hiding. Yoshitsune asks him angrily where Shizuka is, but Tadanobu replies that he does not know. Then another Tadanobu arrives with Shizuka. The Tadanobu who has been her companion says that he is the son of the fox whose skin was used in making the drum carried by Shizuka. Yearning for his parent, he came to Shizuka when she banged the drum. When he tells the story of his parent's tragic death, Yoshitsune is moved and gives him the drum. The overjoyed fox-Tadanobu, in gratitude, lures a bunch a rough priests who were planning to attack the mansion and is instrumental in their capture. Yoshitsune realizes that the priest Kakuhan is the Heike general Noritsune and promises to meet up with him again.

Together with *Sugawara Denju Tenarai Kagami** and *Kanadehon Chūshingura**, this play is one of the three greatest masterpieces of the puppet theatre. The last moments of Tomomori, as he prepares to fling himself into the waters at Daimotsu Beach; the character of Gonta in the *sushi*-shop scene; the vitality of the fox-Tadanobu, whose performance involves a variety of acrobatic tricks *(keren*)*; the three famous narrative recitals *(monogatari*)*—these all contribute to maintaining *Yoshitsune Senbon Zakura*'s vigorous life as one of the most polished and exciting of Kabuki plays.

YOSHIZAWA AYAME I. 1673-1729. One of the greatest *onnagata** actors in Kabuki's history, he performed opposite Yamashita Hanzaemon* in the Kamigata area for much of his professional life. After acting the role of the courtesan Mitsu in *Keisei Asamagatake* in 1698, it became the greatest role of his career. Later, he received the highest praise for his work in *Sanga no Tsu Sōge Igashira* and *Mikuni Murō* and was recognized throughout Japan as the best *onnagata* of his time. He was better in realistic acting than in dance. Extremely important as a perfecter of the *onnagata*'s art, Ayame occupies a special place in Kabuki history. He wrote a famous treatise on the art of female impersonation, the *Ayamegusa,* in which he stated his belief that the *onnagata* must get as close to being a real woman as he can so that he can penetrate the reality of his character and project it with honesty.

Ayame II (1702-1754) was his eldest son, and his fourth son became Ayame III (1720-1774). His third son was Nakamura Tomijūrō I*. Each was an *onnagata.* The line continued up to the fifth Ayame (1755-1810), who was active during the early nineteenth century. Of them all, only the fifth achieved any degree of fame in his lifetime.

YOSOGOTO JŌRURI. "Someplace else *jōruri,*" *sewamono** scenes which use the narrative musical background called *jōruri**, but in which the words of the narrative bear no relation to the action of the drama being enacted. It is sung as though it were taking place somewhere other than in the scene itself. The acting of the scene, though, is based on the rhythms of the music.

YOTEN. An outer kimono notched at the hem on both sides; it is seen in fight scenes and on brave samurai types. Its varieties include the *karaori no yoten,* the embroidered *(nui) yoten,* the colored *(iro) yoten,* and the black *(kuro) yoten.* They differ according to cloth and color. The *gochūshin** messengers who report on battle conditions in history plays—Shigasaki Tarō in *Ōmi Genji Senjin Yakata** and Shirasuga Rokurō in *Honchō Nijūshikō**—wear embroidered *karaori no yoten* with fringes *(baren*)* at the hem. It is also worn by sorcerers and bandits. Besides this there are the black *yoten* worn by the police forces in the *Terakoya* scene of *Sugawara Denju Tenarai Kagami**; the flower *(hana) yoten* worn by the soldiers who appear in the Mount Yoshino scene of *yoshitsune Senbon Zakura** and *Ochiudo**, where they carry flowering branches and spears as weapons (*see also* HANAYARI); and the brightly colored *yoten* worn by police and soldiers in dance plays. The characters who appear in *yoten* often are referred to by the term.

YOTSU TAKE. A bamboo percussion instrument. (*See also* NARIMONO.)

YOUCHI NO SOGA (KARIBA NO AKEBONO). Kawatake Mokuami*. *Jidaimono**. Kabuki. Five acts. June 1881. Shintomi-za, Tokyo.

This play depicts the true story of the Soga brothers, from the attainment of their famous vendetta to their deaths. The main part performed today begins with the break-in in Act IV, although Act III is also performed occasionally.

Among various sources for this play was Mokuami's own *Chō Chidori Soga no Jitsuden*, staged in 1874 at the Ichimura-za*. In the present work's first production, the featured players were Ichikawa Danjūrō IX*, Onoe Kikugorō V*, Nakamura Sōjūrō I*, Ichikawa Sadanji I*, Nakamura Shikan IV*, Ichikawa Kodanji V*, and Iwai Hanshirō VIII*.

The Soga brothers' retainers Omo and Doza beg to accompany their lords on their vendetta mission, but they are refused. The brothers entrust their mother and sister with a keepsake, the latter pair return to their native town, and the brothers depart to take their revenge on the killer of their father (Act III).

The brothers steal into Kudō's temporary residence, and with the guidance of Kametsure, a courtesan, they kill Kudō and then take part in a great battle with Kudō's men. However, Nitta Shirō kills Jūrō, and Gorō is captured (Act IV).

Gorō is brought before Yoritomo, who offers him a fur cushion. Gorō then tells the tale of his revenge. He hears of the last moments of his brother's life from Nitta. He mourns when confronted with his brother's head. Inubomaru, saying that he will avenge his father, strikes Gorō, but the latter perceives that Inubo shares the same lot in life as he and is content to be killed. Admiring the brothers' filial love, Yoritomo grants territory to the brothers' mother (Act V).

The play expertly blends the violence of the fight in Act IV—where ten men are killed and Jūrō dies—with the quietness of Act V, the central feature of which is Gorō's narrative. Its production style is influenced by the "living history" method of the late nineteenth century.

YOUNG MEN'S KABUKI. Known as *wakashu kabuki*, this was an early form of Kabuki. (*See also* ACTORS; IZUMO NO OKUNI.) The actors were handsome young men, and audiences were more interested in their sex appeal than in their artistic ability. When women's Kabuki* was banned in 1629, this form became very popular. However, the behavior of audiences with regard to the overt homosexuality of the actors led to its prohibition in 1652.

YOWA NASAKE UKINA NO YOKOGUSHI. Segawa Jokō III*. Also called *Genyadana, Kirare Yosa.* English title: *Genyadana* (Scott). *Sewamono**. Kabuki. Nine acts, thirteen scenes. January 1853. Nakamura-za*, Edo.

This famous play is based on a storyteller's tale *(kodan)* that was, in its turn, based on a true story. The parts produced today are the *Misome* scene in Act II, the *Mikai* scene in Act III, the *Genyadana* scene in Act IV, and, occasionally, the *Izuya* scene of Act VIII. Ichikawa Danjūrō VIII* and Onoe Kikugorō IV* played the leads in the first production. In this century, one of the greatest casts was composed of Ichimura Uzaemon XV* as Yosaburō, Onoe Matsusuke IV* as Yasu, and Onoe Baikō VI* as Otomi.

At Kisarazu Beach, Yosaburō falls in love at first sight with Otomi, a former Fukugawa geisha who is presently Akama Genzaemon's mistress. Yosaburō, adopted son of the Izuya family, secretly meets with Otomi during Genzaemon's absence, but is found out by Genzaemon. He is cut all over his face and body, wrapped in a bamboo mattress, and, like Otomi, thrown in the sea to drown. Unknown to each other, however, they each are saved. Otomi's savior is Tazaemon, clerk of the Izumi-ya. With his help she goes to live in Edo's Genyadana district. Yosaburō comes to this place. He is now a petty crook who goes by the nickname of Kirare Yosa ("Scarface Yosa"). With his crony, Kōmori ("Bat") Yasu, his purpose is to extort money. Here Yosa meets up again with Otomi. Soon he goes to his adopted parents' house to survey the situation there. Admonished by the servant, Chūsuke, he meets indirectly with his father and sister and then leaves.

The main feature of the scene at the beach occurs when Yosa gazes at Otomi with such rapture that he is not even aware that his jacket has slipped off his shoulders and to the ground. The apex of the entire work is the famous speech by Yosaburō in the Genyadana shop; it begins, "Love and passion have been my worst enemies. . . ." The play is an example of the *kizewamono** variety of late Edo period drama.

YUJŌ KABUKI. *See* COURTESAN KABUKI.

YUKA. "Floor," the place from which the *gidayū** musicians perform. It is a bamboo screened room either on a level above the stage on stage left or below this level on a platform placed on the stage proper. On rare occasions, it is situated on stage right in front of the *geza** room. The *gidayū* music played here is called *yuka*, too. In plays taken from the puppet theatre the parts involving a flow of dialogue between the characters are spoken by the actors, while their emotional and mental stages are expressed by the *gidayū*. Because the *gidayū* master *(tayū*)* marks "*chobo chobo*" in red next to the narrative passages in the script that he uses onstage (the *yuka hon*), the word *chobo* is used to refer to the *gidayū* music and narrative. (*Chobo* is a reading given to the Chinese character meaning *mark.*) There are times when the *chobo* performs in the screened room over the stage and times when, as the *degatari**, it performs in view of the audience.

YUKI. "Snow," a property item prepared by the prop master *(kodōgu kata; see also* PROPERTIES), but manipulated and made to fall onto the stage by the men in charge of the scenery *(ōdōgu kata; see also* SCENERY). Small, triangular pieces of white Japanese paper are placed in bamboo "snow baskets" *(yuki kago)* suspended over the stage. When a rope is pulled, the paper falls through holes in the baskets, giving the impression of a snowfall. Traditionally, the paper has been cut in triangles, but recently squares have been used to save time in preparation. One drawback to this paper snow is that occasional flakes may be seen falling from the area over the stage in scenes that do not call for snow effects. When such items as snow-covered umbrellas are employed, cotton is used to represent the snow. In the realistic new plays of Kabuki, snow is shown by lighting effects or by plastic mixed with paper.

YUMAKI. A cloth that covers the lower half of the body and is worn under the *onnagata*'s* inner kimono *(juban)*. It is of white or scarlet crepe and may differ depending upon the role type and costume. Also called *yugu* and *yumaji*.

YURA NO MINATO SENGEN CHŌJA. Takeda Koizumo, Chikamatsu Hanji*, Takemoto Saburobei, Miyoshi Shōraku, Kitamado Goichi. Also called *Sanshō Dayū, Tori Musume. Jidaimono*. Jōruri**. Three acts. May 1761. Takemoto-za, Osaka.

The material on which this play is based is the legend of Sanshō Dayū, taken directly from Takeda Izumo's I* *Sanshō Dayū Gonin Musume* (1727). Kabuki's first production was in 1784 at Osaka's Kado no Shibai. The events of Act II, *Tori Musume*, still are performed.

Iwaki Masauji's children, Princess Yasu and Zushiomaru, are sold by a slave dealer to Master Sanshō and are engaged in back-breaking slave labor. The Iwaki samurai Tatebe Kanamenosuke comes to pay a visit to the youngsters, but is captured by Sanshō's nephew, Yurami Saburō, and sentenced to death by beheading, along with the young siblings. Osan, Sanshō's daughter—who is in love with Kanamenosuke—turns into a fowl at dawn, a punishment suffered in atonement for her father's sins. The time fixed for the execution is the first crow of the day, but Osan does what she can to prevent the crowing. Ultimately, it is she who raises her voice in a crow, while flapping her wings. She runs around madly, then chews Kanamenosuke's ropes off. The brother and sister are set free and escape, and the samurai confronts Sanshō. The latter, however, recognizes the samurai as the child who was stolen from him years ago; repenting of the crimes that he has committed, he allows his long-lost son to kill him. Kanamenosuke then takes his own life to atone for the act of slaying his father. Osan also commits suicide.

The highlight of the performance is the vision of the mad Osan in the form of a fowl. Sanshō's and his daughter's moral reversal provides a thematic foundation to this unusual work.

YŪSHOKU KAMAKURAYAMA. Suga Sensuke, Nakamura Gyōgan. Also called *Kamakurayama, Sano no Genzaemon. Jidaimono**. *Jōruri**. Eight acts. August 1789. Kita Horie-za, Osaka.

A dramatization of Sano Zenzaemon's hatred of the despotism of Tanuma Okitsugu and his son and of the violence that befell the latter pair in March 1784. The time of the events has been placed in the Hōjō era (twelfth century). Kabuki produced a version of the play several months after the puppet play premiered, in Kyoto, with Arashi Sangorō and Kataoka Nizaemon VII*. An Osaka production, at the Nakayama Fukuzō-za, opened at the same time. A year later, in 1790, the Edo public saw it at the Ichimura-za* with Sawamura Sōjūrō III*. In this century, the role of Genzaemon was a great success for Ichimura Uzaemon XV*.

Miura Yasamura and his son, Arajirō, have planned a rebellion, but Sano Genzaemon's uncle, Tsunekage, has effectively blocked their plans. While hawking one day, Genzaemon concedes the honors to Arajirō, but the latter humiliates him. As a result Genzaemon kills Arajirō within the palace. Genzaemon is ordered to commit ritual suicide *(seppuku)* as a punishment. His family hides at Sano no Watashi and is aided by his loyal retainer, Yūsuke. Yasamura continues to further his plans for rebellion, but Akita Shironosuke puts an end to them. The Sano family is revived with Genzaemon's son, Umenosuke, at its head.

Since the historical figure upon whom this play is based is revered as a Shinto deity, the play was quite popular and was produced in many versions.

YUSURIBA. *See* BLACKMAIL SCENES.

Z

ZAGASHIRA. "Troupe leader," the representative actor of a troupe and the highest-ranking position among actors of leading male roles *(tachiyaku*)*. Instances of *onnagata** serving as *zagashira* are exceedingly rare. The *zagashira*'s name invariably was written last in the program (a practice called *tomefude; see also* KAKIDASHI; NAKAJIKU). Programs known as *mon banzuke* (because they depicted the actor's crest* or *mon; see also* BANZUKE: YAKUWARI BANZUKE) printed his name and his crest in the box that was second down and second in from the right side of the page. The *zagashira*'s entire face and figure was depicted in the center of a group picture on the lower half of the annual *kaomise** program. (*See also* ACTORS.)

ZAMOTO. In Edo the manager or proprietor of a theatre. He was called the *yagura nushi* and *tayūmoto (see also* TAYŪ) as well. He did not necessarily possess financial resources for producing plays and thus differed from the theatrical financiers of today. After the Edo fire of 1652, which destroyed most of the city, there were four Edo *zamoto:* Nakamura Kanzaburō I*, Murata Kuroemon, Yamamura Nagadayū, and Morita Tarobei (later Morita Kanya I*). They had been granted the right to produce plays at Edo's four authorized theatres, and this authority was handed on to their successive generations as an inherited privilege. After the Yamamura-za* was closed down following the 1714 Ejima-Ikushima incident*, Edo had only three licensed theatres. Thus, their power was great. They were honored by being called *tayūmoto*, while the male heir to the position of *zamoto* was called *wakadayū**. (*See also* EDO SANZA.)

In Kyoto and Osaka a theatre proprietor with the authority to produce plays was called the *nadai** (not to be confused with the actor's title of *nadai)*. An actor who wished to produce a play borrowed or rented the title of *nadai* from its owner, and the former then was permitted to put on plays. Later, when this name-renting person gained popularity through public approval of his talents, he produced plays under the cover of his theatre's name. He was now a *zamoto*, or "actor-manager," a title that represented to a Kamigata actor public acknowledgment of his abilities as a performer. For example, in 1701, Sakata Tōjūrō* produced plays in the name of the Kyoto *nadai* Miyako Mandayū at the Miyako Mandayū-za. In the same year, in Osaka, Arashi San'emon I* did the same under the *nadai* Matsumoto Nazaemon at a theatre he called the Arashi-za. It must be understood, then, that the Kamigata *zamoto* was not an authorized producer, theatre proprietor, or theatrical financier—as he was in Edo—but was, rather, the representative actor of his troupe. The role fell to the major star of a company during the early years of Kabuki's history, but in later years it became less important who the *zamoto* actor was, since the position was merely nominal; many later *zamoto* were child actors as a result. The custom continued up to the mid-Meiji era. It should be noted as well that the second character in *zamoto* was spelled differently in Edo and the Kamigata area. (*See also* THEATRE MANAGEMENT.)

ZANGIRI MONO (or KYŌGEN). One of the types of *sewamono** developed during the Meiji era. It took its ideas from the new, Western-influenced customs of the time. Following the Meiji Emperor's Restoration (1868), the wearing of a sword was banned and Western manners were imported. A revolution in social customs took place, including men's cutting off the traditional topknot and changing to short hair. This development gave the genre its name: *zangiri mono,* or "cropped-hair plays." Since the earlier *sewamono* had taken contemporary life for its material, it was natural for new plays to be written depicting the conventions established during the Meiji era. Onoe Kikugorō V* performed in a number of such works created for him by Kawatake Mokuami*. However, only the externals of the new manners and speech were adopted—because the old style of dramatic construction and performance were maintained—so the genre did not really work well and was abandoned about 1882. Representative works still performed are Mokuami's *Shimachidori Tsuki no Shiranami** and *Suitengū Megumi no Fukagawa**. (*See also* PLAY CATEGORIES.)

ZAREGUMA. "Funny *kuma,*" a humorous *kumadori** makeup worn by comical characters. There are a number of variations of the style, the main ones being the *numazu* ("catfish") *guma* worn by the foolish priest in *Shibaraku**; the *Anewa guma* of Anewa Heiji in *Suma no Miyako Genpei Tsutsuji;* the *rokujūsan nichi* ("sixty-three-day") *guma* created by Onoe Kikugorō V*; the *asagao* ("morning glory") *guma,* which is shaped like a morning glory, on the face of Asagao Senbei in *Sukeroku Yukari no Edo Zakura**; and the *tori no guma,* which depicts the rising sun.

ZENSHIN-ZA. A theatre company founded on idealistic principles in 1931 by the Kabuki actors Kawarazaki Chōjūrō IV* and Nakamura Gan'emon

III*; it has produced Kabuki and modern drama since then. Among their controversial actions was the entire company's joining the Communist Party after World War II. They have been quite active in revivals of plays by Chikamatsu Monzaemon* and always seek to reinterpret Kabuki's classics in light of modern ideas.

ZŌHO FUTATSU DOMOE. Kimura Enji. *Jidaimono**. Kabuki. Seven acts. October 1861. Morita-za*, Edo.

This work borrows from the story of the bandit Ishikawa Goemon, as told in a number of earlier plays. The scenes shown today show the reunion of Goemon and his childhood friend Konoshita; Goemon's magic "basket escape" *(tsuzura nuke)*; his arrest in the Fuji Forest; and his execution by being boiled in oil. Goemon was first played by Ichikawa Kodanji IV*.

Kureha Chūnagon, Imperial envoy, is attacked by Goemon, a notorious bandit, and robbed of his possessions. Goemon dresses himself as the envoy and enters the palace of the Shogun Yoshiteru. He is greeted by Konoshita Tōkichi, whom Goemon recognizes as his boyhood friend Tomoichi. The two relax and talk over old times. Presently, Tōkichi brings out a large wicker basket that he says he has bought for Goemon. The latter looks into the basket and sees his stepfather, Jirozaemon. He pays for the basket and is going to leave with it when both his and Tōkichi's swords begin to resonate. This is proof that the swords form a famous pair. A struggle over them ensues. Goemon is surrounded by Tōkichi's men, but he manages to escape through the use of magic. Later, in the Fuji Forest, his pursuers surround him. Though fearing for the safety of his child, Gorōichi, he does battle. Finally, he is captured and boiled in oil.

The play is fascinating in conception and performance. Audiences laugh when the Imperial envoy is stripped bare and are intrigued by such scenes as the two old friends' carousing in the Ashikaga Palace and telling tales of their youth, the performance of magic by Goemon as he enacts the aerial feat of his "basket escape" (he flies through the air supported by wires; *see also* CHŪNORI), and the great fight in the Fuji Forest.

ZŌHO MOMOYAMA MONOGATARI. Kawatake Mokuami*. Also called *Jishin Gatō. Jidaimono**. Kabuki. Five acts, nine scenes. August 1869. Ichimura-za*, Tokyo. The *zōho* version premiered September 1876; Murayama-za, Tokyo.

One of the representative works of the genre known as "living history plays* *(katsureki geki)*, in which Ichikawa Danjūrō IX* specialized during the Meiji era. The supplement *(zōho)* alluded to in the title refers to additions made following the play's first performances. The parts performed today begin with the scene in Katō's mansion and go to the scene at Momoyama Castle. They are part of the original work.

Katō Kiyomasa, having been accused falsely by Ishida Minari, is ordered by Hideyoshi to confine himself to his quarters. One night there is a great earthquake. Concerned for his master's safety, Kiyomasa hastens with the men under his command to the Momoyama Palace. Hideyoshi recognizes the depth of the man's loyalty, but does not pardon him for his alleged crime. Presently, the false charge is explained before Hideyoshi, and Kiyomasa receives his pardon. He also is given a reward and is ordered to lead his troops on an expedition to Korea.

The art of the master storyteller is clearly in evidence in this work, from the curtain raiser—in which the mansion is destroyed—to the appearance of Kiyomasa in armor at Momoyama Palace, where the treachery that he has suffered is exposed.

Danjūrō was so successful in this play that he included it in his *shin kabuki jūhachiban** collection.

APPENDIX I

A Brief Chronology of Kabuki

OVERVIEW OF THE PERIOD	DATES	SUMMARY	OTHER INCLUDING PUPPET THEATRE EVENTS
Pre-Kabuki (late sixteenth to early seventeenth centuries): *Furyū, nyōbo kyōgen, nyōbo nō, yayako odori, kaka odori*, and other performing arts popular among the people are performed, and these become the soil out of which Kabuki sprouts.	1571	July: An unprecedentedly great *furyū* dance is performed in Kyoto.	
	1581	September: *Yayako odori* is performed in Kyoto's Imperial Palace.	
	1582	May: *Yayako odori* and *kaka odori* performed at Kasuga Shrine by two young girls from Kaga Province.	Akechi Mitsuhide assassinates Oda Nobunaga at Honnō Temple.
			1600: Battle of Sekigahara.
Women's kabuki and young men's kabuki** (1603-52): The *kabuki odori* performed in the Kamo River bed by Okuni gains popularity. Imitated by groups of females, it gives rise to the successful *onna kabuki*. When it is banned, *wakashu kabuki*, which features handsome youths, comes to the fore and becomes the fashion.	1603	Around this time, Izumo no Okuni*, renegade priestess of the Izumi Shrine, performs *kabuki odori* (Kabuki dances) in the dry bed of Kyoto's Kamo River.	1603: Founding of Tokugawa Shogunate in Edo.
	1607	Okuni goes to Edo and dances in Edo Castle.	1616: Tokugawa Ieyasu dies.
	1615-23	Kyoto permits seven theatres to operate.	
	1624	Saruwaka (Nakamura) Kanzaburō I* founds a theatre in Edo and begins to present plays in March.	
	1629	*Onna kabuki* is banned in October because of its disruptive social influences. *Wakashu kabuki* takes its place in popularity.	
	1634	The Murayama-za (later the Ichimura-za*) is founded in Edo's Sakai-chō.	May 1639: Policy of national isolationism is declared.
	1642	The Yamamura-za* is founded in Edo.	
	1652	June: *Wakashu kabuki* banned.	
	1653	Kabuki allowed to start over again; mature male *(yarō)* kabuki* begins.	

Period of Dramatic Gestation (late seventeenth century): Period of reform of Kabuki's physical constitution from *wakashu* to *yarō kabuki*. In order to reopen, Kabuki is forced to deepen dramatic contents and to deprive its players of their attractive forelocks. Actors must now appear with a shaven crown in the conventional male coiffure. The development of Kabuki drama begins.	1657	January: Great fire of Edo. Thereafter, only four theatres are officially acknowledged as major Edo playhouses: the Nakamura-za*, the Ichimura-za, the Morita-za*, and the Yamamura-za.*	
	1664	Plays of multiple acts begin, at the Ichimura-za. Multiple-act plays also begin in Osaka at about the same time.	
	1668	The Miyako Mandayū-za of Kyoto is allowed to produce plays.	Sakurai Tanbanojō and others are popular in Edo during these years for their *kinpira jōruri** performances.
	1673	Ichikawa Danjūrō I* performs *Shittennō Osanadachi* at the Nakamura-za in Edo; he plays the part of Sakata Kintoki. Said to be the start of *aragoto** acting.	
	1678	February: Sakata Tōjūrō* plays Izaemon in *Yugiri Nagori no Shōgatsu* at the Araki Yojibei-za and displays the art of *wagoto** acting.	
First Period of Perfection: I. Until this time, Kabuki plays have been simple affairs mainly created by the actors themselves. Playwrights now appear to meet the demands for complex plotting. Various dramatic elements are added to the form. Chikamatsu Monzaemon* is one of these play-	1680	February: Tominaga Heibei declares his profession to be that of a playwright.	
	1684	March: Ichikawa Danjūrō I performs *Narukami**. The same year sees Sakata Tōjūrō achieve renown for his performance in *Yūgiri Shichinenki.*	Takemoto Gidayū founds the Takemoto-za puppet theatre in Osaka. 1685: Chikamatsu's *Shusse Kagekiyo* is staged at the Takemoto-za.

OVERVIEW OF THE PERIOD	DATES	SUMMARY	OTHER INCLUDING PUPPET THEATRE EVENTS
wrights. The Genroku era is the first period of perfection. The actors Ichikawa Danjūrō I and Nakamura Shichisaburō I* flourish in Edo, while Sakata Tōjūrō, Yoshizawa Ayame I*, and Mizuki Tatsunosuke* lead the theatre in the Kamigata area.	1697	Danjūrō I plays *Shibaraku** as part of *Sankai Nagoya* and the role of Fudō in *Tsuwamono Kongen Soga.*	
	1698	Nakamura Shichisaburō I performs at Kyoto's Hoteiya-za with marked success in *Keisei Asamagatake.*	
	1699	January: Chikamatsu's *Keisei Hotoke no Hara* is played at Kyoto's Miyako Mandayū-za, and Tōjūrō and Iwai Sagenta receive great acclaim for their acting. March: An annual actor's critique book (*yakusha hyōbanki**) called the *Yakusha Kuchi Shamisen* is published.	1703: Chikamatsu's *Sonezaki Shinjū** premieres at the Takemoto-za. The Toyotake-za puppet theatre is built this year.
	1704	February: Danjūrō I is murdered by a fellow actor.	
	1709	Sakata Tōjūrō dies.	
First Period of Perfection: II. The puppet theatre begins its golden age, surpassing Kabuki in popular esteem. However, during this time, Kabuki begins to absorb the dramas and theatrical effects of the puppet theatre. The masterpieces of the puppets are quickly adapted for Kabuki and performed. Meanwhile, theatre music prospers and dance drama develops.	1713	April: Danjūrō II* performs the first version of *Sukeroku Yukari no Edo Zakura**	
	1714	February; The Yamamura-za in Edo is abolished following a scandalous affair concerning Lady Ejima and the actor Ikushima Shingorō.	Takemoto Gidayū dies. 1715: Chikamatsu's *Kokusenya Kassen** premieres.
	1717	May: *Kokusenya Kassen* is performed in a Kabuki version in all three Edo theatres.	1720: Chikamatsu's *Shinjū Ten no Amijima** premieres.

	1724	April: All three Edo theatres construct complete roofs, becoming genuine buildings.	
	1731	March: Segawa Kikunojō I* gives the first performance of *Musume Dōjōji**.	
	1732	Miyakoji Bungonojō I comes to Edo, and *bungo bushi** becomes popular there.	
	1733	January: Danjūrō II performs *Sukeroku* using *katō bushi** music.	1734: Three men operate a single puppet for the first time, when *Ashiya Dōman Ōuchi Kagami** is presented. 1746: The puppet play *Sugawara Denju Tenarai Kagami** premieres. 1747 sees the premiere of *Yoshitsune Senbon Zakura**; and 1748, of *Kanadehon Chūshingura**.
	1749	Segawa Kikunojō I dies.	1750: The puppet play *Ichinotani Futaba Gunki** premieres.
Period of Diversification of Kabuki's Contents: This is Kabuki's second period of perfection. Such devices as the revolving stage* and trap lifts, invented by playwright Namiki Shōzō*, come into use. Such playwrights as Namiki Gohei I*, Nagawa Kamesuke*, and Nagawa Shimesuke are active. Meanwhile, theatre music becomes more	1753	December: Namiki Shōzō's *Keisei Ten no Hagoromo* premieres at Osaka's Ōnishi Shibai. The large *seri** trap lift is used here for the first time.	
	1758	December: Premiere at Osaka's Kado no Shibai of Shōzō's *Sanjikokku Yofune no Hajimari*. The revolving stage *(mawari butai)* is used by Kabuki for the first time. Danjūrō II dies this year.	

OVERVIEW OF THE PERIOD	DATES	SUMMARY	OTHER INCLUDING PUPPET THEATRE EVENTS
varied and a mixture of spoken drama with dance drama develops. Actors who appear and flourish include Danjūrōs II and IV*, Sawamura Sōjūrō I*, Nakamura Nakazō I*, Matsumoto Kōshirō IV*, and Nakamura Utaemon I*.			1765: The puppet theatre named Toyotake-za is closed. The puppet play *Honchō Nijūshikō** premieres in 1776, *Ōmi Genji Senjin Yakata** in 1767, and *Shinrei Yaguchi no Watashi** in the same year.
	1779	March: The first performance of the *tomimoto**-music dance drama named *Sono Omokage Asamagatake* at the Ichimura-za.	1722: the puppet theatre, Takemoto-za, is closed.
	1784	The *tokiwazu**-music dance drama entitled *Seki no To** premieres at Edo's Kiri-za.	1780: Premiere of the puppet play, *Shinpan Utazaemon**.
	1788	November: The *tokiwazu*-music dance drama entitled *Modori Kago** premieres at Edo's Nakamura-za. Namiko Shōzō's representative works include *Yadonashi Danshichi Shigure no Karakasa** (1767) and *Kuwanaya Tokuzō Irifune Monogatari* (1770). Nagawa Kamesuke's include *Meiboku Sendai Hagi** (1767) and *Katakiuchi Tengajaya Mura** (1781). Namiki Gohei's include *Sanmon Gosan no Kiri** (1778), *Godairiki Koi no Fujime**	

		(1794), and *Suda no Haru Geisha Kataki* (1796). Nagawa Shimesuke's include *Sumidagawa Gonichi Omokage** (1784).	1795: The Kansei era's reforms begin.
Period of Overripeness and Decadence: Along with the overripeness and decadence of the Bunka era, Kabuki also shows signs of eccentricity. Ghost plays*, murder plays, plays dealing with the exploits of thieves, and various other themes reflecting the popular taste of the time are used in the *kizewamono** dramatic genre, which now makes its appearance. In dance there appears the division of the main role into several so that the leading actor can portray a variety of roles, and quick-change dances become the fashion. Playwrights of the time include Sakurada Jisuke I*, Tsuruya Nanboku IV*, Segawa Jokō III*, and Kawatake Mokuami*. Actors include Matsumoto Kōshirō V*, Iwai Hanshirō V*, Nakamura Utaemon III* and IV*, Onoe Kikugorō III*, Ichikawa Danjūrō VII* and VIII*, Bandō Mitsugorō III* and IV*, and a varied list of others who are active in the *kizewamono* genre.	1796	April: The gabled roof over the stage is removed. July: Osaka's Kado no Shibai premieres Chikamatsu Tokusō's* *Ise Ondo Koi no Netaba**.	1804: Uemura Bunrakuen opens a puppet theatre in Osaka.
	1808	July: Edo's Ichimura-za premieres Tsuruya Nanboku's *Toki wa Ima Kikkyō no Hataage**. Nanboku's works include *Ehon Gappō ga Tsuji* (1810), *Osome Hisamatsu Ukina no Yomiuri** (1813), *Ukiyo Gara Hyoku no Inazuma* (1823), and *Tōkaidō Yotsuya Kaidan** (1825).	1812: Puppet performances begin on the grounds of Inari Shrine in Osaka.
	1818	March: The *kiyomoto**-music dance drama, *Yasuna** premieres as a single section drawn from a longer quick-change piece. Today a number of such dance pieces are all that remain of longer quick-change plays. These include the *nagauta**-music *Shiokumi**, *Echigo Jishi**, *Fuji Musume**, and *Tomoyakko;* the *kiyomoto*-music *Sanja Matsuri**, *Ochiudo**, *Kanda Matsuri**, and *Tobae**; the *tokiwazu*-music *Ukare Bozu, Rokkasen**, and *Toshima.* All of these were first performed during this period.	

OVERVIEW OF THE PERIOD	DATES	SUMMARY	OTHER INCLUDING PUPPET THEATRE EVENTS
	1840	Ichikawa Danjūrō VII* gives the first performance of *Kanjinchō** at Edo's Kawarazaki-za.	
	1841	The theatres are ordered to move to Asakusa as part of the Tenpō era reforms. From 1842 on, the theatres are found in Asakusa's Saruwaka-machi*.	Tenpō era reforms begin.
	1842	Danjūrō VII banished from Edo for breaking sumptuary laws.	American naval commander Perry come to Japan.
	1850	Danjūrō VII pardoned and allowed to return to Edo.	
	1851	August: Segawa Jokō's *Sakura Giminden** premieres.	
	1853	*Yowa Nasake Ukina no Yokogushi** is premiered.	Perry comes to Japan.
	1854	March: Kawatake Mokuami's *Miyakodori Nagare no Shiranami* is premiered at Edo's Kawarazaki-za. Mokuami writes plays for Ichikawa Kodanji IV*, producing many robber plays* *(shiranami mono)* during this period. His major works include *Sannin Kichiza Kuruwa no Hatsugai** (1860), *Aotozōshi Hana no Nishikie** (1862), *Soga Moyō Tateshi no Goshozome** (1864), *Tsuta Momiji Utsunoya Tōge** (1856).	1860: Uprising outside the Sakurada gate, main entry to the shogun's castle. Assassination of il Tairyō, high Shogunate official.

Meiji Period (1868-1912): This period revolves around the great actors Ichikawa Danjūrō IX*, Onoe Kikugorō V*, and Ichikawa Sadanji I*, known collectively as Dan-Kiku-Sa*. Following the death of these actors, one after the other, Kabuki enters a period extending from the late Meiji to the Taishō era; independent playwrights who are not attached to the theatres begin writing what becomes the *shin* ("New") *kabuki**. These Meiji period influences have a definite effect on Kabuki until the conclusion of World War II. (We thus may incorporate even so late a date in our consideration of this period.) Other great actors include Nakamura Utaemon V*, Matsumoto Kōshirō VII*, Ichikawa Chūsha VII*, Nakamura Ganjirō I*, and Ichimura Uzaemon XV*, and then Onoe Kikugorō VI*, Onoe Baikō VI*, and Nakamura Kichiemon I*.	1872	October: The Morita-za moves from Saruwaka-machi to Shintomi-chō. November: The new genre of *zangiri mono**, which incorporates Western-influenced social manners, is represented by the performances of such plays as *Sono Irodori Toki no Koeki* and *Kutsu Naoshi Warabe no Oshie*. Mokuami's *Tōkyō Nichi Shinbun* (1873) and *Shimachidori Tsuki no Shiranami** (1881) are also in this genre.	1868: Restoration of Imperial rule. 1872: The puppet theatre known as the Inari Shibai, which has moved to Osaka's Matsushima, changes its name to Bunraku-za.
	1874	July: The Kawarazaki-za opens in Shiba, Tokyo, and Danjūrō IX presents *Shinbutai Iwao no Kusunoki* in a manner based on historical fact. This kind of drama is termed living history* *(katsureki geki)*. Such works as *Hōjō Kudai Meika no Isaoshi* (1884) and *Nachi no Taki Chikai no Mongaku* (1889) are written and produced in this style.	1877: Satsuma rebellion. 1878: Sudō Sadanori, an Osakan, begins the movement toward a new dramatic form that comes to be known as Shinpa. In 1881, Kawakami Otojirō also helps to launch this new form. 1884: Sino-Japanese War. Shinpa receives a great boost in popularity with Kawakami Otojirō's "war-report" dramas.
	1886	August: Formation of the Engeki Kairyōkai (Association for the Improvement of Drama). September: The *Engeki Kairyō Ron Shiko (Personal Thoughts on the Improvement of the Drama)*, a critique, is published by Toyama Shōichi, followed in October by Suematsu Kenchō's critique entitled *Engeki Kairyō Iken (Ideas on the Improvement of the Drama)*.	

OVERVIEW OF THE PERIOD	DATES	SUMMARY	OTHER INCLUDING PUPPET THEATRE EVENTS
	1887	April: Performance of Kabuki for the Emperor at Inoue Kaoru's Tokyo mansion. Kabuki's social status is greatly enhanced.	
	1889	November: Opening of the Tokyo Kabuki-za*.	
	1893	Kawatake Mokuami, last of the true Edo Kabuki playwrights, dies.	
	1889	*Aku Genta*, a work by an independent playwright, Matsui (Tsubouchi) Shōyō*, is presented by Ichikawa Sadanji I.	
	1902	The Shōchiku* Joint Stock Corporation is founded by the brothers Ōtani Takejirō* and Shirai Matsujirō*; they embark on a venture of producing theatre on modern terms.	
	1903	February: Onoe Kikugorō V dies, followed by Danjūrō IX in September. The following year sees the death of Sadanji I, and the Dan-Kiku-Sa triumvirate of the Meiji period is gone.	
	1904	Tsubouchi Shōyō's historical drama, *Kiri Hitoha**, is produced. Shōyō publishes discussion of the need for dance reforms, *Shingaku Geki Ron (Argument for a New Musical Drama)*, this year.	Outbreak of the Russo-Japanese War.
	1908	November: Tamura Nariyoshi commences	

	management of the Ichimura-za in Shitaya, Tokyo, and gains success with his two young stars, Kikugorō VI and Kichiemon I. Thereafter, the period until about 1921 is known as the "Ichimura-za era."	
1909	November: Sadanji II* and Osanai Kaoru found the Jiyū Gekijō ("Free Theatre"). The modern theatre *(shingeki)* arises.	Bungei Kyōkai, a troupe led by Tsubouchi, is founded. *Hamlet* is staged as their first performance.
1911	March: Japan's first all Western-style theatre, the Teikoku Gekijō*, opens. Its stars include Kōshirō VII, Baikō VI, and Sawamura Sōjūrō V*.	
1913	May: Ichikawa Ennosuke II* and others establish the Waga Goe Kai, an experimental group that is active in the modern theatre movement. Other experimental theatre groups flourish. Among them are Onoe Kikugorō's 1914 Kyōgen-za and Morita Kanya XIII's* Bungei-za. August: Otani Takejirō commences management of the Kabuki-za.	Matsui Sumako's Geijitsu-za gives its first performances.
		1914: World War I erupts. 1919: Geijitsu-za disbanded.
1923	September: Great earthquake hits the Tokyo area and almost all Tokyo theatres are lost.	
		1925: Tsukiji Shō-Gekijō gives its first performances.
1928	July: Ichikawa Sadanji and troupe perform Kabuki in Russia.	

OVERVIEW OF THE PERIOD	DATES	SUMMARY	OTHER INCLUDING PUPPET THEATRE EVENTS
	1930	April: The Nihon Haiyū Gakkō (Japan Actors' School), founded by Kikugorō VI, opens.	
	1931	The Kabuki-za, Meiji-za*, and Shintomi-za come under the management of Shōchiku, and all Kabuki actors sign up with this company. May: the Zenshin-za* troupe is formed with Kawarazaki Chōjūrō and Nakamura Gan'emon III* as its stars.	The Manchurian incident occurs.
			1937: The Sino-Japanese Incident occurs. 1938: National general mobilization ordered.
	1940	February: Death of Sadanji II. August: Death of Ichikawa Shōchō II; September: Death of Utaemon V. During the decade surrounding 1940, the most important Meiji period actors who are still active pass away, while Kikugorō VI and Kichiemon I rise to the apex of Showa Kabuki.	
			1941: War begins with United States and Great Britain.
	1944	In conformity with the general plans laid out for the decisive battles to be fought in the closing years of the war, nineteen theatres are ordered to close. October: The *Kikubatake* scene of *Kiichi Hōgen Sanryaku no Maki** is performed as the final play at the Kabuki-za before the major battles begin.	

The Postwar Period of Kabuki: A new generation of Kabuki, which we should call "modern Kabuki," grows out of a period in which there are few theatres, theatrical art is under the strict control of the Occupation forces, and the leading actors die, one after the other. In this new generation many new works appear, and soon Kabuki is well on the road to economic revival.	1945	The great theatres of Tokyo are destroyed in air raids. October: Onoe Kikugorō VI plays in *Ginza Fukkō* and *Kagamijishi** at Teikoku Gekijō and begins the efforts toward postwar revival of the stage. November: *Terakoya* is scheduled at the Tōkyō Gekijō, but the production is cancelled at the order of the Occupation GHQ. This is followed by strict censorship of Kabuki plays. In November 1947, censorship is lifted.	World War II ends on August 15, 1945.
	1946	June: Ichikawa Ebizō (later Danjūrō XI*) gives his first performance as the lead in *Sukeroku Yukari no Edo Zakura*. This becomes the inspiration for the rise in favor of Kabuki's young stars. November: A hall at the Nihonbashi branch of the Mitsukoshi Department Stores opens as the Mitsukoshi Gekijō. The young stars of Kabuki appear here.	National Constitution proclaimed. Zenshin-za begins tour of entire country. 1948: Bunraku-za splits into two factions, the Mitsuwa Kai and the Chinami Kai.
	1949	January: Kōshirō VII dies, followed by Sawamura Sōjūrō VII* in March and Kikugorō VI in July. Experimental theatre productions, starring Nakamura Senjaku II* and Bandō Tsurunosuke (now Nakamura Tomijūrō V*) and directed by Takechi Tetsuji, begin.	1950: Korean War begins.
	1951	January: Tokyo's Kabuki-za, having been rebuilt, opens. March: Funabashi	Japan-U.S.A. Security Treaty signed.

OVERVIEW OF THE PERIOD	DATES	SUMMARY	OTHER INCLUDING PUPPET THEATRE EVENTS
		Seiichi's dramatization of the *Genji Monogatari* premieres. This actually rings the knell on postwar Kabuki. Jitsukawa Enjaku II* dies in February.	
	1954	September: Deaths of Nakamura Kichiemon I and Bandō Jūsaburō. The old Meiji-Taishō generation has been completely superseded by a new generation.	
	1955	Ichikawa Ennosuke (En'o I*) performs in Communist China. The Zenshin-za appears there in 1960, and Kabuki makes its first tour of the United States during the same year. Overseas tours begin to be popular.	
	1957	August: Matsumoto Kōshirō VIII* joins the Bungaku-za troupe and stars in *Akechi Mitsuhide.* This becomes the spark for Kabuki actors to begin to appear in other forms of theatre.	Successful launching of a satellite by U.S.S.R.
	1961	February: Kōshirō VIII and others sign a contract to join the Tōhō* Company and leave Shōchiku. November: Bandō Mitsugorō VII* dies.	
	1963	June: Ichikawa En'o dies.	Formation of the Bunraku Kyōkai.
	1964	March: Nakamura Kanzaburō XVII* stars in *Richard III.* April: Onoe Shōroku II* stars in *Cyrano de Bergerac.*	Tokyo Olympics.

1965	November: Danjūrō XI dies.	The Shinpa star Hanayagi Shōtarō dies.
1966	November: The Kokuritsu Gekijō (National Theatre of Japan*) opens. Its purpose is to perform and preserve classical theatre art and to train successors to the old traditions.	
1969	Film versions and modern theatre versions of Kabuki plays flourish. October: Sadanji III* dies. December: Ōtani Takejirō dies.	
		1970: Suicide of the author Mishima Yukio.
1973	Onoe Kikunosuke takes the name of Onoe Kikugorō VII*.	
1975	Theatre world celebrates fifty years of Shōwa Kabuki. Deaths of Bandō Mitsugorō VIII* and Morita Kanya XIV*.	

APPENDIX II
Major Plays

1. Plays are listed by their current formal titles; dance dramas are given by their popularized titles, followed by their more formal titles in parentheses. The listing is selective. Many plays have additional titles not given in this book.
2. The following abbreviations are used to signify the major categories of plays: ka = Kabuki, jo = *jōruri* (here meaning a work originally written as a puppet play), bu = *buyō* (dance drama).
3. For many entries the most popular title is given in parentheses following the formal title.
4. *Shin kabuki** plays are not included in this list.

	A	AUTHOR
ka	*Akegarasu Hana no Nureginu**	Sakurada Jisuke III* (1851)
ka	*Ami Moyō Toro no Kikukiri*	Kawatake Mokuami* (1865)
ka	*Ansei Kibun Tsukuda no Yo Arashi*	Yoshikawa Shinsui (Morita Kanya XII*) (1914)
ka	*Ansei Mitsugumi Sakazuki*	Kawatake Shinshichi III* (1893)
ka	*Aotozōshi Hana no Nishikie* (Benten Kozō)*	Kawatake Mokuami (1862)
bu	*Asazuma Bune (Nami Makura Tsuki no Asazuma)*	Sakurada Jisuke II* (1820)
jo	*Ashiya Dōman Ōuchi Kagami**	Takeda Izumo II* (1734)
bu	*Ataka no Shinseki (Odoke ni Waga Ataka no Shinseki)*	Kawatake Mokuami (1865)
bu	*Awamochi (Hana no Hoka ni Waka no Kyokutsuki)*	Sakurada Jisuke III* (1845)
jo	*Awa no Naruto**	Chikamatsu Hanji*, etc. (1768)
bu	*Ayatsuri Sanbasō* (Yanagi ni Ito Hikuya Go Hiiki)* (See *Sanbasō**)	Minekoto Hachijūrō (1853)

	B	
ka	*Banzui Chōbei Shōjin no Manaita* (Manaita no Chōbei)*	Sakurada Jisuke I* (1803)

C

jo	*Chikagoro Kawara no Tatehiki* (Horikawa)*	Tamegawa Sōsuke, etc. (1782)
ka	*Chūshin Renri no Hachime (Uekiya)*	Namiki Gohei I* (1794)

D

jo	*Daikyōji Mukashi Goyomi* (Osan Mohei)*	Chikamatsu Monzaemon* (1715)
jo	*Dan no Ura Kabuto Gunki* (Akoya no Kotozeme)*	Matsuda Bunkodō, Hasegawa Senshi (1732)
ka	*Date Kurabe Okuni Kabuki (Sendai Hagi; Kasane no Miuri)*	Sakurada Jisuke I* (1778)
jo	*Date Musume Koi no Higanoko* (Yagura no Oshichi)*	Suga Sensuke, etc. (1773)

E

bu	*Echigo Jishi* (Osozakura Teniha no Nanamoji)*	Shinoda Kinji I (1811)
ka	*Edo Sakura Kiyomizu Seigen*	Kawatake Mokuami (1858)
ka	*Edo Sodachi Omatsuri Sashichi* (Omatsuri Sashichi)*	Kawatake Shinshichi III (1898)
jo	*Ehon Taikōki (Taikōki)*	Chikamatsu Yanagi, etc. (1779)

F

ka	*Fujibita Itsukuba no Shigeyama*	Kawatake Mokuami (1877)
ka	*Fuji Musume**	Katsui Gonpachi (1826)
bu	*Funa Benkei**	Kawatake Mokuami (1885)
ka	*Fune Uchikomu Hashima no Shiranami* (Ikake Matsu)*	Kawatake Mokuami (1866)
bu	*Futa Omote (Shinobu Kusa Koi no Utsushie)*	Kawatake Shinshichi I (1775)
jo	*Futatsu Chōchō Kuruwa Nikki**	Takeda Izumo II, etc. (1749)

G

bu	*Geki Zaru*	Anonymous (1824)
jo	*Genpei Nunobiki no Taki* (Sanemori Monogatari)*	Namiki Sōsuke, etc. (1749)
bu	*Genroku Hanami Odori**	Takeshiba Hyōsuke (1878)
jo	*Gion Sairei Shinkōki* (Kinkakuji)*	Nakamura Akei, etc. (1757)
jo	*Goban Taiheiki**	Chikamatsu Monzaemon (1706)
ka	*Godairiki Koi no Fūjime**	Namiki Gohei I (1794)
jo	*Gokusai Shiki Musume Ogi*	Chikamatsu Hanji, etc. (1760)

bu	*Gonpachi (Sono Kouta Yume Mo Yoshiwara)*	Fukumori Kiusuke (1816)
bu	*Goro* (Yae Kokonoe Hana no Sugata E)*	Mimasuya Nisōji (1841)
jo	*Goshō Zakura Horikawa Youchi* (Benkei Jōshi)*	Matsuda Bunkodō, etc. (1737)
jo	*Gotaiheiki Shiraishi Banashi* (Shiraishi Banashi)*	Utei Enba, etc. (1780)

H

jo	*Hachijin Shugo no Honjō**	Nakamura Gyōgan, etc. (1807)
ka	*Hachiman Matsuri Yomiya no Nigiwai* (Chijimaya Shinsuke)*	Kawatake Mokuami (1860)
jo	*Hade Kurabe Ise Monogatari* (Ise Monogatari)*	Nagawa Kamesuke (1775)
jo	*Hade Sugata Onna Maiginu* (Sakaya)*	Takemoto Saburobei (1772)
bu	*Hagoromo**	Kawatake Shinshichi III (1898)
jo	*Hakata Kojōrō Nami Makura**	Chikamatsu Monzaemon (1718)
jo	*Hakone Reigen Izari no Adauchi* (Izari no Adauchi)*	Shiba Shisō (1801)
bu	*Hamamatsu Kaze (Hamamatsu Kaze Koi no Kotonoha)*	Anonymous (1785)
jo	*Hana no Ueno Homare no Ishibumi* (Shidodera)*	Shiba Shisō, etc. (1788)
bu	*Hane no Kamuro* (Haru wa Mukashi Yukari no Hanabusa)*	Anonymous (1785)
bu	*Harugoma (Taimen Hana no Harugoma)*	Masuyama Kinpachi (1791)
bu	*Hashi Benkei**	Kineya Kangorō III (1868)
jo	*Heike Nyogo no Shima* (Shunkan)*	Chikamatsu Monzaemon (1719)
jo	*Hibariyama Hime Sudematsu* (Chūjō Hime)*	Namiki Sōsuke (1740)
jo	*Hidakagawa Iriai Zakura**	Chikamatsu Hanji, etc. (1759)
ka	*Higashiyama Sakura Zōshi*	Segawa Jokō III (1851)
jo	*Hikosan Gongen Chikai no Sukedashi* (Keyamura)*	Umeno Shitakaze, etc. (1786)
jo	*Hiragana Seisuiki* (Seisuiki)*	Matsuda Bunkodō, etc. (1739)
ka	*Hōjō Kudai Meika no Isaoshi (Takatoki*)*	Kawatake Mokuami (1884)
jo	*Honchō Nijūshikō (Nijūshikō)*	Chikamatsu Hanji, etc. (1766)
jo	*Horikawa Nami no Tsuzumi*	Chikamatsu Monzaemon (1707)
ka	*Hoshi Yadoru Tsuyu no Tamagiku*	Kawatake Shinshichi III (1900)
ka	*Hototogisu Date no Kikigake*	Kawatake Mokuami (1876)
ka	*Hyakunin Machi Ukina no Yomiuri (Suzuki Mondo)*	Sakurada Jisuke III (1852)
jo	*Hyoshimaru Wakaki no Sakura*	Chikamatsu Yanagi (1801)
bu	*Hyōtan Namazu (Nijiri Gaki Nanatsu Iroha)*	Segawa Jokō II (1818)

I

bu	*Ibaraki**	Kawatake Mokuami (1883)
jo	*Ichinotani Futaba Gunki* (Kumagai Jinya)*	Namiki Sōsuke, etc. (1751)
jo	*Igagoe Dōchū Sugoroku* (Igagoe)*	Chikamatsu Hanji, etc. (1783)
ka	*Igagoe Norikake ga Tsuba*	Nagawa Kamesuke (1777)
bu	*Ikioi (Kikujo no Kusazuri)*	Anonymous (1787)
jo	*Ikudama Shinjū*	Chikamatsu Monzaemon (1715)
jo	*Imoseyama Onna Teikin**	Chikamatsu Hanji, etc. (1771)
bu	*Inaka Genji Tsuyunoshi no Nome (Inaka Genji)*	Sakurada Jisuke III (1867)
ka	*Iroha Gana Shijū Shichi Moji*	Nagawa Shimesuke (1791)
ka	*Ise Ondo Koi no Netaba**	Chikamatsu Tokusō (1796)
ka	*Ittō Ryū Narita Kakegaku*	Takeshiba Kisui (1897)

J

ka	*Jiraiya Gōketsu Monogatari*	Kawatake Mokuami (1852)
ka	*Jitsugetsu Seichūya no Oriwake*	Kawatake Mokuami (1859)
ka	*Jitsugetsu Seikyōwa Seidan*	Kawatake Mokuami (1876)

K

ka	*Kachizu Mō Ukina no Hanabure*	Tsuruya Nanboku IV* (1810)
bu	*Kagamijishi* (Shunkyō Kagamijishi)*	Fukuchi Ōchi (1893)
ka	*Kagamiyama Gonichi no Iwafuji*	Kawatake Mokuami (1860)
jo	*Kagamiyama Kokyō no Nishikie* (Onna Chūshingura)*	Yō Yodai (1782)
jo	*Kagamiyama Sato no Kikigaki*	Nakamura Gyōgan (1796)
ka	*Kagekiyo*	Sakurada Jisuke I (revision, 1778)
ka	*Kagotsurube Sato no Eizame**	Kawatake Shinshichi III (1888)
bu	*Kagoya (Kanadehon Chūshingura)*	Sakurada Jisuke III (1847)
ka	*Kaidan Botan Dōrō* (Botan Dōrō)*	Kawatake Shinshichi III (1892)
bu	*Kairaishi (Mata Arata Mitsu Gumi Sakazuki)*	Sakurada Jisuke II (1824)
jo	*Kajiwara Heiza Homare no Ishikiri (Ishikiri Kajiwara)* (See *Miura no Ōsuke Kōbai Tazuna*)*	Matsuda Bunkodō, Hasegawa Senshi (1730)
bu	*Kakubei (Nochi no Tsuki Shuen no Shimadai)*	Segawa Jokō III (1888)
jo	*Kamagafuchi Futatsu Domoe*	Namiki Sōsuke (1737)
jo	*Kamakura Sandaiki* (Sandaiki)*	attr. Chikamatsu Hanji (1781)
jo	*Kamiko Jitate Ryōmen Kagami*	Suga Sensuke (1768)
ka	*Kami no Megumi Wagō no Torikumi* (Megumi no Kenka)*	Takeshiba Kisui (1890)
jo	*Kanadehon Chūshingura* (Chūshingura)*	Takeda Izumo II, etc. (1748)
ka	*Kanadehon Suzuri no Takashima*	Kawatake Mokuami (1858)

bu	*Kanda Matsuri* (Shimero Yare Iro no Kakegoe)*	Mimasuya Nisōji III (1839)
bu	*Kanjinchō**	Namiki Gohei III (1840)
ka	*Kanjin Kanmon Tekuda no Hajimari (Tojin Goroshi)*	Namiki Gohei I (1789)
ka	*Kanzen Choaku Nozoki Karakuri (Murai Chōan)*	Kawatake Mokuami (1862)
bu	*Kappore (Hatsukasumi Sora mo Sumiyoshi)*	Kawatake Mokuami (1888)
jo	*Karukaya Dōshin Tsukushi no Iezuto*	Namiki Sōsuke, etc. (1735)
bu	*Kasane* (Iro Moyō Chotto Karimame)*	Matsui Kozō II (1823)
bu	*Kashima Odori (Shiki no Nagame Yosete Mitsudai)*	Segawa Jokō II (1813)
ka	*Kasuga no Tsubone*	Fukuchi Ōchi (1891)
ka	*Katakiuchi Tengajaya Mura* (Tengajaya Mura)*	Nagawa Kamesuke II (1781)
jo	*Katakiuchi Tsuzure no Nishiki (Daian Jizu Tsumi)*	Matsuda Bunkodō, Miyoshi Shōraku (1736)
jo	*Katsuragawa Renri no Shigarami* (Obiya)*	Suga Sensuke (1776)
ka	*Keian Taiheiki**	Kawatake Mokuami (1870)
jo	*Keisei Hangonko**	Chikamatsu Monzaemon (1708)
ka	*Keisei Setsugekka* (Kari no Tayori)*	Kanezawa Ryūgyoku (1830)
ka	*Keisei Tamata Zuna*	Kanezawa Ryūgyoku (1837)
ka	*Kenuki**	Tsuuchi Hanjūrō (1742)
ka	*Kichi Sama Mairu Yukari no Otozure*	Kawatake Mokuami (1869)
jo	*Kiichi Hōgen Sanryaku no Maki (Kikubatake; Ichijō Okura Kyo)*	Matsuda Bunkodō, Hasegawa Senshi (1731)
bu	*Kikujidō*	Kawatake Shinshichi III (1852)
ka	*Kinmon Gosan no Kiri* (See *Sanmon Gosan no Kiri**)	Namiki Gohei I (1778)
bu	*Kioijishi* (Kioijishi Kabuki no Hanakago)*	Segawa Jokō III (1851)
jo	*Kishi Hime Matsu Kutsuwa Kagami*	Toyotake Ōritsu, etc. (1762)
ka	*Kiwametsuki Banzui Chōbei* (Yudono no Chōbei)*	Kawatake Mokuami (1881)
ka	*Kiyomasa Seichu Ryoku*	Kawatake Shinshichi III (1897)
ka	*Koi Bikyaku Yamato Orai*	Namiki Shōzō (1757)
jo	*Koi Musume Mukashi Hachijō*	Matsu Kanshi, Yoshida Kadomaru (1775)
jo	*Koi Nyōbo Somewake Tazuna* (Shigenoi Kowakare)*	Yoshida Kanshi, etc. (1751)
bu	*Kokaji**	Kimura Tomiko (1939)
ka	*Koko ga Edo Kode no Tatehiki*	Kawatake Mokuami (1863)
ka	*Kokoro no Nazo Toketa Iroito*	Tsuruya Nanboku IV (1810)
jo	*Kokusenya Kassen**	Chikamatsu Monzaemon (1715)
jo	*Komochi Yamanba* (Yaegiri Kuruwa Banashi)*	Chikamatsu Monzaemon (1712)
ka	*Komonki Osanago Koryaku*	Kawatake Mokuami (1877)
bu	*Komori* (Yamatogana Tamuke no Itsumoji)*	Nasuyama Kinpachi (1823)

ka	*Konoma no Hoshi Hakone no Shikabue*	Chikamatsu Monzaemon (1808)
jo	*Konoshita Kage Hazama Kassen (Takenaka Torido)*	Wakatake Fuemi, etc. (1789)
ka	*Kore wa Hyōban Ukina no Yomiuri* (Choinose no Zenroku)*	Sakurada Jisuke III (1862)
ka	*Kosode Soga Azami no Ironui* (Izayoi Seishin)*	Kawatake Mokuami (1859)
ka	*Kotobuki Shiki Sanbasō (See Sanbasō*)*	Kineya Rokuemon (music, 1856)
ka	*Kumo ni Magō Ueno no Hatsuhana (Kochiyama to Naozamurai)*	Kawatake Mokuami (1881)
bu	*Kumo no Ito Azusa no Yumihari*	Kanai Sanshō (1765)
bu	*Kumo no Kyoshimai (Wagase Ko ga Koi no Aizura)*	Sakurada Jisuke (1781)
bu	*Kuramajishi (Meoto Sake Kawaranu Nakanaka)*	Nakamura Jūsuke I (1777)
ka	*Kuramayama*	Kawatake Mokuami (1856)
bu	*Kurozuka**	Kimura Tomiko (1939)
ka	*Kuruwa Bunshō* (Yoshidaya Yūgiri Izaemon)*	Chikamatsu Monzaemon (1808)
bu	*Kusazuri Biki* (Shōfudatsuki Kongen Kusazuri)*	Anonymous (1814)
jo	*Kusunoki Mukashi Banashi*	Namiki Sōsuke, etc. (1746)
ka	*Kusunoki Ryū Hanami no Makubari (Marubashi Chūya)*	Kawatake Mokuami (1870)
ka	*Kyōkaku Harusame Gasa (Harusame Gasa)*	Fukuchi Ōchi (1897)
bu	*Kyō Ningyō (Haroiri Ayame Ningyō)*	Sakurada Jisuke III (1843)

M

bu	*Makasho (Kangyō Yuki no Sugatami)*	Sakurada Jisuke II (1820)
bu	*Masakado* (Shinobi Yoru Koi wa Kusemono)*	Takarada Jusuke (1836)
jo	*Meiboku Sendai Hagi* (Sendai Hagi)*	Nagawa Kamesuke, etc. (1777)
jo	*Meido no Hikyaku* (Koi Bikyaku Yamato Orai)*	Chikamatsu Monzaemon (1711)
ka	*Mekura Nagaya Ume Ga Kagatobi* (Kagatobi)*	Kawatake Mokuami (1886)
bu	*Migawari Zazen**	Okamura Shikō (1910)
bu	*Mitsumen Komori (Hana Nichō Magaki no Urareme)*	Tsuuchi Jihei II (1824)
bu	*Mitsu Ningyō* (Sono Sugata Hana no Utshishi E)*	Sakurada Jisuke III (1819)
jo	*Miura no Ōsuke Kōbai Tazuna* (Ishikiri Kajiwara)*	Matsuda Bunkodō, Hasegawa Senshi (1730)
ka	*Miyakodori Nagare no Shiranami*	Kawatake Mokuami (1854)

bu	*Mochizuki*	Kineya Kangorō IV (1870)
bu	*Modori Bashi* (Modori Kage Koi no Tsunc Moji)*	Kawatake Mokuami (1876)
bu	*Modori Kago* (Modori Kago Iro ni Aikata)*	Sakurada Jisuke I (1788)
bu	*Momijigari**	Kawatake Mokuami (1887)
bu	*Munekiyo (Onai Hitome no Sekimori)*	Nagawa Motosuke (1828)
bu	*Musume Dōjōji* (Kyōganoko Musume Dōjōji)*	Fujimoto Tōbun (1753)
ka	*Musume Gonomi Ukina no Yokogushi* (Kirare Otomi)*	Kawatake Mokuami (1864)
jo	*Musume Kagekiyo Yashima Nikki (Hyūga Shima)*	Wakatake Fuemi, etc. (1764)

N

jo	*Nagamachi Onna no Harakiri*	Chikamatsu Monzaemon (1712)
jo	*Nanbantetsu Gotō no Menuki* (Yoshitsune Koshigoejō)*	Namiki Sōsuke (1735)
ka	*Narukami**	Tsuuchi Hanjūrō, etc. (1742)
jo	*Nasu no Yoichi Saikai Suzuri*	Namiki Sōsuke, etc. (1734)
ka	*Natori Gusa Heike Monogatari* (Shigemori Kangen)*	Kawatake Mokuami (1876)
jo	*Natsu Matsuri Naniwa Kagami* (Natsu Matsuri)*	Namiki Sōsuke, etc. (1745)
jo	*Nebiki no Kadomatsu**	Chikamatsu Monzaemon (1718)
jo	*Nigatsudō Rōben Sugi no Yurai**	Kako Chikajō (1887)
ka	*Ningen Banji Kane Yo no Naka**	Kawatake Mokuami (1879)
bu	*Ninin Bakama*	Fukuchi Ōchi (1894)
bu	*Ninin Shōjō (Kotobuki Ninin Shōjō)*	Kawatake Shinshichi III (1874)
ka	*Ninjō Banashi Bunshichi Motoyui* (Bunshichi Motoyui)*	Enokido Kenji (1902)
ka	*Noriaibune* (Noriaibune Eho Manzai)*	Sakurada Jisuke III (1843)

O

bu	*Ochiudo* (Michiyuki Tabiji no Hanamuke)*	Mimasuya Nisōji (1833)
ka	*Ōgibyoshi Ōoka Seidan*	Kawatake Mokuami (1875)
bu	*Ohan (Michiyuki Shian no Hoka)*	Sakurada Jisuke II (1819)
bu	*Oharame (Kaketate Matsuru Iro no Ukioe)*	Segawa Jokō II (1810)
jo	*Ōmi Genji Senjin Yakata* (Moritsuna Jinya)*	Chikamatsu Hanji, etc. (1769)
bu	*Omiwa (Negai no Ito Enishi no Oda Maki)*	Takarada Jusuke (1833)
bu	*Ōmori Hikoshichi**	Fukuchi Ōchi (1897)
bu	*Onatsu Kyōran**	Tsubouchi Shōyō (1914)
bu	*Oniji Hyōshimai (Tsuki no Kao mo Naka Natori Gusa)*	Kineya Masajiro I (1793)
jo	*Onna Goroshi Abura no Jigyoku* (Abura no Jigyoku)*	Chikamatsu Monzaemon (1721)

bu	*Onna Modori Kago (Sugata no Hana Torii no Irozashi)*	Sakurado Jisuke I (1805)
jo	*Ono no Tōfū Aoyagi Sugiri (Ono no Tōfū)*	Takeda Izumo II (1754)
ka	*Ōsakazuki Shusen no Tsuwamono*	Kawatake Mokuami (1881)
jo	*Ōshū Adachigahara* (Sodehagi Saimon, Adasan)*	Chikamatsu Hanji, etc. (1762)
ka	*Osome Hisamatsu Ukina no Yomiuri* (Osome no Nanayaku)*	Tsuruya Nanboku IV (1813)
bu	*Osome no Michiyuki* (Michiyuki Ukina no Tomodori)*	Tsuruya Nanboku IV (1825)
jo	*Ōtō no Miya Asahi no Yoroi (Migawari Ondo)*	Takeda Izumo I (1723)
bu	*Otsue (Namo Otsue Kabuki no Mazebari)*	Kawatake Mokuami (1875)

R

bu	*Renjishi**	Kawatake Mokuami (1872)
bu	*Rokkasen* (Rokkasen Sugata no Irodori)*	Matsui Kōji (1831)
bu	*Ryōkan to Komori**	Tsubouchi Shōyō (1929)

S

bu	*Sagi Musume* (Yanagi ni Hina Shochō no Saezuri)*	Mimasuya Nisōji (1762)
ka	*Sakura Giminden* (Sakura Sōgo)*	Segawa Jokō III (1851)
jo	*Sakuratsuba Urami no Samezaya* (Unagidani)*	Anonymous (1774)
bu	*Sanbasō**	(Various versions)
ka	*Sandai Banashi Koza no Shinsaku*	Kawatake Mokuami (1863)
bu	*Sanja Matsuri* (Yayoi no Hana Asakusa Matsuri)*	Segawa Jokō II (1832)
jo	*Sanjūsan Gendō Munagi no Yurai* (Yanagi)*	Wakatake Fuemi, etc. (1760)
ka	*Sanmon Gosan no Kiri* (Kinmon Gosan no Kiri)*	Namiki Gohei I (1778)
bu	*Sannin Katawa**	Takeshiba Kisui (1898)
bu	*Sannin Kichiza Kuruwa no Hatsugai**	Kawatake Mokuami (1860)
bu	*Sannin Namayoi (Sekku Asobi Koi no Tenarai)*	Takarada Jusuke (1833)
bu	*Sanzesō Nishiki Bunshō**	Sakurada Jisuke III (1857)
bu	*Sarashime* (Mata Koko ni Sugata Hakkei)*	Sakurada Jisuke II (1813)
ka	*Satomi*	Sakurada Jisuke III (1852)
bu	*Seki no To* (Tsumoru Koi Yuki Seki no To)*	Takarada Jurai (1784)
jo	*Sekitori Senryō Nobori (Senryō Nobori)*	Chikamatsu Hanji (1767)
jo	*Sesshū Gappō ga Tsuji* (Gappō)*	Suga Sensuke, Wakatake Fuemi (1773)
ka	*Shibaraku**	Mimasuya Hyōgo (1697)

bu	*Shichiya no Kura (Shichiya no Kura Kokoro no Irekai)*	Kawatake Mokuami (1876)
ka	*Shikorobiki*	Kawatake Mokuami (1872)
ka	*Shimachidori Tsuki no Shiranami* (Shimachidori)*	Kawatake Mokuami (1881)
ka	*Shimoyo no Kane Jūji no Tsujiura*	Kawatake Mokuami (1880)
jo	*Shinjū Ten no Amijima* (Kamiji)*	Chikamatsu Monzaemon (1720)
jo	*Shinjū Yoi Gōshin**	Chikamatsu Monzaemon (1722)
bu	*Shin Nanatsumen*	Fukuchi Ōchi (1893)
jo	*Shinpan Utazaemon* (Nozaki Mura)*	Chikamatsu Hanji (1780)
jo	*Shinrei Yaguchi no Watashi**	Fukuuchi Kigai (1770)
ka	*Shin Sarayashiki Tsuki no Amagasa* (Sakanaya Sogorō)*	Kawatake Mokuami (1883)
bu	*Shin Shakkyō (Botan Chō Ōgi no Irodori)*	Kawatake Mokuami (1878)
jo	*Shinshu Kawanakajima Kassen* (Terutora Haizen)*	Chikamatsu Monzaemon (1721)
jo	*Shin Usuyuki Monogatari**	Matsuda Bunkodō, etc. (1741)
ka	*Shiobara Tasuke Ichidaiki**	Kawatake Shinshichi III (1892)
ka	*Shiokumi* (Shichimai Tsuzuki Hana no Sugatae)*	Sakurada Jisuke II (1811)
ka	*Shirami Monogatari*	Kawatake Mokuami (1853)
ka	*Shisenryō Goban no Umenoha**	Kawatake Mokuami (1885)
bu	*Shitadashi Sanbasō* (Mata Kuru Haru Suzuna no Tanemaki)* (See *Sanbasō*)*	Sakurada Jisuke II (1812)
ka	*Shōchiku Bai Yuki no Akebono*	Kawatake Mokuami (1856)
bu	*Shōjō (Shōjō Yuki no Eizame)*	Sakurada Jisuke II (1820)
jo	*Shō Utsushi Asagao Nikki* (Asagao Nikki)*	Yamada Anzanshi (1832)
bu	*Shūjaku Jishi* (Hanabusa Shūjaku Jishi)*	Anonymous (1754)
ka	*Soga Moyō Tateshi no Goshozome* (Gosho no Gorozō)*	Kawatake Mokuami (1864)
ka	*Soga no Taimen* (Kotobuki Soga no Taimen)*	Kawatake Mokuami (1676; revision, 1903)
jo	*Some Moyō Imose no Kadomatsu*	Suga Sensuke (1767)
jo	*Sonezaki Shinjū**	Chikamatsu Monzaemon (1703)
ka	*Sono Mukashi Koi no Edo Zome (Yaoya Oshichi)*	Fukumori Kyūsuke (1809)
ka	*Suda no Haru Geisha Katagi (Ume no Yoshibei)*	Namiki Gohei (1796)
jo	*Sugawara Denju Tenarai Kagami**	Takeda Izumo, etc. (1746)
ka	*Suitengū Megumi no Fukagawa* (Fudeya Kōbei)*	Kawatake Mokuami (1885)
bu	*Sukeroku (Hana Goyomi Iro no Showake)*	Sakurada Jisuke III (1839)
ka	*Sukeroku Yukari no Edo Zakura**	Tsuuchi Jihei II (1713)
bu	*Suma (Imayō Suma no Utsushie)*	Sakurada Jisuke II (1815)
jo	*Suma no Miyako Genpei Tsutsuji* (Ogiya Kumagai)*	Matsuda Bunkodō, Hasegawa Senshi (1730)
bu	*Sumidagawa**	Yamazaki Shikō (1919)

ka	*Sumidagawa Gonichi no Omokage* (Hokaibō)*	Nagawa Shimesuke (1784)
ka	*Sumidagawa Hana no Goshozome*	Tsuruya Nanboku IV (1814)
bu	*Sumi Nuri Onna*	Takeshiba Kisui (1907)
bu	*Suō Otoshi* (Suō Otoshi Nasu no Katari)*	Fukuchi Ōchi (1892)
ka	*Suzugamori* (Ukiyozuka Hyoku no Inazuma)*	Tsuruya Nanboku IV (1823)

T

bu	*Tachi Nusubito**	Yamazaki Shikō (1917)
bu	*Tadanobu (Itsu no Kikuchō Hatsune no Michiyuki)*	Segawa Jokō II (1808)
jo	*Taiheiki Chūshin Kōshaku (Chūshin Kōshaku)*	Chikamatsu Hanji, etc. (1766)
ka	*Taiko no Oto Chū no Sanryaku* (Sakai no Taiko)*	Kawatake Mokuami (1873)
bu	*Takasago (Meoto Matsu Takasago Tanzen)*	Kineya Matajirō I, music (1785)
jo	*Tamamono Mae Asahi no Tamoto* (Tamasan)*	Chikamatsu Baishiken, etc. (1806)
bu	*Tamausagi (Tsuki Yuki Hana Nagori no Bundai)*	Sakurada Jisuke II (1820)
bu	*Tamaya (Odoke Niwaka Shabon no Tamatori)*	Segawa Jokō II (1832)
bu	*Tenaraiko (Kakitsubata Nanae no Someginu)*	Masuyama Kinpachi (1792)
ka	*Tenjiku Tokubei Ikoku Banashi**	Tsuruya Nanboku IV (1804)
bu	*Tobae* (Ōnnagori Oshie no Mazebari)*	Sakurada Jisuke II (1819)
ka	*Tōkaidō Yotsuya Kaidan* (Yotsuya Kaidan)*	Tsuruya Nanboku IV (1825)
ka	*Toki wa Ima Kikkyō no Hataage* (Badarai no Mitsuhide)*	Tsuruya Nanboku IV (1808)
bu	*Tokusa Kari (Sugata no Hana Aki no Nanakusa)*	Kineya Matajirō I, music (1796)
ka	*Tomigaoka Koi no Yama Biraki (Futari Shinbei)*	Namiki Gohei (1798)
bu	*Tomoyakko (Nijiri Gaki Nanatsu Iroha)*	Segawa Jokō II (1828)
bu	*Tonbi Yakko (Manete Mimasu Shiki no Waza Ogi)*	Kineya Rokusaburō IV, music (1814)
bu	*Toshima (Hana Goyomi Iro no Showaka)*	Sakurada Jisuke III (1839)
jo	*Tsubosaka Reigenki**	Kako Chikajō (revision, 1887)
bu	*Tsuchigumo**	Kawatake Mokuami (1881)
ka	*Tsuki no Kakezara Koiji no Yoshiyami*	Kawatake Mokuami (1865)
bu	*Tsuki no Maki (Tsuki Yuki Hana Makie No Sakazuki)*	Sakurada Jisuke II (1827)
bu	*Tsuri Onna* (Ebisu Mōde Koi no Tsuribari)*	Kawatake Mokuami (1883)
ka	*Tsuta Momiji Utsunoya Tōge* (Bunya Goroshi)*	Kawatake Mokuami (1856)

ka	*Tsuta Moyo Chizome no Goshuin*	Kawatake Shinshichi III (1889)
ka	*Tsuyu Kosode Mukashi Hachijō* (Kamiyui Shinza)*	Kawatake Mokuami (1873)

U

bu	*Ukare Bozu (Shichimai Tsuzuki Hana no Sugatae)*	Sakurada Jisuke II (1812)
ka	*Ukiyozuka Hyoku no Inazuma (Sayaate; Suzugamori*)*	Tsuruya Nanboku IV (1823)
ka	*Uraomote Chūshingura*	Mimasuya Nisōji, etc. (1833)
bu	*Urashima (Nigirigaki Nanatsu Iroha)*	Segawa Jokō II (1828)
bu	*Utsubo Zaru* (Hana Butai Kasumi no Saru Hiki)*	Takarada Jusuke (1838)
ka	*Uwabami Oyoshi Uwasa no Adauchi*	Segawa Jokō III (1866)

W

jo	*Wada Gassen Onna Maizuru (Hangaku)*	Namiki Sōsuke (1736)
ka	*Wakagi no Adanagusa* (Ranchō)*	Kiyomizu Senkatsu (1855)
bu	*Wankyū (Midare Gokoro Sato no Tegoto)*	Sakurada Jisuke III (1839)

Y

ka	*Yadonashi Danshichi Shigure no Karakasa**	Namiki Shōzō (1767)
bu	*Yakko Dako (Yakko Dako Sato no Harukaze)*	Kawatake Mokuami (1893)
bu	*Yakko Dōjōji (Dōjōji Koi Hakusemono)*	Matsumoto Kōji (1829)
bu	*Yamagaeri (Yamagaeri Makenu Kikyō)*	Sakurada Jisuke II (1823)
bu	*Yamanba* (Takigi Ō Yukima no Ichikawa)*	Mimasuya Nisōji (1848)
jo	*Yamatogana Ariwara Keizu* (Ranpei Monogurui)*	Asada Itchō, etc. (1752)
bu	*Yami no Ume Hyaku Monogatari*	Kawatake Shinshichi II (1800)
ka	*Yanone* (Yanone Goro)*	Fujimoto Tōbun (revision, 1740)
jo	*Yari no Gonza Kasane Katabira**	Chikamatsu Monzaemon (1717)
bu	*Yasuna* (Miyama no Hana Todokane Edaburi)*	Shinoda Kinji (1818)
jo	*Yoshitsune Koshigoejō (Gotō)*	Namiki Eisuke (1754)
jo	*Yoshitsune Senbon Zakura* (Senbon Zakura)*	Takeda Izumo II, etc. (1747)
bu	*Yoshiwara Suzume (Oshiegusa Yoshiwara Suzume)*	Sakurada Jisuke I (1768)
ka	*Youchi no Soga Kariba no Akebono**	Kawatake Mokuami (1881)
ka	*Yowa Nasake Ukina no Yokogushi* (Kirare Yosa)*	Segawa Jokō III (1853)

jo	*Yura no Minato Sengen Chōja* (Sanshō Dayū)*	Chikamatsu Hanji, etc. (1761)
jo	*Yūshoku Kamakurayama* (Sano no Genzaemon)*	Suga Sensuke, etc. (1789)

Z

bu	*Zatō (Kaesu Gaesu Nagori no Bundai)*	Katsui Genpachi (1826)
jo	*Zōho Chūshingura*	Takeshiba Genzō (1902)
ka	*Zōho Futatsu Domoe**	Kimura Enji (1861)
ka	*Zōho Momoyama Monogatari**	Kawatake Mokuami (1876)

APPENDIX III
Variant and Popularized Play and Act Titles

1. This appendix includes titles commonly used for Kabuki plays (and parts of plays) performed today. The listing is selective.
2. The alphabetical list on the left contains short, variant, and popular forms of titles both for full plays and for particular acts, scenes, and parts of scenes. The pertinent full play titles appear on the right.
3. The numeral following some full play titles refers to the act in which the part indicated on the left occurs. For instance, *Terakoya* is one scene of *Sugawara Denju Tenarai Kagami*'s fourth act, but specific parts of this scene have their own titles, such as *Genzō Modori* and *Iroha Okuri.*
4. For dance play titles, see Appendix II.

A

Abegawa	*Hiza Kurige**
Abura Bōzu	*Abura Bōzu Yamiyo no Sumizome*
Abura no Jigyoku	*Onna Goroshi Abura no Jigyoku**
Aburaya	*Ise Ondo Koi no Netaba** (final scene), *Shinpan Utazaemon** (1)
Adasan	*Ōshū Adachigahara**
Ageya	*Gotaiheiki Shiraishi Banashi** (7), *Kuruwa Bunshō**, *Meiboku Sendai Hagi** (3)
Aiaigasa	*Igagoe Dōchū Sugoroku** (8)
Aibara	*Shin Usuyuki Monogatari** (2)
Ainoyama	*Ise Ondo Koi no Netaba** (1), *Keisei Hangonkō** (2)
Aitashi Kosuke	*Shinpan Utazaemon** (2)
Ajiyariba	*Wada Gassen Onna Maizuru* (4)
Akagaki	*Kanadehon Suzuri no Takashima*
Akama Bessō	*Yowa Nasake Ukina no Yokogushi** (2)
Akamon Mae Torimono	*Mekura Nagaya Ume ga Kagatobi** (6)
Akasaka Namiki	*Hiza Kurige**
Akashi Funa Wakare	*Shō Utsushi Asagao Nikki** (2)
Akegarasu	*Akegarasu Hana no Nureginu**
Akitsushima, Akitsushima Harakiri	*Sekitori Nadai Kagai* (2)
Akizuki Yashiki	*Shō Utsushi Asagao Nikki** (2)
Akogi, Akogi ga Ura	*Seishū Akogi ga Ura (Tamuramaro Suzuka Gassen)* (4)

Akoya no Kotozeme	*Dan no Ura Kabuto Gunki** (3)
Amagasaki Kankyō	*Ehon Taikōki** (10)
Amagawaya	*Kanadehon Chūshingura** (10)
Amanagori	*Heike Nyogo no Shima** (2)
Amida ga Mine	*Kiyomasa Seichū Roku* (2)
Anahori	*Sumidagawa Gonichi no Omokage** (2)
Anchin Kiyohime	*Hidakagawa Iriai Zakura** (4)
Anjitsu	*Sakurahime Azuma Bunshō* (3), *Tōkaidō Yotsuya Kaidan** (final scene)
Annaka Soza	*Haruna no Ume Kaoru Uchiwae*
Aoba no Fue	*Ichinotani Futaba Gunki** (3)
Aoyama Yakata	*Banshū Sarayashiki* (2)
Araki Mataemon	*Nippon Bari Iga no Adauchi*
Arima no Neko	*Arima Tsuzome Sumō no Yukata*
Asagao Nikki	*Shō Utsushi Asagao Nikki**
Asahina Yōshi	*Kishinohime Matsu Kutsuwa Kagami* (3)
Asakusa Kaminari Mon	*Gotaiheiki Shiraishi Banashi* (6)
Asakusa Kamon Gakudō	*Tōkaidō Yotsuya Kaidan** (1)
Ashigarayama	*Komochi Yamanba** (4)
Ashikaga Yakata	*Konoshita Kage Hazama Gassen* (10)
Atagoyama	*Toki wa Ima Kikkyō no Hataage** (3)
Atakemaru	*Zokusetsu Bidan Komonki*
Atsumori Saigo	*Ichinotani Futaba Gunki** (2)
Awa Batake	*Yura no Minato Sengen Chōja** (1)
Awadaguchi	*Awadaguchi Kiwame no Orikami*
Awaji Machi Kameya Uchi	*Meido no Hikyaku** (3)
*Awa no Naruto**	*Keisei Awa no Naruto*
Awazu	*Hachijin Shugo no Honjō** (9)

B

Baba Saburobei	*Ōsakazuki Shusen no Tsuwamono*
Badarai no Mitsuhide	*Toki wa Ima Kikkyō no Hataage** (3)
Benchō	*Kichisama Mairu Yukari no Otozure*
Beni Nagashi	*Kokusenya Kassen** (3)
Benizara Kakesara	*Tsuki no Kakezara Koiji no Yoiyami*
Benkei Jōshi (Benjō)	*Goshō Zakura Horikawa Youchi** (3)
Benten Kozō	*Aotozōshi Hana no Nishikie**
Benten Musume Meono no Shiranami	*Atotozōshi Hana no Nishikie**
Bōzu Yosa	*Tsuki no Enmasu no Igaguri*
Bukkoji	*Sakura Giminden**
Bun Tsukai	*Kanadehon Chūshingura**
Bunri Hitoe	*Sannin Kichiza Kuruwa no Hatsugai**
Bunya Goroshi	*Tsuta Momiji Utsunoya Tōge**

C

Chasen Zake	*Sugawara Denju Tenarai Kagami** (3)
Chawanaya	*Hiyoshimaru Wagaki no Sakura* (1)
Chayaba	*Kanadehon Chūshingura** (9)
Chijimiya Shinsuke	*Hachiman Matsuri Yomiya no Nigiwai**
Chikubujima	*Genpei Nunobiki Taki** (3)
Chikushō Zuka	*Musume Gonomi Ukina no Yokogushi** (2)
Chimori	*Hana no Yuki Koi no Tenarai*
Chōhachi, Chō Hanagata	*Chō Hanagata Meika no Shimadai* (8)
Choinose no Senroku	*Kore wa Hyōban Ukina no Yomiuri**
Chōkichi Goroshi	*Akanuzome no Naka no Kakureido*
Chongare	*Shinjū Ten no Amijima** (3)
Chūjōhime Yukizeme	*Hibariyama Hime Sudematsu** (3)
Chūku	*Kanadehon Chūshingura** (9)
Chūroku, Chūsan, Chūshi, Chūshichi	*Kanadehon Chūshingura** (6, 3, 4, 7)
Chūshingura	*Kanadehon Chūshingura**
Chūshin Kōshaku	*Taiheiki Chūshin Kōshaku*
Chūya Torimono	*Keian Taiheiki** (final scene)

D

Daianji	*Katakiuchi Tsuzure no Nishiki* (1)
Daiba Goroshi	*Tsuta Momiji Utsunoya Tōge** (final scene)
Daibutsu Kuyō	*Shusse Kagekiyo* (5)
Daichōji	*Shinjū Ten no Amijima** (3)
Daidaikō	*Ise Ondo Koi no Netaba** (2)
Daihōji Machigomeya	*Futatsu Chōchō Kuruwa Nikki** (4)
Daijo	*Kanadehon Chūshingura** (1)
Daikyōji	*Daikyōji Mukashi Goyomi**
Daimonjiya	*Kamiko Jitate Ryōmen Kagami* (2)
Daimotsu no Ura	*Yoshitsune Senbon Zakura** (2)
Daishichi	*Sumidagawa Gonichi no Omokage** (1)
Daitokuji	*Sangoku Busō Hisago no Gunbai*
Dakki no Ohyaku	*Zenaku Ryōmen Kōno Degashiwa*
Dantokusen	*Ichinotani Futaba Gunki** (2)
Denba Machi Tairō	*Shisenryō Koban no Umenoha** (6)
Denbōya	*Igagoe Norikake Gappa* (9)
Denchū	*Kanadehon Chūshingura** (3)
Dengaku Mai	*Hōjō Kudai Meika no Isaoshi (Takatoki*)*
Denjuba	*Sugawara Denju Tenarai Kagami** (1)
Demura Tamaya	*Tomigaoka Koi no Yamabiraki*
Dobashi	*Meiboku Sendai Hagi** (6)
Dōchū Hizakurige	*Hiza Kurige**

Dōchū Sugoroku	*Igagoe Dōchū Sugoroku*, Koi Nyōbō Somewake Tazuna* (10)
Dōgū Nagashi	*Imoseyama Onna Teikin** (3)
Dōgen Uchi	*Mekura Nagaya Ume ga Kagatobi** (3)
Dōgūya	*Natsu Matsuri Naniwa Kagami** (4)
Dōjō	*Gotaiheiki Shiraishi Banashi** (1)
Dokucha no Tansuke	*Banzai Okuni Kabuki*
Dokumanjū no Kiyomasa	*Kiyomasa Seichū Roku*
Dokushu no Kiyomasa	*Hachijin Shugo no Honjō** (4)
Domo Mata	*Keisei Hangonkō** (3)
Dōmyōji	*Sugawara Denju Tenarai Kagami** (2)
Donburiko	*Kusunoki Mukashi Banashi* (3)
Dondoro	*Kuni Namari Futaba no Oizuru*
Doroba, Dorojiai	*Natsu Matsuri Naniwa Kagami** (7)
Dote no Oroku	*Kakitsubata Iromoedozome*

E

Echigoya	*Meido no Hikyaku** (2)
Efurin	*Ningen Banji Kane Yo no Naka**
Egara no Heitai	*Hoshizuki Yoken Monjitsuki, Wada Gassen Onna Maizuru* (2)
Ehen Bassari	*Tsuyu Kosode Mukashi Hachijō** (1)
Eitai Hashi Bashizume	*Kanadehon Chūshingura* (3)
Enkakuni	*Jitsugetsu Seikyōwa Seidan*
Enmadō	*Tsuyu Kosode Mukashi Hachijō* (final scene)
Enmeiin	*Igagoe Dōchū Sugoroku** (3)
Enuke	*Keisei Hangonkō** (3)

F

Fudekō	*Suitengū Megumi no Fukagawa*
Fuinkiri	*Meido no Hikyaku** (2)
Fuji Bashi	*Jiraiya Gōketsu Monogatari*
Fujigawa	*Hiza Kurige**
Fuji Imondayū	*Zo Kusetsu Bidan Imonki*
Fuji no Mori	*Kamagafuchi Futatsu Domoe*
Fujigawa	*Hiza Kurige**
Fujisawa Nyūdō Yakata	*Wada Gassen Onna Maizuru*
Fujō Mon	*Ōgibyoshi Ōoka Seidan* (4)
Fuka Shichi Jōshi	*Imoseyama Onna Teikin** (4)
Fukkodera	*Sakura Giminden** (5)
Fukujima	*Hiragana Seisuiki** (3)
Fumizukai	*Kanadehon Chūshingura** (3)
Funa Ikusa	*Yoshitsune Senbon Zakura** (2)
Fune Okayama	*Meiboku Sendai Hagi** (1)
Fune Wakare	*Shō Utsushi Asagao Nikki, Yura no Minato Sengen Chōja** (2)

Fūrin Soba	*Dediaki Yawata Matsuri*
Furudera	*Hiza Kurige** (final scene), *Inaka Genji Tsuyu no Shinonome*
Furuteya Hachirobei	*Fuzuki Urami*
Futaba Gunki	*Ichinotani Futaba Gunki**
Futami ga Ura	*Ise Ondo Koi no Netaba** (1)
Futa Omote	*Sumidagawa Gonichi no Omokage** (3)
Futatsu Tama	*Kanadehon Chūshingura** (5)
Fuwa Nagoya	*Ukiyozuka Hiyoku no Inazuma*

G

Ga no Iwai	*Sugawara Denju Tenarai Kagami** (3)
Gappō	*Sesshū Gappō ga Tsuji** (1)
Gebasaki	*Kanadehon Chūshingura** (3)
Genjidana	*Yowa Nasake Ukina no Yokogushi** (3)
Genkan	*Kumo ni Magō Ueno no Hatsuhana** (3)
Genta Kandō	*Hiragana Seisuiki** (2)
Genyadana	*Yowa Nasake Ukina no Yokogushi** (3)
Genzō Modori	*Sugawara Denju Tenarai Kagami** (4)
Gion Ichiriki Jaya	*Kanadehon Chūshingura** (7)
Gisaku Seppuku	*Hana no Kumo Sakura no Akebono* (1)
Goban Tadanobu	*Chitose Soga Genji no Ishizue*
Godairiki	*Godairiki Koi no Fūjime**
Godanme	*Kanadehon Chūshingura** (5)
Godate	*Gion Sairei Shinkōki** (4)
Gojō Bashi	*Kiichi Hōgen Sanryaku no Maki** (5), *Suma no Miyako Genpei Tsutsushi** (2)
Gokinzū Yaburi	*Shisenryō Koban no Umenoha**
Gokurakuji Sanmon	*Aotozōshi Hana no Nishikie** (5)
Gonpachi no Tachibara	*Shirai Gonpachi Yoshiwara ga Yoi*
Gonshirō Uchi	*Hiragana Seisuiki** (3)
Goroichi Urei	*Kamagafuchi Futatsu Domoe* (2)
Gorosuke Sumika	*Hiyoshimaru Wakaki no Sakura* (3)
Goshiki no Iki	*Sugawara Denju Tenarai Kagami** (4)
Gosho no Gorozō	*Soga Moyō Tateshi no Goshozome**
Goshōsan	*Goshō Zakura Horikawa Youchi** (3)
Goten	*Imoseyama Onna Teikin** (4), *Meiboku Sendai Hagi** (6)
Gotō no Sanba, Gotō no Teppō	*Nanbantetsu Gotō no Memyki** (3)
Gozabune	*Genpei Nunobiki Taki** (3), *Hachijin Shugo no Honjō** (4)

H

Hachidanme	*Kanadehon Chūshingura** (8)
Hachijin	*Hachijin Shugo no Honjō**
Hachi no Su no Heiemon	*Ura Omote Chūshingura* (3)

Hachirō Monogatari	*Shinrei Yaguchi no Watashi** (2)
Haire no Gonsuke	*Kachizumō Ukina no Hanabure*
Haisho	*Sugawara Denju Tenarai Kagami** (4)
Hakkenden	*Arameyama Ume no Yatsubusa*
Hako Tataki	*Toki wa Ima Kikkyō no Hataage** (3)
Hakoya Goroshi	*Tsuki to Umegaoru Oboryo*
Hamabe	*Hiragana Seisuiki** (3)
Hamachō Gashi	*Shinzō Tsuribune Kidan* (final scene), *Tsuki to Umegaoru Oboryo* (final scene)
Hamamatsu Koya	*Shō Utsushi Asagao Nikki** (4)
Hamamatsuya	*Aotozōshi Hana no Nishikie**
Hamazutai	*Kokusenya Kassen** (2)
Hana Bishiya	*Musume Kagekiyo Yashima Nikki* (3)
Hana Bome	*Ichinotani Futaba Gunki** (3)
Hanai Oume	*Tsuki to Umegaoru Oboryo*
Hanakago, Hana Kenjō	*Kanadehon Chūshingura** (4)
Hanami	*Kagamiyama Kokyō no Nishikie** (6), *Shin Usuyuki Monogatari** (1)
Hanamizu Bashi	*Meiboku Sendai Hagi** (3)
Hana Watashi	*Imoseyama Onna Teikin** (3)
Hangakumon Yaguri	*Wada Gassen Onna Maizuru* (2)
Hangan Seppuku	*Kanadehon Chūshingura** (4)
Haniyū Mura	*Meiboku Kasane Monogatari* (1)
Harada Kai	*Hototogisu Date no Kikigaki*
Harusamegasa	*Kyōkaku Harusamegasa*
Hashimoto	*Futatsu Chōchō Kuruwa Nikki** (6)
Hataya	*Ashiya Dōman Ōuchi Kagami** (4)
Hatchō Tsubute no Kiheiji	*Yumihari Zuki Genke no Kaburaya*
Hattaija	*Hade Kurabe Ise Monogatari** (6)
Hayashi Sumika	*Ichinotani Futaba Gunki** (2)
Hebiyama Anshitsu	*Tōkaidō Yotsuya Kaidan** (final scene)
Heiji Sumika	*Tamuramaro Suzuka Gassen* (4)
Heisaku Uchi	*Igagoe Dōchū Sugoroku**
Heitarō Sumika	*Sanjūsan Gendō Munagi no Yurai** (3)
Hibariyama	*Hibariyama Koseki no Matsu*
Higaki	*Ichijō Ōkura Monogatari* (4) (See *Kiichi Hōgen Sanryaku no Maki**)
Higo no Komageta	*Katakiuchi Higo no Komageta*
Hikiage	*Kanadehon Chūshingura** (11)
Hikimado	*Futatsu Chōchō Kuruwa Nikki** (8)
Hikyakuya	*Meido no Hikyaku** (1)
Hime Modori	*Imoseyama Onna Teikin** (4)
Hina Nagashi	*Imoseyama Onna Teikin** (3)
Hinin no Adauchi	*Katakiuchi Tsuzure no Nishiki* (3)
Hinokiyama Sōdō	*Kōdan Hinokiyama Jikki*
Hinokuchi	*Tenjiku Tokubei Ikoku Banashi** (2)

Hinomi Yagura	*Date Musume Koi no Higanoko** (6), *Sannin Kichiza Kuruwa no Hatsugai** (5)
Hirofureyama	*Shō Utsushi Asagao Nikki** (4)
Hirozumi Yakata	*Yamatogana Ariwara Keizu** (1)
Hidakagawa	*Hidakagawa Iriai Zakura** (4)
Hitsubō Denju	*Sugawara Denju Tenarai Kagami** (1)
Hiyoshimaru	*Hiyoshimaru Wakaki no Sakura* (3)
*Hiza Kurige**	*Tōkaidō Dōchū Hiza Kurige*
Hōbiki	*Ichinotani Futaba Gunki** (3)
Hokaibō	*Sumidagawa Gonichi no Omokage**
Honnōdera	*Ehon Taikōki** (2), *Toki wa Ima Kikkyo no Hataage** (3)
Horagatake	*Hime Komatsu Nenchi no Asobi* (3)
Horibata	*Keian Taiheiki** (1), *Shisenryō Koban no Umenoha* (1)*
Horikawa	*Chikagoro Kawara no Tatehiki** (2)
Horikawa Yakata	*Yoshitsune Senbon Zakura** (2)
Horikawa Youchi	*Goshō Zakura Horikawa Youchi**
Hōryukaku	*Satomi Hakkenden* (6)
Hoshiaidera Ishikiri	*Miura no Ōsuke Kōbai Tazuna** (3)
Hōsho Jiai	*Nihon Bare Iga no Adauchi*
Hosogawa no Chidaruma	*Tsuta Moyō Chizome no Goshuin*
Hotaru Gari	*Shō Utsushi Asagao Nikki** (1), *Tōkaidō Yotsuya Kaidan** (final scene)
Hototogisu	*Kamakura Sandaiki** (7)
Hototogisu Goroshi	*Soga Moyō Tateshi no Goshozome** (3)
Honzō Shimo Yashiki (Honshimo), Hosogawa no Kaji	*Zōho Chūshingura*
Hyaku Domairi	*Honchō Nijūshikō** (2)
Hyakuman Tsubo	*Zenaku Ryōmen Kono Degashiwa* (5)
Hyaku Monogatari	*Yami no Ume Hyaku Monogatari*
Hyokura Yashiki	*Shinrei Yaguchi no Watashi** (3)
Hyōtan Dana	*Hikosan Gongen Chikai no Sukedachi** (7)

I

Ichihara no Danmari	*Ichihara no Tsuki no Nagame*
Ichiko no Kuchiyose	*Hiza Kurige**
Ichinotani	*Ichinotani Futaba Gunki**
Ichiriki Jaya	*Kanadehon Chūshingura** (7)
Ichiwaka Seppuku, Ichiwaka Uijin	*Wada Gassen Onna Maizuru* (3)
Ido Gae	*Imoseyama Onna Teikin** (4)
Iemon Rōtaku	*Tōkaidō Yotsuya Kaidan** (2)
Igagoe	*Igagoe Dōchū Sugoroku**, *Igagoe Norikake Kappa*
Igagoe Jitsuroku	*Nippon Bare Iga no Adauchi*

Igami no Gonta	*Yoshitsune Senbon Zakura** (3)
Iihara Hyoe Yashiki	*Kishi no Hime Matsu Kutsuwa Kagami* (3)
Ikake Matsu	*Fune e Uchikomu Hashima no Shiranami**
Ikari Tomomori	*Yoshitsune Senbon Zakura** (2)
Ikka	*Ōshū Adachigahara** (4)
Ikutama	*Some Moyō Imose no Kadomatsu** (3)
Imo Arai Kanjinchō	*Gohiiki Kanjinchō**
Imorizaki	*Karukaya Dōshin Tsukuchi no Iezuto* (3)
Imoyama	*Imoseyama Onna Teikin** (3)
Inaba Kozō	*Inaba Kozō Ame no Yo Banashi*
Inaka Genji	*Inaka Genji Tsuyu no Shinonome*
Inari no Mori	*Yoshitsune Senbon Zakura** (2)
Inasegawa Seizoroi	*Aotozōshi Hana no Nishikie** (4)
Inga Kozō, Inga Monoshi	*Ryō to Mimasu Takane no Kumo Kiri*
Inga Numa	*Sakura Giminden** (2)
Iriya	*Kumo ni Magō Ueno no Hatsuhana** (4)
Iroha Okuri	*Sugawara Denju Tenarai Kagami** (4)
Iruka Goten	*Imoseyama Onna Teikin** (4)
Isawagawa	*Nichiren Shōnin Minori no Umi* (3)
Ise Monogatari	*Hade Kurabe Ise Monogatari**
Ise no Saburō	*Mibae Genji Michi no Kuni Tsuki*
Ise Ondo	*Ise Ondo Koi no Netaba**
Ishibe no Shuku	*Katsuragawa Renri no Shigarami** (1)
Ishidan	*Kichirei Kotobuki Soga*
Ishidōmaru	*Karukaya Dōshin Tsukushi no Iezuto* (5)
Ishikawa Goemon	*Kamaguchi Futatsu Domoe, Konoshita Kage Hazama Gassen, Sanmon Gosan no Kiri**
Ishikiri Kajiwara	*Miura no Ōsuke Kōbai Tazuna**
Ishiya	*Ichinotani Futaba Gunki** (3)
Isobe Yashiki	*Shin Sarayashiki Tsuki no Amagasa** (3)
Isshin Taisuke	*Midashi Yanagi Medori no Matsumae*
Itaniya Misesaki	*Tsuta Momiji Utsunoya Tōge** (2)
Itō Yashiki	*Tōkaidō Yotsuya Kaidan** (2)
Iwado no Kagekiyo	*Arigata Yamegumi no Kagekiyo*
Iwakura Sōgen	*Kikuchi Ōtomo Konrei Kagami* (4)
Izari Katsugorō	*Hakone Reigen Izari no Adauchi**
Izayoi Seishin	*Kosode Soga Azami no Ironui**
Izumi Saburō Yakata	*Nanbantetsu Goto no Menuki** (3)

J

Jigyoku Meguri	*Sanzesō Nishiki Bunshō** (4)
Jigyoku Yado	*Tōkaidō Yotsuya Kaidan** (1)
Jijūtarō Yakata	*Goshō Zakura Horikawa Youchi* (3)
Jikiso	*Sakura Giminden** (4)
Jinmon	*Ichinotani Futaba Gunki** (2)
Jirosaku Sumika	*Tsuyu Kosode Mukashi Hachijō**

Jishin Katō	*Zōho Momoyama Monogatari** (1)
Jisshukō	*Honchō Nijūshikō** (4)
Jitsuroku Sendai Hagi	*Hototogisu Date no Kikigaki*
Jōkanya	*Gion Sairei Shinkōki** (3)
Jūban Giri	*Youchi Soga Kariba no Akebono**
Jūdanme, Jūichidanme	*Kanadehon Chūshingura** (10, 11)
Jūnin Giri	*Ise Ondo Koi no Netaba** (final scene)
Junrei Uta	*Awa no Naruto** (8)
Jūraku Machi	*Akamizome no Naka no Kakureido*
Jūrobei Sumika	*Awa no Naruto** (8)
Jūtarō Ba	*Taiheiki Chūshin Kōshaku*

K

Kabuto Aratame	*Kanadehon Chūshingura** (1)
Kadan	*Kiyoshimaru Kaki no Sakura* (3)
Kaeru Tobi	*Ono no Tōfū Aoyagi Suzuri* (2)
Kagamiyama	*Kagamiyama Kokyō no Nishikie**
Kagatobi	*Mekura Nagaya Ume ga Kagatobi**
Kagekatsu Geta, Kagekatsu Jōshi	*Honchō Nijūshikō**
Kagekiyo	*Shusse Kagekiyo*
Kago Yaburi no Gonpachi	*Shirai Gonpachi Yoshiwara ga Yoi*
Kaheiji Sumika	*Toki wa Ima Kikkyō no Hataage** (final scene)
Kaina	*Genpei Nunobiki no Taki** (3)
Kajima Mura	*Yoshitsune Senbon Zakura** (2)
Kajiwara Yakata	*Hiragana Seisuiki** (2)
Kajiya	*Shin Usuyuki Monogatari** (3)
Kakegoi	*Imoseyama Onna Teikin** (2)
Kakinoki Kinsuke	*Keisei Kogane no Shiyachi Hoko*
Kamabara	*Iroha Shijūshichi Moji* (6)
Kamagafuchi	*Kamagafuchi Futatsu Domoe* (3)
Kamakura Kashi	*Edo Sodachi Omatsuri Sashichi** (7)
Kamakurayama	*Yūshoku Kamakurayama**
Kamasan	*Kamakura Sandaiki** (3)
Kameya Misesaki	*Meido no Hikyaku** (1)
Kamiiri	*Kamagafuchi Futatsu Domoe* (3)
Kamiji	*Shinjū Ten no Amijima** (2)
Kamisuki	*Tōkaidō Yotsuya Kaidan** (2)
Kamisuki Gonpachi	*Gonjō**
Kamiya Uchi	*Shinjū Ten no Amijima** (2)
Kamiyui Shinza	*Tsuyu Kosode Mukashi Hachijō**
Kamiyui Tōji	*Sandai Hanashi Kōza no Shinsaku*
Kamo Tsuzumi	*Sugawara Denju Tenarai Kagami** (1)
Kanpei Harakiri, Kanpei Sumika	*Kanadehon Chūshingura** (6)
Kane	*Kosenjo Kane Kake no Matsu* (2)
Kanefū Yakata	*Komochi Yamanba** (3)
Kanki Yakata	*Kokusenya Kassen** (3)

Kansaku Sumika, Kansuke Monogatari	Honchō Nijūshikō* (3)
Kantō Ba, Kanzaki Ageya	Hiragana Seisuiki* (2, 4)
Kappo no Kichizō	Zokusetsu Bidan Kōmonki
Kara Nako	Kokusenya Kassen* (3)
Karasu Naki	Kagamiyama Kokyō no Nishikie* (7)
Kari no Tayori	Keisei Setsugetsukka*
Karukaya	Karukaya Dōshin Tsukushi no Iezuto
Kasamori Osen	Kaidan Tsuki no Kasamori
Kasane Miuri	Meiboku Sendai Hagi* (8)
Kashi Tsukejō	Shisenryō Koban no Umenoha* (5)
Kashi Zashiki	Katakiuchi Tengajaya Mura* (2)
Kasuga Mura	Hade Kurabe Ise Monogatari* (3)
Kasumigaseki	Kanadehon Chūshingura* (4)
Katami no Katasode	Goshō Zakura Horikawa Youchi* (3)
Katami Okuri	Jūni Toki Kaikei Soga (5), Youchi Soga Kariba no Akebono* (3)
Kataoka Chūgi	Nihon Kenjō Kagami (10)
Katsu Okatami	Tsuyu Kosode Mukashi Hachijō* (1)
Katsuragawa Rikizō	Yagura Daiko Narita no Adauchi
Katsuyori Seppuku	Honchō Nijūshikō* (2)
Kawaba	Imoseyama Onna Teikin* (3)
Kawabara no Goroshi	Ōmi Genji no Tatehiki (2)
Kawagoe Tarō Jōshi	Yoshitsune Senbon Zakura* (1)
Kawanakajima	Kawanakajima Azuma Nishikie
Kawashō	Shinjū Ten no Amijima* (1)
Kawa Tabi	Some Moyō Imose no Kadomatsu (3)
Kawatsura Yakata	Yoshitsune Senbon Zakura* (4)
Keian Taiheiki*	Hana Shōbu Keian Jikki
Keimasa Goroshi	Koi Nyōbō Somewake Tazuna (7)
Keisei Tadanori	Ichinotani Futaba Gunki* (4)
Kenchōji	Kanadehon Chūshingura* (2)
Kenjō, Kenjō Yakata	Ōshū Adachigahara* (3)
Kenka	Sugawara Denju Tenarai Kagami* (3)
Kenka Ba	Kanadehon Chūshingura* (3)
Kenshi Batake	Gion Sairei Shinkōki* (2)
Kenshin Yakata	Honchō Nijūshikō*
Keshō Yashiki	Nasu no Yoichi Saikai Suzuri (3)
Keyamura	Hikosan Gongen Chikai no Sukedachi* (9)
Kezori	Hakata Kojōrō Nami Makura* (1)
Kikaigashima	Heike Nyogo no Shima* (2)
Kikubatake	Kiichi Hōgen Sanryaku no Maki* (3)
Kikyō ga Hara	Honchō Nihūshikō* (3)
Kimon no Zenbei	Osome Hisamatsu Ukina no Yomiuri* (Osome no Nanayaku)
Kimyōin	Murekiyo Taki Hiiki no Seiriki
Kinai Sumika	Taiheiki Chūshin Kōshaku (7)

Kinden	Imoseyama Onna Teikin* (4)
Kinkakuji	Gion Sairei Shinkōki* (4)
Kin Kanban no Kankurō	Kin Kanban Tateshi no Hondana
Kinpachi	Ōmi Genji Senjin Yakata* (8)
Kinugawa Mura Kankyō	Kamakura Sandaiki* (7)
Kinugawa Zutsumi	Kesakake Matsu Narita no Riken (Iro Moyō Chotto Karimame*) (2), Meiboku Sendai Hagi* (final scene)
Kinuta Byōshi	Kusunoki Mukashi Banashi* (3)
Kirare Otomi	Musume Gonomi Ukina no Yokogushi*
Kirare Yosa	Yowa Nasake Ukina no Yokogushi*
Kiriki no Saitō Tarozaemon, Kiriko Ondo	Ōtō no Miya Asahi no Yoroi (3)
Kisarazu Mozome	Yowa Nasake Ukina no Yokogushi* (1)
Kishihime	Kishi no Hime Matsu Kutsuwa Kagami (3)
Kishin no Omatsu	Shinban Koshi no Shiranami
Kishu Shirabe	Ogibyōshi Ōoka Seidan* (6)
Kisshōin	Sannin Kichiza Kuruwa no Hatsugai* (4)
Kitano no Mori	Ichinotani Futaba Gunki* (1)
Kita Saga	Sugawara Denju Tenarai Kagami* (4)
Kita Saga Anjitsu	Yoshitsune Senbon Zakura* (1)
Kitsuji no Kuruwa	Igagoe Norikake Gappa (7)
Kitsune	Yoshitsune Senbon Zakura* (4)
Kitsunebi	Honchō Nijūshikō* (4)
Kitsune Tadanobu	Yoshitsune Senbon Zakura* (4)
Kitsune Wakare	Ashiya Dōman Ōuchi Kagami* (4)
Kiyari Ondo	Sanjūsan Gendō Munagi no Yurai* (3)
Kochiyama	Kumo ni Magō Ueno no Hatsuhana*
Koharu Jihei	Shinjū Ten no Amijima*
Koijū	Koi Nyōbō Somewake Tazuna* (10)
Koika	Kanadehon Chūshingura* (1)
Koisogahara	Keisei Soga Kuruwa Kagami
Koito Sashichi	Edo Sodachi Omatsuri Sashichi*, Kokoro no Nazo Toketa Iroito
Koi Tsukami	Araki Butai Kiyomizu Mode
Kojirō Senjin	Ichinotani Futaba Gunki*
Kojo Ochiku	Futatsu Chō Iro no Dekiaki
Kokingo Uchijini	Yoshitsune Senbon Zakura* (3)
Kokusenya	Kokusenya Kassen*
Komakiyama Jochū	Hiyoshimaru Wakaki no Sakura (3)
Koman Gengobei	Godairiki Koi no Fūjime*
Kome Arai (Kome Togi)	Kamakura Sandaiki* (7)
Komeya	Futatsu Chōchō Kuruwa Nikki* (4)
Kōmonki	Zokusetsu Bidan Kōmonki
Kōnen no Inori	Sakura Giminden* (5)
Konoma no Hoshi	Konoma no Hoshi Kakone Shikabue
Konomi	Yoshitsune Senbon Zakura* (3)

Kōnoyama	*Karukaya Dōshin Tsukushi no Iezuto* (5)
Konpira Rishōki	*Hana no Ueno Homare no Ishibumi**
Konrei, Kōriyama	*Igagoe Dōchū Sugoroku** (5)
Kosan Kingorō	*Ōedo Meibutsu Nishikie Hajime*
Koshirō Onai	*Ōmi Genji Senjin Yakata** (8)
Kosode Monogatari	*Ashiya Dōman Ōuchi Kagami** (2)
Kotatsu	*Shinjū Ten no Amijima** (2)
Kotatsu Yagura	*Honchō Nijūshikō** (3)
Kotozeme	*Dan no Ura Kabuto Gunki** (3)
Kotsuyose	*Kagamiyama Gonichi ni Iwafuji*
Kowakare	*Sakura Giminden** (3)
Koyoshi Sumika	*Hade Kurabe Ise Monogatari** (6)
Kozaru Shichinosuke	*Ami Moyō Tōro no Kikukiri*
Kubi Jikken	*Ichinotani Futaba Gunki** (3)
Kudanme	*Kanadehon Chūshingura** (9)
Kumagai Jinya, Kumagai Monogatari	*Ichinotani Futaba Gunki** (3)
Kumi Uchi	*Hiza Kurige*, Ichinotani Futaba Gunki** (2)
Kumokiri Gonin Otoko	*Ryū to Mimasu Takane no Kumokiri* (3)
Kuramae	*Aotozōshi Hana no Nishikie** (3), *Some Moyō Imose no Kadomatsu* (3)
Kurosuke Sumika	*Genpei Nunobiki no Taki** (3)
Kurotegumi Sukeroku	*Kurotegumi Kuruwa no Datehiki*
Kuruwa Monogatari	*Komochi Yamanba** (3)
Kuruma Ba, Kuruma Biki	*Sugawara Denju Tenarai Kagami** (3)
Kusa Wakare	*Ashiya Dōman Ōuchi Kagami** (4)
Kusemai	*Kiichi Hōgen Sanryaku no Maki** (4)
Kutsukake	*Koi Nyōbō Somewake Tazuna** (7)
Kuzu no Ha Kowakare	*Ashiya Dōman Ōuchi Kagami** (4)
Kyōo	*Kyōkaku Harusamegasa*

M

Magobei Uchi	*Tōkaidō Yotsuya Kaidan** (4)
Mago Kiri	*Sanzenryō Kogane no Kurairi*
Mamakozeme	*Kamagafuchi Futatsu Domoe* (2)
Mamataki	*Meiboku Sendai Hagi** (6)
Mamushi no Jirokichi	*Hototogisu Mizuni Hibikune*
Mamushi no Oichi	*Chūshingura Gonichi no Tatemae*
Manaita no Chōbei	*Banzui Chōbei Shōjin Manaita**
Manju Musume	*Igagoe Dōchū Sugoroku**
Manzai	*Imoseyama Onna Teikin** (2)
Mariko no Shuku	*Tsuta Momiji Utsunoya Tōge**
Marubashi Chūya	*Keian Taiheiki**
Maruzukayama	*Satomi Hakkenden* (5)
Masaemon Yashiki	*Igagoe Dōchū Sugoroku** (5)

Masakiyo Honjō	*Hachijin Shugo no Honjō**
Masamune Uchi	*Shin Usuyuki Monogatari** (3)
Masaoka Chūgi	*Meiboku Sendai Hagi** (6)
Masui	*Goku Zaishiki Musume Ōgi* (5)
Masu Otoshi	*Nebiki no Kadomatsu** (2)
Matsudaira Chōshichirō	*Sanzenryō Kogane no Kurairi*
Matsuda no Kenka	*Ittōryū Narita no Kakegaku*
Matsuemon Uchi	*Hiragana Seisuiki** (3)
Matsue Yakata	*Kumo ni Magō Ueno no Hatsuhana**
Matsukiri	*Kanadehon Chūshingura**
Matsumaeya	*Medashi Yanagi Midori no Matsumae* (4)
Matsunami Kenhyō Biwa	*Genpei Nunobiki no Taki** (4)
Matsuō Kubi Jikken	*Sugawara Denju Tenarai Kagami** (4)
Matsuō Shimo Yashiki	*Zōho Sugawara Denju Tenarai Kagami* (4)
Matsura no Taiko	*Shin Butai Iroha Kakisome*
Matsushita Sumika	*Misuka Taiheiki* (9)
Megumi no Kagekiyo	*Arigataya Megumi no Kagekiyo*
Megumi no Kenka	*Kami no Megumi Wagō no Torikumi**
Mekura Hyōsuke	*Goku Zaishiki Musume Ogi* (8)
Mekura Kagekiyo	*Musume Kagekiyo Yashima Nikki*
Mekura Nagaya	*Mekura Nagaya Ume ga Kagatobi**
Memekiya	*Nanbantetsu Gotō no Menuki**
Mennai Chishima	*Kanadehon Chūshingura** (7), *Koi Bikyaku Yamato Ōrai* (3)
Mibu Mura	*Konoshita Kage Hazama Gassen* (9), *Yamatogana Ariwara Keizu** (4)
Micharu Yakata	*Tamamono Mae Asahi no Tamoto** (3)
Michitose Naozamurai	*Kumo ni Magō Ueno no Hatsuhana**
Michizure Kohei	*Shiobara Tasuke Ichidaiki**
Midaroku Sumika	*Ichinotani Futaba Gunki** (3)
Migawari	*Shinrei Yaguchi no Watashi** (4)
Mikage no Matsubara	*Ichinotani Futaba Gunki** (3)
Mikazuki Nagaya	*Ami Moyō Tōro no Kikukiri* (4)
Mimiguri Dote	*Sumidagawa Gonichi no Omokage** (2)
Minato Machi	*Kotobuki Renri no Matsu* (3)
Miroku Machi	*Musume Gonomi Ukina no Yokogushi** (2)
Mito Kaidō	*Hototogisu Date no Kikigaki* (1)
Miura Wakare	*Kamakura Sandaiki** (7)
Miuraya Kōshisaki	*Kurotegumi Kuruwa no Tatehiki* (3), *Sukeroku Yukari no Edo Zakura**
Miuri	*Kanadehon Chūshingura** (6)
Miyagi no Shinobu	*Gotaiheiki Shiraishi Banashi** (7)
Miyajima no Danmari	*Chobanzei Araki no Shimadai*
Mizuiri	*Sukeroku Yukari no Edo Zakura**
Momijimayama	*Genpei Nunobiki no Taki** (4)
Momonoi Yakata	*Kanadehon Chūshingura** (2)

Mongaku	*Nachi no Taki Chikai no Mongaku, Sesshū Watanabe no Hashi Kuyō*
Monomi	*Ehon Taikōki** (10)
Monso	*Sakura Giminden** (1)
Monsoto	*Kanadehon Chūshingura**
Moritsuna Jinya (Moritsuna)	*Ōmi Genji Senjin Yakata** (8)
Morokoshi Bune	*Kokusenya Kassen** (2)
Motobune	*Hakata Kojōrō Nami Makura** (1)
Muhitsu no Kakioki	*Sakuratsuba Urami no Samezaya**
Muken no Kane	*Hiragana Seisuiki** (4)
Munetō Monogatari	*Ōshū Adachigahara*
Murai Chōan	*Kanzenchōaku Nozoki no Karakuri*
Murayamaza	*Kiwametsuki Banzui Chōbei**
Muromachi Gosho	*Honchō Nijūshikō**
Myōjinji	*Ehon Taikōki** (6)
Myokichi Goroshi	*Hachijin Shugo no Honjō**

N

Nagamachi	*Shinpan Utazaemon** (3)
Nagamachi Miyoya	*Hade Sugata Onna Maiginu** (3)
Naga Tsubone	*Kagamiyama Kokyō no Nishikie** (7)
Nagamachi Ura	*Natsu Matsuri Naniwa Kagami** (7)
Nanba Ura	*Futatsu Chōchō Kuruwa Nikki** (5)
Nanbei Tsuru Koroshi	*Ōshū Adachigahara**
Nanyokei Sumika	*Futatsu Chōchō Kuruwa Nikki** (5)
Naozamurai	*Kumo ni Magō Ueno no Hatsuhana**
Narita no Adauchi	*Yagura Daiko Narita no Adauchi*
Nashi no Edo	*Ichinotani Futaba Gunki** (2)
Natsu Matsuri	*Natsu Matsuri Naniwa Kagami**
Nezumi Kozō	*Nezumi Komon Haru no Shinkata*
Nichirenki	*Nichiren Shōnin Minori no Umi* (3)
Nichō Soba	*Kumo ni Magō Ueno no Hatsuhana** (4)
Nidanme	*Kanadehon Chūshingura* (2)
Nigatsudō	*Nigatsudō Rōben Sugi no Yurai**
Nihon Zutsumi	*Kumo ni Magō Ueno no Hatsuhana** (2)
Nijōjō	*Ehon Taikōki** (1)
Nijūshikō	*Honchō Nijūshikō**
Ningyōya	*Katakiuchi Tengajaya Mura** (4)
Ninin Kuzo no Ha	*Ashiya Dōman Ōuchi Kagami** (4)
Ninin Shinbei	*Tomigaoka Koi no Yamabiraki*
Ninin Yakko	*Ashiya Dōman Ōuchi Kagami** (4)
Ninjō	*Kanadehon Chūshingura** (3), *Meiboku Sendai Hagi**
Ninokuchi Mura	*Meido no Hikyaku** (3)
Nomitori	*Natsu Matsuri Naniwa Kagami** (7)

Nozaki Mura	*Shinpan Utazaemon** (2)
Nozarashi Gosuke	*Suibo Daigo Dōno Nozarashi*
Numazu	*Igagoe Dōchū Sugoroku** (6)
Nunobiki	*Genpei Nunobiki no Taki**
Nuosan	*Genpei Nunobiki no Taki** (3)
Nuregappa	*Kanadehon Chūshingura** (4)
Nyonindō	*Karukaya Dōshin Tsukushi no Iezuto* (5)

O

Obiya	*Katsuragawa Renri no Shigarami** (3)
Ocha no Suidote	*Mekura Nagaya Ume ga Kagatobi** (1)
Ochiudo	*Kanadehon Chūshingura** (3)
Odosha	*Sono Mukashi Koi no Edozome* (1)
Ōgiya, Ogiya Kumagai	*Suma no Miyako Genpei Tsutsuji** (2)
Oguri Hangan	*Oguri Hangan Kuruma Kaidō*
Oguri no Umakichi	*Jitsugetsu Seikyō Waseidan*
Ohan Chōemon	*Katsuragawa Renri no Shigarami**
Ohatsu Tokubei	*Sonezaki Shinjū**
Ōigawa, Oiso Ageya	*Shō Utsushi Asagao Nikki** (5, 2)
Oiwa no Kaidan	*Tōkaidō Yotsuya Kaidan**
Ōka Yakutaku	*Ōgibyōshi Ōoka Seidan*
Okazaki	*Igagoe Dōchū Sugoroku**
Okazaki no Neko	*Ozuma Kudari Gojūsan Tsugi*
Okiku Kaeri Uchi	*Hikosan Gongen Chikai no Sukedachi** (6)
Okoma Saiza	*Koi Musume Mukashi Hashijo*
Okon Mitsugi	*Ise Ondo Koi no Netaba**
Okoyo Genzaburō	*Yume Musubu Chō ni Iorioi*
Ōkuchi no Ryō, Ōkuchiya Nikai	*Kumo ni Magō Ueno no Hatsuhana** (4, 2)
Okudaya	*Hakata Kojōrō Nami Makura* (1)
Okuden	*Kiichi Hōgen Sanryaku no Maki** (4)
Okuniwa	*Honchō Nijūshikō**, *Kagamiyama Kokyō no Nishikie** (7), *Kiichi Hōgen Sanryaku no Maki** (3)
Ōkura Kyō	*Kiichi Hōgen Sanryaku no Maki** (4)
Omatsuri Sashichi	*Edo Sodachi Omatsuri Sashichi**, *Kokoro no Nazo Toketa Iroito*
Ōmi Genji, Ōmi Hakkei	*Ōmi Genji Senjin Yakata**
Omiwa	*Imoseyama Onna Teikin** (4)
Onatsu	*Goku Zaishiki Musume Ōgi* (8)
Onatsu Seijūrō	*Kotobuki Renri no Matsu*
Onbōbori	*Tōkaidō Yotsuya Kaidan** (3)
Oni Azami	*Kosode Soga Azami no Ironui**
Oniō Hinka	*Kichirei Kotobuki Soga*
Onna Chūshingura	*Kasamiyama Kokyō no Nishikie*
Onna Danshichi	*Shinzō Tsurifune Kidan*

Onna Kiyoharu	*Sumidagawa Hana no Goshozome*
Onna Narukami	*Zōho Onna Narukami*
Onna Sadakurō	*Chūshingura Gonichi no Tatemae*
Onna Shibaraku	*Arigata Shinzei Genji*
Onna Shōsei	*Fuji Bitai Tsukuba no Shigeyama*
Onoe Heya, Onoe Jigai	*Kagamiyama Kokyō no Nishikie** (7)
Onogawa	*Arima Tsuzome Sumō no Yukata*
Ōoka Seidan	*Ōgibyōshi Ōoka Seidan* (2)
Ōrō	*Shisenryō Koban no Umenoha** (6)
Oryū Wakare	*Sanjūsan Gendō Munagi no Yurai** (3)
Osakabe Yakata	*Chō Hanagata Meika no Shimadai* (8)
Osakayama	*Irohagana Shijū Shichi Moji*
Ōsakazuki	*Ōsakazuki Shusen no Tsuwamono**
Osan Goroshi	*Ōgibyōshi Ōoka Seidan** (1)
Osan Mohei	*Daikyōji Mukashi Goyomi**
Osayo Kurobei	*Konoma no Hoshi Hakone no Shikabue*
Oshishi Kichizō	*Date Musume Koi no Higanoko** (6)
Oshizu Reiza	*Keisei Soga Kuruwa Kagami*
Oshun Danpei	*Chikagoro Kawara no Tatehiki**
Osome Hisamatsu	*Kore wa Hyōban Ukina No Yomiuri**, *Shinpan Utazaemon**, *Some Moyō Imose no Kadomatsu*
Osome no Nanayaku	*Osome Hisamatsu Ukina no Yomiuri**
Osono Rokuzō	*Sanzesō Nishiki Bunshō**
Osono Shuttatsu	*Hikosan Gongen Chikai no Sukedachi** (5)
Otomi Yosaburō	*Yowa Nasake Ukina no Yokogushi**
Otosa	*Sono Mukashi Koi no Edozome* (1)
Otowayama	*Genpei Nunobiki no Taki** (4)
Otsu	*Hiragana Seisuiki** (3)
Otsuma Hachirōbei	*Sakuratsuba Urami no Samezaya**
Ōuchi	*Sugawara Denju Tenarai Kagami** (1)
Ōuchi Yakata	*Karukaya Dōshin Tsukushi no Iezuto* (3)

R

Ranchō	*Wakaki no Adan gusa**
Ranpei Monogurui	*Yamatogana Ariwara Keizu** (4)
Rantō Ba	*Hiza Kurige**
Renga	*Toki wa Ima Kikkyo no Hataage** (3)
Renshōbō	*Renshō Monogatari*
Rikiya Shisha	*Kanadehon Chūshingura** (2)
Rōbarai	*Natsu Matsuri Naniwa Kagami** (3)
Rōben Sugi	*Nigatsudō Rōben Sugi no Yurai**
Rōka	*Kagamiyama Kokyō no Nishikie** (7)
Rokkakudō	*Katsuragawa Renri no Shigarami** (3)
Rokudanme	*Kanadehon Chūshingura** (6)
Rokurōdayū Sumika	*Miura no Ōsuke Kōbai Tazuna**

Rokurō Kubi	*Kasa no Rokurō Ukina no Nureginu*
Rokusuke Sumika	*Hikosan Gongen Chikai no Sukedachi** (9)
Rokuyata Monogatari	*Ichinotani Futaba Gunki** (4)
Rōmon	*Kokusenya Kassen** (3)
Rōnuke	*Ansei Kibun Tsukuda no Yoarashi* (1)
Rōyaburi no Kagekiyo	*Kiku Gasane Sakae no Kagekiyo*

S

Sabu Uchi	*Natsu Matsuri Naniwa Kagami** (2)
Sadasuke Gonpachi	*Shirai Gonpachi Yoshiwara ga Yoi*
Saifu no Shōkō	*Kanadehon Chūshingura** (11)
Saikai Suzuri	*Ōgi no Mato Saikai Suzuri*
Saisaki Yakata	*Shin Usuyuki Monogatari** (2)
Sakanaya Sōgorō	*Shin Sarayashiki Tsuki no Amagasa**
Sakaro	*Hiragana Seisuiki** (3)
Sakaya	*Hade Sugata Onna Maiginu** (3)
Sakura no Miya Monogurui	*Nigatsudō Rōben Sugi no Yurai** (2)
Sakuramaru Seppuku	*Sugawara Denju Tenarai Kagami** (3)
Sakura Mochi	*Miyakodori Nagare no Shiranami** (2)
Sakura Sōgorō	*Sakura Giminden**
Sanemori Monogatari	*Genpei Nunobiki no Taki** (3)
Sanjūsan Gendō	*Sanjūsan Gendō Munagi no Yurai**
Sankaku Yashiki	*Tōkaidō Yotsuya Kaidan** (4)
Sankichi Mago Uta, Sankichi Urei	*Koi Nyōbō Somewake Tazune** (10)
Sanmon	*Sanmon Gosan no Kiri**
Sannin Jyōgo	*Genpei Nunobiki no Taki** (4), *Hakone Reigen Izari no Adauchi** (11)
Sannin Kichiza	*Sannin Kichiza Kuruwa no Hatsugai**
Sannin Warai	*Shin Usuyuki Monogatari** (2)
Sano Genzaemon	*Yūshoku Kamakurayama**
Sano Jirozaemon	*Kagotsurube Sato no Eizame**
Sano Yatsuhashi	*Kakitsubata Iromoedozome*
Sanshō Dayū	*Yura no Minato Sengen Chōja**
Sanza Rotaku	*Ukiyozuka Hiyoku no Inazuma* (1)
Sanzesō	*Sanzesō Nishiki Bunshō**
Sarayashiki	*Banshū Sarayashiki*
Saru Mawashi	*Chikagoro Kawara no Tatehiki** (2)
Sasabiki	*Hiragana Seisuiki** (3)
Sasaki Monogatari	*Kamakura Sandaiki** (7)
Sashi Kago	*Ashiya Dōman Ōuchi Kagami** (4)
Sata Mura	*Sugawara Denju Tenarai Kagami** (3)
Satomi Isuke	*Meisaku Kiri Kono Akebono*
Satsuta Tōge Hitotsuya	*Musume Gonomi Ukina no Yokogushi** (2)
Sawaichi Uchi	*Tsubosaka Reigenki** (1)
Saya-ate	*Ukiyozuka Hiyoku no Inazuma* (2)
Seiriki Tomigorō	*Murekiyo Taki Hiiki no Seiriki*

Sekisho	*Igagoe Dōchū Sugoroku** (7)
Senbetsu	*Hakone Reigen Izari no Adauchi** (10)
Senbon Matsubara	*Igagoe Dōchū Sugoroku** (6)
Senbon Zakura	*Yoshitsune Senbon Zakura**
Sendai Hagi	*Meiboku Sendai Hagi**
Sendan Jō Michiyuki	*Kokusenya Kassen** (4)
Sengi	*Shin Usuyuki Monogatari** (2)
Senjin Mondō	*Hiragana Seisuiki** (2)
Senō Jurō Sengi	*Genpei Nunobiki no Taki** (3)
Senrigatake	*Kokusenya Kassen** (2)
Senryō Nobori	*Sekitori Senryō Nobori*
Setta Naoshi	*Yume Musubu Chō no Torioki*
Seyama	*Imoseyama Onna Taikin** (3)
Shaberi (Shaberi Yamanba)	*Komochi Yamanba** (3)
Shiai	*Kagamiyama Kokyō no Nishikie** (6)
Shibai Kido Mae	*Kami no Megumi Wagō no Torikumi** (2)
Shibaroku Sumika	*Imoseyama Onna Teikin** (2)
Shichidanme	*Kanadehon Chūshingura** (7)
Shichimise	*Kumo ni Magō Ueno no Hatsuhana** (1)
Shicho no Kakioki	*Jūni Toki Kaikei Soga* (6)
Shidōji (Shidodera)	*Hana no Ueno Homare no Ishibumi** (4)
Shiga no Sato	*Nigatsudō Rōben Sugi no Yurai** (1)
Shigemori Kangen	*Natori Gusa Heike Monogatari**
Shigenoi Kowakare	*Koi Nyōbō Somewake Tazuna** (10)
Shigi Hamaguri	*Kokusenya Kassen** (2)
Shihei no Nanawarai	*Tenmangū Natane no Gokū* (2)
Shiji Miuri	*Nezumi Komon Haru no Shingata*
Shijō Kawara	*Chikagoro Kawara no Tatehiki** (2)
Shikagawa no Soga	*Fujito Mimasu Suehiro Soga*
Shika Goroshi	*Imoseyama Onna Teikin** (2)
Shikishima Kaidan	*Kōshoku Shikishima Monogatari*
Shikitae Shisha	*Ōshū Adachigahara** (3)
Shimachidori	*Shimachidori Tsuki no Shiranami**
Shima no Tametome	*Yumi Harizuki Genke no Kaburaya*
Shimazakirō	*Kami no Megumi Wagō no Torikumi**
Shimizu Ikkaku	*Chūshin Iroha Jikki*
Shinai Uchi	*Kagamiyama Kokyō no Nishikie** (6)
Shinbei no Watashi	*Sakura Giminden** (2)
Shingen Yakata	*Honchō Nijūshikō** (2)
Shinigami	*Mekura Nagaya Ume ga Kagatobi** (5)
Shin Kiyomizu Hanami	*Kagamiyama Kokyō no Nishikie** (6)
Shinmachi Ageya	*Futatsu Chōchō Kuruwa Nikki** (3), *Meido no Hikyaku** (2)
Shinmotsu Ba	*Kanadehon Chūshingura** (3)
Shinobu no Sōta	*Miyakodori Nagare no Shiranami*
Shinoki, Shinokiri	*Yoshitsune Senbon Zakura** (3, 4)
Shinseimachi	*Hakata Kojōrō Nami Makura** (2)

Shinseki	*Igagoe Dōchū Sugoroku** (7)
Shinutsubo	*Yaoya no Kondate*
Shin Yoshiwara Ageya	*Gotaiheiki Shiraishi Banashi** (7)
Shinza Uchi	*Tsuyu Kosode Mukashi Hachijō** (2)
Shiobara Tasuke	*Shiobara Tasuke Ichidaiki**
Shiomochi	*Sugawara Denju Tenarai Kagami** (2)
Shirafuji Genta	*Kachi Zumo Ukina no Hanabure*
Shiraishi Banashi	*Gotaiheiki Shiraishi Banashi**
Shiranami Gonin Otoko	*Aotozōshi Hana no Nishikie**
Shiranui	*Shiranui Monogatari*
Shiratama Gonkurō	*Kurotegumi Kurowa no Tatehiki*
Shiroake Watashi	*Kanadehon Chūshingura** (4)
Shirokiya	*Koi Musume Mukashi Hachijō* (4)
Shirokoya Misesaki	*Hachijin Shugo no Honjō** (10)
Shōgen Kankyō	*Keisei Hangonkō* (1)
Shōgi	*Nebiki no Kadomatsu** (2)
Shōjiki Shōdayū	*Ise Ondo Koi no Netaba ** (2)
Shōjō Nagori	*Sugawara Denju Tenarai Kagami** (2)
Shō Konsha	*Shimachidori Tsuki no Shiranami* (final scene)
Shundō Yashiki	*Katakiuchi Tsuzure no Nishiki* (2)
Shunkan	*Heike Nyogo no Shima** (2)
Shunkan Shima Monogatari	*Hime Komatsu Nenohi no Asobi* (3)
Sobaya	*Kumo ni Magō Ueno no Hatsuhana** (4)
Sodehagi Sanmon	*Ōshū Adachigahara** (3)
Soga no Shikikawa	*Youchi Soga Kariba no Akebono** (6)
*Soga no Taimen**	*Kotobuki Soga no Taimen*
Sōgen Anjitsu	*Kikuchi Ōtomo*
Sōkaba	*Taiheiki Chūshin Kōshaku* (6)
Sōma Daisaku	*Kōdan Hinoki Yama Jikki*
Sonobe Yakata	*Shin Usuyuki Monogatari**
Soshō	*Sugawara Denju Tenarai Kagami** (3)
Sotoba	*Ono no Tōfū Aoyagi Suzuri* (3)
Sugi no Mori	*Ehon Taikōki** (7)
Sugi Sakaya	*Imoseyama Onna Teikin** (4)
Suikoden	*Suikoden Yuki no Danmari*
Sukeroku	*Kamiko Jitate Ryōmen Kagami, Sukeroku Yukari no Edo Zakura**
Suma no Ura	*Hikosan Gongen Chikai no Sukedachi** (6), *Ichinotani Futaba Gunki** (2)
Sumiya	*Shiobara Tasuke Ichidaiki** (4)
Sumiyoshi	*Natsu Matsuri Naniwa Kagami** (1)
Sumōba	*Futatsu Chōchō Kuruwa Nikki** (2), *Sekitori Senryō Nobori* (2)
Sumō Goya	*Kami no Megumi Wagō no Torikumi** (4)
Sumō na Adauchi	*Yagura Daiko Narita no Adauchi* (2)
Susaki Dote	*Ami Moyō Toro no Kikukiri* (3)
Sushiya	*Yoshitsune Senbon Zakura** (2)

Suzugamori	*Banzui Chōbei Shōjin Manaita**, *Koi Musume Mukashi Hanchijō** (5)
Suzuki Mondo	*Sumidagawa Tsui no Kagamon*
Suzume Odori	*Nanbantetsu Gotō no Menuki** (3)

T

Taigyūrō	*Satomi Hakkenden* (8)
Taijū	*Ehon Taikōki** (10)
Taiketsu	*Date Kurabe Okuni Kabuki (Meiboku Sendai Hagi**) (final scene)
Taikōki	*Ehon Taikōki**, *Mitsuka Taiheiki*
Taimen	*Soga no Taimen**
Takada no Baba	*Katakiuchi Takada no Baba*
Takano Chōei	*Yume Monogatari Rosei no Sugatae*
Takechō Shichi Mise	*Mekura Nagaya Ume ga Kagatobi** (3)
Takeda Kaidō	*Kiyomasa Seichū Roku* (4)
Takehori	*Honchō Nijūshikō** (3)
Takenaka Toride	*Konoshita Kage Hazama Gassen* (7)
Takeni Suzume (Takesu)	*Imoseyama Onna Teikin** (4)
Takenoma	*Meiboku Sendai Hagi** (6)
Takenoshi	*Honchō Nijūshikō** (3)
Takeyabu	*Igagoe Dōchū Sugoroku** (7), *Yoshitsune Senbon Zakura** (3)
Taki	*Hakone Reigen Izari no Adauchi** (10)
Takidashi Kichiburō Uchi	*Kami no Megumi Wagō no Torikumi** (3)
Takozakana	*Kanadehon Chūshingura** (7)
Tamagiku	*Hoshi Yadoro Tsuyu no Tamagiku*
Tamaki no Miya Aki Goten	*Ōshū Adachigahara** (3)
Tamamizu Buchi	*Hade Kurabe Ise Monogatari** (5)
Tamamono Mae, Tamasan	*Tamamono Mae Asahi no Tamoto**
Tamatori	*Karukaya Dōshin Tsukushi no Iezuto* (3)
Tamiya Bōtarō	*Hana no Ueno Homare no Ishibumi**
Tanba no Yosaku	*Koi Nyōbō Somewake Tazuna**
Tango no Sekku	*Kusonoki Mukashi Banashi* (3)
Taroya Osen	*Meisaku Kiri Kon Akebono*
Tatazu no Mori	*Yamatogana Ariwara Keizu** (2)
Tatsugorō Uchi	*Kami no Megumi Wagō no Torikumi** (3)
Taue	*Gotaiheiki Shiraishi Banashi** (4)
Tenbō Masamune	*Shin Usuyuki Monogatari** (3)
Tengajaya	*Katakiuchi Tengajaya Mura**
Tengu Mai	*Hōjō Kudai Meika no Isaoshi (Takatoki**)
Tenichibō	*Ōgibyōshi Ōoka Seidan*

Tenjiku Tokubei	*Tenjiku Tokubei Ikoku Banashi**
Tenjin no Mori	*Katakiuchi Tengajaya Mura** (3)
Tenmokusan	*Honchō Nijūshikō** (5)
Tennichibō	*Azuma Kudari Koju Santsugi*
Ten no Amijima	*Shinjū Ten no Amijima**
Tennōji	*Katakiuchi Tengajaya Mura** (1)
Tennoji Mura Heisuke Uchi	*Gokuzai Shiki Musume Ōgi* (8)
Tenpaizan	*Sugawara Denju Tenarai Kagami** (4)
Tenshu Kaku	*Hachijin Shugo no Honjō** (8)
Tentoku	*Tenjiku Tokubei Ikoku Banashi**
Terairi	*Sugawara Denju Tenarai Kagami** (4)
Teraka Setsubuku	*Chūshin Nidome no Kiyogaki*
Terakoya	*Sugawara Denju Tenarai Kagami** (4)
Teremen	*Kasa no Rokuro Ukina no Nureginu*
Terutora Haizen	*Shinshū Kawanakajima Kassen** (3)
Tetsubō Ba	*Nanbantetsu Gotō no Menuki**
Tetsubō Goroshi	*Honchō Nijūshiko**, *Kanadehon Chūshingura** (5)
Tobari Kyū	*Genpei Nunobiki no Taki** (4)
Tobiume	*Sugawara Denju Tenarai Kagami** (4)
Tōdaiji	*Nigatsudō Rōben Sugi no Yurai** (3)
Toda no Yashiki	*Shiobara Tasuke Ichidaiki** (2)
Tōfū Kai	*Imoseyama Onna Teikin** (4), *Kamakura Sandaiki** (7)
Tōfuya	*Meiboku Sendai Hagi** (4)
Tōfu Yakata	*Ono no Tōfu Aoyagi Suzuri* (2)
Tōge	*Tsuta Momiji Utsunoya Tōge**
Toitagaeshi	*Tōkaidō Yotsuya Kaidan** (3)
Tōji Kashi Zashiki	*Katakiuchi Tengajaya Mura** (2)
Tōji Ura	*Ono no Tōfu Aoyagi Suzuri* (2)
Tokaiya	*Yoshitsune Senbon Zakura** (2)
Tokudayū Sumika	*Kusunoki Mukashi Banashi* (3)
Tokuri no Wakare	*Kanadehon Suzuri no Takashima*
Tōmegane	*Igagoe Dōchū Sugoroku** (7)
Tomoe Ikedori	*Hiragana Seisuiki** (1)
Tonda	*Gion Sairei Shinkōki** (3)
Tonbei Uchi	*Shinrei Yaguchi no Watashi** (4)
Tora no Maki	*Kiichi Hōgen Sanryaku no Maki** (3)
Tora Taiji	*Kokusenya Kassen** (2)
Torime no Ikkaku	*Ōedo Meibutsu Nishikie Hajime*
Tori Musume	*Yura no Minato Sengen Chōja**
Tosamachi	*Tsubosaka Reigenki** (1)
Tōtenkō	*Sugawara Denju Tenarai Kagami** (2)
Totoya no Chawan	*Hototogisu Mizuni Hibikune*
Tōyama Seidan	*Tōyama Seidan Ryōmen Kagami*, *Tōyama Zakura Tenbō Nikki*

Tōyama Zakura	*Tōyama Zakura Tenbō Nikki*
Toyata Monogatari	*Goshō Zakura Horikawa Youchi** (4)
Toyonari Yakata	*Hibariyama Koseki no Matsu* (3)
Tsubosaka	*Tsubosaka Reigenki**
Tsubosaka Dera	*Tsubosaka Reigenki** (2)
Tsue Sekkan, Tsuiji	*Sugawara Denju Tenarai Kagami** (2, 1)
Tsuji Hoin	*Hiragana Seisuiki** (4)
Tsukigomeya	*Futatsu Chōchō Kuruwa Nikki** (4)
Tsukudajima Rō Yashiki, Tsukuda no Yoarashi	*Ansei Kibun Tsukuda no Yoarashi*
Tsumahachi	*Sakuratsuba Urami no Samezaya**
Tsumasaki Nezumi	*Gion Sairei Shinkōki** (4)
Tsuri Tenjō	*Utsu no Miya Nishiki no Tsuri Yogi*
Tsurube Zushi	*Yoshitsune Senbon Zakura** (3)
Tsurugaoka	*Kanadehon Chūshingura** (1)
Tsuru Goroshi	*Ōshū Adachigahara** (2)

U

Uba Arasoi	*Nasu no Yoichi Saikai Suzuri* (3)
Uchiiri	*Kanadehon Chūshingura** (11)
Ude no Kichisaburō	*Koko ga Edo Kode no Tatehiki*
Udonya	*Shisenryō Kōban no Umenoha** (4)
Uegiya	*Chūshin Renri no Hachiue* (3)
Uji no Sato	*Nigatsudō Rōben Sugi no Yurai** (2)
Ukai no Kansaku	*Nichiren Shōmin Minori no Umi* (3)
Ukamuse	*Futatsu Chōchō Kuruwa Nikki** (1), *Shinjū Kamiya Jihei* (1)
Ume Chū	*Meido no Hikyaku**
Umekichi Uchi	*Mekura Nagaya Ume ga Kagatobi**
Ume no Yubei	*Akanezome no Naka no Kakureido, Sumida no Haru Geisha Katagi*
Ume to Sakura	*Kanadehon Chūshingura** (2)
Umeyoshi	*Sumida no Haru Geisha Katagi*
Unagidani	*Sakuratsuba Urami no Samezaya**
Uramon, Uramon Gatten	*Kanadehon Chushingura** (3)
Uratahō	*Tōkaidō Yotsuya Kaidan** (1)
Urazato Tokijirō	*Akegarasu Hana no Nureginu**
Utsunoya Tōge	*Tsuta Momiji Utsunoya Tōge**
Uwabami Oyoshi	*Uwabami Oyoshi Uwasa no Adauchi*

W

Wadabei Jōshi	*Ōmi Genji Senjin Yakata** (8)
Wakoku Bashi no Tōji	*Sandai Banashi Kōza no Shinasaku*
Warai Gusuri	*Shō Utsushi Asagao Nikki** (4)
Watakuri Uma	*Genpei Nunobiki no Taki** (3)

Watanabe Kazan	*Yume Monogatari Rosei no Sugata E*
Watashi	*Shinrei Yaguchi no Watashi** (4)
Watonai	*Kokusenya Kassen**

Y

Yabuhara Kengyō	*Narita Michi Hatsune no Yabuhara*
Yadoya	*Shō Utsushi Asagao Nikki** (4), *Tsuta Momiji Utsunoya Tōge** (1)
Yaegiri Kuruwa Banashi	*Komochi Yamanba** (3)
Yaguchi no Watashi	*Shinrei Yaguchi no Watashi** (4)
Yagura no Oshichi	*Date Musume Koi no Higanoko** (6)
Yagyū Tajima no Kami	*Medashi Yanagi Midori no Matsumae*
Yaji Kita	*Hiza Kurige**
Yakan no Michiyuki	*Ashiya Dōman Ōuchi Kagami** (4)
Yakata Sōdō	*Kanadehon Chūshingura** (3)
Yaki Gote	*Natsu Matsuri Naniwa Kagami** (6)
Yakiri Mura	*Awada Guchi Kikime no Orikami* (6)
Yakoe no Tori	*Ichinotani Futaba Gunki** (4), *Sugawara Denju Tenarai Kagami** (2)
Yama	*Imoseyama Onna Teikin** (3), *Yura no Minato Sengen Chōja** (2)
Yamanaya	*Akegarasu Yuki no Akebono*
Yamashina Kankyō	*Kanadehon Chūshingura** (9)
Yamato Bashi	*Sanzenryō Kogane no Kurairi, Shinjū Ten no Amijima** (3)
Yamazaki Kaidō	*Kanadehon Chūshingura** (5)
Yamazaki Yojibei	*Nebiki no Kadomatsu**
Yanagi	*Sanjūsan Gendō Munagi no Yurai** (3)
Yanagiwara Dote	*Edo Sodachi Omatsuri Sashichi** (3)
Yanone	*Ōshū Adachigahara** (3)
Yaoya	*Date Musume Koi no Higanoko** (6), *Shinjū Yoi Gōshin** (1), *Yaoya no Kondate*
Yaoya Oshichi	*Date Musume Koi no Higanoko**
Yasaku no Kamabara	*Irohagana Shijūshichi Moji* (6)
Yasuna Monogurui, Yasuna Uchi	*Ashiya Dōman Ōuchi Kagami** (2, 4)
Yatsu Yamashita	*Kami no Megumi Wagō no Torikumi** (1)
Yawata no Sato	*Futatsu Chōchō Kuruwa Nikki** (8)
Yodanme, Yoichibei Sumika	*Kanadehon Chūshingura** (4, 6)
Yojirō Uchi	*Chikagoro Kawara no Tatehiki** (2)
Yōjiya	*Hiragana Seisuiki** (2)
Yorikaze Kandō	*Ono no Tōfū Aoyagi Suzuri* (2)
Yoshida Shatō	*Sugawara Denju Tenarai Kagami** (3)
Yoshidaya	*Kuruwa Bunshō**
Yoshikata Saigo	*Genpei Nunobiki no Taki** (2)
Yoshinokawa	*Imoseyama Onna Teikin** (3)
Yotsune Jaya	*Shiobara Tasuke Ichidaiki** (3)

Yotsuya Kaidan	*Tōkaidō Yotsuya Kaidan**
Youchi Soga	*Youchi Soga Kariba no Akebono**
Yuagari no Kasane	*Okuni Gozen Keshō Kagami*
Yudono Chōbei	*Kiwametsuki Banzui Chōbei**
Yūgaodana	*Ehon Taikōki** (10)
Yukashita	*Meiboku Sendai Hagi** (6)
Yukie Yashiki	*Igagoe Dōchū Sugoroku** (2)
Yukihime Nezumi	*Gion Sairei Shinkōki** (4)
Yukihira Yakata	*Yamatogana Ariwara Keizu** (4)
Yuki Kokashi	*Kanadehon Chūshingura** (9)
Yume no Ichizō	*Nihon Bare Iga no Adauchi*
Yumishi Tōshirō Uchi	*Keian Taiheiki** (2)
Yura no Minato	*Yura no Minato Sengen Chōja**
Yutono no Chōbei	*Kiwametsuki Banzui Chōbei** (2)

Z

Zama Yashiro	*Shinpan Utazaemon** (1)
Zangiri Otomi	*Tsuki no Enmasu no Igaguri*
Zatō Goroshi	*Tsuta Momiji Utsunoya Tōge**
Zenni Yakata	**Wada Gassen Onna Maizuru** (3)
Zesai Uchi	*Gion Sairei Shinkōki** (3)
Zōriuchi	*Kagamiyama Kokyō no Nishikie** (6)
Zundohei	*Katakiuchi Osana Bundan* (5)

APPENDIX IV
Actors' Genealogies

The names following those in capitals are other names held by the actor during his career. When only one name appears, it is understood that the family name is that given in the main entry. Thus, Ebizō is Ichikawa Ebizō. Family trees have been simplified.

ICHIKAWA DANJŪRŌ I
Ebizō
Son of Horikoshi Juzō
Died September 19, 1704

|

DANJŪRŌ II
Kuzō
Ebizō II
Died September 24, 1758

|

DANJŪRŌ III
Suketarō
Shogorō
Son of Mimasuya Sukejūrō
Pupil of Danjūrō I
Adopted son of Danjūrō II
Died February 27, 1742

|

DANJŪRŌ IV
Matsumoto Shichizō
Matsumoto Kōshirō II
Ebizō III
Matsumoto Kōshirō II (again)
Adopted son of Matsumoto Kōshirō I
Actual son of Danjūrō II
Died February 25, 1778

|

DANJŪRŌ V
Umemaru
Matsumoto Kozō
Matsumoto Kōshirō III
Ebizō
Son of Danjūrō IV
Died October 30, 1806

DANJŪRŌ VI
Tokuzō
Ebizō IV
Adopted son of Danjūrō V
Died May 1, 1799

DANJŪRŌ VII
Kotama
Shinnosuke I
Ebizō (written with syllabic letters)
Ebizō V (written with Chinese characters)
Adopted son of Danjūrō VI
Died March 23, 1859

DANJŪRŌ VIII
Shinnosuke II
Ebizō VI
Eldest son of Danjūrō VII
Died August 6, 1854

DANJŪRŌ IX
Kawarazaki Chōjurō
Kawarazaki Gonjūrō
Kawarazaki Gonnosuke
Fifth Son of Danjūrō VII

DANJŪRŌ X
Horikoshi Fukusaburō
Ichikawa Sanshō
Adopted son of Danjūrō IX
Died February 1, 1956

DANJŪRŌ XI
Matsumoto Kintarō
Komazō IX
Ebizō IX
Adopted son of Danjūrō X
Eldest son of Matsumoto Kōshirō VIII (See Matsumoto Kōshirō genealogy)
Died February 10, 1965

EBIZŌ X
Natsuō
Shinnosuke VI
Eldest son of Danjūrō XI
Born August 6, 1946

MATSUMOTO KŌSHIRŌ I
Hisamatsu Kōshirō
Koshirō (spelled differently)
Pupil of Hisamatsu Tashirō
Died March 1730

KŌSHIRŌ II
(later Ichikawa Danjūrō IV)
Adopted son of Kōshirō I

KŌSHIRŌ IV
Segawa Kingo
Segawa Kinji
Ichikawa Takejūrō
Ichikawa Somegorō I
Ichikawa Komazō II
Omegawa Kyōjūrō
Pupil of Kōshirō II
Died June 1802

KŌSHIRŌ III
(Later Ichikawa Danjūrō V)

KŌSHIRŌ V
Ichikawa Junzō
Ichikawa Komazō III
Son of Kōshirō IV
Died October 1838

KŌSHIRŌ VI
Kinko
Ichikawa Komazō V
Kinshō
Son of Kōshirō V
Died February 1849

KŌSHIRŌ VII
Toyokichi
Ichikawa Kintarō
Ichikawa Somegorō IV
Ichikawa Komazō VIII
Pupil of Ichikawa Danjūrō IX
Died January 27, 1949

KŌSHIRŌ VIII
Junzō
Ichikawa Somegorō V
Second son of
Kōshirō VII
Brother of Danjūrō XI
Born July 7, 1910

ONOE SHŌROKU II
Toyo
Third son of Kōshirō
Pupil of Kikugorō VI
Born March 28, 1913

ICHIKAWA DANJŪRŌ XI
(See Ichikawa
Danjūrō genealogy)

NAKAMURA KICHIEMON II
Mannosuke
Second son of Kōshirō VIII
Born May 22, 1944

ICHIKAWA SOMEGORŌ
Kintarō
Eldest son of Kōshirō VIII
Born August 18, 1942

ONOE TATSUNOSUKE I
Sakin
Eldest son of Shōroku II
Born October 26, 1946

SAWAMURA SŌJŪRŌ I
Fujinojō
Someyama Kijūrō
Kigorō
Sōjūrō
(spelled with a different Chinese character for *Sō* than that used in the final form of the name)
Chōjūrō III
Suketakaya Takasuke
Disciple of Sawamura Chōjūrō II
Died January 1756

SŌJŪRŌ II
Toyozawa Naganosuke
Takenaka Utagawa
Takinaka Utagawa
Utagawa Shirogorō
Adopted son of Sōjūrō I
Died August 1770

SŌJŪRŌ III
Tanosuke I
Second son of Sōjūrō II
Died March 1801

SŌJŪRŌ IV
Gennosuke
Eldest son of Sōjūrō III
Died December 1812

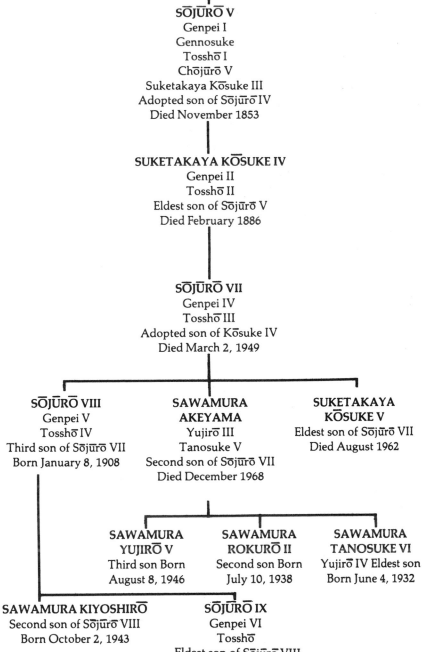

SŌJŪRŌ V
Genpei I
Gennosuke
Tosshō I
Chōjūrō V
Suketakaya Kōsuke III
Adopted son of Sōjūrō IV
Died November 1853

SUKETAKAYA KŌSUKE IV
Genpei II
Tosshō II
Eldest son of Sōjūrō V
Died February 1886

SŌJŪRŌ VII
Genpei IV
Tosshō III
Adopted son of Kōsuke IV
Died March 2, 1949

SŌJŪRŌ VIII
Genpei V
Tosshō IV
Third son of Sōjūrō VII
Born January 8, 1908

SAWAMURA AKEYAMA
Yujirō III
Tanosuke V
Second son of Sōjūrō VII
Died December 1968

SUKETAKAYA KŌSUKE V
Eldest son of Sōjūrō VII
Died August 1962

SAWAMURA YUJIRŌ V
Third son Born
August 8, 1946

SAWAMURA ROKURŌ II
Second son Born
July 10, 1938

SAWAMURA TANOSUKE VI
Yujirō IV Eldest son
Born June 4, 1932

SAWAMURA KIYOSHIRŌ
Second son of Sōjūrō VIII
Born October 2, 1943

SŌJŪRŌ IX
Genpei VI
Tosshō
Eldest son of Sōjūrō VIII
Born March 8, 1933

ICHIMURA UZAEMON III
(theatre manager)
Died July 1687

UZAEMON V
(Name is spelled with different Chinese characters than customary for this name)
Ichimura Takematsu Pupil of Uzaemon IV

TAKENOJŌ IV
Nephew and adopted son of Uzaemon III
Died October 1718
Was first manager at the Murayama-za after it became the Ichimura-za

TAKENOJŌ VI
Takematsu
Son of Uzaemon V
Died December 1686

TAKENOJŌ VII
Chōtarō
Adopted son of Uzaemon V
Died April 1698

UZAEMON VIII
Takenojō
Pupil of Uzaemon VII
Died May 1762

UZAEMON IX
Manzō
Kamezō
Died August 25, 1785

UZAEMON X
Shichijūrō
Kamezō II
Son of Uzaemon IX
Died February 15, 1799

UZAEMON XI
Manjirō
Adopted son of Uzaemon X

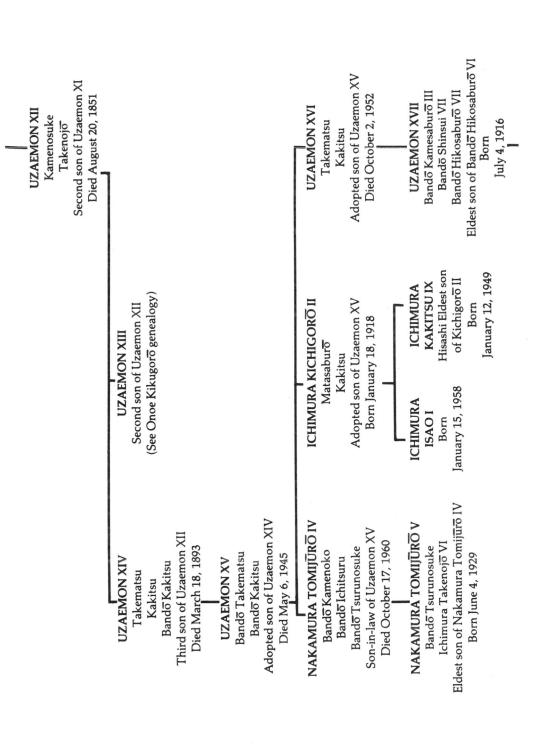

UZAEMON XII
Kamenosuke
Takenojō
Second son of Uzaemon XI
Died August 20, 1851

UZAEMON XIV
Takematsu
Kakitsu
Bandō Kakitsu
Third son of Uzaemon XII
Died March 18, 1893

UZAEMON XIII
Second son of Uzaemon XII
(See Onoe Kikugorō genealogy)

UZAEMON XV
Bandō Takematsu
Bandō Kakitsu
Adopted son of Uzaemon XIV
Died May 6, 1945

NAKAMURA TOMIJŪRŌ IV
Bandō Kamenoko
Bandō Ichitsuru
Bandō Tsurunosuke
Son-in-law of Uzaemon XV
Died October 17, 1960

ICHIMURA KICHIGORŌ II
Matasaburō
Kakitsu
Adopted son of Uzaemon XV
Born January 18, 1918

UZAEMON XVI
Takematsu
Kakitsu
Adopted son of Uzaemon XV
Died October 2, 1952

NAKAMURA TOMIJŪRŌ V
Bandō Tsurunosuke
Ichimura Takenojō VI
Eldest son of Nakamura Tomijūrō IV
Born June 4, 1929

ICHIMURA ISAO I
Born
January 15, 1958

ICHIMURA KAKITSU IX
Hisashi Eldest son
of Kichigorō II
Born
January 12, 1949

UZAEMON XVII
Bandō Kamesaburō III
Bandō Shinsui VII
Bandō Hikosaburō VII
Eldest son of Bandō Hikosaburō VI
Born
July 4, 1916

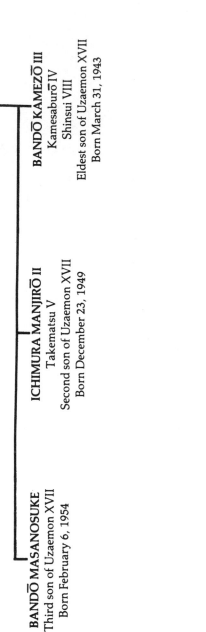

BANDŌ MASANOSUKE
Third son of Uzaemon XVII
Born February 6, 1954

ICHIMURA MANJIRŌ II
Takematsu V
Second son of Uzaemon XVII
Born December 23, 1949

BANDŌ KAMEZŌ III
Kamesaburō IV
Shinsui VIII
Eldest son of Uzaemon XVII
Born March 31, 1943

NAKAMURA UTAEMON I
Utanosuke
Utashishi
Kagaya Kashichi
Third son of the artisan, Ōzeki Shunzan
Died October 1791

UTAEMON II
Mizuki Tōzō
Tōzō
Tōzō (again)
Mizuki Tōzō (again)
Pupil of Utaemon I
Died March 1798

UTAEMON III
Kagaya Fukunosuke
Shikan I
Tamasuke I
Son of Utaemon I
Died July 1838

UTAEMON IV
Hirano Kichitarō
Fujima Kamesaburō
Fujitarō Tsurusuke
Shikan II
Adopted son of Utaemon III
Died February 1852

SHIKAN IV
Tamatarō
Fukusuke I
Adopted son of Utaemon IV
Died January 1, 1899

UTAEMON V
Kotarō
Fukusuke IV
Shikan V
Adopted son of Shikan IV
Died September 12, 1940

UTAEMON VI
Kotarō
Fukusuke VI
Shikan VI
Second Son of Utaemon V
Born January 20, 1917

FUKUSUKE V
Kotarō
Eldest son of Utaemon V
Died August 1, 1933

SHIKAN VII
Kotarō
Fukusuke VII
Eldest son of Fukusuke V
Born March 11, 1928

KOTARŌ
Eldest son of Shikan VII
Born October 29, 1960

MATSUE V
Kagaya Hashinosuke
Adopted son of Utaemon VI
Born January 1, 1948

FUKUSUKE VIII
Kagaya Fukunosuke
Adopted son of Utaemon VI
Born August 2, 1946

JITSUKAWA GAKUJŪRŌ I
Asao Yaozō
Nakamura Yaozō
Asao Yūjirō
Pupil of Asao Kuzaemon I
Died November 1835

GAKUJŪRŌ II
Asao Mankichi
Asao Ensaburō
Ensaburō
Adopted son of Gakujūrō I
Died February 1867

ENJAKU I
Enji
Nakamura Enjaku
Onoe Baikō
Enjirō
Adopted son of Gakujūrō II
Died September 1885

ENJAKU II
Enjirō
Eldest son of Enjaku I
Died February 22, 1951

ENJAKU III
Enjirō II
Eldest son of Enjaku II
Born January 3, 1921

NAKAMURA UTAEMON IV
(first to use the *haiku* pen name of Ganjaku)

GANJAKU II
Ichimura Kitsuzō
Bandō Kitsuzō
Adopted son
Died January 1861

GANJAKU III
Arashi Tamazō
Adopted son
Died February 1881

GANJIRŌ I
Jitsukawa Ganjirō
Pupil of Jitsukawa Enjaku I
Son of Ganjaku I
Died February 1, 1935

NAKAMURA GANJIRŌ II
Hayashi Yoshio
Senjaku I
Shijaku IV
Son of Ganjirō I
Born February 17, 1902

HAYASHI MATAICHIRŌ II
Hayashi Chōsaburō
Eldest son of Ganjirō I
Died December 1967

SENJAKU II
Mitsutarō
Second son of Ganjirō II
Born December 31, 1931

KŌTARŌ
Second son of Senjaku II
Born December 1960

TOMOTARŌ
Eldest son of Senjaku II
Born February 6, 1949

ONOE KIKUGORŌ I
Taketarō
Son of Otowaya Hanji
Son-in-law of Bandō Hikosaburō I
Died December 29, 1783

KIKUGORŌ II
Ushinosuke
Son of Kikugorō I
Died July 12, 1787

KIKUGORŌ III
Shingorō
Shinsaburō
Eisaburō I
Matsusuke II
Baikō III
Ōgawa Hashizō
Adopted son of Matsusuke I
Died April 24, 1849

KIKUGORŌ IV
Nakamura Kachō
Kikueda
Eisaburō III
Baikō IV
Son-in-law of Kikugorō III
Died June 28, 1860

KIKUGORŌ V
Kuroemon
Ichimura Uzaemon XIII
Ichimura Kakitsu
Grandson of Kikugorō III
Son of Ichimura Uzaemon XII and Kikugorō IV's second daughter
Died February 18, 1903

BAIKŌ VI
Nishikawa Einosuke
Eisaburō V
Adopted son of Kikugorō V
Died November 8, 1934

KIKUGORŌ VI
Ushinosuke
Eldest son of Kikugorō V
Died July 10, 1949

BAIKŌ VII
Ushinosuke IV
Kikunosuke III
Illegitimate son of
Kikugorō VI
Born August 31, 1915

KUROEMON II
Sakin
Eldest son of Kikugorō VI
Born January 22, 1922

KIKUGORŌ VII
Ushinosuke V
Kikunosuke IV
Son of Baikō VII
Born October 2, 1942

- **NAKAMURA KAROKU I**
  Moshio
  Pupil of Utaemon III
  Died July 1859
  - **KAROKU II**
    Shutarō
    Moshio II
    Second son of Karoku I
    Died 1881
  - **KAROKU III**
    Yonekichi
    Umeeda I
    Tokizō I
    Third son of Karoku I
    Died May 1919
    - **KANZABURŌ XVII**
      Yonekichi III
      Moshio IV
      Third son of Karoku III
      Born July 29, 1909
      - **KANKURŌ V**
        Eldest son of Kanzaburō XVII
        Born May 30, 1955
    - **TOKIZŌ III**
      Yonekichi II
      Second son of Karoku III
      Died July 11, 1959
      - **KAZUO**
        Fifth son of Tokizō III
        Born April 23, 1938
      - **KINNOSUKE**
        Fourth son of Tokizō III
        Born November 20, 1932
      - **TOKIZO IV**
        Umeeda IV
        Shijaku VI
        Second son of Tokizō III
        Died January 1962
      - **NAKAMURA KASHŌ II**
        Kogawa Kichio
        Nakamura Shutarō
        Eldest son of Tokizō III
        Born July 15, 1925
        (Left the profession)
    - **KICHIEMON I**
      Eldest son of Karoku III
      Died September 5, 1954
      - **KICHIEMON II**
        Grandson of Kichiemon I
        (See Matsumoto Kōshirō genealogy)

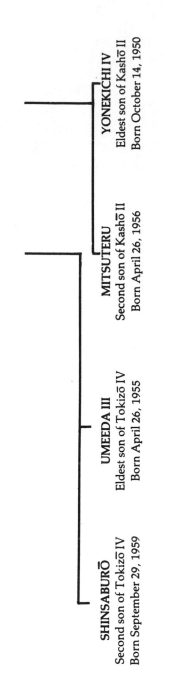

SHINSABURŌ
Second son of Tokizō IV
Born September 29, 1959

UMEEDA III
Eldest son of Tokizō IV
Born April 26, 1955

MITSUTERU
Second son of Kashō II
Born April 26, 1956

YONEKICHI IV
Eldest son of Kashō II
Born October 14, 1950

BANDŌ MITSUGORŌ I
Takeda Inosuke
Adopted son of Bandō Sanpachi
Brother of Uzaemon VIII
Died April 1782

MITSUGORŌ II
Onoe Tōzō
Onoe Monsaburō
Ogino Isaburō
Pupil of Mitsugorō I
Died October 1828

MITSUGORŌ III
Mitahachi I
Inosuke
Morita Kanjirō
Minosuke I
Son of Mitsugorō I
Died December 1831

MITSUGORŌ IV
Minosuke II
Morita Kanya XI
Adopted son of
Mitsugorō III
Died November 1863

MITSUGORŌ V
Tamanosuke
Tamasaburō
Shūka (spelled with Chinese characters)
Shūka (spelled with syllabic letters)
Adopted son of Mitsugorō III
Died March 1855

MORITA KANYA XII
Jusaku
Adopted son of
Bandō Mitsugorō IV
Died August 21, 1897

MITSUGORŌ VI
Kichiya
Son of Mitsugorō V
Died September 1873

MORITA KANYA XIII
Mitahachi III
Third son of Kanya XII
Died June 16, 1932

MITSUGORŌ VII
Hachijūrō II
Eldest son of
Morita Kanya XII
Died November 1961

MORITA KANYA XIV
Bandō Tamasaburō IV
Bandō Shūka III
Adopted son of
Kanya XIII
Died 1975

BANDŌ KŌTARŌ I
Sawamura Kentarō
Adopted son of
Morita Kanya III
Born May 4, 1911

MITSUGORŌ VIII
Yasosuke III
Minosuke VI
Adopted son of Mitsugorō VII
Died 1975

KICHIYA II
Son of Kōtarō I
Born June 21, 1937

MINOSUKE VII
Mitsunobu
Yasosuke IV
Adopted son of Mitsugorō VIII
Born May 14, 1929

SHŪKA IV
Inoue Kuzō
Onoe Matsuya
Adopted son of
Morita Kanya XIV
Born June 11, 1950

TAMASABURŌ V
Kinoji
Adopted son of
Morita Kanya XIV
Born April 25, 1950

YASOSUKE V
Eldest son of Minosuke VII
Born January 23, 1956

KATAOKA NIZAEMON I
Fujikawa Isaburō
Pupil of Yamashita Hanzaemon I
Died November 1715

NIZAEMON II
(Died young)
Son of Nizaemon I

FUJIKAWA HAN'EMON
(NIZAEMON III)
Fujikawa Hansaburō
Married to younger sister of
Nizaemon II

NIZAEMON IV
Fujikawa Seishō
Fujikawa Hansaburō II
Adopted son of
Fujikawa Han'emon
Died 1758 (?)

FUJIKAWA HANSABURŌ
(NIZAEMON V)
Yamamoto Shichisaburō
Yamamoto Shichizō
Relative of Nizaemon IV

MIOKI GIZAEMON II
(NIZAEMON VI)
Died September 1787

NIZAEMON VII
Nakamura Matsusuke
Asao Kunigorō II
Pupil of Asai Kunigorō I
Died March 1, 1837

NIZAEMON VIII
Ichikawa Shinnosuke
Mimasu Iwagorō
Arashi Kitsujirō
Gatō
Gadō
Adopted son of
Nizaemon VII
Died February 16, 1863

NIZAEMON IX
Mimasu Umemaru
Matsunosuke II
Gatō II
Adopted son of
Nizaemon VIII
Died November 1871

NIZAEMON X
Tsuchinosuke
Matsuwaka
Gadō
Third son of
Nizaemon VIII
Died April 16, 1895

NIZAEMON XI
Kishutarō
Gatō IV
Fourth son of
Nizaemon VIII
Died October 16, 1934

NIZAEMON XII
Tokichi
Tsuchinosuke II
Gadō XII
Son of Nizaemon X
Died March 16, 1946

NIZAEMON XIII
Sendainosuke
Gatō
Third son of Nizaemon XI
Born December 15, 1904

KATAOKA ROEN VI
Osuke
Third son of Nizaemon XII
Born November 16, 1926

ICHIMURA KICHIGORŌ II
(See Ichimura Uzaemon genealogy)

GADŌ XIII
Hitoshi
Roen
Eldest son of Nizaemon XII

TAKAO I
Third son of
Nizaemon XIII
Born March 14, 1944

HIDETARŌ II
Shunin
Second son of
Nizaemon XIII
Born September 13, 1941

GATŌ V
Shuko
Eldest son of
Nizaemon XIII
Born January 7, 1935

SHINNOSUKE
Eldest son of Gatō V
Born September 7, 1967

Selected Bibliography

BOOKS ON KABUKI IN ENGLISH

Arnott, Peter D. *The Theatres of Japan.* New York, 1969.

Bowers, Faubion. *Japanese Theatre.* New York, 1952.

Brandon, James R. *Kabuki: Five Classic Plays.* Cambridge, Mass., 1975.

______, ed. *Traditional Asian Plays.* New York, 1972.

______, William P. Malm, and Donald Shively. *Studies in Kabuki: Its Acting, Music, and Historical Context.* Honolulu, 1978.

Dunn, Charles J., and Bunzo Torigoe, trans. and ed. *The Actor's Analects [Yakusha Rongo].* Tokyo and New York, 1969.

Ernst, Earle. *The Kabuki Theatre.* Rev. ed. Honolulu, 1974.

______. *Three Japanese Plays from the Traditional Theatre.* New York, 1959.

Gunji Masakatsu. *Buyo: The Classical Dance.* Translated by Don Kenny. New York and Tokyo, 1970.

______. *Kabuki.* Translated by John Bester. Tokyo, 1968.

Halford, Aubrey S., and Giovanna M. Halford. *The Kabuki Handbook.* Tokyo, 1952.

Hamamura, Yonezo, et al. *Kabuki.* Translated by Fumi Takano. Tokyo, 1956.

Japanese National Commission for UNESCO. *Theatre in Japan.* Tokyo, 1963.

Kawatake Mokuami. *The Love of Izayoi and Seishin.* Translated by Frank T. Motofuji. Tokyo, 1966.

Kawatake Shigetoshi. *Kabuki: Japanese Drama.* Tokyo, 1958.

Kawatake Toshio. *A History of Japanese Theatre.* Vol. II, *Bunraku and Kabuki.* Tokyo, 1971.

Keene, Donald. *Chūshingura: The Treasury of Loyal Retainers.* New York, 1971.

______. *Major Plays of Chikamatsu.* New York, 1961.

Kikuchi Kwan. *Tōjūrō's Love and Four Other Plays.* Translated by Glenn W. Shaw. Tokyo, 1925.

Kincaid, Zoe. *Kabuki: The Popular Stage of Japan.* New York, 1925.

Komiya Toyotaka, comp. and ed. *Japanese Music and Drama in the Meiji Era.* Translated and adapted by Donald Keene and Edward G. Siedensticker. Tokyo, 1956.

Leiter, Samuel L., trans. with commentary. *The Art of Kabuki: Famous Plays in Performance.* Berkeley, 1979.

Malm, William P. *Japanese Music and Musical Instruments.* Tokyo, 1959.

______. *Nagauta: The Heart of Kabuki Music.* Tokyo, 1964.

Pronko, Leonard. *Guide to Japanese Drama.* Boston, 1974.

______. *Theatre East and West: Perspectives Towards a Total Theatre.* Berkeley, 1967.

Richie, Donald, and Miyoko Watanabe, trans. *Six Kabuki Plays.* Tokyo, 1963.

Scott, A.C. *The Kabuki Theatre of Japan.* London, 1955.

______, trans. *Kanjinchō: A Japanese Kabuki Play.* Tokyo, 1953.

______, trans. *Genyadana: A Japanese Kabuki Play.* Tokyo, 1953.

Shaver, Ruth. *Kabuki Costume.* Tokyo, 1966.

Toita Yasuji. *Kabuki: The Popular Stage.* Translated by Don Kenny. Tokyo and New York, 1971.

Tsubouchi Shoyo and Yamamoto Jiro. *History and Characteristics of Kabuki.* Translated by Ryuzo Matsumoto. Yokohama, 1960.

Yamamoto Yuzo. *Three Plays.* Tokyo, 1957.

Yoshida Chiaki. *Kabuki.* Tokyo, 1971.

SELECTED JAPANESE SOURCES

Many Japanese sources have been consulted in preparing the English adaptation of *Kabuki Jiten.* A brief list of some of the most helpful follows.

Engeki Hyakka Daijiten. 6 vols. Tokyo, 1960-1962.

Kagayama Naozō. *Kabuki no Kata.* Tokyo, 1957.

Kanazawa Yasutaka. *Kabuki Meisaku Jiten.* Tokyo, 1971.

Kawarazaki Shigetoshi, ed. *Nihon Gikyoku Jiten.* Tokyo, 1964.

Sōga Tetsuō. *Banyū Hyakka Daijiten, Vol. III, Ongaku, Engeki.* Tokyo, 1974.

Subject Guide to Main Entries

In this subject guide all entries in the encyclopedia are arranged according to the following categories: Actors, Actors' World, Architecture and Permanent Scenic Devices, Costumes, Dance Schools, Makeup, Music, Performance Terms, Play and Scene Categories, Plays, Playwrights, Playwriting Terms, Props, Role Types, Scenic Techniques and Stage Equipment, Theatre Expressions, Theatre Management, Theatres, and Wigs. Certain terms have been categorized arbitrarily as they might have been placed under another heading with some justification. A few terms appear in more than one category. *Only terms that have main entries in the book are listed here.* If a term is not found in this guide, very likely it can be located in the general index.

ACTORS

ACTORS' WORLD

ARCHITECTURE AND PERMANENT SCENIC DEVICES (*See also* SCENIC TECHNIQUES AND STAGE EQUIPMENT)

COSTUMES

DANCE SCHOOLS

MAKEUP

MUSIC

PERFORMANCE TERMS

PLAY AND SCENE CATEGORIES

PLAYS

PLAYWRIGHTS

PLAYWRITING TERMS

PROPS

ROLE TYPES

SCENIC TECHNIQUES AND STAGE EQUIPMENT (*See also* ARCHITECTURE AND PERMANENT SCENIC DEVICES)

THEATRE EXPRESSIONS

THEATRE MANAGEMENT

THEATRES

WIGS

Index

Prepared by Marcia Leiter

About the Author

Samuel L. Leiter is Professor of Theatre at Brooklyn College, Brooklyn, New York. He is the author of *The Art of Kabuki: Famous Plays in Performance,* in addition to many articles published in scholarly journals. He is also a professional actor and director and is currently writing a book on the great stage directors of the twentieth century.